Everyman's Astronomy

A volume in
Everyman's Reference Library

The Contributors

Dr. S. V. M. Clube
Senior Principal Scientific Officer
Royal Observatory, Edinburgh

Professor David S. Evans
F.R.S.S.Af., F. Inst. P., *University of Texas*

Dr. D. Emerson
University of Edinburgh

Professor Z. Kopal
University of Manchester

Professor M. W. Ovenden
F.R.S.E., *University of British Columbia*

Dr. T. W. Rackham
Nuffield Radio Astronomy Laboratories
Jodrell Bank

Dr. V. C. Reddish
F.R.S.E., *Senior Principal Scientific Officer*
Royal Observatory, Edinburgh

H. Seddon
Principal Scientific Officer
Royal Observatory, Edinburgh

R. H. Stoy
Deputy Director, Royal Observatory, Edinburgh
Honorary Professor, University of Edinburgh

Everyman's Astronomy

Edited by R. H. Stoy
C.B.E., F.R.S.E., F.R.S.S.Af.
formerly H.M. Astronomer at the Cape

J. M. Dent & Sons Ltd London

Made in Great Britain at the
Aldine Press Letchworth Hertfordshire for
J M Dent & Sons Limited
Aldine House Albemarle Street London

First published 1974

ISBN 0 460 03024 8

Preface

The information explosion of the past few decades has automatically ensured that any book that attempts to give a general picture of a modern science is out of date before it is published. Nevertheless the present has its roots in the past, and to appreciate each fresh discovery as it is reported in the press or on the radio it is essential to have some understanding of the existing core of knowledge out of which it has grown. It is such a core of currently accepted astronomical fact and theory that we have tried to present in this book in a form which we hope will be comprehensible to the well-informed general reader. It consists of eleven chapters each of which was written, and can be read, independently of the others. To save unnecessary repetition some of the general concepts have been gathered together in the first chapter which also provides a short guide to the night sky and indicates how typical examples of the various celestial objects may be located there. In the same way instrumental and observational matters which are common to several chapters have been collected in Chapter 11.

If in reading any chapter it be found that a subject has been introduced with what appears to be insufficient explanation, consultation of the glossary and index may provide a clue to the missing information or give a reference to another chapter in which the subject is treated in rather greater detail. All distances, masses and quantities dependent on them have been given in metric units with some attempt to restrict these to the International System of Units (SI). This has not been done uniformly throughout, however, and in some places CGS units have been retained when they seemed more appropriate. Frequent use has been made of powers of 10 to avoid writing long strings of noughts (e.g. 10^8 for 100,000,000), or to emphasize the order of magnitude of the quantities involved.

Although this book was planned to be a new edition of Dr Martin Davidson's *Astronomy for Everyman* published in 1953, its bias is different. That book was written by leading members of the British Astronomical Association, all of them keen and able amateur astronomers who wrote from a deep love of their subject and a long experience of practical observing with small instruments. Twenty years have altered the astronomical background but it has in no way altered the truth or the felicitousness of their descriptions of what can be seen or done with relatively simple equipment. It is a great pity that that book is now unobtainable and that it has not been possible to bring more of it forward into the present work. In this edition the authors have been working professional astronomers who, though they love their chosen subject fully as much as do the amateurs, necessarily write from a different experience. Their endeavour has been to give a balanced view of their subject at the time of writing and to indicate how such knowledge as is firmly established was acquired. It was in 1960 that Dr Michael J. Smyth of the University of Edinburgh was first invited to prepare a new edition of Dr Davidson's book and it was he who determined the general form of the present book and commissioned several of its chapters. Unfortunately, owing to the pressure of other work, he had to abandon the project. When it was restarted in 1969, those chapters which had already been written were revised by their authors or, in two cases where this was not possible, completely rewritten. Thus the epoch of the book as a whole is approximately 1970. To reduce overlapping and to increase homogeneity some of the contributions have been rather more extensively edited than is usual in such compilations.

It is a pleasure to acknowledge the debt that this book owes to all those who, consciously or unconsciously, have helped in its preparation and in particular:

To Dr M. J. Smyth who started it

To the contributors who having, as they thought, finished their assignments, willingly revised them and cheerfully accepted editorial alterations

To those who, whether mentioned in the formal list of acknowledgments or not, have freely granted permission for the use of material for which they are responsible

To Professor H. A. Brück, Astronomer Royal for Scotland, and my colleagues at the Royal Observatory, Edinburgh, on whose knowledge and experience I have frequently drawn

To Mrs M. Fretwell who plotted the star charts in Chapter 1 and who prepared many of the diagrams

To Mrs C. A. McLachlan who typed much of the final copy for press

To the publishers, and especially to Donald Ross, and also Jocelyn Burton of their editorial staff for their constant encouragement, their patience in the face of many delays, and the great care with which they have prepared the manuscript and illustrations for the press.

Editing this book has proved a longer job than I originally imagined but it has given me considerable pleasure and caused me to discover much that I did not know before. I can only hope that it will bring something of the same kind of pleasure and enlightenment to some of those who may chance to read it.

1974 R. H. STOY

Acknowledgments

The Directors of
Armagh Observatory (Plate 18); Australian National Radio Observatory (Plate 47b); Hale Observatories (Plates 6*a*, 15, 23*b*, 24, 25*a*, 25*b*, 31*a*, 31*b*, 32, 33, 35, 41, 43, 44, 45*b* and Figure 10.2); Harvard Observatory (Plates 42*a*, 42*b* and Figure 10.1); International Latitude Observatory (Figure 3.6); Leiden Observatory (Plate 47*a*); Lick Observatory (Plates 22*b*, 40*a*, 40*b*); Lowell Observatory (Plates 9, 10, 11, 16); Lund Observatory (Plates 36, 37); Pic du Midi Observatory (Manchester Lunar Programme) (Plate 5); University of Michigan Observatory (Plates 28*b*, 29); Yerkes Observatory (Plates 6*b*, 45*a*)
The British Astronomical Association (Tables 5.2, 5.3)
The Department of the Environment (Plate 1)
The European Space Research Organization (Figure 11.18)
The Journal of the Optical Society of America (Figure 11.12)
The National Aeronautics and Space Administration (Plates 4, 7*a*, 7*b*, 7*c*, 8*a*, 8*b*, 13, 14, 21*b*)
The Publications of the Astronomical Society of the Pacific (Figure 5.10)
The Science Research Council and the Directors of the various institutions under their control (Plates 21*a*, 21*c*, 23*a*, 27, 28*a*, 30*a*, 30*b*, 38, 39*a*, 39*b*, 48*a*, 48*b* and Figures 11.13, 11.19)
The United States Navy (Plate 17*a*)
E. M. I. Electronics Ltd (Figure 11.4)
Messrs Grubb-Parsons (Plates 46*a*, 46*b*)
Professor W. Becker (Figures 9.5, 11.17 based on diagrams which appeared in the *Zeitschrift für Astrophysik*, Volume 58, page 207 and Volume 41, page 53)
Professor D. E. Blackwell (Plate 20)
Mr C. A. Cross (Plate 12)
Dr W. Gliese (Figure 8.8 based on a diagram that appeared in the *Zeitschrift für Astrophysik*, Volume 39, page 14)
Professor J. D. Kraus (Figure 11.14)
Dr D. McLean (Plate 19)
Professor J. H. Oort (Plate 34 and Figure 9.3)
Dr M. J. Smyth (Figure 11.16)
Mr R. L. Waterfield (Plates 17*b*, 22*a*)
Professor R. Wilson (Plate 28*a*, and Figure 11.19)

Contents

Plates

between pages 240 and 241

between pages 272 and 273

between pages 288 and 289

between pages 376 and 377

between pages 416 and 417

between pages 448 and 449

Unfortunately it is not possible to give an idea of the vast range in size of the various objects illustrated in these plates, since in many cases their exact distances are unknown. The best that can be done is to indicate the size they appear on the celestial sphere by giving the angular equivalent in the sky of one centimetre on the plate, as reproduced here, expressing this either in degrees, minutes or seconds of arc. The angular diameter of the Sun and of the Moon as seen from the Earth is approximately $\frac{1}{2}°$, or 30′ or 1800″.

Chapter One
The night sky

I have loved the stars too fondly
To be fearful of the night.
(*From* 'The Old Astronomer' by Sarah Williams, 1841–68)

One of the abiding joys of mankind is the sight of the night sky unobscured by cloud or by city lights. To many who have little astronomical knowledge and to some who have, the contemplation of the stars has brought tranquillity and companionship. These feelings are enhanced if one can recognize some of the stars by name and know when and where to look for them as the night sky gradually changes with the progress of the Earth's annual journey round the Sun.

It is not difficult to get to know the principal stars and constellations if one sets about it systematically. The best time to begin is when the Moon is just about half full and its light sufficient to blot out many of the fainter stars. This makes it easier to recognize the patterns formed by the brighter stars which are all that are shown in the simple star charts that are published monthly in the better papers. One thing that is confusing at first is the vast difference in scale between a constellation as seen in the sky and as represented on the chart; one looks so huge, the other so small. This ceases to be a difficulty, however, as soon as two or three constellations are clearly recognized in the sky and it becomes possible to use the chart to work round the sky from one constellation to the next. Charts intended to assist in the recognition of the principal stars and constellations are given later in this chapter but they will be more comprehensible if we first consider how the positions and brightnesses of the stars are usually indicated.

The constellations originated as convenient groupings of adjacent stars into memorable figures so that the individual stars could be the more easily identified. They are analogous to the squares, streets, and lanes into which the houses of a town or village are grouped for the benefit of the postman. A few of the constellations, like Scorpio, actually resemble the creature or object for which they are named, but the great majority do not. In the analogous case, few of the squares and streets named in honour of Queen Victoria resemble her in appearance, although some of the Broad Streets are broad and the Long Streets long. There are 88 constellations which are now officially recognized. Their boundaries were fixed some fifty years ago by a special commission of the International Astronomical Union, and between them they cover the whole area of the sky. These boundaries are a series of straight lines, or rather great circles, and were arranged to include as far as possible the ancient star grouping of the constellation after which the new area is called. Consequently the various constellations differ greatly in size and shape. A list of them is given in Table 1.1. The first column gives the official three-letter abbreviation by which the constellation is usually known and which is the same for all languages. The third column gives the Latin name and the fourth column the genitive (possessive) form of this name which is used when a star is being identified by its constellation letter or number. The last column gives the English equivalent of the name, but this is very rarely used in practice. The second column indicates on which of the five charts of the sky given at the end of this chapter the whereabouts of the constellation will be found, even if, as in several cases, the constellation does not contain a star sufficiently bright to be indicated on these particular charts.

Different civilizations have grouped the stars differently. Most of the northern constellations as we now know them in the western world have been handed down to us from the ancient peoples of the Fertile Crescent via the Greeks and, to some extent, were frozen into their present form in the early seventeenth century. It was at this time that Johann Bayer published his *Uranometria*, a series of star maps in which the individual stars in the constellations were designated by Greek letters, followed by Latin ones when there were more than 24 stars to be named in the constellation. An alternative nomenclature was introduced by Flamsteed, the first Astronomer Royal, who numbered the stars in each constellation, the numbers being approximately in order from west to east. Bayer's letters supplemented by Flamsteed's numbers are still in use, though professional astronomers more frequently refer to a star by its number in some specialized catalogue. The constellations in the southern polar cap were formulated in the eighteenth century after La Caille's expedition to the Cape of Good Hope. Most of these are named in honour of various pieces of scientific or artistic equipment which, with the possible exception of Triangulum Australe, they do not in the least resemble. One notable exception is Mensa, more properly Mons Mensae, which was named in honour of Table Mountain which had dominated the scene of La Caille's labours at the Cape. The Larger

TABLE 1.1. THE CONSTELLATIONS

Symbol	*Chart*	*Name*	*Genitive*	*English Name*
1	*2*	*3*	*4*	*5*
And	A, C, E,	Andromeda	Andromedae	Andromeda
Ant	D	Antlia	Antliae	Air Pump
Aps	B	Apus	Apodis	Bird of Paradise
Aqr	E	Aquarius	Aquarii	Water Carrier
Aql	E	Aquila	Aquilae	Eagle
Ara	B	Ara	Arae	Altar
Ari	C	Aries	Arietis	Ram
Aur	A, C	Auriga	Aurigae	Charioteer
Boo	A, D	Boötes	Boötis	Bear Driver
Cae	B, C	Caelum	Caeli	Graving Tool
Cam	A	Camelopardalis	Camelopardalis	Giraffe
Cnc	D	Cancer	Cancri	Crab
CVn	A, D	Canes Venatici	Canum Venaticorum	Hunting Dogs
CMa	C	Canis Major	Canis Majoris	Larger Dog
CMi	C, D	Canis Minor	Canis Minoris	Smaller Dog
Cap	E	Capricornus	Capricorni	Sea Goat
Car	B	Carina	Carinae	Keel
Cas	A	Cassiopeia	Cassiopeiae	Cassiopeia
Cen	B, D	Centaurus	Centauri	Centaur
Cep	A	Cepheus	Cephei	Cepheus
Cet	C	Cetus	Ceti	Whale
Cha	B	Chamaeleon	Chamaeleontis	Chameleon
Cir	B	Circinus	Circini	Compasses
Col	B, C	Columba	Columbae	Dove
Com	D	Coma Berenices	Comae Berenices	Berenice's Hair
CrA	E	Corona Australis	Coronae Australis	Southern Crown
CrB	D, E	Corona Borealis	Coronae Borealis	Northern Crown
Crv	D	Corvus	Corvi	Crow
Crt	D	Crater	Crateris	Cup
Cru	B	Crux	Crucis	Cross
Cyg	A, E	Cygnus	Cygni	Swan
Del	E	Delphinus	Delphini	Dolphin
Dor	B	Dorado	Doradus	Goldfish
Dra	A	Draco	Draconis	Dragon

Symbol	*Chart*	*Name*	*Genitive*	*English name*
1	*2*	*3*	*4*	*5*
Equ	E	Equuleus	Equulei	Little Horse
Eri	B, C	Eridanus	Eridani	River
For	C	Fornax	Fornacis	Furnace
Gem	C, D	Gemini	Geminorum	Twins
Gru	B, E	Grus	Gruis	Crane
Her	A, E	Hercules	Herculis	Hercules
Hor	B, C	Horologium	Horologii	Clock
Hya	D	Hydra	Hydrae	Water Snake
Hyi	B	Hydrus	Hydri	Sea Serpent
Ind	B	Indus	Indi	Indian
Lac	A, E	Lacerta	Lacertae	Lizard
Leo	D	Leo	Leonis	Lion
LMi	D	Leo Minor	Leonis Minoris	Smaller Lion
Lep	C	Lepus	Leporis	Hare
Lib	D, E	Libra	Librae	Scales
Lup	B, D, E	Lupus	Lupi	Wolf
Lyn	A, D	Lynx	Lyncis	Lynx
Lyr	A, E	Lyra	Lyrae	Lyre
Men	B	Mensa	Mensae	Table Mountain
Mic	E	Microscopium	Microscopii	Microscope
Mon	C	Monoceros	Monocerotis	Unicorn
Mus	B	Musca	Muscae	Fly
Nor	B	Norma	Normae	Level
Oct	B	Octans	Octantis	Octant
Oph	E	Ophiuchus	Ophiuchi	Serpent Holder
Ori	C	Orion	Orionis	Orion
Pav	B	Pavo	Pavonis	Peacock
Peg	C, E	Pegasus	Pegasi	Pegasus
Per	A, C	Perseus	Persei	Perseus
Phe	B, C	Phoenix	Phoenicis	Phoenix
Pic	B	Pictor	Pictoris	Easel
Psc	C	Pisces	Piscium	Fishes
PsA	E	Piscis Austrinus	Piscis Austrini	Southern Fish
Pup	B, C, D	Puppis	Puppis	Stern
Pyx	D	Pyxis	Pyxidis	Mariner's Compass
Ret	B	Reticulum	Reticuli	Net
Sge	E	Sagitta	Sagittae	Arrow

Symbol	*Chart*	*Name*	*Genitive*	*English name*
1	*2*	*3*	*4*	*5*
Sgr	E	Sagittarius	Sagittarii	Archer
Sco	D, E	Scorpius	Scorpii	Scorpion
Scl	C, E	Sculptor	Sculptoris	Sculptor's Tools
Sct	E	Scutum	Scuti	Shield
Ser	D, E	Serpens	Serpentis	Serpent
Sex	D	Sextans	Sextantis	Sextant
Tau	C	Taurus	Tauri	Bull
Tel	B	Telescopium	Telescopii	Telescope
Tri	C	Triangulum	Trianguli	Triangle
TrA	B	Triangulum Australe	Trianguli Australis	Southern Triangle
Tuc	B	Tucana	Tucanae	Toucan
UMa	A, D	Ursa Major	Ursae Majoris	Great Bear
UMi	A	Ursa Minor	Ursae Minoris	Little Bear
Vel	B, D	Vela	Velorum	Sails
Vir	D	Virgo	Virginis	Virgin
Vol	B	Volans	Volantis	Flying Fish
Vul	E	Vulpecula	Vulpeculae	Fox

TABLE 1.2 THE GREEK ALPHABET

A, α	Alpha	I, ι	Iota	P, ρ	Rho
B, β	Beta	K, κ	Kappa	Σ, σ	Sigma
Γ, γ	Gamma	Λ, λ	Lambda	T, τ	Tau
Δ, δ	Delta	M, μ	Mu	Υ, υ	Upsilon
E, ϵ	Epsilon	N, ν	Nu	Φ, ϕ	Phi
Z, ζ	Zeta	Ξ, ξ	Xi	X, χ	Chi
H, η	Eta	O, o	Omicron	Ψ, ψ	Psi
Θ, θ	Theta	Π, π	Pi	Ω, ω	Omega

Magellanic Cloud represents the 'Table Cloth' which so often forms on the top and over the face of that mountain during the summer time.

There are some people who feel that when they look at the stars they should be able to see the constellations as fanciful figures somewhat similar to those in Plate 2–3, which is taken from Bode's *Uranographia.* Only those with a vivid imagination can hope to do this; for others some memories of these beautiful figures do linger in the mind and they tend to see Orion as a giant confronting a charging bull whose red, fiery eye is represented by Aldebaran. It will be noticed that Plate 2–3 includes a number of constellations that have now been discarded. There are many of these, most of them completely forgotten though the names of a few sometimes occur, e.g. in the Quadrantids, a meteor shower having its radiant in the former constellation of Quadrans Muralis which was between Hercules and Boötes. Perhaps the best known of these former groups is Argo, the great ship which has now been divided into four: Carina, the Keel; Puppis, the Stern; Vela, the Sails; and Pyxis, the Mariner's Compass.

Star positions While constellations are useful for indicating the approximate whereabouts of a star or other celestial object, some more systematic method of specifying its precise position is clearly necessary, just as on the Earth the position of a place can be defined by its longitude and latitude. This is a particular case of spherical coordinates in which the equator is taken as the principal circle, and Greenwich to define the zero of longitude. The analogous spherical coordinates for celestial objects, right ascension and declination, are based on the celestial equator as the principal circle. This is the circle in which the plane of the terrestrial equator cuts the celestial sphere. Right ascensions are measured eastwards along this circle from the point where it is crossed from south to north by the apparent annual path of the Sun through the heavens, i.e. by the ecliptic. This point, which is frequently denoted by γ, is called the 'First Point of Aries' even though because of the phenomenon known as the precession of the equinoxes it now lies in Pisces. Right ascension and declination are clearly very closely associated with terrestrial longitudes and latitudes; in fact, at times when the First Point of Aries is crossing the Greenwich meridian, the right ascension and declination of a star are equal to the longitude and latitude of the sub-stellar point, i.e. of the point at which the line joining the star to the centre of the Earth cuts its surface. Some time later when the Earth has turned about its axis through an angle θ, the stars that were on the Greenwich meridian will be on the meridian whose longitude is θ west of Greenwich, and the stars on the Greenwich meridian will be those having a right ascension θ.

But we usually measure the rotation of the Earth in time, defining the day of 24 hours or 360° as the interval between successive transits of some selected object across the appropriate meridian. For most purposes the selected object is the Sun, or more precisely a mathematical fiction called the Mean Sun, since its light and heat control our daily lives. The solar day begins at noon, though for civil purposes it is convenient to add twelve hours and begin the calendar day at midnight. When we are dealing with the stars, however, it is more convenient to use sidereal time which is measured by the angle through which the Earth has rotated since the First Point of Aries crossed the meridian. Sidereal time and solar time are not the same since, as seen from the Earth, the Sun is gradually moving round the sky in the same direction as the Earth is turning. Consequently after the Earth has made a complete revolution relative to the stars, it has still to turn a little further to overtake the Sun which, during the day that has elapsed since the last transit has moved forward $(360/365\frac{1}{4})°$. This takes about four minutes and makes the solar day longer than the sidereal day by this amount. A result of the Sun's motion is that there is one fewer solar than sidereal day in the tropical year, i.e. in the time interval between successive transits of the Sun through the First Point of Aries. Thus $366\frac{1}{4}$ sidereal days must equal $365\frac{1}{4}$ solar days.

At any instant the solar and sidereal times at any place differ by the right ascension of the Sun. This is zero at the time of the March equinox and increases at approximately two hours per month. Consequently the sidereal time at midnight is approximately 12 hours on 21 March, 14 hours on 21 April, 16 hours on 21 May, and so on throughout the year. Starting from these times and using the fact that sidereal time gains four minutes a day on normal civil time, it is easy to compute the approximate sidereal time at midnight on any day of the year, and thus at any instant during that day.

Knowing the sidereal time, we can predict the aspect of the heavens. All objects with right ascensions equal to the sidereal time will be on the meridian, those with smaller right ascensions will be to the west of the meridian, and those with larger, to the east. Which stars will be above the horizon depends on the latitude of the place of observation. As may be seen from Figure 1.1, the height above the horizon of the celestial pole, i.e. of the point where the prolongation of the axis of the Earth cuts the celestial sphere and about which all the stars in their diurnal motion appear to circle, is equal to the latitude. The highest and lowest altitudes that any star attains in the sky are when it is crossing the merid-

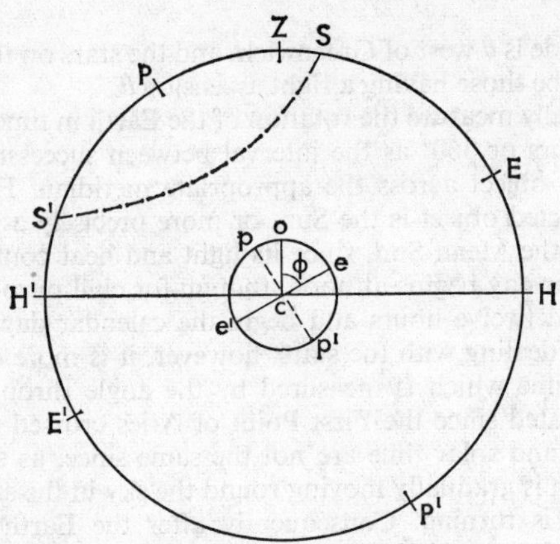

Figure 1.1 The terrestrial and celestial spheres

The figure represents the meridian section of the terrestrial and celestial spheres through the place of observation, o, of which the lattitude is ϕ. c represents the centre of the Earth, ee′ the equator and pp′ its axis of rotation. The radius of the celestial sphere is effectively infinite. Z marks the zenith point, HH′ the horizon as seen from o, EE′ the celestial equator and PP′ the celestial poles. SS′ denotes the diurnal track of a star of declination δ

ϕ = angle eco = angle EZ = angle PH′
$90°-\phi$ = angle HE = angle ZP = angle H′E′
δ = angle ES = angle E′S′

Hence

angle HS = angle HE+angle ES = $90°-\phi+\delta$
angle H′S′ = angle E′S′−angle E′H′ = $\delta-90°+\phi$

ian. These altitudes are $\delta - \phi + 90°$ and $\delta + \phi - 90°$, where ϕ denotes the latitude of the place and δ the declination of the star. Consequently if $\delta > 90° - \phi$, the star never goes below the horizon and is said to be circumpolar. Similarly if $\delta < \phi - 90°$, the star never rises above the horizon and is therefore never visible from that place. If $\phi = \delta$, the star passes directly overhead, i.e. through the zenith. On the equator, where $\phi = 0$, the celestial poles lie on the horizon and all the stars of the sky are visible for twelve hours at a time. At the poles, where $\phi = 90°$, one celestial pole is directly overhead and all the stars in that hemisphere are circumpolar, their diurnal motions being in horizontal circles. In an intermediate latitude, say 50° N, the north celestial pole is at an elevation of 50° and all the stars with declination north of + 40° are circumpolar, while those with declinations south of – 40° are always invisible. From 30° S, stars with declinations north of + 60° will be invisible, while those with declinations south of – 60° will be circumpolar.

The brightness and colours of the stars By long-established convention, the brightness of a celestial body is expressed in magnitudes. This system goes back at least as far as the Greeks who divided the stars visible to the naked eye into six classes according to their brightness. The twenty brightest stars were said to be of the first magnitude, the next sixty of the second magnitude, and so on down to the sixth magnitude which contained all those stars which were just visible to the naked eye under the best conditions. During the early part of the nineteenth century, when astronomers were beginning to measure the light of the stars with photometers based on sound physical principles, it was found that the stars that had been assigned to the first magnitude were on the average 100 times brighter than those assigned to the sixth, while for the magnitude classes in between, the stars of class n were on the average 2.5 times brighter than those in class n + 1. The old conventional magnitude system was therefore rationalized by defining the magnitude difference between two stars whose luminosities are L and L_0 as

$$m - m_0 = 2.5 \log_{10} (L_0/ L)$$

This definition ensures that when the luminosities differ by a factor of 100, the magnitudes differ by 5, and also that the ratio of the luminosities between successive magnitudes is the fifth root of 100, i.e. 2.512. This definition also has two extra advantages in that it provides a continuous scale that can take into account small changes in brightness, and that its scale can be extrapolated to all objects however bright or however faint. The zero point of the new system was chosen so as to agree as far as possible with the mean of the old conventional magnitude classes. The magnitudes of the very brightest stars come out negative as do those of the Sun (– 26.8), the Moon (–12.5 when full), and the brighter planets. The magnitude of the faintest star that can be detected with the 200-inch telescope is about magnitude + 24, just about as faint when compared with Sirius as Sirius is compared with the Sun. In each case the light ratio is about 10^{10}.

The brightness ratios corresponding to magnitude differences of 0.5 are given in the following table which can be extended indefinitely by making use of the fact that a factor of ten in brightness means an addition of 2.5 in magnitude, e.g. a magnitude difference of 4.0 corresponds to a brightness ratio of 39.80.

Magnitude difference	*Brightness ratio*
0.0	1.000
0.5	1.585
1.0	2.512
1.5	3.980
2.0	6.310
2.5	10.000

Colour differences between the brighter stars can be recognized by the naked eye which quickly learns to detect which are blue stars like Rigel, white stars like Vega, yellow stars like Capella, and red stars like Betelgeuse. A telescope accentuates the colours and reveals some stars so deep in colour that they look like drops of blood. These differences in colour arise mainly from the different surface temperatures of the stars which also largely determine their spectra. In spite of minor individual variations, these stellar spectra can be arranged in a single sequence of which the principal classes are now denoted by the letters O, B, A, F, G, K, and M, the earlier classes referring to the hot blue stars, the later ones to the relatively cool red stars. For a finer sub-division each of these major spectral classes is divided into ten.

The spectral class, or type, provides a qualitative indication of the colour distribution of the radiation as it leaves the star; what is observed is the colour distribution of the radiation as it arrives at the Earth, sometimes after having suffered considerable selective absorption on the way. The general colour distribution of the radiation received from a star can be indicated numerically by comparing its apparent magnitudes as measured in two different ranges of wavelength. By combining various filters with the appropriate types of photographic plates or photoelectric cells, a wide selection of such ranges of wavelength are now available, but the two most frequently used are those denoted by V and B. The V range corresponds to that used in the traditional visual observations, while B approximates to the use of ordinary blue-sensitive photographic plates with a refracting telescope. The zero point of the B magnitude system has been so adjusted that the B and V magnitudes are, on the average, the same for stars of spectral class AO. Thus B–V gives a measure of colour which is negative for blue stars and positive for red ones. It is called 'the B–V colour index', or more frequently 'the colour index', of the star.

This subject is dealt with further in Chapter 8, and illustrated in Plate 29.

The brightest stars Table 1.3 lists the 22 stars which can be considered as being of the first magnitude and which provide useful reference points when locating the various constellations. All of them have names but those given in parentheses are rarely used and should probably be ignored. Thus Rigil Kentaurus, or Rigil Kent, is much better known as Alpha Centauri. The right ascensions and declinations given in the fourth and fifth columns of Table 3 are for the year A.D. 2000. The sixth and seventh columns give the visual magnitudes and colours as measured on the V, B–V system.

A star may appear to be bright either because, like the Sun, it is relatively close or because it is intrinsically very much brighter than the general run of stars. We can only tell which is the case by determining the actual distance of the star and then computing what its magnitude would be if the star were moved to some standard distance from us. The last column of Table 3 gives such a measure of intrinsic brightness. It is the absolute visual magnitude, i.e. the magnitude the star would appear to be if it were at a distance of 10 parsecs or 32.6 light years, and has been computed from the V magnitude given in the eighth column and the distance in light years given in the ninth column. The corresponding absolute magnitude for the Sun, like Alpha Centauri a G2 V star, is + 4.8.

The eighth column gives the spectral type which consists of two parts, a letter indicating the spectral class which has already been mentioned and a Roman numeral indicating what is called the luminosity class. Most stars, including the Sun, are of luminosity class V and are said to belong to the 'main sequence'. These stars have absolute magnitudes which range down from about − 3 for the very blue stars to fainter than + 10 for very red stars. The second most numerous class is III which contains mostly yellow and red stars with absolute magnitudes between − 1 and + 1. These stars are usually called giants and are several magnitudes brighter than stars of class V having the same colours. Since their emission of radiation per unit area of surface must be similar, the greater brightness of the class III stars must arise form their having a greater surface area than the corresponding stars of class V. Thus Capella, which does not differ greatly in colour from the Sun, is intrinsically 4.7 magnitudes brighter, i.e. it emits nearly 100 times more light. Its surface area must therefore be about 100 times greater, and its radius 10 times greater than that of the Sun, which is itself about 100 times that of the Earth. Though well represented in Table 3, stars of luminosity classes I and II are very rare in space. They have absolute magnitudes of the order of − 5 and are usually referred to as supergiants. That this name is fully justified can be seen by considering the amount of radiation that is being poured out by the red, rather cool

TABLE 1.3 THE BRIGHTEST STARS

	Star		*R.A.*	*(2000) Dec.*	V	B–V	Sp	d (l.y.)	M_V
1	*2*	*3*	*4*	*5*	*6*	*7*	*8*	*9*	*10*
1	α CMa	Sirius	06^h45^m	− 16°43′	− 1.42	0.00	A1 V	8.6	+ 1.4
2	α Car	Canopus	06 24	− 52 41	− 0.72	+ 0.16	FO II	185	− 4.5
3	α Cen	(Rigil Kentaurus)	14 40	− 60 50	− 0.28	+ 0.72	G2 V	4.3	+ 4.7
4	α Boo	Arcturus	14 16	+ 19 11	− 0.06	+ 1.24	K2 III	36	− 0.3
5	α Lyr	Vega	18 37	+ 38 47	0.00	0.00	AO V	26	+ 0.5
6	α Aur	Capella	05 17	+ 46 00	+ 0.06	+ 0.81	G8 III	32	+ 0.1
7	β Ori	Rigel	05 15	− 08 12	+ 0.18	− 0.03	B8 Ia	680	− 6.4
8	α CMi	Procyon	07 39	+ 05 14	+ 0.36	+ 0.42	F5 IV	11	+ 2.7
9	α Eri	Achernar	01 38	− 57 15	+ 0.48	− 0.16	B5 IV	140	− 2.6
10	β Cen	(Hadar)	14 04	− 60 22	+ 0.62	− 0.24	B1 II	180	− 3.1
11	α Ori	Betelgeuse	05 55	+ 07 24	+ 0.7	+ 1.86	M2 Iab	170	− 2.9
12	α Cru	(Acrux)	12 27	− 63 06	+ 0.76	− 0.25	B1	200	− 3.2
13	α Aql	Altair	19 51	+ 08 52	+ 0.78	+ 0.22	A7 V	16	+ 2.3
14	α Tau	Aldebaran	04 36	+ 16 30	+ 0.8	+ 1.55	K5 III	68	− 0.8
15	α Sco	Antares	16 29	− 26 26	+ 0.9	+ 1.83	M1 I	590	− 5.4
16	α Vir	Spica	13 25	− 11 09	+ 0.98	− 0.23	B1 V	160	− 2.4
17	β Gem	Pollux	07 45	+ 28 01	+ 1.13	+ 1.00	KO III	35	+ 1.0
18	α PsA	Fomalhaut	22 58	− 29 37	+ 1.16	+ 0.09	A2 V	22	+ 2.0
19	α Cyg	Deneb	20 41	+ 45 16	+ 1.25	+ 0.09	A2 Ia	530	− 3.5
20	β Cru	(Becrux)	12 48	− 59 42	+ 1.25	− 0.24	BO IV	290	− 4.8
21	α Leo	Regulus	10 08	+ 11 58	+ 1.35	− 0.12	B7 V	84	− 0.7
22	ε CMa	(Adhara)	06 59	− 28 58	+ 1.50	− 0.20	B2 II	270	− 3.1

11 Betelgeuse varies between 0.4 and 1.3 approximately. 14 Aldebaran varies between 0.7 and 1.0. 15 Antares varies between 0.9 and 1.8.

Antares. This star must be so huge that if it were placed with its centre coinciding with that of the Sun, its surface would lie well out beyond the orbit of Mars.

Perhaps the most interesting feature of Table 1.3 is the large range in the intrinsic luminosity from the absolute magnitude of -6.4 for Rigel to $+4.7$ for Alpha Centauri, which at a distance of 4.3 light years is the Sun's nearest neighbour. This 11.1 magnitude range in absolute magnitude corresponds to a 30,000-fold range in brightness; but this is not the total range since the sample of stars represented in Table 3 is not typical. The intrinsically very bright stars are over-represented and the fainter ones correspondingly under-represented; in fact, the very numerous low luminosity stars and the white dwarfs are not represented at all. When these fainter, telescopic stars are taken into account, the range in intrinsic brightness from Alpha Centauri, and the Sun, downwards is almost as great as it is upwards.

The data given in Table 3 were the best available at the time of writing. It may be that some of them will be found to differ slightly from those given elsewhere in somewhat similar tables. These differences are not to be attributed to 'mistakes' but to the difficulty in measuring some of the quantities involved, even for these, the brightest stars in the sky. Moreover, many of these stars may well be slightly variable in magnitude as Betelgeuse, Aldebaran and Antares undoubtedly are.

The star charts given at the end of this chapter are intended to show all stars in the Astronomical Ephemeris list for which the visual magnitude is 4.0 or brighter. These should include most of those stars that are easily visible to the naked eye from a 'dark' spot within a modern city; many more will, of course, be visible from the country on a clear dark night. Charts C, D, and E show the equatorial band which is equally visible from the northern and southern hemispheres. Charts A and B show the polar caps which contain stars that are circumpolar from the one hemisphere and invisible from the other. To keep the charts as uncluttered as possible, only the Bayer or Flamsteed designations of the stars have been given, the constellations have been indicated by their official three-letter abbreviations, and the great circles drawn in restricted to those marking the celestial equator, the ecliptic, and the galactic equator. The latter, which is the central line of the Milky Way, is shown as a dotted line. The band of sky of 8° on either side of the ecliptic is known as the Zodiac and it is within this band that the Sun, Moon and brighter planets will be found.

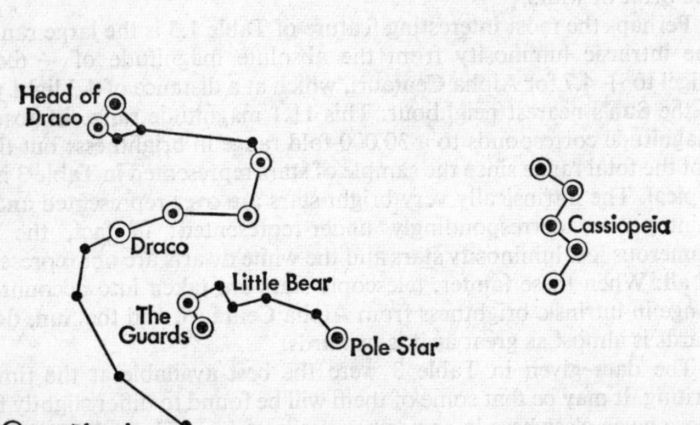

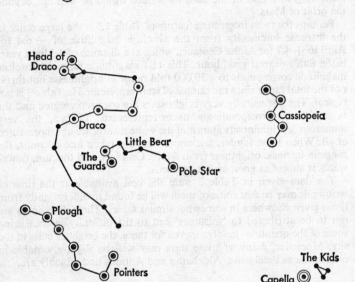

Figure 1.2 The north polar stars

The north polar stars Figure 1.2 is a key to the principal constellation figures in the north polar cap. While it does not include all the stars on Chart A, it does include some extra ones which are fainter than 4.0 but which are required to complete the outlines of what have become conventional star groupings.

The best-known grouping of all is the Plough which is formed by seven of the brightest stars in Ursa Major, the Great Bear. All the seven stars but one are of the second magnitude and as they are on the average about 6° apart they spread over quite a large area of the sky and form a very conspicuous figure which, once it is recognized, can never be completely forgotten. It is circumpolar for all places north of latitude 42° N and can be seen at any time by looking towards the north. It will be high or low in the sky according to the season and time of night. Figure 1.2 shows the position for sidereal time 21 hrs, i.e. at midnight on

7 August, 10.00 p.m. on 7 September, 8 p.m. on 7 October, and so on. It will be at its highest in the sky at sidereal time 12 hrs (midnight on 21 March, 10.00 p.m. on 21 April, etc.), when, as seen from the United Kingdom, it passes overhead.

The 'seven bright shiners' that form the Plough have always been taken together to form one figure, though it has received various names at different times and places, e.g. Charles's Wain or, in the United States, the Big Dipper. All the individual stars have names but these are not in common use except perhaps for that of Zeta Ursae Majoris, the mid star of the handle, which is called Mizar. Mizar is the brighter component of a naked eye double, i.e. people with keen eyesight, or a pair of binoculars, can see that there is a fainter star only 12 minutes of arc away from it. This is 80 UMa or Alcor, which forms with Mizar what the North American Indians called the Horse and Rider. Mizar is also notable as being the first star to be recognized as a telescopic double. This discovery was made in 1650 when Riccioli of Bologna found that it really consisted of two stars about 14 seconds of arc apart. In 1889 it was noticed at the Harvard College Observatory that the spectrum of one of these stars showed a periodic doubling of the absorption lines which implied that this star consisted of two components revolving fairly rapidly round each other and so close together that they cannot be seen separately even in the most powerful telescopes. This was the first such spectroscopic binary to be discovered. Many more have since been found including the other component of Mizar. Thus, in addition to forming a naked eye double with Alcor, Mizar is itself a telescopic double in which each component is a spectroscopic double.

Alpha and Beta Ursae Majoris are known as the Pointers because a line through them extended for about five times its length leads to a fairly isolated second magnitude star. This is Alpha Ursae Minoris, better known as Polaris the Pole Star, which, for all practical purposes, marks the north celestial pole round which all the other stars appear to revolve. Polaris also marks the end of the tail of the Little Bear whose principal stars form the group which is known in the United States as the Little Dipper. The other two brightish stars in this group, Beta and Gamma Ursae Minoris, are sometimes called the Guards or Guardians of the Pole.

On the opposite side of Polaris from the Plough and at about the same distance from it is another smaller, but still conspicuous configuration. This is the Great W formed by Beta, Alpha, Gamma, Delta, and Epsilon Cassiopeiae, the five principal stars of the constellation of Cassiopeia which lies in the Milky Way. The Plough and the Great W dominate two opposite quarters of the circumpolar sky. The intermediate quarters are marked by two bright first magnitude stars, Capella and Vega, which lie on a line through the pole almost at right angles to that joining the Plough and the Great W and at very much the same distance from the pole as these groups. Capella is distinctly yellow in colour and Vega bluish-white. Though not very bright, Draco is an interesting constellation that can be traced winding its way between the Big and Little Bears. The most conspicuous part is the head formed of Beta, Gamma, Xi, and Nu Draconis. Alpha Draconis, which on account of the precession of the equinoxes was the pole star at the time of the building of the pyramids, is about two thirds the way along the body towards the tail and will be found about midway between Mizar and the Guards. It is possible that this star was brighter in the past than it is now. Another of the fainter polar constellations is Cepheus which lies between Cassiopeia and Draco. Probably its best-known star is Delta Cephei which has given its name to one of the most important classes of variable stars, the cepheids. These are intrinsically very bright stars whose actual brightness is closely related to their period of variability, which can be relatively easily determined however faint and distant the star may be. Cepheids are consequently extremely useful as distance indicators. Delta Cephei itself varies between magnitude 3.8 and 4.6 with a very regular period of 5.37 days,

Direction finding in the northern hemisphere is simply a matter of locating Polaris which marks true north; when facing it, east is to the right and west to the left. The northern stars can also be used for roughly estimating the sidereal time from which normal solar time can be deduced. Polaris can be regarded as the centre of a 24-hour clock dial, and the line joining it to Beta Cassiopeiae as the hour hand. When this hand is vertically upwards, i.e. on the meridian, the sidereal time is 0 hrs; when it is horizontal and pointing westwards, the sidereal time is 6 hrs; and so on. It must be noted that this clock goes round in an anti-clockwise direction. Alternatively, the sidereal time can be roughly estimated by remembering that it is approximately 0, 6, 12, or 18 hrs according to whether the Great W, Capella, the Plough, or Vega is highest in the sky.

The south polar stars Figure 1.3 provides a key to the principal stars in the south polar cap and is orientated for 10 hrs sidereal time. Although, as may be seen from Chart B, the immediate region of the south pole is devoid of bright stars so that there is no star comparable with Polaris, the south polar cap as a whole is richer in bright stars than the north and contains no fewer than six of the first magnitude. Four of these are

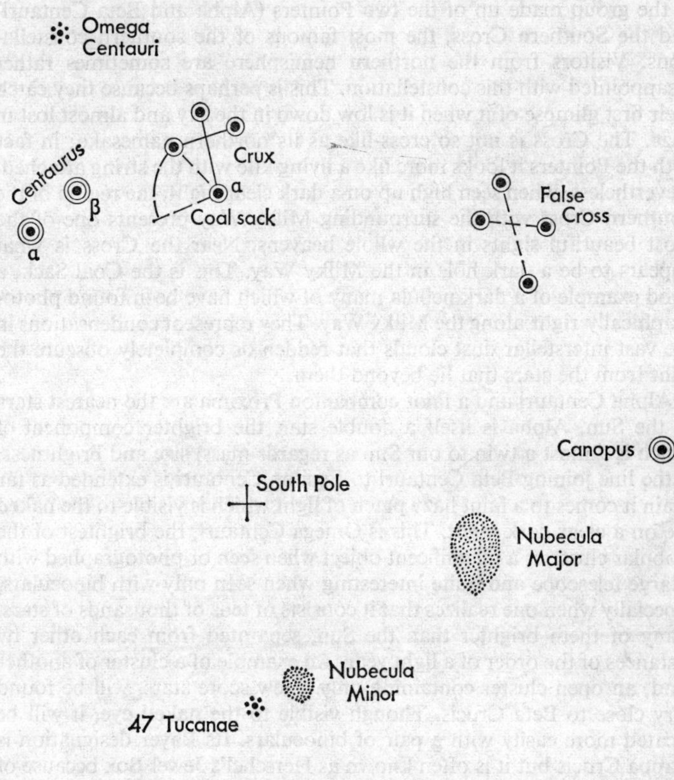

Figure 1.3 The south polar stars

in the group made up of the two Pointers (Alpha and Beta Centauri) and the Southern Cross, the most famous of the southern constellations. Visitors from the northern hemisphere are sometimes rather disappointed with this constellation. This is perhaps because they catch their first glimpse of it when it is low down in the sky and almost lost in haze. The Cross is not so cross-like as its northern namesake; in fact with the Pointers it looks more like a flying kite with the string attached. Nevertheless, when seen high up on a dark clear night, the region of the Southern Cross with the surrounding Milky Way presents one of the most beautiful sights in the whole heavens. Near the Cross is what appears to be a dark hole in the Milky Way. This is the Coal Sack, a good example of a dark nebula many of which have been found photographically right along the Milky Way. They represent condensations in the vast interstellar dust clouds that redden or completely obscure the light from the stars that lie beyond them.

Alpha Centauri and a faint companion Proxima are the nearest stars to the Sun. Alpha is itself a double star, the brighter component of which is almost a twin to our Sun as regards mass, size and brightness. If the line joining Beta Centauri to Epsilon Centauri is extended as far again it comes to a faint hazy patch of light which is visible to the naked eye on a clear dark night. This is Omega Centauri, the brightest of the globular clusters; a magnificent object when seen or photographed with a large telescope and quite interesting when seen only with binoculars, especially when one realizes that it consists of tens of thousands of stars, many of them brighter than the Sun, separated from each other by distances of the order of a light year. An example of a cluster of another kind, an open cluster containing only a few score stars, will be found very close to Beta Crucis. Though visible to the naked eye, it will be located more easily with a pair of binoculars. Its Bayer designation is Kappa Crucis but it is often known as Herschel's Jewel Box because of the varied colours of the stars when viewed through a big telescope.

The Southern Cross is very much to the south what the Plough is to the north. It too can be used for locating the pole which lies on the line joining Gamma and Alpha Crucis extended for about five times this length. It is sometimes easier, however, to visualize the south celestial pole as being the intersection of the line joining Gamma and Alpha Crucis with the perpendicular bisector of the line joining Alpha and Beta Centauri. The southern sky regarded as a celestial clock goes round clockwise; the length of the Cross can be taken as an hour hand which indicates 12 hrs sidereal time when high up on the meridian.

On the opposite side of the south pole from Beta Centauri and at about the same distance from it is Alpha Eridani or Achernar, a bright blue first magnitude star which marks the end of the long river that winds its way right across the southern sky. Approximately at right angles to the line joining Achernar and Beta Centauri and at the same distance from the pole is a very bright star. This is Alpha Carinae or Canopus, the second brightest star in the sky, a super-giant that owes its apparent brightness more to its own intrinsic luminosity than to its relative closeness. Two objects of special interest are the Nubeculae Major and Minor, the Large and Small Magellanic Clouds (Plates 37, 42) which look like detached pieces of the Milky Way and which at distances of approximately 160,000 light years are the nearest extra-galactic systems to our own Milky Way, of which they are a smaller version. Immediately to the west of the Small Magellanic Cloud and almost appearing part of it is another little hazy patch. This is 47 Tucanae, a globular cluster that is almost as big and bright as Omega Centauri.

A feature of the southern sky is the way in which the bright blue stars cluster towards the Milky Way. Amongst them in what used to be known as Argo are the four stars Epsilon Carinae, Iota Carinae, Delta Velorum, and Kappa Velorum which together make up the False Cross, so named because it bears a distinct resemblance to the brighter but smaller Crux. Both asterisms are in the Milky Way and have their arms similarly orientated. Two small constellations which will also be fairly easily recognized are Musca, the Fly, and Triangulum Australe. The former lies directly between Crux and the pole, while the latter is to the south-east of Alpha Centauri.

November evenings Figure 1.4 provides a key to some of the constellations that are visible from both hemispheres near 0 hrs sidereal time, e.g. in the evenings of early November. The key, which covers parts of Charts C and E, was drawn with the northern hemisphere in mind and will appear upside down to southern viewers. In the northern hemisphere this quadrant is dominated by the Great W of Cassiopeia. Some 20° south of it is a remarkable series of second, or near second, magnitude stars running in a great smooth arc across the sky with about 15° separation between each star and its neighbour. Running from west to east these are Beta Pegasi, Alpha Andromedae, Beta Andromedae, Gamma Andromedae, and Alpha Persei. At the western end is the Great Square of Pegasus formed of Alpha Andromedae, Beta Pegasi, Alpha Pegasi, and Gamma Pegasi. Beta Andromedae, Gamma Andromedae, and Alpha Persei form with Beta Trianguli and Beta Persei what may be called the Greater W, a configuration with sides approximately parallel to those of the Great W. Beta Persei is also known as Algol, the Demon,

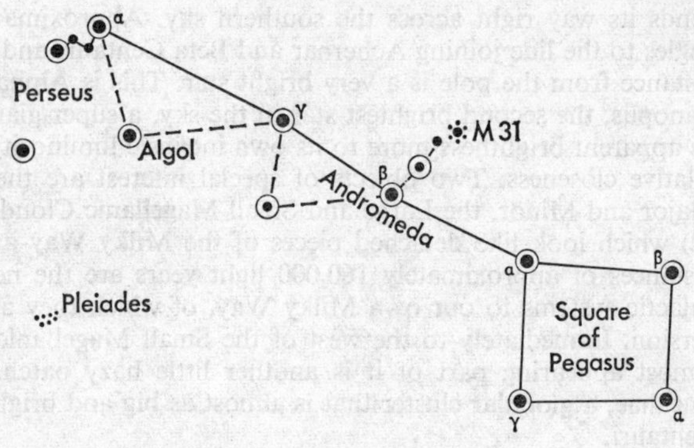

and was the first discovered example of an eclipsing binary, i.e. of two stars revolving round each other in a plane passing very close to the Sun so that, as seen from the Earth, each star eclipses, or partially eclipses, the other. In the case of Algol, the magnitude remains more or less constant at 2.2 for 2½ days, fades to 3.5 for some hours and then returns to its former brightness, this phenomenon being repeated in a period of 2.87 days with great regularity.

A line from Beta Andromedae through Mu extended for its own length leads to a hazy patch of light just visible to the naked eye which one early astronomer likened to a candle shining through horn. This is the Great Nebula in Andromeda (Plate 33) which is the largest and best known of the spiral nebulae, an extragalactic system which is probably very similar in form and content to our own Milky Way system from which it is separated by about two million light years.

The diagonal of the Square of Pegasus formed by Gamma Pegasi and Beta Pegasi extended westward for twice its length leads to the constellation of Cygnus, the Swan, of which the principal stars form the Northern Cross. Beyond it to the west is the brilliant Vega and its accompanying constellation of Lyra. Apart from Vega, the only two stars in Lyra brighter than 4.0 are Beta and Gamma Lyrae. Between these two stars is Messier 57, the well known Ring Nebula in Lyra, which can be

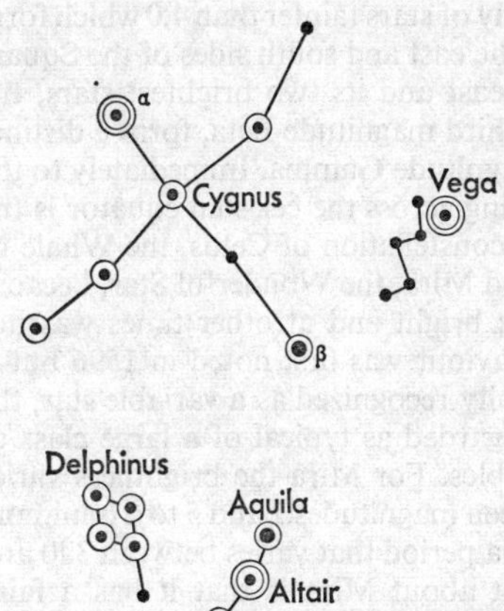

Figure 1.4 The stars visible during November evenings

seen in quite a small telescope. It is a planetary nebula and consists of a small, clear-cut shell of nebulosity surrounding a relatively faint central star which provides the ultraviolet radiation necessary to stimulate the emission of the nebular light. The first magnitude star at the head of the Northern Cross is called Deneb, from the Arabic word meaning tail, since this star marks the tail of the Swan. The length of the Cross, defined by Deneb and Beta Cygni, is parallel to the central line of the Milky Way and points in the general direction of Aquila, the Eagle, of which the principal star is the first magnitude Altair. Altair, or Alpha Aquilae, can be easily recognized by its brightness and by the two stars, Beta and Gamma Aquilae, which are about 2° on either side and form with it a straight line that is somewhat reminiscent of Orion's Belt, though the stars in this case are not of equal brightness.

A line along the west side of the Square of Pegasus, i.e. from Beta Pegasi to Alpha Pegasi, extended southwards for about 3½ times its own length leads to a first magnitude star, Alpha Piscium Austrini or Fomalhaut. Fomalhaut is the most southerly first magnitude star visible from Britain, but for the southern observer it passes almost overhead. Directly south of it is Grus, the Crane, a constellation that can be fairly easily identified from the scrawled Y made by its five principal stars. A line along the east side of the Square of Pegasus, i.e. through Alpha Andromedae and Gamma Pegasi, extended southwards for its own length leads almost to the First Point of Aries. This point is now in Pisces, a constellation formed mainly of stars fainter than 4.0 which form a large V-shaped figure enclosing the east and south sides of the Square of Pegasus. Aries itself is further east and its two brightest stars, the second magnitude Alpha and the third magnitude Beta, form a distinctive small triangle with the fifth magnitude Gamma. Immediately to the south of Alpha Arietis and sprawling across the celestial equator is the large but relatively inconspicuous constellation of Cetus, the Whale or Sea Monster. Omicron Ceti is called Mira, the Wonderful Star, because sometimes it appeared to be quite bright and at other times was not visible to the naked eye. This behaviour was first noted in 1596 but it was not till 1638 that Mira was fully recognized as a variable star, the first such to be found and now regarded as typical of a large class of long period, rather irregular variables. For Mira the brightness varies from a maximum somewhere between magnitudes 2 and 5 to a minimum between magnitudes 8 and 10 with a period that varies between 320 and 370 days. Another interesting fact about Mira is that it has a faint companion which is a white dwarf, i.e. a star comparable in mass and temperature to the Sun but so much smaller in size that its average density is of the order of 10^5 g c^{-3}, that is one hundred thousand times that of water.

Following Pisces and Aries along the Zodiac is the constellation of Taurus, the Bull, which lies about 60° to the east of the Square of Pegasus. Prominent in this constellation are two of the nearest and best known open clusters, the Hyades and the Pleiades. The brighter stars in the Hyades form a distinctive V with the orange-red first magnitude Aldebaran at the end of one of its arms. The Pleiades, or Seven Sisters (Plates 30*b* and 40*b*), form a compact group of stars of which from six to eleven are visible to the naked eye depending on the darkness and transparency of the night. Tennyson said very aptly that they 'Glitter like a swarm of fire-flies tangled in a silver braid' and they inevitably attract the attention of anybody who looks at the night sky at all carefully. They are probably the most studied group of stars in the sky and certainly the most frequently referred to in literature from the Chinese annals of 2357 B.C. onwards.

February evenings But Taurus as a whole belongs to the section of the sky that is centred on 6 hrs sidereal time for which Figure 1.5 provides a key. This is the quarter of the heavens which in the northern hemisphere is marked by Capella, but for both northern and southern hemispheres the dominant constellation is the large bright figure of Orion. This consists of a large quadrilateral formed by Betelgeuse (Alpha),

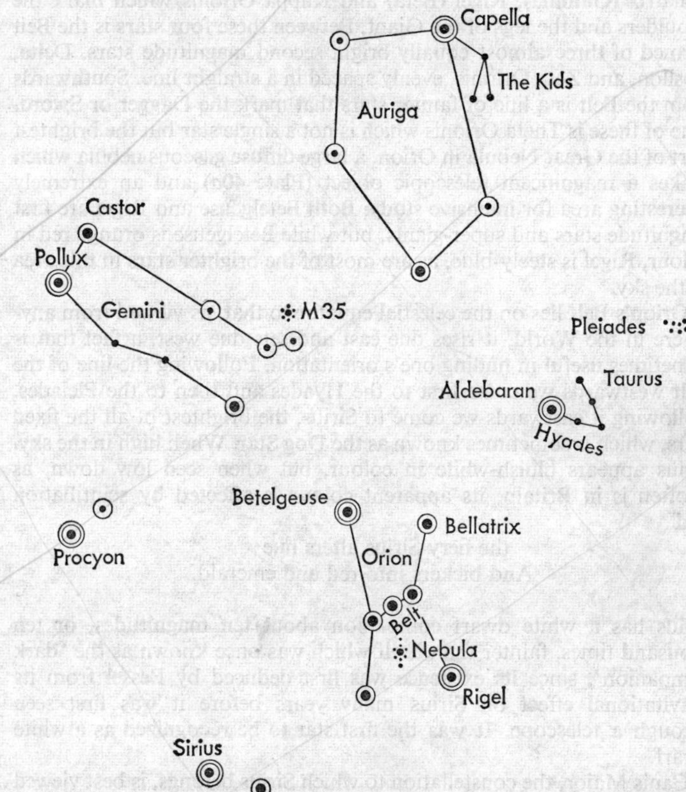

Figure 1.5 The stars visible during February evenings

Bellatrix (Gamma), Rigel (Beta) and Kappa Orionis which mark the shoulders and the legs of the Giant. Between these four stars is the Belt formed of three almost equally bright second magnitude stars, Delta, Epsilon, and Zeta Orionis, evenly spaced in a straight line. Southwards from the Belt is a line of fainter stars that mark the Dagger or Sword. One of these is Theta Orionis which is not a single star but the brightest part of the Great Nebula in Orion, a large diffuse gaseous nebula which makes a magnificent telescopic object (Plate 40*a*) and an extremely interesting area for intensive study. Both Betelgeuse and Rigel are first magnitude stars and super-giants, but while Betelgeuse is orange red in colour, Rigel is steely-blue, as are most of the brighter stars in this area of the sky.

Orion's Belt lies on the celestial equator so that, as viewed from anywhere in the World, it rises due east and sets due west, a fact that is sometimes useful in finding one's orientation. Following the line of the Belt westwards we come first to the Hyades and then to the Pleiades. Following it eastwards we come to Sirius, the brightest of all the fixed stars, which is sometimes known as the Dog Star. When high in the sky, Sirius appears bluish-white in colour, but when seen low down, as it often is in Britain, its apparent colour is affected by scintillation and

> the fiery Sirius alters hue
> And bickers into red and emerald.

Sirius has a white dwarf companion about ten magnitudes, or ten thousand times, fainter than itself which was once known as the 'dark companion', since its existence was first deduced by Bessel from its gravitational effect on Sirius many years before it was first seen through a telescope. It was the first star to be recognized as a white dwarf.

Canis Major, the constellation to which Sirius belongs, is best viewed from the southern hemisphere where its bright stars merge with those of Puppis and Vela in high-lighting the general course of the Milky Way from Orion to the rich regions of Carina and Crux. Epsilon, the second brightest star in Canis Major, is on the border line between first and second magnitude. Almost due south of Sirius is Canopus, so situated that a line joining these two bright stars if extended southwards for an equal length will lead to the south celestial pole, a useful way of approximately locating this point when the Southern Cross is either not available or too low in the sky. Returning to Orion, it will be noticed that there is a third magnitude star just to the north west of Rigel (Beta Orionis). This star does not belong to Orion but is Beta Eridani which marks the beginning of the long river that winds its way from here right across the southern sky to Achernar in the South Polar Cap. Once more starting from Orion, a line from Rigel through Betelgeuse leads to the constellation of Gemini, the Heavenly Twins, of which the most prominent stars are the second magnitude Castor (Alpha) and the first magnitude Pollux (Beta). Two lines of stars stretching out south-westwards from Castor and Pollux indicate where the Twins lie side by side, their feet being represented by the line of stars formed by Zeta, Gamma, Mu, and Eta Geminorum. A line from Bellatrix through Betelgeuse if prolonged leads to a pair of stars not unlike Castor and Pollux except that the distance between them is slightly less and their difference in magnitude rather more marked. These are Alpha and Beta Canis Minoris which the Arabs sometimes called the Short Cubit in contrast to the Long Cubit formed by Castor and Pollux. Alpha Canis Minoris is of the first magnitude and is called Procyon, the Announcer, because in northern latitudes its rising presages that of Sirius.

Directly to the north of Orion and, in the northern hemisphere, high in the sky is Capella which is closely accompanied by three fainter stars, Epsilon, Zeta and Eta Aurigae, which are known as the Kids. Capella is the brightest star in the constellation of Auriga, the Charioteer, in which the principal figure is the large pentagon formed by Alpha (Capella), Beta, Theta, and Iota Aurigae and Beta Tauri. This latter star marks the tip of the northern horn of the Bull; the tip of the southern horn is Zeta Tauri, close to which is Messier 1, the Crab Nebula (Plate 32*b*). This is the remains of a super-nova, a star that blew itself to pieces on 4 July A.D. 1054 and is now a powerful radio source and the location of a pulsar whose radiation has been observed to vary with the extremely short period of a fraction of a second not only in the radio region but, in this case, in the optical as well.

May evenings Figure 1.6 is a key to some of the constellations that are visible at about 12 hrs sidereal time, a part of the sky which in the northern hemisphere is dominated by the Plough. A line through the Pointers in the direction away from the pole leads to the constellation of Leo, the Lion. This will be recognized by the six stars which form the Sickle that is the forepart of the Lion, and the three stars forming a right-angled triangle that marks its rear quarters. The first magnitude star at the base of the Sickle is Alpha Leonis or Regulus, while the second magnitude star at the eastern tip of the triangle is the tail star, Denebola, or Beta Leonis. Counting from Aries, Leo is the fifth Zodiacal constellation; the fourth one, Cancer, the Crab, which lies between Leo and Gemini, is not very bright and its most interesting

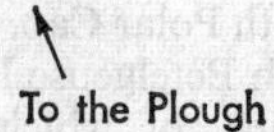

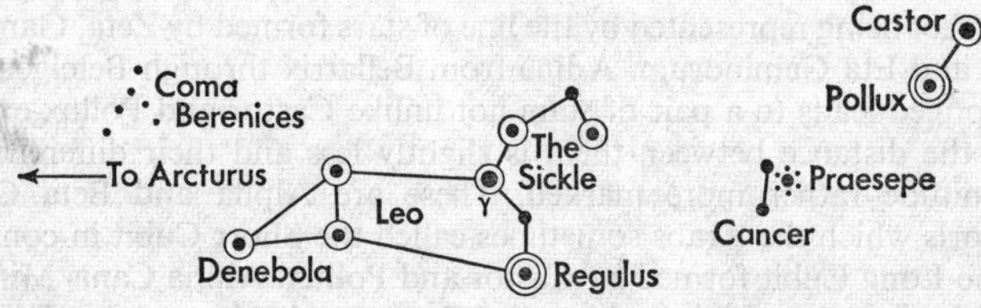

Figure 1.6 The stars visible during May evenings

object lies midway between Pollux and Regulus. This is Epsilon Cancri, better known as Messier 44, the open cluster Praesepe, which is also known as the Beehive.

If the curve of the handle of the Plough is extended for about 30° it leads to a bright yellowish-red first magnitude star. This is Alpha Boötis or Arcturus. To the south, and forming a large equilateral triangle with Arcturus and Denebola, is another first magnitude star. This is Spica, the brightest star in the sixth Zodiacal constellation of Virgo, the Virgin. To the south-west of Spica is the small constellation of Corvus, the Crow, whose four principal stars, Beta, Delta, Gamma, and Epsilon Corvi, form a compact, relatively conspicuous quadrilateral. Some 40° south of Spica are the numerous bright stars of Centaurus and Lupus marking out the northern boundary of the Milky Way in that part of the sky. A long winding constellation of which the head is 15° south of Praesepe and the tail 20° south-east of Spica is Hydra, the Water Snake, whose modern boundaries make it the constellation with the largest area of all. In its tail and immediately south of Spica is R Hydrae, a crimson red, long period variable star which ranges in magnitude from about 3.6 to 11 in a period of about 387 days.

Returning to the northern sky it will be noticed that the last five stars of the Plough, Gamma to Eta Ursae Majoris, lie approximately on a circular arc, and that the centre of the circle of which this arc forms a part is marked by a fairly isolated third magnitude star. This is Alpha Canum Venaticorum, or Cor Caroli, being so named by Halley when Astronomer Royal because it was said to have been especially bright at the time of the Restoration of King Charles II. Between it and Denebola is the constellation of Coma Berenices made up of faint stars many of which belong to one of the nearest open star clusters. Telescopically this region is notable for the large number of extragalactic nebulae it contains.

August evenings Figure 1.7 provides a key to some of the stars that can be seen at about 18 hrs sidereal time when, in the northern hemisphere, Vega is high in the sky. In the southern hemisphere, the outstanding constellation is Scorpio which with the magnificent curl of its tail is so like the creature for which it is named that it is easy to recognize the one from the other. The heart of the Scorpion, and the brightest star in it, is Alpha Scorpii or Antares, a red first magnitude star which is flanked by Sigma and Tau Scorpii in much the same way that Altair is by its two companions. Antares is so named because of its resemblance to the planet Mars, the God of War, for whom the Greek name is Ares. Scorpio is the eighth Zodiacal constellation, the seventh, Libra, being between it and Virgo. Libra, the Scales, is supposed to have been so named when the September equinox, now in Virgo, was in it. It is a constellation that would more naturally form the claws of the Scorpion. The other Zodiacal constellations that follow Scorpio are Sagittarius, Capricornus and Aquarius. Sagittarius, like Scorpio, contains many bright blue stars and it is in these two constellations that the Milky Way is at its broadest and brightest. As will be seen in Chapter 9, the direction to the centre of the whole Milky Way system is in Sagittarius.

Returning once more to the sky as seen from the northern hemisphere, it will be seen that Arcturus, now in the western part of the sky, is at the base of a big Y of which the arms are formed by Gamma and Epsilon Boötis and Alpha Coronae Borealis. This latter is the brightest star in the regular circular arc of stars that make up the Northern Crown. Between it and Vega lies the large and not very conspicuous constellation of Hercules in which, between Eta and Zeta, is Messier 13, the brightest globular cluster visible in the northern hemisphere. To the south of Corona Borealis is the head of Serpens, the Serpent that is being carried by Ophiuchus. The tail is in an isolated piece of the constellation on the other side of Ophiuchus. Ophiuchus itself extends over the ecliptic and ought really to be included in the Zodiacal constella-

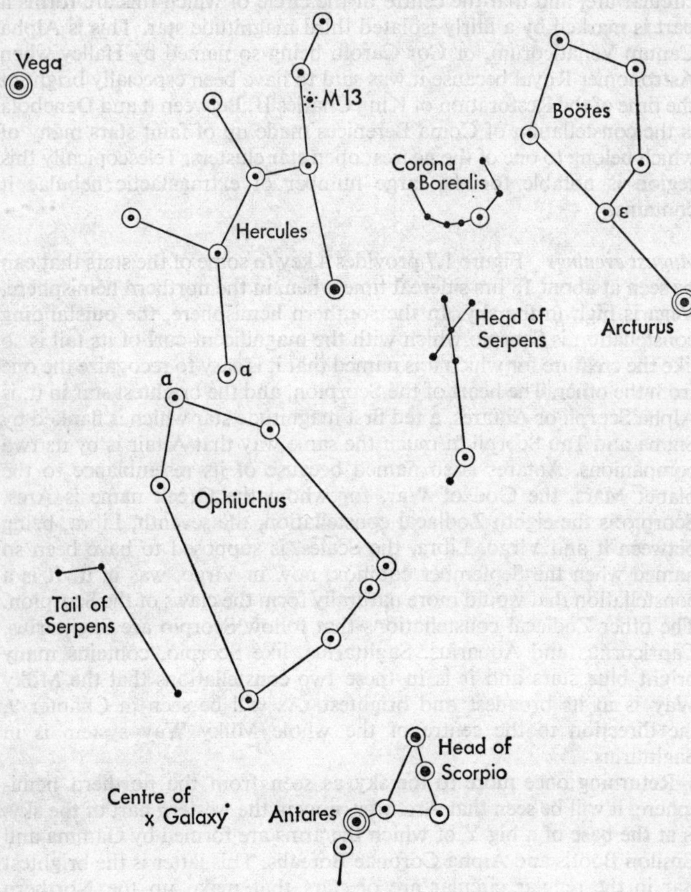

Figure 1.7 The stars visible during August evenings

tions but, by long tradition, these are confined to the twelve that can be remembered by the little jingle:

The Ram, the Bull, the Heavenly Twins,
And next the Crab, the Lion shines,
The Virgin and the Scales,
The Scorpion, Archer, and the Goat,
The man who holds the watering pot
And Fish with glittering tails.

Finally, attention must be drawn to those objects that appear in the sky and which may be mistaken for stars. These include the five bright planets, Mercury, Venus, Mars, Jupiter, and Saturn, whose general appearance and apparent motions are described in Chapter 5. There are also the brighter artificial satellites whose numbers are constantly increasing. The nearer ones move so quickly that they are easily detectable as such, but the more distant ones have to be watched carefully for some minutes before their nature becomes apparent. Other infrequent but sometimes quite spectacular phenomena such as those provided by comets and meteors are described in later chapters.

It is hoped that the foregoing will be sufficient to serve as an introduction to the night sky and some of the fascinating objects it contains. Those who wish to obtain a deeper knowledge of the constellations will need more elaborate star charts than it is possible to give in a book of this size. The best small star atlas is undoubtedly that prepared originally by A. P. Norton and recently reissued with an enlarged introduction by Patrick Moore and others. More elaborate, but still quite practical, is A. Becvar's *Atlas Coeli 1950.0* published in Czechoslovakia. A comprehensive guide to the sky for the naked eye astronomer is provided by D. H. Menzel's *A Field Guide to the Stars and Planets*, while owners of small telescopes will probably find E. J. Hartung's *Astronomical Objects for Southern Telescopes* a useful companion. The title is somewhat misleading for, though written in the southern hemisphere, it does cover both hemispheres. The author is a former professor of chemistry in the University of Melbourne and this book enshrines his own experiences as an amateur astronomer. For those who wish to pursue the rather involved history of constellation and star names, the best book is the scholarly, but rather heavy, *Star Names and Their Meanings* by R. H. Allen, originally published in 1899.

tions but, by long tradition, they are confined to the twelve that can be remembered by the little jingle:

The Ram, the Bull, the Heavenly Twins,
And next the Crab the Lion shines,
The Virgin and the Scales;
The Scorpion, Archer, and the Goat,
The man who holds the watering pot,
And Fish with glittering tails.

Finally, attention must be drawn to those objects that appear in the sky and which may be mistaken for stars. These include the five bright planets, Mercury, Venus, Mars, Jupiter, and Saturn, whose general appearance and apparent motions are described in Chapter 5. There are also the brighter artificial satellites, whose numbers are constantly increasing. The nearer ones move so quickly that they are easily detectable as such, but the more distant ones have to be watched carefully for some minutes before their nature becomes apparent. Other infrequent but sometimes quite spectacular phenomena such as those provided by comets and meteors are described in later chapters.

It is hoped that the foregoing will be sufficient to serve as an introduction to the night sky and some of the fascinating objects it contains. Those who wish to obtain a deeper knowledge of the constellations will need more elaborate star charts than it is possible to give in a book of this size. The best small star atlas is undoubtedly that prepared originally by A. P. Norton and recently reissued with an enlarged introduction by Patrick Moore and others. More elaborate, but still quite practical, is A. Becvar's *Atlas Coeli 1950.0* published in Czechoslovakia. A comprehensive guide to the sky for the naked eye astronomer is provided by D. H. Menzel's *A Field Guide to the Stars and Planets*, while owners of small telescopes will probably find E. J. Hartung's *Astronomical Objects for Southern Telescopes* a useful companion. The title is somewhat misleading for, though written in the southern hemisphere, it does cover both hemispheres. The author is a former professor of chemistry in the University of Melbourne and this book embodies his own experiences as an amateur astronomer. For those who wish to pursue the rather involved history of constellation and star names the best book is the scholarly, but rather heavy, *Star Names and Their Meanings* by R. H. Allen, originally published in 1899.

Star charts

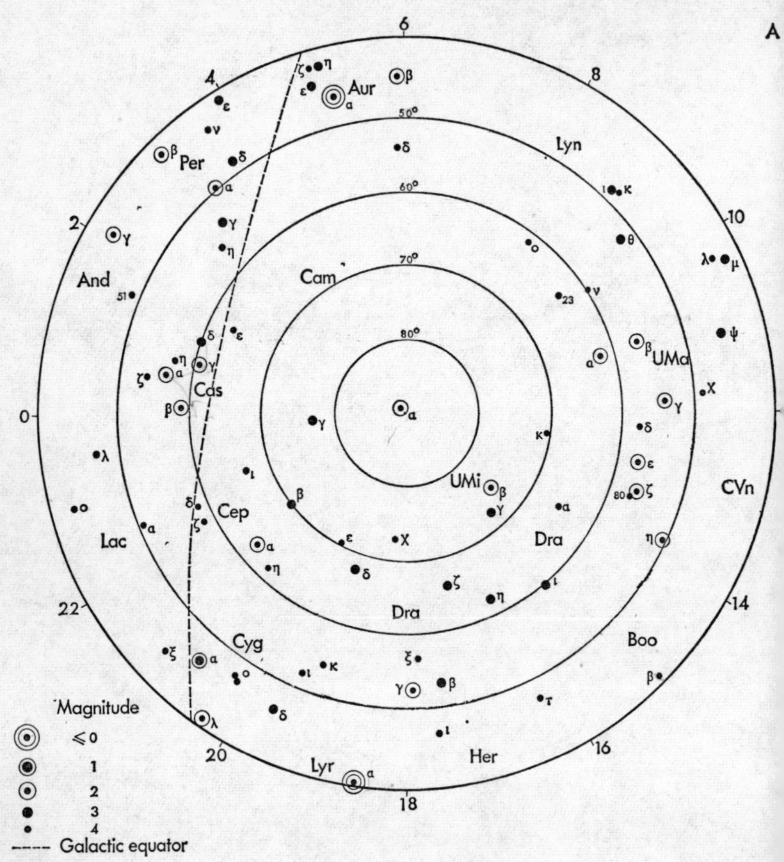

A The north polar cap

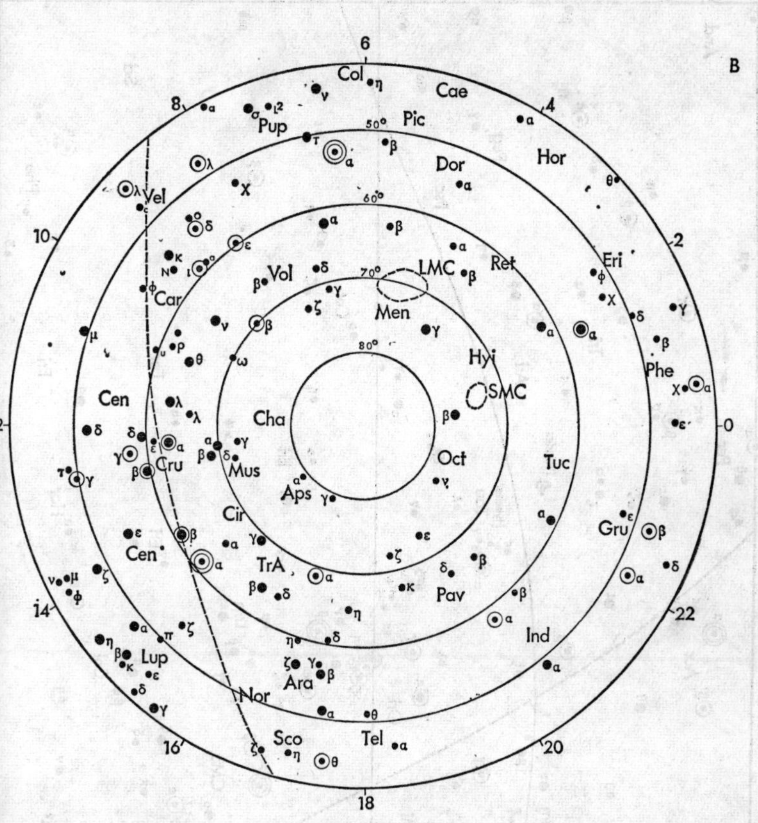

B The south polar cap

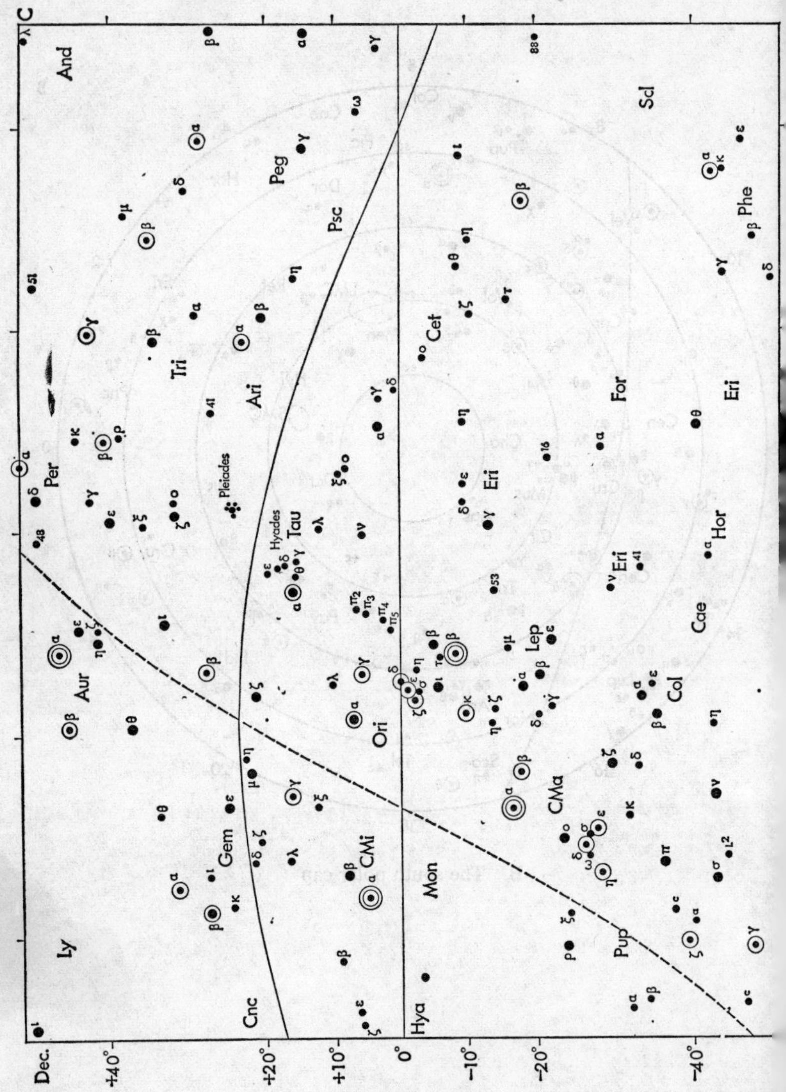

C The equatorial band 0 to 8 hours R.A.

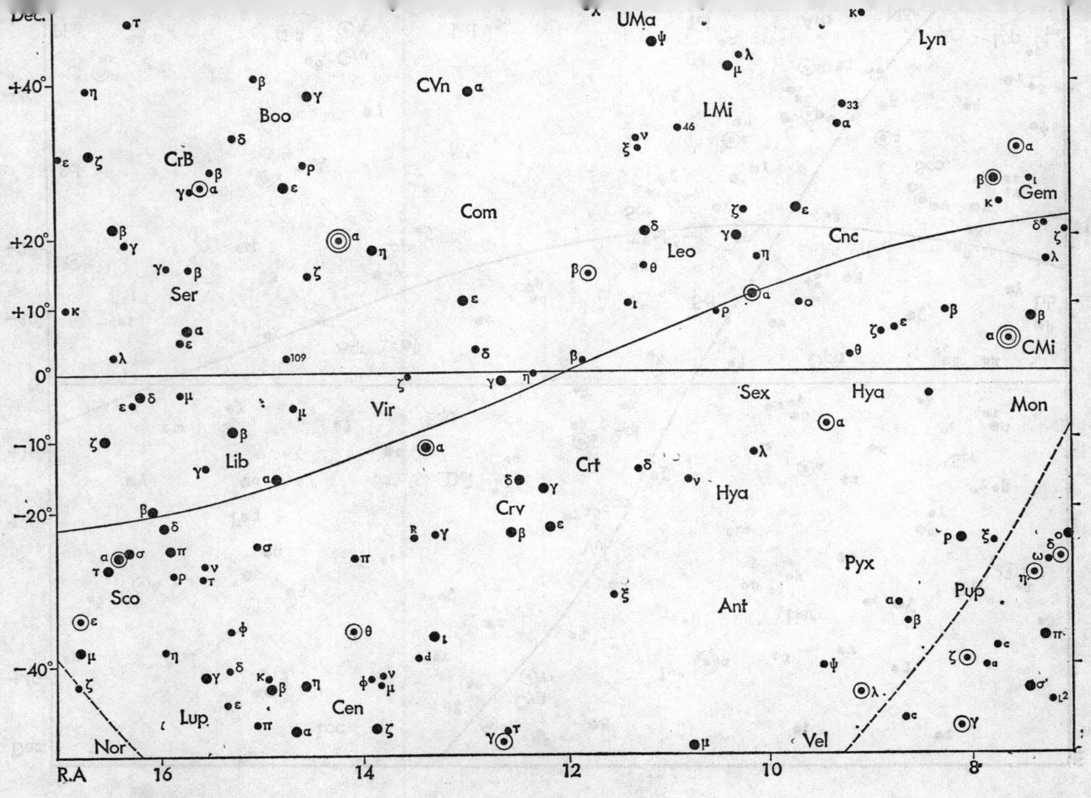

D The equatorial band 8 to 16 hours R.A.

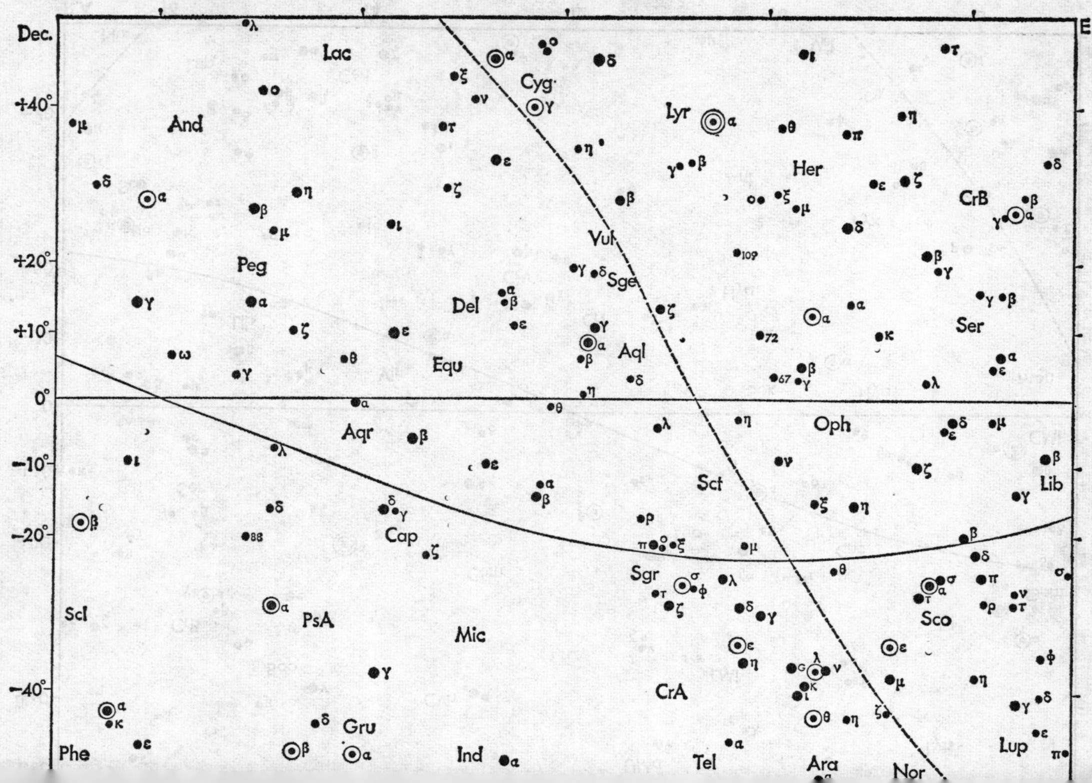

E The equatorial band 16 to 24 hours R.A.

Chapter Two

The growth of astronomy

M. W. Ovenden

Prehistoric beginnings Astronomy can justly claim to be the oldest of the sciences, for we can trace its origins back to before recorded history. Ten thousand years or more ago, Man began to change from a nomadic hunter following the herds of animals upon which he preyed, to a sower of seeds and a reaper of harvests. He noted the pattern of the stars, and came to recognize familiar groups. He noticed, too, how the Sun, while rising and setting each day, moved higher in the sky during the summer, and how it remained low in the sky during winter. He thus came to rely upon the Sun and the stars to tell him when to sow and when to reap.

The directions on the horizon of the rising and setting Sun change throughout the year. At the equinoxes (about 21 March and 22 September) the Sun sets due west. During the summer, the setting point is north of west, being furthest north at the summer solstice (about 21 June). In the winter, it is south of west, being furthest south at the winter solstice (about 22 December). To measure accurately the exact times when, for example, the Sun set furthest north, distant mountains could be used, behind which the setting of the Sun could be observed. Early Man left behind large standing stones (often 10 or 12 feet high) to mark the places where these observations could be made; sometimes a line of stones would be set up to mark the direction of the setting Sun at midwinter or midsummer.

It is probable that such megalithic monuments as Stonehenge (the earliest form of which dates back to about 2000 B.C.) had some such astronomical purpose. With isolated sites of a simple nature, it is difficult to be sure of the significance of an approximate astronomical orientation. But scattered over Great Britain and Europe there are many sites of standing stones, which reveal that their builders had a surprising knowledge of geometry, and if these sites are carefully surveyed, their orientations can be examined statistically. This has been done for a large number of sites in the north and west of Scotland, as for

Callanish, Isle of Lewis (Plate 1), and it is quite beyond doubt that a great many of these standing stones are orientated towards the setting-points of the midwinter and midsummer Sun. Indeed, it is possible to estimate when these stones were set up because the positions of the setting-points of the Sun change slightly over long periods, at a rate that can be calculated theoretically from the law of gravitation. These Scottish sites date back to about 2000 B.C.

Some of the standing stones indicate the rising points of bright stars. These can also be used to measure the passage of the year. For, although the direction of setting or rising of a bright star does not change, it is possible to observe the morning on which, for example, a given bright star can first be seen rising before the Sun (the Sun appears to move eastwards against the background of the stars, so that on the previous morning the star would rise when the light of the Sun was already too bright for the star to be observed). These 'heliacal risings' were the basis of the calendars used, for example, by the ancient Egyptians.

We can find evidence of prehistoric astronomy not only from the physical artefacts left behind by the early astronomers, but also in the astronomical tradition that we have inherited from the past. Traditionally, the sky was supposed to be divided up into areas, or constellations, with mythological figures associated with each area (Plate 2–3). At first sight, these constellations seem to be little more than the idle fancies of a primitive people. Yet a closer look shows that the constellations are arranged in some sort of pattern symmetrical about a single point in the sky. This point proves to be the position of the north pole of the sky about 2600 B.C. (the position of the pole moves because the Earth's axis of rotation changes its direction in space; this *precession* is explained in Chapter 3). An examination of the earliest accounts of the constellations (written down about 500 B.C.) shows that the astronomical traditions associated with the constellation figures were developed in the middle of the third millenium B.C. These traditions are closely associated with navigation on the sea, and it is reasonable to suppose that the division of the sky into the constellations as we know them was made as an aid to navigation.

The earliest developments of astronomy, then, were for practical purposes—time-keeping and navigation. But these practical activities also came to have associated with them an aura of myth and primitive religion. In the earliest Babylonian legends, we find the creation of the Universe, and its development, described in terms that seem strange to us. The Universe is supposed to have begun as a watery chaos, with Earth (i.e. matter) being born of the merging of the sweet waters with the bitter waters. A quasi-human personality was attributed to each and

Plate 1 An early astronomical observatory: the Standing Stones at Callanish, Isle of Lewis, Scotland

Plate 2–3 A sheet from Bode's *Uranographia* published in 1801

Such figures as Harpa Georgii are no longer regarded as constellations

Plate 4 U.S. astronaut Ed Aldrin on the lunar surface, 20 July 1969

the development of the Universe from this chaotic beginning is described in terms of the clash of personal powers.

At first sight, these myths seem to have no rational basis. But again a closer look shows that they have at least one feature in common with many later, truly scientific, theories. This is the element of analogy. When a physicist describes the behaviour of a gas in terms of the motions and collisions of a large number of atoms, each behaving like a small, elastic billiard ball, he is drawing an analogy between the behaviour of a gas and the behaviour of familiar, everyday objects. Similarly our early ancestors in the valleys of the great rivers attempted to understand the Universe by analogy with their everyday experiences —experiences as human beings in a society that indeed evolved from the clash of personal powers, in a land whose rivers could be seen, year after year, to be silting up at their estuaries.

The trouble with these early mythological cosmologies was that they were useless for the purpose of predicting how the Universe would behave in future. One feature of the Universe that cried out for 'prediction' was the motion of the planets, or 'wanderers', the bright luminaries that, while partaking of the daily rotation of the celestial sphere, seemed to move (often in complicated looped paths) against the background of the stars (early Man included the Sun and Moon in the term 'planets'). Tables of predictions of the positions of the Moon and planets have been found on clay tablets from Mesopotamia, in the characteristic cuneiform script of the Sumerian-Babylonian peoples. While these tablets date back only to a few centuries before Christ, the extreme accuracy of prediction that the authors of these tables could attain testifies to many centuries of careful observation. These tablets have been deciphered, and the methods of their construction elucidated (even to the extent of being able to detect errors on the part of the original scribes). The interesting thing is that these tables were calculated using a complicated rule-of-thumb arithmetic, refined to a remarkable degree by a long process of trial and error, and did not depend at all upon any theory of *why* the planets should move as they do. Thus it was possible for these accurate predictions to be made by men who held the most mythological of cosmological views.

Greek astronomy The first attempts to combine a quantitative description of the behaviour of the Universe with a rational cosmology seem to have been made by the Greeks. During the seventh century B.C. Greek science emerged in Asia Minor, in close contact with the Sumerian-Babylonian civilization (which had survived as a culture many conquests by alien peoples, including the Persians—at that time the dominant power). The founder of the Ionian school was Thales of Miletus (624–545 B.C.). Our knowledge of these early philosophers is entirely second- or third-hand, and much that has been attributed to Thales is almost certainly of Babylonian origin. For example, Thales acquired great fame for the prediction of an eclipse of the Sun; yet, in so far as he could have made such a prediction, it would have been by Babylonian methods. But the Ionian philosophers brought to science an invaluable psychological factor—the belief that Man by his own efforts could aspire to understand the cosmos. This sturdy humanism was to be the mainspring of Greek science for many centuries.

As relations between Greece and Persia became strained (to culminate in the Graeco-Persian wars) the centre of Greek science moved to southern Italy. There, in 532 B.C., the philosopher, mathematician and astronomer Pythagoras founded his school. Pythagoras was born on the island of Samos, in Ionia, and the influence of Babylonian thought on his ideas is clear. Babylonian science was a science of secrecy—a priestly science, concerned with the ritual of the temple. Pythagoras himself seems to have held the view that knowledge was power, and his followers undertook a pledge of secrecy, leaving nothing in writing. For this reason, our knowledge of the Pythagoreans is fragmentary, depending upon later accounts by writers not always sympathetic to their viewpoint. Nevertheless, if attention is concentrated on those features of the Universe that would have been most obvious to them, it is possible to appreciate the Pythagoreans' ideas as rational pictures of the Universe.

Pythagoras was fascinated by the relationship between the tones emitted by a plucked string and its length. He conceived that at the root of the phenomena of the observed world lay the properties of numbers. To him, astronomy, music, geometry and arithmetic were all different aspects of the same fundamental relationships. And so, the work of the Pythagoreans was largely the search for underlying harmonies among the apparently irregular phenomena of everyday experience. Not unnaturally, the complicated motions of the planets early attracted their attention as being in need of explanation in terms of regular, harmonic behaviour. Pythagoras himself seems to have been the first to maintain that the Earth was a sphere, together with the Sun, Moon and other planets. In the middle of the fifth century B.C., a later Pythagorean (known as Philolaos) had a brilliant flash of insight. He realized that the apparent motion of the Sun was caused by a combination of the Sun's motion, and the motion of the observer on the Earth. But, knowing nothing about the relative size of the Earth and the distances of the planets, he thought, not of an Earth rotating on its axis, but of an Earth moving around a central point.

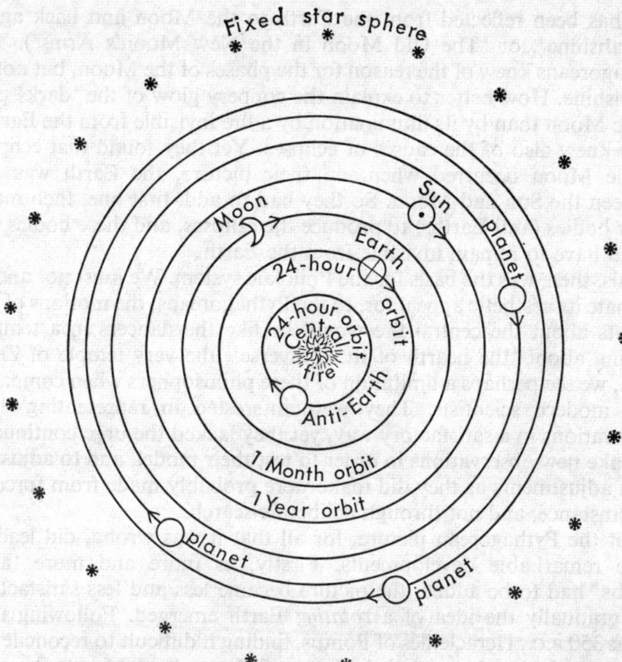

Figure 2.1 The cosmological system of Philolaos

The Philolaic system is shown, in outline, in Figure 2.1. It is drawn as a plane figure, although the system must have had the orbit of the Earth inclined to that of the Sun and planets. The Earth moved in a period of 24 hours, about the central fire. The apparent rotation of the star sphere was regarded as being a reflection of the motion of the Earth, and the more complicated motions of the Sun and planets as combinations of their own circular motions with that of the Earth. Between the Earth and the central fire was an anti-Earth, moving with a period of 24 hours, and always invisible from the inhabited part of the Earth, which is turned away from the central fire.

Why the central fire? If one looks at the Moon when it is a few days old, one will see the 'dark' part of the Moon illuminated by sunlight that has been reflected from the Earth to the Moon and back again ('Earthshine', or 'The Old Moon in the New Moon's Arms'). The Pythagoreans knew of the reason for the phases of the Moon, but not of Earthshine. How better to explain the coppery glow of the 'dark' part of the Moon than by its illumination by a fire invisible from the Earth? They knew also of the causes of eclipses. Yet they found that eclipses of the Moon occurred when, on their picture, the Earth was not between the Sun and Moon. So they had to add, first one, then many other bodies (anti-Earths) to produce the eclipses, and these bodies too would have to remain invisible from the Earth.

This, then, was the basis for the Philolaic system. We must not underestimate its aesthetic appeal for, to the Pythagoreans, the motions of the planets about the central fire would be like the dancers in a temple, moving about 'the hearth of the Universe', the very temple of Zeus. Here, we see perhaps a limitation of these philosophers when compared with modern scientists. They were interested in representing their observations in a satisfactory way, yet they lacked the urge continually to make new observations in order to test their model, and to adjust it. Such adjustments as they did make were probably made from force of circumstance, and not through deliberate search.

Yet the Pythagorean picture, for all that it was wrong, did lead to some remarkable developments. Firstly, as more and more 'anti-Earths' had to be added, the picture became less and less satisfactory and gradually the idea of a *rotating* Earth emerged. Following this, about 350 B.C., Heracleides of Pontus, finding it difficult to reconcile the picture with the changing brightness of Venus (and Mercury), made these planets move in circles about the Sun, while the Sun was still conceived as moving about the Earth. It is even possible that Heracleides made *all* the planets move in circles about the Sun, the Sun moving around the Earth. This is the picture put forward nineteen centuries later by Tycho Brahe, and known as the Tychonic system. Finally, about 280 B.C., Aristarchos of Samos proposed the scheme shown in Figure 2.2. In this the planets *and the Earth* moved about the Sun in circles, the apparent motion of a planet being a combination of its own motion and that of the Earth. This, essentially, was the picture put forward in the middle of the sixteenth century A.D. by Copernicus. The early philosophers had started on the right track.

Why was the system of Aristarchos not accepted? It failed precisely as, eighteen centuries later, the Copernican system appeared to fail, for it seemed to conflict with everyday experience. If the Earth is rotating, why are we not flung off it? If the Earth moves around the Sun, why are we not left behind? And, most important of all, if the Earth moves, then

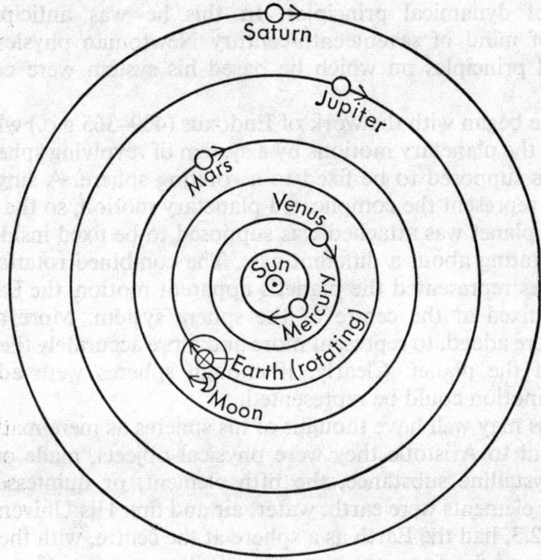

Figure 2.2 The cosmological system of Aristarchos

the nearby stars should appear to show an apparent motion against the background of more distant stars (a 'parallax effect'). With modern instruments we can measure the actual parallaxes of the nearer stars, but these are far too small to be detected by the naked eye. Aristarchos' contemporaries were familiar with the idea that the stars must be very remote compared with the size of the Earth, since the horizon seems to divide the star sphere exactly in two. But to suppose that the stars were very remote compared with the size of the Earth's *orbit* was just too big a jump for their imagination.

In the face of these objections, Aristarchos' system could not compete with the grand and in many ways compelling cosmology of Aristotle. The world-pictures hitherto considered are only *descriptions* of the Universe; they contain no element of *explanation*. In this respect, they are similar to the Babylonian arithmetic, although manipulating geometrical rather than arithmetical concepts. Aristotle (384–322 B.C.) conceived the grand idea of a *dynamical* model of the Universe, in which the motions of the Sun, Moon planets and stars were consequences of dynamical principles. In this he was anticipating the attitude of mind of seventeenth-century Newtonian physics, but the dynamical principles on which he based his system were completely different.

Aristotle began with the work of Eudoxus (409–365 B.C.) who sought to explain the planetary motions by a system of revolving spheres. Each planet was supposed to be fixed to a rotating sphere. A single sphere could not represent the complicated planetary motion, so the sphere to which the planet was attached was supposed to be fixed inside another sphere, rotating about a different axis. The combined rotations of the two spheres represented the planet's apparent motion, the Earth being supposed fixed at the centre of the sphere system. More and more spheres were added, to represent more and more accurately the observed motion of the planet. Clearly, if enough spheres were added, any observed motion could be represented.

Eudoxus may well have thought of his spheres as mere mathematical devices, but to Aristotle they were physical objects, made of a transparent crystalline substance, the fifth element, or quintessence. The other four elements were earth, water, air and fire. His Universe, shown in Figure 2.3, had the Earth as a sphere at the centre, with the elements water, air and fire forming concentric shells around it. If any of these elements were disturbed from their natural places, they returned to them. A clod of Earth that is thrown up falls to the ground; water that gets into the air falls back as rain; and the flames of a fire seem to move upwards. The celestial objects did not fall down; instead, they moved eternally in circles, or combinations of circular motion. While matter beneath the sphere of the Moon was subject to decay, celestial matter was everlasting and unchanging.

Such a brief summary cannot do justice to a picture of the Universe that served to represent many features of everyday experience, on the basis of dynamical principles in a partially quantitative way. Aristotelian cosmology had a profound influence on medieval Europe, where it became elevated to something approaching theological dogma, in a spirit entirely alien to that of Aristotle himself.

After the conquests of Alexander the Great, the centre of Greek science moved to Alexandria. Here worked Aristarchos, and Eratosthenes who, about the year 200 B.C., measured the size of the Earth. The greatest astronomer of antiquity, Hipparchos (190–120 B.C.), observed from the island of Rhodes, but may have visited Alexandria. He made an accurate star catalogue, and, by comparing his observations with earlier ones, found how the pole of the sky moves among the stars as a precession. Hipparchos was, in fact, the founder of systematic observa-

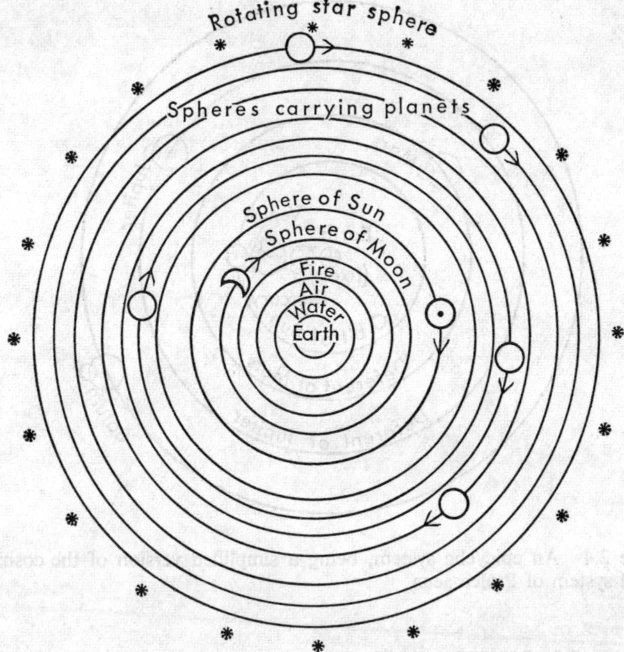

Figure 2.3 A simplified version of the world-picture of Aristotle

tional astronomy, in connection with which he also developed the necessary theory of the geometry of a sphere.

Naturally, he also turned his attention to the representation of the apparent motions of the planets. Some fifty years earlier, the mathematician Apollonius had suggested that, instead of using the clumsy Eudoxian spheres, the planetary motions could be represented by combinations of circular motions, either (i) a circular orbit with the Earth not quite at the centre (eccentric) or (ii) a small circular orbit, or epicycle, the centre of which moved in a large circular orbit (the deferent), which might be centred on the Earth, or eccentric. Hipparchos developed the use of these methods to represent the planetary motions tolerably accurately.

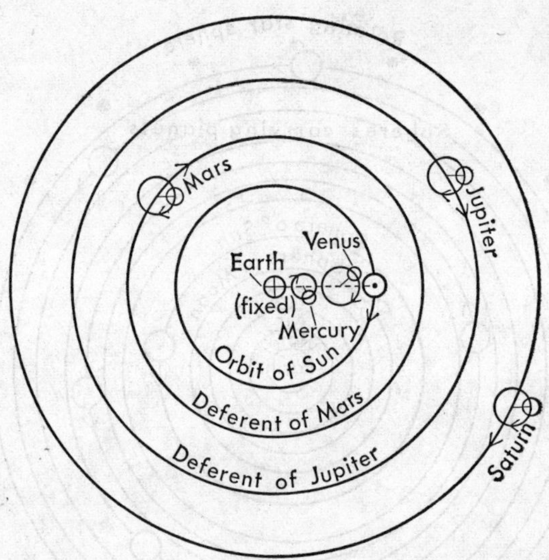

Figure 2.4 An epicyclic system, being a simplified version of the cosmological system of Ptolemaeus

Figure 2.4 shows the simplest possible epicyclic theory, with one epicycle for each planet. Such a picture is often called 'The Ptolemaic System', after the last of the Alexandrian astronomers, Claudius Ptolemaeus (*c.* A.D. 140). Actually, the Ptolemaic System was vastly more complicated, having numerous eccentrics and epicycles. It was based on Hipparchos' work, and then modified to take into account later observations. In fact, the epicyclic theory is capable of representing any observed motion whatsoever, provided enough epicycles are used. Herein lies its strength, and its weakness; as a description of the planetary motions, it is adequate, even efficient—but as a *theory* it is useless.

The later Alexandrians seemed not to seek for a theory, for Greek science had lost its essential spark. There are doubtless many reasons, social and political, for this change, but the nature of the Aristotelian cosmology was a contributing factor. If celestial objects are different in kind from terrestrial ones, what hope can there be for understanding the Universe on the basis of terrestrial experience? While Aristotle may not have subscribed to this view, there is no doubt that, in his successors, the motive for a scientific formulation was to 'save the phenomena' (i.e. represent observations accurately), rather than to understand them.

The Copernican awakening The works of the Greek scientists, especially of Aristotle and Ptolemy, were inherited by the Arabs. These great craftsmen improved the art of astronomical observation by developing a sighting instrument, described by Ptolemy, into the medieval astrolabe, at its best an instrument of high precision. Their theoretical work was less inspired, being largely confined to adding more and more epicycles to Ptolemy's picture to represent their own refined observations. Knowledge of the great cosmologists of the past came to the awakening scientific consciousness of medieval Europe from the Arabs through their outposts in Spain. With the coming of printing, there was a revival in the study of the classics, and the Greek scientists were read again in their own language, and not only in poor translations from the Arabic.

One of the first astronomical fruits of this new interest in science was the resurrection by Nicholas Copernicus (originally Koppernigk) (1473–1543) of the Sun-centred picture of the planetary system given by Aristarchos of Samos. This simple system could not represent the accurate observations then available; to improve it, Copernicus added eccentrics and epicycles exactly as in the Ptolemaic theory. Indeed, the only part of the Copernican system that still survives is the heliocentric concept due to Aristarchos. The Copernican system met the same objections as its predecessor, and was no more able to give any answer. While it required fewer epicycles, it was not in principle essentially simpler than the Ptolemaic, and no better at representing the observations. Indeed, the two theories, so far as predicting planetary positions is concerned, are mathematically identical. To the astronomer, the Sun-centred system had the advantage that observation fixed the relative distances of the planets, while on the Ptolemaic theory the orbits could be any size provided that the sizes of the epicycles were suitably adjusted. This was a small gain for having to contradict common-sense experiences, as well as having to envisage the stars almost infinitely remote compared with the Earth's orbit. Small wonder then that the Copernican theory was not immediately accepted.

It is interesting to note that the science of the Renaissance began by first recapitulating the philosophy of the ancients. So it was also with Johannes Kepler (1571–1630), who was an assistant to the last great pre-telescopic observer, Tycho Brahe (1546–1601). Tycho developed accurate sighting instruments, and increased the accuracy of the observations of the positions of the stars and especially the planets by a factor of five or more, as compared with his predecessors. Two fields of observation by Tycho had great influence on medieval thought. He showed that the 'new star' of 1572 had no measurable parallax, and therefore belonged to the realm of the fixed stars; the celestial regions were *not*, therefore, unchanging. He also showed that the comets, hitherto thought to be fiery emanations of the Earth's atmosphere, were not only beyond the atmosphere, but were moving through interplanetary space. Where now were the quintessential spheres? Such were the observations that toppled the edifice of Aristotelian cosmology! Yet Tycho himself, because he was unable to measure any stellar parallax, never accepted the Copernican system. He proposed that the planets moved around the Sun, which moved in an eccentric circle about the Earth (a development of the theory of Heracleides of Pontus).

Kepler, on the other hand, had accepted the Copernican theory, for reasons that can best be described as mystical. Kepler had a reverence for the Sun, and believed that the centre of the system was the only fit place for such a luminary. He was strongly influenced by Pythagorean thought, and began his researches on the structure of the solar system with a question that seems strange to modern minds: why are there only six planets? Kepler thought that he had found the answer in pure geometry. A regular solid is one having all its faces similar regular polygons (e.g. a regular tetrahedron has four faces, each an equilateral triangle). Now it is possible to construct five types of regular solid, and five only. So Kepler supposed that the orbits of the planets lay on spheres. The sphere of Mercury lay inside an octahedron, touching its faces. The same octahedron fitted inside the sphere of the orbit of Venus, which touched the inside faces of an icosahedron, and so on. Using each regular solid once, there was room for only six planets, and these planets would have definite relationships between their distances. Encouraged by early approximate successes with this method, Kepler turned to the accurate observations of Tycho Brahe to improve his model. He found that he had to take his spheres as having thickness, as the planets' distances from the Sun are not constant.

Finding it increasingly difficult to make his model work, Kepler decided to investigate the nature of the planetary orbits by working directly from the observations, instead of thinking of a possible shape and seeing if it worked. Starting with observations of the planet Mars, he was able by ingenious arguments to show that the orbits of the Earth and Mars about the Sun are ellipses, with the Sun at one focus, and he later showed the same to be true of the other planets. He also established the law governing the rate of movement of a planet in its elliptical orbit.

Finally, after an incredible amount of intricate calculation, his search for 'harmony' in the Universe was rewarded by his harmonic law, which relates the distances of the planets from the Sun to their periods about it, a consummation that would have gladdened the heart of Pythagoras.

The Newtonian contribution Kepler's laws mark, in a sense, the birth of modern science, for in Kepler's picture of the solar system we have, essentially, the picture that we hold today. More significantly, it was the attempt to understand Kepler's laws as a consequence of laws of dynamics that later led Newton (1642–1727) to formulate his famous law of gravitation, and to develop the application of mathematics to scientific investigation, a development upon which the whole of modern physical science depends.

In 1609 Galileo used the first astronomical telescope. By modern standards it was small and crude. But the very first observations had a most important effect. For the telescope showed that the planet Venus passes through a complete set of phases, like the Moon, from thin crescent to full disk. Venus, therefore, shines by reflecting the light of the Sun. Yet, on the Ptolemaic theory, it could never be seen as more than a thin crescent—so this theory could no longer be held (the observations did not prove that the Sun was the centre of the planetary system, for on Tycho's picture 'full Venus' is also possible). The planets were seen as disks, with markings showing that they were rotating. If the planets rotate, why not the Earth? Galileo also saw the brighter moons of Jupiter, which accompanied the planet in its motion about the Sun, as though some force of attraction were being exerted by Jupiter on the satellites. Might not a similar force serve to keep the planets moving about the Sun?

Galileo also conducted experiments on the motions of bodies, which helped to pave the way for the great synthesis made by Newton in his laws of motion and theory of universal gravitation. In Aristotle's dynamics, a body could move only if a force continually acted upon it; in the absence of such a force, the body would come to a stop. This is the behaviour of a body moving against a resistance (for example, a body falling through a tube containing a sticky liquid). It is not surprising that Aristotle came to this conclusion, for in everyday life we usually meet objects moving against some resistance. To take a modern example—a car will stop, from friction on the road and air resistance, if a push is not continually provided by the engine. However, Newton realized that if all resisting forces could be removed a body would not stop, but would continue to move in a straight line with a constant speed. If a body does not move in this way, then a force must be acting on it. A stone whirled around at the end of a string is subjected to a force by the pull of the string, and similarly exerts a pull on the string, which can be felt by the hand holding the string. Should the string break, the stone will go off into space in a straight line.

If, then, we find a body moving in a curved path, but without any string, we must suppose that a force is acting upon it without the medium of a material connection. The planets moving around the Sun must be attracted to the Sun by an invisible force—the force of gravitation. Likewise, the planets must also attract the Sun. That the Sun moves much less than the planets is because the Sun is much more massive, and requires a greater force to move it. Newton generalized this into the law of universal gravitation—that any massive body attracts any other massive body by a force proportional to the product of their masses, and inversely proportional to the square of the distance between them.

Newton's achievement was not only to formulate such a concept—others of his contemporaries had very similar ideas—but also to develop the mathematical techniques necessary to put the ideas on to a precise basis, and to show that the selfsame law of gravitation that governed the falling of bodies at the Earth's surface could equally well explain precisely the motion of the Moon about the Earth, and the motions of planets about the Sun according to Kepler's laws. With Newton we have reached what is essentially modern science, a method of looking at the Universe that is essentially our own. For, with all the wide range of developments of modern physical science, we still use methods of mathematical analysis, and methods of thought itself, that stem directly from Newton.

Indeed, the history of astronomy throughout the eighteenth and most of the nineteenth century is almost entirely the tale of the application of Newtonian gravitation to an ever-widening sphere—to the motions of planets allowing for their mutual attractions in addition to the attraction of the Sun (a problem that is still by no means completely solved), to the motions of comets and of double stars. In the present century, it has been applied to the orbital motion of stars in the Galaxy and of artificial satellites about the Earth. Perhaps the greatest triumph of the theory of gravitation came with the discovery of the planet Neptune in 1846. Observations of the planet Uranus (discovered by chance by Herschel in 1781) showed that, even after allowing for the attractions of Jupiter and Saturn, the planet did not follow the path predicted by the theory of gravitation. The suggestion was made that Uranus was being perturbed by the attraction of an unknown planet further from the Sun.

Adams in England and Le Verrier in France independently calculated the position of the unknown planet, which was discovered by Galle close to the predicted position.

The telescopic era The telescope was gradually applied to instruments of precision for the measurement of the position of stars and planets. Already by the end of the seventeenth century, the opening up of the American continent had produced an urgent need for accurate astronomical data and accurate timekeepers to make sea navigation practicable. The provision of the appropriate data for navigation is still an important part of the work of national observatories. Throughout the eighteenth century, experience was gained in the working of lenses and mirrors, and in the accurate mounting of telescopes. But it was Friedrich Bessel (1784–1846), above all others, who developed methods of measuring positions to a fraction of a second of arc. He was therefore able, for the first time, to measure the parallax of a star directly and to establish the motion of the Earth about the Sun beyond any reasonable doubt.

In position-measuring instruments, the telescope is used mainly as an accurate pointer. The telescope produces enlarged images of planets and the Moon, but it is as a light-gatherer that the telescope is most important in astronomy. A star is so far away that, even through the largest telescope, its image is still effectively a point. But, because the telescope collects much more light than the eye, the star's image is much brighter. For example, the 200-inch telescope collects a million times as much light as the unaided eye. A telescope, therefore, enables us to observe much fainter stars than those visible to the naked eye.

The first astronomer to use the light-gathering power of a telescope systematically to investigate the Universe was Sir William Herschel (1738–1822). His main problem was to determine the distribution of the stars in space. At that time, no stellar distance had been measured directly but he realized that if two identical stars were at different distances, the further would appear the fainter, and the relative distances of the two stars could be calculated, assuming that the intensity of a source of light falls off as the square of its distance. Now Herschel appreciated that all the stars were not identical and that some might give out much more light than others, but he had sufficient statistical insight to know that if some average luminosity is assumed to apply to all stars, the average distance deduced will be correct even though the distance might be wrong in any individual case. The picture of the Universe built up in this way should be reasonably reliable since many hundreds of thousands of stars are visible through a telescope.

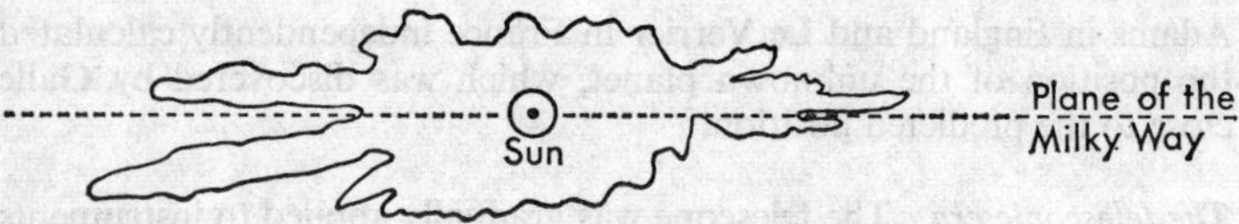

Figure 2.5 The Galaxy as conceived by Sir William Herschel
The diagram shows a cross-section perpendicular to the plane of the Milky Way

Herschel made a systematic count of the numbers of stars of different brightnesses in different areas of the sky, including the Milky Way (which even Galileo's crude telescope had shown to consist of large numbers of faint stars). This monumental task was extended into the southern sky by his son, Sir John Herschel (1792–1871). The picture built up by the Herschels was of a flattened system, the principal plane of the system being the plane of the Milky Way. The system was more or less circular in outline, parallel to the Milky Way, but it had a very irregular outline, for there were areas of the sky ('holes in the heavens', as William called them) where there were few faint stars. The Sun was in the main plane, more or less in the middle of the system.

The Herschels' system illustrated in Figure 2.5 is greatly different from the modern view of the structure of our Galaxy described by Dr Reddish in Chapter 9. The cause of this difference lies, not in the principle of the Herschels' method, which is quite sound, but in the fact that, between the stars, there is a widespread but irregular distribution of interstellar matter, which absorbs starlight, so that a star may appear faint, not because it is far away, but because there is a lot of interstellar matter between it and us. The 'holes in the heavens' are caused by particularly thick interstellar clouds, near us in space, hiding the light of the more distant stars.

A telescope sees faint stars because it collects more light. But a telescope could be made more efficient if the light that it does collect is observed with an instrument more sensitive than the human eye. The photographic plate is one such device because it is able to build up an image by long exposure. Photography has therefore played, and still plays, an important role in observational astronomy.

As early as 1840, daguerreotypes were taken of a solar eclipse, and of the Moon and Sun. By 1850, the first daguerreotypes of bright stars had been made. But the development of photography in astronomy had to wait for the coming of the dry plate. It was quickly realized that the blackness of the image of a star on a photographic negative could be used to measure the relative brightnesses of stars, and this became one of the standard methods of measuring stellar apparent magnitudes. The relative positions of stars in the sky can also be obtained accurately from the positions of their images on a photographic plate. The methods of photographic astrometry are still paramount where relative positions of stars are required, such as in the measurement of stellar parallax and proper motion.

As soon as the power of photography in astronomy was fully realized, the need for larger and larger telescopes became apparent. With these, our own Galaxy has been revealed as only one among many thousands of millions of similar systems. In view of this rapid expansion of our ideas of the size of the Universe, it is interesting to reflect that it was not until the 100-inch telescope was able to reveal individual variable stars in the Andromeda nebula that the extragalactic nature of the spiral nebulae was definitely established.

Astronomers have always been concerned with improving the efficiency of their light-detectors, so that the use of the photo-conductive cell for measuring stellar brightnesses was investigated soon after their discovery. In such a cell, the electrical resistance of a bar of metal (selenium) varies according to the amount of light falling on to it, so that the star's brightness is measured by the current passing through the bar under an applied voltage. The early forms of this cell were not sensitive enough to be of much use in astronomy where, even with large telescopes, the intensity of starlight is very small by laboratory standards. Following this pioneer work, photoelectric cells were investigated. In these, light falling upon a sensitive metal surface causes the ejection of charged particles (electrons), which give rise to an electric current. The difficulty at first was that the current was so small that it had to be amplified and spurious currents generated in the valves of the amplifier ('noise'), were usually larger than the signal to be measured. The general introduction of photoelectric methods into astronomy had to wait for the emergence, under the pressures of the technological requirements of the Second World War, of easily available noise-free, self-amplifying, photoelectric cells, called photomultiplier tubes. With photomultipliers, photoelectric photometry has come into its own, and, while photographic methods of measuring stellar brightness are still extensively used for programmes requiring large numbers of observations, photoelectric methods now provide the most accurate magnitudes for stars measured one at a time. At the present time, astronomers are interested in the possible use of photoelectric 'image tubes', which have the advantage of photoelectric accuracy and efficiency but can record many images simultaneously.

The growth of astrophysics But astronomy aims at more than merely recording the positions and brightnesses of the stars. It aims at understanding their physical natures. While Newtonian mechanics broke down the Aristotelian barrier between celestial and terrestrial objects as far as their movements were concerned, there still seemed a barrier to our understanding of their physical nature, because, unlike the chemist or physicist in the laboratory, an astronomer cannot experiment; he can only observe the objects that interest him. Early in the nineteenth century it was still possible for sensible people (e.g. the philosopher Auguste Comte) to believe that we should never be able to learn of what the stars are made.

Yet could not its light contain clues to the nature of a star? While a chemist may analyse an unknown substance by comparing its properties with those of known substances, could not an astronomer compare the nature of the light of a star with the light emitted by known elements and compounds in the laboratory? Newton had shown how the light of the Sun could be split into its component colours by a prism to form a rainbow-band or spectrum. Wollaston (1766–1828) and Fraunhofer (1787–1826) observed that there were certain colours missing in the Sun's spectrum which appeared, when the light was first passed through a slit before entering the prism, as dark lines in the coloured band. The spectra of incandescent solids in the laboratory do not show these dark lines. But the light of a gas, excited by heat or an electrical discharge, is concentrated in a few discrete colours. The work of Kirchhoff (1824–87) showed several important facts about these spectra. Firstly, the bright lines occurred at places in the spectrum that were characteristic of the elements and compounds present in the gas, so that observation of the gas spectrum enabled a chemical analysis of the gas to be made. Secondly, he found that the lines in the spectra of some stars coincided in position with the bright lines of some gases, e.g. the yellow lines of sodium, seen in the spectrum when common salt is placed in a flame. Thirdly, he showed that when light from a hot source is passed through a gas (which, by itself, would give certain bright lines), the bright lines become dark lines.

These laboratory results of Kirchhoff were quickly applied to astronomy, especially by Huggins (1824–1910), and Lockyer (1828–1920). At first it was believed that the differences between one spectrum and another arose from the different chemical compositions of the stars, but as the science of atomic physics developed, it became clear that the stars were all of very similar composition, and that the differences of spectra were due primarily to differences of temperature. The various elements are able to cause dark lines only under certain specific conditions of temperature and pressure, and thus, by spectrum analysis, the chemical and physical properties of the outer layers of a star can be determined.

Perhaps the most remarkable developments in the present century have come from the application to astronomy of principles of physics developed in the laboratory. It is now possible to investigate the internal structure of a star, and how it generates its energy by nuclear reactions at its centre; to calculate (with the help of modern high speed computers) how a star will change with time, and to relate such theories of stellar evolution to observations of star clusters, so as to determine their different ages. By observing, in the Universe, matter under extreme conditions of temperature and pressure that cannot be reproduced in the laboratory, astronomy in turn has provided important information to check theories of physics. So rapid indeed has been this integration of astronomy with physics that today it is perhaps best looked upon as a specialist branch of physics.

Recent developments Within the last quarter of a century, a completely new branch of astronomy has been developed. The end of the Second World War saw a large number of scientists who had been trained in electronics looking for fresh fields to conquer, and a wide range of government surplus radio equipment. In a number of centres research schools were set up, with a view to investigating the various radio waves that were received on earth from distant objects. Radio waves from the Milky Way had first been detected by Jansky in 1931, but his work was not followed up until after the end of the war. This was the beginning of radio astronomy, which has been pursued with such vigour ever since that it sometimes appears to outshine the more conventional optical astronomy. However, radio and optical astronomy are not really competing rivals but complementary methods of studying the same celestial universe. The most significant results have been obtained by combining the two, e.g. the elucidation of the structure of our own Milky Way system, the recognition of the existence of those intriguing quasars, etc. Each method has its own particular advantages. One of the more important of the radio observations is their ability to detect objects which appear to be at much greater distances than anything accessible to the largest optical telescope, objects which on account of their great distances are of special interest in the study of the structure and evolution of the Universe as a whole.

Light and radio waves travel through space at a speed of about 186,000 miles per second. The objects that emit them may be so far away that the waves take thousands of millions of years to reach us.

Before they fall on our telescopes, they have to pass through the Earth's atmosphere. In this last thousandth of a second of their journey, they are distorted almost beyond recognition. For many of these radiations are completely absorbed by the Earth's atmosphere, and even those that get through are often seriously affected by it. As a result of the latest developments astronomical observations are now being made from above the Earth's atmosphere both from rockets and from satellites. The instruments now in orbit are quite small but plans are being made for telescopes with apertures as large as 100 inches to be launched. These will operate automatically, transmitting their observations back to the ground. In due course, we can expect to have manned observatories in orbit or on the airless Moon. It is not only ultraviolet and infrared light that can be observed from above the Earth's atmosphere but also X-rays and gamma rays from distant parts of the Universe.

There can be no doubt that these observations will have the most profound effect upon our whole view of the Universe. In a thousand years from now it may well be that the astronomy of today will seem as strange and primitive as the physics of Aristotle, the harmonies of the Pythagoreans or the myths of Babylon seem to us. For such is the history of Astronomy.

Chapter Three

The Earth

R. H. Stoy

To Everyman the Earth is home and as such the most important body in the Universe. Astronomically it is just one of several planets revolving round the Sun, a comparatively insignificant star in a system containing a hundred thousand million such stars and itself but one of many million comparable systems. Nevertheless the Earth has a special interest for the astronomer since it is the base from which he must explore the Universe and the only part of it he can examine in his laboratories. It is a matter of faith that the laws of physics and chemistry that he finds there will be equally applicable throughout space, but, on the whole, observation does seem to justify this faith and to indicate that the Earth is in no way unique but a typical example of the material of which the physical universe is composed.

Several sciences are entirely devoted to the study of one or more aspects of the Earth and many of their findings are relevant to astronomy. From this vast wealth of material this chapter must try to select those facts which best describe the Earth as an astronomical body, which help to interpret the observations that can be made of other planets, or which provide the means by which the physical universe can be measured in terms of the metre, kilogram, and second.

Origin There is as yet no certain knowledge as to how the Earth originated or of its exact age. The most generally accepted theory is that it was formed simultaneously with the Sun and the rest of the solar system by condensation from cold, widely diffused matter very similar in constitution to the interstellar clouds described by Dr Reddish in Chapter 9. How such diffuse clouds divide up into proto-stars and how some of these proto-stars in ridding themselves of excessive angular momentum become surrounded by proto-planets is not yet fully understood. Once such condensations have begun to form, however, their subsequent development can be fairly confidently predicted. The gravitational energy released by their contraction appears as heat. If the condensation is small, such as may later form the nucleus of a comet, what little heat is produced can escape without raising the temperature of the material appreciably, If, on the other hand, the condensation is a large one, very much more heat is developed and a considerable fraction of it is trapped in the material, particularly near the centre. The temperature there begins to rise and will continue to rise until the contraction is halted by the increasing outward pressure of the compressed heated central material. If the condensation exceeds a certain critical mass, this balance will not be achieved before the central temperature has risen so high that nuclear energy is released and the condensation has become a star similar to those whose formation and development are treated by Dr Clube in Chapter 8. If the condensation is large, but less than this critical mass, it condenses into what, for want of a better word, can be described as a planet. Though the rise in temperature towards the centre will not be sufficient to trigger off nuclear reactions, it will be sufficient to melt and even vaporize the central region of the condensing material. After the initial contraction has been halted the central store of heat will no longer be appreciably augmented by the release of gravitational energy though there may be some further heating by normal radioactive decay. The centre will slowly cool as its heat is gradually dispersed through the general body of the proto-planet, which, during this process, will consist of a hot compressed core surrounded by a less dense envelope whose temperature and density steadily decrease from the centre outwards until they just match those of surrounding space. There will be a steady loss of material from this envelope into space if the outside temperature exceeds a certain limit set by the prevailing force of gravity. In the case of proto-planets orbiting round a proto-sun the temperature of the outer layers is determined partly by the heat leaking from the inside and partly by the heat received by radiation from the proto-sun. This latter radiation will be small at first but will gradually increase as the surface of the proto-sun warms up to its final steady state. In the case of the Earth and the other terrestrial planets it is believed that some 99.8 per cent of the original material in the proto-planet, including most of the hydrogen and the helium, leaked or was blown away into space before a steady state was reached. What remained was still molten throughout and had been in this state sufficiently long for the material, originally fairly homogeneous, to have become partially segregated by the heavier constituents sinking towards the centre to form a core and the less heavy rising towards the surface to form a mantle. In time as the temperature slowly fell, the liquid Earth began to solidify, possibly from the base of the mantle outwards, since the temperature of the melting point of the material from which it is thought to be composed increases rapidly with pressure. When once the mantle had started to solidify, transport of heat through it by convection effectively ceased and the heat trapped in the core could leak away only by conduction, an extremely slow process when long distances are involved. Consequently the core is likely to have remained hot and part of it at least to be still liquid. Even the inner parts of the mantle may be still so warm that its state there may be better described as slightly plastic rather than as completely rigid.

With the solidification of the light residue that floated to the top of the mantle and which now forms the crust of the Earth, geological history began. Studies of the radioactivity of the oldest known rocks suggest that this was just over three thousand million years ago, while the period between the initial condensation of the proto-planets and the time when the first rocks were formed has been estimated as about one thousand million years.

At this stage we must leave the story of the development of the Earth to the geologists and turn to consider the Earth as we find it today.

The size and shape of the Earth The Pythagoreans taught that the Earth was spherical and this was accepted by Aristotle who pointed out that the Earth must be a sphere since the edge of the Earth's shadow on the Moon at the time of a lunar eclipse is always a circle of approximately the same radius whatever the relative positions of the Earth and the Sun. Aristotle was also well aware of the two arguments usually advanced to show that the Earth is convex, viz. the way in which a ship departing from land gradually disappears from sight, the deck going first and the top of the masts last, and the way in which the pole star rises or sinks in the night sky according to whether one is travelling north or south. The first known attempt to measure the size of the Earth was made some years after Aristotle's time by Eratosthenes of Alexandria who lived from 276 to 194 B.C. He noted that at the time of the summer solstice the Sun passed directly overhead at Aswan whereas at Alexandria, which lay some 5000 stadia to the north, it passed $7\frac{1}{4}°$ south of the zenith. He assumed that the Sun was so far away that its rays were effectively parallel and deduced that the circumference of the Earth must be $(360 / 7\frac{1}{4}) \times 5000$ stadia, a distance that works out tolerably close to the presently accepted value.

The principle of this method has been used from the seventeenth century onwards to determine the size and shape of the Earth. An extended arc on the Earth's surface is measured by triangulation from an accurately established base line, and the distance between points on this arc compared with the differences between their latitudes and longitudes as determined by astronomical observation, i.e. with the angles between the directions of gravity at the points. In this way it was found that the length of a meridian arc that corresponds to one degree of latitude varies with the latitude, being least at the equator and greatest at the poles, and thus that the overall shape of the Earth is an oblate spheroid as was predicted by Huygens and Newton as a necessary consequence of the fact that the Earth was rotating. This trigonometrical method of determining the size and shape of the Earth can only be applied to land areas which taken all together cover less than half its surface. An alternative method of determining its shape is provided by a detailed study of how the Earth's gravitational field differs from that of a uniform sphere or of a body made up of a series of uniform spherical shells. The variation of the Earth's gravitational field from place to place can be easily measured with a gravimeter while its absolute strength at any place can be determined by swinging suitable compound pendulums. These observations can be made at sea as well as on the land so that investigations of the force of gravity can cover the whole Earth. The shape so determined is called the geoid and is conceived as being the surface that the top of a shallow sea covering the whole Earth would take up under the joint action of the Earth's gravitational attraction and the effects of its rotation. This surface has only a theoretical existence over land, where it may be conceived as being defined by the surface of water in a canal directly connected with the oceans. It is an oblate spheroid with small local deviations caused by variations in the Earth's gravity.

As in many other fields, the coming of artificial satellites has made possible new and more powerful methods. Simultaneous observation of a chosen satellite from a number of stations provides the means for an absolute trigonometrical determination of the relative positions of these stations in three dimensions quite independently of any assumptions about the exact figure of the Earth, while a study of the perturbations of the orbits of various satellites defines variations in the Earth's gravitational field more accurately and completely than has previously been possible. The presently accepted equatorial radius of the mean spheroid is 6378.16 km and its polar radius 6356.78 km, the corresponding oblateness being 1 / 298.25. Local variations from this mean spheroid do not exceed 80 m and their distribution shows no clear connection with that of the continental land masses. This is in accord with the theory of isostasy which visualizes the lighter continental material floating on an underlying denser layer.

Mass and density The first attempts to measure the mass of the Earth were based on a suggestion made by Newton that it could be derived by observing the deviation in the direction of gravity produced by an isolated mountain. One such experiment was carried out in 1774 by the fifth Astronomer Royal, Neville Maskelyne, who chose Schiehallion, a Scottish mountain which is formed by a high, very regular hog-back ridge running approximately east and west. Two stations were chosen on the same meridian, the one being just north of the mountain, the other just south. The difference in their latitudes as determined from astronomical observations was 53 arc seconds, whereas the difference as determined by triangulation and the assumed radius of the Earth was only 41 arc seconds. Thus the mass of the mountain produces a deviation of 6 arc seconds in the direction of the vertical so that

$$G.m / d^2 = (G.M / R^2) . \tan 6''$$

or

$$M = m . (R^2 / d^2) . \cot 6''$$

where m denotes the mass of the mountain, M that of the Earth, d the distance of the station to the centre of the mountain, R the radius of the Earth, and G the gravitational constant. m and d were found as accurately as possible by a geological survey of the mountain, including deep borings into its strata. The mass found by Maskelyne corresponded to a mean density for the whole Earth of 4.71 that of water, while the best modern determinations of mass give 5.976×10^{24} kg corresponding to a mean density of 5.517 g cm^{-3}. Modern determinations of the Earth's mass are derived from a comparison of the observed value of the acceleration due to gravity with its calculated value. The principle of the method can be illustrated by assuming that the Earth is spherically symmetrical of mass M and radius R so that g, the acceleration due to gravity, is given by

$$g = G . M / R^2$$

Thus if g and G are determined by laboratory experiments and R is known, M can be derived. g is found from the time of oscillation of a suitable compound pendulum and G from some variation of the experiment performed by Cavendish in 1798 in which the attraction between two large and two small spheres was measured in terms of the torsion it produced in the fine wire supporting the two small spheres.

The interior of the Earth The average density of the outer layers of the Earth is less than 3 so to compensate for these there must be a considerable volume of the interior in which the density exceeds 5.5, the

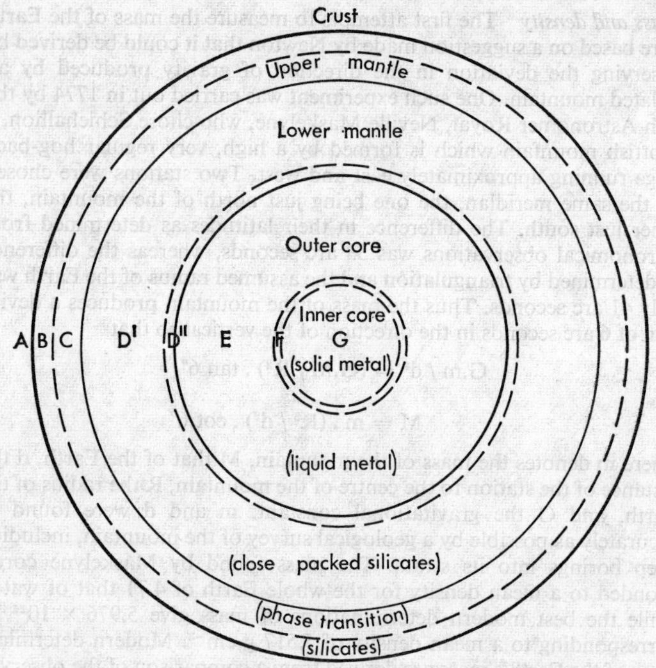

Figure 3.1 Provisional model for the interior of the Earth

mean for the whole. Unfortunately we have no direct knowledge of the interior and must be content with constructing a plausible model of it. Such a model must conform to what is already known, e.g. the conditions at the surface, the total mass, the mean density, and the moment of inertia as derived by comparing the observed rate of precession of the equinoxes with its predicted rate. Moreover, as the Earth appears to have achieved a fairly stable state, both the temperature and the pressure must increase steadily towards the centre, while the central pressure will have to be of the order of three or four million atmospheres in order to support the overlaying weight. But the most extensive clues to the state of the interior have come from the study of earthquakes and of the ways in which the resulting seismic waves are refracted and reflected as they travel through the Earth. These waves are of

TABLE 3.1 PROVISIONAL MODEL FOR THE INTERIOR OF THE EARTH

	Region	*Depth in km*	*Density*
A	Crust	0 – 40	Variable
	Mantle		
B	Upper mantle (silicates)	40 – 400	3.3 – 3.6
C	Upper mantle (phase transition)	400 – 1000	3.6 – 4.7
D′	Lower mantle (close packed silicates)	1000 – 2700	4.7 –
D″	Transition	2700 – 2900	5.7
	Core		
E	Outer core (liquid metal)	2900 – 5000	9.4 – 11.5
F	Transition	5000 – 5100	
G	Inner core (solid metal)	5100 – centre	(15)

Estimated mass of the		
	core	1.9 $\times 10^{24}$ kg
	mantle	4.1
	crust	0.024
	ocean	0.0014
	atmosphere	0.0000051

various kinds of which two have received special attention, the P (principal, pressure, or compressional) waves for which the speed of propagation depends on the degree of incompressibility, the rigidity, and the density of the material, and the S (secondary, shear, or shake) waves for which the speed depends only on the rigidity and the density. Using some very elegant mathematical methods it has proved possible to analyse the very extensive earthquake data and to determine the variations in the velocities of the P and S waves down to a depth of 5000 km. The velocity of the P waves increases from about 5 km s^{-1} near the surface to a maximum of 14 km s^{-1} at a depth of 2900 km. Down to this same depth the S waves travel with about two-thirds the velocity of the P waves. Just below this depth the S waves disappear indicating that the material is virtually liquid.

One of the earliest discoveries made from the study of earthquakes was that the Earth has a central 'core' about 3500 km in radius whose properties are distinctly different from those of the 'mantle' surrounding it. Another early discovery was that made in 1909 by Mohorovičić of the discontinuity which now bears his name and which separates the 'mantle' from the 'crust'. This discontinuity is only about 8 km below the floor of the deepest oceanic regions but dips to some 30 to 40 km below the surface of the continental land masses and is deepest of all under the large mountain ranges. The seismic data indicate a remarkable degree of spherical symmetry in the Earth's interior apart from some irregularities relatively close to the surface. No earthquake centre has been found below 800 km and the great majority of them occur in the first 80 km. Table 3.1 and Figure 3.1 show a provisional model (for which we are indebted to K. E. Bullen) of the density distribution within the Earth which is consistent with the data now available. Layers A–D are solid and their rigidity increases with depth until it is about four times that of steel. Going from layers D to E, that is from the mantle to the core, there is little change in the degree of incompressibility but there is an abrupt change in both the density and the rigidity. This latter is so reduced that the material in E can be expected to behave like a fluid. The state of the material in G, the inner core, is somewhat uncertain but the indications are that it is solid and that its rigidity lies between twice and four times that of steel.

There is little evidence as to the chemical composition of the interior of the Earth but it seems probable that the upper mantle consists mainly of silicate rock such as olivine, an iron-magnesium silicate mineral. There is also a very widely held opinion, based largely on the composition of meteorites, that the core is predominantly iron mixed with a certain amount of nickel. There is also very little known about the internal temperature of the Earth. Near the surface the temperature increases with depth with an average rate of about 20 degrees Centigrade per kilometre, but the actual rate depends on the thermal conductivity of the surrounding rocks. Part of this temperature gradient is due to heat flow from the interior and part to the heat generated from radioactive materials which seem to have become concentrated towards the surface. The rate of increase of temperature with depth probably decreases with depth and it is possible that the central core is effectively isothermal with a temperature of not less than 2000°K and not more than 10,000°K.

The atmosphere Unlike the interior, the atmosphere of the Earth is accessible to direct observation though it is only relatively recently that balloons, rockets, and artificial satellites have made access to its upper reaches possible. The ever-changing weather and a wide variety of natural phenomena are a constant reminder that the atmosphere is a complex system and very far from being the simple, homogeneous layer of gas that we sometimes tend to imagine the atmosphere of other planets to be. In spite of its complexity, however, the general behaviour of the atmosphere is determined by relatively simple physical considerations. The normal gas laws apply and also the mechanical principle that the pressure at any point equals the weight of the atmosphere above that point. In theory, the simplest condition is an isothermal atmosphere in a uniform gravitational field. In this case, the pressure and density both decrease exponentially with height, i.e. if the pressure and density are at 1/10 of their ground level value at a height h, they will be at 1/100 of their ground level value at height 2h, at 1/1000 of these values at height 3h, and so on. 'h' is called the 'decimal scale height' and for this theoretical atmosphere varies directly as the absolute temperature, which by supposition is uniform throughout, and inversely with the strength of the gravitational field and with the mean molecular weight. For air at 288°K (15°C) the decimal scale height is 19.4 km. Theoretically an isothermal atmosphere should extend to infinity but in practice it can be regarded as extending until its density falls so low that it equals that of the surrounding space, or until the collisions between the molecules become so rare that the statistical gas laws no longer apply. Because of the dependence of the decimal scale height on molecular weight, the composition of an isothermal atmosphere consisting of a mixture of gases varies with height, the lighter gases being relatively more abundant at great heights than at ground level.

Although parts of the terrestrial atmosphere are approximately isothermal, the atmosphere as a whole is not, since it is constantly receiving heat from the Sun. Of the solar radiation not reflected directly back into space, the ultraviolet and infrared portions are absorbed in the upper atmosphere, while the remainder, which carries the greater part of the energy, penetrates to ground level. Here it is absorbed and warms the surface which, in turn, warms the air close to it, partly by conduction but mainly by the radiation that it emits. This is concentrated in a portion of the infrared that is efficiently absorbed by atmospheric gases, particularly by water vapour and carbon dioxide. Part of this energy absorbed by the lower atmosphere is re-emitted as infrared radiation, the portion travelling downwards being reabsorbed by the surface which is thereby kept considerably warmer than it would otherwise be. The heating of the lower atmosphere reduces its density compared with that of its surroundings and sets up convection currents. Once a volume of air starts to rise through the atmosphere, however, it gets cooler, unless heat is fed into it to counterbalance the energy it uses up in expanding against the decreasing pressure to which it is subjected. In the same way, a descending volume of air gets warmer unless it can lose heat fairly rapidly by one means or another. If no heat is being fed in at all, i.e. if the motion of the volume of air is completely adiabatic, the temperature will decrease with height at a rate of 9.8 degrees Centigrade per kilometre. This is the 'lapse rate' that one might expect to find in a perfectly dry atmosphere. If the ascending volume of air contains some moisture, the expected lapse rate will be smaller for, as the temperature falls below the dew point, water vapour condenses to liquid or to ice and in doing so releases a considerable amount of latent heat.

The way in which the temperature does vary with height in the actual atmosphere is shown in Figure 3.2. The ordinate in this figure is calibrated both as the height in kilometres and as pressure in millibars, which, as it equals the weight of the atmosphere above the height in question, indicates the mass distribution. It will be noticed that the atmosphere can be divided into a number of layers according to the way in which the temperature varies. In the lowest layer, which is called the troposphere, the temperature decreases with increasing height with a lapse rate of about six degrees Centigrade per kilometre. This is the layer in which most of the weather occurs. Its top, where the temperature stops decreasing, is known as the tropopause; above it is the stratosphere, in which the temperature remains fairly constant in the lower portion but increases with height in the upper, until it reaches a maximum of about 0°C at the stratopause which occurs at a height of about 50 km. The reason for the increase of temperature in the upper part of the stratosphere is the absorption of ultraviolet solar radiation by ozone. The fact that the temperature increases upwards inhibits vertical currents in the stratosphere and makes it a very stable layer. Above the stratopause comes the mesosphere, or middle sphere, another layer in which the temperature falls off with increasing height to reach a minimum of about 180°K at the mesopause, some 85 km above the ground. The average lapse rate is thought to be about half that in the troposphere, but knowledge of these higher reaches of the atmosphere is still very incomplete. Above the mesopause comes the thermosphere in which the temperature once more begins to increase with increasing height until it reaches the temperature of interplanetary space, which may be about 1500°K at sunspot maximum and 1000°K at sunspot minimum. The mechanism by which this very tenuous upper atmosphere is heated is the absorption of part of the ultraviolet radiation from the Sun, particularly by the oxygen molecules. These can absorb the radiation with wavelength shorter than 2420 Å and are thereby split into oxygen atoms; if the wavelength of the radiation is shorter than 1800 Å, at least half of the oxygen atoms so produced will be in an excited state. The absorption of the shorter wave radiation at these higher levels also results in a considerable amount of ionization and thus of a significant number of free electrons. The region above

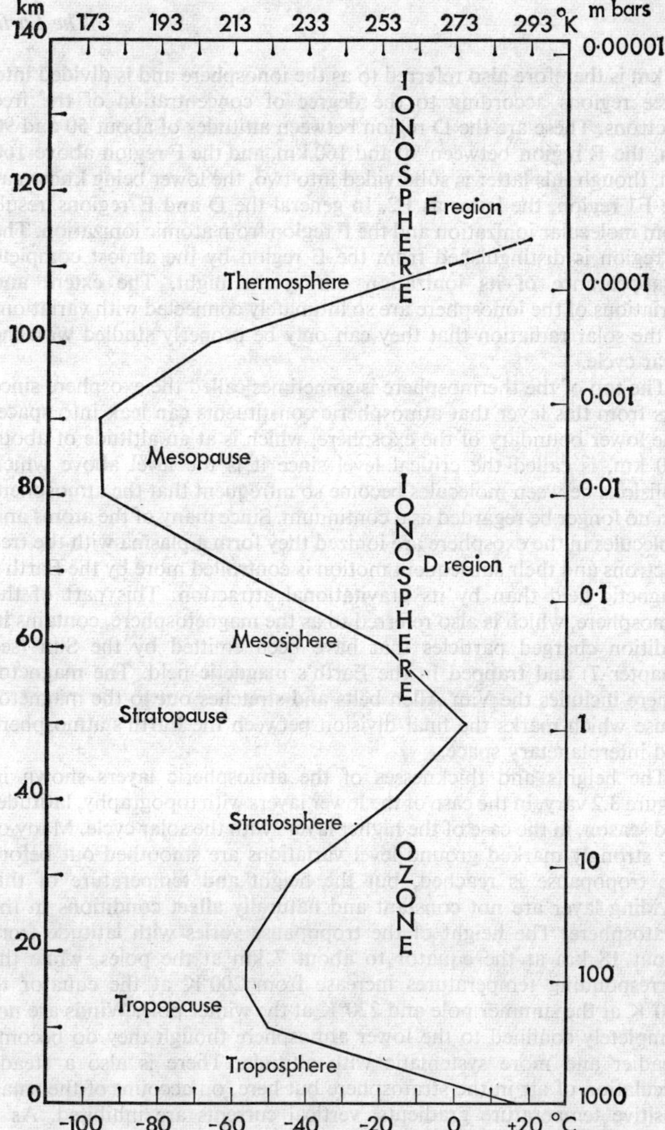

Figure 3.2 Variation of atmospheric temperature with height

50 km is therefore also referred to as the ionosphere and is divided into three regions according to the degree of concentration of the free electrons. These are the D region between altitudes of about 50 and 90 km, the E region between 90 and 160 km, and the F region above 160 km, though this latter is subdivided into two, the lower being known as the F1 region, the latter as F2. In general the D and E regions result from molecular ionization and the F region from atomic ionization. The D region is distinguished from the E region by the almost complete disappearance of its ionization during the night. The extent and variations of the ionosphere are so intimately connected with variations in the solar radiation that they can only be properly studied with the solar cycle.

The top of the thermosphere is sometimes called the exosphere since it is from this layer that atmospheric constituents can leak into space. The lower boundary of the exosphere, which is at an altitude of about 500 km, is called the critical level since it is the level above which collisions between molecules become so infrequent that the atmosphere can no longer be regarded as a continuum. Since many of the atoms and molecules in the exosphere are ionized they form a plasma with the free electrons and their subsequent motion is controlled more by the Earth's magnetic field than by its gravitational attraction. This part of the atmosphere, which is also referred to as the magnetosphere, contains in addition charged particles that have been emitted by the Sun (see Chapter 7) and trapped in the Earth's magnetic field. The magnetosphere includes the Van Allen belts and stretches out to the magnetopause which marks the final division between the Earth's atmosphere and interplanetary space.

The heights and thicknesses of the atmospheric layers shown in Figure 3.2 vary, in the case of the lower layers with topography, latitude, and season, in the case of the higher layers with the solar cycle. Many of the strongly marked ground level variations are smoothed out before the tropopause is reached, but the height and temperature of this dividing layer are not constant and naturally affect conditions in the stratosphere. The height of the tropopause varies with latitude from about 18 km at the equator to about 7 km at the poles, while the corresponding temperatures increase from 200°K at the equator to 230°K at the summer pole and 220°K at the winter pole. Winds are not completely confined to the lower atmosphere though they do become steadier and more systematic with altitude. There is also a steady circulation of air in the stratosphere but here, on account of the small positive temperature gradients, vertical currents are inhibited. As a consequence fine dust and the debris from atomic explosions once

TABLE 3.2 CHEMICAL COMPOSITION OF THE LOWER ATMOSPHERE

Constituent		*Molecular weight*	*Amount (atmo-cm)*	*Percentage of dry air by volume*	*Percentage of dry air by weight*
Nitrogen	N_2	28	624000	78.08	75.52
Oxygen	O_2	32	167400	20.95	23.14
Water vapour	H_2O	18	800 to 22000		
Argon	Ar	40	7450	0.93	1.28
Carbon dioxide	CO_2	44	260	0.03	0.05
Neon	Ne	20	14.6		
Helium	He	4	4.2		
Methane	CH_4	16	1.2		
Krypton	Kr	84	0.91		
Carbon monoxide	CO	28	0.05 to 0.8		
Sulphur dioxide	SO_2	64	1		
Hydrogen	H_2	2	0.4		
Nitrous oxide	N_2O	44	0.4		
Ozone	O_3	48	0.25		
Xenon	Xe	131	0.07		

injected into the stratosphere take a long time to settle. The major eruptions of the equatorial volcanoes Krakatoa and Mount Agung blew clouds of fine dust into the stratosphere which gradually spread all over the world and for many months caused outstandingly beautiful purple-red sunrises and sunsets. In the case of Krakatoa, the initial dust cloud moved steadily westwards at an average speed of 117 km per hour and, keeping within the equatorial zone, circled the Earth several times before meridional currents gradually spread it out to cover the whole globe. Observed from outside the Earth such a phenomenon might well recall the behaviour of markings on the equatorial zones of Jupiter and Saturn. The motion of the dust cloud from Krakatoa led to the belief that the equatorial regions of the stratosphere were dominated by winds blowing from east to west, but continuous observations from about 1955 suggest that the direction of flow alternates from east-to-west to west-to-east with a period of about 26 months. The cause of this phenomenon is still obscure.

The chemical composition of the lower atmosphere is shown in Table 3.2, the amount of each constituent being given in 'atmo-cm' which is the thickness in centimetres of the layer it would form if it were all at the standard temperature and pressure (S.T.P.), i.e. if it were at 0°C and

1013.25 millibars (760 mm of mercury). It seems probable that the present oceans and atmosphere have very largely evolved from vapours escaping from the interior in the long interval since the crust first began to form. Vast quantities of gas are still pouring forth from volcanic regions and it is likely that this flow was even more abundant in the past. Steam and carbon dioxide are the principal constituents of these volcanic vapours but many other gases are also present including carbon monoxide, hydrogen sulphide, hydrogen chloride, ammonia, methane, hydrogen, argon, nitrogen, etc. The present atmosphere is, however, not simply an accumulation of volcanic gases but is the result of a dynamical balance between many continuous processes. Water vapour that diffuses into the upper atmosphere is dissociated by ultraviolet solar radiation. Much of the resulting hydrogen escapes into space while the oxygen accumulates. Some of it is used at ground level for supporting animal life and various forms of combustion. On the other hand, free oxygen is restored to the atmosphere by vegetable life as a result of photosynthesis. This same process absorbs carbon dioxide but some of this is returned by the respiration of the plants, by their decay, and when they are used as food by animals. The rate of removal of carbon dioxide from the air and of its return is so rapid that the whole carbon dioxide content of the atmosphere could pass through the cycle in a decade or so; the period of the corresponding cycle for oxygen is of the order of 3000 years. The solar radiation with wavelengths shorter than 2420 Å which dissociates oxygen molecules into oxygen atoms is completely absorbed by the oxygen above an altitude of 20 km. Some of the resulting oxygen atoms combine with oxygen molecules to form ozone which has its maximum concentration between the 20 and 30 km levels. Diffusion and convection currents carry some of this ozone down to ground level where it is removed since it is a powerful oxidizing agent. Some is also broken down in the higher levels of the atmosphere by solar radiation with wavelengths shorter than 3000 Å. From the human point of view this is perhaps the most important function of ozone since it ensures that none of this lethal radiation reaches ground level.

As regards the other atmospheric constituents, argon (40), which is very much more abundant than argon (36), is produced by the radioactive decay of potassium (40) and can accumulate indefinitely. Helium is also the product of radioactivity but can escape into space. Methane (marsh gas) and nitrous oxide result from organic decay but are decomposed by sunlight, while carbon monoxide is a major product of industrial processes and in particular of internal combustion engines, but some of it is destroyed by soil micro-organisms. It is possible that the chemically inert gases, neon, argon (36), krypton and xenon were once part of the gaseous atmosphere of the proto-planet, but if this is so it appears probable that only one part in 10^7 of the krypton and xenon originally present has survived and only one part in 10^{11} of the much lighter neon.

In the upper atmosphere gravitational diffusion tends to enrich the relative proportions of the lighter gases like hydrogen and helium; also, since the density is very low and the flow of ultraviolet solar radiation relatively strong, molecules tend to split up into their component radicals or atoms. Some of these are excited or even ionized by radiation or by particle collision. As they return to normal they emit light which is so faint that normally it is only visible on dark clear moonless nights as a faint grey luminous background to the stars. This airglow is difficult to observe from the ground because it has first to be separated from scattered starlight and also, in some parts of the sky, from the zodiacal light and gegenschein and from polar aurorae. These latter are themselves partially an atmospheric phenomenon being largely due to oxygen atoms in the high atmosphere that have been stimulated to emit by collision with charged particles coming from the Sun.

The airglow can be examined from the ground using specially designed spectrographs but it is much more effective to mount the appropriate apparatus into a rocket which can fly right through the various layers involved in the emissions. The signal strength due to such an emission increases as the rocket rises, reaches a maximum as the rocket passes through the layer and then drops sharply as the rocket climbs still higher. The strongest emissions are in the infrared and come from hydroxyl radicals in a layer at about 90 km up. Oxygen molecules at the same height emit in the violet and ultraviolet, while higher up oxygen atoms give their usual auroral spectrum, a single line in the green at 5577 Å and a doublet in the red at 6300 Å and 6364 Å. These lines are both the results of forbidden transitions and so can be emitted only when the density is very low. As the upper level of the 5577 Å line has a half life of 0.74 seconds while the upper level of the 6300 Å doublet has a half life of 110 seconds, the green line can be emitted at higher densities than can the red. In the air glow the green line is emitted at a height of 90 km while the red line does not appear below 300 km. Other atomic emissions in the airglow are the Lyman alpha and Balmer alpha lines of hydrogen; the former is, of course, in the far ultraviolet and so not visible from the ground. The airglow is not uniformly bright; the individual emissions vary with the local time, with the season of the year, with latitude, and with solar and magnetic activity. A study of these variations is likely to throw considerable light on the structure of the upper reaches of the atmosphere and on the complex reactions taking place there. Especially interesting are the differences between the day and night time emissions and how certain emissions, like the yellow lines of sodium, are greatly enhanced during twilight when the Sun's radiation is nearly parallel to the emitting layers and so traverses great distances in them.

Precession of the equinoxes Somewhere about 120 B.C., Hipparchos noticed that the length of the year as measured by the interval between successive vernal equinoxes was about twenty minutes shorter than the year as measured by the interval between successive returns of the Sun to the same place in the heavens relative to the stars. The first of these intervals could be determined by observing when the Sun rose precisely in the East, while the second had to be determined by observing the heliacal rising of the stars, i.e. by noting which were the last stars that could be seen to rise before the Sun. The difference between these two kinds of year, now known as the tropical and sidereal year respectively, was too small to be observed by the naked eye during a single year, but the effect is cumulative and becomes obvious to anyone who, like Hipparchos, compared observations made over a long interval of time. Although the right ascensions and declinations of the stars are changing continuously, the actual position of the ecliptic scarcely alters relatively to the stars, nor does the angle between it and the celestial equator. What is happening, in fact, is that the axis of rotation of the Earth is describing the surface of a cone with an angle of about 23½° about the normal to the plane of the ecliptic. This causes the equinoctial points, i.e. the intersections of the celestial equator and the ecliptic, to move slowly backwards along the ecliptic, the circuit being completed in a period of approximately 25,800 years.

The explanation of this phenomenon had to await the development of Newtonian mechanics in the eighteenth century. It is a particular case of a general property of rotating systems, viz. if a couple is applied to a rotating body, the body does not move in the direction that it would if it were not rotating but tries instead to align its axis of rotation with the axis of the applied couple. The strength of the forces involved can be vividly realized by anyone who is holding a spinning bicycle wheel by its axle and tries to change the direction of that axle. It is of course this effect which helps to keep the rider balanced on a moving bicycle or motor cycle. Another common example is provided by a spinning top such as that illustrated in Figure 3.3 and which is in steady conical motion about the vertical. The top is subject to a disturbing couple produced by its weight acting downwards through the centre of gravity

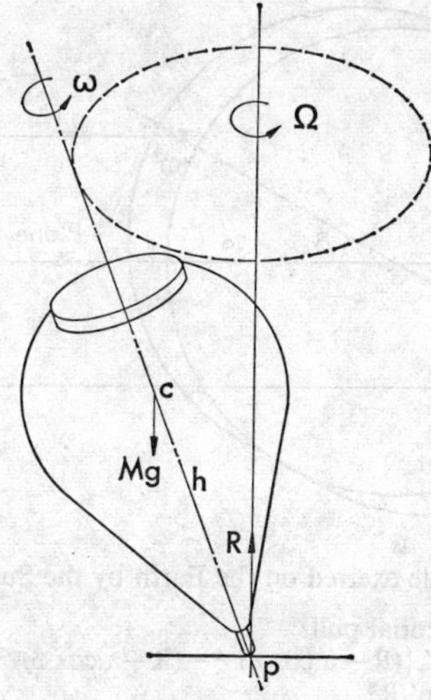

Figure 3.3 Motion of a spinning top

and the equal, but opposite, reaction of the ground acting upwards through the peg. The axis of this couple is at right angles to the vertical plane through the axis of the top. Consequently this latter axis is always trying to move into a horizontal direction at right angles to itself. The result is that it 'precesses' about the vertical with an angular velocity given by M.g.h / I.ω, where M is the mass of the top, g the acceleration due to gravity, h the distance between the centre of gravity and the peg, I the moment of inertia of the top about its axis, and ω the angular velocity of the spin about this axis which is assumed to be large compared with the other quantities concerned.

The rotating Earth is subject to the disturbing couples produced by the differential gravitational attractions of the Sun and the Moon on its equatorial bulge. Consider first the effect of the solar couple which is illustrated in Figure 3.4. This acts in the plane through the axis of the Earth and the centre of the Sun and its moment is approximately proportional to M . sin 2δ / R^3, where M denotes the mass of the Sun, R its distance, and δ its declination. The moment of this couple varies from a maximum at the solstices to zero at the equinoxes and also, to a lesser

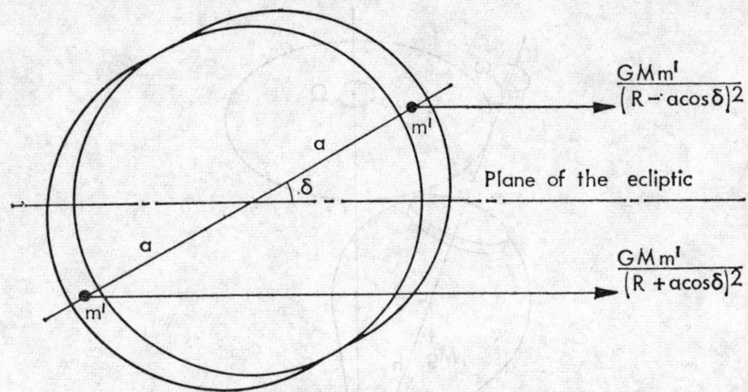

Figure 3.4 The couple exerted on the Earth by the Sun

Moment of the differential pull
$= 2a. \sin \delta.G.M.m'.\{(R-a.\cos \delta)^{-2}-(R+a.\cos \delta)^{-2}\}$
$= 4a. \sin 2\delta.G.M.m'/R^3$

extent, throughout the year on account of the varying distance between the Earth and the Sun. Its direction, however, remains the same, viz. it tries to make the Earth's equatorial plane coincide with the ecliptic. Consequently this couple causes the axis of the Earth to precess about the normal to the plane of the ecliptic. The couple produced by the Moon, whose mass is m and distance r, acts in a similar way to the solar couple but is stronger since $m / r^3 > M / R^3$ and it causes the axis of the Earth to precess with a variable speed about the normal to the plane of the Moon's orbit. But this normal is itself precessing with a period of 18.6 years about the normal to the ecliptic to which it is inclined at an angle of 5° since the Moon and the Earth orbiting round each other form a system having considerable angular momentum and subject to a solar couple trying to turn their orbital plane towards the ecliptic. Moreover, the ecliptic itself is not quite stationary in space, but is moving slightly under the disturbing influence that the attractions of the various planets have on the rotating system formed by the Moon and the Earth orbiting round the Sun.

The resultant motion of the Earth's axis is consequently rather complex, but it is possible to regard it as being compounded of a steady precessional motion of a 'mean' position and of a relatively small variable

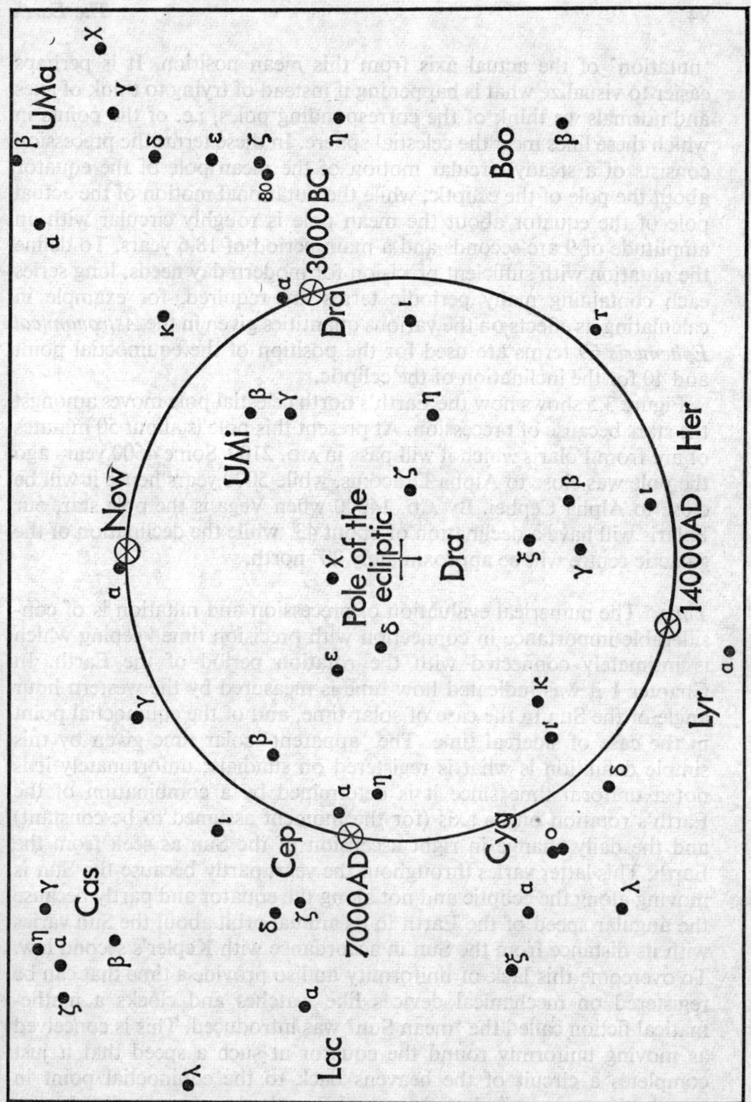

Figure 3.5 Because of precession the north celestial pole describes a circle of radius $23\frac{1}{2}°$ around the pole of the ecliptic in 25,800 years

'nutation' of the actual axis from this mean position. It is perhaps easier to visualize what is happening if instead of trying to think of axes and normals we think of the corresponding poles, i.e. of the points in which these lines meet the celestial sphere. In these terms the precession consists of a steady circular motion of the mean pole of the equator about the pole of the ecliptic, while the nutational motion of the actual pole of the equator about the mean pole is roughly circular with an amplitude of 9 arc seconds and a main period of 18.6 years. To define the nutation with sufficient precision for modern day needs, long series each containing many periodic terms are required, for example in calculating its effects on the various quantities given in the *Astronomical Ephemeris* 69 terms are used for the position of the equinoctial point and 40 for the inclination of the ecliptic.

Figure 3.5 shows how the Earth's north celestial pole moves amongst the stars because of precession. At present this pole is about 50 minutes of arc from Polaris which it will pass in A.D. 2100. Some 4600 years ago the pole was close to Alpha Draconis, while 5000 years hence it will be close to Alpha Cephei. By A.D. 14000 when Vega is the pole star, our Polaris will have a declination of about 43° while the declination of the galactic centre will be approximately 20° north.

Time The numerical evaluation of precession and nutation is of considerable importance in connection with precision time keeping which is intimately connected with the rotation period of the Earth. In Chapter 1 it was indicated how time is measured by the western hour angle of the Sun in the case of solar time, and of the equinoctial point in the case of sidereal time. The 'apparent' solar time given by this simple definition is what is registered on sundials; unfortunately it is not a uniform time since it is determined by a combination of the Earth's rotation on its axis (for the moment assumed to be constant) and the daily change in right ascension of the Sun as seen from the Earth. This latter varies throughout the year, partly because the Sun is moving along the ecliptic and not along the equator and partly because the angular speed of the Earth in its annual orbit about the Sun varies with its distance from the Sun in accordance with Kepler's second law. To overcome this lack of uniformity and so provide a time that can be registered on mechanical devices like watches and clocks a mathematical fiction called the 'mean Sun' was introduced. This is conceived as moving uniformly round the equator at such a speed that it just completes a circuit of the heavens back to the equinoctial point in exactly the same period as the actual Sun. Its hour angle gives 'mean solar time' and differs from apparent solar time by a quantity which is

TABLE 3.3 LOCAL MEAN SOLAR TIME OF NOON

Date	*1*	*11*	*21*
January	12 03.5	12 07.9	12 11.3
February	12 13.6	12 14.3	12 13.7
March	12 12.5	12 10.2	12 07.4
April	12 04.0	12 01.2	11 58.8
May	11 57.1	11 56.3	11 56.5
June	11 57.7	11 59.4	12 01.6
July	12 03.6	12 05.3	12 06.3
August	12 06.3	12 05.2	12 03.2
September	12 00.1	11 56.7	11 53.2
October	11 49.8	11 46.9	11 44.7
November	11 43.6	11 44.0	11 45.8
December	11 48.9	11 53.1	11 58.0

usually called 'The Equation of Time'. Its variation throughout the year is indicated in Table 3.3 which gives the local mean solar time of transit of the actual Sun, i.e. the local clock time corresponding to noon or twelve o'clock sundial time. It will be noticed that the Equation of Time can be as large as 16 minutes. As sundials are now mainly ornamental, the chief practical use of the Equation of Time is for determining the instant of noon when the shadow cast by a plumb line gives a true north–south line, a very simple and reliable way of establishing the meridian.

So far, only local time has been considered, i.e. time as measured at the place in question. At any given instant the local times as measured at two places differ by their difference in longitude, an idea with which radio has made us very familiar, e.g. when it is noon in London it is only 7.00 a.m. in New York. Longitudes in atlases are usually given in degrees and minutes but can easily be converted into hours and minutes if it is remembered that 24 hours is equivalent to 360° so that 1 hour = 15°, 1 minute = 15′, and 1 second of time = 15 seconds of arc. Up to about the middle of the last century each place kept its own local time but, with the coming of the railways and the introduction of the electric telegraph, it began to be very inconvenient that every station along the line was using a different time. 'Railway time' was introduced, but this was gradually replaced by 'standard time' which was the local mean solar time as measured on a chosen standard meridian. An international conference held at Washington in 1884 selected the meridian of the

Greenwich Observatory as longitude zero and suggested that the meridians selected as standard for time keeping should be those whose longitude as measured from Greenwich was either a whole number of hours or half hours.

As the mean Sun is a mathematical fiction mean solar time cannot be directly observed, but has to be deduced from the sidereal time which is determined from observations of the right ascensions of a number of stars and thus ultimately from the instantaneous position of the true equinoctial point. On account of nutation this point is moving at an irregular rate along the ecliptic and the equator and consequently the sidereal day as previously defined is not of constant length. The effect of nutation is small and was tacitly ignored until clocks achieved a sustained accuracy of rate of the order of 0.01 seconds per day as they did with the introduction of the Shortt free pendulum clocks in the 1920s. The crystal clocks of the 1930s and their modern successors controlled by caesium beam oscillators do far better than this and maintain rates that make a microsecond per day significant. Nutation must therefore be taken into account and use must be made of mean sidereal time, the analogue of mean solar time. The difference between this time and the observed apparent sidereal time is the nutation in right ascension or, as it is now more usually called, The Equation of the Equinoxes. For convenience it is divided into the long and short period terms, the latter including all those terms with periods less than 35 days. The major term has a period of 18.6 years and an amplitude of ± 1.2 seconds of time. The amplitude of the short period terms does not exceed ± 0.020 seconds of time and their principal period is approximately 15 days.

Mean sidereal time as defined above would be completely satisfactory for regulating clocks if the Earth revolved uniformly round an axis which remained fixed relatively to its surface. Neither of these conditions are strictly true. That the surface of the Earth does move relatively to the axis of rotation was demonstrated towards the end of the nineteenth century when it was found that precise astronomical determinations of the latitude of a given spot varied with time, the variations being of the order of 0.3 arc seconds. These variations were of similar amount for places in the same vicinity but differed from vicinity to vicinity in such a way that a decrease on one side of the world was accompanied by an increase of approximately equal amount on the other. It thus became clear that the north and south poles were not fixed points on the surface of the Earth but wandered somewhat irregularly over a small area. This was not altogether unexpected, as Newton had pointed out in his *Principia* that if a body is rotating round an axis which is not one of its three principal axes of inertia the body slowly alters its position relatively to the axis of spin, and vice versa. In the case of the Earth, the axis of spin defines the astronomical pole and the axis of figure the geographical pole. These can normally be considered as being coincident, but if for any reason, e.g. an earthquake, the coincidence of the two axes is upset, the one pole will rotate slowly round the other until the motion is gradually damped out by the general frictional forces. In 1765 Euler showed that the period of this rotation would be approximately ten months if the Earth behaved as a perfectly rigid body. In the 1890s a special chain of observing stations was established along the 39° 08′ north parallel to keep this variation of latitude and thus the motion of the pole under continuous observation. Figure 3.6, which is based on the 1969 report from these stations, shows the polar motion between 1962 and 1968 as deduced from observations made at Carloforte (Italy), Gaithersburg (Maryland, U.S.A.), Ukiah (California, U.S.A.), Mizusawa (Japan), and Kitab (Uzbek, U.S.S.R.). It will be noticed that the motion is a rather complicated spiral with an average semi-amplitude of about 0.3 arc seconds which is equivalent to about 9 metres on the surface of the Earth. The motion can be resolved into at least two components: one with a 14-month period and a variable amplitude, the other with a yearly period and an almost constant amplitude of about 0.2 arc seconds. The amplitude of the first has varied between 0.5 arc second in 1910 to 0.1 arc second in 1926 and seems to have some relation to the degree of earthquake activity. Its period also seems to vary slightly with the amplitude of the motion, growing slightly longer as the amplitude increases. That this period is approximately 14 months and not the 10 months expected from Euler's theoretical work can be explained by supposing that the Earth is not completely rigid but has a rigidity about twice that of steel. The effects of the annual cycle of meteorological conditions are a possible explanation for the second component of the polar motion.

The wandering of the pole alters not only the astronomical latitudes but also the whole system of longitudes. To take account of the effect of this variation on observations made for the determination of time, it is necessary to calculate how the instantaneous longitude of the place of observation differs from its mean value. To do this it is convenient to define the zero of longitude at any instant as being not the meridian passing through Greenwich itself but the meridian passing through the point whose coordinates on the mean system are longitude zero, latitude zero. With this convention the changes in longitude resulting from polar motion are zero on the equator and elsewhere, along any given meridian, vary as the tangent of the latitude. Thus the amplitude of the longitude

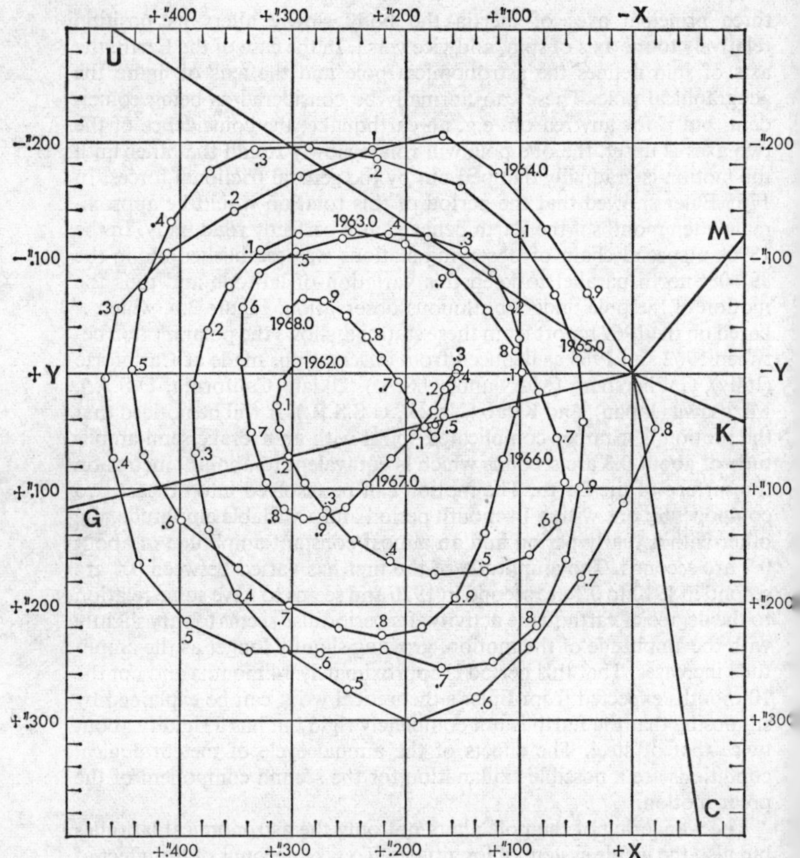

Figure 3.6 The motion of the pole between 1962 and 1968
M Mizusawa K Kitab C Carloforte G Gaithersburg U Ukiah

variation in latitude 45° is of the order of ± 0.3 arc seconds, or ± 0.02 seconds of time.

It was realized during the 1930s that certain small differences that had been found between the observed and the computed positions of the Sun, Moon, Mercury and Venus, and which were obviously related, were really due to variations in the adopted unit of time, i.e. in the period of rotation of the Earth. The recognition of this fact led to the introduction of 'ephemeris time' which was conceived as a measure of the uniform time inherent in Newtonian gravitational theory. Although convenient for celestial mechanics this time is not suitable for everyday use, since it can only be determined by fairly complicated calculations from the observed motions of the solar system and of the Moon in particular. This lack of practicability is reflected in the formal definition of its unit, the ephemeris second, as being (1 / 31 556 925 . 9747) of the length of the tropical year in 1900. In 1972 its difference from mean solar time, with which by definition it coincided in 1900, was just over 42 seconds.

The increasing precision in time-keeping rendered possible by the steady improvement in crystal clocks and their control by caesium beam oscillators showed up these variations in the rotation period of the Earth even more clearly, and indicated that there were also small quasi-regular seasonal variations whose integrated effect over the year was to make the actual time vary from the mean time with an amplitude of the order of $\pm$ 0.025 seconds.

As the introduction of railways produced a need for standard time, so the coming of the airways and the world wide use of radio produced a need for 'universal time' (U.T.), a time that should be the same all over the world at the same instant. The first form of this universal time, U.T.0., was computed by a certain agreed formula from the mean sidereal time as observed at Greenwich. It was a refined version of the mean solar time at Greenwich with 12 hours added to make the U.T. day begin at midnight in accordance with normal civil practice. U.T.0. ('U.T. nought') was improved by introducing a correction to allow for the effect of the polar motion on the longitude of the place of observation. This gave U.T.1 which was later improved to U.T.2 by introducing a further correction to take into account as far as possible the seasonal fluctuations in the rotational period of the Earth. U.T.2 should be a uniform time and as such suitable for comparison with the best crystal clocks. It was so used for a number of years but it did not prove sufficiently good in practice for the very high precision clocks now in use. Consequently it was decided that from 1 January 1972 the Earth would no longer be regarded as the standard time keeper. This function was taken over by a number of clock installations in various parts of the world which are all carefully intercompared and coordinated by the Bureau International de l'Heure in Paris. The result is an atomic time which is called Coordinated Universal Time, U.T.C., and which rigidly adheres to the definition of the second adopted in 1967, viz. the duration of 9 192 631 770 periods of the radiation corresponding to the transition between the two hyperfine levels of the ground state of the caesium-133 atom.

U.T.C. is to be kept in step with time as determined by the rotation of the Earth by inserting or dropping a 'leap' second as necessary at midnight on 30 June and 31 December. For the benefit of surveyors, navigators, astronomers, and others who may be interested, the precision radio signals also give the difference between U.T.1 as defined above and U.T.C. This difference, which is denoted by D.U.T.1, is given only to 0.1 seconds as this is regarded as sufficiently accurate for most non-electronic survey and navigational purposes. Normally D.U.T.1 does not exceed 0.7 seconds. The extremely precise time signals are used for various purposes of which the most important at present is the control of radio frequencies, especially those that are used in distance measurements or in navigational aids like Decca and Loran whose utility depends on the radio frequencies involved being kept absolutely constant.

Chapter Four
The Moon

Z. Kopal

The Moon, the only natural satellite of our Earth and its faithful companion since the days of its formation, holds a unique position among the bodies in the solar system in several respects. Its size and mass render it a body of the order of magnitude of minor terrestrial planets, rather than of the many smaller satellites revolving around Jupiter or Saturn. Its close proximity to the Earth makes it possible to study the various characteristics of a cosmic mass of this order in considerable detail, particularly its surface features, unprotected by any atmosphere and exposed, since time immemorial, to all the rigours of interplanetary climate. The very unchangeability of the lunar face under these conditions renders the visible fossil record wrought by time on its wrinkled old face a priceless scientific document of inestimable value; for it bears, without doubt, the scars (long obliterated on the Earth) produced by events that took place in days long gone by. Much of it may, in fact, be traced to the events not distant in time from the days of the formation of the solar system itself. The aim of the present chapter will be to summarize some of the principal characteristics of our satellite in this light, and to outline their significance within the general framework of the astronomy of the solar system as a whole.

Distance, size and orbit When we begin to inquire about the properties of any celestial body, the first characteristic, in order of importance of its implications, is its distance. For a body as close to us in space as the Moon, this can be determined by triangulation and checked (in recent days) by the timing of the time of return of the radar or laser echoes sent out by terrestrial transmitters and reflected from the lunar surface. The astronomical triangulation using the known diameter of the Earth as a baseline, or the echo timings relying on the known velocity of propagation of the radio signals in a vacuum, revealed that the relative orbit of the Moon around the Earth is an ellipse (disturbed slightly by the gravitational attraction of the Sun and other neighbouring bodies of the solar system), characterized by a mean eccentricity of 0.055, which causes the distance to the Moon to vary between 356 and 407 thousand kilometres. The mean distance of the Moon during the course of a month is 384,405 kilometres, equal to 60.27 times the Earth's radius, or 0.00257 times the mean distance separating us from the Sun. Thus the Moon's distance is only about one per cent of that separating us from our other two nearest celestial neighbours, Venus and Mars, at the time of their closest approach. Light or radio signals can traverse this distance in 1.28 seconds; and space vehicles such as the Russian Luniks and American Rangers can reach the Moon after free flight lasting two to three days.

The orbit of the Moon around the Earth is inclined to the ecliptic, i.e., the plane in which the Earth revolves around the Sun, by a little more than 5°; this is why we do not have lunar eclipses each month, but only at such times (usually once a year) as Full Moon happens to take place at a time when the lunar orbit intersects the ecliptic. Its mean orbital period is equal to 27.32166 days; this period, based as it is on century-long series of observations, is known now to some 12 decimal places, and represents one of the most accurately measured quantities known to human science.

The mean apparent diameter of the lunar disk at its average distance amounts to $1865''.2$ (or just over half a degree), oscillating by $102''.4$ between perigee and apogee, and corresponds to a diameter of 3476 kilometres for the essentially spherical globe of the Moon. The Moon is, therefore, about one-quarter of the Earth in size. It rotates around an axis with a uniform angular velocity in exactly the same period as it revolves, thus showing us each month almost the same face, but not exactly so for several reasons. First, since the velocity of revolution in an elliptical orbit varies inversely with the square of the radius-vector, the rotation of the Moon is sometimes ahead, and sometimes behind the orbital motion (by as much as $7^{\circ}.7$), giving rise to the libration in longitude, as a result of which actually more than one-half of the Moon's surface can be seen from the Earth. Secondly, the axis of rotation of the lunar globe is not exactly perpendicular to the plane of its orbit, the angle between them being approximately $6^{\circ}.5$; which means that in the course of one month we can see again sometimes more of one polar region, and sometimes more of the other. This gives rise to a libration in latitude. Again, when the Moon is rising for the observer on the Earth, we look over its upper edge—seeing a little more of that part of the Moon than if we were observing it from the centre of the Earth; and when the Moon is setting the converse is true. This diurnal, or parallactic, libration (not of the Moon, strictly speaking, but of the observer) amounts to about 1°, and superposes on all other librations to enable us to see considerably more than one-half of the Moon from the Earth. On the whole, not less than 59 per cent of the entire lunar globe can be seen, at one time or another, from the surface of the Earth; only 41 per cent being permanently invisible (except from space vehicles) and 41 per cent never disappearing.

The next quantity in order of interest, which should offer a clue to many fundamental characteristics of our satellite, is its mass. The mass of the Moon, like that of any other celestial body, can be found only from the effects of its attraction on another nearby body of known mass; and in the case of the Moon, this will be our Earth. The oft-repeated statement that our planet revolves around the Sun in an ellipse is not sufficiently precise, for in actual fact it is the centre of gravity of the Earth-Moon system (and not the Earth's centre) that describes this ellipse; while both the Earth and the Moon revolve together around their common centre of gravity in orbits that are exactly alike in form, but whose absolute radii are in inverse proportion to their masses.

The Earth does not, therefore, roll around the Sun in an ellipse; it rather wobbles around it; and the necessary result of this monthly wobbling is a slight apparent oscillation, on the celestial sphere, of every astronomical object in the sky, around the place this object would occupy if the Earth had no satellite and its motion were governed by the Sun alone. In the case of the stars (or more distant planets) this displacement is not detectable; but it can be measured in the apparent motion of the Sun, or, better still, of one of the nearer planets or asteroids.

From extensive observations of this kind it has been found that the radius of the monthly orbit of the Earth's centre (i.e., the mean distance between the centre of the Earth and the common centre of gravity of the Earth-Moon system) is 4670 kilometres. This places, therefore, the centre of gravity of the Earth-Moon system well into the interior of the Earth (though nearer to its surface than to its centre), and represents about 82.31 times the mean distance from the Earth to the Moon. By elementary principles of mechanics it follows then that the mass of the Moon is $1/(82.30-1) = 1/81.30$ times that of the Earth.

There exists another gravitational method by means of which the ratio of the Moon's mass to the Earth's can be independently ascertained; and that consists of interpreting the observed rate at which the axis of rotation of the Earth (inclined to the ecliptic by 66°.6) precesses in space like a spinning top in a period of just over 25,800 years under the combined gravitational attraction of the Sun and the Moon. This method confirms that the Earth is, very approximately, 81.3 times as massive as the Moon. The Moon weighs, therefore, little more than one per cent of the terrestrial mass; and as the latter is known to amount to 5.976×10^{24} kilograms, the mass of the Moon results as 7.35×10^{22} kilograms or over 73 trillion tons. This figure may seem immense when we first encounter it, but on the cosmic scale it represents but a relatively tiny speck.

Dividing next this mass of the lunar globe by the volume of a sphere 3476 kilometres in diameter, we find that its mean specific gravity comes out to be 3.34, i.e., only a little higher than that of the common rocks constituting the Earth's mantle. What can be said about possible density variation inside the Moon, and about the internal structure of the lunar globe as a whole? It is unlikely that the Moon is very much compressed anywhere in its interior. The relatively small mass of the Moon gives rise to an internal pressure of not more than 50 thousand atmospheres at its centre, which is exceeded at a mere 150 kilometres below the surface of the Earth; and pressures of this order, easily attainable in laboratories, are not sufficient to do much harm to the crystal lattice of the common silicate rocks subjected to them. On the basis of all evidence we now possess it is reasonable to surmise that the actual density of lunar surface material is close to 3.28 g cm^{-3}, and increases by compression to 3.41 g cm^{-3} near the Moon's centre. The relatively low mean density of the Moon precludes, therefore, the existence of any heavy core inside it; and its body should not be appreciably magnetized, an expectation borne out by measurements made aboard the space vehicles that recently paid close calls on our satellite.

Interior Does the Moon then represent a solid and nearly homogeneous rock, or is it partly molten in its interior? The answer is inseparably connected with the problem of the internal temperatures of the Moon, on which considerable light was thrown in recent years, in particular by Urey. In the present state of research it appears probable that the Moon, as well as all other solid bodies of the solar system, originated by an agglomeration of solid particles and dust at relatively low temperatures, decidedly lower than those required for complete volatilization. It does not seem possible to envisage a physical process which could lead to the formation of the planetary bodies—let alone the Moon—by a condensation of gas at high temperature. Therefore, the view prevalent today among serious students of the subject assumes that the original mass of the Moon accumulated from pre-existent smaller solid particles not less than some 4.6×10^9 years ago, and that the temperatures of this initial agglomeration (which may have formed, under favourable conditions, in a surprisingly short time) was moderate, between $-100°$ and 0°C.

Once, however, the body of the Moon grew up by coalescence of such particles at low temperatures, its subsequent thermal history became quite interesting. Heat was continuously being generated in the Moon's interior by spontaneous decay of such traces of radioactive elements (like potassium 40, thorium 232, or uranium 235 and 238) as are expected to be present in lunar matter by analogy with the Earth or with meteoritic material: that debris of solid particles in the space around us, left over from the days of the formation of the solar system, and intercepted by the Earth on its perpetual journey around the Sun. The amount of heat liberated by such elements is known from terrestrial laboratory measurements, and so is the rate of decay, generally of the order of 10^9–10^{10} years. The heat so generated in microscopic amounts throughout the entire mass of the Moon then flows outwards towards the cool surface, but is impeded by the low thermal conductivity of the rocks, which renders this cooling an exceedingly slow process.

The solution of the problem, at the hands of Urey and other investigators, led recently to the realization that the bulk of the mass of the Moon must, at present, be maintained at an internal temperature in excess of 700°C; and, in central parts of the Moon, the temperature may become so high (1,200–1,400°C) as to lead to at least partial melting. The Moon may, therefore, possess at present a small plastic core, chemically homogeneous with the rest of its mass. Moreover, the core is likely to grow slowly with time, for the Moon is at present very gradually warming up, and its central temperature increasing.

This gradual increase of lunar internal temperatures brings several interesting consequences: one of them is the inevitable desiccation and degassing of its interior. If the Moon originated, as we now believe, by an accumulation of essentially cold matter, this matter was bound to contain also a certain percentage of volatile compounds (such as H_2O, SO_2, etc.) which could, at low temperatures, have been absorbed into the crystal lattice of many minerals (hydrates, etc.) and thus be present in the initial Moon in solid state. However, at temperatures above 700°C, water vapour would be expelled from almost all hydrates, and penetrate, as superheated steam, through any crack or cavity in the interior towards the outer and cooler layers, where it could condense into liquid and eventually freeze. Some of it may have even made its way to the surface of our satellite to escape into space, or to hide itself in a variety of ways awaiting discovery. Whatever the case may be, there seems no escape from the conclusion that, as a result of gradually increasing internal temperature of the Moon (caused by radioactive heating) in the past 4,600,000,000 years, the bulk of its mass must have largely become desiccated by a gradual expulsion of all its volatile compounds which must, in turn, have considerably enriched the outer layers of the lunar globe. The evidence that this has indeed taken place will be examined when we inspect the visible surface of our satellite, and try to understand the nature of the forces and processes that have been shaping this face in the past.

Surface appearance Even to the naked eye, the face of the Moon is an interesting object, diversified with many markings. The most cursory glance through a telescope—or, better still, at a photograph of the Full Moon (Plate 5)—reveals that the lunar landscape consists of essentially two different types of surface. One type, rough and broken, is comparatively light in colour, reflecting, in places, as much as 20 or 30 per cent of incident sunlight; the other is darker, reflecting on the average but 6–7 per cent of incident sunlight, much smoother, and frequently quite flat. The first type of surface we generally call the 'mountains'. They occupy large continuous areas—particularly in the southern hemisphere of the Moon—and cover, on the whole, about two-thirds of the entire visible face of our satellite. The flatlands, 'seas' (or *maria*) as they were misnamed in the past, before the true nature of the lunar surface was properly understood, occupy the rest. They are, on the whole, remarkably uniform in reflectivity and general appearance, be they small or large.

A closer look at the Moon with the aid of a more powerful telescope reveals an almost bewildering array of formations and structures, no two of which are exactly alike. However, the dominant type of formation among them, and by far the most numerous in any part of the Moon, appears to be ring-like walled enclosures commonly called the craters. They occur almost everywhere on the Moon, in mountainous regions as well as in the seas, in truly prodigious abundance, giving the lunar surface an appearance of a pock-marked face. The number of craters with diameters exceeding one mile is estimated to be more than 100,000 on the visible face of the Moon alone; and those smaller still are too many to be counted.

The largest of these craters attain dimensions in excess of 200 km and representative samples are shown in the plates. The greatest walled plain of all visible on the near face of our satellite, the crater Clavius, 230 km in diameter, is shown in close-up in Plate 6*a*. The maximum height of its ramparts is only 1600 m above the surrounding landscape, but some 4900 m above the lowest point of its depressed floor. These heights are so small—and the dimensions of the crater so large—that an observer standing in the middle of its floor would not see even the rim of its ramparts at all—the considerable curvature of the relatively small lunar globe would lower them below his horizon!

There are altogether five such craters on the visible face of the Moon whose dimensions exceed 200 km; and an additional thirty-two objects with diameters between 100 and 200 km. Thus on the shores of a plain bearing the name of Mare Nectaris we find an impressive group of craters, the largest of which, Theophilus, possesses a diameter of just over 100 km; and the rugged landscape surrounding it is beautifully shown on a sunset photograph reproduced in Plate 6*b*. The maximum height of the ramparts of Theophilus above this landscape does not exceed 1200 m; but they tower some 4400 m above its floor and the central mountain rises to an altitude of 2200 m above its immediate surroundings.

On the opposite quadrant of the Moon, the extensive plains of the 'Ocean of Tempests' are dominated again by a magnificent solitary crater bearing the name of Copernicus (Plate 7), 90 km across, whose ramparts rise only 1000 m above the outer surroundings but 3300 m above the inner bowl. The central peak attains a modest relative altitude of 1200 m. Many other specimens of similar formations can be seen on the same photographs; and their description could continue almost without end.

No two mountains on the Moon are exactly alike; nevertheless they possess many characteristics in common. First, the heights of their ramparts prove, in general, to be very small in comparison with their absolute dimensions (Figure 4.1). Secondly, their floors appear systematically to be depressed below the surrounding surface, and the volume of the depressions seems in many cases to be closely equal to the volume of the ramparts around them, suggesting that the material of the rims may have been displaced from the crust by the forces that produced the crater pit. Very small craters appear to possess hardly any ramparts at all, and represent mere pits sunken in the lunar surface. The craters on the Moon thus hardly deserve the name of real mountains, and most of them have no obvious terrestrial counterpart.

Perhaps the most surprising result of recent morphological studies of such formations has been the realization, so contrary to earlier impressions based on visual inspection rather than measurement, that there appear to be no really steep slopes, of appreciable size, anywhere on the Moon; all slopes of crater walls or mountains whose gradients have so far been measured seem inclined to the horizontal direction by less than

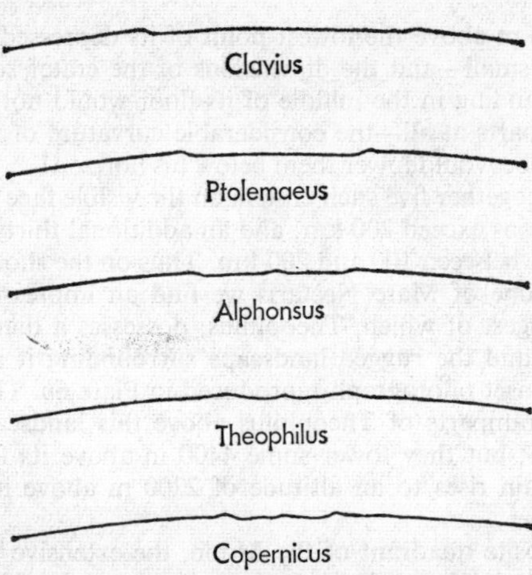

Figure 4.1 Profiles of five large lunar craters on the same scale as the curvature of the Moon. In order to bring the outline of the craters into perceptible relief the vertical scale has been made twice that of the horizontal. The actual craters are thus even flatter than these profiles suggest.

10°. The impression of ruggedness gathered by telescopic observation, or cursory glances at photographs, of the sunrise or sunset on the Moon largely disappears when the very low altitude of the Sun above the horizon (not readily apparent to inspection) is duly taken into account. When, in addition, we recall the large curvature of the relatively small lunar globe, which will effectively hide from view any but the nearest or highest landmarks—for example, a mountain 3000 metres high would completely disappear below the horizon at a distance of a mere 100 kilometres—we cannot escape the conclusion that the horizontal panorama visible from most points on the Moon would be quite flat and unimpressive, offering but a few points on which the eye of the explorer on the spot could safely rest in search of orientation.

Besides the craters and the maria, the surface of the Moon exhibits a great many other interesting features—chains of mountains, domes, rilles, rays—which may offer further significant clues to its past. But there is no room for doubt that the craters and the maria, by their number as well as the area occupied by them, constitute the most distinct morphological characteristics of the surface of our satellite; and any effort to reconstruct the past history of its composite fossil record will have to clarify the problem of their origin before lesser details are ripe for interpretation.

Origin and age of the craters What can we say at present about the origin of the lunar craters? A glance at an almost bewildering array of such formations, as shown in Plates 6 and 7, shows it to be unlikely that all originated in the same way or at the same time. In fact, the most reasonable approach to our problem can probably be made if, to begin with, we ask ourselves the question: what are the principal physical processes that could conceivably have been operative on the surface of our satellite? When we formulate the problem in this way, we meet at once the two principal contending theories of crater origin: the external theory, invoking the effects produced by impacts of other celestial bodies (asteroids, meteorites, or even comets) on the lunar surface, and the alternative theory, relying on the internal processes connected with the gradual defluidization and degassing of the lunar globe.

To begin with the theory of external impacts, it is necessary to remember that the interplanetary space through which the Earth with the Moon continues to circle around the Sun is not entirely empty, but contains a wide variety of ingredients of all weights and sizes, from the ubiquitous gas and plasma extending from the Sun, through microscopic specks of dust and larger meteoritic debris to major meteorites, asteroids and comets whose orbits through space may occasionally intersect the path of the Moon and collide with it. The frequency with which the surface of the Moon—like that of the Earth—may suffer direct hits by major chunks of cosmic matter in the form of asteroids or comets is difficult to assess with any accuracy at the present time, let alone what it could have been in a more distant past. As, however, in the past 4.6×10^9 years a certain number of such hits must undoubtedly have been scored, it is important to realize the consequences that such an event would bring about.

In an attempt to visualize these, let us consider a large meteorite, possibly a rock weighing a million tons and moving relative to the Moon with a velocity of (say) 30 km s^{-1}. The total kinetic energy of such a body would be such that if it were to crash against the surface of the Moon, it would penetrate into the crust like an armour-piercing bullet and get buried well underneath the surface before coming to a complete stop. The kinetic energy which the meteorite possessed before impact cannot, however, get lost. Its entire amount must re-appear in other guises to which it has been converted in accordance with known

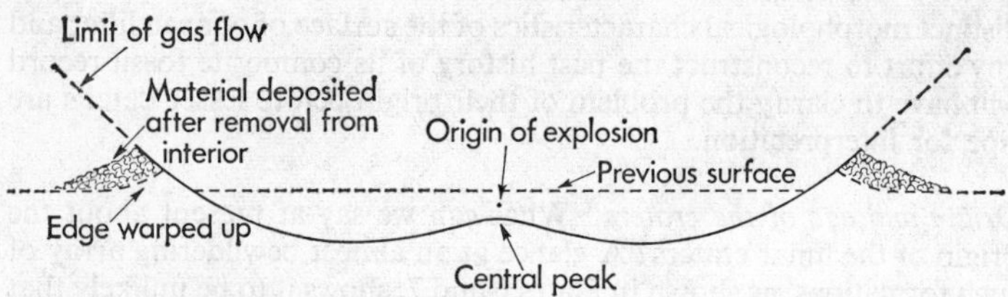

Figure 4.2 Schematic representation of a hypothetical lunar impact crater (after Gold). Vertical scale exaggerated.

laws of physics, mainly as heat, which would be sufficient completely to volatize the whole impinging mass and convert it into an extremely hot gas bubble at a temperature of the order of a million degrees.

Needless to say, so large a quantity of such extremely hot gas could not be contained for an instant by the weight of the overlying debris. It would immediately explode, and the expanding gas would affect severely a surrounding region very large in comparison with the size of the original missile. The main effect of such an explosion would, therefore, be essentially similar to that of a point-charge; and the initial direction of approach of the impinging body need not have had much influence on the geometry of the surface markings produced by the explosion. The probable result is shown on Figure 4.2, which represents the expected cross-section of a hypothetical lunar impact crater. The amount of actual solid material left around by the intruder would be negligible since most of it would evaporate and escape back into space, or get dispersed over a large part of the adjacent lunar surface.

Various terrestrial experiments with explosive charges detonated in suitable media have indeed been found to produce local surface effects closely simulating the ramparts of some types of lunar craters; but it is difficult to match in this way all known types of such formations. Besides, the weight of circumstantial evidence based on this analogy should not be overestimated; for the difference in scale and total energy of the terrestrial experiments and their hypothetical lunar analogues amounts to many orders of magnitude and necessitates a wide extrapolation. It is also still rather uncertain just what kind of partition of the incident kinetic energy to expect between heat and mechanical effects, some of which should be transmitted in the form of seismic waves through the entire lunar globe. Moreover, any effort to explain the principal features of the lunar surface by impact of solid bodies would be quite incomplete without simultaneous consideration of the effects produced by collisions with other known denizens of interplanetary space such as comets. These are as yet little explained or understood.

Having taken a brief stock of the principal external agents which can mutilate significantly the lunar face over long intervals of time, let us turn next to examine the internal processes whose action can possibly affect the surface of our satellite in a similar manner. These processes are, in general, connected with the gradual build-up of internal heat by radioactive decay, forcing all gases and volatile compounds to make their way from the Moon's interior to the surface, to accumulate there or to escape into space. This gradual defluidization and degassing, which must be continuously operative in the Moon as it has been in the Earth may, in turn, have produced (by upwelling and withdrawal of a molten rock column) local surface areas of subsidence, akin to the terrestrial 'calderas of collapse'. This is quite consistent with what is perhaps the most striking characteristic of lunar craters already mentioned, namely, the fact that their floors are systematically depressed below the level of the surrounding landscape. In the face of all these facts and considerations, it is very difficult to escape the conclusion that both types of formative process, external impacts as well as internal defluidization and degassing, had their hand in shaping the present face of our Moon. While some conspicuous 'ray craters' like Tycho or Copernicus (Plate 7) are very probably due to impacts, Clavius (Plate 6*a*) and others like it may again represent lunar calderas of collapse. As far as the flatlands or maria are concerned, greater uncertainty prevails. Many serious students of the subject consider them as solidified lava flows. As to the origin of this lava, Urey seeks its origin in large-scale melting caused by low-velocity impacts of solid planetesimals; Kopal points out a possible relevance of cometary impacts in this connection; while Green regards them as extensions of basaltic material which accompanied the process of defluidization, and Gold again as depositories of large amounts of dust removed by gradual abrasion of lunar highlands.

It is as yet impossible to discriminate among these various alternatives with any finality; but once we admit that different processes may have co-operated in shaping the face of the Moon as we see it today, the question arises about their timing. Can we fit the origin of the principal lunar surface features in any kind of reasonable time sequence? Absolute dating seems, unfortunately, impossible so far; but relative comparisons can indeed be attempted with some success.

Of various indications of the relative age of the craters (or of the maria), the 'principle of overlap' is perhaps the most dependable one.

If there are two craters that overlap each other—and the plates show several examples of such overlaps—then the one with the unbroken rim must be younger than the one whose rim was damaged or entirely removed. In the case of two overlapping craters of comparable dimensions, such as Theophilus and Cyrillus (Plate 6*b*), there is no room for doubt that Cyrillus must be the older formation of the two. But the same principle can also be extended to cases in which a large crater contains smaller ones within its enclosures; an example of such a situation is the Hale photograph of the crater Clavius in Plate 6*a*. No kind of process that raised the ramparts of the large formation could have left the small interior craters intact; hence, the latter must have been formed subsequently. If so, however, Clavius must be considerably more ancient than all other smaller craters—at least forty of them—which can at present be seen on its floor; and the greater the number of smaller craters inside a large one, the greater their presumed disparity in ages.

Crater overlaps of great multiplicity can be found in certain parts of the lunar surface; and it is occasionally possible thus to arrange five or six craters in a time sequence. Another relative age criterion is afforded by the streaks, or 'rays', of bright material which are seen to diverge in all directions from certain craters (Tycho, or Copernicus, for instance), sometimes to a great distance. As these rays must obviously have originated at the same time as the crater at their convergent point, the latter must obviously be younger than any features overlaid by the ray. Such rays represent, indeed, a system of tentacles spreading widely over certain sections of the lunar surface, and enabling us to extend our system of relative dating wherever they reach.

The main importance of these age criteria lies, however, in their application to the dating of the maria. If we accept the foregoing premises, there seems to be no escape from the conclusion that the oldest parts of the visible lunar surface are those which are most rugged and contain the greatest number of craters or other mountains per unit area. For irrespective of whether the rate of accretion of craters on the Moon, by whatever process, has been uniform or diminishing with time, the oldest parts of its surface should obviously have suffered the greatest number of scars. If this is indeed so, then the oldest parts of the visible surface of the Moon are without doubt the regions surrounding its south pole—the lunar Antarctic—which may indeed record an unbroken chain of events that have affected it since the days of the formation of our satellite. But as the density of craters in most of the great dark plains of the lunar surface is much less than that encountered near the south pole, it follows that the maria must be very much younger

Plate 5 The Moon when full showing the maria and ray systems

Plate 6*a* The crater Clavius near the time of sunset. Being seen relatively close to the edge it is foreshortened. Actually it is a circular walled mountain 230 km in diameter and the largest of its type on the near side of the Moon.
Hale Observatories

Plate 6*b* Sunset over the shores of Mare Nectaris. The principal craters are Theophilus (centre), Cyrillus and Catharina (above). Their approximate diameters are 100, 90 and 90 km.
Yerkes Observatory

Plate 7 The crater Copernicus as seen from the Earth and from Lunar Orbiter 2

The oblique view of this 90 km-diameter crater shown in Plate *a* (upper left) was taken on 23 November 1966 when the Orbiter was close to the position marked A on *b* (upper right), while *c* (below) shows a high resolution view taken from a point 46 km above B. USAIS-NASA

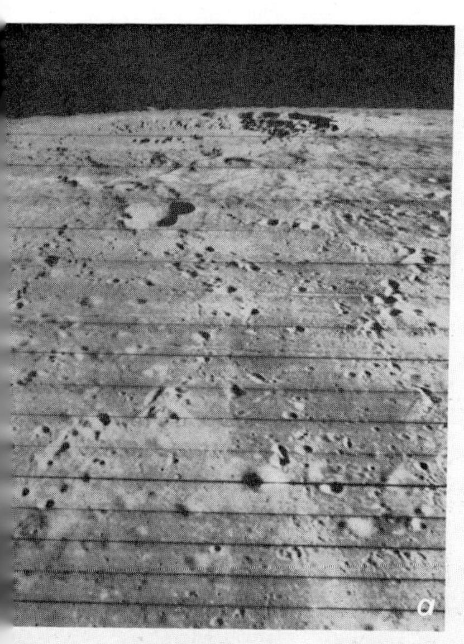

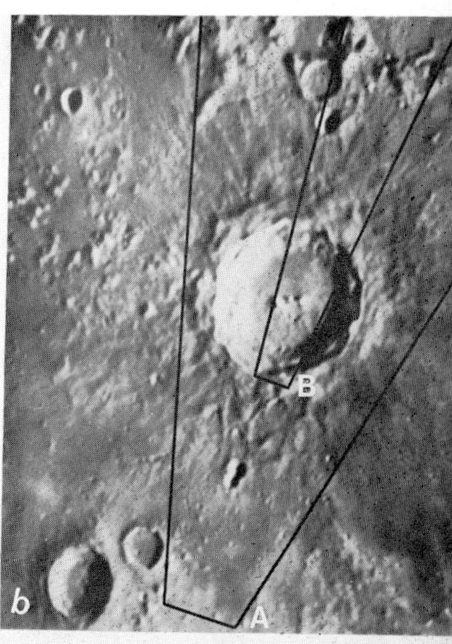

Plate 8 *a* Planet Earth photographed from Apollo 17, December 1972

A large part of the Earth, and particularly the southern hemisphere, is covered with cloud, but in the north Arabia and the Red Sea, the Gulf of Aden, the Horn of Africa and Madagascar can be seen clearly. USAIS-NASA

b Man's footprint on the Moon. USAIS-NASA

than the mountainous regions; and some of the great craters like Copernicus, Kepler, or Aristarchos, which spread the tentacles of their bright rays over large parts of the surrounding maria, must be younger still. They represent, quite probably, the latest large-scale addition to the full exhibit of lunar surface features engraved there, perhaps, in the past one hundred million years.

Surface temperature and radiation This should conclude our brief survey of the strange world of the Moon as we can see it from the Earth through our telescopes. As is well known, the limit imposed by atmospheric unsteadiness on the resolving power of even the largest terrestrial telescopes precludes us from discerning on the lunar surface objects smaller than a few hundred metres in size, i.e., relatively coarse features if viewed on the spot. In order to learn more about the finer structure of the lunar surface and its physical properties, we must turn now to study the information contained in the light of the Moon, and examine the message carried by its photons, those nimble-footed messengers which continuously reach us from the Moon at top speed unencumbered by the shackles of universal gravitation. All photons travel with the same speed, but there is great diversity in the amount of energy they carry. Not all of them can, moreover, penetrate through our own atmosphere; many fall prey to the terrestrial atoms or molecules lying in wait to absorb them before they can reach the ground-based astronomer at his telescope. The astronomer can, therefore, inspect and analyse only such variety of lunar photons as can actually reach him through available atmospheric windows; and these fall, by and large, in two distinct groups, the optical (light) and the radio parts of the spectrum. In what follows, we shall examine these in turn.

Of what does the optical light of the Moon really consist? As is known to every school-child these days, most of the moonlight is nothing but sunlight incident on the Moon and scattered by the lunar surface in the direction of the Earth. The amount of light scattered by the Moon at different phases, i.e. different altitudes of the Sun above the lunar horizon, offers in turn a possibility of finding out about the small-scale structure of the scattering surface—for instance, its degree of roughness. An appropriate analysis of photometric observations of the Moon at different phases, undertaken by many investigators, thus reveals that the average lunar surface material is likely to be porous rather than smooth on the centimetre scale; while the degree of polarization caused by scattering discloses that this rough surface must be covered by at least a thin layer of fine dust, whose grains are, on the average, between one or two micrometres in size.

We shall have more to say about this dust later on, in connection with the thermal conductivity of the lunar surface. For the present we wish to stress that this surface is, on the whole, a rather poor reflector. Only about 7 per cent of incident light is scattered by the Moon as a whole; although the actual amount fluctuates somewhat from spot to spot. The balance of incident sunlight is absorbed by the lunar surface, and converted into heat. But any 'black' body—and the lunar surface behaves very much like one—must re-emit all the radiation it has absorbed; and the distribution in frequency of this emission will be controlled solely by the prevailing absolute temperature, in accordance with what physicists call Planck's law. For the Sun, whose temperature is about 5400°C on the surface, most of the radiation is emitted between the violet and the red ends of the visible spectrum, with a maximum in the yellow, giving a total impression of what we call 'white light'. This is also the colour of reflected moonlight; but the lunar radiation proper is of a very different kind.

The sole, and sufficient, reason for this is the fact that the temperature of the lunar surface is much lower than that of the Sun. The Moon, like the Earth, receives virtually all its surface heat from the Sun; and as their average distances from it amount to 214 solar radii, each square centimetre of lunar surface (unprotected by any atmosphere) receives only one $(214)^2$th or the 46,000th part of the heat flux passing through each square centimetre of the surface of the Sun. As this flux is (for a black body) known to be proportional to the fourth power of the temperature above absolute zero (−273°C), it follows that (when the Sun is directly overhead and its rays fall perpendicularly on the illuminated surface) the temperature of the sunlit lunar landscape should be $\sqrt{214}$ or about 15 times lower than that of the Sun, or approximately 110°C. Now Planck's law discloses that, at this temperature, the radiation emitted by a black body will be very different from white light; most of it being in the deep infrared (with a maximum around the wavelength of 10 micrometres or 0.01 mm). Light of this colour is quite invisible to the human eye, and incapable of impressing the photographic plate. It will, in addition, experience considerable difficulty in penetrating the terrestrial atmosphere. However, that part of it which does get through can be detected and, in fact, quite accurately measured, by its thermo-electric effect.

There exists, moreover, still another way in which the lunar surface can transform incident sunlight into a characteristic light of its own; and that is by a process of non-thermal emission commonly called luminescence. As is well known, luminescence represents the ability of certain substances to absorb photons (or mechanical stimulus by corpuscular radiation) of relatively high energy, and re-emit it by instalments at certain discrete lower frequencies; for example, to absorb ultraviolet light and to re-emit the energy as visible light. Now in the absence of any protective atmosphere to speak of, the lunar surface is continuously exposed to sunlight of all frequencies from radio waves to X-rays—and also to a continuous bombardment by charged particles, mostly photons and electrons, evaporating from the Sun and blowing past the Moon (sometimes in gusts) as a 'solar wind'. There are several indications that this stimulating radiation causes the lunar surface to return part of it, at lower frequencies, as fluorescent light. Such light is particularly in evidence during the partial phases of eclipses of the Moon; but even out of eclipses the contribution of localized fluorescence to the total light of the Moon may amount to a few per cent.

However, it is proper to stress again that all light reaching us from the Moon is nothing but sunlight, original or transformed. Most of this light falls on the Moon directly, and the rest indirectly by way of sunlit Earth. A few per cent of this light is scattered from the rough lunar surface back into space, with its white colour essentially unchanged; and the fluctuation of the scattering power (albedo) from place to place, caused no doubt by different types of lunar surface material, endows the apparent disk of the Moon with its characteristic patchy appearance. This is the component of moonlight visible to the naked eye, and responsible for the term the 'silvery moon' of our songs and romance. Most of the incident sunlight is, however, absorbed by the lunar surface and re-emitted as infrared frequencies that are invisible to the human eye. This moonlight cannot be seen or photographed, and for this reason we do not readily recognize its existence; but thermo-electric detectors leave no room for doubt that we are, in fact, living under an 'infrared' rather than 'silvery' moon, notwithstanding all poetical fiction.

How does the infrared emission by the Moon vary in the course of a lunar day, and to what surface temperatures does it correspond? Repeated careful thermo-electric measures of lunar radiations from selected areas of the surface have indicated that, at the subsolar point in the lunar tropics—when the Sun stands directly overhead—the predicted temperatures, as high as 110°C, are indeed attained each day. In the course of the afternoon on the Moon, as the altitude of the Sun decreases, the local temperature declines steadily to well below freezing at the time of sunset, and continues further to decline in the course of the night down to a minimum between −160° and −170°C. The total range of day-to-night variation in temperature of the Moon amounts, therefore, to little less than 300°C, and ranges from a temperature above that of boiling water at noon down to that of liquid air at dawn.

The mean surface temperature of the lunar globe appears to be well below the freezing-point of water; but it is the extremes that concern us in the first place: why does the Moon behave so differently from the Earth in this respect? For both the Earth and the Moon the principal source of heat on the surface is, of course, sunlight, in comparison with which the outward flow of heat from the interior is almost negligible; and as our planet and its satellite are, on the average, equally far from the Sun, both are bound to receive equal shares. But their particular properties allow them to husband their energy in essentially different ways. The absence of any appreciable atmosphere around the Moon precludes the trapping, as on the Earth, of its thermal radiation from the surface in a surrounding gaseous mantle; all of it is bound to escape into space; and the very small heat capacity of its rocky surface (so different from that of the terrestrial oceans) causes it to become very hot during the daytime and cold again at night. In one respect, however, the lunar climatic changes are not as drastic as the extremes alone may indicate; for although the temperature range is so great, the duration of the lunar day—lasting 27.32 days or 656 hours of our own time—is again so long that the rate of change of the temperature is, in fact, less than 9 degrees per hour. It is the persistence of this change over so many hours of rise and fall which makes the extremes in temperature so wide.

There exists, however, a time when the temperature changes on the Moon become very much more rapid: and that is during the relatively brief intervals of lunar eclipses when approximately twice a year (or every six lunar days), the Moon passes through the shadow of the Earth for a period of a few hours. Thermo-electric measurements reveal that, during this brief spell of time, the lunar surface experiences virtually as large a variation in temperature as between day and night. In particular, the egress of the Moon from the shadow brings about so frantic a 'heat wave' that the temperature on the surface rises by almost 200 degrees within less than one hour. This constitutes virtually a rock-breaking temperature gradient, which can do the surface rocks much more damage than the more frequent, but less rapid, daily temperature changes.

It should, however, be stressed that these large climatic variations appear to be limited to the outermost layer of the lunar surface, exposed to outer space, and become very much smaller immediately beneath it—as has been recently disclosed by observations of the thermal emission of the lunar globe in the domain of radio frequencies. In the preceding paragraphs we have mentioned already that the moderate absolute temperature of the lunar globe will cause most of its own thermal radiation to lie in the far infrared (with a maximum around 10 micrometres wavelength) and to fall off gradually towards longer wavelengths. Most of this moonlight will be absorbed in our atmosphere up to a wavelength of approximately one millimetre, but beyond this limit the atmosphere becomes transparent again to afford us a new view of the Moon and other celestial bodies in a truly strange light.

Measurements of the thermal emission of the Moon in the microwave range (i.e., at frequencies between 3,000 and 100,000 megahertz) revealed that, surprisingly enough, the range of the corresponding temperature variation turns out to be considerably less than in the near infrared—becoming the more reduced, the longer the wavelength. Secondly, the maxima or minima of the microwave temperature curves do not follow in phase the altitude of the Sun above the horizon, but lag behind it, again by amounts increasing with the wavelength. Thus, in light of 1–2 millimetres wavelength, Sinton found the temperature of the lunar surface to vary only between $-100°$ and $+ 30°$C, following the amount of surface insolation, with a phase-lag of 2–3 hours. Piddington and Minnett, working at a wavelength of 12.5 millimetres, found the extreme of the temperature variation reduced to about a third of its surface value, with a phase-lag of more than three days; while Denisse, working at a still longer wavelength of 33 centimetres, found the flux of the lunar thermal radiation to be constant day and night, and equal to $-50° \pm 30°$C.

Nature of the surface What is the cause of all these phenomena? The basic clue to their understanding is the fact that the thermal radiation of the Moon at different frequencies does not originate at the same depth, but the longer wavelengths come, in general, from deeper layers. In other words, the surface of the Moon—opaque to visible and infrared light—becomes partially transparent in the domain of microwaves; and the lower their frequency, the deeper inside we can penetrate in their train. In the decimetre range (still observable by existing instruments) we can manage to penetrate almost one yard beneath the surface in tracing the flow of heat caused by daily exposure to the Sun. As sunshine on the Moon is, moreover, never interrupted by clouds, the insolation of its surface proceeds each day with clock-like regularity, and the heat incident upon it makes its way inwards in accordance with the well-known properties of heat flow in solids.

If the daily variation of microwave temperatures decreases as rapidly with depth (and continues to lag in phase behind the variation on the surface) as the existing observations appear to indicate, the reason can only be a very low thermal conductivity of the surface layers. The calculated coefficient of heat conduction matching the observed facts turns out to be so low as to make it quite clear that most of the visible lunar surface cannot consist of bare solid rock, but must be covered by a fine dust, of an average grain size of the order of a few micrometres, letting heat flow only through areas where the individual dust grains are actually in contact. This conception is completely in agreement with the polarization properties of scattered moonlight, when the surface of our satellite is illuminated by the Sun at different angles.

That the lunar surface should be covered by dust was, perhaps, only to be expected; for no bare solid rock could stand indefinitely the strenuous day-by-day heating and cooling to which the lunar surface is exposed, particularly the violent temperature changes experienced during lunar eclipses. Under such conditions all rocks are bound to keep cracking into increasingly smaller bits; and solar ultraviolet and corpuscular radiation as well as cosmic rays may do further significant damage to the crystalline structure of smaller fragments.

This 'native' dust produced by inevitable gradual cracking of the lunar surface must, furthermore, be freely intermingled with the 'cosmic' dust swept up by the Moon on its perpetual journey, with the Earth, through interplanetary space. This dust and meteoric debris (which represent, probably, the left-overs from the formation of the solar system) is, of course, being intercepted by the Earth as well, and the rate of its infall is established experimentally by a variety of methods. If we assume, reasonably enough, that the rate of deposition of cosmic dust on the Moon is approximately constant, we are led to expect that the total deposit on the lunar surface in the past 4,500 million years should add up to nearly one metre. Unless, perchance, this rate of deposit was very much higher in the past than it seems to be now, more could scarcely have fallen on the Moon from outside even throughout its entire astronomical past; and as to the indigenous dust produced by gradual disintegration of lunar rocks, once a few inches have been formed on the top, the rocks beneath should be completely shielded from any further temperature or radiation damage. No more dust than (at most) a metre could thus be locally produced (or accumulated) anywhere on the Moon; unless, of course, the dust, once formed, could move to another place and thus expose the parent rock to continued erosion.

But how could anything move over the dead and inert landscape of the Moon? There is certainly not enough atmosphere around it to give rise to any appreciable wind; and apart from occasional disturbances produced by meteor impacts, the only physical agent ever present to provide gentle stirring is the random (Brownian) motion of dust grains activated by the prevailing temperature. Dust of an average grain size of 1–2 micrometres cannot, however, be stirred by temperature agitation alone to form a dust 'atmosphere' more than a fraction of a millimetre scale height even at lunar high noon; and so minute a layer cannot, in turn, provide any effective means for the transport of dust from one place to another in the daytime, let alone at night.

This argument may, however, be altered somewhat when we turn to consider the electrostatic forces arising from electrical charges, which the lunar dust is almost certain to accumulate. In order to explain this point, let us consider some basic facts of lunar electrodynamics. We have mentioned before that, in the absence of a protective atmosphere, the solid surface of the Moon is bound to be daily exposed to the full blast of undiluted sunlight; and this produces many interesting consequences. Not only, as we have already seen, will the 'lunar auroral zone' be relegated on to the solid surface, but the 'lunar ionosphere' as well. For, on the surface, the solar ultraviolet and X-ray (as well as corpuscular) radiation will meet, on the whole, a much greater proportion of the elements, such as Si, Mg, Fe, Al, Ca, Na, etc., with weakly-bound outer electrons than in the terrestrial upper atmosphere; and, as a result, this radiation should produce much more intensive ionization than that encountered in the E- or F-layers of our own atmosphere, where the same undiluted sunlight meets only gases relatively difficult to ionize. As a result, the photo-ionization caused by the solar ultraviolet and X-rays, together with the impact of solar and cosmic corpuscular radiation (both consisting essentially of protons), is bound to keep charging the lunar surface positively in the course of time.

How long, however, can this charge keep building up? For it is obvious that a growing positive charge on the surface is bound to retard (or prevent altogether) any escape of electrons below a certain energy threshold, thus gradually slowing down the growth of the charge—and, besides, the surface charge must also be lessened by sweeping up of free electrons from the interplanetary space, i.e. the extension of the Sun's corona. The actual density and extent of an electron envelope surrounding the lunar surface will be the resultant of a contest between these mutually antagonistic processes; but their combined effect should envelop at least the sunlit face of the Moon with a space charge (or transient atmosphere) of free electrons, whose density and height should fluctuate in the course of the day. Its actual quantitative analysis is made difficult by the fact that several crucial factors (such as the actual electron density in space, or the electron emission of the lunar surface) are as yet uncertain within fairly wide limits; but the observed occulations of radio sources (such as the Crab Nebula) by the Moon indicate that this density may be of the order of 10^4 electrons per centimetre, i.e. about 100 to 1000 times as large as the density of interplanetary electrons around us.

However, coming back to the surface dust, many of these free electrons may be temporarily captured by (or released from) the dust grains lying on the surface or hovering low above it as a result of their random (Brownian) motion, and the electrostatic repulsion thus produced may stir the dust against gravity in a much more effective manner than any Brownian motion maintained by the prevailing temperature. If so, an electrostatically charged dust atmosphere might indeed attain an appreciable height above the sunlit lunar surface, or experience some kind of wind as the noon meridian travels around the lunar equator. Even then, however, the actual mass of the dust which could be transported across the lunar surface remains uncertain and largely conjectural.

The missing atmosphere To conclude our description of the conditions prevailing on the surface of our satellite (as far as they can be reconstructed on the basis of available telescopic observations), some words may be added concerning possible gas content of a hypothetical lunar atmosphere. In all our previous discussion we disregarded the existence of such gas altogether; but how sure are we that this is indeed the case? First, the kinetic theory of gases discloses that the low gravitation of the Moon (less than one-sixth of that of the Earth) and the consequent relatively low velocity of escape (2.38 km s^{-1}) from the surface makes it very difficult to retain permanently any free atomic or molecular gas around it at daytime temperatures; the feeble gravity on the Moon does not make its surroundings sufficiently 'air-tight' for any gas of low molecular weight. Hydrogen or helium would, for instance, dissipate into space in a matter of days. Free oxygen, nitrogen, water vapour or carbon dioxide would escape more slowly on account of their greater molecular weight. but would still be lost from the Moon in a time very short in comparison with the lunar age—not to speak of the fact that reactive gases (like oxygen or sulphur dioxide) would react also with the lunar surface rocks and thus soon be bound in solid chemical compounds. But even apart from this, the rate of thermal disspation into space of all but the heavier gases (which are, again, cosmically very scarce) from the Moon is so high that we should not expect to find any appreciable permanent atmosphere around it; and this expectation seems indeed to be borne out by all aspects of the observational evidence available to us so far.

The most sensitive evidence of this type is the complete absence of the twilight phenomena on the Moon, or the elongation of its cusps beyond 90° caused by scattered sunlight, which should be detectable by its polarization. Lyot and (later) Dollfus proved, in this way, that the absence of detectable polarization imposes an upper limit for the density of neutral gas above the lunar surface equal to some 10^{-9} of the atmospheric density at sea-level on Earth; how much smaller its actual density may be remains largely conjectural.

A gas density of this order of magnitude (attained, incidentally, in our own atmosphere at an altitude of 180 km) represents a pretty hard vacuum, in fact, embarrassingly hard; for one would have expected that the 'inert' gases like argon, krypton, or xenon, which for reasons of their atomic structure do not normally enter into compounds, and are at the same time heavy enough for their rate of escape from the gravitational field of the Moon to be moderately slow, would add up altogether to more; and their absence seems to confront us with a new problem.

The case of argon is particularly interesting, because, quite apart from any quantity of this element with which the Moon may have been endowed at the time of its origin, its supply must be continually replenished by radioactive decay of the heavy isotope of potassium (K^{40}). If, as is highly likely, the chemical composition of the Moon is similar to that of the outer mantle of the Earth, potassium should constitute about 0.12 per cent of it by weight. The total mass of the Moon (which is 7.35×10^{22} kg) should then contain about 8.8×10^{19} kg of potassium; and of this about 9.7×10^{14} kg should be radioactive K^{40} decaying into the common isotope of argon A^{40}.

The total disintegration of all lunar radioactive K^{40} should, therefore, create 9.7×10^{14} kg or 1.5×10^{40} atoms of argon, as compared with some 10^{44} gas particles that now constitute the terrestrial atmosphere. Just how much of this argon may have succeeded in escaping to the surface from the bulk of the lunar mass by its gradual degassing (caused by the rising internal temperature) remains still conjectural; but on almost any reasonable estimate the amount of free argon now present around the Moon should add up to more than the upper limit for the lunar air density that is consistent with the absence of perceptible twilight phenomena.

How are we to explain this apparent discrepancy? One way out of the dilemma was recently indicated by Herring and Licht, who pointed out that a good many atoms of heavy gases contained in whatever primordial atmosphere the Moon may once have had (or created there by radioactive decay as well as by nuclear disintegrations arising from the impact of cosmic rays) can be 'blown off' into space by collisions with the corpuscular radiation emitted from time to time (and sometimes in considerable gusts) by the Sun. The existence of such gusts, usually associated with flares and other disturbances of the solar surface, is well known and attested by such terrestrial phenomena as the polar aurorae and magnetic storms. Herring and Licht argue that the knocking-off power of this 'solar wind' should be sufficient to remove most of the argon and other gases from the proximity of the lunar surface, and thus to despoil it of even such exceedingly tenuous traces of gas vesture as the feeble lunar gravity would manage to retain.

More recently, however, Öpik and Singer pointed out another and more effective way of gas removal from the lunar surface; namely, by ionization. As long as gas remains neutral, its atoms or molecules can be removed only by collisions, be it with other molecules, or particles of the 'solar wind'. Should, however, the gas particles become ionized and thus acquire positive electric charge (and Öpik with Singer has shown how easily this can happen to lunar argon and heavier inert gases), the positive charge of the sunlit hemisphere of the Moon acquired by photo-ionization of the light elements in its crust can remove ions by repulsion far more effectively than could be accomplished by the collisions with particles of the solar wind.

Such gases as are left by these processes to cling to the lunar surface for a limited time do not, therefore, constitute any real atmosphere (in which individual gas particles are balanced up by mutual collisions) but rather a transient *exosphere* in which the individual atoms or ions describe essentially free-flight trajectories in the prevailing gravitational or electrostatic field. Each planetary atmosphere is bound to peter out into such an exosphere on its outer fringe bordering on interplanetary space; but on the Moon this exosphere apparently reaches down to the solid surface itself. As to its probable chemical composition, owed partly to captures from interplanetary space and partly to degassing of the lunar surface layers, Öpik estimated recently that it contains approximately 5×10^5 particles per cm^3 among which are about 1.2×10^4 molecules of hydrogen, 1.4×10^5 molecules of water; a comparable number of the molecules of carbon dioxide; and not more than 1×10^4 atoms of inert gases.

If, moreover, the Moon possesses no detectable atmosphere, it cannot, of course, maintain any liquid on its surface. Near the poles, to be sure, depressions may exist which are never reached by direct sunlight and which are illuminated at best by sunlight scattered from adjacent slopes. In such regions, condensed volatile substances may possibly be present in the form of some kind of a permafrost; but should they ever evaporate, they are apt to be lost in a very short time. Hence, no liquid—or even solid—water can be present at any spot on the Moon which can be reached by sunlight. The surface of the Moon must, therefore, be regarded as bone-dry; with none of its visible features formed, or even modified, by running water; or by freezing and melting water. With both hydrosphere and atmosphere effectively absent as disturbing agents, the fossil record of the lunar surface should possess a *vastly greater degree of permanence* than anything known to us on Earth: later in this chapter we shall disclose the facts furnished by the Apollo 11 mission confirming that this is indeed the case.

If the Moon cannot possess any permanent atmosphere to speak of, could it, perchance, have acquired at times a transient atmosphere, which could have shielded its surface at least temporarily; and thus have enabled (for instance) the existence of fluid flow for at least limited periods of the long lunar past? The answer to this question cannot so far be an unqualified no; for, regardless of any possible past period of temporary volcanism or degassing, a temporary atmosphere could also have been 'imported' from outside whenever the Moon suffers a collision with a comet.

Chemical composition Having thus described the principal types of large-scale structural characteristics of the lunar surface and at least some features of their environment, let us turn to the chemical and mineralogical composition of the material constituting it, the first samples of which we received in terrestrial laboratories from manned spacecraft (Apollo 11 and 12) in 1969. By atomic content the most abundant constituents of the material brought back by Apollo 11 from Mare Tranquillitatis are oxygen (40–60 per cent by weight), aluminium (4–7 per cent), titanium (4–6 per cent) and magnesium (4–6 per cent)—to list only elements present in amounts exceeding one per cent. The ranges indicated for each element refer to the respective abundances in different samples. The samples returned by Apollo 12 from the Oceanus Procellarum in November 1969 were found to be of a broadly similar composition with some differences such as a lower titanium content.

The molecular composition of lunar matter was found to consist predominantly of silica (SiO_2; 38–43 per cent) followed by FeO (16–21 per cent), Al_2O_3 (9–13 per cent), CaO (9–12 per cent), TiO_2 (7–11 per cent) MgO (7–10 per cent) and other constituents amounting to less than one per cent by weight. The bearing strength of the surface amounts to a few pounds per square inch (i.e., about 0.3 N cm^{-2}), increasing rapidly with depth; and the bulk density of the fine-grain component of the material is between 1.5 and 1.6 g cm^{-3}. Since the densities of the individual compact grains were found to range between 3.1 and 3.5 g cm^{-3}, it follows that about half of the volume of the bulk of the material lifted from the topmost layer of the surface is empty space. This accounts for the relatively low bearing strength of the material, as well as for its low effective dielectric constant. Therefore, the bulk of the material covering the lunar surface, as we see in Plate 4, and in which the astronauts made imprints of their footsteps (Plate 8*b*) consists of loosely packed silicate material, predominantly silica.

How do these results compare with previous expectations? That the surface of the Moon is covered with loosely packed material of very low thermal conductivity and radar reflectivity we knew before from ground-based observations on Earth; and its relatively low bearing has been previously disclosed by the Surveyors. However, as regards the chemical composition of lunar material, prior to the return of the Apollo samples two schools of thought were abroad; one expected the Moon to possess a chemical composition akin to that of the terrestrial mantle, which should have been the case if the Moon's mass was ever detached from the Earth; while the other—regarding the Moon as a primary object possibly older than our planet—anticipated a similarity between the composition of the Moon and that of the solar atmosphere. The latter should approximate as closely as anything within observational (i.e. spectroscopic) reach to the unadulterated composition of primordial matter from which the solar system originated; unadulterated because, on one hand, the large mass of the Sun would have prevented any selective escape of the elements from its gravitational field; and, on the other hand, its temperature is too low to cause nuclear transformations on any appreciable scale.

The observational verdict delivered by the lunar spacecraft confounded both these views, and presented the Moon to us in a much more enigmatic light, for chemically the Moon proved to be quite different from both the Sun and the Earth. For example, its content of titanium (and also chromium, zircon and others) is very much higher than in the Sun or the Earth's crust; whereas other elements, like nickel and sodium, potassium or europium, are again very much less abundant. In particular, the ratio of iron-to-nickel in the Moon appears to be larger than that encountered in any other sample of cosmic matter we know (the Earth's crust; solar atmosphere; meteorites) and the common elements like carbon or nitrogen appear to be conspicuously absent from the compounds found so far in the lunar crust.

What kind of rocks have been found on the Moon? All those brought back so far are *igneous*, of generally *basaltic composition*; and numerous minerals of this type well-known from the Earth, such as olivine, plagioclase, feldspar, ilmenite, and others, have been identified in many samples. In point of fact, only three new minerals, not known previously from the Earth, have been found in lunar rocks so far. Their crystalline structure and chemical properties indicated, moreover, that lunar rocks solidified at temperatures between 1000–1200°C under highly reducing conditions (the partial pressure of available free oxygen had to be less than 10^{-13} of an atmosphere to account for the virtual absence of higher states of oxidation). Moreover, many rocks exhibit evidence of shock metamorphism, which is strongly suggestive of effects of the passage of intense shock waves through solids, such as can be produced on the Moon by meteoric impacts from space. All rocks brought back from the Moon so far are, therefore, igneous; but we should not jump to a conclusion equating 'igneous' with 'volcanic'. All rocks we call 'volcanic' on the Earth are, to be sure, igneous; but the converse is not necessarily true. Lunar rocks we possess do indicate the effects of heat treatment; but no rocks of the same structure ever passed through the crater of any terrestrial volcano!

What could, then, be their origin; and what is the origin of the Moon as a whole? In the present state of research it is probable that the Moon —like most other bodies of the solar system—came into being by an agglomeration of solid pre-existing particles. It does not seem possible to envisage a workable process which could lead to the formation of planetary bodies, let alone of mass as small as that of the Moon, by condensation of gas at moderate or high temperature. Therefore, the view prevalent today is that the Moon accumulated from pre-existing solid particles more than 4000 million years ago; and it is at least possible that some of these particles may have been heated up to temperatures well above their melting point by the Sun which at that time may have been in the last stage of its contraction towards the Main Sequence, and very much larger than now; possibly of dimensions comparable with those of the present orbits of the inner planets.

At this stage, the Sun would have been somewhat cooler than today; but dust clouds exposed to it at a shorter range could have been heated to several hundred degrees or even more. If any particles evaporated during this heat treatment, the gas thus produced would have dissipated beyond retrieval; but particles which only melted could have cooled off again quite rapidly in a condensing swarm, in which the individual particles shield each other by their shadows from the scorching sunlight. It is, therefore, possible that not only the surface material, but the bulk of the Moon's mass may have acquired its igneous (basaltic) nature *before* the original swarm of solid particles coalesced into the lunar globe as we know it today; and that the source of heat responsible for this conversion need not have been any radioactively heated sub-surface volcanic 'pockets', but radiant energy of the youthful Sun.

Age of lunar rocks Perhaps the most important scientific result which we owe to the Apollo missions has been a determination of the time which has elapsed since the solidification of the lunar rocks now in our hands. As is well known, this can be ascertained from continuous ticking of atomic clocks embedded in most minerals occurring in nature, in the form of radioactive elements spontaneously disintegrating at a known rate. The particular atomic clock best suited for measurements of long intervals of time is radioactive potassium (^{40}K), which disintegrates (by β-decay) into one kind of argon (^{40}Ar) at a constant rate. Laboratory measurements have disclosed this rate to be such that one-half of potassium 40 will decay into argon in a time close to 1,270 million years, which is quite independent of the physical conditions (temperature, pressure) to which solid minerals are exposed. The decay product, argon, is a gas which would escape freely from a liquid, but becomes imprisoned in the crystal lattice of a mineral from the moment when it solidifies. If, at a later time, we grind a sample to powder and expel gas from it by heating, the ratio of the decay produce (^{40}Ar) to its mother substance (^{40}K) will indicate as a hand of a cosmic clock the time that has elapsed since the respective sample solidified; and neither temperature, nor pressure to which rocks can be exposed will alter in the least the regularity of its march. Other radioactive methods (based on the determination of uranium-lead, or strontium-rubidium ratios) have been developed for the same purpose and led to closely concordant results.

When this method was applied for the determination of the age of crystalline lunar rocks which the Apollo 11 astronauts brought back to the Earth from Mare Tranquillitatis, the potassium-argon clock indicated that *these rocks must have crystallized 3000–4000 million years ago*; with the average age close to 3700 million years. On the other hand, similar finds picked up by Apollo 12 at its landing place in Oceanus Procellarum proved to be only 2000–3000 million years old, their average age being thus more than one milliard years less. The dispersion in age within each group is no doubt real; and testifies to the fact that not all rocks found now in the same place on the Moon actually solidified *in situ*. The local finds represent rather a mixture of rocks which may have been transported there (by impact throw-outs) from different parts of the Moon. A difference between the average age of the majority of rocks brought back from Mare Tranquillitatis and Oceanus Procellarum is probably due to a difference of more than one milliard years between the events which gave rise to these formations; Mare Tranquillitatis being the older of the two.

However, perhaps the most interesting result which has come about so far from radioactive dating of lunar rocks is the fact that on each landing site investigated by Apollos 11 and 12 the smaller debris was found to exhibit substantially greater age. The time which elapsed since the solidification of these small 'fines' proved, in fact, to cluster around 4.6 milliard years in *both* localities, making their ages virtually identical with those of the oldest known meteoritic material. A lighter colour, i.e. higher albedo, of many of these small chips lends some weight to a conjecture that these chips solidified in the *continental* regions of the lunar surface, and were subsequently transported to their present localities by mechanical action of meteoritic impacts.

Whatever may have been the case, however, these chips constitute an irrefutable testimony that *solid matter existed on the lunar surface already 4.6 milliard years ago*, which has not been melted since; while the substantially younger age of dark rocks characteristic of the lunar mare ground from the plains of Mare Tranquilitatis or Oceanus Procellarum discloses that later solidification of material in these localities must have been the result of subsequent but isolated events. This is indeed what we inferred earlier from the stratigraphy of the lunar face; and the radioactive dating of the rocks collected at two localities so far has provided our previous time-scale with absolute calibration. Even before the Apollo flights we surmised the great age of the stony relief of the lunar surface from the number of its disfiguring pockmarks. Now we know that the continental land masses may have solidified while the Sun was in the last throes of its Kelvin contraction towards the Main Sequence.

Nothing of comparable age can certainly be found anywhere on the Earth, or (as far as we know) elsewhere in the solar system. In contrast with the Moon, our mother Earth exhibits to the outside world a cosmic face of almost eternal youth, rejuvenated as it is continuously by geological processes such as erosion and denudation of its land by joint action of air and water; or, more important, by continental drifts operative in its mantle and driven by the internal heat engine of the Earth. Very few parts of the terrestrial continents or ocean floors are older than a few hundred million years. In contrast, the Moon (on account of its small mass and heat capacity) can afford none of these means of cosmic cosmetics to make up her face. The latter truly mirrors, therefore, the ages gone by and preserves a reflection of events that occurred long before our own terrestrial continents were formed; and long before the first manifestation of life on Earth flickered in our shallow waters. As a monument of the past, the Moon constitutes the most important fossil of the solar system; and in interpretation of the hieroglyphs engraved by Nature on its stony face reveals indeed a fascinating story.

A search for the presence of unstable nuclides in the lunar crust produced by cosmic rays led, moreover, to an interesting by-product in the form of a determination of the rate at which the lunar surface is being 'ploughed over' by meteoritic infall. Microchemical analysis of samples of lunar rocks from Mare Tranquilitatis brought back by Apollo 11 disclosed the presence in them, not only of many stable elements present elsewhere in nature, but also of certain unstable elements (like ^{26}A1), which are known to be produced by impact of hard corpuscular radiation commonly referred to as 'cosmic rays'. These rays are of partly solar, partly galactic origin; and their flux remains roughly constant in time.

The penetrating power of cosmic rays but seldom exceeds about one-half to one metre of the lunar crust. If, therefore, we find rocks on the Moon showing signs of exposure to cosmic rays (such as the presence of nuclear spallation products which do not otherwise occur in Nature) at some depth underground, it follows that these rocks must once have been exposed to cosmic rays closer to the surface. Moreover, from the state of decay of these spallation products we can infer the length of time which elapsed since the gradual underground burial of such rocks.

A determination of such 'cosmic ray exposure ages' of lunar rocks brought back by Apollo 11, or of such rocks as we see lying exposed on the surface in Plates 4 and 8*b*, has shown that *these rocks must have been within one metre of the surface for periods ranging between 20 and 160 million years*—with an average of close to a hundred million years. Cumulative effects of mechanical disturbances associated with cosmic impacts on the Moon over longer intervals of time may bury rocks underground to sub-surface depths to which cosmic rays can no longer penetrate in appreciable flux; but a topmost layer about one metre in depth seems to be 'ploughed over' by cosmic erosion in a time-interval of the order of 100 million years, i.e. about the time separating us from the cretaceous geological period on the Earth.

It is indeed a sobering thought to consider that the footprints, which Apollo astronauts and their followers will have left in the soft lunar ground, may possess a degree of permanence comparable with footprints of the dinosaurs in the soft ground of the cretaceous period, preserved for us by fossilization. Should, perchance, human civilization perish tomorrow by some disaster and trips to the Moon be not resumed until millions of years later, our distant descendants of that age could find footprints there still much the same as we see them now in Plate 8*b*. These footprints, and other marks of human activity on the Moon may, therefore, yet prove to be a better claim to immortality of the intrepid travellers who impressed them than all the fleeting glory of the Earth.

Note added in press It must be stressed that this and the following chapter are two of those mentioned in the Preface as being written several years ago and revised before the more recent Apollo, Luna, Mars, Pioneer and Venus flights. Though these are rapidly adding to our knowledge of the Moon and nearer planets, they have not, as yet, indicated any significant deletions that ought to be made from these two chapters.

R. H. S.

Chapter Five

The planets

T. W. Rackham and R. H. Stoy

Discovery In Chapter 2 Professor Ovenden has traced the development of man's ideas about the brighter planets up to the time that their motions were explained in terms of Newton's Laws of Motion and of Universal Gravitation. He also mentioned how Uranus was discovered serendipitously in 1781 by William Herschel in the course of one of his systematic surveys of the sky, and how deviations of this new planet from its computed orbit led Adams and Leverrier independently to deduce the existence and approximate position of Neptune. The discovery of this planet by Galle at Berlin in 1846 was universally acclaimed as one of the greatest triumphs of the human intellect. As there is no known reason why there should not be other planets beyond Neptune, various astronomers were encouraged by this triumph to see if the feat of Adams and Leverrier could be repeated. Unfortunately, though it was agreed that the observations of Uranus and Neptune did not fit the computed orbits exactly, neither the observations nor the theory were extensive enough for these deviations to be determined with sufficient certainty to provide adequate data to locate precisely any further planets. Amongst those who worked on this problem was Percival Lowell, whose calculations led to the systematic search of a large part of the sky at the Lowell Observatory and the resulting discovery of Pluto in 1930 by Clyde W. Tombaugh.

Though the effect of a trans-Plutonian planet on the orbits of the major planets might be small, its effect on a comet passing close to it could be large, but this effect is not likely to be noticed unless the comet is a periodic one which has already completed three or more circuits of its orbit. Moreover this orbit would have to extend out well beyond the orbits of Neptune and Pluto. This limits the known periodic comets which would be at all suitable for this investigation to three, of which Comet Halley is the best observed. It has been known for a long time that the orbit of this comet as derived from observations made during one apparition does not exactly fit the observations made during the previous or subsequent apparitions. Recently J. L. Brady has shown that an orbit can be derived that satisfies the observations made during all the apparitions since 1456 if it be assumed that there is another planet at a distance of about twice that of Neptune, having a mass three times that of Saturn, and moving in an orbit which is inclined at 120° to the ecliptic.

If such a planet exists it may be expected to appear about the 13th or 14th magnitude and, being as bright as this, would have been picked up during the search for Pluto made at the Lowell Observatory were it not that its large inclination had carried it well away from the Zodiac and thus right outside of the area then investigated. Systematic searches of the appropriate part of the sky made at the Royal Greenwich and Lick Observatories since the publication of Brady's paper have so far failed to locate Planet X, while theoretical astronomers have advanced alternative explanations of the variations between successive orbits of Halley's Comet. It has also been pointed out that so massive a planet moving in an orbit inclined at so great an angle to the ecliptic would produce easily observable effects on the remainder of the solar system, effects of which no trace appears to exist.

The planets in general

Kepler's laws While the motions of the planets round the Sun and of satellites round their primaries conform accurately to Newton's laws, they approximately obey three simple rules which can be deduced from these laws but which were first inferred by Kepler from Tycho's observations. These three laws of Kepler, which are sufficient to solve many planetary and satellite problems, can be stated as follows:

1. The path or orbit of a planet is an ellipse with the Sun in one focus.
2. The radius vector, i.e. the line joining a planet to the Sun, sweeps out equal areas in equal times.
3. For any two planets the squares of the periods of revolution are in the same proportion as the cubes of their mean solar distances.

Astronomical distances The immensity of the Universe cannot be gauged by the human mind any more than the globe of the Earth can be appreciated by an intelligent ant. The mile and the kilometre satisfy most of our everyday terrestrial needs and a thousand miles represents a considerable distance even in this day and age. Puck to 'girdle the Earth' would have made a 40,000 kilometre journey before returning breathlessly to his starting position, but it is doubtful if his immortal creator would have been able to visualize so large a span. Multiply this length a hundred times and we have a measuring rod that is still too short to plumb the distances between the Earth and her nearest sister planets. How then may we make an appraisal of such vast dimensions? One time-hallowed method, that has some merits as well as limitations, is to present interplanetary distances in model form: whatever analogy is used we can never hope to be able to appreciate fully the massive scale of the solar system, but the comparative distances of the planets from their primary can be understood with the help of such devices.

For many purposes the most convenient measuring rod for the solar system is the astronomical unit which is defined as the mean distance between the centres of the Earth and the Sun and is approximately equal to 149.6×10^9 m. Another convenient measure that has astronomical applications is the distance that light travels in a given length of time. Again it is useless to try to imagine anything that can traverse a distance of 2.998×10^8 m in the short interval of one second, Puck's 'girdling of the Earth in forty minutes' pales into insignificance in comparison to the speed of electro-magnetic waves that can accomplish the same journey seven times in one second! To measure distances in this way is to use the method beloved by commuters who can more conveniently indicate the distances to their places of work by the durations of the time intervals involved in getting to them rather than by the actual mileages. The speed of light measure is no less effective than the others and what it lacks in directness is made up by its property of being applicable to both planetary and stellar systems. Above all it permits us to appreciate the isolation of the solar system from the rest of the Universe. For example, if we assume that the orbit of Pluto represents the outer extremity of the solar system—this is not strictly true, for comets with highly elliptical orbits travel to greater distances from the Sun—light requires some eleven hours to cross the solar system from side to side. We may imagine the plight of a future astronaut in the vicinity of Pluto who sends a radio message back to the Earth and has to wait over ten hours for the reply!

To the denizens of the Earth these distances are terrible to contemplate, but on the cosmic scale they are immeasurably small, and the few hours that the Sun's light requires to reach the outer confines of the solar system are but a minute percentage of a period of more than four years that it needs to complete a journey to the nearest of the stars.

The size of the solar system Table 5.1 shows the mean distance of the planets from the Sun in (1) gigametres, i.e. in millions of kilometres, (2) light minutes, and (3) astronomical units (A). It also gives the periods of the planets' orbits round the Sun in sidereal years (T) and in solar days. The last two columns, which show A^3 and T^2, illustrate how far Kepler's third law, which refers to massless planets going round a massive sun, is satisfied when the solar system is considered as a whole and all the complicated effects of the mutual gravitational attractions of its individual parts are taken into account.

The *sidereal periods* of the planets given in the fifth and sixth columns of Table 5.1 are the times it takes them to move round the Sun, as seen from the Sun against the stellar background. The *synodic periods* relative to the Earth, which are given in column seven, are the times it takes the planets to move from a given configuration relative to the Sun and Earth, e.g. opposition, round the Sun and back to the same relative configuration. The synodic period (S) and the sidereal period (P) are connected by the relation

$$1/S = 1/P - 1/E \quad \text{for an inferior planet}$$

and

$$1/S = 1/E - 1/P \quad \text{for a superior planet,}$$

E being the sidereal period of the Earth, i.e. the sidereal year. The truth of this relation can be easily comprehended if one considers the mean angular velocities of the planet and the Earth about the Sun. These are $2\pi/P$ and $2\pi/E$. The relative angular velocity of the planet relative to the Earth as seen from the Sun is the difference between these two velocities, i.e. $2\pi(1/P \sim 1/S)$. But this relative angular velocity is by definition also equal to $2\pi/S$. This simple relation is very important because it allows the sidereal period, which cannot be directly observed, to be deduced from the synodic period, which it is possible to observe, e.g. by noting the mean interval between successive oppositions of the planet.

Once the sidereal periods of the planets are known, somewhat sophisticated celestial mechanics, of which Kepler's third law is a simplification, provide a scale model of the solar system in terms of the astronomical unit. The evaluation of this unit in kilometres has been one of the major problems of practical astronomy since the seventeenth century. Quite often this problem is referred to as being that of the determination of the solar parallax which, being defined as the angle subtended by the Earth's equatorial radius at the centre of the Sun, is in circular measure the radius of the Earth divided by the distance to the Sun. This angle, which is about 8.8 arc seconds, is much too small to be measured directly with sufficient proportional accuracy, and conse-

TABLE 5.1 DISTANCES AND PERIODS OF THE PLANETS

	Mean distance from the Sun			Period				
				Sidereal		Synodic		
Name	*Gigametres*	*Light minutes*	*Astronomical units* (A)	*Sidereal years* (T)	*Solar days*	*Solar days*	A^3	T^2
1	*2*	*3*	*4*	*5*	*6*	*7*	*8*	*9*
Mercury	57.91	3.2	0.39	0.241	88.0	116	0.059	0.058
Venus	108.21	6.0	0.72	0.615	224.7	584	0.373	0.378
Earth	149.60	8.3	1.00	1.000	365.3		1.000	1.000
Mars	227.94	12.7	1.52	1.881	687.0	780	3.512	3.538
Jupiter	778.34	43.3	5.20	11.862		399	140.608	140.660
Saturn	1427.01	79.4	9.54	29.457		378	868.251	867.892
Uranus	2869.6	160.0	19.18	84.013		370	7055.79	7057.68
Neptune	4496.7	250.0	30.06	164.783		367	27162.32	27159.04
Pluto	5910	330.0	39.52	248.420		367	61723.5	61702.6

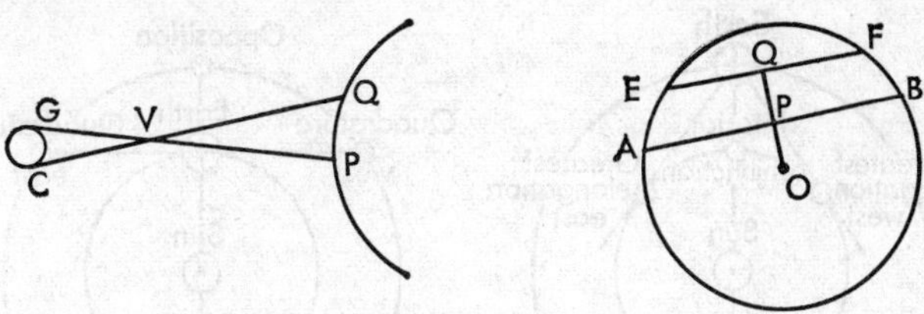

Figure 5.1 Determination of the solar parallax from a transit of Venus

To illustrate the principle of the method suppose that APB represents the track of Venus across the face of the Sun as seen from Greenwich (G), and EQF the track as seen from the Cape of Good Hope (C). Since we already know the length of GC from a survey of the Earth, and the ratio of GV : VP from Kepler's third law, a knowledge of PQ in angular measure will enable us to solve the triangles completely. Halley pointed out that the lengths of the chords AB and EF could be found easily and accurately by timing the interval between the first and last contacts of Venus with the Sun. The lengths of AB and EF being known, that of PQ follows from the geometry of the circle.

quently astronomers have tried to determine it indirectly by measuring the parallax, or distance, of one of the other members of the solar system when they are at their closest to the Earth. Venus at inferior conjunction, Mars at opposition, certain minor planets of which Eros is the best known, have all been used for this purpose. Particularly noteworthy historically are the elaborate national campaigns that were mounted during the eighteenth and nineteenth centuries to observe the rather rare transits of Venus across the Sun in 1761, 1769, 1874 and 1882 from points widely spaced upon the Earth (Figure 5.1). It was while he was on the 1769 expedition that Captain Cook explored the east coast of Australia. The last of the big international efforts to determine the value of the solar parallax was the Eros campaign of 1930–1, and though the results were more accurate than any previously obtained they have been completely superseded in the past few years by direct determinations of the distance to Venus made by radar.

Before leaving the subject of the distances of the planets from the Sun it may be of interest to point out an approximate relationship between them which was first noticed in the eighteenth century by Titius of Wittenberg but which is usually known as Bode's law since it was he who first gave it prominence in 1772. It is this: the approximate distances of the planets in astronomical units are given by the series of numbers

$$0.4 + 0.3 \times 2^n$$

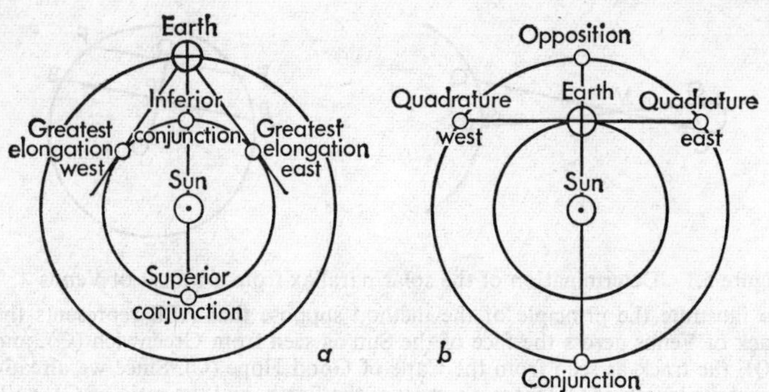

Figure 5.2 Planetary configurations *a* of an interior (or inferior) planet, and *b* of an exterior (or superior) planet

Mercury corresponding to $n = -\infty$, Venus to $n = 0$, the Earth to $n = 1$, Mars to $n = 2$, Jupiter to $n = 4$ and Saturn to $n = 5$. When Uranus was discovered, its distance was found to correspond to $n = 6$, while the discovery of the asteroids seemed to fill the gap at $n = 3$. It will be noticed that Neptune is somewhat closer, and Pluto very much closer, than Bode's law would indicate for $n = 7$ and 8.

Planetary configurations Figure 5.2 indicates the meaning of some of the terms that are used in describing the various planetary configurations as seen from the Earth, *a* referring to the *inferior* planets, i.e. those having orbits lying entirely within that of the Earth, and *b* to *superior* planets whose orbits lie entirely outside that of the Earth.

The *elongation* of a planet is defined as the angle between the lines joining the Earth to the Sun and to the planet. For an inferior planet this angle reaches a maximum when the line from the Earth to the planet is tangential to the planet's orbit. When this is the case, the planet is said to be at *greatest elongation* east or west of the Sun, as the case may be. It is of course at such times when the planet is furthest away from the glare of the Sun that it will be most easily visible, in the evening sky at eastern elongations and in the mornings at western. When the elongation is zero, i.e. when the Earth, Sun and planet are in line, an inferior planet is said to be in *superior conjunction* if it is on the far side of the Sun from the Earth, and in *inferior conjunction* when it lies between the Sun and the Earth. As the planets, like the Moon, are visible only by the light they receive from the Sun, they will show

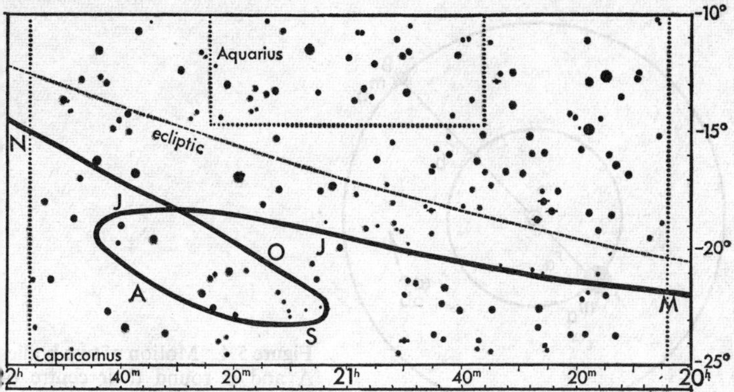

Figure 5.3 Apparent path of Mars during the 1971 opposition

The positions of Mars on 1 May, 1 June, 1 July, 1 August, 1 September, 1 October and 1 November are denoted by M, J, J, A, S, O and N The actual opposition took place on 10 August, and the stationary points were reached on 13 July and 11 September.

phases as seen from the Earth. As can be seen from Figure 5.2, inferior planets pass through all the same phases as does the Moon, full planet being at superior conjunction when the planet is at its furthest and its apparent diameter a minimum, new planet at inferior conjunction. Thus when the planet is at its nearest and apparently largest, it is invisible. Maximum brightness occurs fairly close to the times of maximum elongation. The change of size with phase is well illustrated in the case of Venus by Plate 9.

For a superior planet, the elongation may take any value between 0° and 180° east or west of the sun. When the elongation is 0°, the planet is said to be in *superior conjunction*, or, more simply, in *conjunction*. The planet is then at its furthest from the Earth and cannot be seen because it is hidden by the glare of the Sun. When the elongation is 180° the planet is said to be in *opposition*. It is then ideally placed for observation, being at its closest to the Earth, fully illuminated and on the meridian at midnight, and consequently visible throughout the night. When the elongation is 90° the planet is said to be at *east* or *west quadrature*. Superior planets away from opposition are not fully illuminated when viewed from the Earth, but the phase is always gibbous and only in the case of Mars is the change in phase appreciable.

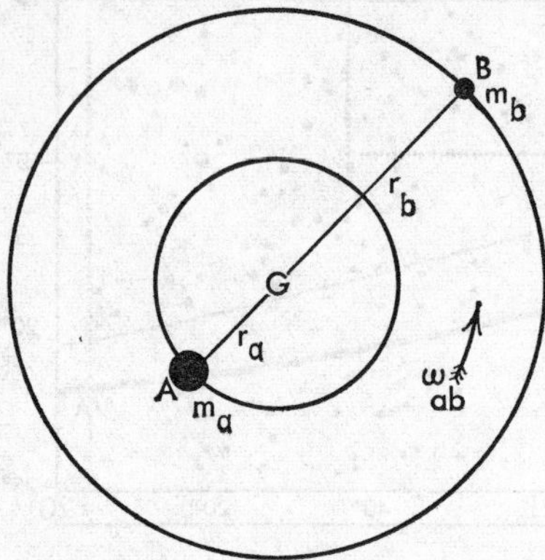

Figure 5.4 Motion of two bodies A and B round their centre of gravity G.

The apparent motion of a superior planet against the stellar background is normally *direct* or eastwards. Near the time of opposition, however, when the Earth, owing to its faster orbital velocity, is overtaking and passing the planet, this direct motion slows down and eventually stops. The planet then appears to *retrograde*, moving westward amongst the stars with a speed which gradually increases to a maximum at the time of opposition. After opposition, as the Earth passes on, the retrograde motion of the planet becomes slower until it finally stops altogether and the planet begins once more its steady eastward journey through the stellar background. The places at which the planet's apparent motion stops are known as *stationary points* and their distance apart, which defines the size of the loop in the apparent orbit, varies inversely as the distance of the planet. That is, the loop in the apparent orbit at the time of opposition is largest for Mars and smallest for Neptune and Pluto. Figure 5.3 illustrates the loop for Mars for the 1971 opposition.

Masses of the planets The masses of the planets are found, as are those of other celestial bodies, by their gravitational effects on the motion of nearby bodies. The determination is comparatively simple and certain when the body has an orbiting satellite. The principle of the method can be easily understood by considering the simplest case of two bodies moving in circular orbits round their centre of gravity under the action of their mutual gravitation.

In Figure 5.4 let A and B represent two such bodies of mass m_a and m_b and G their centre of gravity round which they are circling with angular velocity $\omega_{ab} = 2\pi/T_{ab}$, where T_{ab} is the periodic time. If r_a, r_b and r_{ab} represent the distances AG, BG and AB respectively, we have

$$r_{ab} = r_a + r_b$$

and

$$m_a.r_a = m_b.r_b$$

also the mutual gravitational pull on each body towards the centre of gravity is

$$G.m_a\ .m_b/r_{ab}^2$$

where G is Newton's constant of universal gravitation. Now the acceleration of A towards G is $r_a\ \omega_{ab}^2$ and the force necessary to produce this is $m_a.r_a.\omega_{ab}^2$ which must just be equal to the gravitational attraction towards B since the two bodies are orbiting in a steady state. Hence

$$r_a.\omega_{ab}^2 = G.m_b/r_{ab}^2$$

Similarly by considering the motion of B,

$$r_b.\omega_{ab}^2 = G.m_a/r_{ab}^2$$

Adding these two equations

$$(r_a + r_b).\omega_{ab}^2 = G.(m_a + m_b)\ /r_{ab}^2$$

or

$$\omega_{ab}^2 = 4\pi^2/T_{ab}^2 = G.(m_a + m_b)\ /r_{ab}^3$$

That is

$$r_{ab}^3/T_{ab}^2 = (G/4\pi^2).(m_a + m_b)$$

which in the particular case when m_a is much greater than m_b, e.g. if A is the Sun and B a planet, is equivalent to Kepler's third law.

If C and D be two other bodies also moving freely in space in circular motion under their own gravitation, we shall have

$$r_{cd}^3/T_{cd}^2 = (G/4\pi^2).(m_c + m_d)$$

and hence, by dividing these last two equations,

$$(r_{ab}^3/T_{ab}^2) : (r_{cd}^3/T_{cd}^2) = (m_a + m_b) : (m_c + m_d)$$

If now we take A and B as a planet and its satellite, C and D as the Sun and the Earth, and if we measure the distances in astronomical units and the time in sidereal years, we get

$$(r_{ab}^3/T_{ab}^2) = (m_a + m_b)/(m_c + m_d)$$

For most purposes m_b will be negligible compared with m_a, and m_d with m_c, so that we get

$$m_a = (r_{ab}^3/T_{ab}^2).m_c$$

which gives the mass of the planet, m_a, in terms of the mass of the Sun, m_c.

In the case of those planets without satellites, Mercury, Venus and Pluto, the masses have had to be derived from the rather small perturbations their masses produce in the motions of their neighbouring planets, and consequently could not be determined with great certainty. In the case of Venus a definitive mass has now been derived from the motions of the various space probes that have passed near it, circled it or landed on it.

Numerical data In the following pages we will be considering each of the planets in turn, but before doing so it may be well to consider them as a family. Tables 5.2 and 5.3 summarize for easy reference their principal physical and dynamical characteristics and, also, those of their satellites. The values given, most of which have been taken from similar tables in the 1973 Handbook of the British Astronomical Association, have been gathered from various sources. They are of varying degrees of reliability and some, particularly the data referring to the fainter satellites, are very uncertain. Only the mean values have been given for quantities that are known to vary, e.g. the inclination of the Moon's orbit is given as 23°.4 though it actually varies between 18°.3 and 28°.5. The inclinations given for the satellite orbits are those referred to the equatorial plane of the primary and, as for the inclination of this equatorial plane to the plane of the planet's orbit, values greater than 90° indicate that the motion is retrograde.

The quantities given in the last three lines of Table 5.2 require some explanation. The 'velocity of escape' indicates the probability of whether or not the planet can retain any particular gas in its atmosphere. It is the minimum velocity with which a particle at the surface of the planet would have to be moving in order to escape from its gravitational field. It appears from the dynamical theory of gases that if the mean-square velocity of the molecules of a gas exceeds one quarter of the velocity of escape, that gas will leak away from the planet in a relatively short time, but that if it is less than one-fifth of this velocity, the gas will be retained in the planet's atmosphere almost indefinitely. The mean-square velocity of the molecules is defined as that velocity whose square is equal to the mean of the squares of the velocities of the individual molecules. It is proportional to $(T / \mu)^{\frac{1}{2}}$, where T° is the absolute temperature of the gas and μ its molecular weight. The mean-square velocity in km s^{-1} is given in Table 5.4 on page 144, for a number of gases likely to occur in planetary atmospheres.

[*continued on page 145*

TABLE 5.2 PLANETARY DATA

	Mercury	Venus	Earth	Mars	Jupiter	Saturn	Uranus	Neptune	Pluto
Eccentricity of orbit	0.206	0.007	0.017	0.093	0.048	0.056	0.047	0.009	0.248
Inclination of the orbit to the ecliptic	7°.0	3°.4	0°.0	1°.9	1°.3	2°.5	0°.8	1°.8	17°
Inclination of planet's equator to its orbit	0°	178°	23°27′	24°46′	3°04′	26°44′	97°53′	28°48′	?
Mean orbital velocity ($km\ s^{-1}$)	47.88	35.02	29.79	24.12	13.05	9.64	6.81	5.44	4.74
Visual magnitude at mean greatest elongation	0.0	−4.4							
mean opposition				−2.0	−2.6	+0.7	+5.5	+7.8	+14.9
Apparent diameter at mean inferior conjunction (arc seconds)	10.98	60.32							
mean opposition				17.87	46.86	19.27	3.57	2.30	0.21
Equatorial diameter (km)	4880	12100	12756	6790	142800	119300	47100	48400	5900
Polar diameter			12714	6750	133500	107700	43800	47400	
Equatorial diameter (Earth = 1)	0.383	0.949	1.000	0.532	11.20	9.36	3.70	3.79	0.47
Volume (Earth = 1)	0.055	0.857	1.000	0.150	1318.7	743.7	47.1	53.7	0.10
Mass (Earth = 1)	0.054	0.815	1.000	0.107	317.89	95.17	14.6	17.2	0.08
Density (Water = 1)	5.5	5.25	5.517	3.94	1.33	0.71	1.71	1.77	4.5
Rotation period	$58^{d}.7$	$243^{d}.0$*	$23^{h}56^{m}04^{s}$	$24^{h}37^{m}23^{s}$	$9^{h}50^{m}30^{s}$	$10^{h}14^{m}$	$10^{h}49^{m}$	$15^{h}48^{m}$	$6^{d}.39$
Surface gravity (Earth = 1)	0.38	0.903	1.000	0.380	2.643	1.159	1.11	1.21	0.43
Velocity of escape ($km\ s^{-1}$)	4.3	10.36	11.18	5.03	60.22	36.26	22.5	23.9	4.2
Albedo	0.06	0.76	0.36	0.16	0.73	0.76	0.93	0.84	0.14
Maximum surface temperature (°K)	633	464	394	319	173	127	90	72	63

* Rotation of Venus is retrograde

TABLE 5.3 SATELLITE DATA

Planet and satellite		*Discoverer*	*Mean distance from Primary* (*in 0.001 AU*)	*Mean distance from Primary* *Angular at mean opposition*	*Mean sidereal period (days)*
Earth					
	Moon		2.5695		27.321661
Mars					
I	Phobus	Hall, 1877	0.0625	0′24.″6	0.318910
II	Deimos	Hall, 1877	0.1570	1 01.8	1.262441
Jupiter					
V		Barnard, 1892	1.2099	0 59.4	0.498179
I	Io	Galileo, 1610	2.8193	2 18.4	1.769138
II	Europa	Galileo, 1610	4.4857	3 40.1	3.551181
III	Ganymede	Galileo, 1610	7.1552	5 51.2	7.154553
IV	Callisto	Galileo, 1610	12.5845	10 17.6	16.689018
VI		Perrine, 1904	76.723	62 45	250.5662
X		Nicholson, 1938	78.345	64 05	259.2188
VII		Perrine, 1905	78.455	64 10	259.6528
XII		Nicholson, 1951	142	116	631
XI		Nicholson, 1938	151	123	692
VIII		Melotte, 1908	157	129	744
IX		Nicholson, 1914	158	130	758
Saturn					
X	Janus	Dollfus, 1966	1.06	0 25.5	0.749
I	Mimas	W. Herschel, 1789	1.2406	0 30.0	0.942422
II	Enceladus	W. Herschel, 1789	1.5916	0 38.4	1.370218
III	Tethys	J. D. Cassini, 1684	1.9703	0 47.6	1.887803
IV	Dione	J. D. Cassini, 1684	2.5235	1 01.0	2.736916
V	Rhea	J. D. Cassini, 1672	3.5241	1 25.1	4.517503
VI	Titan	Huyghens, 1655	8.1660	3 17.3	15.945448
VII	Hyperion	W. C. Bond, 1848	9.9115	3 59.4	21.276657
VIII	Iapetus	J. D. Cassini, 1671	23.798	9 35	79.33085
IX	Phoebe	W. H. Pickering, 1898	86.575	34 51	550.337
Uranus					
V	Miranda	Kuiper, 1948	0.872	9.9	1.41349
I	Ariel	Lassell, 1851	1.2820	14.5	2.520384
II	Umbriel	Lassell, 1851	1.7860	20.3	4.144183
III	Titania	W. Herschel, 1787	2.9303	33.2	8.705876
IV	Oberon	W. Herschel, 1787	3.9187	44.5	13.463262
Neptune					
I	Triton	Lassell, 1846	2.3747	0 16.9	5.876844
II	Nereid	Kuiper, 1949	37.1797	4 23.9	359.881

TABLE 5.3 SATELLITE DATA—*continued*

Planet and satellite	*Inclination*	*Eccentricity*	*Estimated diameter (km)*	*Reciprocal mass (planet = 1)*	*Density (water = 1)*	*Mean visual mag. at opposition*
Earth						
Moon	23°.4	0.0549	3476	81.30	3.3	— 12.7
Mars						
I	1.1	0.0210	23	?	?	11.6
II	1.8	0.0028	13	?	?	12.8
Jupiter						
V	0.4	0.003	200	?	?	13.0
I	0.0	0.000	3659	26,200	2.82	4.8
II	0.5	0.0001	2900	40,300	3.7	5.2
III	0.2	0.0014	5000	12,200	2.4	4.5
IV	0.2	0.0074	4500	19,600	2.0	5.5
VI	28	0.1580	100	?	?	13.7
X	29	0.1074	20	?	?	18.6
VII	28	0.2072	30	?	?	16.0
XII	147	0.169	20	?	?	18.8
XI	163	0.207	20	?	?	18.1
VIII	148	0.410	20	?	?	18.8
IX	157	0.275	20	?	?	18.3
Saturn						
X	0.0	0.0	300	?	?	14.0
I	1.5	0.0202	500	15,000,000	1	12.1
II	0.0	0.0045	600	7,000,000	1	11.8
III	1.1	0.000	1000	910,000	1.1	10.3
IV	0.0	0.0022	1000	490,000	3.2	10.4
V	0.3	0.0010	1300	250,000	2.0	9.8
VI	0.3	0.0292	4800	4,150	2.3	8.4
VII	0.6	0.1042	500	5,000,000	3	14.2
VIII	14.7	0.0283	1100	300,000	3	11.0
IX	150	0.1633	200	?	?	16.5
Uranus						
V	0.0	0.00	300	1,000,000	5	16.5
I	0.0	0.0028	800	67,000	5	14.4
II	0.0	0.0035	600	170,000	4	15.3
III	0.0	0.0024	1100	20,000	6	14.0
IV	0.0	0.0007	1000	34,000	5	14.2
Neptune						
I	159.9	0.000	3700	750	5.1	13.5
II	27.7	0.7493	300	?	?	18.7

[*continued overleaf*

TABLE 5.3 (cont.) DIAMETER OF SATURN'S RINGS

		Kilometres	*Ratio*	*Angular diameter at mean opposition (arc seconds)*
Ring A	Outer diameter	272,300	1.0000	43.96
	Inner diameter	239,600	0.8801	38.69
Ring B	Outer diameter	234,200	0.8599	37.80
	Inner diameter	181,100	0.6652	29.24
Crepe Ring	Inner diameter	149,300	0.5487	24.12

Note. The Cassini division comes between Rings A and B and is therefore about 2700 kilometres wide. There is no prominent line of demarcation between Ring B and the Crepe Ring.

TABLE 5.4 MEAN-SQUARE VELOCITIES FOR SOME ATMOSPHERIC GASES (km s^{-1})

		Molecular weight (μ)	*Temperature* (T) 50°K −223°C	100°K −173°C	200°K −73°C	300°K 27°C	400°K 127°C	600°K 327°C
Hydrogen	H_2	2	0.78	1.11	1.56	1.93	2.22	2.72
Helium	He	4	0.56	0.79	1.12	1.38	1.58	1.94
Methane	CH_4	16	0.28	0.40	0.56	0.69	0.79	0.98
Ammonia	NH_3	17	0.28	0.39	0.55	0.67	0.78	0.95
Water	H_2O	18	0.27	0.38	0.54	0.65	0.76	0.93
Nitrogen	N_2	28	0.21	0.30	0.42	0.51	0.60	0.73
Carbon monoxide	CO	28	0.21	0.30	0.42	0.51	0.60	0.73
Oxygen	O_2	32	0.20	0.28	0.39	0.48	0.56	0.68
Argon	Ar	40	0.18	0.25	0.36	0.43	0.50	0.61
Carbon dioxide	CO_2	44	0.17	0.24	0.34	0.41	0.48	0.58

The albedo of a planet is the fraction of the incident solar radiation falling on it that is directly reflected or scattered back into space. It varies considerably with wavelength and with varying conditions in the planet's atmosphere or on its surface. In general it is small when the planet has no atmosphere at all or only a thin one, and large when the planet has a very thick atmosphere or one which supports an almost continuous cloud layer. The values given in Table 5.2 refer to normal visual light which range of radiation includes the maximum of the solar emission.

The maximum surface temperatures given in the last line of Table 5.2 should not be taken as anything more than a very rough indication of the actual temperatures we may expect to find on the various planets. As we know in the case of the Earth, no single temperature can satisfactorily represent the actual complex and ever changing temperature distribution that exists not only over the surface of the Earth but also at different heights in its atmosphere. The temperatures given are those that would be taken up by insulated plane black surfaces normal to the direction of the Sun at the distances of the various planets. Perfectly black conducting spheres placed at the same distances will take up temperatures that are 0.707 of these. These latter temperatures are probably a better approximation to the actual average temperatures of the planets, though they too will tend to be too high because they are based on the assumption that all the solar radiation is absorbed, i.e. that the albedo is zero. The figure given for the maximum surface temperature of the Earth in Table 5.2 is 394°K or 121°C. This is above the boiling point of water and at first sight seems absurdly high. However the reading of a black bulb thermometer exposed to the midday sun in the middle of a desert will approximate to it. A fairer comparison is with the sunlit side of the Moon which is observed to attain temperatures of the order of 100°C.

The planets are usually divided into two groups: Mercury, Venus, Earth and Mars, being comparable in size and density, are known as the *terrestrial* planets; while Jupiter, Saturn, Uranus and Neptune, which are much greater in size but of considerably lower density, are referred to as the *major* planets. Pluto stands out; its remoteness from the Sun links it with the major planets, but its dimensions suggest that it ought to be classified as terrestrial. As will be seen later, it has been suggested that Pluto is not really a foundation member of the planetary system but a satellite of Neptune that has broken free. The relative sizes of the Sun and planets are shown in Figure 5.5. It will be noticed that as regards size the planets tend to occur in pairs, viz. Jupiter and Saturn, Uranus and Neptune, Venus and Earth. An examination of the proper-

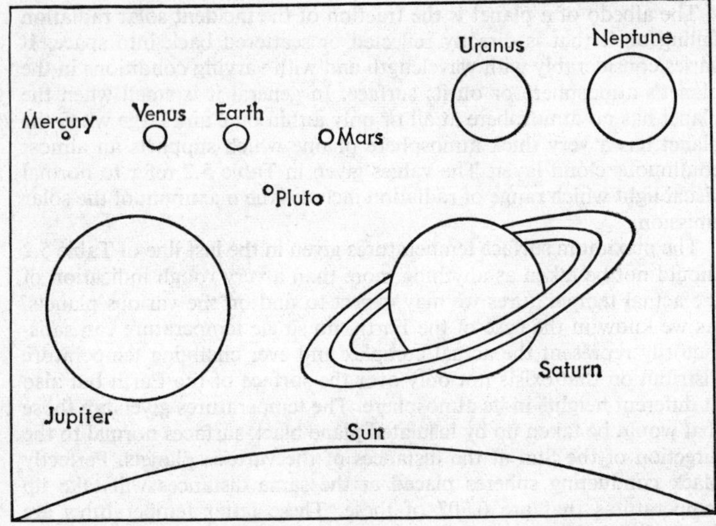

Figure 5.5 The relative sizes of the Sun and planets

ties of these planets confirms that each member of these pairs resembles the other more closely than it does the rest of the planets.

The data collected in Tables 5.2 and 5.3 make it appear highly improbable that the solar system is just a casual collection of bodies held together by gravitation. On the contrary it gives every indication of being a strongly unified system having a common origin and development. The system is isolated in space; all the planets go round the Sun in orbits that are very nearly circular and coplanar and in the same direction as the Sun itself rotates; moreover this same pattern is continued in the regular system of satellites that accompany Jupiter, Saturn and Uranus. What the common origin may have been and how the solar system actually developed is, in spite of the very many and varied theories that have been advanced, still a mystery. The problem of the formation of the solar system seems now to be regarded as a particular case of the more general problem of the formation of stars out of pre-existing nebulosity, a phenomenon that still seems to be occurring in such regions as the Orion Nebula. How such condensations start and develop is still far from clear; when the condensation took place in the case of the solar system seems, however, to be fairly definite since the age of the system is the same as that of the Earth, viz. about five thousand million years.

If this general hypothesis is correct, the solar system is no more likely to be unique than the Sun is to be a unique star. Many other planetary systems are likely to exist and to contain bodies on which conditions are similar to those on Earth and favourable for the development of life as we know it. This, however, is pure speculation; what is not speculation, as we shall see when we study each of the planets in turn, is that the Earth is the only member of the solar system on which life is likely to exist.

Mercury

The planet Mercury, on account of its proximity to the Sun and its small size, is an elusive and disappointing object to observe telescopically for it must be viewed either during broad daylight or low in the sky just before sunrise or just after sunset. The most favourable periods for observation are near the times of maximum elongation, the western, or morning, elongations being slightly the better since then the observer can take advantage of the reduced turbulence that often occurs at the end of a night before the Sun's morning rays begin to warm the atmosphere. Although fairly bright, Mercury is not easily noticed by the casual observer in European latitudes, since it tends to get lost in the bright twilight and, because of its rapid motion, is only in a position close to maximum elongation for a few days at a time. Such an observer feels that Mercury is well named after the fleet messenger of the gods who also possessed the gift of invisibility. In the tropics, however, Mercury can be more easily seen, as near times of maximum elongation it rises or sets while the sky is still quite dark.

Mercury orbits the Sun at a mean speed of nearly 48 km s^{-1}. The planet not only travels faster through space than any other, but its orbit is also more eccentric than any except that of Pluto. In consequence the distance between Mercury and the Sun varies from 46.0 gigametres at perihelion to 69.8 gigametres at aphelion. As indicated by Kepler's second law, there is a correspondingly large range in the speed of the planet which made it a suitable test object for Einstein's theory of relativity which predicted a change of mass with speed. An observable effect of this change of mass is to alter the rate at which the direction of the perihelion of the orbit changes. Another effect of the eccentricity is that the greatest elongation ranges from 18° to 28° Thus greatest elongations, which occur about 22 days before and after inferior conjunction, are not all equally favourable for observation. At a particularly favourable elongation, Mercury may appear as bright as Sirius, while at others it is more comparable with Aldebaran. The planet is most easily seen as an evening star when eastern elongations occur in March or April and as a morning star at such western elongations as occur in September and October. Even at best, Mercury never rises or sets much more than two hours before or after the Sun.

Mercury's sidereal period about the Sun is 88 days and its synodic period with respect to the Earth averages 116 days. Three synodic periods average 348 days so that in most calendar years there will be three morning and three evening elongations, though very occasionally there will be a total of seven elongations. During a synodic period, the distance of Mercury from the Earth increases from a minimum, never less than 77 gigametres, at inferior conjunction to a maximum, never greater than 222 gigametres, at superior conjunction. In the same way, its apparent angular diameter, which varies inversely as the distance, changes from about 13 arc seconds to less than 5 arc seconds. At maximum elongation the angular diameter of Mercury is about 9 arc seconds, that is, about the angular diameter of a new ten pence piece at 500 metres. A powerful telescope would be required to read the print on the coin at that distance; the same is true of the elusive detail on Mercury.

Transits As its orbit is inclined at 7° to that of the Earth, Mercury usually passes north or south of the Sun at inferior conjunction. When, however, as in Figure 5.6, inferior conjunction happens when Mercury is close to the node of its orbit, i.e. the point where its orbit intersects the plane of the Earth's orbit, it will be seen to cross the disk of the Sun as a tiny black spot taking up to a maximum of about 8 hours to do so. Such transits are of interest since they provide an opportunity of checking the planet's orbit and of measuring its diameter. The Earth passes the nodes of Mercury's orbit on 7 May and 9 November so that transits can only occur near these dates. Mercury is nearer the Sun for the November transits than for the May ones, consequently such transits are nearly twice as numerous and may take place only 7 years apart, but more usually the interval is 13 years. These intervals can be derived by considering how many synodic periods of Mercury make an exact number of terrestrial years; 22 synodic periods nearly equal 7 years; 41, much more nearly equal 13 years, while 145 almost exactly equal 46 years. Thus a series of transits of Mercury across the Sun's disk

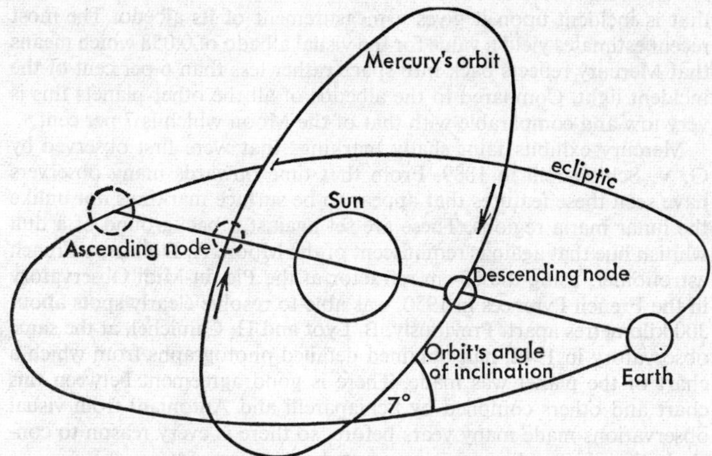

Figure 5.6 Transits of the Sun by Mercury. These can occur only when Mercury is near the ascending or descending nodes of its orbit.

may be expected to repeat almost exactly with a period of 46 years. The actual dates of transits occurring in the second half of this century are

1953 November 14
1957 May 5
1960 November 7
1970 May 9
1973 November 10
1986 November 13
1993 November 6
1999 November 15

Physical characteristics We would be breaking with tradition if we made no attempt to compare the dimensions of the planets with those of the Earth but, in the case of Mercury, it would be more apt to make the comparison with the Moon for the two bodies have certain properties in common. In the first place Mercury has a diameter which is approximately one-and-a-half times the diameter of the Moon and, secondly, like the Moon, it reflects back into space only a small percentage of the total radiation that it receives from the Sun. The percentage of the light that is reflected away from a planet compared to the total that is incident upon it gives a measurement of its albedo. The most recent estimates yield a value for the visual albedo of 0.058 which means that Mercury reflects back into space rather less than 6 per cent of the incident light. Compared to the albedos of all the other planets this is very low and comparable with that of the Moon which is 7 per cent.

Mercury exhibits faint shady markings that were first observed by G. V. Schiaparelli in 1889. From that time onwards many observers have seen these features that appear to be surface markings not unlike the lunar maria regions. These are set against a background of a dull whitish hue that again is reminiscent of the Moon. A. Dollfus, a French astronomer, using the 60-cm refractor at the Pic-du-Midi Observatory in the French Pyrenees in 1950, was able to resolve clearly spots about 300 kilometres apart. Previously, B. Lyot and H. Camichel, at the same observatory in 1942, had obtained detailed photographs from which a chart of the planet was made. There is good agreement between this chart and others compiled by Schiaparelli and Antoniadi from visual observations made many years before, so there is every reason to conclude that the markings are permanent.

Axial rotation It was long believed that the rotation period of Mercury about its own axis was exactly equal to the sidereal period of its orbit about the Sun, that is that Mercury kept one side permanently turned towards the Sun in the same way that the Moon keeps one side turned towards the Earth. Quite recently this was shown not to be the case. Radio observations obtained with the 1000-foot diameter radio telescope at Arecibo, Puerto Rico (Figure 11.14) suggested a sidereal period of 59 days which is about two-thirds of the orbital period round the Sun. Subsequent radar and optical observations have confirmed that the ratio is exactly two thirds, and this is explained by the assumption that the Sun's gravitational control on a tidally deformed body would tend to synchronize its axial rotation into a simple resonance, in this case 3/2, with its period about the Sun.

The Sun's control on the rotation of a planet will be most effective when the planet is closest to it, that is, at perihelion. Thus there will be a tendency, especially when the orbit is very eccentric, for the planet's speed of rotation about its own axis, which is effectively uniform, to get into step with its mean angular velocity round the Sun at the time of perihelion. Now, by Kepler's second law, we have for any planet

$$\tfrac{1}{2}\, r^2\omega = \text{constant} = \pi a.b/T$$

where r denotes the distance of the planet from the Sun, ω its angular velocity about the Sun, a and b the semi-major and minor axes of its orbit and T its periodic time. As $b = a(1-e^2)^{\frac{1}{2}}$ and $r = a(1-e)$ at perihelion, the angular velocity of the planet about the Sun there will be

$$\omega_p = (2\pi/T) \, . \, (1-e^2)^{\frac{1}{2}}/(1-e)^2.$$

Thus the ratio of the angular velocity of a planet about the Sun at the time of perihelion to its mean angular velocity for the whole orbit $(2\pi/T)$, is

$$(1-e^2)^{\frac{1}{2}} /(1-e)^2$$

For Mercury e, the eccentricity, is approximately 0.2 so that this ratio becomes

$$(0.96)^{\frac{1}{2}} /(0.8)^2 = 0.98/0.64 = 1.53$$

which is very approximately 3/2. We should not really be surprised, therefore, that if the rotational period of Mercury approached 2/3 times its orbital period, the Sun's gravitational control would take over and lock it into an exact 3/2 resonance.

This resonance has some interesting consequences. The Mercurial meridian that faces the Sun at one perihelion will again face the Sun at the next perihelion but one, after Mercury has made two complete orbits round the Sun. The meridian that faces the Sun at the intermediate perihelia is 180° from the first. In the same way the meridians that are at 90° from these will face the Sun at alternating aphelia, while intermediate pairs of meridians will face the Sun alternately at specific points in the orbit. This results from the fact that Mercury's 'mean solar day' is exactly twice its sidereal year, i.e. its orbital period about the Sun, and three times its sidereal day.

To see that this is so, take ω as the constant angular velocity of rotation of Mercury on its axis, so that the length of its sidereal day is $2\pi/\omega$, and of its sidereal year $3\pi/\omega$. The mean angular velocity of the Sun's apparent motion about Mercury is equal to the mean angular velocity of Mercury about the Sun, i.e. $2\omega/3$. Hence, relative to a point fixed on the surface of Mercury, the Sun's apparent mean angular velocity across the sky from east to west is $\omega-2\omega/3 = \omega/3$ so that the length of the Mercurial mean solar day is $2\pi/(\omega/3) = 6\pi/\omega$

= three times the length of its sidereal day
= twice the length of its sidereal year
= 176 terrestrial solar days.

Because of the eccentricity of the orbit, the angular rate of the Sun's apparent motion across the Mercurial sky varies very considerably. For a short while near perihelion it is actually faster than the sidereal rate of rotation of Mercury on its axis, so that at such times the Sun will appear to move backwards from west to east. This curious phenomenon will be most spectacular at points on the equator approximately 90° from the sub-solar point at the time of perihelion. Here the Sun will be close to either rising or setting. Instead of rising simply, the Sun will appear above the horizon for a short interval, set where it rose and then, after another short interval, rise again to remain above the horizon for nearly a Mercurial year after which it would set twice in a manner similar to its rising.

Temperature The eccentricity of the orbit has another and rather more important effect. The Sun's diameter as seen from Mercury changes between perihelion and aphelion in the ratio 1.53 : 1, and the intensity of radiation received in the ratio 2.34 : 1. This means that the temperature at the subsolar point will be very much higher at perihelion than at aphelion. Infrared measures which are not yet definitive indicate temperatures of about 420°C at perihelion and 285°C at aphelion. The temperatures on the night side of Mercury will fall rapidly as there appears to be little atmosphere to provide a blanketing effect and to act as a transferrer of heat from the sunlit side. Observations suggest that the night temperatures might fall as low as −130°C.

Atmosphere Mercury is massive enough to retain an atmosphere consisting of the heavier gases, but no certain indications of an appreciable atmosphere have yet been observed. The velocity of escape is only 4.2 km s^{-1} but the surface temperature can rise quite high. During the crescent phase the horns do not extend beyond their geometric limits as they would if there were any appreciable atmosphere and as they do in the case of Venus. A. Dollfus, has, however, found a slight excess in the polarization of light at the cusps which might be due to the presence of an atmosphere of not more than 1/300 that of the Earth in extent.

Further evidence of the lack of an atmosphere is the low albedo of the planet which is close to that of the Moon, which Mercury seems to resemble in so many ways. As their surfaces reflect and scatter light of all wavelengths very similarly and have similar radar albedos and roughness measures, it seems possible to conclude that they are of a similar nature and in particular that the surface of Mercury is fairly rough and may be covered with craters.

One point in which Mercury does not resemble the Moon needs stressing, since it may be a significant clue to the way in which the solar system was formed. The mean density of Mercury, which is fairly well established as being 5.4, is considerably greater than that of the Moon which is only 3.3.

Venus

Venus, the second planet out from the Sun, is the only planet mentioned by Homer, who describes it as the most beautiful star in the firmament, calling it Hesperos when an evening star and Phosphoros when a morning star. In the case of Mercury it was pointed out that many people go through life without ever consciously noticing it; with Venus, however, the situation is completely reversed. Every living person, given reasonable eyesight, must have noticed Venus at one time or another as the most conspicuous 'star' in either the western evening or the eastern morning sky. In the darkness of the countryside the light from Venus can project shadows of nearby trees on to white walls or similar objects. Even in daylight with the Sun high in the sky, Venus may be seen with the naked eye near the times of its maximum brightness provided the observer knows where to look. This latter condition is not always necessary. Several sightings of 'flying saucers' reported to observatories in recent years have turned out to be of Venus during the daytime as a tiny, shining, silver disk seen against the clear blue sky.

Venus moves round the Sun at a mean distance of about 108 gigametres in an orbit that is so nearly circular that its orbital speed varies little from its average of 35 km s^{-1}, while the heat and light received from the Sun remain nearly constant at about twice that received by the Earth on an equal area. The orbital period about the Sun, or sidereal year, is a little under 225 terrestrial solar days while its mean synodic period, the interval from one inferior conjunction to the next, is about 584 days, subject to a variation of about 4 days either way. It will be noticed that 13 cytherean sidereal years are nearly equal to 8 terrestrial years so that all the phases, elongations and conjunctions in any 8-year period will be repeated in the next but about 2 or 3 days earlier. This interval is also 5 synodic periods, so that in it the sequence of phenomena will be repeated 5 times. Of the 584 days that make up one synodic period, only 144 are spent passing from the evening elongation through inferior conjunction to the morning elongation, while it takes 440 days for Venus to pass from there through superior conjunction back to an evening elongation.

Angular size and phases At superior conjunction, when the Sun is between us and Venus, the distance between the two planets is 258 gigametres: at inferior conjunction Venus can come within 42 gigametres of the Earth. Such vast changes of distance are reflected in the apparent variations of the diameter of the planetary disk that can shrink to about 10 arc seconds—roughly the diameter of Mercury at a maximum elongation—and increase to 64 arc seconds thus presenting a disk, albeit averted, that is greater than any other planetary disk that can be seen from the Earth.

The phases of Venus were first seen by Galileo and the nearer crescent phases are easily discerned with a small telescope or binocular. Like the Moon and Mercury, Venus displays, for the benefit of terrestrial observers, a series of waxing and waning phases (Plate 9), and soon after inferior conjunction the thin, large-diameter crescent of Venus can be observed. Often the cusps or points of the crescent seem to continue faintly all around the darkened disk, indeed this phenomenon has been photographed and yields ample proof of an atmosphere that can transmit light from the illuminated hemisphere to the darker regions. As the planet recedes from the Earth the illuminated area takes up a greater percentage of the disk until exactly one half is illuminated: this is the condition of dichotomy. It so happens in the case of Venus that dichotomy occurs at approximately the same time as maximum elongation, which is between 45° and 47°.

As the planet moves away from us round the Sun its apparent brightness or magnitude changes as a function of the apparent area of the illuminated disk as seen from the Earth. The radiant flux that reaches the planet from the Sun is substantially constant but during the early crescent phases most of this light is reflected away from the Earth. The brightness builds up very rapidly and when Venus is a morning star it reaches its brightest about one month before greatest elongation: as an evening star the converse is true and the planet's maximum brightness occurs approximately one month after greatest elongation. At these times the planet is about magnitude −4.4, that is some twelve times as bright as Sirius, the brightest of all the so-called fixed stars. At its faintest, Venus is about magnitude −3.3, over four times brighter than Sirius and still the most conspicuous object in the sky after the Sun and the Moon.

Axial rotation In spite of its great brilliance and closeness to the Earth, Venus is most disappointing telescopically. Normally the brightness of the crescent or gibbous image shades smoothly off towards the terminator without a trace of any detail. What is seen, in fact, is simply sunlight reflected from the top of a dense almost uniform cloud layer, as was realized long ago from the high albedo of 0.76. Under the most favourable conditions, however, faint and ill-defined markings are sometimes seen, which, as F. E. Ross showed in 1927, are more conspicuous in the ultraviolet. These markings change greatly from day to day and are evidently some form of cloud formation.

The absence of definite markings renders it impossible to determine the rotation period of Venus by direct visual or photographic observation. If the period of rotation were of the order of twenty days or less, there might be some hope of measuring it spectrographically by determining the difference of radial velocity on opposite sides of the disk. Such observations have been tried at a number of observatories and all agree that the rotation is too slow to be measured in this manner. Because it was slow, there was a tendency amongst some astronomers to assume that Venus must keep the same face towards the Sun, as does the Moon to the Earth, and as Mercury was long thought to do. Radio observations have shown that this is not the case.

The same radar Doppler technique that was used successfully for measuring the rotation period of Mercury can be applied with greater ease and certainty to the larger and nearer disk presented by Venus when near inferior conjunction. In addition there is an alternative method of determining the rotation period that depends on the fact that it has been found possible to distinguish a few fixed features on the surface of Venus that produce distinctive effects on the radar echoes. The rotation period obtained from three such features observed at the times of inferior conjunctions in 1962, 1964, 1966 and 1967 agrees closely with that obtained from the radar Doppler method and indicates that Venus is rotating slowly in a retrograde direction about an axis which is inclined at approximately 6° to the normal to its orbital plane with a sidereal period of 242.982 ± 0.04 days. Before this period was determined with such certainty it had been noticed that a retrograde period of 243.16 days would give a resonance with the synodic period of the Earth and Venus in that an observer on Venus would experience exactly five cytherean solar days of 117 terrestrial days length* between conjunctions with the Earth. The closeness of this resonance period of rotation to the observed value gave rise to the speculation that the Earth might exert enough influence to control the rotation of Venus, though this seemed very unlikely unless Venus has a marked axial asymmetry. Of this there is no indication and the period of rotation as now determined is sufficiently clear of the critical period to make the real existence of such a gravitational coupling between the rotation of Venus and the Earth extremely doubtful.

Physical characteristics In visible wavelengths the upper cloud layer of Venus diffusely reflects some 76 per cent of the incident light from the Sun back into surrounding space. Radar investigations show that the

* The length C of the cytherean solar day is given by the relation

$$1/C = 1/243 + 1/225.$$

surface, which is smoother than those of the Moon and Mercury, only returns 12 per cent of the incident radar power. Large reflective areas have been detected and these may be associated with mountain chains on the surface. In fact it is now possible to make radar pictures of the planet and R. Jurgens was the first to succeed using the 1000-foot radio telescope at Arecibo. Radar techniques also provide the means of determining accurate measurements of the diameters of the planets and M. E. Ash, I. I. Shapiro and W. B. Smith published in 1967 a number of revised astronomical constants extracted from radar data during the years 1959 to 1966 and from optical data from the U.S. Naval Observatory over the years 1950 to 1965. Among these is a value of 6056 $\pm$ 1 km for the radius of Venus, and where there seem to be discrepancies between this and other values it must be remembered that optical measurements include at least part of the depth of the atmosphere.

Although the spectrograph failed to detect any acceptable period of axial rotation of Venus it did furnish information about the chemical constituents of the outer layers of the atmosphere. Certainly there seemed to be no measurable quantity of oxygen present, but J. Strong of the Johns Hopkins University found evidence favouring small amounts of water vapour. Long before, W. S. Adams and T. Dunham of the Mount Wilson Observatory had conducted spectrographic analyses in the infrared region of the spectrum and had discovered that the most abundant gas was undoubtedly carbon dioxide, the amounts above the cloud layer being very much more than their counterparts in the Earth's atmosphere. Traces of other chemical compounds such as hydrochloric acid and hydrogen fluoride have also been detected by French astronomers.

The space probes A major breakthrough took place on 14 December 1962, when the American Mariner II (launched 26 August 1962) passed by Venus at a distance of 34,800 km and relayed back to Earth, some 59.5 Gm away, new and hitherto unsuspected information about the planet. The scientists at the Jet Propulsion laboratory of the California Institute of Technology were able to announce that the magnetic field of Venus was less than 1/30 of that of the Earth and that the probe was unable to detect any evidence supporting the existence of Van Allen belts. Perhaps the most important item was that the planet's surface was very hot and there seemed to be no breaks in the cloud cover; neither could any decrease in temperature be detected when an infrared scanner swept across the terminator from the sunlit hemisphere into the area of darkness.

Since Mariner II several other space-probes have visited Venus. Russian scientists were the first to attempt the landing of a parachuted instrumented package there. The Russian Venus 4 space-probe entered the atmosphere at about the same velocity as a similar object would return to Earth—somewhat less than 11 km s^{-1}. Atmospheric braking took place and the 836-pound instrumented 'soft-lander' was ejected to float down to the surface. During this phase of operations its radio transmitter was returning to the Earth important information relating to the composition, pressure and temperature of the cytherean atmosphere. There is some doubt as to whether the ejected canister's transmitter failed before reaching the surface, at any rate the highest temperature recorded was 280°C. It seems not improbable that the canister was crushed like an egg-shell by the atmospheric pressure that was estimated to be around 18 atmospheres near the surface. There were also problems with the probe's radio altimeter and Soviet scientists cannot be sure that the probe did drop 26 km in 94 minutes. Interesting as these results were found to be, it has to be admitted that the figures did not fit into the theoretical models that predicted higher temperatures and pressures. The Venus 4 probe also sent back data suggesting that 90 per cent of the atmosphere was carbon dioxide.

In view of the partial failure and uncertainty of the findings of Venus 4, the Russian scientists returned to their drawing boards to design improved equipment that would withstand the rigours of the cytherean atmosphere. The American Mariner V arrived in the neighbourhood of Venus only 34 hours after Venus 4. No attempt was made to eject an instrumented canister to the surface but the spacecraft encircled the planet at a distance of 4000 km and detected concentrations of carbon dioxide ranging from 72 to 87 per cent, which is in excellent agreement with the estimate made by Venus 4. No traces of oxygen were found but at high altitudes hydrogen was present. Evidence favouring the existence of an ionosphere was discovered on the sunlit hemisphere. Mariner V also measured the magnetic field of Venus and found that it was about 1/300 of that of the Earth.

The Russian Venus 5 and Venus 6 arrived on 16 and 17 May 1969 to continue the studies begun by Venus 4. This time, however, the parachuted probes were designed to survive pressures some 50 per cent greater than the Venus 4 probe could withstand, and they were constructed to resist forces amounting to 450g. This was necessary because of the greater velocities of the probes' entries into the atmosphere. Each descent module was about 1 metre in diameter, weighed 405 kg, and was enclosed in a heat resisting outer shield capable of withstanding temperatures of some 10,000°C.

Each probe was designed to sample the atmosphere twice. With Venus 4 the first sample was taken shortly after the opening of the parachute and indicated a pressure of 0.6 atmospheres and a temperature of 25°C. The second analysis was conducted at a lower level in a pressure of 5 atmospheres and a temperature of 150°C. The corresponding measurements made by Venus 6 indicated 1 atmosphere at 60°C, and 10 atmospheres at 225°C. The full ranges of pressures and temperatures encountered were, respectively, 0.5 to 27 atmospheres and 25° to 320° Centigrade. Notwithstanding this there are some uncertainties relating to these results, particularly with the heights to which these pressures and temperatures are thought to refer. Despite these it would appear that the pressure of the atmosphere at the surface of Venus is in the range 60 to 140 atmospheres and the corresponding temperatures from 400°C to around 530°C.

The preliminary analysis of the atmosphere supports previous findings that there is a high concentration of carbon dioxide so it can be assumed that some 95 per cent of the cytherean atmosphere is made up of this gas. Nitrogen and inert gases account for another 3 per cent while oxygen does not exceed 0.5 per cent.

Only traces of water vapour have been found so far and this means that Venus possesses an unimaginable aridity that together with the high temperatures suggests an environment where violent dust storms prevail most of the time.

Mars

Visibility Of all the planets none has excited the imagination and curiosity more than Mars. The reason for this is not difficult to understand, for when it comes close to us a wealth of detail near the limit of visibility tantalizes the observer who sees many features strongly reminiscent of the Earth. The best time to observe Mars is when it is near opposition but, as can be seen from Figure 5.7 which shows the oppositions between 1963 and 1990, all oppositions are not equally favourable. The main reason for this is the relatively large eccentricity of the orbit of Mars which is exceeded only by the eccentricities of the orbits of Mercury and Pluto. The most favourable opposition, that is the one in which the Earth and Mars are at their closest, will occur when the Earth is near aphelion and Mars near perihelion. The Earth is at aphelion early in July while the line joining the Sun to Mars at its perihelion is in the direction from the Sun in which the Earth is on

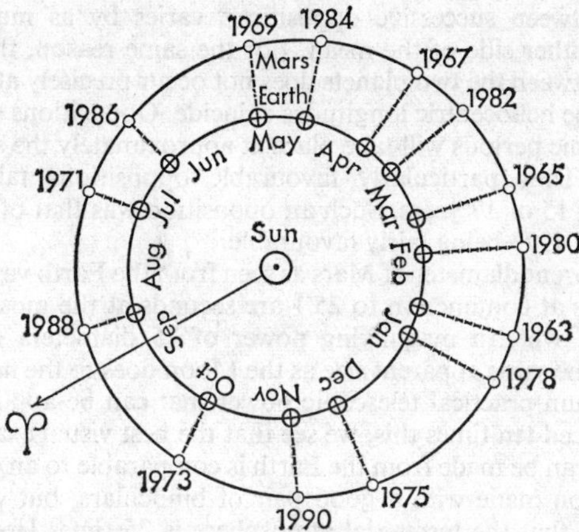

Figure 5.7 Oppositions of Mars as seen from the Earth, 1963 to 1990

The relative distances at opposition are shown by the lines joining the orbits. The terrestrial months in which the oppositions take place are indicated. Mars is north of the equator for oppositions taking place between September and March.

23 August. The most favourable oppositions take place, therefore, in August. At such a time Mars is only about 55.5 gigametres from the Earth, while at the least favourable oppositions this distance is 101.2 gigametres. At conjunction, when the Earth and Mars are on opposite sides of their orbits, the average distance between them is 378 gigametres. It follows that the apparent brightness of Mars as seen from the Earth varies greatly; at the most favourable oppositions it is of magnitude −2.8, while at an unfavourable opposition its magnitude is −1.1, and when near conjunction only 1.6. That is, at a favourable opposition Mars outshines all celestial bodies except the Sun, the Moon and Venus; at an unfavourable opposition, it still outshines Sirius, but is not so bright as Jupiter; while near conjunction it becomes relatively inconspicuous and is easily mistaken for just another bright star.

The sidereal period of Mars in its orbit round the Sun is 687 days, to which the corresponding synodic period is 780 days, or slightly less than two and one-seventh years. This should be the interval between successive oppositions, but due to the ellipticity of the two orbits, the actual interval between successive oppositions varies by as much as three weeks on either side of the mean. For the same reason, the minimum distance between the two planets does not occur precisely at opposition, i.e. when the heliocentric longitudes coincide. Oppositions separated by seven synodic periods will take place at approximately the same time of the year. Thus particularly favourable oppositions take place at intervals of 15 or 17 years. Such an opposition was that of 1971; those of 1969 and 1973 being fairly favourable.

The apparent diameter of Mars as seen from the Earth varies from 3.5 arc seconds at conjunction to 25.1 arc seconds at the most favourable opposition, when a magnifying power of 75 diameters will make it appear as the same apparent size as the Moon does to the naked eye. As the maximum practical telescopic power that can be applied does not greatly exceed ten times this, we see that the best visual examination of Mars that can be made from the Earth is comparable to an examination of the Moon made with a good pair of binoculars, but with the disadvantages that the terrestrial atmosphere is 75 times less steady and that the visibility of the martian features is often greatly reduced by the planet's own atmosphere. It is not surprising, therefore, that skilled and diligent observers did not always agree about the precise details of the finer features on the martian surface which are so close to the limit of visibility. Photography has not yet fully caught up with the human eye for recording such fine and elusive detail under comparable conditions, but the photographs taken from the American Mariners 4, 6 and 7 as they flew by Mars in 1965 and 1969 far surpass any observations that can be made from the surface of the Earth. The best of these photographs show martian features only 300 metres across and thus compare with the best photographs of the Moon yet taken from the Earth.

Telescopic appearance A small telescope show Mars as a small ruddy-orange disk on which there are a number of dusky blue-green markings and quite often a brilliant white patch marking the polar cap. Near opposition the disk is circular but becomes markedly gibbous near quadrature when its shape resembles that of the Moon three days from full. Its general appearance is well illustrated by the Lowell Observatory photographs reproduced at the top of Plates 10 and 11 which were taken through red, orange, or yellow filters and thus show red 'deserts' as light patches and blue-green 'oases' and 'maria' as dark. The conspicuous white spot at the top of each photograph is the south polar cap. The maps in the lower parts of the plates, which were prepared at the Lowell Observatory, indicate the principal surface features. The nomenclature is essentially that introduced by Giovanni Schiaparelli of

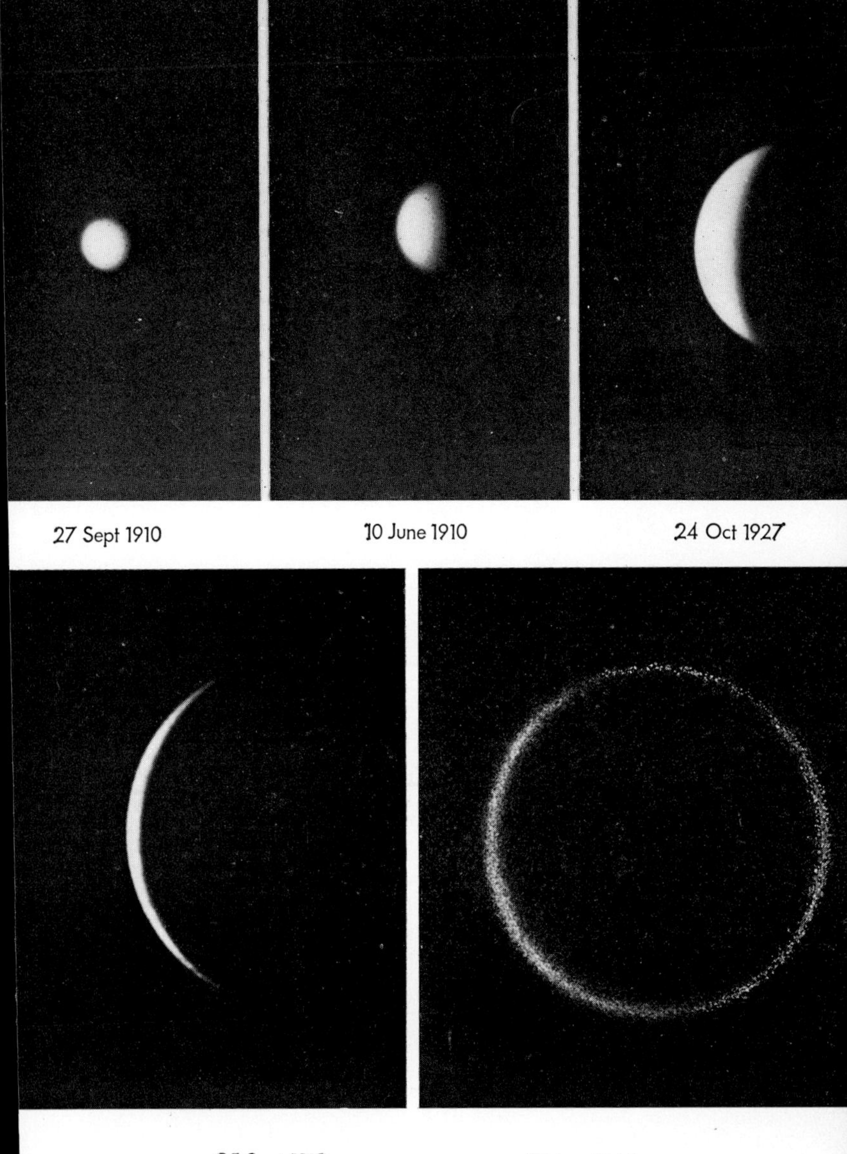

Plate 9 Venus at various phases displaying relative sizes. The photograph at inferior conjunction (1964) shows the complete atmospheric ring that appears at such times. Lowell Observatory

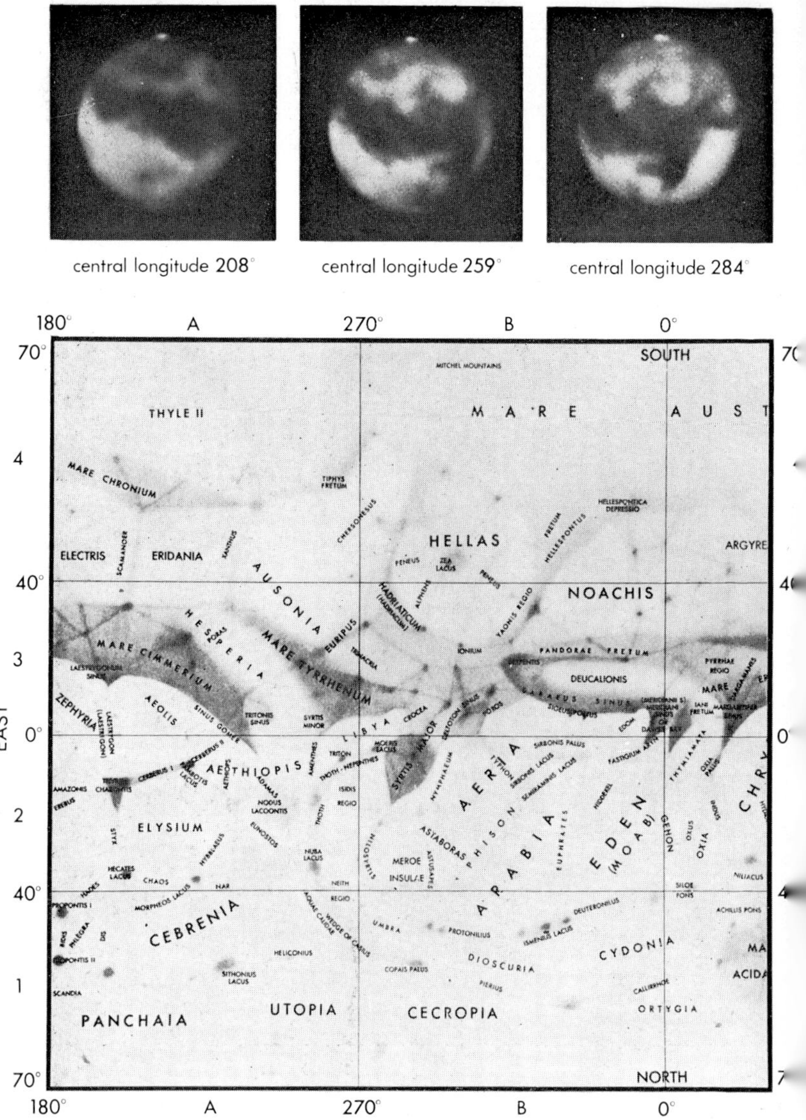

EASTERN HEMISPHERE

Plate 10 Reference map of Mars. These charts provide a key to the names of the principal permanent surface features of Mars. It was compiled from observations made at many favourable oppositions and gives a false impression of the ease and distinctness with which the individual features can be seen. A more realistic idea of how Mars actually appears through a telescope at any time is given by the reproductions of six actual photographs

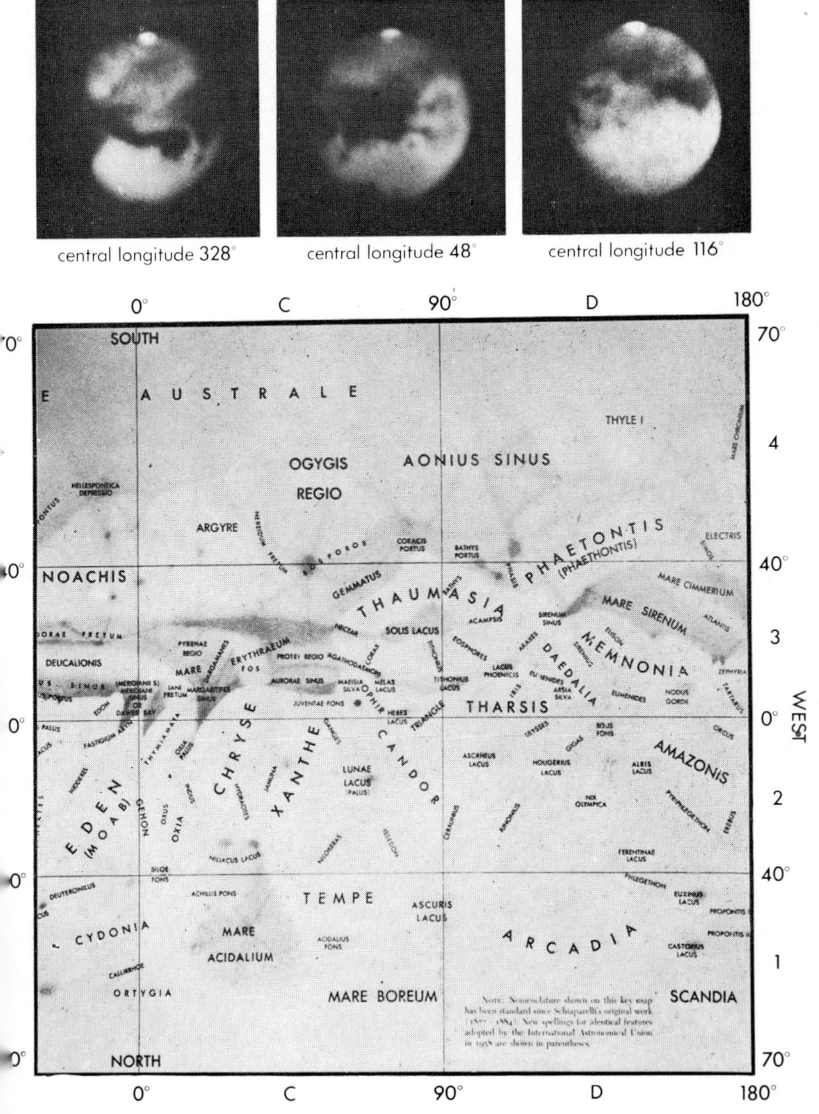

WESTERN HEMISPHERE

Plate 11 Reference map of Mars. The longitude of the central meridian of Mars at the time each photograph was taken is given and indicates the portion of the chart with which it should be compared. Light areas indicate the red deserts and dark markings the maria and oases. The most conspicuous features are the white south polar cap, the Syrtis Major (284°) and the double forked Meridiani Sinus feature at 0°. Lowell Observatory

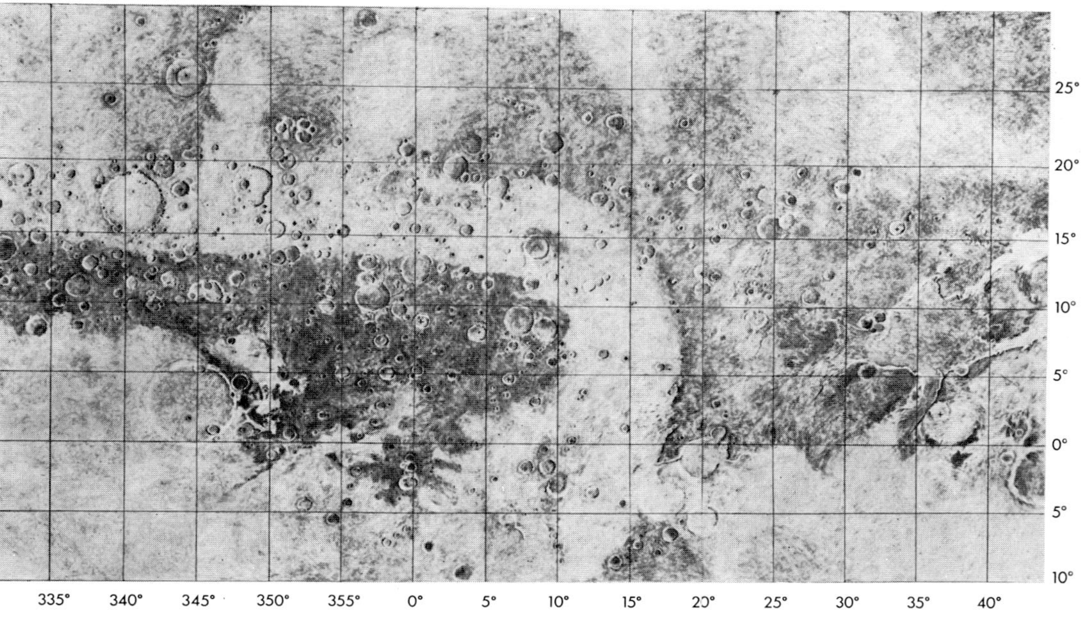

Plate 12 Chart of the Meridiani Sinus Region compiled by Charles A. Cross from wide angle near-encounter photographs taken by Mariner 6 in July 1969. The most striking feature is the number of craters, strongly reminiscent of those on the Moon. The 'chaotic' terrain centred at 34° west, 8° south is a depressed area of jumbled ridges and troughs. Other surface features are described on pages 164 and 165. Scale: 5° longitude = 300 km

Milan between 1877 and 1884 which is derived partly from names in the Bible and classical mythology and partly from ancient place names of the Mediterranean region. Many of Schiaparelli's names were officially recognized by the International Astronomical Union in 1958 but for others alternative names or spellings were adopted. The more important of these alternatives are shown on the maps in parentheses. The features shown on the map are permanent in that they can be recognized from year to year though many of them are subject to seasonal changes. Except for the effect of clouds or other obscuration in the martian atmosphere, the reddish areas show little change, the blue-green areas considerable change, and the polar caps conspicuous changes with the martian seasons. These changes will be discussed in more detail later.

One of the most conspicuous of the blue-green surface markings is the Syrtis Major (in martian longitude 285° and just north of the equator) which was first drawn by Christian Huygens, the celebrated Dutch scientist, in 1659. A comparison of his drawings with modern observations gives a very accurate determination of the martian sidereal day, 24 hours 37 minutes 23 seconds, only slightly longer than that of the Earth. This means that a marking which is visible near the centre of the planet's disk one night will be seen on the following night at about the same hour in the same position, and will be so visible for several nights. Because the martian day is slightly the longer, the region of its surface observable at a fixed hour from a fixed place on the Earth changes slowly and it takes approximately forty days for the region first observed to pass out of sight and to return again to its original position. From the observed motion of the surface markings it is possible to deduce that the axis of rotation of Mars is inclined at an angle of 23° 59′ to the normal to the plane of its orbit round the Sun. This is remarkably close to the inclination of the Earth's axis, 23° 27′, so that the seasons on Mars will be very similar to those on the Earth. On account of the greater eccentricity of its orbit, however, the lengths of these seasons are more markedly unequal. Thus the southern spring or northern autumn is 146 terrestrial days long, the southern summer 160 days, the southern autumn 199 days, and the southern winter 182 days. Mars, like the Earth, passes its perihelion during the southern summer so that the southern hemisphere has a shorter warmer summer and a colder longer winter than does the northern, a fact which is clearly demonstrated by the differing seasonal behaviours of the polar caps.

These behave similarly in that they both begin to form during the corresponding martian autumn, are largest and of almost constant size throughout the winter, and then shrink steadily and almost uniformly from the beginning of spring to the end of summer. But the southern cap grows to a larger size, extending to about 3000 km from the pole as compared with 2500 km for the northern. Moreover the southern cap disappears completely towards the end of the southern summer, whereas the northern cap never completely vanishes. William Herschel suggested that the caps were composed of snow and it seems clear that if they are not frozen water, they are at least of some substance that melts or evaporates when the temperature reaches a certain value in spring and precipitates again as soon as the temperature falls. Measured temperatures and the composition of the martian atmosphere indicate that this substance might well be carbon dioxide. The same substance may well be responsible for the white areas that are sometimes observed near the sunrise limb and which disappear as they come more fully into sunlight, just as on Earth hoar-frost that has formed during the night vanishes during the morning. The polar caps are sometimes covered with mist or low lying clouds which lend a greater brightness to these areas and thus suggest that the surface below is not completely covered with 'snow'. In any case, it is clear from the rate at which the caps form and melt that their thickness must be small. Another interesting observational phenomenon is the fact that as the caps recede they leave behind isolated white patches which persist for several days. These patches occur in the same place year after year and probably indicate the existence of craters or extended areas considerably higher than their surroundings. A conspicuous example of this is provided by the south polar cap of which the last remaining portion as it melts is not at the pole but some 7° away from it.

With the melting of a polar cap many of the dark markings in that hemisphere become more prominent and in some cases may even change their colour from chocolate brown to blue-green. They regain their original appearance, however, as autumn approaches. These general changes are also shown by many of the fine details that can only be glimpsed under the very best conditions. Amongst these finer details are the so-called 'canals' which appear as fine dark lines criss-crossing the red deserts in all directions. According to Percival Lowell, who spent a great deal of his life studying Mars, these canals are faint or invisible during the martian spring and increase in prominence as the polar cap shrinks, those nearest the pole darkening first about the time of the summer solstice, whilst those in lower latitudes, with the oases connected with them, follow successively the 'wave of quickening' which advances from latitude 70° to the equator and beyond at the rate of about 80 kilometres per day. Half a year later, when this effect has very nearly faded out, a fresh 'wave of quickening' starts from the opposite pole. There was for many years much argument as to the nature of these canals. One extreme view, which captured the public imagination because it implied intelligent life on Mars, was that these features were actually artificial channels intended to bring water from the melting polar caps to irrigate the desert wastes; what was observed being not the watercourse itself but the vegetation growing alongside, comparable, for example, with the green strip irrigated by the waters of the Nile. A more conservative view, which the Mariner probes seem to have proved correct, is that the apparent appearance of the canals as straight lines is an optical illusion produced by the human eye working near the extreme limit of visibility and connecting up a series of isolated dots into a continuous feature.

The Mariner space probes Up to the end of 1970 three Mariner space probes had been successfully flown by Mars, precursors of more elaborate probes to be flown during the near approaches of Mars in 1971 and 1973. The first flyby was by Mariner 4 which was launched on 28 November 1964 and passed within 9800 km of Mars on 14 July 1965 when Mars and the Earth were separated by 216 Gm. This was followed four years later by the twin Mariners 6 and 7 which were launched on 24 February 1969 and 24 March 1969 respectively and which passed within 3000 km of Mars on 31 July 1969 and 5 August 1969 when the distances between Mars and the Earth were 95 and 99 Gm. Each of these probes carried several experiments but the most spectacular were the cameras which photographed the surface of Mars during the flyby. Comparison of Plate 12 with the corresponding portion of Plates 10 and 11 (long. 0°, lat. 0°) shows the essential accuracy of the latter but emphasizes the vast increase in detail provided by the Mariner photographs. The improvement in technique between 1965 and 1969 can be gauged from the fact that in 1965 each picture took 8½ hours to transmit back to Earth whereas in 1969 this time had been reduced to 5½ minutes. Mariner 4 was fitted with a single camera which was limited to 22 exposures, the sequence starting when the probe was about 17,000 km from Mars. Not all the 22 photographs were completely successful but they were sufficient to show a pock-marked cratered surface quite different from that of the Earth and not dissimilar to that of the Moon. Mariners 6 and 7 each carried two cameras, a wide-angle one covering a field 11° × 14° and a telescope one covering a field of only 1°.1 × 1°.4 but with much greater resolution. The wide-angle photographs were taken through red, green and blue filters, but all the high resolution ones were taken through a yellow filter to reduce the effect of any haze there might be in the martian atmosphere. In all 200 photographs were obtained, 74 by Mariner 6, mostly of the equatorial zone, and 126 by Mariner 7, mostly of the south polar region. The maximum resolution achieved was 300 metres, i.e. objects with dimensions bigger than 300 metres could be detected on the surface of Mars. Plates 13 and 14 give some idea of the enormous amount of detail recorded on these Mariner photographs. Both are reproductions of near encounter photographs taken with the high resolution camera on Mariner 6 and refer to part of the bright area Deucalionis (long. 330°, lat. 15°S). Plate 13, which shows how the initial television pictures are improved by subsequent computer analysis and enhancement, is of a large flat-bottomed crater about 40 km across which, with the slump terraces on the inside of the crater walls and the radial gullies, is very similar to a typical large crater on the Moon. On the crater rim is another smaller crater with a recognizable central peak. This crater and the still smaller one close to it on the floor of the main crater seem to have been formed after the main crater. The smallest craters shown are comparable in size to Meteor Crater in Arizona. Plate 14 represents an area of 72 × 83 km and was taken from a distance of about 3,460 km at an angle of 15° from the zenith when the Sun's zenith distance was 76°. The large crater that it shows is superimposed on the rim of a much larger crater whose walls can be traced from the bottom centre to the upper left. The wrinkle ridges that run vertically up the middle of the photograph are reminiscent of the Moon.

In a preliminary report on the Mariner photographs, the investigators stress the resemblance to the Moon in the abundance, form, arrangement, and sizes of the craters, but point out some subtle and possibly highly significant differences. These lie in the subdued relief of many of the martian craters, their flatter floors, fewer central peaks, absence of obvious secondary craters and rays, and also in the presence of a greater abundance of 'ghost' craters.

There is a striking change in surface morphology between the elongated dark area of Hellespontus (long. 325°, lat. 45°S) and the large, circular bright area of Hellas (long. 300°, lat. 45°S), Plate 10. Hellespontus and the intervening scarped and ridged transition zone show numerous craters of good size but the floor of Hellas is virtually free of craters except within a marginal zone where they are faintly visible. Small craters disappear even earlier, being unrecognizable in the transition zone and on the near edge of Hellespontus, even in high resolution photographs. This disappearance of craters from the photographs does not appear to be the result of atmospheric haze or fog but of a real surface difference possibly caused by some form of erosion.

The part of the surface covered by the near encounter photographs taken by Mariners 6 and 7, about one-sixth of the total surface of Mars, seems to be divisible into three main types of terrain: the cratered, the chaotic, and the featureless (Plate 12). Cratered terrains appear to be widespread in the southern hemisphere. Chaotic areas show no signs of cratering but are a jumble of short ridges and depressions, from 2 to 10 km long and from 1 to 3 km wide. Such chaotic areas do not occur all together but form an irregular pattern. They appear to be lower and have a higher reflectivity than adjacent cratered areas. The largest example of a featureless terrain is the bright desert Hellas which is entirely devoid of craters down to the 300 m limit of visibility. No area of comparable size or smoothness is known on the Moon. Some of the 'oases' observed from the Earth, such as Juventae Fons (long. 70°, lat. 4°S), have been identified with single, large, dark-floored craters, and others, like Oxia Palus (long. 15°, lat. 5°N), with groups of such craters. Classical 'canals', such as Gehon (long. 0°, lat. 30°N), have been found to coincide with quasi-linear alignment of several dark-floored craters. Others appear to be composed of irregular dark patches and it seems probable that most 'canals' will eventually prove to be associated with a variety of physiographic features and will cease to be regarded as a distinctive class. The superficial appearance of the south polar cap as photographed by Mariner 7 is that of a clearly visible, moderately cratered surface covered with a varying thickness of 'snow'. The principal effect seen at the edge of the cap is a marked enhancement of crater visibility resulting from the tendency for the snow to lie preferentially on the poleward facing slopes. The cap itself shows distinct variations in reflectivity mostly related to moderately large craters. Often a crater appears to have a darkened floor and a bright rim, and in some craters having central peaks, these peaks are unusually prominent.

Atmosphere The existence of an atmosphere on Mars is most clearly demonstrated by comparing photographs taken in different colours. Those taken in red light usually show the surface details clearly, while those taken in blue rarely show any but the most prominent of these markings and at best only vaguely. Photographs taken through narrow band filters indicate that the martian atmosphere is almost opaque for wavelengths shorter than 4500 Å, but nearly transparent for those longer than 5000 Å. The portion of the atmosphere that is responsible for this effect is usually known as the 'violet layer', but as Öpik has pointed out, it could better be called the 'red haze' since from the view point of some one on the surface of Mars it transmits red light and makes the heavens look red. A remarkable and still unexplained phenomenon connected with this layer is its sudden disappearance for short periods. At these times of 'blue clearing' the surface of Mars can be photographed almost as clearly in blue light as in red. Also unexplained is the behaviour of this layer during the flights of Mariners 6 and 7 when photographs taken from them through blue filters showed craters and other surface details, even near the limb and terminator where atmospheric effects are at their strongest, though, as judged from terrestrial observations, no blue clearing was in progress.

Some idea of the depth of the martian atmosphere can be obtained from the extent of the twilight arc which is most pronounced when Mars is near quadrature and its shape distinctly gibbous. At such times the equatorial width of the visible portion of the planet's disk is greater than it should be when calculated by simple geometric theory from the length of the polar diameter by an amount which indicates that the sunlit portion is encroaching by about 8° on the dark. The part of the atmosphere that reflects sunlight strongly enough to be observed must therefore be about 0.01 of the planet's radius in height, that is about 30 km. Because of the smaller force of gravity, the density of the atmosphere will change more slowly with height on Mars than on the Earth. Consequently it is possible for the martian atmosphere to contain less material and exert a smaller pressure on the planet's surface than does the terrestrial atmosphere and yet have its rarefied upper layers rise higher.

Three main types of cloud have been observed on Mars and are referred to as being yellow, blue or white. The yellow clouds seem to be vast dust storms stirred up by winds and confined to the lower portion of the atmosphere below the violet layer. At times, and sometimes for days or even weeks at a time, they obliterate all surface detail. They spread at a rate which implies wind speeds of the order of 30 km per hour. The blue or violet clouds can only be detected when viewed through an appropriate colour filter. They are very tenuous and are most frequent on the equator near sunrise and sunset, disappearing in the middle of the day. It has been suggested that they are associated with the violet layer and that they are comparable with the terrestrial mother-of-pearl clouds that are occasionally photographed in polar regions at an altitude of about 30 km. Like them, the blue clouds are probably caused by the condensation into small crystals of gaseous products in the atmosphere. This may possibly also be true of the white clouds which are less tenuous than the blue and which may be composed of rather larger crystals. There is usually a thin veil of these white clouds over the polar caps and short lived ones frequently occur on other parts of the disk, especially near the sunrise and sunset limbs. They are most conspicuous when they are seen as bright spots protruding beyond the illuminated part of the planet. An intensive study of clouds has been made at the Lowell Observatory. Several thousand photographs were analysed and the detailed histories of 95 clouds were deduced. About half of these appeared to be relatively stationary, but others moved with a speed of the order of 5 km per hour, the most common direction of motion being eastwards, particularly at high latitudes. There was a tendency for the clouds to avoid the relatively darker areas of the martian surface, and more occurred in the northern than in the southern hemisphere, while certain regions seemed to be more favoured than others. There were a few cases of clouds recurring in the same positions as though they were connected with certain topographical features.

The appearance and disappearance of the blue and white clouds probably depends on the prevailing temperatures. Some indication of what these may be was obtained from sensitive thermocouple observations made in the 1920s. These gave noon surface temperatures of between 10°C and 20°C for the bright tropical areas, from 20°C to 30°C for the tropical dark areas and from 0°C to 20°C for high latitudes in winter. These temperatures refer to the sun-warmed surface; with the thin dry martian atmosphere lacking any greenhouse effect, the corresponding air shade temperatures are probably much lower and the nights very cold indeed. These early results have been confirmed by later infrared measurements which indicate a temperature range from above 20°C just after noon at the subsolar point to a sunrise minimum well below −80°C. The dark maria appear to be always warmer than the bright desert areas but the difference in temperature nearly vanishes during mid morning. It rises to a maximum of about 15 degrees centigrade in the evening and lingers on throughout the night. The rates of heating and cooling suggest that the average particle size of the martian soil is between 20 μm and 40 μm in the light areas and between 100 μm and 300 μm in the maria. Measurements made in the centimetre radio range, which will indicate the mean temperature a short way below the solid surface, give a figure near to −70°C, which is of the same order as the temperature calculated from a consideration of the solar radiation received and the appropriate albedo.

More detailed measurements of variations in the surface temperature of Mars were obtained from the infrared instruments carried by the Mariner space probes. Those from Mariner 6 which flew along the equator fully confirmed the observations previously made from the Earth. The results from Mariner 7, which swept over the polar cap, were rather more interesting. Just before the polar cap was reached the indicated temperature was −48°C; as the polar cap was reached and traversed this dropped abruptly to below −110°C and finally reached a minimum of −120°C. As the frost temperature of carbon dioxide under martian atmospheric conditions is of the order of −125°C, this Mariner 7 observation can be interpreted as indicating that the major constituent of the polar caps is solid carbon dioxide.

The determination of the composition of the martian atmosphere has proved to be an unexpectedly difficult problem. Before the days of spectroscopic observation, it was usually assumed that the atmosphere of Mars was very similar to that of the Earth and in particular, because of the way in which clouds were observed to come and go and the polar caps to wax and wane, that it contained appreciable quantities of water vapour. The velocity of escape seemed to be sufficiently high for Mars to be able to retain an atmosphere of oxygen, nitrogen and possibly even water vapour as well as all the heavier gases. After the introduction of the spectrograph it was thought that these conclusions would be readily verified; but it was not so.

Light from Mars gives a spectrum which is that of normal sunlight on which are superimposed the absorption features that it acquires during its passage through the martian and terrestrial atmospheres. If these atmospheres are of similar composition, it will be difficult to sort out the specifically martian absorptions unless they are at least comparable in strength to the terrestrial ones. This was quickly found not to be the case for absorption features in the normal spectral range. One way of eliminating the terrestrial atmospheric effects is to compare the spectra of Mars and the Moon taken at equal altitudes; any difference between the two spectra can be ascribed to the martian atmosphere. This method produced no certain results except to place an upper limit on the quantity of oxygen and water vapour in the martian atmosphere, an upper limit that implied that only minute quantities of these gases could be present. Another, and rather more sensitive, method of separating out the martian and terrestrial absorptions is provided by the Doppler shift between them caused by the radial velocity of Mars relative to the Earth. This shift, which is at a maximum when Mars is at quadrature, is relatively small so that the method can be applied only with high dispersion spectrographs. It has in fact given reliable results only within the last few years and with such powerful equipment as the coudé spectrographs on the big reflectors. It appears that there is some water vapour in the martian atmosphere, but only a minute quantity. Under average conditions, the total amount of water vapour in the whole atmosphere could be condensed into a few cubic kilometres of water. The observations appear to indicate that the amount of water vapour in the martian atmosphere varies with time and with location on the planet in a way that suggests that the water cycles through the polar caps and thus that these consist at least partly of frozen water, most probably mixed with a very much larger quantity of solid carbon dioxide. The temperature and pressure conditions on Mars are such that ice sublimes directly to vapour so that the presence of any liquid water is highly doubtful, though some astronomers have pointed out the possibility of it occurring in concentrated solutions of strongly deliquescent salts.

The first constituent of the martian atmosphere to be definitely identified was carbon dioxide, the identification of which was made by Kuiper in 1947 from absorption bands in the infrared near 1.6 μm and 2.0 μm. With improving instrumentation other features in the spectrum of carbon dioxide have been observed. Its abundance can be most easily deduced from measures of the weaker bands at 0.87 μm and 1.05 μm, while measures of the strong bands at 1.6 μm and 2.0 μm can be used to deduce the pressure of the atmosphere as a whole. It appears that the average total amount of carbon dioxide present in the martian atmosphere is equivalent to a layer 78 m thick under normal terrestrial atmospheric temperature and pressure, while the total atmospheric pressure at the surface of Mars is in the range 5 mbar to 10 mbar, i.e. less than one per cent of that at the surface of the Earth. As this only slightly exceeds the pressure due to carbon dioxide alone, any other atmospheric constituents must be relatively rare. As in the case of water vapour, there are indications of seasonal changes in the amount of atmospheric carbon dioxide, the maximum abundance being when the northern polar cap has finished the major portion of its annual shrinking and the minimum when this cap begins to reform as a polar haze in the northern autumn. Another interesting result obtained from these spectroscopic observations of carbon dioxide is the apparent change of atmospheric pressure at different parts of the surface of Mars as though the elevation of this surface varied over the planet by amounts of the order of 10 km. Such changes of elevation are also indicated by radar observations and the two completely different methods yield results which are in substantial agreement. The Syrtis Major, for example, appears to be very high, but these elevation differences do not, in general, seem to be correlated with the bright and dark markings as was suggested by some of the earlier astronomers who regarded the dark areas as 'maria' or seas lying at a lower elevation than the bright bare uplands.

The only other constituent of the lower atmosphere of Mars that has yet been identified is carbon monoxide, its total being equivalent to a layer about 56 mm thick at normal terrestrial atmospheric temperature and pressure. Search has been made, of course, for other gases and it is possible to say that if oxygen is present, its total amount is equivalent to a layer less than 200 mm thick, and similarly if ozone is present, its equivalent layer is less than 2 μm thick.

The upper atmosphere of Mars was investigated during the flyby of Mariners 6 and 7 by observations of the day-glow made with the ultraviolet spectrograph with which each Mariner was equipped. Ultraviolet emissions from carbon dioxide, carbon monoxide, atomic hydrogen and atomic oxygen were observed, but there were no similar indications of either molecular or atomic nitrogen, nor of nitric oxide, all of which have prominent emissions in the corresponding spectra of the Earth's upper atmosphere.

Information about Mars's ionosphere was obtained during the Mariner flybys. Soon after the time of its nearest approach each Mariner, as seen from the Earth, was occulted by Mars. As it passed behind the planet, and again as it emerged, the radio signals received from its transmitter were traversing the martian atmosphere and the resultant changes in them depended on the structure of that atmosphere. The Mariner 4 observations placed the maximum electron density at about 160 km above the planet's surface and made it about equal to the highest electron density found in the Earth's ionosphere at night. The observations made with Mariners 6 and 7 indicated that the peak ionization occurred at 130 km and had an electron density some 50 per cent greater than that observed with Mariner 4. The differences in the two results can probably be explained partly by the greater solar activity in 1969 and partly by the Sun being nearer the zenith at the points of observation. Incidentally, all three Mariners failed to detect any trace of an appreciable magnetic field associated with Mars or anything analogous to the Van Allen belts, and indicated that the magnetic moment of Mars is probably less than 0.0002 that of the Earth. A knowledge of the orbits followed by the Mariners combined with a careful timing of the beginnings and ends of the occultations gave an accurate determination of the dimensions of the solid body of Mars. An accurate determination of its mass was also obtained from the deviations it produced in the orbits of the Mariners at the times of closest approach.

Satellites Mars has two small satellites: Phobos (Fear) and Deimos (Panic) named after the chariot horses of the God of War. They were discovered by Asaph Hall in 1877 using the 26-inch telescope of the U.S. Naval Observatory in Washington. Because they are so small and so close to Mars they can be seen only with powerful telescopes at times when Mars is at a favourable opposition. They are of interest as being the subject of one of the most remarkable prophecies made in literature. Writing some 150 years before their discovery, Dean Swift recorded in *Gulliver's Travels* that the Laputan astronomers had

> discovered two lesser stars, or satellites, which revolve about Mars, whereof the innermost is distant from the centre of the primary planet exactly three of his diameters, and the outermost five; the former revolves in the space of ten hours and the latter in twenty-one and a half.

The corresponding distances and periods for the actual satellites are one and a half and three and a half diameters, and 7.65 and 30.3 hours. Their orbits are nearly circular and almost in the planet's equatorial plane. They are so close to the planet that they cannot be seen from its polar regions.

Phobos, the inner and brighter satellite, is the only natural satellite in the solar system that orbits its primary in a shorter period than the latter takes to rotate. Consequently it rises in the *west*, and sets in the *east* about 5½ hours later. Deimos, on the other hand, rises in the east but remains in the sky for 66 hours, that is for nearly three days, before it slowly sinks in the west. During this time it displays to an observer on Mars two sets of phases similar to those we associate with our own Moon. Because of the difficulty of observing them, their actual size was until recently purely a matter of conjecture based on their known brightness and an assumed albedo. The estimated diameters were 16 km for Phobos and 8 km for Deimos. With these dimensions, Phobos as seen from a point of the equator immediately beneath it would appear about one-third the diameter of our own full moon and about one twenty-fifth as bright, while Deimos would be forty times fainter still and have a diameter of only eighty arc seconds; it would look much the same as Venus does to us. Images of Phobos in transit across the martian disk were recorded on three of the photographs taken by Mariner 7 when its distance from Mars was 130,900 km. Preliminary measurements indicate an elongated shape for Phobos, 18 km by 22 km, not greatly different from the estimated size given above.

Jupiter

Ever since 1610, when Galileo turned his first telescope upon it, Jupiter has been a favourite object for small telescopes. Even the smallest will show the disk of the planet crossed by dusky belts and the ever changing pattern of the four bright inner satellites. The naked-eye observer has little difficulty in recognizing the bright golden object whose unchanging light is noticeably steadier than that of the stars in general. Jupiter, the largest and nearest of the major planets, is larger than all the rest of the planets put together. Its diameter is about eleven times that of the Earth, but while its volume is over thirteen hundred times greater, its mass is only just over three hundred times as great. This means that the average density is less than one quarter that of the Earth, or about one and one-third times that of water. The structure of Jupiter must therefore be fundamentally different from that of the four terrestrial planets, a difference which can probably be explained in terms of a very extensive atmosphere composed of hydrogen and helium. This deep atmosphere prevents our seeing down to any solid surface there may be and such features as are observed are due to clouds which show relative motion and continual change.

Orbit The sidereal period of Jupiter's motion about the Sun is 11.86 years and its synodic period 399 days, or about 13 months. It is easily visible throughout the year, except for a month or so on either side of opposition. It progresses steadily round the sky at the rate of about one zodiacal constellation per year. The regular observer can confidently predict its position without recourse to an ephemeris, for Jupiter has none of the elusiveness of Mercury. Its mean distance from the Sun is 5.2 astronomical units, so that its distance from the Earth varies from an average of 4.2 astronomical units at opposition to 6.2 astronomical units at conjunction. Taking into account the eccentricities of the orbits, the actual opposition distances vary from 3.97 to 4.43 astronomical units, the closest oppositions taking place in October and the furthest in April. The resulting changes in the apparent brightness of the planet are from magnitude −2.5 at an October opposition, or from −2.1 at an April one, to −1.4 at conjunction, that is, except near opposition, Jupiter is considerably brighter than Sirius. Its apparent diameter varies from 50 arc seconds at an October opposition to 32 arc seconds at conjunction. A magnifying power of forty diameters is sufficient to show the disk in more detail than the Moon can be seen with the naked eye. Its distance is sufficiently large for it to show no appreciable phases, though at quadrature the edge furthest from the Sun shows a slight darkening.

Telescopic appearance The general telescopic appearance of Jupiter is well shown in Plates 15*a* and *b* which are reproductions of photographs taken with the 200-inch Hale Telescope, the former in red, the latter in

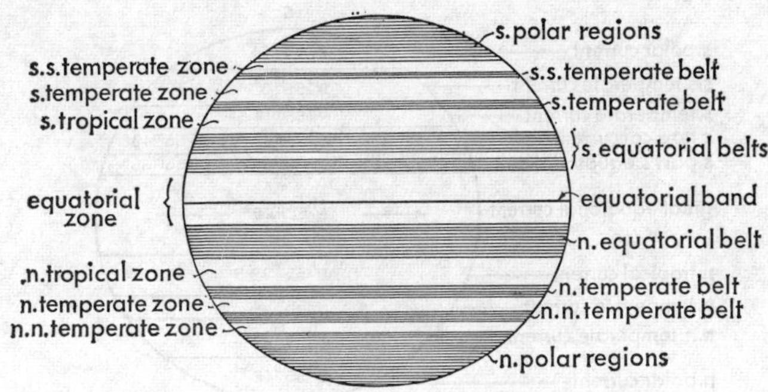

Figure 5.8 The belts and zones of Jupiter and Saturn

blue light. The disk is noticeably elliptical and falls off in brightness towards the edge. The cause of the ellipticity is the rapid rotation which gives its figure an oblateness of about 1/15, while the darkening towards the limb results from that part of the jovian atmosphere that overlies the reflecting layer. Aligned parallel to the major axis of the ellipse are a series of alternating dusky brownish-red 'belts' and bright light yellow 'zones', the principal ones of which are illustrated in Figure 5.8. The belts and zones are not nearly as regular in intensity, shape or width as the diagram suggests, and are, moreover, constantly changing. Both belts and zones are variegated with irregular dark and bright spots and streaks of different tints and sizes. At various times a great range of colour is seen: shades of brown, red, pink, orange, yellow, green, blue and purple have been recorded as well as grey and white. Frequent changes in the ragged, wispy edges of the belts and in the spots vividly indicate the underlying atmospheric turmoil. Regular colour changes in the equatorial belts corresponding to the jovian year have been suspected by some careful observers, but, as the axis of rotation of the planet is inclined at only 3° to that of the orbit, no marked seasonal variations can be expected.

Rotation A careful watch on such distinctive features as the spots will reveal the planet's rapid rotation. New details come into view on the following limb as others disappear at the edge of the preceding one. The period of rotation found from the observation of such features varies

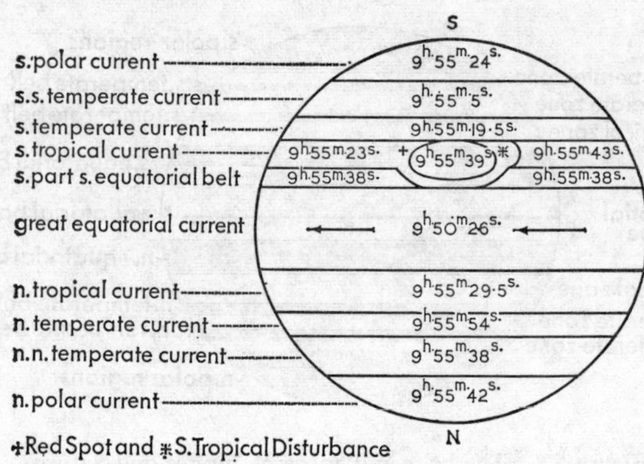

Figure 5.9 The various rotation periods of Jupiter: Red Spot, South Tropical Disturbance, and the chief atmospheric currents on Jupiter. From diagram by T. E. R. Phillips.

with their position on the disk, being about 9 hours 50 minutes at the equator and 9 hours 55 minutes in the higher latitudes. These varying speeds of rotation, which are shown diagrammatically in Figure 5.9, result from a combination of the 'solid body' rotation and the various atmospheric currents. What the period of the solid body rotation is may be indicated by the radio emissions, which show a fixed periodicity of 9 hours 55 minutes 29.75 seconds. It was found during the 1950s that Jupiter is a source of non-thermal radio waves in both the 13-metre band and the 10-centimetre band. The former are emitted in short, sharp bursts, not unlike the static associated with terrestrial thunderstorms, but vastly more powerful. They appear to be associated with certain areas of Jupiter's surface and seem in some way, which is not yet understood, to be influenced by Io, the innermost of the four bright satellites, and to a lesser extent by Europa, the next closest satellite. The radiation in the 10 centimetre band is emitted continuously and appears to be due to electrons trapped in a strong magnetic field comparable to, but much stronger than, the Van Allen belt that surrounds the Earth. The variation that is observed in this radiation is that of the plane of polarization, which changes steadily, presumably because of a 10° difference in the directions of the magnetic and rotational axes of Jupiter.

The Red Spot It is not possible in a brief account of Jupiter to describe the ever-changing cloud patterns. The number of belts, their breadth and detailed arrangement, vary continuously but tend to conform to a general pattern which seems to be imposed by atmospheric currents flowing in circles of latitude. The equatorial zone is usually light and the polar regions are not so noticeably banded as the rest of the planet and tend to be more uniformly shaded. Among these ever-changing features there are a few which seem to be semi-permanent. Most conspicuous of these is the Red Spot, which being red is clearly shown as a dark marking in the blue photograph (Plate 15*b*). This, or its prototype, was noted by Hooke in 1664; it disappeared and reappeared several times until it was lost to sight in 1713. The Red Spot of today was drawn by Schwabe in 1831 and has been observed regularly ever since. By 1878 it had developed into an ellipse stretching 50,000 km in jovian longitude and 11,000 km in latitude and having an area comparable to that of the whole of the Earth's surface. Its colour also seems to have reached its maximum intensity about that time, having changed from pale pink to deep brick red. Since 1882 it has often taken the shape of a capsule with pointed ends and has faded at times almost into invisibility, but it is still observable as an oval spot with a varying depth of colour. It was particularly conspicuous during the 1968–9 apparition.

The Red Spot does not remain fixed relative to its surroundings. Between 1831 and 1938 it moved 1046° in longitude, which is equivalent to nearly three circuits round the planet. The motion is not uniform since the Spot moved forward 477° between 1891 and 1910, backward 313° between 1910 and 1929, then forward 81° but with oscillations between 1929 and 1938. It follows that the Red Spot cannot be attached to the solid surface but must float in the atmosphere, though its semi-permanence indicates a greater solidity than the surrounding cloud. Wildt has suggested that it finds its level in much the same way as a balloon finds its 'ceiling' in the terrestrial atmosphere. Peek, one of the most assiduous observers of Jupiter, has extended this idea a little further by supposing that the buoyancy of the Red Spot relative to its surroundings changes from time to time, sometimes allowing it to be observed and at other times letting it sink below the level of visibility. As the Red Spot rises or falls, its speed relative to the visible surface will alter and Peek concludes that a vertical movement of only nine kilometres would be sufficient to explain the varying appearances and motions of the Red Spot since 1831.

The Red Spot is surrounded by the 'Hollow', a lighter region located on the southern side of the South Equatorial Belt and easily visible in Plate 15*b*. Often, as happened in 1955–6, the Red Spot virtually disappears leaving the Hollow as a conspicuous feature. In the same latitude as the Red Spot and the Hollow is, or rather was, the South Tropical Disturbance. This curious feature was first noted by Molesworth in February 1901 and its activities were followed until it disappeared in about 1940. Starting as a dark marking across the zone, it rapidly expanded in longitude and thereafter showed great variations in shape, extent and motion. It was rarely less than 100° of longitude long and at times was over 200°. Its rotation period, though irregular, was shorter than that of the Red Spot which it overtook at intervals of from two to four years. At such times the Disturbance pushed the Red Spot forward while flowing round or below it. In years when the Disturbance, the Hollow, and much of the South Equatorial Belt were inconspicuous, the Red Spot was most prominent.

Physical constitution The observed spectrum of Jupiter is that of sunlight on which are superimposed a number of absorption features due to the passage of the light through the terrestrial atmosphere and its double passage through that part of the jovian atmosphere that lies above the reflecting cloud layer. Strong bands due to this latter cause have long been known to be present in the orange and red but it was not until 1932 that Wildt identified them as being due to methane (CH_4) and ammonia (NH_3). Spectroscopic technique and the range of spectrum observed have been greatly extended since then but the only other gas that has so far been identified is molecular hydrogen (H_2). The estimated abundances of the observed gases depend to some extent on theoretical assumptions. If these are correct, the amount of molecular hydrogen above the cloud deck is the equivalent of 68 km of the gas at normal terrestrial atmospheric pressure and temperature. The corresponding amounts of methane and ammonia are of the order of 150 m and 10 m respectively, while the temperature of the cloud deck is between 140°K and 150°K. At this temperature most of the ammonia present will be frozen solid and the 10 m equivalent of ammonium vapour that is observed represents about all that the observable portion of Jupiter's atmosphere can contain. Since the hydrogen is relatively so abundant it seems reasonable to assume that it has combined with all the carbon, nitrogen and oxygen present. The water resulting from this last combination will almost all be frozen and sunk beneath the cloud deck. Even so, traces of water vapour will be present in the observable atmosphere, but only in quantities which are ten thousand times less abundant than can be detected by the present spectroscopic methods. Similarly, there is as yet no direct test to verify the presence of helium, which may well be there, since it is so abundant throughout the greater part of

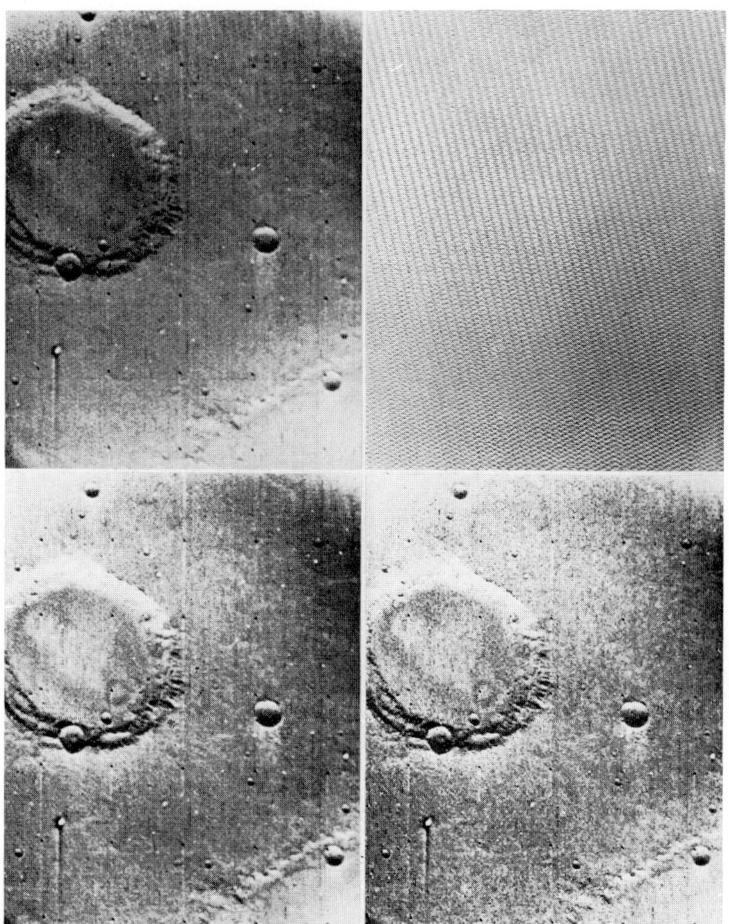

Plate 13 Mars from Mariner 6: refinement of pictures

Television pictures of Mars from the two Mariner spacecraft are improved through computer analysis and enhancement. Features such as the gullies in the lower rim of the large crater and minute indentations in the surrounding surface gradually appear sharper. The frame at upper left has a general 'softness' and a faint 'basket-weave' pattern caused by electronic 'pickup' in the sensitive camera system. Computer analysis revealed the 'pickup' pattern at upper right. The appropriate value, determined from the pattern, was then subtracted from each of the 658,240 elements of the picture to produce the picture at lower left. Two further computer programmes produced the refinement at lower right. The large crater in this Mariner 6 picture is about 38 kilometres in diameter. IPS photograph

Plate 14 Close up narrow-angle view of Mars from Mariner 6

The photograph spans an area of 72 × 83 kilometres. The large crater at the south edge with a prominent smaller crater on its floor is about 24 kilometres across. Camera distance is about 3,460 kilometres. IPS photograph

Plate 15 Jupiter *a* in red light, showing the satellite Ganymede and its shadow on the upper surface and *b*, below, in blue light, showing the Red Spot. Hale Observatories

Plate 16 Various aspects of Saturn, 1933–40, photographed at Lowell Observatory

These six photographs, taken in yellow light, display various aspects of the ball and the ring system seen from the north side of the ring plane (1933–34) and the south (1937–40). In 1936 the plane of the rings passed through the Earth. There is an obvious change in the markings on the ball between 1933 and 1934; especially noteworthy are the single dark belt and large whitish cap over the southern polar regions in 1934. In 1940 the equatorial bright zone is much narrower and brighter than normal the universe. Since methane is still gaseous at 150°K, it seems reasonable to suppose that the visible cloud layer is composed of floating crystals of frozen ammonia, just as terrestrial cirrus clouds consist of floating ice crystals. Wildt has suggested that some of the colours they show may be due to sodium and potassium which form intensely coloured solutions with liquid ammonia.

Information about Jupiter's atmosphere can be obtained from observations made on those relatively rare occasions when Jupiter occults a bright star. The rate at which the light of the star appears to diminish in intensity as the planet moves in front of it indicates the way in which the density of the jovian atmosphere varies with height. From such observations and from theoretical interpretations of spectroscopic data it appears that the mean molecular weight of Jupiter's upper atmosphere is about 2.6. Since the molecular weight of hydrogen is only 2.0 it follows that the atmosphere must contain an appreciable quantity of heavier gases, presumably mostly helium of which the molecular weight is 4.0.

Knowledge of the internal composition of Jupiter can be obtained by studying a series of theoretical models, starting from the simplest and modifying it stage by stage until one is evolved that, where it can be tested, matches the actual planet. The simplest model is a sphere composed entirely of cool hydrogen in equilibrium under its own gravitation. The hydrostatic pressure within such a sphere increases steadily towards the centre to a maximum value which will depend only on the total mass of the sphere. The external radius of the sphere and the internal distribution of density will be determined by the way in which hydrogen behaves under the immense pressures that will exist within spheres of planetary dimensions. Well established theory indicates that up to a critical pressure of about 800,000 atmospheres hydrogen retains its molecular form, but its density increases steadily up to 0.35 g cm^{-3}. At the critical pressure there is a phase change; the hydrogen becomes 'metallic' and the density suddenly increases to 0.77 g cm^{-3}. Further increases of pressure cause the density to increase so that by 30,000,000 atmospheres it exceeds 3 g cm^{-3}.

Taking the mass of the Earth as unity, no hydrogen planet of mass lower than 88 will have a metallic core, whereas if the mass exceeds 95 there must be such a core. For still higher masses the relative size of the metallic core increases as does the concentration of density towards the centre and the mean density of the planet as a whole. This results in the rather curious relation between the radius of a hydrogen planet and its mass which is shown in the following table taken from a paper by W. H. Ramsey.

TABLE 5.5 THE RELATION BETWEEN MASS, RADIUS AND DENSITY FOR HYDROGEN PLANETS

Mass ($M_E = 1$)	*Radius* (km)	*Mean density* (g cm^{-3})
10.7	46,000	0.16
60	73,000	0.22
97	75,600	0.32
208	77,100	0.65
317	79,400	0.90
623	82,600	1.57
1000	84,500	2.36
1400	83,700	3.42
1800	83,000	4.53

The radius increases slowly with increasing mass to a maximum corresponding to a mass one thousand times that of the Earth and thereafter decreases. The hydrogen planet having a mass equal to that of Jupiter has a radius slightly greater and a density of only 0.9 g cm^{-3}. To get a model in better agreement with the actual planet, heavier elements have to be introduced, and in particular helium. A plausible model can be constructed in which 95 per cent of the mass is a homogeneous mixture of one atom of helium to every twenty-two of hydrogen, while the other five per cent consists of helium and the heavier elements and is concentrated towards the centre. In this model most of the hydrogen is in the metallic state for this phase extends from the centre outwards for six-sevenths of the radius.

Satellites The essential details of the twelve known satellites of Jupiter are given in Table 5.3. They are designated by Roman numerals, the first four being assigned in order of distance from Jupiter to the four bright satellites discovered by Galileo, and the remaining eight to the faint satellites in order of their discovery, The first four also have proper names, being respectively Io, Europa, Ganymede (Plate 15*a*) and Callisto. As may be seen from Table 5.3 or from Figure 5.10, which shows the arrangement of the orbits, the twelve satellites form three distinct groups. The first consists of Satellites I–V which form a compact, regular system close to Jupiter, and move in circular orbits which lie virtually in its equatorial plane and have periods ranging from one half to sixteen days. The second group, which is formed by Satellites VI, VII and X, is considerably further from Jupiter, and its members move in eccentric orbits inclined at about 30° to the equatorial plane with

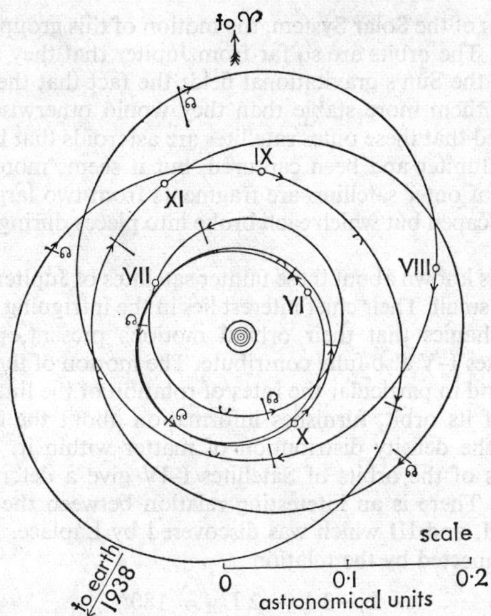

Figure 5.10 The orbits of the satellites of Jupiter

This diagram, prepared by Seth B. Nicholson, shows the position and orbits of the first eleven satellites as they were at the time of the 1938 opposition. Each orbit is shown as in its own plane and, in the case of the outer satellites, the nodes, or points in which it intersects the plane of the ecliptic, are indicated by short lines and the ascending node by ☊. The arrows which show the direction of motion are confined to that part of the orbit that lies north of the ecliptic. The small semicircles concave to Jupiter mark the position of perijove.

The first five satellites form a compact regular system with circular orbits lying in the equatorial plane. Satellites VI, VII and X form a second group considerably further from Jupiter and move in eccentric orbits inclined at about 30° to this plane. Satellites VIII, IX and XI form a third group still further from Jupiter and having retrograde eccentric orbits. It is to this last group that Satellite XII belongs.

periods of the order of eight months. Satellites VIII, IX, XI and XII are even further from Jupiter and have orbital periods of the order of two years. These orbits are also eccentric but the most interesting thing about them is that they are inclined at an angle of approximately 150° to the planet's equatorial plane; that is, in marked contrast to most other motions of the Solar System, the motion of this group of satellites is retrograde. The orbits are so far from Jupiter that they are strongly perturbed by the Sun's gravitational field; the fact that they are retrograde makes them more stable than they would otherwise be. It has been suggested that these outer satellites are asteroids that have strayed too close to Jupiter and been captured, but it seems more likely that both groups of outer satellites are fragments from two larger satellites that nearly escaped but which each broke into pieces during the process of recapture.

Very little is known about these fainter satellites of Jupiter except that they are very small. Their chief interest lies in the intriguing problems in celestial mechanics that their orbital motions present, problems to which Satellites I–V also fully contribute. The motion of the innermost, Satellite V, and in particular the rates of rotation of the lines of apsides and nodes of its orbit, furnishes information about the ellipticity of Jupiter and the density distribution of matter within it. The mutual perturbations of the orbits of Satellites I–IV give a determination of their masses. There is an interesting relation between the motions of Satellites I, II, and III which was discovered by Laplace. Their longitudes are connected by the relation

$$L_{I} - 3\,L_{II} - 2\,L_{III} = 180°$$

which means that they cannot all come into conjunction at one time, or into simultaneous opposition or conjunction with the Sun.

If it were not for their closeness to Jupiter the first four satellites would be quite conspicuous objects and easily visible to the naked eye on a dark moonless night. I and II are similar in size, mass, and density to our own Moon, while III and IV are larger in size than Mercury but less massive. Their albedos decrease with distance from Jupiter, that for I and II being 0.6, for III 0.34, and for IV 0.15. Even the smallest of these is twice that of our Moon, so that while it may be tempting to think of I and II as being similar in composition to the Moon, they must differ from it in having a coating of some highly reflecting substance. This may be a layer of frozen gases, but how these gases were originally acquired is not clear, for these satellites are too small to have held a free atmosphere of their own unless they have always been very cold. The lower densities of III and IV may result from their carrying relatively greater depths of these frozen gases. All four satellites show markings on their surface and appear to keep the same face turned constantly towards Jupiter as does the Moon to the Earth.

The fact that the orbits of I–IV are so slightly inclined to the planes in which the Earth and Jupiter orbit the Sun gives rise to a continuous

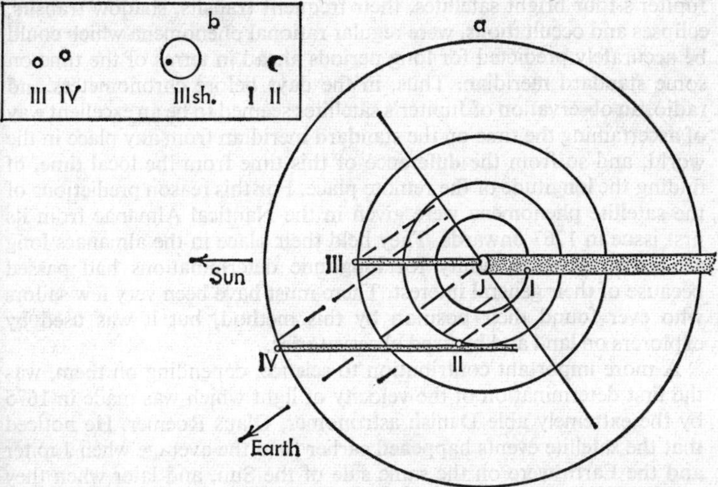

Figure 5.11 The geometry of the phenomena of Jupiter's satellites

A hypothetical situation of the Galilean satellites: *a* in plan—radii of orbits approximately to scale (28 : 45 : 72 : 126); *b* as seen from the Earth: shadow of III in transit; I eclipsed by Jupiter; II partially eclipsed by IV (large aperture could show this).

series of interesting phenomena in which the satellites, or their shadows, transit the planet's disk, while the satellites are eclipsed by Jupiter's shadow or occulted by its disk. The geometry of the phenomena is illustrated in Figure 5.11. When Jupiter is in opposition its shadow lies directly away from the Earth and no eclipses are seen. When Jupiter is at or near quadrature, however, its shadow projects so far to one side that the whole eclipse of II, III, and IV can be seen. At other times only the beginning or end of an eclipse is visible. Plate 15 shows a shadow transit of III in progress, III itself being still clear of the planet. The shadow appears so much larger than the satellite itself because it includes both the umbra and the penumbra. The fact that the shadow looks so dark indicates that the surface of Jupiter is not, as at one time supposed, self luminous. Satellite transits are not so conspicuous unless they happen to be across one of the dark bands.

It was quickly noticed that the rapidly changing configuration of

Jupiter's four bright satellites, their frequent transits, shadow transits, eclipses and occultations, were regular rational phenomena which could be accurately predicted for long periods ahead in terms of the time on some standard meridian. Thus, in the days before chronometers and radio, an observation of Jupiter's satellites seemed to be an excellent way of ascertaining the time on the standard meridian from any place in the world, and so from the difference of this time from the local time, of finding the longitude of the remote place. For this reason predictions of the satellite phenomena were given in the Nautical Almanac from its first issue in 1767 onwards. They held their place in the almanacs long after their possible utility for longitude determinations had passed because of their general interest. There must have been very few sailors who ever found their position by this method, but it was used by explorers on land and by fixed observatories.

A more important contribution to science, depending on them, was the first determination of the velocity of light which was made in 1675 by the extremely able Danish astronomer, Olaus Roemer. He noticed that the satellite events happened earlier than the average when Jupiter and the Earth were on the same side of the Sun, and later when they were on opposite sides, the extreme differences being about 8 minutes on either side of the mean. He explained these observations in terms of what at that time was a completely new and revolutionary idea, namely that the velocity of light was finite and that it took approximately 16 minutes to traverse the diameter of the Earth's orbit.

Saturn

To the naked eye Saturn is a first magnitude star shining with a steady pale yellow light; seen through a good telescope it is one of the most beautiful objects in the sky, especially when the ring system is fully open. The photographs reproduced in Plate 16, which were all taken in yellow light, give an impression of the appearance of the planet in various parts of its orbit, but, being in black and white, they fail to do justice to Saturn's striking appearance when seen under the best conditions. These probably occur during twilight when there is just sufficient light in the sky to provide a deep blue background to set off the golden yellow ball of the planet and the shimmering white rings surrounding it.

Orbit Saturn takes $29\frac{1}{2}$ years to complete its orbit, which is inclined at $2\frac{1}{2}°$ to the ecliptic and which is slightly more eccentric than that of

Jupiter. The perihelion and aphelion distances are approximately 9 and 10 astronomical units so that its distance from the Earth varies from 8 astronomical units at the most favourable oppositions to 11 astronomical units at the furthest conjunctions. The former occur in December when Saturn is high in the northern sky and provide the best opportunities for observing the planet, especially as the ring system then presents its most open aspect. The most favourable opposition for some years took place on 22 December 1973, but as the synodic period only exceeds a year by 13 days other fairly favourable oppositions take place for some years before and after 1973. Between the times of perihelion and aphelion the ring system gradually closes and then opens up again to display the other side of the rings. As observed from the Sun, the rings appear edgeways on at alternate intervals of $13\frac{3}{4}$ and $15\frac{3}{4}$ years, the uneven interval being due to the eccentricity of the planet's orbit. The Earth's own orbital motion introduces complications, and on such occasions our planet may pass through the plane of the rings three times in fairly quick succession, and there will be periods of a few months during which the Earth and the Sun are on opposite sides of the plane of the rings.

The apparent diameter of the ring system varies between approximately 46 arc seconds at a favourable opposition and 32 arc seconds at the more distant conjunctions, the corresponding diameters for the planet itself being 20 and 14 arc seconds. The variations in total brightness depend as much on the aspect of the ring system as on the distance of the planet since the rings when most open, which happens also to be the times of perihelion and aphelion, reflect about 60 per cent more light than does the ball of the planet. Thus it happens that the visual magnitude at the time of opposition is −0.4 at the time of perihelion, 0.2 at the time of aphelion, and only 0.9 at times when the ring system is edgeways on. The corresponding conjunction magnitudes are 0.3, 0.8 and 1.5. Thus the total range in the apparent magnitude of Saturn is from −0.4 to 1.5 and at a December opposition when the planet is at its brightest it outshines all the stars except Sirius and Canopus.

Physical properties Apart from its rings, Saturn bears a fairly close resemblance to Jupiter, though it is smaller and, being further from the Sun, cooler. There is the same falling off in brightnesss towards the edge of the planetary disk and a similar array of belts parallel to circles of latitude, but the surface markings are not quite so complex and the variations in them not so conspicuous nor so rapid. Changes do take place, however, as may be seen from Plate 16, by comparing the photographs taken in 1933 and 1934 with those taken later. Very occasionally spots appear that are sufficiently well defined to permit a determination of the period of rotation. Short lived white spots which appeared near the equator in 1876, 1891–4, and in 1933 gave a rotation period of approximately 10 hours 14 minutes, while spots appearing away from the equator in 1876, 1903 and 1960 gave a period of about 10 hours 38 minutes. Spectroscopic observations made when the rings were nearly invisible showed that the rotation period increases steadily towards the higher latitudes and is fully an hour longer in latitude 57° than at the equator. The 1933 spot was first seen by Will Hay, a keen amateur astronomer, but better known as a film comedian. At first it was oval in shape and about one-fifth of the planet's diameter in length. It increased rapidly in length and had more than doubled its initial length before it merged into the general bright equatorial band.

The rapid rotation of Saturn is demonstrated by its marked oblateness which is greater than that of any other planet. The difference between the polar and equatorial diameters is over 10 per cent and is greater than can be explained by the speed of rotation unless the mass of the planet is concentrated towards the centre. The average density is very much smaller than that of any other planet and is less than that of water. Referring to Table 5.5, it will be noticed that a planet composed of pure hydrogen and having the mass of Saturn would have a radius of 75,600 km and a density of only 0.32 since only a small portion of hydrogen in the centre will be in the metallic phase. But as Saturn has a mean radius of 56,800 km and a density of 0.71, it can be concluded that, like Jupiter, Saturn contains in addition to hydrogen a considerable fraction of helium and a rocky core which may be even bigger than that in Jupiter. Direct spectroscopic evidence of the presence of large quantities of molecular hydrogen in the planet's atmosphere has been obtained. The only other gas that has, as yet, been certainly identified is methane, which produces strong absorption bands in the spectrum, stronger even than those in the spectrum of Jupiter. This may result from the lower temperature of Saturn's atmosphere, which from radiometric observations is estimated to be about 94°K, at which temperature essentially all of the water and ammonia vapour will have been frozen out of the atmosphere and in its solid form have sunk to the bottom.

The rings The rings are the particular glory of Saturn. They were first observed in July 1610 by Galileo, who was greatly mystified to see what he thought were two small spheres, one on either side of the disk of the planet. He was even more astonished in the following years to see these appendages diminish, disappear completely and then come back, grow to a maximum and fade away again. Galileo's surprise can have been

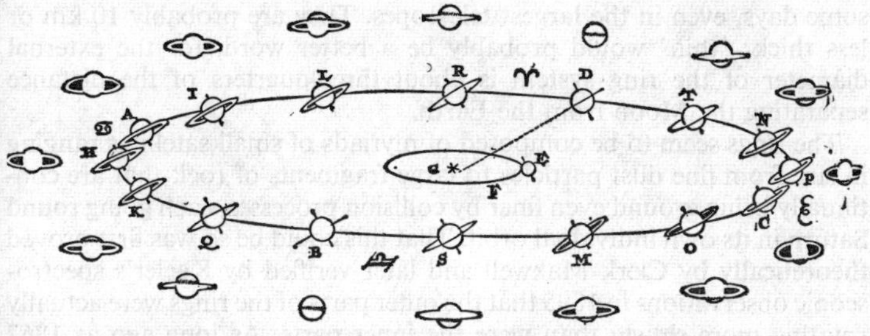

Figure 5.12 Phases of Saturn's Rings according to Christiaan Huygens, *Systema Saturnium*, 1659

matched only by his chagrin at having such a feeble instrument with which to study the phenomenon. Many seventeenth-century astronomers studied Saturn but their telescopes did not have sufficient resolving power to provide them with an easy clue to the mystery. This was finally solved by Christiaan Huygens who, in his book *Systema Saturnium* published in 1659, clearly states that 'Saturn is surrounded by a thin flat ring not touching it anywhere, which is oblique to the ecliptic'. Figure 5.12, a photograph of a diagram given in Huygens's book, explains more clearly than can many words the changing appearance of the rings as seen from the Earth as Saturn moves round the Sun. The plane of the rings is inclined to the ecliptic at 28° so that when the rings are most fully open, as happens when Saturn is in the direction of Taurus or Sagittarius, they have the form of an ellipse in which the minor axis is just under half the length of the major axis.

The ring system consists of three main parts: a greyish-white outer ring, usually referred to as A; a bright white middle ring known as B; and a rather faint, somewhat indefinite inner ring, C, blue-grey or slate in colour, which is sometimes called the 'crepe ring'. Between rings A and B there is a definite gap known as 'Cassini's Division' after the Parisian astronomer who first described it in 1675. There is no such marked division between rings B and C, though the bright B fades into the rather dull C somewhat abruptly. A narrow dark line that occasionally appears on ring A and which suggests a narrow gap has been named 'Encke's Division'. The observed diameters of the rings are given in Table 5.3. The rings appear to be very flat and very thin, for at the times when they are edgeways on to the Earth they become quite invisible for some days, even in the largest telescopes. They are probably 10 km or less thick; 'thin' would probably be a better word, for the external diameter of the ring system is about three-quarters of the distance separating the Moon from the Earth.

The rings seem to be composed of myriads of small satellites ranging in size from fine dust particles to large fragments of rock that are continually being ground even finer by collision processes, each going round Saturn in its own individual orbit. That this could be so was first proved theoretically by Clerk Maxwell and later verified by Keeler's spectroscopic observations in 1895 that the outer parts of the rings were actually rotating more slowly than were the inner parts. As long ago as 1867 Kirkwood studied the gravitational effects of the saturnian satellites upon the ring system and concluded that orbits for which the periodic time was a simple fraction of the periods of revolution of the inner satellites were unstable, and that particles travelling in them would relatively quickly be removed to other more stable orbits. The distances at which the period would be one-half that of Mimas, one-third that of Enceladus and one-quarter that of Tethys, all fall within Cassini's Division, while the boundary between rings B and C corresponds to particles having periods one-third that of Mimas, and Encke's Division to particles with three-fifths of this period. Over the years several observers have drawn attention to what they took to be other divisions in the rings, but according to Kuiper, who made a study of Saturn with the 200-inch telescope at Mount Palomar under near-perfect observing conditions, such divisions are either minor intensity ripples or illusions. In 1921 Goldsborough continued the work begun by Kirkwood and showed that both the divisions and the 'tores', that is the thickening of the rings near the divisions, could have been formed by the perturbing influence of the inner satellites. His work was amended and extended by Jeffreys who showed that there is a tendency for particles near the edge of ring B to move into ring C and that another 'crepe' ring ought to be forming outside ring A. Such a faint dull ring has been reported several times since the beginning of the century and recently still another very faint ring inside C has been discovered at the Pic du Midi Observatory.

Some clues to the nature of the rings can be gathered from a variety of observations, some of which will now be discussed. The opportunity for one set of these arises on the rather rare occasions when Saturn passes in front of a bright star. One such occultation was watched under ideal conditions by three very reliable and experienced South African amateur astronomers in March 1920. The star in question was orange-red in colour and thus in sharp contrast with the white of the rings and the pale yellow of the planet. As the star passed behind ring A its light was only slightly dimmed, but as soon as it touched ring B its light gradually faded by about half a magnitude. It remained like this for a few seconds before flickering, that is the light would suddenly almost go out, but not quite. The light of the star continued to fluctuate very considerably but was never fainter than a magnitude below its original brightness. It reached the planet's limb when it was still only two-thirds the way across ring B but instead of disappearing immediately, its light gradually got dimmer until it was about two and one-half magnitudes below its original brightness. The final disappearance appeared to take place well within the limb of the planet and, although sudden, had not the 'snap' that occurs when a star is occulted by the Moon. This observation demonstrates the transparency of the rings and, since the star flickered but was never completely occulted, indicates that there cannot be many particles in the rings that subtend at the Earth an angle greater than does the disk of the star. Taking this latter as being of the order of 0.0001 arc seconds, the corresponding limiting size for the particles is about 0.6 km. This is far larger than the average particle is likely to be for consideration of the greater reflecting power of ring B, and the fact that its total mass is so small as to be gravitationally insignificant leads to the conclusion that the average particle must be very small indeed, possibly comparable in size to fine white flour.

Observations that demonstrate the partial transparency of the rings can be made at times when the rings are nearly edgeways on with the Sun and Earth on opposite sides of their plane. At such a time the side illuminated by direct sunlight is not visible from the Earth, but the other side is and can be seen to be faintly illuminated partly by sunlight reflected from the surface of the planet and partly by sunlight that has found its way through the rings. The rings appear as a relatively faint, narrow, elongated ellipse which shows up as a dark band where it crosses the more strongly illuminated surface of the planet. Away from the planet, and on each side of it, the ellipse brightens up in two places, the inner brightenings corresponding to ring C and the outer to the Cassini Division and the adjacent portions of ring B.

Another type of observation that can yield information about the particles forming the ring is the careful photometry of the change in the brightness of the rings as the phase angle changes from 0° at opposition to 6° at quadrature. When the rings are invisible the light from the planet itself shows little variation with phase angle, indicating that the reflecting surface of the planet is effectively smooth. On the other hand, when the rings are visible there is a considerable change in brightness with phase angle; when the rings are fully open, the light reflected from them is diminished by about 35 per cent for a change in phase angle of only 6°. At opposition, when the Earth is directly in line between the Sun and Saturn, each particle in the ring hides its own shadow and the whole surface of the ring appears bright. But when the phase angle is even a degree or two, the Earth is out of the direct line by this amount and the shadow of each particle begins to come out from behind it and to obscure the particles beyond it that were previously visible. Thus the multitude of these tiny shadows diminishes the brightness of the ring as a whole. From the observed light curve, Seeliger concluded that, on the average, the particles occupied about one-sixteenth of the whole volume of rings A and B, but later Schönberg made the fraction much less and deduced that the larger particles are accompanied by much fine dust.

An observation of some interest concerning the physical constitution of the rings was made in 1969 by observers from the University of Arizona's Lunar and Planetary Laboratory, who used a more powerful spectrograph than was previously available to record the spectrum of the rings in the range from one to four microns. They found eight major absorption bands which were not present in the spectrum of the planet itself, but which all matched up with laboratory spectra of water ice at a temperature of −190° C, i.e. 83° K.

Satellites Saturn has ten known satellites, of which the names and relevant data are given in Table 5.3. Unlike those of Jupiter, they are usually referred to by name rather than by number since there does not seem to be complete agreement as to whether the numbering system should be in order of discovery or in order of distance from the primary. The names are those assigned by Sir John Herschel for the seven known in his time, and by the discoverers for the three that have been found since. Titan, the largest of the satellites, was seen by Huygens in 1655; Janus, the innermost one, was only discovered by Dollfus in 1966 at a time when the rings, to which it is very close, were edgeways on and practically invisible. Titan and the six satellites interior to it form a very regular, compact system in that their orbits are practically circular and lie in, or very close to, the equatorial plane of the planet, which is also the plane of the rings. Their periods range from three-quarters of a day up to sixteen days and their size increases with increasing distance from the planet. Hyperion, the next satellite, may also be regarded as belonging to this system since it is not very much further out than Titan and its orbit lies in very much the same plane as that of the others. On the other hand, Hyperion is very much smaller than Titan and its orbit is noticeably eccentric. The other two satellites are very much further out and quite clearly do not conform to the regular pattern of the rings and the inner satellites. Iapetus takes 79 days to complete its orbit which is inclined at 15° to the equatorial plane of Saturn, while Phoebe takes 550 days to move, like the four outer satellites of Jupiter, in a retrograde direction round an orbit inclined at 30° to that of most of the others.

As in the case of Jupiter, it has been possible to estimate the masses of most of the satellites from the mutual perturbations of their orbits. Only the diameter of Titan is sufficiently large to be directly measured, though that of Rhea has been estimated from the time it takes to enter or leave the planet's shadow at the time of an eclipse. The diameters of the others have to be derived either from the brightness, guessing the albedo, or from the mass, guessing the density. It seems that the two estimates can only be reconciled by assuming that the satellites have, as compared with our own Moon, a relatively low density and a high albedo comparable with that of freshly fallen snow. Titan is of the same order of size as the Galilean Moons of Jupiter but the other satellites are considerably larger than the comparable jovian bodies. It must be remarked, however, that if Saturn has a number of satellites comparable in size to Jupiter's VII–XII, they will be extremely faint as seen from the Earth and could quite easily have escaped detection.

Titan is the only satellite in the solar system on which an atmosphere has been found. It was discovered at the McDonald Observatory in 1944 by Kuiper who observed the absorption bands of methane in considerable strength in its spectrum. It may seem somewhat surprising that Titan should have an atmosphere whereas Ganymede, which is somewhat larger and more massive, shows no trace of one. The explanation appears to lie in the considerably lower temperature of Titan, for Kuiper has calculated that if its temperature were raised only as high as 200° K (i.e. −73°C) it would completely lose all its methane.

Several of the satellites as they move round their orbits show regular variations in brightness which clearly indicate that they keep the same face turned towards their primary, as does the Moon towards the Earth. In the case of Titan and Rhea, the total range of brightness is of the order of 25 per cent, but in the case of Iapetus the range is far greater than this, the brightness as seen from the Earth being some five times greater at maximum than at minimum. This means that one side of this extraordinary body must reflect light over five times more efficiently than does the other.

Uranus

Under very good conditions Uranus is just visible to the naked eye, to which it appears like any of the neighbouring stars. In a telescope it shows a small blue-green disk never more than 4 arc seconds in diameter. Various observers have reported extremely faint belts reminiscent of those on Jupiter, but no distinct markings permitting direct observations of rotation have yet been observed. When suitably placed the disk can be seen to be markedly elliptical, suggesting that the planet is in rapid rotation. The rate of this rotation has been measured both spectroscopically and by observing the periodic fluctuations in the light of the planet. Both methods give a rotation period of about $10\frac{3}{4}$ hours, but neither gives any indication as to whether the surface rotates like a solid body or shows a differential rotation with latitude like Jupiter and Saturn. So far five satellites have been discovered. These form a very regular, compact system, reminiscent in size and arrangement of the inner satellites of Saturn, though it must be remembered that some of the data given in Table 5.3, e.g. the rather high densities, must be treated with some reserve since they are based partly on extremely difficult measures and partly on plausible assumptions. The orbits of the satellites lie in the equatorial plane of the planet and are traversed in the same direction as the planet rotates.

One of the most interesting things about this system is that this equatorial plane is inclined at an angle of 98° to the plane of the planet's orbit round the Sun, which is itself very close to the plane of the ecliptic. That is, the motion of the system is retrograde and the polar axis of Uranus lies very close to the plane in which the planet goes round the Sun. Consequently there are times during the 84-year period, such as 1903 and 1945, when Uranus as seen from the Earth is 'pole-on'. The disk then appears as a perfect circle with the pole in the centre while the satellite orbits are seen 'in plan' as nearly perfect circles. At other times, such as 1924 and 1966, the planet's visible disk is a projection on to a meridian plane and appears noticeably elliptical with the apparent polar compression a maximum. The satellite orbits are then seen 'edge-on' so that the satellites appear to move backwards and forwards along straight lines. In intermediate years conditions between these two extremes pertain.

The mass of the planet is well determined but its small and faintly illuminated disk is difficult to measure so that the diameter given in Table 5.2, about 4 times that of the Earth, is not so accurate as those given for the nearer planets. The derived density of 1.70 is considerably greater than those of Jupiter and Saturn and about 10 times greater than that of a purely hydrogen planet having the same mass. To account for this high density and for the concentration of mass towards the centre implied by the observed oblateness and by the motion of the satellites, we must assume that Uranus contains a considerable core of rocky material surrounded by a very extensive atmosphere of hydrogen and helium. Since Uranus is sufficiently massive to retain a hydrogen atmosphere it is something of a mystery that it should contain less hydrogen in proportion than do Jupiter and Saturn.

The high albedo suggests a deep atmosphere, and the spectrum shows the absorption bands of methane in great strength, the depth of the equivalent layer at normal atmospheric pressure and temperature being about 3.5 km. The quadrupole lines of molecular hydrogen indicate that the hydrogen atmosphere is optically semi-infinite, that is, that the lines are as strong as they can get when the penetration of the visible and near infrared radiation into the atmosphere is limited only by Rayleigh scattering. At the very low prevailing temperature, thought to be about 60°K, all the ammonia and water vapour will be completely frozen out and will have settled to the bottom. We might expect, therefore, that few clouds will be visible. This expectation has been partially confirmed by some remarkable high-resolution photographs of Uranus taken with the 36-inch balloon-borne Stratoscope II telescope of the Princeton University Observatory. These show a well defined, slightly flattened disk with distinct limb darkening but with no indication of any pattern of belts or bands.

Neptune

Neptune appears to be a twin of Uranus but, being further away, is more difficult to observe. Of magnitude 7.8, it is too faint to be seen with the naked eye, but it can be glimpsed with field glasses and in a powerful telescope shows a small greenish disk little more than 2 arc seconds in diameter. It follows an almost circular orbit round the Sun with a period of 165 years and a radius of 30 astronomical units, which is considerably smaller than the 38.8 astronomical units predicted by Bode's law. The mass can be found both from the planet's effect on the orbit of Uranus and from the motion of its own satellites. The diameter cannot be found so easily or with such certainty because of the smallness and intrinsic faintness of the disk. Measures can be made with the ordinary filar micrometer or with a special instrument called a disk meter. This provides within the field of the telescope an artificial planetary disk that can be made to match exactly, in brightness, size and shape, the disk of the planet as seen through the main instrument. A completely different method of measuring the diameter is available from time to time when Neptune, in the course of its orbital motion, occults, that is, passes in front of, a star. Such an occultation took place in 1968 and was carefully observed from Japan, Australia, and New Zealand. The diameter of Neptune was deduced from the length of time that the star was occulted at each observing point and the known rate of the planet's motion. The mean density resulting from the adopted value of the diameter is 2.26, which is significantly greater than that found for Uranus; while the albedo, the estimated value of which also depends on the adopted diameter, is 0.84, slightly less than that of Uranus.

Neptune shows no definite surface markings from which its rotation can be directly observed, but spectroscopic observations indicate a direct rotation with a period of approximately 16 hours, twice that of the observed light fluctuations. The oblateness indicated by the difference between the polar and equatorial diameters given in Table 5.2 is not directly observed but is deduced partly from the rate of rotation of the planet and partly from the rate of precession of the orbit of its larger satellite, Triton. This is a large satellite comparable with Titan and the Galilean Moons of Jupiter. Its circular orbit, however, is not in the equatorial plane of Neptune but is inclined to it at an angle of approximately 20°. What is perhaps more surprising is that Triton goes round this orbit in a *retrograde* direction with a period of approximately 6 days. The mass of Triton has been determined by Alden from precise photographic observations of the orbital motion of Neptune and Triton about their common centre of gravity, a very difficult series of observations to make and measure because the displacement of Neptune is so small. Nereid, Neptune's other known satellite, is very much further away from Neptune and takes just over a year to complete its orbit. From its brightness it appears comparable with the smaller satellites of Saturn, but its chief interest is the highly eccentric orbit, which is, however, direct and not retrograde like that of Triton.

The spectrum of Neptune shows the absorption bands of methane in very great strength, so strong that they almost blot out all the red light and so give the planet its characteristic greenish hue. The equivalent layer of methane, at normal terrestrial atmospheric temperature and pressure required to produce such an intensity, is not less than 40 km thick.

Pluto

This, the most remote of the planets, is named after the God of the Infernal Regions that dwelt in an obscure and gloomy place. The name is a happy choice in that its first two letters are the initials of Percival Lowell who initiated the long search that led to its discovery in 1930, and they have been combined to form the planet's conventional symbol ♇. The choice was perhaps not so appropriate if it was meant to indicate that Pluto dwelt in the outer cold and darkness. Even at aphelion Pluto receives from the Sun over 200 times the light we receive from the full moon, while at perihelion it receives nearly four times as much again; all this in spite of the fact that the size of the Sun as seen from Pluto approximates to that of Venus as seen from the Earth.

Pluto, which varies in visual magnitude between 13.6 at perihelion and 15.8 at aphelion, can only be observed with a fairly large telescope and the disk is so small that it can scarcely be distinguished from a faint star. It orbits the Sun once in 248 years in a highly eccentric orbit which is inclined at 17° to the ecliptic. Its distance from the Sun varies between 30 and 50 astronomical units so that for some years before and after perihelion, which next occurs in 1989, Pluto is nearer to the Sun than is Neptune. The large mutual inclination of their orbits ensures that there is no danger of a collision between the two planets. Pluto's mean distance from the Sun is 39.5 astronomical units, which is close to the 38.8 astronomical units predicted by Bode's law for the distance to Neptune.

From the time of its discovery onwards Pluto has been a puzzling object, which is perhaps not surprising when one considers its faintness, the difficulty of collecting relevant data and the fact that it has only traversed a small section of its orbit since the first pre-discovery observation in 1914. The mass can be found from the observed perturbations in the orbits of Uranus and Neptune but these are not yet definitively determined. Nicholson and Mayall in November 1930 and, later, Wylie in 1942 considered this problem and came to the conclusion from the observations then available that the mass of Pluto was similar to that of the Earth. Assuming that the density was also similar, the apparent diameter should be 0.4 arc seconds, which is nearly twice the value observed both at Meudon and at Mount Palomar where in 1950 Kuiper used his disk meter on the 200-inch telescope. Accepting these observed values for the mass and diameter would imply a mean density for Pluto of about 8 times that of the Earth or 40 times that of water, which did not seem at all credible since the planet is far too small to have developed a very high density core of degenerate matter. Many ingenious explanations designed to avoid this conclusion of a very high density were put forward. It was suggested, for example, that the surface of the planet was smooth enough to reflect light specularly in the same way as does a polished steel ball bearing. In this case the observed diameter would pertain to the solar image rather than to the planet as a whole. Öpik suggested in 1950 that Pluto was covered by an ocean of nitrogen and oxygen with enough dissolved impurities to enable the gases to remain in liquid form at the estimated temperature of 50°K, and, using the optical properties of liquid oxygen, deduced that the diameter of the planet was 20,000 km and that its mean density was about that of water. The resulting albedo, however, appeared to be impossibly small.

Such special explanations are no longer necessary since more reliable observational data have become available. An upper limit to the diameter of Pluto was determined in April 1965 when a possible occultation of a 15th magnitude star by Pluto was observed from a number of observatories in North America. Unfortunately no occultation took place at any of the observatories concerned, but it was possible to deduce that the nearest approach between the light centres of star and planet was 0.125 arc seconds. Accepted at its face value this implies a maximum diameter for Pluto of 5800 km, or, if we allow for the maximum effect of likely errors concerned in this observation, 6800 km. There has also been a new and more reliable determination of the mass by astronomers at the U.S. Naval Observatory who are engaged on a re-examination of the orbits of Uranus, Neptune and Pluto, using all observations up to 1968. Preliminary results indicate a mass for Pluto of only 0.11 that of the Earth, which taken with the diameter limits indicated above imply a mean density of 0.88 that of the Earth. Thus Pluto seems to be about the same size as Mars, with a similar albedo and density. Its period of rotation as deduced from fluctuations in its light is 6.39 days. Partly because this period is so much longer than those of Jupiter, Saturn, Uranus and Neptune, and partly because of its very eccentric orbit, it has been suggested that Pluto originated as a satellite of Neptune. But this would make it by a factor of seven or more the most massive satellite in the solar system. Another suggestion is that Pluto is but the first of another belt of small planets outside Neptune's orbit analogous to the belt of asteroids between the orbits of Mars and Jupiter. It is possible that in the future further faint and more distant planets will be discovered, but, considering all the difficulties of observation, it does not seem likely that the effort involved in their discovery will throw as much new light on all the many unsolved problems of the solar system as would the same effort devoted to the observation of the nearer and brighter members of the system.

Chapter Six

The debris of the solar system

R. H. Stoy

This chapter deals with the innumerable small bodies of the solar system which, like the planets, move in orbits round the Sun and are dominated by its gravitational attraction. Though insignificant in size, these bodies produce some of the most spectacular and awe inspiring of the celestial phenomena. The largest of these bodies, the minor planets, are the least conspicuous; only one of them is ever faintly visible to the naked eye, yet their break up probably provides the raw material for the meteorites. A really large meteorite could easily cause havoc comparable to that of the most powerful hydrogen bomb. Fortunately such large meteorites are very rare. The smaller ones were until recently the only source of extraterrestrial matter available to the chemist, and even now are cheaper and more abundant than lunar material. The comets tend to be smaller than the minor planets and are more conspicuous. They possibly come from the outermost part of the solar system. Their decay is the source of innumerable meteors while some of the material they bring from the outer regions may drift down to us virtually unaltered along with other micrometeorites. The small fragments from the break up of the minor planets and comets gradually drift towards the Sun and we see the sunlight reflected from them as the zodiacal light and the gegenschein.

The minor planets

Discovery Kepler pointed out the large gap between the orbits of Mars and Jupiter and speculated on the possibility of there being another planet between them. This hypothesis was never completely forgotten and it was rendered increasingly plausible first by the publication in 1772 of Bode's law and then by the discovery nine years later of Uranus whose orbit was found to conform exactly with that law. In Germany von Zach formed his 'celestial police', each member of which undertook to search systematically part of the zodiacal band for the missing planet. They were, however, forestalled by an Italian astronomer, Piazzi, who was engaged on compiling a catalogue of stars at the Palermo Observatory in Sicily. On the evening of 1 January 1801, that is on the first evening of the nineteenth century, Piazzi examined a region in Taurus and noted amongst others a seventh magnitude star. Re-examining the field the following evening he was surprised to see that this star had moved; from then on he watched its motion from night to night for six weeks until he was forced to give up observing because of serious illness. Like Herschel when he discovered Uranus, Piazzi thought at first that he was watching a comet though he could see no coma. Piazzi informed other astronomers of his find but the means of communication were then so slow that the object had passed out of the evening sky and was hidden by the glare of the Sun before its existence could be verified. It might not have been found again for several years, even by the celestial police, had it not been for a young German mathematician, Gauss, who on this occasion devised his method of deriving the elements of an elliptical orbit from three observations only. He found that Ceres, as the object was named after the titular goddess of Sicily, had a mean distance from the Sun of 2.767 astronomical units as compared with the 2.8 predicted by Bode's law.

Ceres was relocated by the German astronomers at the end of 1801 and in 1802 one of them, Olbers, discovered a second object, subsequently called Pallas, in Virgo quite close to where Ceres had been. Its orbit, too, was derived by Gauss who found that Pallas had nearly the same mean distance from the Sun as had Ceres. This, and the unexpectedly small sizes of these two new objects as compared with the older planets, gave Olbers the idea that Ceres and Pallas were only two fragments of a planet that had exploded. In this case there should be other fragments waiting to be found and, whatever the eccentricities and inclinations of their orbits might be, they should, if the fragments all had a common origin, have the same mean distance from the Sun and pass through two points on opposite sides of the sky. Olbers therefore suggested that attention should be concentrated on the two regions of the sky, the one in Virgo the other in Cetus, where the orbits of Ceres and Pallas intersect. It was close to the expected spot in Cetus that the third minor planet, Juno, was found by Harding, one of the celestial police, in 1804, while Olbers himself found Vesta, the fourth and brightest, while searching the Virgo area in 1807. No more minor planets, or asteroids as they were called by Sir William Herschel on account of their star-like appearance, were discovered until 1845, partly because of the difficulty of searching for new objects without having adequate star charts and partly because the searchers did not realize how much fainter the other minor planets were than the first four discovered. In that year Hencke found a tenth magnitude object now called Astraea. Hencke was an amateur astronomer who had spent fifteen years examining the fainter stars in the hopes of making just such a discovery. Three more were found in 1847 and from that time on they have been discovered at an ever increasing rate. Over three hundred had been located visually before photographic methods of searching were introduced by Max Wolf of Heidelberg in 1891.

Minor planets are now normally observed photographically with fast astrographs which cover a fairly wide field. Exposures of the order of one hour are given and, provided the astrograph has been driven at the normal sidereal speed, the stars give point-like images while any sufficiently bright minor planets that may be in the field show up as short trails, the length of the trail indicating the extent of orbital motion during the time of exposure. Fainter objects can be recorded by driving the astrograph at the expected rate of motion of the minor planets in the region of the zodiac under observation. In this case the star images are trailed while the images of the minor planets are very much shorter trails or even round dots. A single plate will usually contain several minor planet trails, some belonging to objects which are already known and some to objects which are not yet identified. As all minor planets look alike on a photographic plate except as regards brightness, the only certain identification is from the orbit being pursued. On account of the perturbations by Jupiter and the other planets, the orbits of the minor planets are not simple ellipses but ellipses which are being constantly modified. Precise orbits have been calculated for relatively few, approximate orbits for nearly two thousand. The observed positions of the minor planets on a plate have first to be compared with the ephemerides of these known orbits before those which refer to new objects can be identified.

When a new minor planet is first located it is given a provisional designation consisting of the year followed by two letters, the first letter of which denotes the half month in which it was found. Thus 1930 EB is the second minor planet discovered in the first half of March 1930. This system allows for an average rate of discovery of two per day. Many objects receive provisional designations each year but to qualify for a numbered place on the recognized list of minor planets the object must have been observed during two oppositions and the elements of its orbit must represent its observed places satisfactorily. When these conditions have been met and it is certain that the object is new, the director of the International Minor Planet Centre assigns to it a serial number and the discoverer has the right of naming it. The names of the first minor planets were taken from mythology and were mainly female but as mythological sources became exhausted the names of states, cities, colleges, etc. were used and there is now a tendency to name them after famous astronomers. It is customary to refer to a minor planet by its number followed by its name, e.g. (1691) Oort. The International Minor Planet Centre, which was formerly at the Recheninstitut in Berlin, is now at the Cincinnati Observatory in the United States of America. Another important centre for work on minor planets is the Institute for Theoretical Astronomy of the Academy of Sciences of the U.S.S.R. which each year publishes a complete list of the known minor planets with their magnitudes, elements of their orbits and short ephemerides giving their positions near the time of opposition. It also indicates which minor planets are most in need of observation. The number of fully identified minor planets included in the list for 1972 is 1779, but of these Nos 864 and 1078 are identical. The tremendous amount of computation involved in keeping tabs on so many minor planets has only been made practicable by the use of modern high speed electronic computers. Even so, the number of identified minor planets is but a small fraction of the 40,000 odd that Baade estimated could be photographed with the 100-inch telescope.

Orbits All the minor planets that have been observed so far move round the Sun in direct elliptical orbits which tend to be more eccentric than those of the major planets and to be inclined at greater angles to the ecliptic. With very few exceptions the orbits lie completely between those of Mars and Jupiter, i.e. between 1.5 and 5.2 astronomical units from the Sun. Most of the orbits are confined within considerably narrower limits than these. Of the 1778 orbits in the 1972 list, 96 per cent have semimajor axes (i.e. mean distances from the Sun) between 2.1 and 3.1 astronomical units, eccentricities between 0.0 and 0.25, and inclinations between 0° and 25°. The distribution of the orbits is not completely random. As early as 1866, when orbits for only about 100 minor planets were known, Kirkwood noticed that when the orbits were arranged in order of period there were marked gaps at those periods which were simple fractions of Jupiter's, those near 1/2, 3/7, 2/5, and 1/3 being the most conspicuous. The effect can be seen quite clearly in Figure 6.1, which shows the distribution of the numbered minor planets according to their mean daily motion about the Sun, i.e. according to the reciprocals of their periods. As more and more orbits

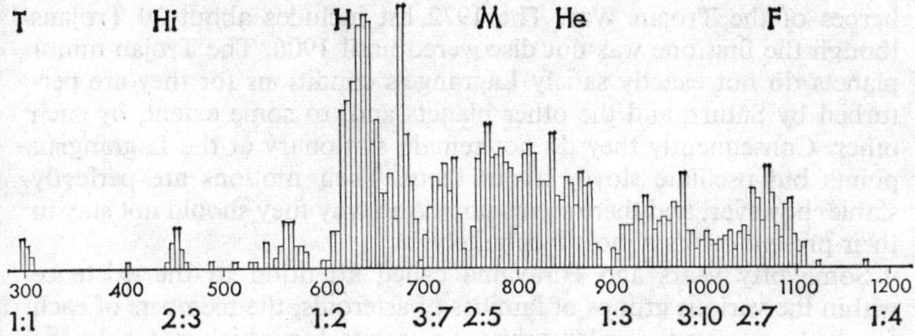

Figure 6.1 Distribution of minor planets according to period

The actual plot is number of minor planets against the mean daily motion in seconds of arc; the corresponding ratio of Jupiter's motion is indicated below, while the letters above locate the more conspicuous groups, viz. the Trojan group (T), Hilda group (Hi), Hecuba group (H), Minerva group (M), Hestia group (He), and Flora group (F). After Yusuke Hagihara.

have become available these Kirkwood gaps have remained conspicuous and something of a puzzle. Although they are obviously connected with the gravitational influence of Jupiter and are in some ways analogous to the gaps in Saturn's rings, a simplified mathematical argument originally due to Bessel and Newcomb indicates that there should be orbit groupings at the places where the gaps are observed, and this actually appears to be the case for the ratios 2/3 and 1/1.

As Figure 6.1 suggests, the minor planets can be divided into a number of groups according to their periods or, what is equivalent, their distances from the Sun. Some of the more conspicuous of these groups have received names,

Over one quarter of the known minor planets belong to the Hecuba group, and large numbers to both the Minerva and the Hestia groups. The smallest, but dynamically perhaps the most interesting, is the Trojan group which contains those minor planets having the same period as Jupiter itself. In 1772 Lagrange showed that a large body (the Sun), a smaller body (Jupiter) and a very small body of negligible mass (a minor planet) will, if situated at the vertices of an equilateral triangle, remain in that relative position while revolving about the centre of gravity of the system. There are two Lagrangian points, the one leading, the other following Jupiter by 60°. A number of minor planets have been found near each and have been named after the heroes of the Trojan War. The 1972 list includes about 30 Trojans though the first one was not discovered until 1906. The Trojan minor planets do not exactly satisfy Lagrange's conditions for they are perturbed by Saturn and the other planets and, to some extent, by each other. Consequently they do not remain stationary at the Lagrangian points but oscillate slowly about them. Their motions are perfectly stable, however, and there seems no reason why they should not stay in their present orbits almost indefinitely.

Some fifty years ago Hirayama called attention to the existence within the various groups of families of asteroids, the members of each family having very similar orbits, i.e. orbits for which not only the periods but also the eccentricities and inclinations cluster round certain specific values. Hirayama himself identified 9 such families but later work by Brouwer and more recently by Arnold have identified 37 families to which 712, or 42 per cent, of the 1697 orbits he examined, belonged. The three largest families, those for which the first members are (43) Ariadne, (24) Themis, and (221) Eos, have 73, 67 and 66 members assigned to them. In the case of the Themis family, the semimajor axes are all between 3.09 and 3.20 astronomical units, the eccentricities between 0.12 and 0.19, and the inclinations between $0^{\circ}.7$ and $2^{\circ}.5$, while the Eos family have orbits which are only slightly smaller than these, but which are noticeably more eccentric and have greater inclinations. It has been suggested that Hirayama's families result from collisions between fairly massive bodies; the larger visible fragments ejected with comparatively low relative velocities will continue to have similar orbital elements. It is perhaps significant that the intrinsically fainter minor planets show a greater tendency to family associations than do the brighter ones.

Such collisions could have taken place at any time during the history of the solar system. The perihelia and the longitudes of the nodes of the resulting orbits would have precessed at slightly different rates so that in the course of time, possibly of the order of 10^5 years, they would have become completely distributed at random. On the other hand, certain first order invariants based on these two parameters would not have changed so quickly and it should be possible to recognize a grouping in them throughout a period of the order of 10^8 years. Recently Alfvén and Arnold have examined the orbital elements of the numbered asteroids to seek out those for which not only the semimajor axes, eccentricities and inclinations are similar, but also the longitudes of the perihelia and the nodes, or rather two functions of these latter quantities. Alfvén found three such series of minor planets which he termed 'jet streams'. Arnold found nine. The largest and best established to which he attributed 32 members is associated with the Flora group. It must be stated that neither Alfvén nor Arnold are completely satisfied that these jet streams result from relatively recent collisions, but they have not yet been able to formulate a satisfactory alternative explanation.

A number of individual minor planets deserve special mention on account of their exceptional orbits. Amongst these are those on the inner and outer fringes of the normal asteroid belt and those which approach exceptionally close to the Earth. The outermost asteroid yet known is (944) Hidalgo discovered in 1920. Its orbit, with a semimajor axis of 5.82 astronomical units and an eccentricity of 0.656, stretches almost from Mars to Saturn, but there are no close approaches of Hidalgo to these planets because of the large inclination (42°.5) of its orbit. The innermost asteroid known is (1566) Icarus discovered in 1949. The semimajor axis of its orbit is only 1.08 astronomical units but, on account of the extremely high eccentricity of 0.83, Icarus passes inside the orbit of Mercury and outside that of Mars. At its opposition in 1968 Icarus came within six megametres of the Earth and, though even then a faint object, was intensively observed.

The most famous of the minor planets that come close to the Earth is (433) Eros which was discovered in 1898 and which was intensively observed during its near approaches to the Earth in 1901 and 1931 for the determination of the solar parallax. Its mean distance from the Sun is 1.458 astronomical units but the eccentricity of its orbit, 0.223, is sufficiently large for Eros to be well within the minor planet belt at aphelion and within 22 megametres of the Earth's orbit at perihelion. Close approaches to the Earth occur in pairs, 7 years apart, at intervals of 37 or 44 years. The last pair of close approaches was in 1931 and 1938; the next will be in 1975 and 1982, but they are not likely to attract very much attention since the solar parallax is now well known from other methods of observation.

The three minor planets known to have approached the Earth most closely are Apollo, Adonis and Hermes. Apollo was found in 1932 when it was passing within 3 megametres of the Earth; Adonis in 1936 when within 1.6 megametres, and Hermes in 1937 when within 0.6 megametres. These three minor planets were observed at one opposition only and so do not qualify for numbering. Their periods are less than three years but the only hope of finding them again is their chance rediscovery when they are once more passing close to the Earth.

Physical properties The only minor planets for which the diameters have been directly measured are (1) Ceres, (2) Pallas, (3) Juno, and (4)

Vesta though even for these the visible disks are too small for the filar micrometer measures to be thoroughly reliable. Taking the measures at their face value, they imply diameters of 770 km for Ceres, 490 km for Pallas, 200 km for Juno and 420 km for Vesta, the uncertainty in these diameters being of the order of 50 km. The corresponding albedos are 0.06 for Ceres, 0.07 for Pallas, 0.12 for Juno and 0.22 for Vesta, that is, Ceres and Pallas reflect about the same proportion of incident light as does the Moon. The albedo of Vesta seems to be high for a planet without an atmosphere, but the micrometric measures of its diameter have been essentially confirmed by interferometric measures made in Paris and by recent measures made at Meudon with a double image micrometer.

The mass of Ceres has been deduced from its gravitational effect on Pallas, which has very nearly the same period. Observations made between 1803 and 1968 were analysed and the resulting mass for Ceres was 6.7×10^{-10} that of the Sun, or 2.2×10^{-4} that of the Earth. In the same way, but with rather less certainty, the mass of Vesta was deduced from its effect on (197) Arete. The value found was 1.2×10^{-10} that of the Sun or 4×10^{-5} that of the Earth. These masses imply that Ceres has very much the same mean density as the Earth, while that of Vesta is 10 per cent higher but considerably lower than that of iron.

Considerable information about the nature of the minor planets can be obtained from photometric observations of their light made in several colours, though the scope of all such studies is greatly restricted by the faintness of the light available. The variation of the polarization and reflectivity with colour for individual objects will in time, as more data are accumulated, give a clue to the nature of their surfaces. Most of the minor planets that have been sufficiently observed have light curves that vary regularly with time and which indicate that the bodies are rotating with periods ranging between about 2 and 12 hours. The way in which the shape of the light curve varies with the relative position of the minor planet and the Earth allows the direction about which the minor planet is spinning to be determined. If the amplitude of the light curve is relatively small and different for different colours, it is probable that the basic cause of the light variation is due to areas with different reflectivities on the surface of the planet; if, on the other hand, the amplitude of the light curve is the same in all colours, relatively large and with two nearly equal minima per period, the basic cause of variation is probably the irregular shape of the minor planet. Examples of both types of light curve are common, the first type being the more frequent for the bigger minor planets, the second type for the smaller ones. Of these latter (433) Eros is the one that has been most intensively observed, over one hundred light curves of it having been determined since 1901. An analysis of these light curves suggests that Eros is like a huge rough brick rotating about an axis nearly perpendicular to its greatest dimension in a period of 5¼ hours. During the close approach of 1931, van den Bos and Finsen, two very experienced double star observers, were able with the big refractor at Johannesburg to measure its size and to watch it rotate in the same direction as the planets. From the observed size, the length of the 'rough brick' must be about 22 km and its cross-section about 6 km. Minor variations in the light curve from period to period indicate that the surface of Eros is not smooth but very irregular.

As we cannot measure the individual dimensions of every minor planet the only practical way to compare one with another is through their brightness when seen under standard conditions. The apparent brightness of any minor planet varies inversely both as the square of its distance from the Earth and as the square of its distance from the Sun. It also depends on the phase angle, that is on the angle between the lines joining the minor planet to the Sun and to the Earth, for like the surface of the Moon, the minor planets look brighter when directly illuminated than when illuminated from the side. The standard conditions chosen for comparing the minor planets with one another are distances of one astronomical unit from both the Sun and the Earth and with the phase angle zero. The apparent magnitude under such hypothetical conditions is known as the 'absolute magnitude' of the minor planet and is usually denoted by 'g'. (It is not to be confused with the 'absolute magnitude' of a star or other self-luminous body for which the standard distance is ten parsecs.) The apparent magnitude, m, will then be given by

$$m = g + 5 \,.\, \log r \,.\, \rho + F(\alpha)$$

where r denotes the distance from the Sun, ρ the distance from the Earth and $F(\alpha)$ a function of the phase angle. Except for the very few minor planets that come close to the Earth, the maximum brightness occurs when the minor planet is in opposition, that is when $r = a$, the semimajor axis of the orbit, and $\rho = (a-1)$. For the great majority of the minor planets for which a lies between 2.1 and 3.1 astronomical units, the opposition magnitude, m_0, will usually be between one and two magnitudes fainter than the absolute magnitude. In the case of the Trojan group for which a is close to 5.1 astronomical units, m_0 is over three magnitudes fainter than g.

Table 6.1 shows the distribution with absolute photographic magnitude of the 1778 minor planets for which particulars are given in the

1972 list. The distribution for minor planets Nos. 1–990 is given separately from that for Nos. 991–1779 to demonstrate how complete the present data appear to be for the brighter objects. Inspection of the table suggests that nearly all the minor planets with photographic absolute magnitudes brighter than 11.0 have already been found; for fainter absolute magnitudes the data are obviously incomplete.

TABLE 6.1 DISTRIBUTION OF MINOR PLANETS WITH ABSOLUTE MAGNITUDE

Absolute magnitude	*Number* 1–990	991–1779	*Total*
< 5.9	3	0	3
6.5	6	0	6
7.5	19	0	19
8.5	82	0	82
9.5	175	8	183
10.5	283	44	327
11.5	219	186	405
12.5	115	251	366
13.5	72	184	256
14.5	12	96	108
15.5	0	14	14
16.5	3	4	7
> 17.0	0	2	2

The five minor planets with the brightest photographic absolute magnitudes are (1) Ceres 4.1; (4) Vesta 4.3; (2) Pallas 5.2; (15) Eunomia 6.3; and (3) Juno 6.4. The absolute magnitudes of (433) Eros and (1566) Icarus are 12.4 and 17.7, while those of Apollo, Hermes and Adonis are 18.0, 19.0, and 21.0.

To extend the statistics for minor planets to fainter objects a special survey was recently made by astronomers from Leiden, Cincinnati, and Tucson using plates taken with the 48-inch Schmidt telescope at Mount Palomar. The plates were exposed during three successive months on a part of the zodiac near the vernal equinox where the density of the star background is a minimum and the chance of picking up faint minor planets a maximum. Over 2000 faint minor planets were discovered and provisional orbits derived for 1800 of them. The distribution of these fainter minor planets is very similar to that of the brighter ones. The same Kirkwood gaps appear and some 42 per cent of the total are members of recognized groups and families. Although new members of the Trojan group were found there was no trace of any faint minor planet beyond the orbit of Jupiter. (944) Hidalgo remains unique.

Combining the results from the surveys of faint minor planets with the data given in Table 6.1 makes it apparent that the number of minor planets with given absolute magnitude increases steadily up to about magnitude 11, remains nearly constant for about a magnitude, and then increases steadily until the observational limit is reached. The distribution curve might be described as being Gaussian for the brighter members and grading into logarithmic for the fainter ones. It has been suggested that the first part represents the distribution of the original condensations and the second that of fragments resulting from subsequent collisions. There is no indication that the observable minor planets do not grade off into smaller and smaller fragments, the fragments getting ever more numerous as they decrease in size.

From this distribution curve and the known masses of Ceres and Vesta it is possible to estimate that the total mass of the minor planets is of the order of 2×10^{-9} solar masses, that is 1/1600 that of the Earth or about 1/20 that of the Moon. Most of this mass is concentrated in the five largest minor planets.

Comets

Unlike the minor planets, comets have been known since antiquity. A bright comet must always have been a magnificent and compelling spectacle, especially in the days before artificial street lighting had hidden the night sky. Although major comets are relatively rare several appear during the average lifetime. They come unheralded, are conspicuous for a short while, and then fade away into the obscurity from which they came. With this mixture of temporary grandeur and mystery it is not surprising that our ancestors regarded comets with awe, as signs of divine wrath and as warnings of evil to come.

> When beggars die, there are no comets seen;
> The heavens themselves blaze forth the death of princes

wrote Shakespeare, and some seventy years later Defoe in his *Journal of the Plague Year* wrote of the comet of December 1664 as being faint, dull, languid in colour, and in its motion very heavy, solemn and slow so that it foretold 'a heavy judgement, slow but severe, terrible and frightful, as was the Plague'. This same comet caused the commander at the then recently established settlement at the Cape of Good Hope to introduce strict regulations for keeping the Sabbath so as 'to ward off the punishment that hangs over our heads, of which we are warned by the long-rayed star . . . a terrible sign of vengeance which threatens us nightly from the heavens'. Perhaps the most interesting thing for the astronomer about this comet of 1664 is the suggestion made by Borelli in 1665 that it was travelling in a parabolic orbit. Many years before Tycho Brahe had shown that the comet of 1577 was more distant than the Moon and in his geocentric scheme had allotted it a circular orbit outside that of Venus. Kepler considered that comets moved through space along straight lines. It was in 1705 that Halley published his treatise on comets and showed that they moved round the Sun in accordance with Newton's recently propounded theory of Universal Gravitation. He calculated the orbits of 24 bright comets that had been sufficiently observed in the past and noticed that three of them, those of 1531, 1607, and 1682, were very similar. This led him to believe that they were really the same comet and that this comet would return to the neighbourhood of the Sun and Earth in 1758. It did. This comet, now named for Halley, is the most famous of all, and all its regular returns but one since 240 BC have been noted in historic records. Its last appearance was in 1910 and the next one is due in 1986, when the perihelion passage should be early in February.

Not all comets are brilliant objects like Halley's. Most of them, in fact, are never seen except as a faint fuzzy patch on a long-exposed photographic plate somewhat similar to Comet Candy 1961 II as it appears in plate 17*a*. Whether the fuzzy patch, or coma as it should more properly be termed, grows into a bright comet depends partly on its previous history and partly on how closely it approaches the Sun. If it does, the normal sequence is for the coma to become rapidly brighter and to increase in size until about two astronomical units from the Sun. At this stage some mechanism depending on solar radiation begins to change the physical state of the coma and to drive part of it backwards away from the Sun to form a tail or tails. Approaching perihelion, the tail increases in size and brightness, sometimes attaining a length that can be measured in millions of kilometres. The comet is usually at its brightest soon after passing perihelion and thereafter fades as it recedes, the tail shrinking in size and the general sequence of events being the reverse of those observed during the approach. The coma, or head as it is called when there is a tail present, remains the brightest part of the comet throughout. Quite often, especially when close to the Sun, there can be seen immersed in it an almost stellar nucleus. In several of the brighter, more active comets bright jets have been observed issuing from the sunward side of this nucleus and, under some strong repulsive action from the Sun, being bent round to form a series of hollow shells as the material in the jets is brushed back to form the head of the tail that is streaming far back into space. Plate 17*b* shows a photograph of Comet Bennett 1969 i taken by H. J. Hendrie and R. L. Waterfield on 4 April 1970 which illustrates the general appearance of a fully developed comet. It will be noticed that there are two distinct tails, a narrow Type I gas tail and a broader Type II dust tail, and that these tails are approximately at right angles to the direction of motion of the comet which is indicated by the star trails.

It is not possible to identify an individual comet by its appearance since this changes so much with its distance from the Sun; the only characteristic by which one can tell one comet from another is by its orbit and even this is likely to be drastically changed if it makes a near approach to one of the planets, especially to Jupiter.

Discovery of comets About 600 different comets have been observed since 239 BC, of which about 100 have, like Comet Halley, appeared on more than one occasion. It is not possible to base any worth-while statistics on these figures since the discovery of faint comets is largely a matter of chance and the number of these discovered has naturally risen with the increasing use and power of photographic instruments. Fresh comets are continually being sighted, usually in one of three main ways: by pure chance; by dedicated amateur astronomers systematically sweeping the sky for new comets; and by professional astronomers searching a limited portion of the sky for the expected reappearance of a comet whose orbit is already approximately known. Discoveries made by pure chance include those that are first found as small faint patches on astronomical photographs taken for other purposes, and also those which, by reason of their orbits, have approached the Sun undetected and then suddenly become visible when so bright that they cannot be missed even by the most inattentive 'man-in-the-street', or, in these days, by the navigators of high flying aircraft. Such comets usually appear in the western sky just after sunset, or in the eastern sky just before sunrise. It is therefore these areas that most comet seekers sweep with their wide-field, relatively low-power telescopes, even though comets may appear in any part of the sky. On average, the systematic amateur comet seeker seems to sight one new comet for every two hundred hours of sweeping, a rate of success that makes it clear that this form of observing is suitable only for those who possess much enthusiasm and great perseverance.

New comet sightings are provisionally designated by the name of the discoverer and by the year followed by a letter indicating its order of discovery in that year, e.g. Comet Bennett 1969 i was the ninth comet sighting made in 1969, the discoverer being J. C. Bennett, a well-known

South African amateur astronomer who was at the time engaged on a systematic search for comets. Later, when the orbits of all recent comets have been derived, a more permanent designation is given. This depends on the order in which the comets come to perihelion and is in the form of the year followed by a Roman numeral. Thus Comet Bennett 1969 i is now more properly referred to as Comet Bennett 1970 II. If the comet is known to be periodic, its name is preceded by P/. It often happens that a bright comet is discovered independently by several different people. If some order of priority can be established, the comet may bear the names of the first three, e.g. Comet White-Ortiz-Bolelli 1970 f. This was a bright comet discovered independently by G. L. White, an Australian college student; by E. Ortiz, a member of the crew of Air Madagascar Flight 281 from St Denis de la Réunion to Tananarive; and by C. Bolelli, a night assistant at Cerro Tololo Inter-american Observatory. If there are more than three people with equal claims to priority, no name is given to the comet, but it may well be referred to as, for example, the Great Comet of 1882. During 1969, which was fairly typical, five new comets were found and four periodic comets recovered. All four of the periodic comets were picked up by professional astronomers who were looking for them. Of the five new ones, three were discovered by amateurs engaged on systematic comet sweeping and two by accident. The first of these was found on spectral plates taken with the 80-cm Schmidt Telescope of the Hamburg Observatory; the second on plates taken at the Alma-Ata Observatory during the search for the expected return of a periodic comet. During October 1969 there were seven comets in the sky bright enough to be easily observed with a small telescope, four of them being short period comets. 1970 was well above average for cometary astronomy, the number of new sightings being 17, plus another one which was given a preliminary designation but which was not confirmed. Of the 17, 6 were new and 11 recoveries of periodic comets. With the inclusion of comets still observable from previous years, the number of comets under observation was 27. In addition, Comet Bennett 1970 II turned out to be the most spectacular comet since 1910 and Comet White-Ortiz-Bolelli 1970 VI was also a bright naked-eye comet.

As M. P. Candy, himself a successful comet seeker, has pointed out, every telescope user is a potential comet discoverer and should be aware of what to do should he be lucky enough to find one. The first thing is to check that the suspected object is really a comet, the crucial test being that it shows motion relatively to the nearby stars. As this test requires time, two other tests may be made during the waiting period, the first to ensure that what is seen is not the flare from a bright object just outside the field of the telescope; the second to verify from a star atlas that the object is not a known nebula or star cluster. It was for this purpose that Messier compiled his famous list of nebulosities nearly two hundred years ago. When it has been established that the object is almost certainly a comet, the nearest observatory or astronomical society should be contacted without delay so that they can cable the information—the time of discovery, position, direction of motion, and approximate magnitude—to the International Astronomical Union's Central Bureau for Astronomical Telegrams. This used to be housed at the Copenhagen Observatory but is now at the Smithsonian Astrophysical Observatory in Cambridge, Massachusetts 02138, U.S.A. The Bureau will then circulate all interested parties by telegram or announcement card.

The orbits of long-period comets A vast amount of data concerning comets has been accumulated, much of it consistent with the hypothesis that they have their origin in a reservoir of appropriate material on the confines of the solar system. Some of this material has accreted into lumps with dimensions of the order of a few kilometres and masses in the range 10^{13}–10^{18} kilogrammes. These lumps, the nuclei of potential comets, consist of a conglomerate of various icy materials such as water, ammonia, methane, carbon dioxide, cyanogen, etc. in which are mixed dust and particles of meteoric matter in a wide range of sizes. Like the material from which they accreted, the lumps move in very long-period orbits about the Sun, relatively few of which have their perihelion distance less than 50 astronomical units. Every now and again, however, some of these orbits are perturbed, either by mutual action or by the action of passing stars, so that the lumps travelling in them will pass sufficiently close to the Sun to become visible to us as comets.

Comets are usually divided into two classes according to their orbital period, those with periods less than 200 years being known as short period, the remainder as long-period comets. For these latter the orbits are very nearly parabolic and it is therefore usual for the preliminary orbit of a new comet to be calculated on this assumption. In many cases it is only after a comet has been well observed over a period of some months that it becomes possible to establish that it is travelling in a very elongated ellipse and not a parabola. After due allowance has been made for the perturbing effect of the planets it is found that all the orbits in which well observed comets have approached the inner portion of the solar system are either definitely elliptical or sensibly parabolic; no case has yet been found of such an orbit being hyperbolic. That is, there is no known case of a comet coming from outside the solar system.

Definitive elliptical orbits have been calculated for about 120 long period comets. The periods of these range from 250 to 30,000,000 years, with over half of them being longer than 6000 years. If it be assumed that elliptical orbits would also have been found for the parabolic comets if these had been sufficiently well observed, the best guess for the average period of the long period comets is of the order of 10^6 years, corresponding to an aphelion distance of about 20,000 astronomical units. Because of Kepler's second law the comets spend the greater part of their time in the aphelion section of their orbits, that is at great distances from the Sun.

The orbits of the long-period comets are inclined at all angles to the ecliptic and about equal numbers of them are direct and retrograde. Their arrangement may not be completely random, however, for a detailed examination of the distribution on the celestial sphere of the perihelion points of 448 orbits indicates a very slight preference for the galactic plane and a rather more marked one for the direction in which the Sun is moving relatively to the nearby stars. The perihelion points also show a distinct tendency to cluster into small compact groups and for some of these groups the orbital elements of the corresponding comets are closely similar. The best known of these is the 'Sungrazing Group' originally studied by Kreutz and containing the Great Comet of 1668, 1843 I, 1880 I, 1882 II, 1887 I, 1945 VII, 1963 V, 1965 VIII, 1970 VI and possibly one or two others. These comets all have very small perihelion distances and have actually passed through the Sun's corona, some of them within 500,000 km of the solar surface. They have all been very bright and when near perihelion have been visible during daylight within a few degrees of the Sun. The orbital periods found for 1843 I, 1882 II, 1963 V, and 1965 VIII were 512, 761, 1111 and 929 years respectively, so it is clear that these comets, though travelling in similar orbits, are not the same. It seems certain, however, that they are portions of a single comet that has been disrupted. A detailed examination of this group was made in 1967 by Marsden who came to the conclusion that there are two distinct sub-groups resulting from a split in the original parent comet some ten or twenty revolutions ago. Tracing back the orbits of Comets 1882 II and 1965 VIII he found that they had almost certainly separated from each other at their previous perihelion passage when together they may have been the Great Comet of AD 1106 The nucleus of Comet 1882 II was itself observed to split into four parts which separated at such a rate that they can be expected to return as four separate comets about a century apart. It is perhaps surprising that the comets of this group have not disintegrated entirely during their perihelion passage during which they complete with a velocity of over

400 km s^{-1} some 250° of their orbit in about six hours. The tidal strain during such an encounter must be very large, and though the nuclei do seem to shed some fragments during the perihelion passage, they seem to have sufficient cohesion to survive not only one but a whole succession of perihelion passages.

Stefanik has made a study of thirteen comets that have split into components that have themselves persisted as comets. For only three of these—Comet 1889 V (P/Brooks 2) passing very close to Jupiter, Comets 1882 II and 1965 VIII grazing the Sun—does the split appear to be the result of strong tidal action. In the other ten cases, mostly 'new' parabolic comets, the split appears to have happened almost at random at solar distances up to 4.9 astronomical units. In none of the cases was the process at all violent and the velocities of separation averaged only 15 m s^{-1}. As this velocity must exceed the velocity of escape from a comet nucleus, Stefanik was able by assuming unit density for the nuclear material to deduce a maximum mass of 3×10^{16} kgm and an approximate radius of 20 km.

The orbit of a comet can be very seriously perturbed by a single close approach to one of the planets; the same effect can result from a series of less drastic encounters. As a comet passes a planet its velocity will be either decreased or increased according to the circumstances. In the first case the comet's orbit will become less eccentric and its period shortened; in the second case the orbit will become more eccentric and if originally nearly parabolic may quite possibly become hyperbolic, and the comet will be lost to the solar system unless it should suffer a second compensatory encounter before it gets away. The process is irreversible so that there must be a steady loss of comets, the rate of loss being greatest for those that return most frequently to the central neighbourhood of the solar system. Thus we can expect to find that the inner portion of the vast reservoir from which planetary material appears to come has been gradually emptied and that what remains is at a great distance from the Sun.

Although encounters with the planets can result in some comet orbits becoming hyperbolic, they can also result in some of the near parabolic orbits being gradually transformed into elliptical orbits for which the periodic times are relatively short, thus giving rise evenually to the short-period comets.

The orbits of the short-period comets About one-sixth of the known comets have orbital periods less than 200 years and over two thirds of these have periods less than 9 years. These latter form a distinct family dominated by Jupiter. The inclinations of their orbits are relatively small and their motions are all direct; their aphelia are not far from Jupiter's orbit and one of their nodes, that is one of the two points at which their orbits intersect the plane of the ecliptic, is closer still. There seems little doubt that these comets have been captured by Jupiter as a result of a selection effect, since the capture process will be most efficient for comets that are moving in direct orbits lying close to the plane of the ecliptic. As has been pointed out, a parabolic comet passing near Jupiter can be retarded sufficiently for its orbit to become elliptical. From time to time the comet will return to the point where the disturbance took place. If at one of these returns it again encounters Jupiter and suffers a further retardation, the orbit will become smaller still—and so on until the aphelion of the comet falls at such a distance within the orbit of Jupiter that the planet is no longer able to disturb it seriously. The end result will be such as is actually observed, a series of comets with their aphelia near the orbit of Jupiter and with periods about half of his, a typical orbit having an eccentricity of 0.5 and an aphelion distance of 5 astronomical units. Comet 1889 V (P/Brooks 2) provides an example of what a drastic change a single encounter with Jupiter can produce. Before the encounter its periodic time was 29 years; afterwards it was 7.

It is to be noted that comets moving in orbits like that of Halley's, which is retrograde and inclined at an appreciable angle to the ecliptic, are now relatively free from serious planetary perturbations. Such orbits are consequently comparatively stable.

Comet Encke, whose period of 3.30 years is the shortest known, was discovered in 1786. Its motion was studied in the early 1820s by Encke who was surprised to find that it could not be entirely explained by the assumption that the comet was moving freely in empty space under the gravitational action of the Sun and planets. The orbit was getting progressively smaller, just as it would if it were encountering some resistance to its motion. The effect of such a retarding resistance, if it were to continue indefinitely, would be to cause the comet to spiral gradually into the Sun, its orbit growing more circular as it got smaller. Some two dozen orbits later, the motion of Encke's comet was again carefully examined by Backlund who found that the resisting force had decreased, apparently almost abruptly several times, and seemed to occur only in a relatively narrow region not far from perihelion. The motion was once more examined by Marsden who in 1968 made a study of the orbits of 18 short-period comets that had been carefully observed at three or more perihelion passages since 1925. Of these 18, 15 showed definite effects of non-gravitational forces, 7 of them, including Comet Encke, showing secular acceleration and 8 secular retardations. The nature of these non-gravitational forces has not yet been definitely established, but it is not unlikely that the explanation will be that first suggested by Bessel in 1836, viz. that they are reactive forces arising from the expulsion of matter by the nucleus. Opinion is divided as to whether matter is expelled impulsively, particularly near perihelion, or continuously by the gradual sublimation of surface ices, the direction of rotation of the nucleus determining if the net effect is to accelerate or to retard the orbital motion. Marsden has pointed out that the size of the non-gravitational effect appears to be related to the physical appearance of the comet; the comets showing no effect are almost asteroidal in appearance, while the comet showing the greatest effect (P/Honda-Mrkos-Pajdusakova) is extremely diffuse.

The physical structure of comets At a great distance from the Sun, the nucleus and any particles that may be accompanying it on its journey through space shine only feebly by reflected sunlight. Nearer the Sun, as the surface grows gradually warmer, the icy materials begin to sublime, first methane, then carbon dioxide and ammonia, and later cyanogen and water. The vapour and dust thus released diffuse away into the vacuum of space with a velocity of the order of 0.5 km s^{-1} for most of the gaseous molecules, about three times this for hydrogen molecules and very much less for dust. The nucleus consequently becomes surrounded by an expanding, almost spherical coma, densest at the centre and thinning out towards the edges. It shines partly by sunlight reflected from the dust and partly by fluorescence of the gases, or rather of the radicals into which their molecules split. Spectroscopic observations show that the reflected sunlight is most intense towards the centre, while the gaseous emissions come from all parts of the coma. Those bands that can be observed in the normal optical regions are all parts of resonance systems in the spectra of CN, CH, OH, NH, C_2, C_3, and NH_2. Their relative intensities change with distance from the Sun and from comet to comet. Observations of Comet Tago-Sato-Kosaka 1969 g and of Comet Bennett 1969 i made from orbiting satellites show that Lyman alpha, the resonance line of atomic hydrogen at 1216 Å, is very strong and that the visible coma is immersed in a much larger hydrogen one. The red auroral line of oxygen has also been identified as present in coma spectra. Within about half an astronomical unit of the Sun, the coma or head of some comets have shown the yellow emission lines of sodium, while comets of the Kreutz group which have approached even more closely than this, have shown emission lines of iron and nickel. Observations made in 1970 of the infrared spectrum of the coma of Comet Bennett 1969 i showed a clear cut emission peak at 10 microns, similar to that observed in the spectrum of the Orion Nebula which Woolf suggested was due to silicate dust.

For dust particles smaller than about one-third of a micron the repulsion due to solar radiation pressure exceeds the attraction due to solar gravity, while for still smaller particles the relative effect of the radiation pressure is even greater. Consequently as the coma approaches the Sun, the fine dust in it is increasingly repelled from the Sun and forms a tail. As the dust particles are subject only to radial forces from the Sun their angular momentum about it remains constant and they continue to obey the law of equal areas. Consequently the tails formed by dust are curved since the further the dust particles are from the head, the more they will tend to lag behind it. Such dust, or Type II, tails are usually fairly smooth and homogeneous in appearance and their spectrum is mainly that of reflected sunlight. Type I, or ionic, tails, on the other hand, shine by light which is predominantly emitted by CO^+ with some contributions from N_2^+, CO_2^+, CH^+, and OH^+. They are usually long and straight, normally point directly away from the Sun, and seem to be composed of rays which have their origin in the sunward side of the nucleus but which gradually bend round into the tail. Quite often such tails show much fine structure and contain rapidly moving knots and kinks. Type I tails appear to be formed from gaseous radicals in the coma that have become ionized and so able to interact with the solar wind which is very much more powerful in its effects than is normal radiation pressure. The violent changes sometimes observed in comet tails can be attributed to corresponding changes in the solar wind.

A number of comets have shown anomalous tails which for a time appear to be directed towards the Sun. A recent example is Comet Arend-Roland 1957 III. Plate 18 is a reproduction of a photograph taken with a Schmidt telescope at the Armagh Observatory on 25 April 1957, soon after the comet had passed perihelion and when the Earth was passing through the plane of its orbit. The explanation of this phenomenon is probably that shown in Figure 6.2. The spike was really the thin sheet of the Type II dust tail seen edgeways on. After a few days this tail, as seen from the Earth, became wider, fanned out and disappeared.

Dimensions and masses For the many comets that have been observed visually the diameter of the coma has usually been between 50,000 and 250,000 km, though for some the diameter has been as large as 2,000,000 km and for a very few as small as 15,000 km. In interpreting these figures it must be remembered that the comae are continually expanding and that they are brightest at the centre and gradually fade towards the edge so that their diameters are somewhat indefinite and depend to

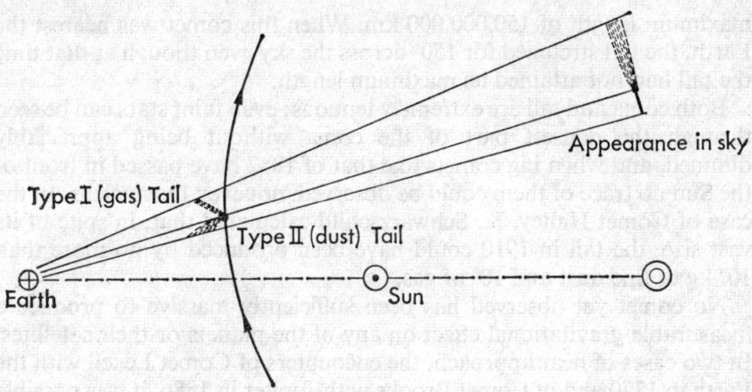

Figure 6.2 Possible explanation of the sunward-pointing spike of Comet Arend-Roland

some extent on the way in which they are observed. Thus, for example, the size as measured in the Lyman alpha emission of hydrogen is likely greatly to exceed that measured in ordinary visible light.

The size of the coma might be expected to be a maximum at the time of perihelion, but visually this is not generally the case. The coma of a comet approaching the Sun is observed to expand and to reach a maximum when the comet is still about $1\frac{1}{2}$ astronomical units from the Sun. From there to perihelion the coma appears to contract; after perihelion it appears to expand again and reaches a second maximum at about the same distance from the Sun as the first. Thereafter it appears continually to contract as the comet recedes from the Sun. This phenomenon is particularly conspicuous in the case of Comet Encke. For Comet Halley the diameter of the coma at perihelion in 1910 as seen visually was about 200,000 km as compared with 350,000 km when the comet was $1\frac{1}{2}$ astronomical units from the Sun and 50,000 km when it was at a distance of just over 4 astronomical units. As Sir John Herschel surmised over a hundred years ago, this apparent change in size is due rather to a change in the physical state of the coma material than to its actual contraction.

The tails of the comets when fully developed are enormous. One visible to the naked eye is seldom less than 10,000,000 km long, while some attain a length of 150,000,000 km or more. The maximum length recorded is 300,000,000 km, or nearly twice the distance of the Earth from the Sun, for the tail of the Great Comet of 1843. In 1910 the tail of Comet Halley was 50,000,000 km long at perihelion and later reached a maximum length of 150,000,000 km. When this comet was nearest the Earth, the tail stretched for 150° across the sky even though at that time the tail had not attained its maximum length.

Both coma and tail are extremely tenuous; even faint stars can be seen through the densest part of the coma without being appreciably dimmed, and when big comets like that of 1882 have passed in front of the Sun no trace of them could be observed, not even the nucleus. In the case of Comet Halley, K. Schwarzschild calculated that, in spite of its vast size, the tail in 1910 could have been produced by no more than 10^9 kg of fine dust and 10^5 of gas.

No comet yet observed has been sufficiently massive to produce a measurable gravitational effect on any of the planets or their satellites. In two cases of near approach, the encounters of Comet Lexell with the Earth in 1770 and of Comet Brooks with Jupiter in 1886, it was possible to assign an upper limit to the mass of the comet. In both cases this limit was of the order of 10^{-4} the mass of the Earth, though the actual masses of the comets were probably very much less.

The fine dust and gaseous material that form the tails and part of the coma dissipate into space and are lost to the main body of the comet which can be expected to become smaller and less conspicuous at each return. The process of dissolution need not be very rapid, however, for Halley's comet has been a most conspicuous object at each of its 29 last apparitions and there is no evidence of its getting any fainter during its last four returns. Actually if the original mass of a comet's nucleus were only 10^{13} kg, i.e. less than 10^{-11} that of the Earth, it could grow 100 tails as big as those of Halley's comet and yet lose only 1 per cent of its mass in the process. Nevertheless, comets do appear to disintegrate and to become less conspicuous as they grow older. 'New' comets travelling in near parabolic orbits produce spectacular tails if they approach close enough to the Sun, while the comets of Jupiter's family at the same solar distance are faint, inconspicuous objects. One such comet, P/Biela, actually seems rather suddenly to have stopped shining. It was observed as a normal faint comet with a $6\frac{3}{4}$ year period in 1772, 1806, 1826 and 1832, but in 1846 it was observed to divide into two. The two separate parts each developed a tail about one half of a degree in length and were seen again in 1852 as twin comets separated by about 2,500,000 km. Neither has ever been seen again, although they must have returned to perihelion many times since then, more than once under favourable conditions for being detected.

The variation in brightness of a comet from apparition to apparition would be simpler to detect if it were possible to assign to a comet an absolute magnitude similar to that assigned to a minor planet, viz. its

Plate 17 Two typical comets. *a* Comet Candy 1961 II as photographed by E. Roemer on 13 January 1961 with the 40-inch reflector of the U.S. Naval Observatory, Flagstaff, Arizona. This gives a good impression of the usual appearance of a faint comet. Official U.S. Navy photograph
b, below, Comet Bennett 1970 II photographed at Woolston by H. J. Hendrie and R. L. Waterfield on 4 April 1970. This was one of the brightest comets of the century

Plate 18 Comet Arend-Roland 1957 III photographed by E. Lindsay on 25 April 1957 with the 30 cm Schmidt camera of the Armagh Observatory, Northern Ireland

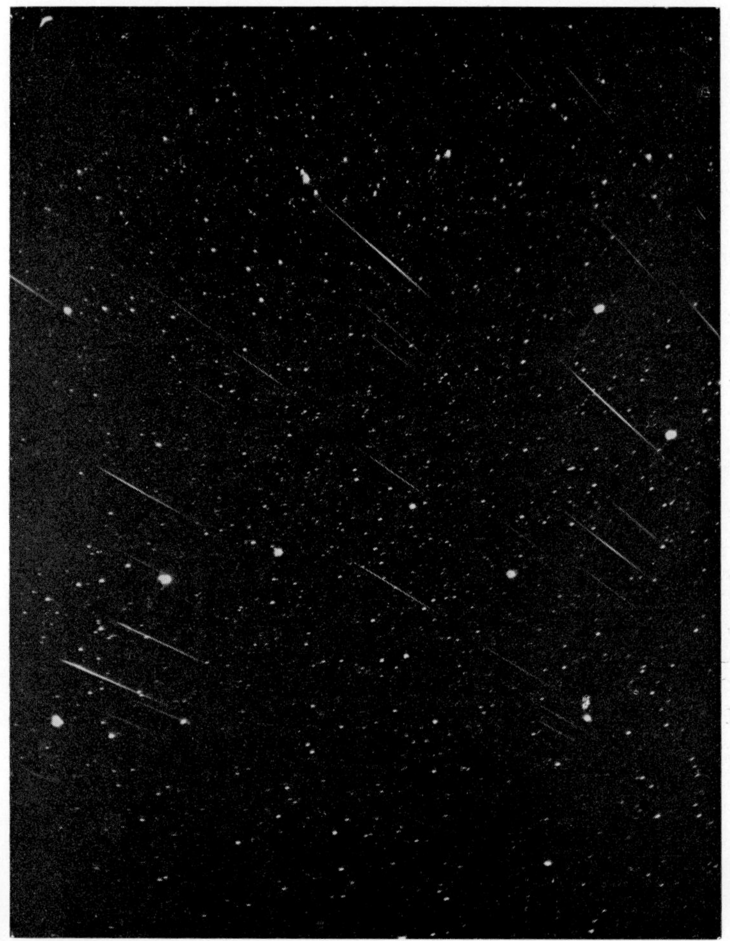

Plate 19 The Great Leonid Meteor Shower of 17 November 1966 as recorded at Kitt Peak, Arizona by D. McLean. The area of the sky photographed is sufficiently large to show the seven stars of the Plough and how the meteor trails appear to diverge from the radiant

Plate 20 The zodiacal light photographed by D. E. Blackwell and M. F. Ingham from Mount Chacaltaya, Bolivia

apparent brightness when at one astronomical unit from both the Sun and the Earth. This is not possible, for although a comet's apparent brightness varies inversely as the square of its distance from the Earth, its intrinsic brightness, which is only partly due to reflected sunlight, varies capriciously with its distance from the Sun. This variation sometimes approximates to r^{-n}, where n varies from 3 to 6 and averages about 4. Adopting such a law it is possible to make a rough comparison of the relative sizes of the comets by comparing their brightness when they are at the same distance from the Sun. The range in size appears to be very large and it turns out that the biggest comet yet observed was that of 1729 which was faintly visible to the naked eye although its perihelion distance was just over four astronomical units. At the same distance the Great Comet of 1882, one of the largest of the really brilliant comets, would have appeared only one-twentieth as bright.

However big its initial nucleus may be, a comet cannot last indefinitely as a comet. Approaching the Sun in a near parabolic orbit, it runs the risk of a close encounter with a planet resulting either in the comet's ejection from the solar system or in its being perturbed into a smaller, less eccentric orbit; it also runs the risk of its nucleus dividing and forming two smaller comets, each of which face the same alternative prospects of ultimate ejection from the solar system or of repeated returns to the Sun. In this latter case, the tail-producing material is gradually exhausted, but the non-volatile particles that are released as the icy materials sublime continue to move through space in orbits very similar to that of the comet's nucleus. Thus, until its ultimate demise, the comet is accompanied by a swarm of particles which, owing to the small relative velocities with which they left the nucleus, will gradually become spread out all round the orbit. Thereafter these particles, together with the remnant of the nucleus, will continue to circulate around the Sun, though prolonged exposure to the perturbing effect of the planets may result in their orbits growing smaller and more circular.

Meteors

Nearly everyone who has been out on a clear dark night will have noticed from time to time a meteor or 'shooting star' streaking across the sky. Meteors are not a rare phenomenon and a careful watcher will normally see from five to ten per hour and, on some occasions, considerably more. They look like stars that have suddenly started to move rapidly across the sky but which fade out within a second or two, before they have got very far. The greater number are relatively inconspicuous but every now and again there is one of the first magnitude, or brighter, which may leave a luminous 'train' behind it which remains visible for a few seconds. Very occasionally there appears one so bright that it lights up the whole sky and is noted by everybody who happens to be out of doors at that time. Such a brilliant meteor is called a fireball or bolide and it may appear to travel right across the sky and leave behind a train that may remain visible for several minutes. Another rare meteor phenomenon which compels general attention is the occurrence of a meteor shower or 'storm' during which meteors can be seen at the rate of many thousands per hour. Several such showers have been noted over the past 2000 years, the earlier ones being briefly, but graphically, mentioned in the ancient records of China, Korea and Japan. Plate 19 is a reproduction of a photograph taken at Kitt Peak in Arizona by D. McLean during the Great Leonid Meteor Shower of 1966. When this shower reached its peak at about 12.00 U.T. on 17 November, meteors were being observed at a rate of about 150,000 per hour. The seven stars of the Plough or Big Dipper will be easily recognized in the plate and it will be noticed how the meteors seem to diverge from a 'radiant point' which lies to the south west in the constellation of Leo. It will also be noticed how much more numerous are the fainter meteors than the brighter ones and how, in general, each trail starts faint, brightens to a maximum, and then fades somewhat abruptly away. There are a number of trails, however, which appear to blaze up suddenly just before their end as though the particle causing the meteor exploded or broke up at that point.

Meteors are caused by relatively small particles, now usually referred to as 'meteoroids', entering the atmosphere at high speed. The air in front of them gets highly compressed and consequently heated. The meteor becomes luminous at a height of about 110 km by which time the meteoroid itself has become very hot. Atoms, molecules and small fragments boil off from its surface and interact with the surrounding atmosphere. A glowing envelope forms round the meteoroid and a long trail of positive ions, electrons and excited atoms is left behind. This process goes on until the meteoroid has been completely consumed, or, in the case of some of the larger ones, until it hits the ground. The surviving fragment in this latter case is known as a 'meteorite'. Very small particles entering the atmosphere do not have sufficient kinetic energy to become completely vaporized before they are slowed down by the atmospheric resistance; thereafter they float gently down to the Earth's surface where they are classed as 'micrometeorites'.

The first step in interpreting the observed phenomena is to consider theoretically what happens when a small spherical body enters the atmosphere at high speed. It is found that the way in which the brightness of the resulting meteor varies along its path is independent of the physical properties of the particle. Maximum light, which occurs when about $\frac{2}{3}$ of the original mass has been consumed, depends on the initial kinetic energy ($\frac{1}{2}mv^2$) of the particle and on the cosine of the angle its motions makes with the zenith. As regards numerical results, a mass of 1 g entering the atmosphere at an angle of 45° to the zenith and at a speed of 30 km s^{-1} produces a meteor which, when viewed from a distance of 100 km, will have an approximate maximum visual brightness of zero magnitude; further this meteor will be visible for about 1.6 seconds over a height range of 35 km. Meteors of similar brightness, but not of similar duration, would be produced by a mass of 2 g travelling at 21 km s^{-1} or of $\frac{1}{2}$ g travelling at 42 km s^{-1}. A different form of light curve is found if it is assumed that the particle breaks into a number of pieces when it encounters the denser layers of the atmosphere, for at the moment of fragmentation the effective atmospheric resistance per unit mass suddenly increases and produces a greatly increased rate of retardation. That is, fragmentation within the atmosphere reduces the duration and path length but increases the brightness.

When observed light curves of meteors are compared with those derived theoretically, it is found that many of those for the brighter meteors agree essentially with the single body curves, while those for the fainter meteors agree better with the curves for the fragmenting model. From this latter fact it can be deduced that the meteoroids that produce the fainter meteors crumble fairly easily, even under pressures as small as 1/50 of normal atmospheric pressure. They can be little more than lightly compressed balls of dust.

As viewed from any given place, the path of a meteor on the celestial sphere is a great circle. Viewed from a second place, the apparent path is also a great circle appreciably different from the first provided that the distance of the meteor is not too large compared with the distance between the two points of observation. The point of intersection of the two great circles is called the 'radiant point' of the meteor, and it marks on the celestial sphere the direction from which the meteoroid has come. Simultaneous observations from two places several kilometres apart can thus determine the direction of motion of a meteoroid, its approximate height and distance at any instant, and thus also its velocity. The first such observations were made visually in 1798 by two Göttingen students and, though not very accurate, served to establish the general nature of meteors. Photographic observations are more reliable than visual ones and are usually made with special cameras of high effective speed; they have rotating sectors mounted in front of them so that any meteor trail that is recorded is chopped into a number of segments from which it is possible to deduce the duration and speed of the meteor. The rate of acquisition of data by such cameras is necessarily slow since even the specially designed Super-Schmidt meteor cameras cannot record meteors fainter than the fourth magnitude. Thus recordable meteors within the area of sky covered by a camera are relatively scarce except during a shower. Photographic observations have now been almost completely superseded by very much more powerful radar techniques which use signals reflected from the train of electrons and ionized particles produced by a meteor. Such techniques can now provide the position and velocity of 10th magnitude meteors with considerable precision and can detect ones of the 15th magnitude, that is meteors over 10,000 times fainter than those that can be seen with the naked eye or recorded photographically. Moreover, radar observations can be made equally well during the day time and in cloudy periods.

The orbit in which a meteoroid was moving before it encountered the Earth can be deduced from the observed direction and speed of the meteor it produces. Many thousand such orbits have now been calculated, the limiting magnitudes of the meteors concerned being + 4 for the photographic observations and + 12 for the radar. The arrangement of these orbits is not completely random. Most—one estimate makes it over 99 per cent—of the meteoroids with masses greater than 10 mg were travelling in direct elliptical orbits round the Sun. Not one was found to be definitely hyperbolic, i.e. there is absolutely no indication of any meteoroid having originated outside the solar system. For the brighter meteors, the orbits tend to have periods of about 5 years, eccentricities of 0.9 and inclinations up to about 30° on either side of the ecliptic, i.e. to resemble those of short-period comets. For the fainter meteors, the orbits are smaller and less elliptical, the most frequent period being about 3 years, though amongst the faintest there is a sizable group for which the orbits have a period of about 1 year, an eccentricity of 0.3 and an inclination of 60°. This has become known as the 'toroidal group' since if the orbits are visualized as being set in all positions round the orbit of the Earth they will be reminiscent of the basket weave or toroidal tuning coils that were used on some of the earlier radio sets.

The resemblance of the orbits of the brighter meteoroids to those of the shorter period comets suggests that most meteoroids had their origin in the gradual dissolution of such comets. This suggestion is rendered even more plausible by a study of the observed orbits which shows that there are streams of meteoroids moving along the tracks of certain comets. The meteors they produce occur in showers near the time when the Earth is close to one or other of the points in which the orbit of the corresponding comet crosses the ecliptic. Usually some meteors belonging to the stream are seen each year near the appropriate date as though in the course of time the comet debris, or meteoroids, have become thinly, but not necessarily uniformly, spread all round the orbit and its immediate neighbourhood. Some years, when the Earth and the central part of the swarm happen to reach the intersection of their orbits at the same time, a brilliant meteor shower or storm may result.

One of the best known of such meteor streams is the Leonids which follows the same orbit as Comet P/Tempel-Tuttle (now lost) which had a period of just over 33 years. Some Leonids are seen in most years, but really spectacular storms occurred in 1799, 1833, 1866 and 1966. Other recorded storms of this stream took place in 934, 1237 and 1533. A similar shower confidently expected in 1899 did not take place because the swarm responsible passed close to Jupiter in 1899 and was deflected away from the Earth. Describing the 1799 storm von Humboldt says he saw 'thousands of meteors and fireballs moving regularly from north to south with no parts of the sky so large as twice the Moon's diameter not filled each instant by meteors'. The relatively short duration, usually less than one hour, of the peak intensity of these great storms indicates that the nucleus of the Leonid swarm is still quite compact even though it must have circled the Sun over thirty times. This compactness means that the maximum of such major storms can be seen from only one side of the Earth.

Another stream that is known to have produced a number of meteor storms is associated with Comet P/Biela which has not been seen since 1852 but which had a period of $6\frac{3}{4}$ years. Small showers of Bielids, or Andromedids as they are more usually called, after the constellation in which their radiant lies, were observed in 1798 and 1892 and strong storms in 1872 and 1885. Perturbations by Jupiter appear to have diverted the main part of the stream away from the Earth. Notable meteor storms that occurred in 1933 and 1946 were due to a swarm associated with Comet P/Giacobini-Zinner and now known as the Draconids. There are a number of streams that provide a regular but not spectacular display of meteors each year. Some of these are listed in Table 6.2. The penultimate column gives the approximate geocentric velocities which all lie, as they should, between the velocity limits defined by the parabolic velocity at the distance of the Earth $\pm$ the Earth's orbital velocity, i.e. between (42 ± 30) km s^{-1}, or between 72 and 12 km s^{-1}. The Beta Taurids shower takes place during the day-time and was discovered by radar.

TABLE 6.2 REGULAR METEOR STREAMS

Name of stream	*Date of maximum*	*Hourly visual rate*	*Date limits of appearance*	*Radiant* R.A.	*Radiant* Dec.	*Velocity* km s^{-1}	*Comet*
Quadrantids	Jan 3	45	Jan 1–Jan 4	$15^h.3$	+48°	40	
Lyrids	Apr 21	5	Apr 19–Apr 24	18.0	+33	48	1861 I
Eta Aquarids	May 4	20	Apr 21–May 12	22.4	00	64	Halley
Beta Taurids	Jun 30	20	Jun 24–Jul 6	5.7	+19	31	Encke
Delta Aquarids	Jul 29	15	Jul 21–Aug 15	22.6	−17	40	
Perseids	Aug 12	50	Jul 25–Aug 17	3.1	+58	60	1862 III
Orionids	Oct 22	20	Oct 18–Oct 26	6.3	+16	66	Halley
Andromedids	Nov 14	2	Nov 3–Nov 22	1.5	+27	16	Biela
Leonids	Nov 17	5	Nov 14–Nov 20	10.1	+22	72	Temple
Geminids	Dec 14	60	Dec 7–Dec 15	7.5	+32	35	
Ursids	Dec 22	5	Dec 17–Dec 24	13.7	+80	37	Tuttle

The regular streams account for only a small proportion of the meteors seen in the course of a year. Most of the others, usually referred to as 'sporadic' or 'non-shower' meteors, presumably had a similar origin but the comets with which they were associated have long since ceased to be visible as such, and the matter formerly concentrated in them dispersed but still subject to the effects of solar radiation. Particles smaller than 0.3 microns, not already consumed in tail making will be repelled from the Sun by radiation pressure. The remainder will be subject to the Poynting-Robertson effect which acts selectively according to size. The particles absorb solar radiation and re-emit its equivalent equally in all directions. Due to a relativity effect, however, the reaction pressure exerted by the emitted radiation is greatest in the direction opposite to that in which the particle is travelling. Consequently the angular momentum of a particle travelling round the Sun is gradually reduced, i.e. its orbit will become smaller and more circular. The particle will therefore gradually spiral in towards the Sun until it gets so close that vaporization sets in and reduces its size to such an extent that radiation pressure can repel the remnants away from the Sun. The size of the Poynting-Robertson effect can be gauged from the fact that it will cause a spherical body of radius a cm and density ρ g cm^{-3} to spiral into the Sun in 7.a.ρ.R^2 million years, where R is the initial distance of the body from the Sun expressed in astronomical units. Thus a ball of rock of radius 1 cm initially travelling in an orbit similar to that of the Earth will spiral into the Sun in only 20,000,000 years. It follows that the central part of the solar system should by now have been swept completely clear of all small particles if it were not for these being continually fed in by the disintegration of the comets and the grinding up of the minor planets. The Poynting-Robertson effect may be the cause of the orbits of the fainter meteors being more circular and having shorter periods than those of the brighter ones, since this effect will be relatively greater on the smaller meteoroids than on the larger.

Although the average number of sporadic meteors remains fairly constant from year to year, the hourly rate fluctuates both diurnally and annually. The diurnal variation is approximately sinusoidal with a maximum at 6.00 a.m. local time when the observer is facing the direction of motion of the Earth about the Sun, and a minimum at 6.00 p.m. when the observer is on the sheltered side of the Earth. Meteor activity is at a minimum during February, March, and April, and at a maximum during June, July, and August. Table 6.3 gives the average hourly rate for the whole year of the meteors that a visual observer might be expected to see under ideal conditions, it being assumed that he normally watches some 5000 square kilometres of the upper atmosphere at a time. The rate given in the second column refers to all meteors as bright as or brighter than the magnitude shown in the first column, while that given in the third column refers to meteors within a single magnitude range of brightness. The ratio of successive values of this latter rate is given in the last column.

TABLE 6.3 HOURLY RATE OF SPORADIC METEORS

Visual magnitude	*Rate per hour*		*Ratio*
$\leqslant 0$	0.025		
1	0.145		
		0.705	
2	0.85		3.4
		2.40	
3	3.25		3.2
		7.75	
4	11.0		3.2
		25.0	
5	36.0		

Since these hourly rates hold all over the world, the daily total of meteors brighter than magnitude 5.0 that enter the atmosphere is of the order of 90,000,000. Taking the average mass of the meteoroids concerned as 0.1 g, the total mass of meteoric matter gained by the Earth daily from these brighter meteors is 9,000 kgm. This is negligible by planetary standards, for if it had continued uniformly since the beginning of the Earth some 4×10^9 years ago, the total mass gained would still be less than one hundred-millionth that of the Earth.

The law of increase in the number of meteors with decreasing brightness implied by Table 6.3, viz. that the number of meteors of magnitude $m + 1$ is approximately 3.2 times the number of magnitude m, appears to hold true for meteors fainter than magnitude 5 at least as far as the faintest ones that have been sufficiently well observed (about + 12). Since the ratio of the masses of the meteoroids producing meteors differing in brightness by one magnitude is the ratio of the corresponding brightnesses, i.e. approximately 2.5, it follows that the total mass of the meteoroids producing meteors of magnitude $m + 1$ will be 3.2/2.5 or 1.3 times that of those producing meteors of magnitude m. Mathematically speaking, this would imply an infinite mass of faint meteoric matter if the same law of increase continued to hold indefinitely for fainter and fainter meteors. This is definitely not the case, however, if for no other reason than that the very fine dust required to produce the extremely faint meteors has been expelled from the neighbourhood of the Earth by solar radiation pressure.

The law of increase in the number of meteors with decreasing brightness implied by Table 6.3 does not hold true for the meteors brighter than magnitude zero. The brighter meteors and fireballs are more numerous than this law would imply. The mass distribution of the bodies causing them appear to follow the same law as that for the meteorites, viz. that the number with mass $\geqslant$ m is proportional to 1/m, which incidentally is also the case for the fainter minor planets.

The difficulty of photographing a meteor trail has been mentioned; the difficulty of photographing the spectrum of a meteor is necessarily much greater. Nevertheless, the spectra of a number of bright meteors have been recorded, mainly during meteor showers when it is possible to point the apparatus, e.g. a camera fitted with an objective prism, in the direction of the radiant where the meteors observed will be seen nearly head-on and thus appear to be moving across the sky more slowly. The spectra show many bright emissions and reveal the presence of iron, calcium, manganese, magnesium, chromium, silicon, nickel, aluminium and sodium.

Meteorites

A body big enough and robust enough for some part of it to survive its fiery passage through the atmosphere produces a fireball that is sufficiently brilliant to attract attention, even in the day time. The train it leaves behind may persist for as long as an hour and is particularly noticeable if the fall happens in the twilight and the Sun brightly illuminates the train when the rest of the sky is dark. The fireball is often followed by a rumbling noise like thunder caused by the shock waves resulting from its passage through the lower atmosphere. The velocity with which a small meteorite hits the ground is not very large and there is usually little difficulty about recovering it once it has been located. About 1500 meteorites of mass 10 kg or more land on the Earth each year of which only about ½ per cent are recovered. Where it has been possible to derive an orbit for the fireball producing a meteorite, it has been found to be direct and to resemble those of the minor planets such as Icarus, Adonis, Apollo, and Hermes, whose orbits come close to that of the Earth. This suggests that meteorites had their origin in the break-up of one or more of the larger minor planets, and all the information we have about them and their composition seems to be consistent with this suggestion. It is noteworthy that no meteorite has been observed to fall in the course of even the most spectacular meteor shower, as might be expected if any of the meteorites had their origin in the comets.

Meteorites enter the atmosphere with a velocity in the range of 15 to 20 km s^{-1} and, unless their mass exceeds 1000 kg, their initial velocity is damped out by the resistance of the atmosphere before the meteorite has reached a height of 20 km; thereafter it falls freely under gravity and reaches the ground with a terminal velocity of about 0.1 km s^{-1}. If the initial mass exceeds 1,000,000 kg, the atmosphere has little power to slow it up at all and the meteorite hits the ground with catastrophic results. Fortunately such massive meteorites are very infrequent, but various craters scattered round the world indicate that they have fallen in the past. Perhaps the most famous of these, but not the biggest, is Meteor Crater near Winslow in Arizona. This has a diameter of 1.2 km and a depth of 175 m, though it was probably deeper than this when it was gouged out some tens of thousands of years ago. No big meteorite has been located in this crater but many thousands of meteoric iron fragments have been collected from the surrounding countryside. Two major falls have occurred so far this century, both of them in Siberia. The first, in 1908, felled several square kilometres of forest and produced a number of craters. The second fell on the snow-covered Sikhote Alin mountain range some 400 km north of Vladivostok at 10.38 a.m. local time on 12 February 1947. It seems to have entered the Earth's atmosphere as a single 70,000 kg mass of iron, but fragmented high up and showered the ground over an elliptical area of about two square kilometres with meteorites of various shapes and sizes. Some of the bigger pieces broke up on striking the rocky ground, but smaller pieces remained intact and many which landed on the soft snow were scarcely damaged by the fall. About 200 craters were formed with diameters ranging up to 30 m and depths down to 7 m. As the sky was completely clear at the time the arrival of this meteorite was witnessed by many hundreds of people. Although it was broad daylight, the bolide was so bright that it cast shadows and appeared blinding to those who looked directly at it. It was a scintillating ball of fire with a luminous tail and as it travelled across the sky it emitted sparks and left behind a grey band of dust which remained visible for several hours. Loud noises, resembling explosions or heavy gun-fire, were heard several minutes after it had disappeared from sight. Airplanes that followed the dust trail quickly located the place where the meteorites had landed. The freshly created yellowish-brown craters stood out in stark contrast to the surrounding snow. This fall has been thoroughly investigated by

Russian scientists who have recovered over 23,000 kg of meteoric matter. Included in this are innumerable very fine particles collected with the help of magnets. Some of these were produced when the bigger fragments broke up, but many are tiny balls with diameters between 10 and 100 μm and appear to owe their origin to the congealing of molten matter blown off from the intensely heated surfaces of the larger meteoric fragments during their journey through the atmosphere. It was such minute solidified droplets that formed the train which persisted for so long after the meteorite's flight. Analysis of the fragments showed that the chemical composition of the meteorite was 93.5 per cent iron, 5.27 per cent nickel, 0.47 per cent cobalt, 0.20 per cent phosphorus, 0.06 per cent sulphur, and minute quantities of other elements. The internal structure of the material suggested that the meteorite had been formed by the pressing together of separate pieces divided from each other by thin layers of schreibersite (a mineral compound of iron and phosphorus). It is this composite structure that accounts for the way in which this particular meteorite broke up so easily into smaller pieces.

Not all iron meteorites fracture so easily. The largest in the Sikhote-Alin shower weighed approximately 1750 kg ; the largest known chunk of meteoric matter weighs over 60,000 kg. It is a solid mass of iron and nickel which lies where it fell near Grootfontein in South-West Africa and protrudes above the surrounding Kalahari limestone into which it only penetrated to a depth of 1.5 m. These large meteorites are, happily, extremely rare. Most meteorites are relatively small bodies ranging in size from the finest dust upwards and with shapes almost as varied. The partial melting they suffer during their passage through the atmosphere tends to round off some of the sharper corners and to smooth out the surface. Chemical analysis shows that they contain nearly all the known elements but not, of course, in any one meteorite. No chemical element has been found that does not occur on the Earth. On the other hand, though most meteoric minerals occur terrestrially, some do not. Incidentally, no trace of any substance that definitely indicates the presence of a living organism has been found.

Meteorites can be divided according to their composition into two main classes, stones and irons, though there are a few that contain a mixture of both. The iron meteorites have, in general, a composition very similar to that of the Sikhote-Alin shower. Their crystal structure indicates that they were formed in the interior of a body at least as big as Ceres, but one that was probably not much bigger. These limits follow from the hypotheses that the parent planet was formed by the accretion of cold particles, that it was big enough for the entrapped radioactivity to melt the interior so that the iron, nickel, etc. could separate out, and yet small enough for this molten core to cool again within the five thousand million years since the birth of the solar system.

The stony meteorites are composed mainly of the mineral forms of the silicates of iron, magnesium, calcium, aluminium and sodium. An examination of their internal structure indicates two main types, the chondrites and the achondrites. The arrangement of the minerals in the chondrites is quite unlike that in terrestrial rocks. They are in a disorderly array of minute fragments in which are imbedded small spherical grains, called chondrules, and small flakes of iron-nickel. The chondrules are of similar composition to their surroundings and vary in size from the microscopic to a few millimetres. The texture of the achondrites is coarser than that of the chondrites; the various minerals are not so jumbled up, there are no chondrules and only very rarely any flakes of nickel-iron. Achondrites are, in fact, rather similar to some terrestrial rocks and for this reason are rather hard to recognize as meteorites unless they have actually been observed to fall. The carbonaceous chondrites are relatively rare; they are fragile, porous, and of considerably lower density than the others. A black, tarlike material, which is presumably a complex polymer, gives them a very dark colour.

The relative abundance of the various types of meteorites can best be estimated from those that have been seen to fall and which were recovered immediately so that there are no complications arising from difficulties of identification. The abundances so found for meteorites of moderate size are stones 90 per cent, irons 10 per cent; of the stones 93 per cent are chondrites, 5 per cent achondrites, and 2 per cent carbonaceous chondrites. For larger meteorites, the irons are relatively more abundant, as might be expected from their greater resistance to crushing and to fragmentation.

The ages of the meteorites can be estimated by various methods based on the rate of radioactive decay. The ages so indicated, that is the times found for the interval since the meteoric material cooled to something below 100° C, are of the order of 4.5×10^9 years. It has also become possible to form some idea of when the meteorites broke into fragments from the cumulative effects of cosmic rays on the surface layers. The times found range from about 2×10^5 to 10^9 years ago, the times of breakup being on the average more recent for the stones than for the irons.

It has been suggested that chondrules were formed by condensation from the nebular cloud that evolved into the solar system and thus represent primordial matter. Gravitation brought them together and as the body grew larger and the internal pressure increased, crushed them into ordinary chondritic material. The achondrites may have formed from chondritic material that was melted and subsequently recrystallized. Thus if we think of the meteorites as being fragments of a planet, the irons can be conceived as coming from the core, the achondrites from the immediately surrounding layer, and the chondrites from the outer shell, the carbonacous chondrites being from near the surface where the pressure crushing the chondritic material together would have been least.

Some reference must be made to tektites, which some people have regarded as being either lunar or meteoric in origin although their texture and composition have little in common with those of ordinary meteorites. They are small glassy objects which are found in great numbers strewn over large areas in Texas, Georgia, Czechoslovakia, Ghana, Australia, the East Indies, and the Philippines. Their shapes suggest that they were once molten and solidified while travelling through the atmosphere or through space. They have the same size range as gravel and, unlike other natural glasses, they show no obvious connection with their surroundings. Their physical and chemical characteristics differ from area to area and radioactive dating shows that this is also true of their ages. It has been suggested that tektites are a by-product of the fall of a really large meteorite, being in fact some of the terrestrial material that was fused and ejected with high velocity during the resulting explosion. The tektites in Ghana are not far from the 10-km diameter meteor crater now filled by Lake Bosumtwi, while those in Czechoslovakia may well be associated with the old, but even bigger, crater at Nordlinger in Germany.

The total mass of meteorites that fall each year is greatly exceeded by that of the micrometeorites. These are particles of the order of a micron in diameter which, because of their small size and low mass, have floated gently down through the atmosphere. As it is difficult at ground level to distinguish them with certainty from the products of industrial contamination, they have been collected in special containers attached to the nose cones of high flying rockets. Many have been captured in this way and have been brought back to earth for examination. The majority have dimensions less than a micron; some show a crystal structure, but most do not. This is rather surprising since all terrestrial dust particles and mineral fragments show a crystal structure, even when they are very finely divided. The captured particles are of three main types: high density spheres with clearly defined surfaces and diameters ranging down to a tenth of a micron; irregular, compacted particles which when magnified look rather like normal meteorites; and irregular, fluffy shaped, non-compacted bodies which appear to be made up of sub-particles about a tenth of a micron in size. These fluffy particles are of particular interest. They are fragile, of relatively low density, and may be typical of the material that makes up the cometary meteoroids; they may in fact be typical of the material out of which the cometary nuclei condensed, and thus of interstellar matter.

The zodiacal light

Most country dwellers will have noticed the zodiacal light from time to time though they may not have recognized its existence as a separate phenomenon. It is visible on clear, moonless evenings just after the end of twilight as a faint diffuse cone of light stretching up from the horizon with its axis following the ecliptic. It is widest and brightest at the horizon and grows fainter and narrower with increasing altitude. The zodiacal light is similarly visible before the morning twilight and is then sometimes referred to as the 'false dawn'. It is most easily seen on spring evenings and autumn mornings when the ecliptic is most nearly perpendicular to the horizon. For the same reason it is more conspicuous in the tropics than in the temperate zones. Plate 20 is from a photograph taken by D. E. Blackwell and M. F. Ingham from high up on the Bolivian Andes.

The spectrum of the zodiacal light indicates that it is sunlight reflected from innumerable small particles—the product of dead comets and ground up minor planets—scattered through a much-flattened ellipsoidal region centred on the Sun and having its greatest diameter in the plane of the ecliptic. These particles can be regarded as an extension of the F-corona of the Sun.

A related phenomenon is the gegenschein or counterglow. This is a feebly luminous elliptical area directly opposite to the Sun which may be seen on very dark, clear nights. It is about 10° long in the direction of the ecliptic and about 7° at right angles to this direction. It may be due to an 'opposition' brightening of the zodiacal light particles, or to an actual accumulation of such particles at about 1.6 gigametres from the Earth near the point corresponding to one of the straight-line solutions of the problem of three bodies, . . . the Sun, the Earth, and the particles.

Chapter Seven
The Sun

D. Emerson

The Sun is a typical star of medium size which has been in existence for perhaps half the lifetime of the Galaxy. Energy is generated near the centre of the Sun by the fusion of hydrogen atoms to form helium atoms and this energy is carried through the outer regions by great stirring motions called convection currents, finally to be radiated away into space from the Sun's surface. The material of the Sun is in a gaseous state so that strictly speaking the Sun has no edge but fades gradually away into the surrounding interplanetary space. However, nearly all the light that reaches the Earth from the Sun comes from a layer that is only a few hundred kilometres thick called the photosphere. Consequently the Sun, as seen from the Earth, appears to have a relatively sharp edge and we can regard the photosphere as being its surface. The region above the photosphere is called the corona and this stretches out far into space. Its density is so low that it would be regarded as a good vacuum in the laboratory, but it has a very high temperature and is perhaps three hundred times hotter than the photosphere. The transition zone between the photosphere and the corona is called the chromosphere. The chromosphere and the corona do not shine very brightly and can only be seen by the naked eye when the overwhelming glare of the photosphere has been blocked out by the Moon during a total solar eclipse. The photosphere, the chromosphere and the corona are collectively known as the solar atmosphere.

The release of energy inside the Sun and its radiation from the various layers of the solar atmosphere are steady processes that have probably gone on at much the same rate for thousands of millions of years. In contrast to these steady processes there are short lived events that occur from time to time in the atmosphere and constitute a sort of solar weather. These events range from cold areas called sunspots and hot areas called plages, which may last for weeks or even months, to violent explosions called flares whose life is measured in hours, if not in minutes. In the case of terrestrial weather we still find considerable difficulty in predicting where and when a particular event, say a rainstorm, is going to happen. We do know, however, that rain is much more likely at certain seasons of the year than at others. In the same way it is found that while individual events of solar weather appear to occur at random, their frequency reaches a maximum at about eleven-year intervals. The various events of solar weather are grouped together under the title of solar activity, and the rise and fall in their number is referred to as the sunspot cycle. They seem to be closely connected with the solar magnetic field and some of them cause disturbances in the Earth's upper atmosphere. When solar activity is at a minimum the Sun is said to be quiet and is then sometimes referred to as the 'Quiet Sun'.

We will begin this survey of the Sun by considering some of its overall features and with a discussion of a theoretical model of its internal structure. The remaining part of the chapter is devoted to various aspects of the solar atmosphere. As our knowledge of these depends almost entirely on the interpretation of the solar spectrum a brief sketch of the radiation properties of hot gases is given before the various layers of the quiet atmosphere are considered. In the same way an outline of the physics of magnetic fields seems a necessary introduction to a survey of sunspots, prominences and the many ramifications of flares. Before we get involved in the details of solar physics, however, it may be of some interest to point out why studies of the Sun are so important.

An understanding of the Sun has immediate practical applications. Solar activity alters the height and strength of the layer in our atmosphere which reflects radio signals from transmitter to receiver, and may, in extreme cases, completely disrupt the world-wide network of telecommunications. High energy particles produced in a major solar flare will certainly endanger space travellers and may possibly put at risk passengers in high-flying supersonic airliners. It is possible, too, that solar activity, through its effect on our upper atmosphere, plays a part in determining terrestrial weather conditions. For astrophysics the importance of the Sun lies in the fact that it is typical of many stars and is the only one of these that can be studied in great detail. For the physicist the Sun provides a laboratory intermediate in scale between those found on the Earth and those provided by the more distant parts of the Universe. As such it has played a significant role in the development of atomic, nuclear and plasma physics.

The interior

Overall characteristics of the Sun It is virtually impossible to probe directly beneath the surface of a star to obtain evidence of its internal structure. All that can be done is to construct a theoretical model, and to compare its predictions with the observable overall characteristics of the star. The most important data for this purpose are the mass, the diameter, the total energy output per second and the age.

The mass of the Sun can be found in terms of that of the Earth by using Newton's theory of universal gravitation, as was indicated in the chapter on the planets. The distance of the Sun and its apparent size in the sky give immediately its linear diameter. The rate of emission of energy, the luminosity, would seem to be a relatively easy quantity to determine. It should be given by combining the known distance of the Sun with a measure of the solar constant, that is, of the total amount of energy per second falling on unit area at the distance of the Earth. There are, however, a number of difficulties in measuring the solar constant. Ideally this should be done with an instrument like a bolometer which is equally sensitive to all wavelengths, but given such a perfect instrument there remains the problem introduced by our atmosphere which absorbs some of the radiation received from the Sun and, at some wavelengths, blocks it out altogether. This difficulty was only really overcome when it became possible to use rockets and satellites to fly instruments above the atmosphere.

The age of the Sun cannot be measured directly but there is a considerable amount of indirect evidence. Fossil algae have been found in rocks whose age appears to be about one hundred million years. These organisms could only have lived if the temperature of the Earth was then within about 20° Centigrade of its present value. This in turn implies that the Sun was shining with its present luminosity at that period. To push further into the past we must turn to estimates of the age of the Solar System. The Earth and other planets could have been formed before, at the same time as, or after the Sun, but it seems most unlikely that the Sun actually picked up a group of planets that had evolved separately some time before. Consequently most modern theories of the formation of the Solar System assume that the Sun and planets came into being together. If this is so, the age of the Earth should give us a good estimate of the minimum age of the Sun. One of the best ways of determining the age of the Earth is by consideration of the relative abundances of long-lived radioactive isotopes. For instance, an isotope of uranium, uranium 238, decays into lead 206 at a constant rate which is such that after four and a half thousand million years half of the uranium 238 has been converted into lead 206. The ratio of the parent (uranium 238) to the daughter (lead 206) in a sample of rock indicates its age if it can be assumed that the rock 'originally' contained none of the daughter isotope, which seems to be the case for certain minerals. The estimates found in this way for the time since the rocks in question crystallized out from a molten state vary considerably, but the indications are that the oldest rocks on the Earth's surface have existed for at least three and a half thousand million years. This figure represents a lower limit for the age of the Earth, for the rocks clearly passed through a long period in the molten state before solidification took place. An alternative method of dating is to measure the average abundance of lead 206 in the Earth's crust as a whole and make some allowance for the amount of lead 206 originally present. This latter amount can be gauged from some of the iron meteorites which appear to contain no parent uranium at all and which were presumably formed at the same time and out of the same material as the rest of the Solar System. The age of the Earth's crust found in this way is about four and a half thousand million years, which is also the age found by radioactive isotope methods for the meteorites themselves. The actual process of dating is, of course, much more complicated than has been indicated here, but the more sophisticated methods agree in indicating that the most probable age of the Solar System is around four and a half thousand million years.

Another general characteristic of the Sun that must be mentioned is its rotation. This can be measured by observing the motion of the sun spots across the face of the Sun (Plate 21*a*). The rotation is in the same direction as the planets rotate around the Sun while the axis of rotation is inclined at about 7° to the normal to the plane of the ecliptic. The Sun does not rotate like a solid body, however, for sunspots at different latitudes move at different speeds. Near the equator they indicate a sidereal period of rotation of 24.65 days; near latitude 20°, of 25.19 days; in latitude 30°, of 25.85 days; and in latitude 35° (beyond which there are very few spots), of 26.63 days. In higher latitudes the rotation period has to be determined by measuring the Doppler shift of the spectrum lines at the east and west limbs. It appears that the rotation period near latitude 75° is about 33 days. This differential rotation is only possible because the Sun is not a solid but a gaseous body.

The relatively slow rotation of the Sun has presented a difficult problem to the formulators of the various theories of the origin of the Solar System, as, despite the fact that the Sun contains most of the mass, the planets have most of the angular momentum of the Solar System taken as a whole. Thus any satisfactory theory of the development of the

Solar System must include some mechanism by which angular momentum can be transferred from the Sun to the planets. Recently it has been suggested that the core of the Sun may be rotating quite quickly, possibly with a period of a day or two, and that it is only the surface envelope that is spinning slowly. This links up with Dicke's gravitational theory and with observations of the solar oblateness which will be discussed in the next section. It is suggested that the whole of the Sun was originally rotating rapidly but that the surface layers were slowed down by the solar wind which blows through the corona and out to beyond the Earth. Observations of young stars in the Pleiades certainly suggest that those of solar mass are still rotating quite quickly.

The pertinent fundamental solar data so far considered can be summarized as follows:

Mass	1.99×10^{30} kg
Distance	1.50×10^{8} km
Radius	6.96×10^{5} km
Luminosity	3.86×10^{33} erg s^{-1}
Minimum Age	4.5×10^{9} years

The gravitational field of the Sun In 1916 Einstein produced his General Theory of Relativity which was essentially a new theory of gravitation. Earlier he had published his Special Theory of Relativity which was concerned with the way in which we measure length, time and energy. This Special Theory has received ample experimental confirmation but the General Theory, while widely accepted on philosophical grounds, has yet to gain decisive experimental proof. The difficulty lies in the fact that Newton's Theory of Universal Gravitation already predicts the motions within the Solar System so accurately that it is inevitable that any new gravitational theory will be almost indistinguishable from Newton's theory in the regions most accessible to observation. At very great distances there are major differences between Einstein's and Newton's theories, but no existing observational evidence of the effects in question is sufficiently reliable to enable us to judge between the two theories. Einstein himself suggested three tests. The first depended on the rate of advance of the perihelion of the orbit of Mercury, which he predicted should be 43 seconds of arc per century different from the value given by Newtonian theory. The actually observed difference is 43 $\pm$ 0.5 seconds of arc per century. Einstein's second proposed test involved the amount of deflection of a light beam by the Sun's gravitational field, which the Special Theory indicates as being twice as great as the deflection predicted by Newtonian theory.

This test depends on measuring the slight displacement in the apparent position of a star when its light passes close to the Sun. As the stars are not normally visible during the day, such observations have to be made during the brief intervals provided by total solar eclipses. The predicted deflection is very small, only 0.87 seconds of arc for a star appearing to be one solar radius from the edge of the Sun's disk. The first measures were made during the total solar eclipse of 1919 and produced a value for the deflection of about the right size, but subsequent analysis of the errors involved in such observations has left little confidence in the result. The third proposed test depends on the prediction that light emitted in a gravitational field has a longer wavelength than it would have were it emitted in a gravity-free region. This effect should show up as a small systematic difference in the wavelengths of the spectral lines emitted by atoms in the strong gravitational field of the Sun when compared with the same spectral lines emitted by the same kind of atoms in a laboratory in the relatively weak gravitational field of the Earth. Experiments along these lines produced somewhat conflicting results, with the solar red shift of a line appearing to depend on which part of the Sun is being examined, an effect which may be due to an inability to correct completely for motions in the solar atmosphere. Recently it has become possible to test the gravitational red shift in the laboratory by using a very narrow gamma ray line. The shift obtained was 1.05 ± 0.10 of the value predicted by Einstein's theory, but this cannot be regarded as a final proof of that theory since other gravitational theories predict a similar effect.

Considerable attention has been paid during the last few years to a development and generalization of Einstein's theory by Brans and Dicke. This new theory predicts a rather smaller value for the rate of advance of the perihelion of the orbit of Mercury than the observed value which, as we have already seen, is in good agreement with the value predicted by Einstein. The new theory would appear therefore to be a non-starter but Dicke has pointed out that part of the advance of the perihelion could be due to a non-spherical distribution of matter inside the Sun. The rotation of the Earth causes it to have a slight equatorial bulge. The Sun appears to be rotating too slowly to have a noticeable bulge, but there could be a small one if the interior is rotating more quickly than the outside. Dicke has made some careful observations and finds a departure from perfect roundness of the solar disk of 5 parts in 100,000 which is just sufficient to explain the discrepancy between the observed value of the rate of advance of the perihelion of the orbit of Mercury and the value predicted by his theory. Needless to say, this result has excited considerable controversy. Attempts have been made to repeat the deflection of light experiments, but using radio waves instead of optical ones. This avoids many of the difficulties inherent in the earlier tests, such as having to wait for a total solar eclipse. The first results from this radio work are in agreement with the predictions based on Einstein's theory, but at the time of writing they are not yet sufficiently accurate to distinguish with certainty between this theory and that of Brans and Dicke.

The source of solar energy In a small object the electrical forces between individual atoms lock them into a rigid structure which is sufficiently strong to withstand the relatively weak gravitational forces. In a large body of electrically neutral material, that is one in which the numbers of positive and negative electrical charges are, as usual, equal, the electrical repulsions and attractions tend to cancel out while the gravitational pulls exerted by the individual particles add. Thus in very large bodies the gravitational forces are dominant and a large isolated body will collapse under the mutual attractions of its constituent particles. As the particles are pulled closer together the gravitational attractions between them become stronger and the collapse will continue at an ever-increasing rate unless something happens to oppose it. In some ways the story of the stars is the story of the ways in which this collapse is resisted. In a hot body like the Sun the pressure exerted by the hot gas opposes collapse in much the same way as a balloon when heated experiences a force tending to make it expand. Consider now a large cloud of fairly cool gas which is collapsing under its own mutual gravitational attractions. The collapse will tend to accelerate, but the in-falling atoms will collide with each other converting some of the energy of the collapse into heat. This heating up will increase the gas pressure which will tend to slow down the collapse, but it can be shown that the heating up is never sufficient to stop the inward movement indefinitely. There must be some other source of energy to provide sufficient heat to raise the temperature high enough to prevent the gravitational collapse, to replace the energy lost by radiation from the outer surface of the cloud, and, in the particular case of the Sun, maintain it in a fairly steady state for over four and a half thousand million years. It was not till 1938 that Bethe and von Weiszäcker were able to outline specific processes of nuclear fusion as the probable source of the necessary energy.

Matter is composed of a number of different types of elementary particles. Five of these are of importance for the present discussion; these are the proton, the neutron, the electron, the positron, and the neutrino. The proton and the neutron are the heavy particles which make up the nuclei of atoms, and are practically identical except for the fact that protons carry a positive electrical charge while neutrons carry no charge at all. The electron and the positron are much lighter and, once again, are almost identical except that electrons carry a negative electrical charge and positrons a positive one. Neutrinos are massless and carry no electrical charge. An atom consists of a nucleus of protons and neutrons round which move a number of electrons. It is these electrons which determine the chemical properties of the atom and the way in which it emits light. An ordinary atom is electrically neutral, the number of surrounding electrons being equal to the number of protons in the nucleus. This number is called the atomic number and defines the element in question. Thus hydrogen has one proton, helium two, lithium three, and so on. The nucleus of a given element can exist in a number of forms with different numbers of neutrons, although the chemical properties of these isotopes, as they are called, are very similar. For instance, hydrogen can exist as ordinary hydrogen with just one proton, or as heavy hydrogen (deuterium) with both a proton and a neutron. Heavy water, in which the ordinary hydrogen atoms are replaced by the deuterium isotope, is very like ordinary water. Similarly ordinary helium has a nucleus consisting of two protons and two neutrons, while the helium 3 isotope has two protons and only one neutron in its nucleus.

The number of neutrons in a nucleus has little effect on the chemical properties of the atom, but is very important in determining the way in which the nucleus is bound together. In general there is a tendency for a nucleus having too many protons as compared with the number of neutrons to convert one of the protons into a neutron, getting rid of the excess positive charge by emitting a positron. In such a case the original nucleus is said to have decayed radioactively into a more stable form. A more detailed discussion of the stability and radioactive decay of nuclei would take us rather further afield than is necessary for the present purpose. All that we need to know is that a helium 4 nucleus is strongly bound together and that it requires energy to split it up. Conversely if two protons and two neutrons are fused together to form a helium 4 nucleus energy will be released. The same conclusion holds if we take four protons, convert two of them into neutrons, and combine the resulting particles into a helium nucleus. This is called a fusion reaction and it is the principal source of the solar energy. It is, incidentally, also the basis of the hydrogen bomb.

Fortunately for us, this reaction does not happen at ordinary temperatures. The positive charges on colliding protons repel each other and it is only when two protons are very close together that the short range nuclear forces can overcome the electrical repulsion. To penetrate the electrical barrier and come to nuclear grips, the protons must collide with a very high relative velocity. This means that the temperature must be very high, of the order of ten million degrees Centigrade. A hydrogen bomb needs a small atomic bomb to detonate it. In the case of the Sun gravitational collapse heated the gas to a temperature at which the fusion reactions could start and supply sufficient energy to prevent further collapse.

It must not be thought that these reactions consist of four protons happening to collide at once and turning into a helium nucleus. Such an event is most unlikely and in practice the basic reactions proceed through several intermediate stages. First two protons fuse together to form a nucleus of heavy hydrogen. This really consists of two reactions, the formation of a helium 2 nucleus and the rapid decay of this unstable nucleus into a deuterium nucleus by the emission of a positron. The next stage is the collision of a proton with a deuterium nucleus to give a nucleus of helium 3. Finally two helium 3 nuclei collide to form a helium 4 nucleus and two protons. The net result of this series of reactions is that four protons have been combined to give one nucleus of helium 4 and two positrons. The energy released appears in the form of the energy of motion of the positrons ejected in the first stage, the energy of motion of the protons from the last stage and the energy of the gamma rays emitted during the reactions. The particles do not travel far before they collide with other particles and the gamma rays are quickly absorbed. Thus the energy released is soon shared amongst the surrounding particles which are heated up. This heating up speeds the rate at which the reactions take place and increases the rate of liberation of energy, still further heating up the central region. It might appear from this that the centre of the Sun would get hotter and hotter indefinitely but the increasing temperature introduces a compensating effect; it causes the pressure of the gaseous material to increase sufficiently not only to overcome the contracting force of the gravitational attraction but also to press the surrounding layers of material outwards. This expansion causes the temperature, and consequently the rate of energy generation, of the central region to fall until a quasi-steady state is attained in which the temperature and rate of energy generation attained is just sufficient to keep the Sun from collapsing and to compensate for the energy that leaks away through the main body of the Sun and which is finally radiated from its surface. In the central regions this outward flow of energy is largely a matter of collisions between the fast moving and very closely packed particles and of the absorption and re-emission of radiation, particularly that of very short wavelength.

Nearer the surface, however, convection, by which the energy is transferred by the actual movement of hot material, sets in. A simple example of convection is provided when a beaker of water is heated by a flame placed under the centre of its bottom. Hot liquid can be seen rising up the middle of the beaker while cold currents descend at the sides. Similarly in the outer layers of the Sun circulating currents are set up with hot rising streams surrounded by cooler descending ones.

It is natural to inquire what evidence there is that the description given above of what happens in the solar interior corresponds with reality. The most convincing, perhaps, is the fact that the theoretical model of a star with the mass and composition of the Sun is predicted to have the radius and luminosity actually observed and a life of about ten thousand million years, which is about twice the present age of the Sun. As will be mentioned in more detail later, the tops of the convective currents near the solar surface can be seen as granulations (Plate 21*b*). A high-resolution picture of the photosphere shows a network of bright cells surrounded by darker areas, which clearly correspond with the hot rising and cold falling currents of the convective system. Direct proof of the nuclear reactions is rather harder to obtain. Although hydrogen is constantly being converted into helium in the centre of the Sun, the convective currents do not reach deep enough into the solar interior to bring the products of the reactions to the surface. Most of the particles and gamma rays produced in the reactions are stopped in the immediate neighbourhood of their creation. However, every time a radioactive decay occurs and a positron is emitted, a neutrino is also ejected. The neutrinos are massless and chargeless and pass through the solar material with very little hindrance. Unfortunately, this same immunity from capture which lets them escape easily from the Sun also makes them very difficult to detect. If our theories of the solar energy generation are correct, thousands of millions of neutrinos should be striking every square centimetre of the Earth every second, but of every hundred thousand million that pass through the Earth only one is likely to be stopped. Neutrinos can be detected by using an inverse form of the type of reaction that formed them. For instance, if a nucleus of chlorine 37 having 17 protons and 20 neutrons is struck by a neutrino there is a very small chance that it will be converted into a nucleus of argon 37 containing 18 protons and 19 neutrons. Argon 37 is radioactive and can thus be detected. Recently Davis in America has attempted to detect solar neutrinos by trying to capture some of them in a tank of one hundred thousand gallons of cleaning fluid which contains chlorine atoms. The tank was placed two thousand metres underground to avoid the confusing events produced by cosmic rays. In 1971 he actually

Plate 21

a The Sun as photographed in white light at the Cape Observatory on 9 April 1947 showing one giant group and a number of more typical spots. The general decrease in brightness towards the edge indicates that the photosphere is gaseous and semi-transparent

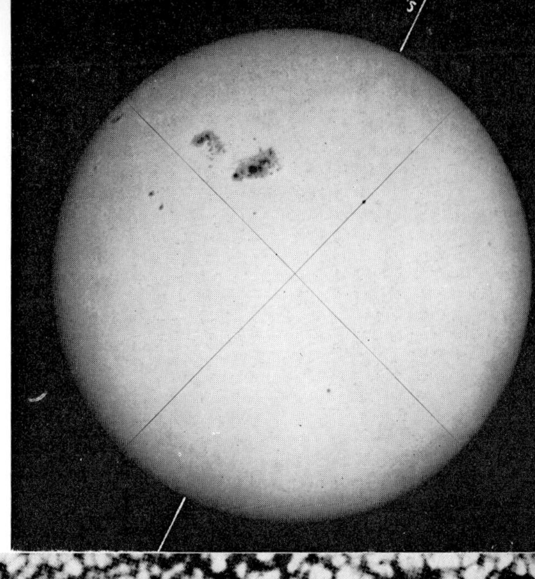

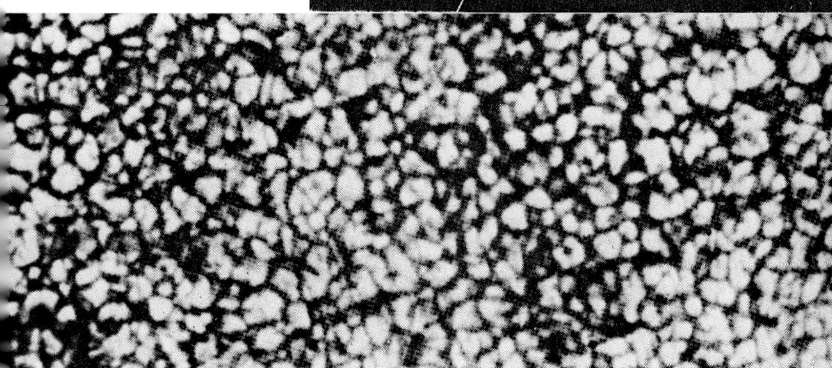

b Photospheric granulation. Enlarged portion of a direct photograph taken with the 12-inch telescope of Project Stratoscope. Princeton Univ., ONR, NSF and NASA

c Large sunspot group. This Greenwich photograph shows the extremely complex structure. The black area (umbra) and the surrounding grey (penumbra) are actually quite bright but, being cooler than the rest of the photosphere, appear dark by contrast. Approximate scale 1 cm = 40,000 km

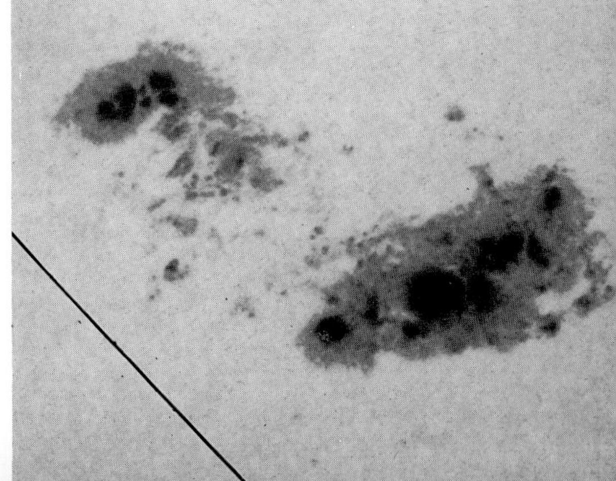

Plate 22 The corona. *a* Near the time of maximum solar activity. Photographed at Chios in Greece by R. L. Waterfield during the eclipse of 19 June 1936

b Near the time of minimum. Photographed during the eclipse of 21 September 1922 by the Lick Observatory expedition to Wallal, Australia

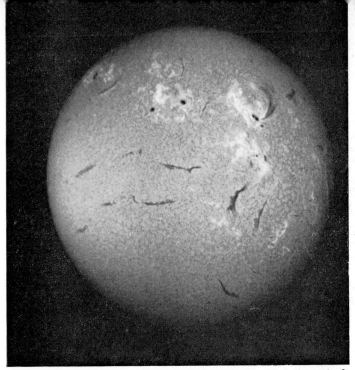

Plate 23 The chromosphere. *a* Photographed with the Lyot Hα heliograph of the Cape Observatory. The brighter areas near the sunspots are called plages

b Portion of an Hα spectroheliogram taken at the Hale Observatories. As in 23*a*, the long dark filaments are prominences silhouetted against the brighter lower chromosphere

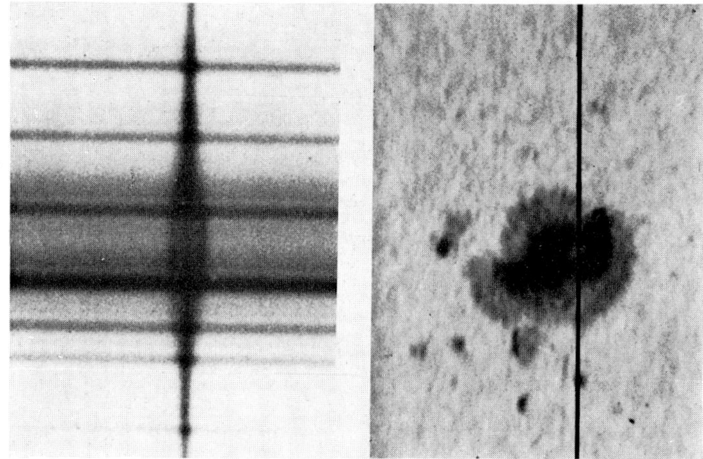

Plate 24 The solar magnetic field. *a* The Zeeman effect near a sunspot (page 262). The black line on the right indicates the position of the spectrograph slit

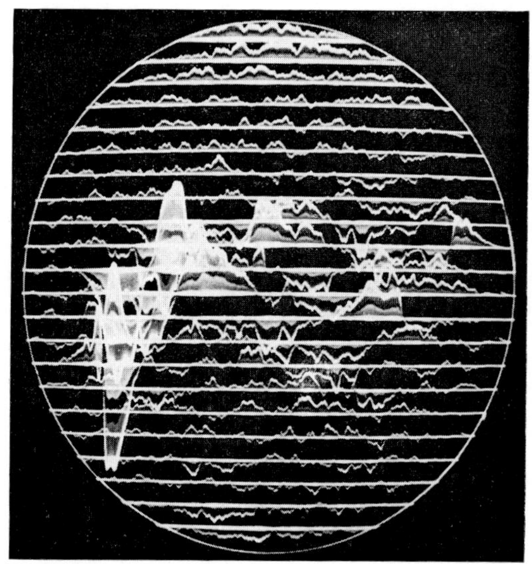

b Magnetogram for 18 July 1953. How such a record of the location and strength of weak magnetic fields is made is explained on page 263. Both Hale Observatories

detected captured neutrinos but their number was smaller than had been expected and may indicate that the temperature in the middle of the Sun is somewhat lower than has been predicted by theory.

The solar atmosphere

The photosphere is the layer of the solar atmosphere from which comes most of the radiation that reaches the Earth in the optical portion of the spectrum, that is in the visible and immediately adjacent ultraviolet and infrared regions. In other words, it is the layer that we actually see when we look at the Sun or when we photograph it under normal conditions. Layers deeper into the Sun are, of course, emitting radiation but this is all transformed during its passage through the photosphere where it is absorbed and re-emitted. Layers higher in the Sun than the photosphere are semi-transparent and contain so few atoms that they can only emit small amounts of radiation. The photosphere itself is a zone a few hundred kilometres thick, with a temperature that falls from 9000° K at the bottom to about 4300° K at the top. The pressure at the bottom of the photosphere is similar to that on the surface of the Earth, but falls by a factor of about one thousand by the time that the top is reached.

From physics we know that the radiation emitted by a black body depends only on its temperature, its total quantity being given by Stefan's law, and its spectral energy distribution by Planck's law. The higher the temperature of a body, the greater the quantity of radiation emitted, and the shorter its average wavelength. These radiation laws only apply when one is dealing with a solid or liquid body or with a sufficiently dense cloud of gas. In the chromosphere and the corona the density is so low that radiation passes through almost unhindered and thus has no opportunity of coming into thermodynamic equilibrium with the gas. In the photosphere the density is still high enough for the radiation laws to hold approximately. In passing it should be noted that, under the circumstances pertaining in the chromosphere and the corona, the intensity of any radiation emitted depends almost entirely on the number of atoms in a suitable state to emit it, since the chance of re-absorption is very low indeed.

As the temperature of the photosphere varies with height, the apparent brightness of a small area of its surface will depend on which layer we are able to see down to, and this is determined by the opacity or 'degree of fogginess' of the photospheric gas. At the centre of the disk we are looking directly down into the Sun, but, as may be seen

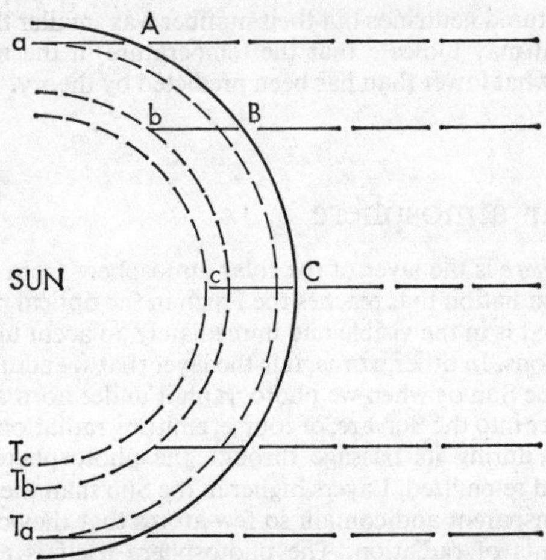

Figure 7.1 Darkening of the solar limb

Lines of sight that penetrate for equal distances through the semi-opaque layers reach different depths below the solar surface. As $T_a < T_b < T_c$, the central portions of the disk appear brighter than the outside

from Figure 7.1, we do not see so deeply into the Sun towards the edge of the disk although we are looking through a similar length of photospheric fog. Consequently, as the temperature is falling from the interior outwards, the radiation we receive from the edge of the disk is characteristic of a lower temperature than that seen at the centre. This 'darkening towards the limb' is clearly visible in the photograph of the Sun (Plate 21*a*), and a detailed investigation of the phenomenon enables us to form some idea of how the temperature varies with height in the photosphere. Taken as a whole, the Sun radiates in the visual region rather like a black body at a temperature of about 5800° K.

For many purposes radiation can be regarded as consisting of discrete quanta which have been emitted as the result of energy transitions in individual atoms, ions or molecules. In the same way the quanta are absorbed individually when they encounter atoms, ions or molecules in the appropriate condition. Thus the net flux of radiation we receive from the photosphere depends on the balance ultimately achieved between myriads of these individual events of emission and absorption.

The amount of absorption determines the opacity of the atmosphere, and at any wavelength depends on what atomic or other transitions are possible. Transitions within an atom emit or absorb at discrete wavelengths and thus lead to a sharp increase in the opacity at those wavelengths. Transitions in which an atom or ion loses or gains an electron can take place over a wide range of wavelengths, but the probability of such a transition varies slowly with the wavelength, resulting in a similar variation in the opacity. These variations in the absorption coefficient with wavelength lead to variations in the layers of the photosphere which we 'see' at any particular wavelength. For consider a photon trying to escape from the lower parts of the atmosphere. It will either pass straight through the upper parts of the atmosphere and escape or it will be absorbed by an atom higher in the atmosphere. The atom so excited will eventually emit another photon, which, if travelling outwards, will in turn either escape or be re-absorbed by an atom still higher in the atmosphere, and so on. The larger the coefficient of absorption for the wavelength involved, the greater the number of such re-absorptions will be, and the higher in the atmosphere the atoms that finally emit the photons that escape. Consequently if the light received from the photosphere is spread out into a spectrum we can expect those wavelengths for which the absorption coefficients are larger than the average to show up as absorption features on an otherwise continuous spectrum, since the light within them comes from higher and therefore cooler layers.

The photospheric spectrum actually observed is a continuous one with maximum intensity in the green and crossed by many dark absorption lines. It is observed in much the same way as a stellar spectrum but, as much more light is available, solar spectrographs are much larger and can detect much finer details. The most elaborate solar spectrographs can separate features in the solar spectrum which are only 0.005 angstroms apart and can detect a depression of 0.1 per cent in the continuous spectrum. The visible spectrum from one of these instruments would spread out over hundreds of metres were it not for the fact that only a small portion of the spectrum is viewed at one time. It is unlikely that any dramatically larger solar spectrographs will be built in the near future, for the very detailed spectra already available show so many lines that their detailed interpretation becomes almost impossible. Already by 1895 the American physicist Rowland had published accurate wavelengths for 14,000 lines in the solar spectrum while in the 1940s an international effort directed by Minnaert produced the Utrecht Atlas of the Solar Spectrum which has become the standard reference book. Tens of thousands of solar lines are known, and work

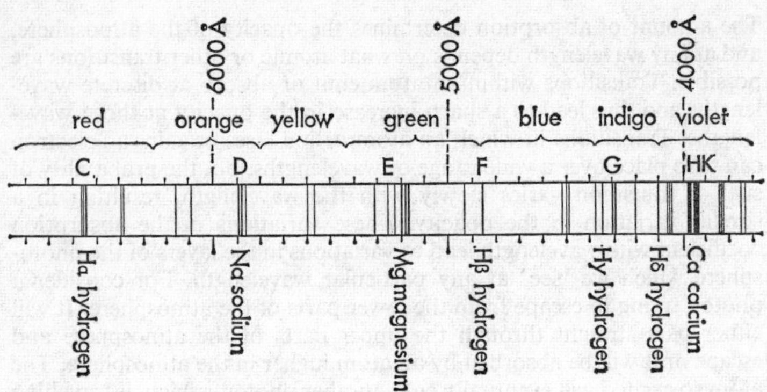

Figure 7.2 The solar spectrum in the visual region

Only a few of the most prominent features are shown, including those lettered by Fraunhofer. His A and B lines in the deep red result from absorption by oxygen molecules in the Earth's atmosphere

on the identification of the elements producing them has continued steadily, particularly at the United States Bureau of Standards. About seventy elements have so far been identified in the Sun. The most prominent lines in the optical solar spectrum are the H and K lines of ionized calcium at 3933 Å and 3968 Å, the lines of the Balmer series of hydrogen and the yellow D lines of sodium. Many of the weaker lines are due to iron and to similar elements like titanium and chromium (Figure 7.2).

The determination of the relative abundances of the various elements present in the solar atmosphere is by no means straightforward. Some elements, such as helium, produce their strongest lines in the ultraviolet and are thus likely to escape detection. Even when the lines of an element are present in the visible spectrum, the strength of the absorption lines depends not only on the quantity of the element present but also on the temperature of the atmosphere and on the intrinsic strength of the line concerned. Most abundance determinations involve comparing the solar spectrum with that of a laboratory 'sun' produced by heating a known quantity of an element to a high temperature. Electric furnaces, arcs and shock tubes have been used but it is not very easy to maintain such very hot gases under controlled conditions. Hydrogen is clearly the most abundant element in the Sun, with helium the next most abundant. Unfortunately helium cannot be seen in the optical spectrum of the photosphere and we have to derive its abundance from an analysis of the solar cosmic ray particles shot out during a major flare. It seems likely that about 90 per cent of the solar atoms are hydrogen, 10 per cent helium, while all the rest of the elements taken together amount to less than 1 per cent. Of these, oxygen, carbon, nitrogen and neon probably have abundances amounting to between 0.1 per cent and 0.01 per cent of the total, although neon, like helium, does not appear in the visible spectrum. These elements are followed by magnesium, silicon, and iron. It is interesting to note that although these three elements represent only a tiny fraction of all the atoms in the Sun, they can have a very considerable effect on the evolution of a star. The composition of the solar atmosphere presumably reflects the composition of the material out of which the Sun was formed, since it seems unlikely that the nuclear processes now taking place in the deep interior of the Sun can have much effect on the surface mixture. It has been suggested that meteorites also provide us with samples of the initial material of the solar system. Unfortunately they differ greatly in their chemical composition, but there is one group of them that does seem to have abundance ratios for the various elements other than hydrogen and helium similar to those in the solar atmosphere.

The intensity distribution in the continuous spectrum of the solar atmosphere in the optical region is approximately that for radiation from a black body of temperature 5800°K. Since hydrogen is so abundant we would expect that most of this continuous light would result from the ionization and recombination of hydrogen atoms and we would predict a rather sharp discontinuity at 3650 Å, the head of the Balmer series. This 'Balmer discontinuity' certainly exists in the solar spectrum but it is much smaller than expected, and it is clear that another process for producing a continuous spectrum must be at work. It was not until 1941 that Wildt suggested that this other process might be based on the hydrogen minus ion, H^-, which is a hydrogen atom that has picked up an extra electron. Such an ion is only just stable and there can be only a very small fraction of the hydrogen in the solar atmosphere in this form. Nevertheless such ions make a very important contribution to the continuous spectrum since they have a very high absorbing and emitting capacity in the visual region.

Thus far we have been discussing the photosphere as though it were a steady unmoving layer of gas. This is far from being the case, for all parts of the solar atmosphere are in motion even at those times when the Sun is described as being quiet. We can study some of these motions by means of the Doppler shifts they produce in the spectral lines. The atoms of the solar atmosphere will be in continuous motion because of the high temperature. Some will be moving towards the Earth as they radiate and some away. The former will emit blue shifted lines, the latter red shifted lines. The net result is that the line actually observed will cover a small range of wavelengths on either side of its normal position. The line is said to be broadened and the amount of broadening indicates how fast the atoms must be moving and hence their temperature. It turns out, however, that the observed broadening is much greater than can be accounted for by the temperature of the solar atmosphere, and we are forced to conclude that in addition to the normal temperature motion there is considerable 'turbulence', that is random motions of small volumes of the solar gas.

This general broadening of the spectral lines is observed when we are viewing large areas of the solar surface at a time. Further information on the nature of the motions causing it can be obtained by examining the Doppler shifts in light originating from small areas of the solar surface. One of the most convenient methods of doing this is due to Leighton who made use of a spectroheliograph to make two maps of the Sun, the one at a wavelength just greater than, and the other at a wavelength just less than, that of an absorption line. Regions moving upward will show up on the blue map, while regions moving downward will show up on the red; regions moving neither up nor down will be identical on both maps. Thus if the two maps are, as it were, subtracted from each other, the moving areas will show up as light or dark patches depending on the direction of their motion. Observations of this kind have established the existence of oscillations in the photosphere. Regions several thousands of kilometres across rise and fall within a period of about five minutes reaching velocities of the order of a kilometre per second.

These oscillations and the turbulence already mentioned are not the only motions in the photosphere. Observed in moments of exceptionally good seeing, the surface of the photosphere has a granulated appearance and has been likened to a bowl of rice grains. The existence of this granulation was firmly established by some remarkable photographs taken by Janssen in 1879, photographs whose quality has only recently been surpassed by those taken from balloons (Plate 21*b*) high above the more turbulent layers of the Earth's atmosphere that are responsible for bad seeing. These photographs show that the photosphere consists of bright granules about 700 kilometres across surrounded by dark lanes, the difference in brightness between the granules and the lanes corresponding to a temperature difference of several hundred degrees. The individual granules have a life time of about ten minutes. The obvious explanation of these granules is that they represent convective cells, the top of the convection system which starts well below the photosphere and which carries much of the energy from the interior to the surface. The bright granules represent the hot material flowing upward and the dark lanes the returning cooled material flowing downward. If this picture is correct we ought to be able to detect the Doppler shifts resulting from the moving streams. The observation is difficult because of the small size of the granules but it does seem that velocities of about one kilometre per second are involved. Even when a number of granules are observed together the effects of the convection currents can still be seen in the line profiles. Were the bright and dark granules of equal temperature and therefore of equal brightness, the only effect of the convective streaming would be to broaden the spectral lines, just as turbulence does, and it would be difficult to distinguish between the two phenomena. But the rising, or blue shifted, stream is hotter and brighter than the descending red shifted one so that the net result is an asymmetric absorption line, which is, indeed, observed.

The chromosphere is the transition region between the photosphere and the corona. It used to be pictured as a layer about ten thousand kilometres thick in which the temperature rose slowly from the temperature minimum of the solar atmosphere of 4300°K to about 10,000°K, and then increased very rapidly to the coronal value of 1,000,000°K. It is now realized, however, that the picture of a uniform layer applies only to the bottom one thousand kilometres and that higher up the chromosphere is very inhomogeneous. Lumps of relatively cool and dense chromospheric material intermingle with regions which have the very low coronal density and the very high coronal temperature. In particular, spikes of chromospheric material called spicules stick far out into the lower corona, shooting up from the lower chromosphere where the local magnetic field is strong. The transition from chromospheric to coronal conditions appears to take place in a very narrow skin round the chromospheric lumps and jets. The uniform chromospheric layer of older theories was the smeared-out effect of these inhomogeneities and it is not surprising that the interpretation of observations sometimes gave contradictory results.

The chromosphere can be viewed in plan over the disk of the Sun, but this requires special instrumentation which will be described later. It can also be seen in side elevation during an eclipse. Normally the bright glare of the photosphere, scattered by our own atmosphere, drowns out the feeble light from the chromosphere. During an eclipse, however, there are a few brief moments before and after totality during which the

Moon blacks out the bright photosphere altogether but leaves the chromosphere as a thin red arc of light. Halley first saw it as a red flash during the total eclipse of 1715 and it is to this characteristic redness that it owes its name of 'coloured sphere'. There was little understanding of the nature of the chromosphere, however, until the 1870s when eclipse phenomena began to be observed spectroscopically. If a series of spectra is taken as totality is approaching, the first ones in the series will show the strong continuous spectrum crossed by dark absorption lines of the photosphere, but later, as the photosphere is gradually blotted out, the spectra recorded change from this absorption spectrum to one consisting of a weak continuous spectrum crossed by bright emission lines. At first these represent the light from the whole height of the chromosphere, but later, as the Moon advances, they refer only to its upper parts. It is in this way that the variation of the properties of the chromosphere with height can be investigated.

The emission lines produced by the chromosphere are similar to those produced by a flame in the laboratory. The early investigators had been puzzled by the absorption lines of the photospheric spectrum and it was the chromospheric spectrum that convinced them that they were looking at a hot gas containing many of the elements found on the Earth. Lockyer made extensive investigations in the 1880s of the spectrum of the chromosphere and of the prominences (which may be regarded as temporary accumulations of chromospheric material in the corona), and began to move towards an understanding of the ionization of atoms at high temperatures. He also found an emission line which he could not identify with that from any known element. It was suggested that this must come from a new element which was called helium, after Helios, the Greek name for the Sun. It was not until 1895 that helium was first isolated in the laboratory by Ramsay. Most of the emission lines in the chromospheric spectrum correspond to the absorption lines in the photospheric spectrum, like the lines of hydrogen and of neutral and ionized iron. The Balmer alpha line of hydrogen is particularly strong and it is this that gives the chromosphere its red colour. The reason why the lines appear in emission is because the chromosphere is optically thin. The radiation emitted by the excited atoms escapes, in general, without interacting with other atoms. Thus the question of absorption does not arise except for the strongest lines and the strength of the radiation emitted at any wavelength depends directly on the number of excited atoms capable of emitting at that wavelength. There are a number of chromospheric lines which are characteristic of gases at rather higher temperatures than those found in the photosphere. Amongst these are the lines of neutral and ionized helium. Unfortunately the helium lines probably come from the transition region between the chromosphere and the corona, and the analysis of this thin skin is so difficult that there is no easy way of obtaining a helium abundance from these lines.

When we turn to the disk 'plan-view' appearance of the chromosphere we find a totally different situation. This is not surprising, since in the side-on eclipse spectrum we are seeing the light emitted by excited atoms of the chromosphere, whereas in the disk plan-view we are seeing what the chromosphere does to alter the flood of radiation pouring out from the photosphere. We have already noted that the stronger the absorbing power of the atoms at any given wavelength, the more opaque the atmosphere was, and the higher we were forced to look. If the atmosphere at some wavelength is very opaque, we will be forced to look at the chromosphere. This happens under three circumstances. The first is near the centre of very strong absorption lines, like the Balmer alpha line of hydrogen or the K line of ionized calcium. Such lines cover a short range of wavelength, the line getting darker as one moves towards the central wavelength. Now we have already seen that one reason for the darkness of absorption lines is the falling temperature of the photosphere and, since the temperature rises again in the chromosphere, one might expect the centres of the strong absorption lines to be bright. This does in fact occur, but the reader should be warned that the rules that applied to the photosphere do not always hold in the low density chromosphere, and that the complete explanation of what happens at the middle of strong absorption lines is rather complicated.

The other circumstances under which we are forced to look at the chromosphere are in the ultraviolet at wavelengths shorter than 1600 Å and in the infrared at wavelengths between 0.1 mm to 1 mm. In both cases the opaqueness of the atmosphere to the continuous spectrum is very high. The steady rise of the temperature of the Sun, inferred from the intensity distribution within the continuous spectrum as one moves into the infrared, reflects the temperature rise of the smoothed out chromosphere. In the ultraviolet the spectrum changes at about 1500 Å from a photospheric spectrum with absorption lines to a chromospheric spectrum with emission lines. Spectra at these sorts of wavelengths have, of course, to be obtained from above the Earth's atmosphere. The emission lines come not only from neutral atoms but also from atoms that have lost up to three electrons. In general, the greater the ionization of an atom, the shorter the wavelengths of the lines that it emits. The presence of all these stages of ionization in the ultraviolet spectrum indicates temperatures ranging from 10,000°K to 70,000°K and it is clear that some of the lines observed must have their origin in the region of the corona-chromosphere transition.

So far we have not discussed the inhomogeneities in the chromosphere. These can best be investigated with the aid of maps of the Sun made in the light of a single wavelength, the wavelength being so chosen that we are forced to look at the chromosphere. One device for making such maps is the spectroheliograph which was developed simultaneously in 1891 by Hale in the United States and by Deslandres in France. A long-focus telescope is used to form an image of the Sun on the slit jaws of a large spectrograph. The slit itself allows light from a narrow strip of the solar image to pass into the spectrograph where it is spread out into a high dispersion spectrum. A second slit in the image plane of the spectrograph permits radiation of just one selected wavelength to fall on a photographic plate and record there an image of the narrow strip of the Sun isolated by the first slit. The image of the Sun on the first slit and the photographic plate behind the second slit are moved across at the same uniform speed and a monochromatic picture of the Sun is gradually built up on the photographic plate. If the selected wavelength be that of the centre of the hydrogen alpha line the resulting photograph is a map of the chromosphere (Plate 23*b*). The one big disadvantage of the spectroheliograph is that it takes an appreciable time to build up a picture of the Sun. The same picture could be obtained more quickly if it were possible to photograph the Sun through a filter having an extremely narrow band pass of the order of one angstrom, or less, wide. Such a filter was developed between 1929 and 1942 by Lyot of the Paris and Meudon Observatories and like the spectroheliograph has been used extensively to study the structure of the chromosphere and also to record the transient phenomena of solar activity (Plate 23*a*).

A spectroheliogram of the chromosphere shows not the smooth even disk that one might expect but a mottled, freckled surface, with here and there more disturbed regions with large bright patches and spiral whirl-shaped features. The more disturbed regions often lie above sunspots and are part of the solar active regions, which we shall be discussing in more detail later on. On close inspection, the freckles fall into a definite pattern of cells, which is known as the chromospheric network. At the centre of the disk each cell appears to be outlined by a border of bright patches sometimes called flocculi. Nearer the edge of the disk the cells look as though they are bordered by dark patches, and as the limb is approached the dark patches give the impression that they are raised above the rest of the chromosphere. When the chromosphere is viewed edge-on, a large number of spikes are seen to be sticking up above the chromospheric layer. These are called spicules, and are the same as the dark patches seen near the limb. Under chromospheric conditions the interpretation of brightness in terms of temperature is not straightforward, but it would appear likely that the flocculi are somewhat hotter than the lower chromosphere, and that the spicules are hotter still, with temperatures of the order of 10,000°K. One of the most important observations about the chromospheric network is that the cell borders appear to coincide with regions of enhanced magnetic field. The spicules seem to occur where fields of 10 gauss or so are seen in the photosphere. Rather stronger fields of 50 gauss or so lead to especially well-developed spicules, and where a large area is covered by a strong field, the cells are filled with the bright plages typical of active regions. If the magnetic field is horizontal the cell structure is replaced by long worm-like features called fibrils which appear to follow the field. Well-developed spicules reach 6000 km or so out into the lower corona but have a thickness of only a few hundred kilometres. Spicules have a life time similar to that of the photospheric granules, that is of the order of ten minutes. The spicular material also appears to be in violent upward motion with velocities of about 30 km s^{-1}. The material seen inside the cells oscillates with a four or five minute period, rather as the upper photosphere does.

Detailed studies of the motions of the upper photosphere and the lower chromosphere by Leighton and his colleagues have shown a pattern of cells with material flowing horizontally outwards from the centre to the borders of the cells with a velocity of about one kilometre per second. This has been interpreted as a 'supergranulation' convective motion, the vertical up-flow at the centre of the cells and the down-flows at the borders remaining undetected. The supergranules are much larger than the ordinary photospheric granules, but coincide closely with the cells of the chromospheric network. It has been suggested that the convective motions of supergranulation force the magnetic field to the edge of the cells, and that it is the magnetic field that allows the formation of spicules at the edge of the cells. The heating of the corona to temperatures of a million degrees or so is still something of a mystery, but at one time it was suggested that the spicules might be the means whereby energy was transferred from the convective motions below the photosphere to the corona. It has since been pointed out that above solar active regions the spicules disappear altogether, but the temperature of the corona is higher than ever. The final solution of these chromospheric problems must await more ultraviolet data from space-vehicles and higher resolution spectroheliograms made at ground level.

The corona is a very high-temperature and low-density extension to the solar atmosphere, stretching far out into interplanetary space. One can even regard the Earth as being immersed in the outer regions of the corona although it is extremely tenuous at the Earth's distance from the Sun. The corona cannot be seen directly because the light from the photosphere is scattered in our atmosphere and makes the sky away from the Sun quite bright and blue. Even on a very clear, dust-free day when the sky looks a very deep blue, the sky brightness is greater than the brightness of the corona. Consequently the early observations of the corona were all made during total eclipses when the photospheric light was blocked out by the Moon (Plate 22). At the time of totality a faint and somewhat irregular glow is visible around the Sun extending out to distances of several times the Sun's own radius. The first recorded observations are probably those of Kepler at the beginning of the seventeenth century, but interest in the corona was not very marked until after the middle of the nineteenth century.

When the light from the corona is analysed spectroscopically it is found to consist of a continuous spectrum on which is superimposed a number of emission lines. The continuous spectrum is believed to be produced by the scattering of photospheric light from free electrons in the corona. This scattering process is a completely different sort of mechanism from the one which gave rise to the photospheric continuous spectrum. Light from the photosphere is deflected by the electrons of the corona so that some of the radiation streaming away from the Sun is turned towards the Earth. If a deflecting electron is some distance from the side of the Sun as seen from the Earth, the scattered light will appear to come from a point high above the Sun's surface. The observed brightness of the corona will depend only on the number of such scattering electrons and not at all on their temperature, for there are too few particles in the corona for it to produce hot body emission of its own, except at the wavelengths of the spectral lines. If the continuous coronal spectrum is produced entirely by scattering we would expect it to be similar to that of the photosphere. Now the latter contains many absorption lines while the coronal continuous spectrum does not. This can be explained if the corona is at a very high temperature so that the scattering electrons are moving at high velocities. This will ensure that the photospheric spectrum suffers a significant Doppler shift as it is scattered. Electrons moving towards the Earth will send on a spectrum shifted to the blue, while those moving away will send on a spectrum shifted to the red. Since we always see the light scattered from a number of electrons moving in random directions, the continuous spectrum observed is the resultant of a large number of photospheric spectra moved by random amounts to both red and blue. The net result is that the absorption lines are so broadened that they are virtually smoothed out altogether.

The zodiacal light (Plate 20), the band of faint light that can be seen on dark nights lying along the ecliptic, is believed to be caused by the scattering of solar radiation by dust particles in interplanetary space. It is presumably present when one looks at the corona during an eclipse. Light observed as coming from a direction close to the Sun may be coming either from electrons near the Sun deflecting the photospheric radiation through large angles towards the observer, or from dust nearer the Earth deflecting the Sun's light through smaller angles. Fortunately it is possible to distinguish the true coronal scattered light from the inner zodiacal light because it is more highly polarized; moreover the spectrum of the zodiacal light retains the photospheric absorption lines, since the scattering dust particles are more massive and do not move so quickly as the coronal electrons. Thus the apparent coronal light can be split into two components, the K-corona produced by electron scattering and the F-corona produced by dust particle scattering. The 'K' designation comes from 'kontinuerliche', the German word for continuous, while the 'F' stands for Fraunhofer and refers to the Fraunhofer absorption lines present in the spectrum.

Once the F and K components have been separated it becomes possible to determine the density of the corona from a comparison of the brightness of the K-corona with that of the photospheric radiation. This gives the fraction of light scattered by a given volume and hence the density of the scattering electrons. It is a fair assumption that this electron density is roughly equal to the number density of the hydrogen ions, since the corona is largely composed of hydrogen which will be almost completely ionized because of the very high temperature and low density.

Ground-based observations during total eclipses have followed the corona out to about ten solar radii. At such times, however, the sky is not perfectly dark because of a certain amount of luminescence from the Earth's own atmosphere, and by observing the eclipse from a high flying aeroplane it has been possible to follow some of the denser structures out to thirty solar radii. At this distance the F-corona is brighter than the K-corona and it becomes impossible to separate out the weaker component. However, the coronal electrons can be traced further out by using radio waves which are not affected by interplanetary dust. If a distant radio point source is observed through the corona, irregularities in the electron density of the corona will spread and smear out its image, in much the same way as bad seeing due to irregularities in our own atmosphere spreads out and distorts the optical images of stars. Thus if a powerful source of radio waves like the Crab Nebula is observed as the Sun passes in front of it, its apparent size increases as the edge of the Sun approaches, while the effect of the irregularities increases with the increasing electron density. In this way the corona has been traced out to about one hundred solar radii, or nearly half way to the Earth. Recently it has become possible to study the corona all the way to the Earth by using space probes to make direct measurements of the electron density, although these measurements are complicated by the fact that the spacecraft's own electrical field affects the charged electrons.

The picture of the corona that results from all these studies is neither perfectly regular nor constant with time. At sunspot maximum (Plate 22*a*) it looks roughly symmetrical and has a fine structure of narrow radial rays. At sunspot minimum (22*b*) the mean density of the corona is lower and it is concentrated in the equatorial plane, while round the poles short tufts, called plumes, stick out. Features with an arch-like form and called fans or helmets are often found above prominences. In the outer corona long radial features called streamers seem associated with active regions on the solar surface. Prominent active regions with flares sometimes produce especially dense and high temperature regions in the corona which are referred to as condensations. Thus the symmetrical appearance of the corona at sunspot maximum is largely due to the blending of the structures over the many active regions present at that time. Indeed some have gone so far as to wonder if the corona would vanish altogether if the Sun were to be completely quiet. The mean coronal density seems to vary from about one to ten million electrons per cubic centimetre at one solar radius above the Sun's surface, to about five electrons per cubic centimetre in the vicinity of the Earth. The first figure represents what by terrestrial standards is a good vacuum while the second indicates one that is almost impossibly good.

We have hinted several times that the corona has a high temperature. The smearing out of the photospheric absorption lines and the enormous extension of the corona both point to a temperature of the order of one million degrees. During the past thirty years it has become possible to observe the radio emission from the corona at metre wavelengths. This is thermal radiation from the corona itself and not just scattered energy from the photosphere. In fact at these long wavelengths radio signals cannot escape from the denser regions of the solar atmosphere. The observed radio brightness indicates a temperature of about one million degrees or so, but the analysis is complicated and somewhat uncertain. Before these radio observations were available it was difficult to believe that the corona had the very high temperature that was indicated by the clues mentioned above. There was, however, another phenomenon pointing in the same direction. As long ago as 1869 Young observed a coronal emission line at 5303 Å and, as the years passed, other coronal emissions were observed which could not be identified with the spectral lines of any known element. Indeed for a long time they were attributed to the unknown element called coronium which it was hoped would eventually be identified on the Earth much as helium had been. A big step forward in the investigation of the coronal spectrum came in the 1930s when Lyot developed his coronagraph and used it to observe the emission lines without waiting for an eclipse. Essentially the coronagraph is a solar telescope which has been extremely carefully designed to avoid scattering or reflecting photospheric light into the coronal image and it has to be used at a location where the atmosphere is very clear such as on the top of a fairly high mountain. Even so the K-corona is fainter than the sky brightness and cannot be observed. The coronagraph enabled the variation of the coronal emissions with the degree of solar activity to be studied, but it did not solve the problem of their identification.

The first effective clue to this came when a coronal line was observed in the spectrum of a nova, that is in a star that was undergoing an explosion. The atmospheres of such stars are known to be very hot and one would expect the atoms in them to be stripped of many of their outer electrons. Now in such highly ionized atoms the remaining electrons are so very firmly bound that changes in their state require a good deal of energy. This means that the normal spectral lines of highly ionized atoms tend to fall in the far ultraviolet. However, a close inspection of the spectrum of an ordinary atom shows that its energy states are often split into two or more levels. An example of the effects of this splitting is that the line of ionized calcium at 3950 Å is divided into two components 30 Å apart. The radiation resulting from transitions between these closely spaced levels is not often observed, partly because the wavelengths lie in the microwave region of the spectrum and partly because such transitions are 'forbidden' by the rules of quantum mechanics, i.e. the transition probabilities between such states are very small. In highly ionized atoms the corresponding levels are further apart and the forbidden jumps produce radiation in the normal optical region. Moreover the very low density of the corona favours the emission of such forbidden radiation, for an ion in an excited metastable state is less likely to be jerked out of that state by collision with another particle before it can return to a lower and more stable state by the emission of a 'forbidden' quantum. In 1939 the Swedish spectroscopist Edlén measured the wavelengths of the permitted spectral lines of Fe X, that is of the iron atom stripped of nine of its electrons. These lie in the X-ray region at about 100 Å. The wavelengths so found were used by Grotian at Potsdam to calculate what the wavelength of the forbidden transition between the lowest metastable states should be. He found that it was 6374 Å, that is exactly the wavelength of one of the most prominent coronal lines. The identification of other coronal lines quickly followed. The green line at 5303 Å was shown to come from Fe XIV, that is from iron atoms that have lost thirteen of their electrons, while others came from the highly ionized atoms of calcium and nickel. Not all of the coronal lines are visible all of the time. The red line from Fe X can be seen when the Sun is fairly quiet; the green line from Fe XIV is found at times of moderate activity, while the yellow line from Ca XV only appears when the Sun is at its most active. These variations indicate variations in the temperature of the corona: the fairly quiet corona is at about 2,000,000°K, while some of the coronal condensations may have temperatures of up to 4,000,000°K.

From what has been said above it is clear that the far ultraviolet permitted lines from coronal ions to be observable from above the Earth's atmosphere. The first ultraviolet spectra of the Sun were obtained soon after the end of the Second World War by Tousey of the U.S. Naval Research Laboratory using captured German V2 rockets. Since then many such spectra have been obtained from rockets and satellites and the wavelengths observed stretch down into the X-ray region. At short wavelengths the radiation from the photosphere becomes insignificant; hundreds of lines in the ultraviolet have been identified although some of them have only been observed during flares. The device ZETA, originally built as a controlled hydrogen fusion power source, has been used as a laboratory 'corona' to assist in the identification of the observed lines. By the end of 1970 twenty-one elements have been recognized as being present, several of them in many different stages of ionization.

So far we have been looking at the corona as an essentially static phenomenon, but this is not the whole story. For many years it has been known that the Sun from time to time ejects streams of particles which produce magnetic disturbances when they reach the Earth. These will be discussed later when we come to consider flares. In the 1950s Biermann showed that the data on the orientation of comet tails strongly indicated that something moving radially outwards from the Sun was pushing the tails off course. In 1958 Parker produced a hydrodynamical model of the corona that demonstrated that a corona fitting the existing data on temperature and density must expand unless there is a strong pressure in interplanetary space holding it back. In 1959 the early Russian space probes seemed to show that there was an outflow from the Sun and this was confirmed beyond any doubt in 1962 by the American Venus probe, Mariner II. This outflow, now known as the solar wind, blows continuously out from the Sun with a velocity of about 450 km s^{-1}, but there are considerable fluctuations in it and at times the velocity may be as high as 900 km s^{-1}. Some of these fluctuations appear to be associated with waves travelling out from flares.

The solar wind has a considerable effect on the nature of the magnetic field in the region between the Sun and the Earth. The 'roots' of this magnetic field are in the Sun and are forced to rotate with it. But the rest of the magnetic field cannot follow this rotation because it cannot cross the direction of a moving ionized gas like the solar wind which is moving radially outwards from the Sun. The magnetic field is therefore wound into a spiral, a phenomenon which is sometimes referred to as the 'garden-hose' effect. We shall return to it later when we come to discuss flares. The solar wind cannot cross the magnetic field of the Earth, so that in the neighbourhood of the Earth the solar wind is divided and passes round the protective shell provided by the terrestrial magnetic field. This shell is known as the magnetopause and on the sunward side of the Earth is at a distance of approximately ten Earth radii. The study of the solar wind and of its interactions with the Earth and other members of the solar system has now become a large and very interesting subject in its own right.

Active regions

The sunspot cycle Certain regions of the solar atmosphere exhibit a disturbed behaviour over periods of weeks or even months. The disturbances take a wide variety of forms, including cold areas in the photosphere called sunspots, hot areas in the chromosphere and corona called plages, and dense ribbons of cold material suspended in the corona called quiescent prominences. Violent explosive events, lasting for an hour or so and called flares, are often associated with these disturbances. A disturbed part of the solar surface of this sort is called an active region. An active region may show only one sort of disturbance like a small plage, or it may present examples of all the various kinds of solar activity, but it always has an associated magnetic field. It is for this reason that it is generally assumed that the magnetic field is the basic cause of the active region and that the sunspots, plages and flares are only symptoms.

We cannot predict when or where an active region will occur, nor can we predict exactly when a flare, say, will occur within a known active region. However, when we examine the yearly totals of the active regions observed on the Sun we find that they rise to a maximum once every eleven years, after which they slowly decline. As sunspots are the most easily detectable aspect of solar activity and as sophisticated instrumentation is needed for the systematic observation of flares and prominences, it is not surprising that the cycle of solar activity has come to be called the sunspot cycle, although from our present point of view flare cycle or prominence cycle would be just as appropriate. The existence of sunspots has been known for many centuries, since the largest ones are visible to the naked eye when the Sun is rising or setting through a heavy bank of mist, but they were not seen with any precision until the invention of the telescope at the beginning of the seventeenth century. Regular records of their numbers have been kept since 1749 and it was from an examination of these records that Schwabe in 1843 first detected the rise and fall of solar activity. The extent of this activity is still usually gauged by the Zürich sunspot number which was introduced by Wolf and which is based on the number of individual spots and of groups of spots that are visible. The Zürich Observatory has provided the longest continuous series of observations of sunspot numbers in the world and now serves as the international centre for collating sunspot number data. An alternative measure of sunspot activity that is sometimes used is the fraction of the solar disk actually covered by the spots, a correction for the foreshortening of the spots near the limb being duly applied. It should perhaps be emphasized that the eleven-year length of the cycle deduced from measurements of this sort is only an average, and that the length of the individual cycles has varied from seven to seventeen years. Near a minimum there will be days when no sunspots at all are visible while near maximum there will usually be a dozen or more spots present. The size of the maximum varies considerably from cycle to cycle, and it has been suggested that there may be a long term eighty-year variation superimposed on the eleven-year cycle.

In 1859 Carrington noticed that, at the beginning of a new cycle, sunspots were to be found away from the solar equator, whereas towards the end of the cycle most spots occurred close to it. Carrington's work was greatly extended and systematized by Spörer who formulated general rules about the variation in the position of the spots during the solar cycle. He pointed out that at any time most sunspots are found within two zones at equal distances north and south of the solar equator. The latitude of these zones changes from about 30° at the beginning of the cycle to about 18° at the time of maximum and to 0° at the end of the cycle. This phenomenon is beautifully shown in Figure 7.3, which reproduces the 'Butterfly Diagram' prepared by Maunder of the Greenwich Observatory many years ago. In it the latitudes of the observed sunspots are plotted against the time of their appearance. It will be noticed that there is some overlap between successive cycles at the time of sunspot minima, the last spots of the old cycle appearing at the equator as the first spots of the new cycle form near latitude 30°. The drift of the zone of sunspots towards the equator during the solar cycle is, of course, matched by similar phenomena with flares and prominences.

Measurements to be discussed later suggest that there is a change in the magnetic character of active regions every eleven years. In circumstances in which in one cycle we find the magnetic field directed away from the Sun, in the next cycle we find it directed into the Sun. This suggests that the basic solar cycle may last twenty-two and not eleven years, for only after the longer period do conditions return completely to the starting point. The magnetic field is so fundamental to studies of the solar active regions that the next section will be devoted to discussing the nature of solar magnetic fields and the ways in which they can be measured. The last part of the chapter is devoted to flares which are at present under intensive study; in between we shall look briefly at the nature of sunspots, plages and prominences. A very large body of observational data concerning these has been gathered, but, in the absence of any clear theoretical understanding, it would be merely confusing to set this data out in detail. Indeed, there is by no means complete agreement on all the experimental 'facts', while on the theoretical side there is as yet no satisfactory answer to such fundamental questions as why sunspots occur, why there is a solar cycle, and how flares release such vast amounts of energy. Thus the reader should be warned of the possibility that some of the features that are omitted here may very well in time turn out to be of fundamental importance.

Solar magnetic fields The magnetic field with which we are most familiar is that of the Earth, and the best known way of detecting it is by using a small magnet as a compass needle. It is convenient to picture this field by imagining a map of the region concerned covered with arrowed lines of force, the directions of which at any point indicate the way in which the north end of a compass needle will point if placed there, while their closeness together shows how strong the magnetic field is. The Earth's magnetic field has a strength of about 0.3 gauss;

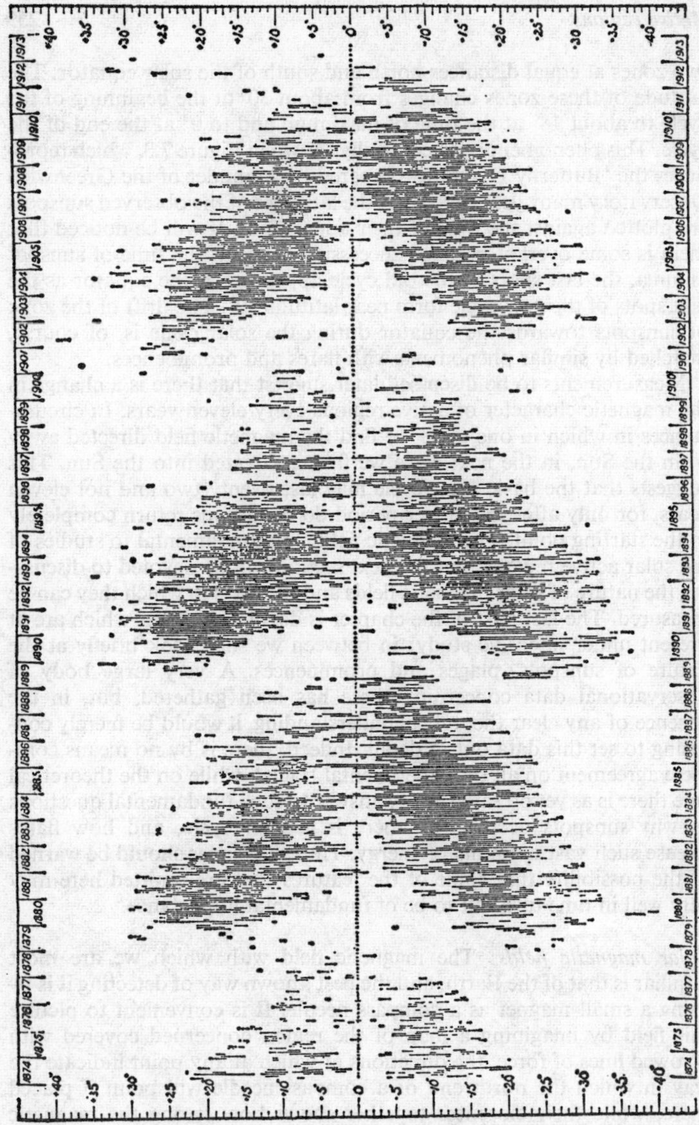

Figure 7.3 Maunder's 'butterfly' diagram

special magnets in a number of laboratories produce fields of the order of 50,000 gauss in volumes a few centimetres across, whilst the biggest field yet produced artificially for any length of time is about 200,000 gauss. The strongest solar fields, found in sunspots, are about 1000 gauss but they sometimes extend over an area ten thousand kilometres or so across. Dynamos, electric motors, and electric magnets have made us familiar with the principal properties of magnetic fields and their interaction with electric currents. When we turn to the Sun, we find that we are no longer dealing with compass needles and copper wire. The Sun is entirely gaseous but, unlike the Earth's atmosphere, most of the gas is ionized, that is, the normally neutral atoms are split up into electrically charged ions and electrons. Such an ionized gas is called a plasma and its properties are so different from those of a neutral gas that some scientists speak of four states of matter, viz. solid, liquid, gas, and plasma. Since moving charged particles constitute an electric current we can expect to find important interactions between the moving plasma and the solar magnetic fields. Charged particles moving along lines of magnetic force experience no opposing or deflecting force, but if they try to move across the magnetic field they experience a force which tends to make them spiral round the lines of force. This is the reason for the striking tendency for the movements of material in certain regions of the solar atmosphere to follow particular curved paths. The plasma is being guided by the local magnetic field. The movement of a magnetic field relative to plasma would tend to generate a voltage. As the conductivity of the plasma is very high, this would produce a very large current, which will in turn produce a magnetic field in such a direction that it reduces the change in magnetic field which started the whole process. The net result of this 'generator' effect is to force the local magnetic field to move with the plasma, and the magnetic field is said to be 'frozen in' to the plasma. Thus we can have a 'motor' effect which forces the solar gases to run along the magnetic field, and a 'generator' effect which forces the magnetic field to move with the gases. In both cases the result is a strong linking of the magnetic field with the plasma; the question is whether the tail wags the dog or the dog wags the tail. Examples of both probably occur on the Sun.

The shape of the structures in the solar atmosphere and the movements of flares and prominences hint at the existence of solar magnetic fields, but for numerical information on the strength of such fields we must make use of the effect of magnetic fields on the lines of the solar spectrum, and in particular of the Zeeman effect (Plate 24*a*). In 1896 the Dutch physicist Zeeman discovered that when a source of light is placed in a magnetic field each of the spectral lines it emits is split up into three components of slightly different wavelengths, the amount of splitting depending on the strength of the field. Moreover this light is polarized. When the light source is viewed from a direction which is at right angles to the direction of the magnetic field, the central Zeeman component is plane polarized in the direction of the magnetic field, while the components on either side are plane polarized in directions perpendicular to the magnetic field. When the light source is viewed along the magnetic field, the middle component disappears altogether and the side components are circularly polarized in opposite senses. Our eyes cannot tell whether light is polarized or not, but there are special materials, such as polaroid, in which a preferred optical direction is built in, that can discriminate and measure the degree of the various kinds of polarization. Thus if a sheet of polaroid is held in a beam of plane-polarized light with its preferred direction at right angles to the plane of polarization, no light will pass through. If now the polaroid is rotated through 90°, the polarized light can pass through it freely. Thus we can measure the extent to which a beam of light is plane-polarized by placing a sheet of polaroid across the beam and rotating it about an axis in the direction of the beam. If, as the polaroid is rotated, the intensity of the light remains constant, the light is not polarized at all, whereas if the beam is completely cut out at some position of the polaroid, then the light is completely plane polarized. Other materials or devices like a Nicol prism can be used in place of the polaroid. To test light that is suspected of being circularly polarized a quarter wave plate is used. This has the property of turning circular polarized light into plane-polarized light, the plane of polarization depending on whether the circularly polarized light rotates clockwise or anticlockwise. The resulting plane-polarized light can be analysed as above.

The first observations of Zeeman splitting in the Sun were made in 1907 by Hale at the Mount Wilson Observatory (Plate 24*a*). These observations were of sunspots in which the magnetic field is fairly large. An image of the Sun was formed and the light from the region of a sunspot was passed through a spectrograph. The Zeeman splitting of suitable spectral lines gave the strength of the magnetic field while its direction was found by analysing the polarization of the Zeeman components by Nicol prisms and quarter wave plates. It should perhaps be emphasized that even now the detailed analysis of the variation of the direction of the magnetic field in different parts of a sunspot presents considerable technical difficulties. An even bigger problem arises when we move from trying to measure the 1000 gauss magnetic fields of the sunspots to the small fields of a few gauss which pepper the solar surface. Individual spectral lines cover a finite range of wavelengths and in small magnetic fields the Zeeman components become blurred together. The apparent result is a single spectral line which is rather broader in wavelength than it would be in the absence of a magnetic field. The only way in this case to separate out the Zeeman components is to make use of their polarization properties. This was done over fifty years ago by Hale and his co-workers at the Mount Wilson Observatory, but the detection of really weak fields only became practicable in the early 1950s when the Babcocks developed the magnetograph at Mount Wilson (Plate 24*b*). This is an instrument for studying the strengths of solar magnetic fields running in the line of sight by using the two circularly polarized side Zeeman components. The principle of its construction is somewhat as follows. Suppose we form the spectrum of a region of the Sun that is free from magnetic fields and position two photocells, one on either side of the position of a selected spectral line. Each photocell produces a voltage which depends on the amount of light falling on them and it is possible to arrange for their difference in voltage to be recorded. Suppose now we move to a region of the Sun in which there is a magnetic field and we let into the spectrograph the light from either the left or the right hand Zeeman component. As we change from one to the other, the broad spectral line will move slightly from one photocell to the other. If the magnetic field is small this will alter the voltage difference slightly, but if the magnetic field is large, jumping from one component to the other will put the spectral line first on one cell and then on the other and the difference in voltage between the two cells will change sign. Thus if we place a quarter wave plate and a rotating piece of polaroid in the solar beam we shall get an alternating voltage from the two cells, the amplitude of which is directly related to the strength of the solar magnetic field (Plate 24*b*). In practice the quarter wave plate and the spinning polaroid are replaced by an electrical device called a Kerr cell and a fixed piece of polaroid.

The magnetograph can detect very weak fields but it can only look at one area of the Sun at a time. To enable the whole surface of the Sun to be surveyed quickly, albeit with less sensitivity to weak fields, Leighton in 1959 produced the magnetoheliograph. This is a modification of the spectroheliograph, which, it will be remembered, is an instrument for making a photograph of the whole of the solar surface in the light of just one wavelength. In the magnetoheliograph the wavelength chosen is just to one side of the magnetically sensitive line. Two beams of light are fed into the apparatus, one beam containing only the light with the polarization of the left Zeeman component and the other only light with the polarization of the right component. If separate photographs of the Sun were to be taken with the two beams, parts of the Sun at which there were no magnetic fields would look the same on both photographs but parts of the Sun where there are strong magnetic fields will look bright on the one photograph and dark on the other, for one Zeeman component will be shifted right onto the wavelength chosen for the spectroheliograph and the other right off it. In practice the two separate photographs are not taken; they are, as it were, differenced and only their difference recorded to give a magnetic map of the Sun on which the magnetic fields stand out from the neutral background.

If we could investigate the Earth from the outside using the kind of apparatus described above, we would easily discover the overall field running from north to south and some of the local distortions. No such overall field is visible on the magnetic maps of the Sun. The most conspicuous features are those associated with active regions in which the magnetic field appears to loop out from the surface. Where there are sunspots occurring in pairs, the field heads out from the Sun in one spot and back again in the other. Cases of this sort are called bipolar magnetic regions. Dotted all over the solar surface there are also weak unipolar magnetic regions whose polarity, north or south, seems to vary in an irregular fashion. Near each geographical pole, however, there is a tendency for magnetic fields of one kind to predominate, the polarities being different in the two hemispheres. Near the equator there appears to be no general pattern in the polarity of these weak fields. It would seem then that one can talk about a general solar magnetic field but it is only of the order of one gauss and results from the combination of a large number of weak, irregular fields with different polarities. At present it rather looks as if the general field decreases to zero at sunspot minimum and changes sign with the new sunspot cycle. Thus, if in one cycle the fields in the northern hemisphere tend to be directed outwards from the Sun they will in the following cycle tend to be directed into the Sun. The effect is not very clear cut, and the two hemispheres seem to switch polarity at rather different times. Much clearer evidence for the change in magnetic character at the end of each sunspot cycle comes from examining the polarities of the bipolar magnetic regions, which are usually coincident with sunspot pairs. During a given sunspot cycle it is found that the polarity associated with the leading spot of a pair is always the same within the same hemisphere but that this polarity is different for the two hemispheres. At the beginning of the next cycle the polarities are interchanged. Incidentally it is observed that the preceding of the two poles (or spots) of a pair is usually slightly nearer the equator than is the following one.

In an attempt to explain some of these phenomena, Babcock has put forward a theory in which he supposes that at the beginning of a cycle the Sun has a general magnetic field running north–south in a thin layer beneath the solar surface. This field will be 'frozen in' to the ionized solar material and, owing to the differential rotation of the solar surface layers, will gradually become twisted. In the zone where the differential rotation is greatest, the lines of magnetic force will eventually become very close together and nearly parallel to the equator. Such a strong field will be unstable, and from time to time loops will break through the surface and manifest themselves as bipolar active regions. Towards the end of the cycle the loops are supposed to break up and the fragments drift towards the poles where they rebuild the general field. Although Babcock's theory explains many of the observed features fairly well, it has still to be worked out quantitatively.

Sunspots, plages and prominences In view of the long history of sunspot investigations it comes as something of a surprise to realize that it is only within the present century that their physical nature has begun to be understood. The observation by Alexander Wilson that as a sunspot goes round the apparent edge of the Sun the near side almost disappears while the far side is enlarged, proved very misleading. It appeared that the sunspots must be pits in the solar surface and that in a sunspot one could look through the hot surface layer of the Sun into the cold and perhaps solid interior. The investigations of Kirchoff showed, however, that both the photospheric and the sunspot spectra were those of a hot gas, while Lockyer noticed that there were many more lines present in the sunspot spectrum. The key development was the electric furnace built by King at the Mount Wilson Observatory which could heat various elements up to about 3000°C. It was possible with this furnace to observe the changes in atomic and molecular spectra as the temperature was raised, and hence to show that a sunspot had a lower temperature spectrum than did the ordinary photosphere. We have already seen how Hale at the same observatory had used the Zeeman effect to demonstrate the strong magnetic fields present in the neighbourhood of sunspots. No dramatic developments have been made recently in our understanding of sunspots, but there has been steady progress both in the detailed study of the spectrum and in the observation of the fine structure of the spots. The investigation of sunspot spectra presents considerable difficulties, partly because both atoms and molecules with their more complex spectra are involved, and partly because the unsteadiness of our own atmosphere pollutes the light from a sunspot with some of the much brighter light from the photosphere. Sunspot spectra have helped with some of the more difficult problems of determining the presence and abundance of certain elements in the solar atmosphere. This is especially the case when the lines of an atom in the photospheric spectrum are blended with those of other atoms. In the sunspot spectrum the lines may be free from these blends or the corresponding molecular spectrum may be seen. To secure the best spectra for such studies and also for studies of the fine structure of sunspots it is necessary to select very carefully the best possible sites for solar telescopes and to use only those photographs that have been obtained during the relatively rare moments of very good seeing.

Spots occur in a great variety of forms with diameters ranging from over 50,000 km down to the smallest we can detect. They usually have a central dark region called the umbra surrounded by a less dark zone called the penumbra. The umbra seems to be about 1600° Centigrade cooler than the photosphere and the penumbra about 500° cooler. The magnetic field is strongest in the core of the umbra where it runs vertically; it is much weaker in the penumbra where it tends to be horizontal. Spot fields are usually less than 3000 gauss, although a field of 4300 gauss has been observed. The material of sunspots appears to be flowing outwards from the umbra to the penumbra with velocities of a few kilometres per second (the Evershed effect), and there is some evidence for a corresponding inflow occurring in the layers above. The umbra shows granulation, but the granules are both smaller and longer lived than those of the photosphere. Long bright filaments are found in the penumbra stretching radially out from the umbral boundary and having the same sort of lifetime as the umbral granules.

Sunspots tend to occur in groups. The most usual form is a pair with opposite magnetic polarity, the preceding spot lying rather closer to the solar equator (Plate 21*c*). Such pairs are often accompanied by a number of smaller spots, but sometimes there are very complex groups which do not fit into any pattern. An active region first shows up as a disturbance in the magnetic field. Plages appear where the magnetic field is strongest, and then pores, which are very small sunspots with magnetic fields of 100 gauss or so. If larger magnetic fields grow in the active region, a single sunspot and then a pair of sunspots may appear, while in big groups subsidiary pores and spots will develop. Finally the spots decrease in size, leaving the magnetic field to disappear last of all, the whole process having taken a month or so.

Most theories of the formation of sunspots follow the suggestion put forward by Biermann in 1941 that the strong magnetic fields of an active region suppress the convective currents in the layers below the photosphere that carry the energy flow from the interior. If these convective motions are inhibited at any place, one would expect to find a cool region on the surface. The vertical umbral field will not affect the vertical movements of the partially ionized gas in the hot and cold streams of the convective system, but it will inhibit the horizontal flows that almost inevitably accompany the vertical motions, and lead to the formation of a sunspot. In Biermann's original theory, the convection was supposed to be halted altogether, but this cannot be correct, for umbral granulation can be observed. However, a partial suppression of the convection would be sufficient to explain sunspot temperatures and would be consistent with the different sort of granules observed in sunspots. The penumbral filaments can also be interpreted as convection in the presence of a horizontal magnetic field, the convection currents effectively circulating around the magnetic lines of force.

We now turn from cold spots in the solar atmosphere to hot ones. In the vicinity of active regions there often occur areas with a higher temperature and density than the surrounding atmosphere. These areas extend right through from the upper photosphere to the corona. We shall refer to them as plages, although strictly speaking this term should be reserved for their chromospheric manifestation. If one looks at an ordinary photograph of the Sun, e.g. Plate 21*a*, one can often see a number of bright areas near the limb, clustered round active regions. These are called faculae and lie in the upper photosphere. They were first described by Hevelius of Danzig in the seventeenth century. Their temperature would seem to be at most a few hundred degrees higher than the surrounding atmosphere, while their strengthening towards the limb indicates that they lie rather higher than the general level of the photosphere.

These bright spots are much more easily observed if we look at the chromosphere proper as photographed by a spectroheliograph in the light of the hydrogen alpha line or in that of the calcium K line. The bright features there depicted are called chromospheric faculae or plages, and are seen surrounded by the bright mottling of the chromospheric network, which, as we have seen, is probably connected with very weak photospheric magnetic fields. As we move upwards in the solar atmosphere, we find similar structures at each level. Thus there are Lyman alpha plages shown in pictures taken in the radiation of this line of hydrogen, radio plages, and X-ray plages. The radio plages are observed at wavelengths of about 20 cm, while the X-ray plages can be observed in the 'soft' X-ray region with wavelengths of around 10 Å, the radio and X-rays presumably originating from features in the corona. Indeed, we can often observe an enhancement of the normal corona over an active region, and coronal condensations show up on white light photographs taken during an eclipse. In this latter case we are dealing with photospheric light scattered by electrons in the corona so that the increased brightness indicates an increased density of electrons. Such coronal condensations also emit the famous yellow line of Ca XV which does not appear in the spectrum of the normal corona and which shows that the temperature in the coronal condensation is much higher.

The various 'plage' features match closely in position and shape, but become steadily more conspicuous as we move outwards. Thus faculae are a minor feature of the photosphere, visible in white light only near the limb of the Sun, whereas the coronal structures associated with solar activity dominate the corona. Indeed, as has already been mentioned, some astronomers have gone so far as to suggest that the whole of the corona is associated with solar activity. Plages seem to occur where there is a small disturbance in the photospheric magnetic field, but it is still not clear why a small disturbance in the magnetic field appears to cause heating in the upper parts of the solar atmosphere, while a large magnetic field causes cooling in the lower parts of the solar atmosphere.

Prominences are masses of material of roughly chromospheric temperature and density suspended in the corona, which is, of course, at a much higher temperature and a much lower density. They are not bright enough to be seen in white light on the disk of the Sun so that most of the early observations refer to prominences standing up above the edge of the Sun during an eclipse. Prominences seem to have been noticed at total eclipses during the Middle Ages, but modern records start with the eclipse of 1842. At first they were thought to be mountains, but by 1851 it was realized that they could only be 'clouds', and in 1868 when the first spectra were observed it was realized that the prominences must be clouds of hot gas. Prominences are quite bright at the wavelengths of certain emission lines and it is possible to see them at the edge of the Sun without waiting for an eclipse by using a fairly high dispersion spectrograph and opening the slit up wide. The spectroheliograph makes it possible to observe prominences on the disk of the Sun, but here they appear dark against the chromospheric background and are often referred to as 'filaments'.

It is convenient to divide prominences into two classes, active and quiescent. Quiescent prominences may endure for weeks or months but active ones last for only an hour or so. It is, however, possible for a quiescent prominence to become activated. Active prominences are generally associated with the explosive events called flares. In spray and surge prominences material is sent outwards from the site of the flare but in coronal rain and loop prominences we seem to be seeing material ejected during a flare falling back to the surface. In these latter types the prominences probably become visible as the falling material cools to the stage where it radiates most efficiently. Active prominences will be discussed in more detail when we come to consider flares.

The quiescent prominences include ordinary filaments and sunspot filaments. On a hydrogen alpha spectroheliogram of the solar disk (Plate 23*b*) the ordinary filaments appear as long dark worm-like structures that are long lived and retain the details of their structure for long periods. The sunspot filaments either curl out from sunspots or lie between a pair of sunspots. They too are long lived but the details of their structure change quite rapidly. Seen in profile on the limb they often give the impression that material is streaming down them into the sunspot. It sometimes happens that a quiescent prominence becomes unstable, perhaps because of a nearby flare. The result is an ascending prominence (Plate 26), a great arch of material that appears to be being blown off from the Sun at a velocity of a few hundred kilometres per second. Two crucial questions arise in connection with the long life of quiescent prominences: how do they manage to stay at constant temperature when surrounded by the much hotter and less dense corona, and what stops them from falling back to the solar surface under their own weight? All spectra of prominences show lines of neutral hydrogen and helium and of ionized calcium, but whereas for active prominences the lines of the ionized metals are weak and a line of ionized helium strong, for quiescent prominences the lines of the ionized metals are strong and the line of ionized helium very weak. Since it requires a much higher temperature to ionize helium than it does to ionize the metals it would seem that active prominences consist mainly of gas at a temperature of 30,000°K with a small admixture of material at a lower temperature of about 10,000°K, while in quiescent prominences the 10,000°K gas predominates. The quiescent prominences can only maintain this temperature for many weeks if the heat input from above and below balances the loss of energy by radiation from the prominence. Most of this energy loss will be through the emission lines of neutral hydrogen and, within limits, the higher the temperature the greater the proportion of the hydrogen atoms in excited states capable of emitting radiation. On the other hand, at temperatures much greater than 10,000°K most of the hydrogen will become ionized and cannot absorb or emit radiation very efficiently. Thus there is a range of temperatures around 10,000°K for which cooling by radiation is efficient and can balance the energy input; outside this range the prominence will heat up rapidly.

The crucial observation relevant to the support problem is that prominences always run along the line of zero magnetic field in the line of sight. On one side of the prominence the field is directed into the Sun, and on the other side out of the Sun. Thus the field is perpendicular to the prominence filament and transverse to the line of sight. If the prominence starts to fall back to the solar surface it will move across the magnetic field and set up forces opposing the motion. Recent observations suggest that this picture may be oversimplified and that electric currents in the prominence may generate internal fields which will, in turn, produce the spiral structure noticed in some prominences.

Flares

Flares are explosive events in the chromosphere or lower corona in which large amounts of energy are released in a small volume over a short period of time. The wide variety in the types of flares and their large range in intensity make it difficult to generalize, but a big flare may involve as much energy as ten thousand million one-megaton hydrogen bombs. Most of the energy appears to be released in a matter of five or ten minutes, although the flare may not completely die away for an hour or so (Plate 27). The heated gas in such a flare appears to occupy a volume of up to 50,000 km in diameter, but there is some evidence that much of the energy release takes place in smaller regions only 1000 km or so across. Flares are always associated with active solar areas and usually occur in the vicinity of a complex sunspot group; flare numbers therefore closely follow the sunspot cycle. The energy released appears in many forms ranging from radio and microwave bursts to visible and X-ray radiation, and often including streams of high energy particles. Particles coming directly or indirectly from solar flares can produce magnetic storms and short-wave radio fadeouts on the Earth. Thus, although the seat of a flare may be a tiny region in the solar atmosphere, the echoes of a major flare eruption reverberate round the whole of the inner solar system.

Optical flares The first flare to be discovered was observed visually by Carrington in 1859. Only the very largest flares are detectable visually or on photographs covering a wide range of colour. Such flares are sometimes called white light flares. Most flares, however, emit light strongly only at the wavelength of certain lines and therefore are not noticeably brighter than the surrounding photosphere on photographs taken in white light. If the Sun is observed at the wavelength of a suitable absorption line, however, a flare stands boldly out above the surrounding atmosphere since it is emitting light at that particular wavelength, while neighbouring regions are only emitting a normal continuum minus the effect of the absorption line. Until fairly recently, most direct observations of flares were made in red light of hydrogen alpha which is normally used to observe the chromosphere and which also turns out to be the line most strongly emitted by flares. Hot spots in the chromosphere like the plages also look bright on the hydrogen alpha photographs, but the flares can be quite easily distinguished by their rapid variations in brightness and shape. The unpredictability and short life of flares make it easy to miss an important event, and in order to prevent this as much as possible continuous records of the Sun's appearance in the light of hydrogen alpha are made at a number of observatories distributed round the world. Normally special flare patrol cameras equipped with Lyot-type filters which let through only the central light of the hydrogen alpha absorption lines are used (Plate 23*a*).

One of the biggest mysteries of solar physics is the reason for the sudden release of such large quantities of energy in flares. One of the most promising methods of attacking this problem observationally is to study the conditions at the point where a flare occurs, just before the start of the flare. The first signs of a flare are often the brightening of small structures in a plage, while quite a number of flares start from an indentation in the umbra of a sunspot. Perhaps the most significant results obtained so far are those of Severny and his co-workers in Russia who compared the sites of flares with magnetic maps of the Sun. Flares seem to occur in between regions of opposite magnetic polarity, that is on the neutral line between a zone in which the magnetic field comes out of the Sun and a zone in which the magnetic field goes into the Sun. The greater the gradient of the magnetic field, the larger the resulting flare. After the flare, the gradient seems to be reduced, but sometimes it gradually builds back to its initial level. This picture fits in with the occurrence of flares near umbral indentations, for the latter tend to form where a region of opposite polarity comes near a sunspot, and also with the association of flares with complex sunspot groups since these provide just the right conditions of fairly steep gradients in the local magnetic fields.

The hydrogen alpha photographs have revealed the great variety of ways in which flares develop. Some flares have what is termed a 'flash phase' in which the brightness and area of the flare increase very rapidly. Others appear to eject material out from the Sun in what is called an 'explosive phase'. Others again show no motion but just brighten on the spot and are termed 'in situ' flares. The flares that move rapidly out from an indentation in the umbra of a sunspot are termed 'sunspot flashes'. In some cases a surface wave has been observed moving out from the flare at 1000 km s^{-1} and producing a ripple in the chromosphere far from the site of the flare. It seems that a flare can trigger off the occurrence of other flares, and on occasions flares seem to have ejected nearby quiescent prominences from the Sun. Perhaps the most difficult observation to explain theoretically is the fact that flares can recur in the same place and nearly in the same form. Small surge flares (Plate 25*b*) can take place from the same point ten times in one day, and even large flares may be repeated a day later. It is possible to imagine that certain arrangements of magnetic fields are unstable and tend to collapse converting magnetic energy into other forms, but it is difficult to visualize the magnetic fields snapping back again after the catastrophe.

Information on the expulsion of material during the explosive phase can best be obtained from flares on the limb of the Sun which we see side-on. Most of these are described as active prominences, although they are quite different in cause from the quiescent and sunspot prominences considered earlier. Large flares often seem to produce a rising ball which breaks up into a spray prominence of small separate clouds of radiating gas moving out in some directions with a velocity of about 1000 km s^{-1}. Very small flares often send out surge prominences which are less broken up and travel more slowly at 100 km s^{-1}. Surges are often repeated at something like hourly intervals, moving out in the same direction. Surges sometimes return to their starting point, sometimes break up, and sometimes return to another point on the solar surface, presumably following the local magnetic field.

After a major flare eruption material is frequently seen falling back to the solar surface in the form of a 'loop' prominence, that is along two oppositely curved pathways, or as 'coronal rain'. This material gives the impression that it appears from nowhere in the corona; presumably it is gas that has previously been ejected into the corona at a temperature above which hydrogen alpha cannot easily be seen because most of the hydrogen atoms will have been ionized; the flare material reappears as it cools on the way back into the solar atmosphere. Thus a surge or spray is material of chromospheric density moving up through the more tenuous corona and just about to become too hot to be seen in visible radiation, while a loop prominence (Plate 25*a*) is the dense material falling back through the corona having just cooled enough to be seen. If this picture is correct, one would expect to be able to detect clouds of relatively dense material at a high temperature in the corona immediately after a violent flare. Such coronal clouds or condensations are actually observed with temperatures considerably higher than those of the quiet corona and possibly reaching up to 4,000,000°K

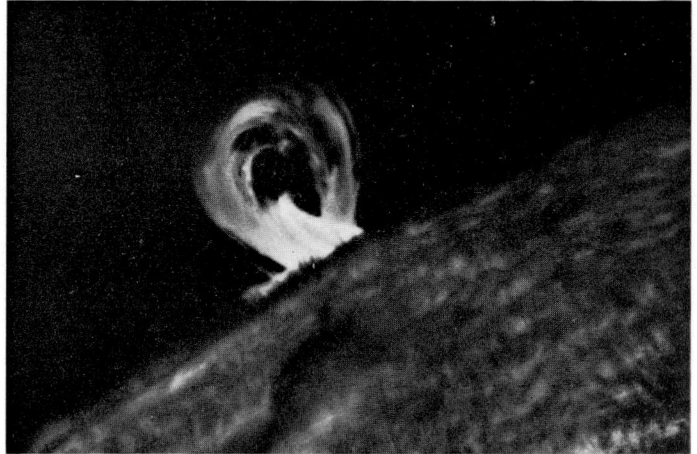

Plate 25 The Sun in action. *a* An eruptive loop photographed at the Big Bear Solar Observatory on 3 August 1970

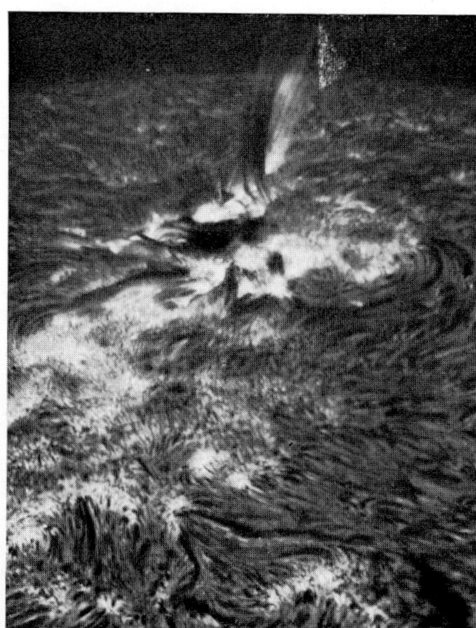

b A surge flare photographed at the Big Bear Solar Observatory on 22 May 1970.
Hale Observatories

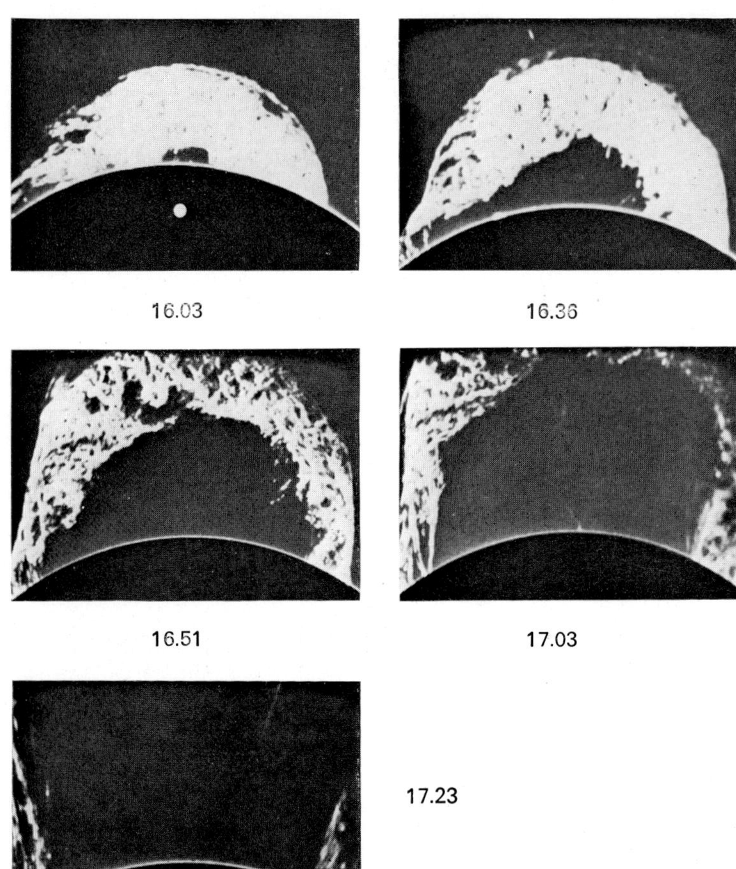

Plate 26 The giant eruptive prominence of 4 June 1946 as photographed in Hα at the High Altitude Observatory, Climax, Colorado, U.S.A. The scale of this violent phenomenon, the largest eruptive prominence yet observed, can be gauged from the white dot which indicates the size of the Earth. Motion pictures showed that the column on the left was in rapid rotation

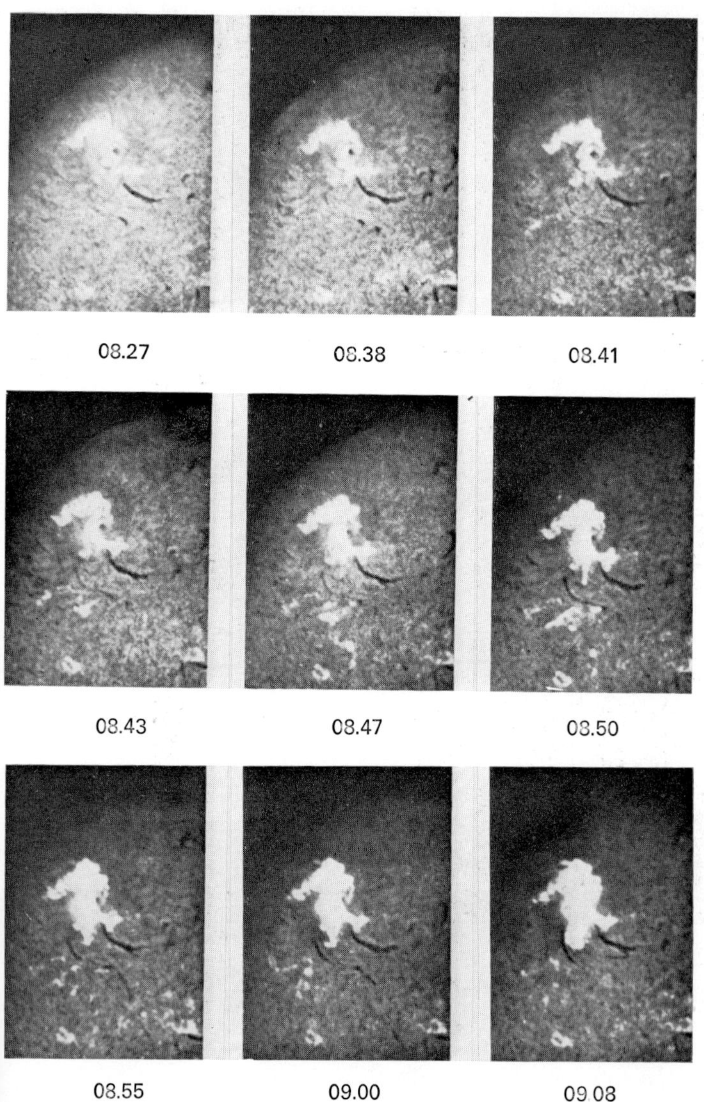

Plate 27 The development of the bright flare of 1 June 1960 as recorded on photographs taken with the Lyot Hα heliograph of the Cape Observatory

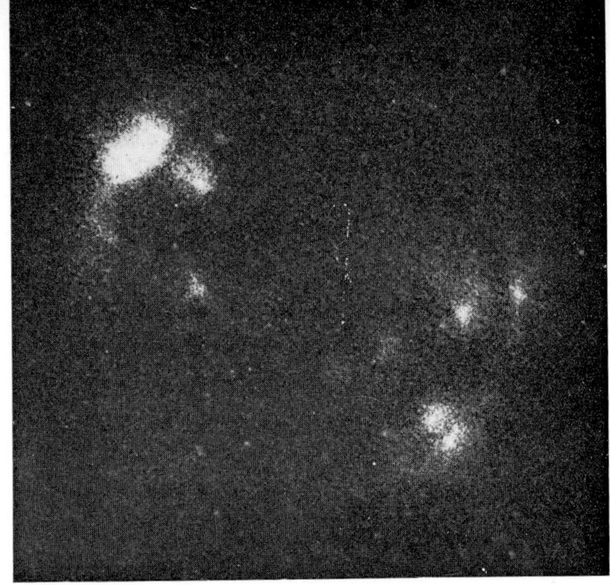

Plate 28 The X-ray Sun. *a* Pinhole camera X-ray photograph taken during a rocket flight, 27 November 1969. Astrophysics Research Unit, Culham Laboratory. *b*, below, Ca II K spectroheliogram taken about ten hours before this flight at the McMath-Hulbert Observatory, University of Michigan

or more. A coronal cloud of this nature will radiate in much the same sort of way as the ordinary corona, producing forbidden lines in the visible region of the spectrum and normal lines in the far ultraviolet, and scattering photospheric continuous light. The intensity of the scattered light is greater than that from the normal corona showing that the cloud is denser than the surrounding medium, while the presence of the yellow forbidden line of calcium XV shows that the temperature is higher.

Space research has made possible dramatic advances in the study of flare phenomena. One such advance was the elucidation of the connection between the flare as seen in hydrogen alpha and the coronal cloud. The United States Naval Research Laboratory recently flew a rocket above the Earth's atmosphere to obtain ultraviolet spectra of the Sun shortly after a flare had passed through its phase of maximum activity. The spectrograph had no entrance slit, and in the resulting spectra each 'line' was a picture of the solar disk. The 'line-disks' tended to overlap but the bright 'lines' in this region of the spectrum are sufficiently far apart for the images to be disentangled. Thus a series of maps of the Sun was obtained, each map being taken in the light of a different ion or atom, and since each ion only exists over a characteristic temperature range the various maps were really maps of the Sun made at different temperatures. The helium images showed those parts of the Sun that were at a temperature of a few ten thousands of degrees, while the iron XVI images showed what the Sun looked like at a temperature of a couple of million degrees. The spectra actually obtained on this particular flight showed a large excited area at low temperatures, a large coronal cloud at high temperatures, and a very bright nucleus which appeared at all temperatures. Clearly more results like these, obtained right through the period of the development of a flare, would enable us to link together the many isolated pieces of information about flares that have so far been collected.

Flares at X-ray and radio wavelengths Another field of flare studies which the availability of rockets and space platforms for observations has opened up is that in the X-ray region (Plate 28). The emission of X-rays during flares has long been inferred from the correlation between disturbances in the Earth's ionosphere and solar flares. The ionosphere is that region of the Earth's atmosphere which stretches from about 80 km to 500 km above the surface and which is partially ionized by solar radiation. The free electrons resulting from this ionization have a considerable effect on short-wave radio signals. At the bottom of the ionosphere lies the D-layer, 60 km to 70 km above the Earth's surface.

Energetic X-rays can penetrate through to this layer and knock further electrons off the atoms and ions, thus increasing the density of the electrons in the D-layer. This causes increased absorption of short-wave radio signals, i.e. those of about 20 MHz, which are usually reflected from the D-layer, and so produces short-wave fade-outs. Rather paradoxically, the enhanced D-layer also acts as a more efficient reflector of the radio noise produced by tropical thunderstorms, a phenomenon known as the sudden enhancement of atmospherics. Most useful of all for the solar physicist is the increased absorption of the radio signals coming from sources outside the solar system. This is referred to as a sudden cosmic noise absorption and provides a convenient method of detecting the occurrence of a major flare, but not, of course, of studying the details of the X-rays produced. For this we are dependent on observations made above the atmosphere. X-rays from a solar active region were detected for the first time by a rocket flight in 1958, but because it is difficult to arrange a rocket flight to coincide with a flare, the X-ray study of flares really started with the satellite experiment of 1962, which, from its orbit round the Earth, could monitor the solar X-ray flux continuously.

There is no qualitative difference between X-rays and light and so the boundary between X-rays and extreme ultraviolet radiation is somewhat vague, depending to some extent on the technique being used to detect the radiation. Generally speaking, radiation with a wavelength shorter than 1 Å is referred to as 'hard X-rays' because such X-rays are very energetic and can penetrate through a considerable thickness of solid material. 'Soft X-rays' cover the region from 1 Å to 20 Å, although radiation with wavelengths up to 60 Å or so is sometimes included in this category. At these very short wavelengths, the use of reflecting mirrors to form images and of reflecting gratings to form spectra is not possible—the X-rays are just not reflected. The identifications of the positions of X-ray sources can only be made by building apparatus which is so designed that only X-rays from a particular direction can enter the detector and then swinging this apparatus in different directions until the source is located. Spectra can be formed by scattering the X-rays inside a suitable crystal, since the direction of scattering depends on the wavelength. Ionization chambers, proportional and Geiger counters, and scintillation counters are used to detect X-rays. The first three make use of the ionization produced by the X-rays in a gas, whereas the fourth counts the flashes of light produced when X-rays pass through certain materials.

The quiet Sun emits soft X-rays while the plages and coronal condensations associated with solar active regions increase the flux, especially at the shorter wavelengths. During a flare two distinct X-ray phenomena occur: a sharp burst of hard X-rays, and a more gradual rise and decline of soft X-rays. The soft X-ray spectrum is that of a continuum with emission lines superimposed upon it, the continuum being approximately what one would expect to see from a hot gas at a temperature of from 20,000,000°K to 30,000,000°K. The emission lines with wavelengths of a few angstroms come from heavy atoms that have been stripped of nearly all their electrons. For example, a line near 1.9 Å has been identified as coming from Fe XXV, that is from iron atoms that have lost all but two of their electrons. The presence of such highly ionized atoms is another indication that the temperature of the gas is of the order of 20,000,000°K. It is interesting to note that the intensity of the less highly ionized Fe XVIII reaches a maximum after that of Fe XXV, suggesting that the initial heating of the gas is almost instantaneous, and that we see the line emission of the gas as it is cooling down with more and more of the electrons recombining with the atomic ions. No lines are observed in the hard X-ray region, and we would not expect them to be, for under hard X-ray conditions all atoms are completely ionized with no circling electrons left to emit or absorb radiation.

The intensity of the bursts of the hard X-ray continuum radiation is such that if it is thermal radiation from a hot gas, that gas must be at a temperature of hundreds of millions of degrees. It therefore seems likely that it has its origin in a 'non-thermal mechanism'. One such mechanism that has been widely suggested to explain the hard X-ray bursts is a stream of high energy electrons being slowed down by collisions with other particles, their energy of motion being thus partially converted into radiation. The intensity and peak wavelength of this sort of radiation are not connected with the temperature of the gas, but with the velocity of the stream of particles and their total number. Radiation produced in this way is sometimes called 'non-thermal bremstrahlung'; bremstrahlung means 'braking radiation' and describes the process by which the radiation is released. The view that the hard X-rays are produced by the retardation of streams of fast particles is supported by the observation that hard X-ray bursts are linearly polarized, that is, that the X-ray waves from a particular flare appear to vibrate in one plane. If the particles producing the radiation were moving at random, as they would be in a hot gas, there would be no reason for one particular plane of vibration to be specially favoured.

The presence of high energy particle streams also seems to be required by observations of the Sun made at microwave wavelengths of between 3 cm and 10 cm, that is in the wavelength range used for radar. Flares produce bursts of microwaves which start simultaneously with the bursts of hard X-rays and which follow fairly closely the rapid rises and falls of the hard X-ray intensity. It is not easy to imagine how a hot gas could simultaneously produce strong bursts of radiation at both very long and very short wavelengths. One possible way in which the stream of particles invoked to explain the hard X-rays could also produce the microwave bursts is by 'synchrotron radiation' which is produced when electrons spiral round the direction of a magnetic field. Such radiation should be circularly polarized, a condition which the observed microwave bursts often seem to obey.

It may be that the streams of high energy electrons, which produce hard X-rays as they are deflected by collisions with other particles and microwaves as they spiral round the local magnetic field, are also responsible in some way for heating up the coronal cloud. The variation in the intensity of the radiation in the emission lines from the hot cloud does not correlate well with that of the microwave bursts; the rise to maximum intensity of the ultraviolet lines from the hot cloud is very much slower than that for the X-rays and the microwave bursts. However, the 'hot cloud emission' at any time does follow rather well the total amount of microwave energy that has been released up to that time. This would be reasonable if the particle streams whose existence is detected by the microwave bursts gradually heated up the coronal cloud, but it must be emphasized that at the moment any such connection is largely speculative.

The first radio observations of flares were made at wavelengths of about one metre. The story is well known of how Hey in England was investigating interference with the radar Early Warning System during the Second World War and noticed that the disturbances were correlated with the position of the Sun. In 1950 an Australian team succeeded in distinguishing between a number of different types of metre radio bursts. These are now classified as Types I to V, of which only Type I does not appear to be directly connected with flares. Bursts of Types IV and V cover a wide range of wavelengths, the short-wave part of Type IV being the microwave emission associated with the hard X-rays that was previously mentioned. On the other hand, radiation from the bursts of Type II and III cover only a narrow range of wavelengths at a given time. The Australians observed Types II and III bursts on a radio receiver which could be tuned very rapidly through a whole range of wavelengths and thus give a radio spectrum of the flare at closely spaced intervals. These radio spectra showed that although at any particular time the radiation from the bursts was confined to a relatively narrow band of wavelengths, this band moved steadily in the direction of increasing wavelength, that is, that the frequency drifted steadily downwards. In Type III bursts this drift is perhaps ten times as rapid as for Type II. It will be recalled that in the section on the corona it was pointed out that the solar atmosphere is more transparent to short radio wavelengths than to long. Consequently if some source of radio signals moves outwards from the Sun, we will at first receive only the shorter wavelengths since these are the only ones that can get out from the bottom of the solar atmosphere; gradually as the source rises higher in the solar atmosphere the longer radio wavelengths will be received. If this is the correct explanation of the behaviour of the bursts of Type II and III, then the sources of the Type II bursts move out from the Sun with a velocity of the order of 1000 km s^{-1}, while those for Type III move out with velocities of the order of 10,000 km s^{-1}. Sometimes a Type III burst starts to drift back upwards in frequency, and one must presume that in an 'inverted U burst' of this kind the source has turned back towards the Sun. Confirmation of this general picture of radio bursts was difficult because at these long wavelengths an enormous radio dish would be required to pinpoint the source of the radio signals with sufficient accuracy. In 1963, however, Wild circumvented this difficulty by using an aerial array arranged as an interferometer and was able to show that the sources of Type III bursts were indeed moving rapidly outwards.

Bursts of Types II and III cannot be attributed to synchrotron radiation like those in the microwave region since this mechanism produces radio signals over a broad wavelength band. A possible clue to the mechanism involved in Type II bursts may be contained in the observed fact that in such bursts a radio signal is often found at a frequency exactly twice that of the main frequency. This phenomenon must be closely analogous to that of harmonics on a musical instrument. The picture here is of a stream of particles (Type III) or a shock wave (Type II) setting the corona into oscillation at its local natural frequency, and of these 'plasma' oscillations in turn producing radio waves. The local natural frequency falls as one moves outwards to less dense parts of the corona accounting for the observed frequency drift. Bursts of Types IV and V could well be due to synchrotron radiation.

Type III bursts are the most common of all, and several brief bursts of this kind often occur right at the beginning of a flare and are followed by a Type V broad band outburst. If the flare is a very big one, a Type II burst may then occur, followed by a broad band Type IV burst which may last for a matter of hours. The Type IV burst starts at microwave wavelengths at the same time as the hard X-ray outburst, and then spreads to longer wavelengths where its rise is less impulsive. Sometimes the source of Type IV bursts also seem to move with a velocity of the order of 1000 km s^{-1}. Thus the requirements for a large flare seem to be very extensive and include an initial production of a stream of very high velocity electrons, some of which spiral in a magnetic field, followed by a second burst of high energy particles some of which are trapped in a magnetic field for a matter of hours, and a shock wave.

Particles and flares The hard X-rays and radio bursts produced by flares seem to require the acceleration of large numbers of particles to high energies. It would seem likely that some at least of these particles escape from the Sun altogether and reach the vicinity of the Earth. Now it has been known for some time that energetic cosmic ray particles can penetrate far down into our atmosphere, knocking off secondary particles in collisions with the atoms of the atmosphere. These secondary particles can be detected at ground level. It turns out that only very rarely does a solar flare produce energetic enough particles to give a ground level effect on Earth, and that most of these energetic cosmic rays come from outside the solar system altogether. Thus it was not until 1942 that Forbush detected an increase in the flux of cosmic ray secondaries at ground level that could clearly be associated with a large flare. These ground level events seem to occur at an average rate of less than one per year.

Less energetic particles from the Sun can cause increased ionization of the Earth's ionosphere in much the same way that hard X-rays can increase the electron density in the D-layer. This increase of ionization can be detected because of the corresponding increase in the absorption of radio signals. The particles from the Sun are charged and are therefore constrained to move along magnetic fields rather than across them. The Earth's magnetic field thus protects the greater part of the ionosphere, but near the poles, where the lines of the magnetic field plunge towards the surface, there are holes through which the solar particles can bombard the ionosphere. The resulting polar cap absorption of radio signals was detected in the late 1940s by using a balloon to carry a radio transmitter above the ionosphere. More recently an instrument called a riometer has been used for this purpose by monitoring the strength of the radio noise coming from outside the solar system. Cosmic noise absorption due to particles can be distinguished from cosmic noise absorption due to X-rays by the fact that the latter affects the whole of the ionosphere on the sunlit side of the Earth, whereas the former affects only the polar regions, both in and out of sunlight. Polar cap absorptions occur with a readily detectable strength about seven times a year on the average, but their frequency tends to follow the sunspot cycle, since such events seem to be associated with flares. Observations of polar cap absorption give no information about the nature of the particles, the direction from which they are coming, or their speed. All such information has come from instruments carried above the atmosphere by balloons and satellites. These have made possible the separation of hydrogen and helium nuclei among the incoming particles, and have demonstrated the existence of electron streams and of very large fluxes of low energy particles. The total number of these lower energy cosmic ray particles coming from the Sun, when averaged over the solar cycle, is actually greater than the total number coming from the Galaxy. The reverse is true when only very energetic particles are considered.

Strong particle events on the Sun seem almost always to occur on its west side. If the particles concerned are moving quickly enough they will not be appreciably deflected by the Earth's magnetic field and will get through to ground level. When such a ground level event is observed from stations all round the Earth it becomes clear that the first particles to arrive appear to come from a point 50° to the west of the Sun. This picture has been amplified and extended by observations made from satellites, and it appears that fast particles travelling from the Sun to the Earth start by heading directly away from the Sun but are bent round to the East by the solar magnetic field which, as we saw when we were considering the solar wind, is wound into a spiral. Thus particles from the east side of the Sun will miss the Earth altogether, while those from the west side will appear to come from a point well west of the Sun. Such indirect paths for the solar particles are confirmed to some extent by their flight times as calculated from their velocities (deduced from the energies with which they arrive) and the assumption that they were emitted during the most violent phase of the associated flare. Not all the particles from solar flares travel directly to the Earth. In some cases particles arrive after journey times which seem to indicate that they have travelled several times the Sun–Earth distance. The sharply directional nature of the arrival of the first fast particles from a flare tends to disappear as later particles arrive, while weak flares that produce particles show no preference for the west side of the Sun. Thus it seems that the particles can in some way be stored in space. Despite its basically spiral nature, the interplanetary magnetic field is rather irregular and it is possible that the lower energy particles are deflected around or scattered by these irregularities, thus increasing their journey time to Earth and tending to make them appear to arrive from all directions. However, this scattering in interplanetary space seems insufficient to explain all the observed facts and it has been suggested that there must be a 'diffusion' zone close to the Sun in which the particles accumulate before being released into space.

The distinction between these solar cosmic ray particles which we have just been discussing, and the charged particles composing the solar wind which we discussed earlier, must be made clear. Although the solar wind varies a good deal in strength, it is continuous and its constituent particles move at the order of 400 km s^{-1}. The fastest solar cosmic rays, which are produced only occasionally by the largest flares, have velocities of the order of 100,000 km s^{-1}, that is one-third the velocity of light. The sort of particles that can be detected by polar cap absorption observations travel at velocities of the order of 40,000 km s^{-1}. Such particles can usually be associated with flares, but sometimes they appear to be produced by regions of continuous particle emission on the solar surface. Particles with velocities intermediate between these and the solar wind can be detected by satellites, but very little is yet known about them.

Fairly sudden changes in the flow of particles in the solar wind are sometimes observed, together with increases in the average velocity of the particles. Some of these events can be attributed to flares, but others must have a different origin. The enhancement of the solar wind cannot be due to particles travelling directly from the flare because the maximum velocity of the particles is less than the observed velocity of the disturbance from flare to Earth. Thus it is necessary to envisage some kind of wave travelling through the solar wind plasma and bunching the particles as it passes. The enhancement of the solar wind is accompanied by an alteration of the local magnetic field and when the disturbances reach the Earth's shielding magnetic field they cause magnetic storms measurable at ground level. The sharp beginning of these magnetic storms, known as 'sudden commencements', provides a useful method of detecting variations in the solar wind. It sometimes happens that a second burst of solar cosmic ray particles arrives almost simultaneously with the sudden commencement and, since the travel time for these fast particles if they came directly from the Sun would be much less than that of the solar wind wave, it has been suggested that the cosmic ray particles have somehow been trapped in the solar wind wave by the associated magnetic irregularities.

The heavier particles that we have been discussing, and which are mainly protons, are not the only ones produced in flares. Electrons can be detected by satellite-borne instruments, though they cannot penetrate down to the Earth's surface or even produce a noticeable polar cap absorption. Electrons travelling very close to the speed of light occur in association with the stronger proton events, and since in such cases the electrons possess similar energies to the protons, it seems likely that the same accelerating mechanism is involved. Less energetic electrons are observed much more frequently, sometimes from flares that produce protons, and sometimes from flares that do not. Thus the low energy electrons would seem to be accelerated by a different process. The flares producing low energy electrons also seem to produce Type III radio bursts, which links up well with the suggestion that Type III bursts are produced by 'plasma oscillations' excited by an outward-moving stream of fast electrons. On the other hand, the flares producing protons and very fast electrons give Type IV bursts, which are, perhaps, synchrotron radiation from the very fast electrons spiralling around a magnetic field.

The cosmic ray particles are all completely ionized, so that it is the nuclei of the various elements that are observed. They have been separated out by mass in observations made from satellites. One might expect that the relative numbers of nuclei of the various elements would reflect their abundances in the solar atmosphere were it not that the acceleration mechanism has also to be considered. The more massive the particle, the more difficult it will be to accelerate, and the larger the electrical charge it carries, the greater the acceleration is likely to be. Thus one would expect nuclei with the same ratio of charge to mass to be accelerated equally efficiently. It is on this assumption that solar abundances for elements like helium and neon, which do not produce easily accessible lines in the solar spectrum, have been derived.

We hope that this chapter has given some slight impression of the variety and scope of current solar research; though much is already known about the Sun, much clearly remains to be discovered.

Chapter Eight
The stars

S. V. M. Clube

It is well known that, even with the world's biggest telescopes, it is impossible to see any star other than as a mere point of light. Nevertheless, it may seem natural nowadays to suppose that stars could be very similar to the Sun and that the apparently minute size is simply due to their enormous distance from us. Such an idea is, of course, entirely in keeping with their virtually unchanging disposition in the sky, even supposing that they move about as rapidly as, for example, the Earth goes round the Sun. The sceptic might argue that such speculations, notwithstanding their wide acceptance, have no firmer foundations in truth than the idea that the stars are due to holes of varying size in an otherwise opaque celestial sphere. But this sceptic is undoubtedly wrong, for such an interpretation, at least in this simple form, does not take into account the host of delicate observations on stars accumulated by astronomers past and present and carefully interpreted by them in the belief that the laws of physics established in our earthbound laboratories extend to all celestial phenomena. The aim of this chapter is to outline the nature of some of these observations and to illustrate the way in which astronomers have evolved our present remarkable picture of the stellar universe. There is, of course, a danger in a short chapter like this that such a picture may seem to represent our knowledge as an orderly progression from honourable ignorance, but our sceptic should be reassured by the fact that such is the rate of growth of astronomical endeavour that this picture is as likely to be as different again fifty years on as it was many centuries ago!

Stellar structure

A common analytical procedure in astronomy, and indeed in many other sciences, is to adopt a specific theoretical model as a preliminary explanation of a set of observations. By examining the differences between the predictions of the hypothetical model and the actual observations, we can tell what simple adjustments have to be made to the model in order to bring it into line with reality. If such adjustments can be made and they are small, we have some confidence in the truth of the adopted model, but if appropriate adjustments cannot be divined or they are large, we are inclined to be suspicious of the model. Astrophysics is peculiar amongst the physical sciences in that usually the factors entering into any model—describing, for example, the behaviour of a star—are considerable in number and outside the usual controls exercised in laboratory experiments. It is often possible therefore to make a variety of inter-related adjustments and ostensibly satisfy a set of observations. There is a need for astronomers to limit the multiplicity of adjustments by gathering together as much observational data as possible and of as wide a variety as possible. Astronomical deduction thereby frequently becomes an exercise in statistics. However, the essence of the procedure is that our understanding tends to advance by inspired guesses (the theoretical model) followed by substantiation, or otherwise by detailed comparison with pertinent observations. In this section our discussion will, to some extent, illustrate this kind of pattern.

We have seen in Chapter 5 that the Sun, which we take to be a fairly typical star, is a hot rotating sphere whose mass, M, is approximately 10^{33} g, whose radius, R, is approximately 10^{11} cm, and which, judging by geological evidence, has lasted for a time, t, approximately 10^{17} seconds, radiating energy into space at a rate, L, which is very approximately 10^{33} ergs s^{-1} from a surface whose temperature, θ, is approximately 10^4 °K. Let us assume that such figures are more or less typical of stars in general and investigate where this hypothesis leads.

By any standards, the maintenance of such a state over such a long period of time may be regarded as a sign of considerable stability—notwithstanding the enormous outflow of energy—and the question of how any object can stay like this poses a real problem. Since heat travels *down* a temperature gradient, we can immediately deduce that a star must be hotter inside than it is at its surface, and that, if it is composed of any of the materials of which the Earth is composed, it is likely to be almost completely gaseous.

Let us now divide a star—in the mind's eye of course—into two equal parts, through its equator for example; we can then picture a force of attraction due to gravity holding these two halves together. Newton's law furnishes us with a rough estimate of the gravitational attraction, viz.

$$F_G \sim \frac{G(^M/_2)\,(^M/_2)}{(^R/_2)^2} \tag{1}$$

in which G represents the Gravitational constant, 6.67×10^{-8} dynes $cm^2\ g^{-2}$, and in which it is presumed that the centres of gravity of each half are separated by a distance of something like half the stellar radius. In order to avoid this force pulling the two halves *into* each other—that is, making the star collapse—the attraction must be balanced by some repulsive force in the opposite direction on each half. Such a force is that exerted by gas pressure over the interface between the two halves, which may be expressed by

$$F_P \sim \pi R^2\, p \tag{2}$$

Neither of these two formulae can be regarded as exact since we do not at first know the way in which the mass of the star is distributed throughout its volume, nor can we expect the pressure (p) exerted to be the same at all depths in the star. Presumably, in fact, the pressure increases towards the middle of the star and the mass is more concentrated there. The formulae therefore express only 'order of magnitude' relationships between the quantities involved, while p is some kind of average pressure through the star. Now if, as we have seen, the material of the star is totally gaseous, we can invoke the well known gas laws to relate pressure to the average temperature (T) of the gas. Thus

$$p = \tfrac{3}{2}\, n\, k\, T \tag{3}$$

where n is the number of independent freely moving particles in a unit volume of the gas, and k is the so-called Boltzmann constant = 1.38×10^{-16} ergs/°K. Let us suppose for the moment that these particles each have an average mass x measured in units of the proton mass, H = 1.66 $\times 10^{-24}$ g, so that we can calculate n from:

$$n \sim \text{(density of the star) / xH} = \frac{M}{\frac{4}{3}\pi R^3} \cdot \frac{1}{x.H} \tag{4}$$

The equilibrium we are examining is described by the simple equation

$$F_G = F_P \tag{5}$$

in which we can substitute the results of the four previous equations and so find that the interior temperature of the star is given by

$$T \sim \frac{8}{9} \cdot \frac{GMH}{kR} \cdot x \sim 10^7\, x\ ^\circ K \tag{6}$$

One might imagine that we are stuck here and cannot derive a suitable value for T in any star without knowing x which must obviously depend on its composition. In fact, however, the enormous temperatures encountered in stellar interiors mean that all known atoms are more or less *totally* ionized, that is, the nuclei are stripped of all their electrons and these electrons are free to move around like the nuclei themselves, virtually unhindered by the electric charges which would otherwise hold them together at normal temperatures. In such a state hydrogen, which is the lightest element, provides one proton and one electron each with an average mass of just over $\frac{1}{2}$H. A heavy element with atomic number Z, on the other hand, provides one nucleus composed of Z protons and roughly Z neutrons together with Z independent electrons, so that each particle here has an average mass of approximately $2ZH/(Z+1)$. If Z is large, as in the case of lead for example, this approximates to 2H, so that within the range of all known elements, x lies between $\frac{1}{2}$ and 2. No great error is therefore made by taking $x \sim 1$ regardless of the possible composition of the star, so deriving its internal temperature to be about 10^7 °K. Since this temperature is so much greater than the surface temperature (θ) of the star, it follows that the central temperature of a star may be somewhat larger than 10^7 °K.

The next question that we may ask is, granted that such temperatures are necessary to explain the fact that we see the star in the state we do, can we be sure that such temperatures will be maintained over periods as long as 10^{10} years $\sim 10^{17}$ seconds? If nothing else were happening and such a hot gas were to cool down at the rate we observe energy pouring out of the Sun, it could not last for anything like this length of time. We are therefore obliged to assume that this energy is being continuously generated in some way inside the star. Surprisingly enough, however, even if the star were made entirely of the most violent chemical explosives known to man, it would not be able to maintain this outflow. Neither would enough energy come from the collapse of the star under its own gravity. It was this dilemma that aroused astronomers' interest in the possibility of nuclear reactions as a source of the energy. Nuclear fusion rather than fission is the more efficient source, the energy being released when two free nuclei get sufficiently close to each other for inter-nuclear forces of attraction to take over. These forces draw such nuclei into one, thereby releasing the stored potential energy, or its mass equivalent, i.e. (radiated energy / (velocity of light)^2, as highly energetic γ-radiation. Nuclear forces are effective only over distances of about 10^{-13} cm, so that free nuclei have to overcome a very considerable barrier caused by repulsion between their respective electric charges (Ze), before the nuclear attraction can take over. In fact, only nuclei with very high thermal energies can be expected to surmount this barrier, which is why a stellar interior provides suitable conditions for such reactions. Even so, at 10^7 °K, only reactions involving light elements (i.e. with low Z) can be expected to be really efficient, and this in itself might be regarded as a good reason for thinking that stars like the Sun are made mostly of hydrogen and helium. In fact, so sensitive is the rate of such reactions to temperature that we might expect greatest activity near the core, while the main bulk of the star is simply acting as a medium for transmitting the generated energy from the core to the surface. The energy sets out from the core largely in the form of γ-rays but emerges from the surface as visible radiation. This is because of successive absorption and re-emission of the radiation on its long journey through the star.

Since nuclear reactions release energy at a rate of some 10^{18} ergs g^{-1}, or ϵ, it is quite possible, if a fair proportion of the star's mass goes through the process, for the star to last some 10^{17} seconds while radiating energy at the rate of 10^{33} ergs s^{-1}. Expressed in symbols, we can say

$$L.t < M.\epsilon$$

It is now possible to hazard a guess at how a typical star may reach this observed state of equilibrium. First of all, we suppose it collapses under self-gravity from a tenuous pre-stellar state—for example, as a cloud of gas and dust—until the kinetic energy so generated raises the interior temperature to a level at which gas pressure resists further contraction. At this stage there is a temperature gradient which drives energy through the star and ultimately out through the surface into space. This loss of energy would result in a cooling of the interior and a subsequent further collapse under gravity to seek a new equilibrium were it not for the fact that energy is continuously supplied by nuclear reactions at the centre of the star. The extreme sensitivity of this rate of generation of energy to temperature simply ensures that any deviation of the star from equilibrium, for example by contraction or expansion, results in forces which oppose these tendencies; and the equilibrium remains stable for immensely long periods until the nuclear fuel is exhausted.

So far, our study of the stellar interior has not indicated any way of calculating the rate at which energy is radiated from the surface, that is the star's luminosity, L. We have already seen, however, that L must depend somehow on the temperature gradient towards the centre of the star, and we might also suppose it depends on the 'resistance' which its constituent materials put in the way of the flow.

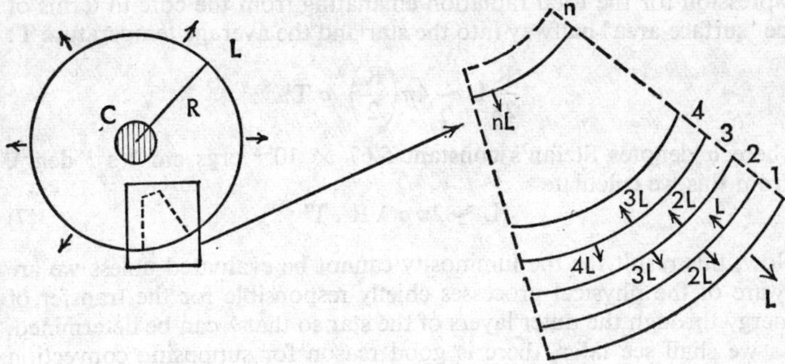

Figure 8.1 Simple model of the interior of a star having a radius R and an energy output L generated in the core C

Consider for simplicity a star such as that illustrated in Figure 8.1 in which the portion outside the core is built in layers like an onion and in which each 'skin' remains in a state of thermal equilibrium—that is, it gives out as much heat as it takes in. Were this not the case, part of the skin of the star would heat up or cool down thereby destroying its equilibrium. Now each layer, we suppose, emits energy uniformly in all directions at a rate dependent on its thermal state. Thus, if the outermost layer emits L into space, a minute part of which is responsible for our seeing the star from the Earth, then it must likewise emit L back into the star. In order to remain in thermal equilibrium, however, this outer layer must be receiving 2L from the next inner layer. Since the layer one in from the outside is emitting 2L outwards and consequently 2L inwards as well, its equilibrium can only be satisfied by receiving 3L from the next inner layer and so on. Halfway into the star, the energy emerging from the 'core' of the star is equal to nL where n is the number of outer layers. Note that in accordance with the idea developed previously, we are imagining that the main part of the star's luminosity is generated in the core where the temperature is highest. The number n is readily estimated since the depth of each layer will correspond roughly to the distance λ each packet of energy travels before being totally absorbed—a distance known as the mean free path. Thus we deduce $n \approx R/2\lambda$. Now, at the temperature of the stellar interior the most efficient mode of energy transport is by radiation, and, if the stellar material behaves like a 'black body', we can write down an expression for the total radiation emanating from the core in terms of the 'surface area' halfway into the star and the average temperature T:

$$\frac{R}{2\lambda} L \sim 4\pi \left(\frac{R}{2}\right)^2 \sigma T^4$$

where σ denotes Stefan's constant 5.67×10^{-5} ergs cm^{-2} s^{-1} deg^{-4}. From this we calculate

$$L \sim 2\pi \sigma \lambda R . T^4 \tag{7}$$

Now, this result for the luminosity cannot be evaluated unless we are aware of the physical processes chiefly responsible for the transfer of energy through the outer layers of the star so that λ can be determined. As we shall see later, there is good reason for supposing convection contributes to the transmission near the surface of some stars, but the dominant process at the prevailing temperatures is generally radiation. If this is indeed the process and if it is the same from star to star, then, without any further assumption, we can guess that the mean free path is inversely proportional to the mean density of the stellar material. Equation (7) then reduces to

$$L \propto M^{-1} . R^4 . T^4 \tag{8}$$

Since we have already found in equation (6) that

$$T \propto M . R^{-1} \tag{9}$$

the substitution of (9) in (8) leads to

$$L \propto M^3 \tag{10}$$

This is a most important result, for its implication is that there should be a strict connection between luminosity and mass for families of stars which are similar in structure and composition, so that the same physical processes may be expected to be occurring in them. This is known as the *mass-luminosity relationship*, and has been the subject of intensive observational effort by astronomers in order to substantiate or otherwise the kind of theoretical arguments we have described. It should be noted that this result depends only on the assumptions of hydrostatic equilibrium (equation (5)) and radiative equilibrium, and was in fact known to astronomers before the discovery of nuclear reactions.

Before leaving this preliminary look at stellar interiors, however, attention should also be drawn to another relationship involving the luminosity L. If stellar luminosities arise from the highly temperature-sensitive nuclear reactions, then perhaps no great error is made in

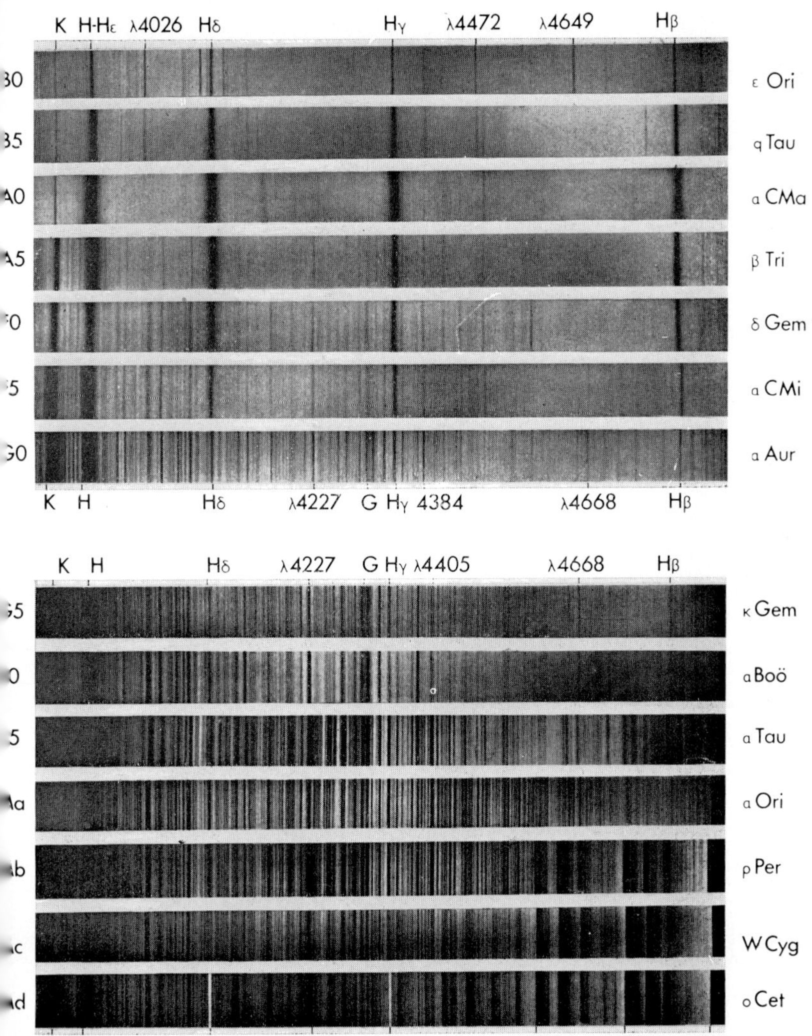

Plate 29 Typical stellar spectra indicating the continuous change in certain key features from Classes B to M. University of Michigan Observatory

Plate 30 Two young open clusters. *a* h and χ Persei, scale 1cm = 4.5′ and *b*, below, the Pleiades, 1cm = 9′. Royal Observatory, Edinburgh

Plate 31 Two old clusters. *a* the globular cluster M 3, scale 1cm = 4.2′ and *b*, below, the open cluster M 67, 1cm = 2.1′. Hale Observatories

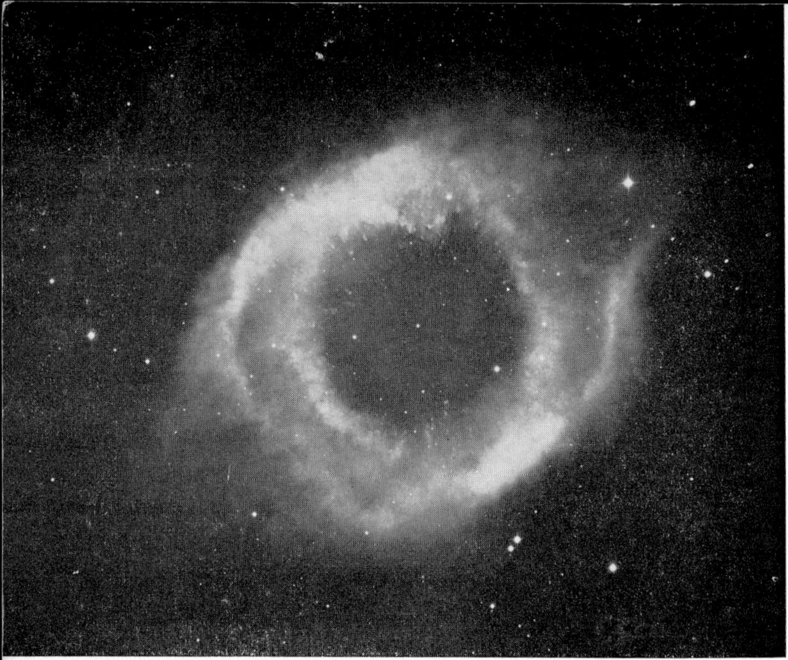

Plate 32 Expanded stars. Hale Observatories red photographs, *a* of the planetary nebula NGC 7293, scale 1cm = 2.2′, and *b*, below, M 1, the Crab Nebula, the remains of the supernova of AD 1054, a strong radio and X-ray source and the location of a pulsar, 1cm = 1′

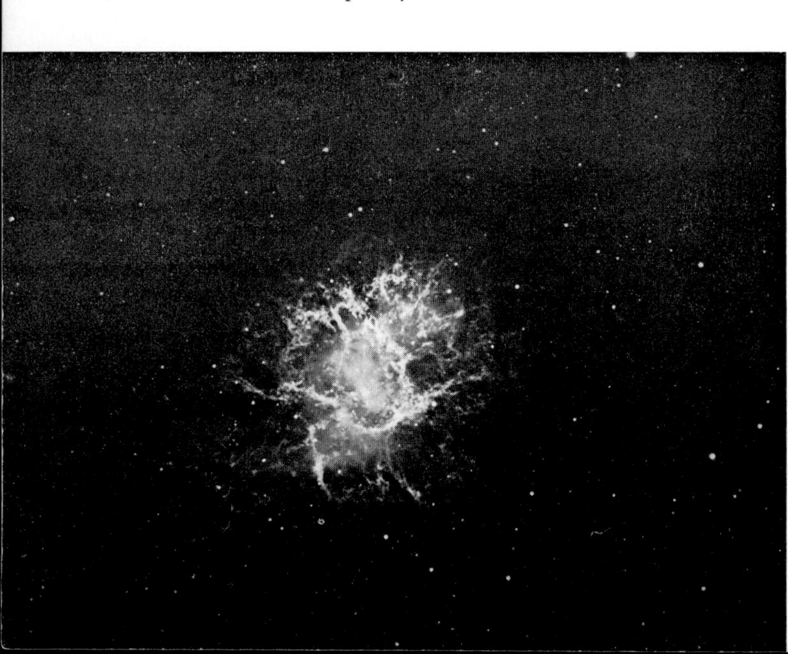

assuming that, for observed stars, a large range in luminosities corresponds to only a small range in average temperatures—that is, equation (9) implies very roughly that $M \propto R$. This in turn gives $L \propto R^3$ from equation (10) and since, at the surface of the star, we know

$$L = 4\pi R^2 \sigma \theta^4 \tag{11}$$

it appears that

$$L \propto \theta^{12} \tag{12}$$

the implication being that for our family of stars, there is also a relationship between luminosity and surface temperature—though, by reason of the assumptions made, we shall set no great store by the exactness of this formula. Indeed, one should perhaps add that there is now reason to believe that a significant change in the type of nuclear reactions going on in the stellar core does occur through the relevant range of temperatures ($\sim 10^7$ °K), thus making our assumption $M \propto R$ rather inadequate. At high temperatures it may well be plausible, however, since one kind of reaction is dominant. The hydrogen burning process known as the proton-proton reaction prevails at $T \sim 10^{6\cdot5}$ °K but it is less sensitive to temperature than the carbon cycle and by $T \sim 10^{7\cdot5}$ °K the latter is dominant. This has the effect of making L less steeply dependent on θ. However, the qualitative result of this analysis of the physical processes occurring in a stellar interior is that we expect that the more luminous a star, the hotter its surface will be. Since 'black body' emitters concentrate their radiation to shorter and shorter wavelengths the hotter they are, so we expect stars more luminous than the Sun to be 'bluer' and those less luminous than the Sun to be 'redder'.

The conclusion drawn from these theoretical investigations of stellar structure is that if objects like the Sun do indeed exist, then we might expect to discover some connection between observable properties of the stars—the so-called colour-luminosity and mass-luminosity relationships. It is understandable, therefore, that astronomers have devoted considerable effort towards seeing whether such relationships do in fact exist. Obviously, the determination of star luminosities, colours and masses must figure a great deal in these investigations, and in subsequent sections we shall see how these quantities are measured for some stars. An essential determinant in many cases is the star's distance, and much of our discussion will be concerned with this particular problem. At first, however, we shall look at some evidence which does not depend on a knowledge of stellar distance. It turns out that, broadly speaking, our observations do confirm the existence of these inter-relationships, and it is this which has inspired an extension of the theory so as to inquire further, especially into how a star evolves.

It would, however, be a real mistake to suppose that this theory could be successfully extended without referring to observations of the stars themselves. To these, therefore, we now turn.

Photometry of stellar clusters

Stars are not uniformly distributed around the sky. Bright stars visible to the naked eye, though scattered more or less at random over the whole sky, show a slight tendency, which is especially marked amongst the blue stars, to concentrate into a band known as Gould's Belt. Through telescopes, however, it is readily observed that the density of the faint stars increases rapidly towards another band around the sky known as the Milky Way. This is seen by the naked eye as a faint but patchy glow. Gould's Belt cuts across the Milky Way at an angle of about 20° in the constellations of Vela and Lacerta. The two lines of sight at right angles to the Milky Way point more or less towards the least densely populated areas of the sky and are believed to be in the directions of the galactic poles (this structure is discussed in Chapter 9). Although the faint stars' density over the sky varies smoothly from the Milky Way to the poles, the detailed distribution is mostly random, save for places where there seem to be special concentrations of stars 'unexpectedly' greater in density than the surrounding area. It is difficult to believe other than that the stars in such *clusters* are physically associated with one another, though there are less readily discerned cases of concentration of stars where astronomers would need further independent evidence to assure themselves that the groups are physically connected rather than statistical accidents. In the cases where such evidence is forthcoming these weaker concentrations are called '*stellar associations*', and most of the members are bright blue stars.

Plates 30 and 31 show some typical clusters, the best known of which is the Pleiades which is easily visible to the naked eye. Several hundred clusters are known and can usually be classified unambiguously as being either 'open' or 'globular'. The open clusters are amorphous in shape, contain from a few score to a few hundred stars, and tend to be found in or near the Milky Way. The globular clusters, on the other hand, contain many thousands of stars, usually give the appearance of being spherical in shape, and tend to occur away from the Milky Way. Clusters are usually referred to by their number in some catalogue or other, the most usual being Dreyer's *A New General Catalogue of*

Nebulae and Clusters of Stars, denoted by NGC, or, for the brightest, most conspicuous objects, Messier's catalogue of 103 nebulous objects and clusters which was compiled in the late eighteenth century and, is denoted by M.

If we believe that clusters are concentrations of related stars—and, as we shall see, this view is amply confirmed by the discovery that member stars share a common motion—it is natural to presume that each member star shares also some kind of common origin with its fellows. Whatever form this origin takes, it is very reasonable to suppose further that each cluster is formed out of some uniform chemical mixture so that its constituent stars have a common composition, and, if their internal structures correspond in any way to the theory we have described, then these clusters of stars will be very useful test-beds for the theory.

The average angular separation of neighbouring clusters of much the same apparent size is observed to be at least ten times their typical cross section. On the grounds that such clusters are characteristically much the same real size, and are more or less uniformly distributed through the solar neighbourhood, we might reasonably argue that all the members of any of the nearest clusters are separated from each other by up to ten per cent of their distance from us. Even if this is not exactly the case for the nearest and brightest clusters such as the Hyades, it is increasingly likely that the members of any fainter cluster can be taken to be nearly at the same distances from us. This means that the light coming from each member star is diminished through distance, with or without intervening absorption, by the same fraction to a very high degree of approximation. *The relative apparent brightness of cluster stars thus reflects their relative true brightness very closely*. This is true for any receiver, whether it be the human eye or a photocell, for example, in spite of passage through the Earth's atmosphere. Ideally an astronomer would like to measure the 'bolometric intensity' of radiation or the total energy throughout the spectrum which corresponds to the 'L' derived theoretically. Selective transmission by the Earth's atmosphere and the telescope, not to mention the restricted response of the receiver, place limitations on such ambitions. But, fortunately, starlight is very often concentrated in the visible region centred on the yellow part of the spectrum and this means that the 'yellow' or 'visual' intensity is quite a good guide to the bolometric intensity.

Let us suppose one receiver records N_B photons per second from a certain star in the blue part of the spectrum, while another records N_V in the yellow part. Similar measurements on another star of identical colour but brighter or fainter would give different counts but the ratio

N_V/N_B would remain unaltered. This ratio can be regarded as an index of colour, for, if yet another star as bright as the first gives a larger value of N_B and a smaller one for N_V, we would recognize it as being bluer, but at the same time it would give a smaller index. The converse is true for redder stars.

Many star clusters have been carefully observed and many reveal a strictly monotonic relationship between N_V and N_V/N_B such that the brighter members are blue and the fainter ones red in accordance with the theoretical prediction. This could be illustrated by plotting N_V against N_V/N_B for these clusters, but, by reason of the techniques employed to obtain these measurements, it is preferable to present these results in the conventional form used by astronomers. This form is largely determined by the history of astronomical photometry and is unfortunately rather cumbersome. The human eye and the photographic plate were the first receivers used to record starlight, and both, in spite of their known limitations, also have many advantages and are still used extensively. The response of each is logarithmic, and it has thus become an established custom to denote apparent star brightnesses by apparent magnitudes m such that

$$m_X = \text{constant} - 2.5 \log_{10} N_X \qquad (13)$$

where N_X is the number of photons received per second in a wavelength interval specified by x. The minus sign simply reflects the fact that decreasing brightness corresponds to increasing magnitude, while the factor 2.5 is an arbitrary constant chosen so that an interval of 5 magnitudes corresponds to a change in N by a factor of 100, roughly equivalent to the visual scale used by astronomers in the distant past. The constant, too, is arbitrary, being a function of the units of energy and the equipment used, and is therefore adopted by international agreement, broadly speaking, so that the very brightest stars have zero apparent magnitude. It is thus possible to define apparent star *magnitudes* in different spectral regions such as

$$m_B = \text{some constant} - 2.5 \log_{10} N_B$$
$$m_V = \text{another constant} - 2.5 \log_{10} N_V$$

and *colour indices* like

$$m_B - m_V = \text{yet another constant} + 2.5 \log_{10} N_V/N_B.$$

A graphical plot of m_V against $m_B - m_V$ thus incorporates the same information as a plot of N_V against N_V/N_B, save for an unspecified origin, and is more closely related to quantities actually measured.

In Figure 8.2 are plotted such diagrams for the four well observed clusters, illustrated in Plates 30 and 31. Both h and χ Persei and the Pleiades are in regions of considerable gas and dust and, as will be seen later, show all the signs of being relatively young. M3 and M67, on the other hand, appear to be relatively old. All four clusters have a 'main sequence' running from the fainter red stars to brighter blue ones. The so-called 'turn-off' point at the top of the sequence occurs at a different colour in each cluster and the stars above it, if any, behave differently. In h and χ Persei there are a few very bright red stars well isolated from the main sequence; in the Pleiades there are no stars beyond the turn-off point; for M3 and M67 there is a continuous 'red giant branch' stretching up from the turn-off point in which the usual trend of magnitude with colour is reversed in that the brighter the star is, the redder it appears. The plot for M3 shows a feature which is characteristic of most globular clusters and which has not been found in any open cluster. This is the 'horizontal branch' of stars joining up at the red end with the red giant branch. The dotted extension of the main sequence of M67 indicates the existence of a few brighter blue stars in this sequence.

It is noticeable that the main sequences for each cluster can be brought into coincidence, especially at the lower end, by very slight shifts parallel to the $m_B - m_V$ axis and quite substantial shifts parallel to the m_V axis. There is therefore a strong suspicion that this line is in fact common to all clusters, since slight shifts along the $m_B - m_V$ axis would correspond to 'reddening' corrections arising from interstellar absorption—as, for example, sunlight is reddened as it traverses the Earth's atmosphere—and large shifts along the other axis to correcting for different distances of the clusters. In Figure 8.3 we see the diagrams brought into coincidence by such shifts. The common sequence of stars and its dotted extension is called the 'zero-age main sequence' (ZAMS), and it is presumed that a star evolves away from this sequence once it has consumed its store of hydrogen fuel in the core.

The choice of origin for the composite sequence shown in Figure 8.3 is arbitrary, and is adjusted first to the values of m_V and $m_B - m_V$ for a cluster whose distance can be determined and for which the reddening is known. The cluster used for this purpose is the Hyades which is discussed later in the chapter. The values of m_V and $m_B - m_V$ are then by common convention scaled to the values they would have if the cluster were placed at a standard distance of 10 parsecs with no intervening absorption. The values of m_V and $m_B - m_V$ so obtained are known as *absolute magnitudes* and *intrinsic colours* and are commonly—though not very logically—denoted by M_V and $(B - V)_0$ respec-

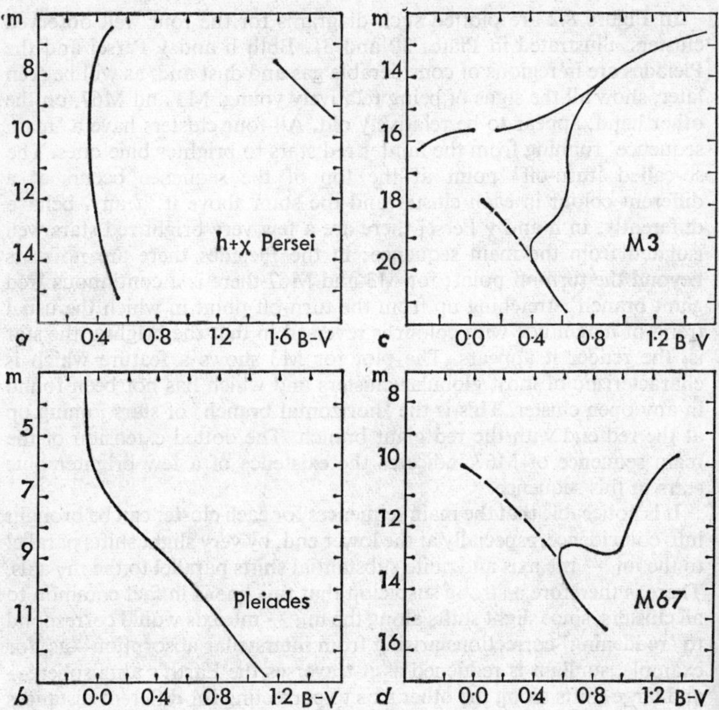

Figure 8.2 Colour-magnitude diagrams for four well observed clusters
a h and χ Persei; *b* the Pleiades; *c* globular cluster M3; *d* old open cluster M67

tively. Clearly the shifts made to bring each observed cluster diagram in line with the standard colour-magnitude diagram give a measure of the reddening correction for, and the relative distance of, the cluster. The reddening which is sometimes called the colour excess

$$E_{B-V} = (m_B - m_V) - (B - V)_0$$

results from differential absorption in the blue and yellow parts of the spectrum. If the process of absorption is known, a relationship between the actual absorption in any one part of the spectrum and the differential absorption can be calculated. However, the state of the interstellar medium is not necessarily well known, and this relationship has to be

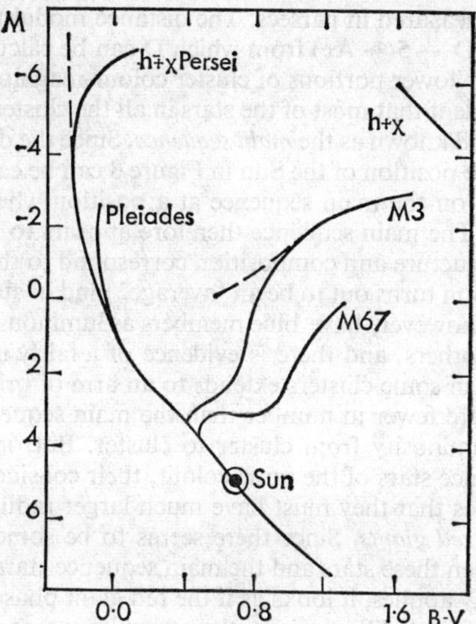

Figure 8.3 Composite magnitude-colour diagram formed by moving the diagrams of Figure 8.2 parallel to the B — V and m axes.

determined observationally (Chapter 9). Very roughly it is found that the visual absorption is given by

$$A_V = 3E_{B-V}$$

so that part of the shift along the m_V axis results from A_V while the remainder can be attributed to distance. The remainder ($m_V - M_V - A_V$) is known as the distance modulus because it can be used to calculate distances in terms of the standard distance introduced above. Thus the number of photons received from certain stars with any particular apparatus is inversely proportional to the square of the distance D: that is

$$N \propto D^{-2} \quad (14)$$

Therefore, in general, equation (13) becomes

$$m_x = \text{constant} + 5 \log_{10} D$$

Introducing the standard distance for absolute magnitude of D = 10 parsecs, we can also say

$$M_x = \text{constant} + 5$$

if distances are measured in parsecs. The distance modulus is therefore equal to ($5 \log_{10} D - 5 - A_V$) from which D can be calculated.

By bringing the lower portions of cluster colour-magnitude diagrams into line, it is evident that most of the stars in all the clusters lie within a fairly narrow band known as the *main sequence*. Since the distance to the Sun is known, the position of the Sun in Figure 3 can be calculated, and it is found to lie on the main sequence at a position where $M_V \approx 4.9$ and $B\text{–}V \approx 0.6$. The main sequence therefore appears to be the family of stars whose structure and composition correspond to the theory outlined, while the Sun turns out to be an 'average' kind of star. Individual clusters do not, however, have blue members as luminous as those that appear in some others, and there is evidence of a fairly marked 'turn-off point' which in some clusters extends to an arm of bright red stars. These red stars are fewer in number than the main sequence stars and differ in their luminosity from cluster to cluster. But, in comparison with main sequence stars of the same colour, their considerably greater luminosity implies that they must have much larger radii and they are therefore called *red giants*. Since there seems to be some kind of discontinuity between these stars and the main sequence stars to which the theory apparently applies, it looks as if the red giant phase corresponds to some fundamental difference in the structure or composition (or both) of these stars from the model examined.

The question arises: why do some clusters not have bright blue members? There would appear to be three possible answers to this question. Either such stars have not yet been formed in the cluster if they are going to be formed at all, or else it is not possible for them to exist because of instabilities, or else they have existed in the past and have since evolved to some other state. The second possibility can reasonably be discounted since, though such stars do not exist in some clusters, they certainly do so in others. As a guide to choosing between the remaining alternatives we can return to the model star and imagine that it evolves first by condensing 'on the main sequence' from its pre-stellar tenuous state under self-gravity. If the gas out of which a star cluster condenses is of uniform density σ, then individual stars will collapse through a distance r, say, which is proportional to $M^{\frac{1}{3}}$, while the time taken for this collapse can be estimated from

$$r \approx \tfrac{1}{2}\,at^2 \approx \tfrac{1}{2}\frac{G.M}{r^2}\cdot t^2$$

whence

$$t^2 \approx \tfrac{3}{2}\,.\,\pi\, G\, \sigma \qquad (15)$$

where a is the acceleration experienced by a surface 'particle' during contraction.

To a first approximation, then, stars of any mass arrive at the equilibrium state on the main sequence more or less simultaneously if all the stars start to condense at the same instant. Thereafter the time they spend on the main sequence may be estimated as before from

$$t \sim M\epsilon/L \tag{16}$$

since $L \propto M^3$, $t \propto M^{-2}$ or $t \propto L^{-\frac{2}{3}}$, which means that stars more massive than the Sun use up their available fuel more rapidly. It appears that a good reason for bright blue members being absent from some clusters is that they have evolved. Since the discontinuity is such that the main sequence connects at its upper end with the red giant branch it appears also that main sequence stars evolve into red giants—the reason for this will be discussed shortly.

The relative luminosities of the brightest blue stars in h and χ Persei (Plate 30*a*), for example, and the Sun are about ten magnitudes, or a factor of about 10^4. Very roughly, this means that these stars can only survive on the main sequence for about 10^{-3} of the Sun's lifetime on it, which in turn implies that such stars must have formed well within the Earth's lifetime. Stellar evolution is thus a continuing process and there is no question of all the stars in the Galaxy being formed at the same time. These ideas have led us to suspect that the turn-off point on the main sequence is a guide to the age of a cluster, since with advancing age less and less luminous stars exhaust their fuel and evolve off it. Because such clusters have giant branches which are not coincident we further suspect that the somewhat sparsely populated giant branches are 'snapshot' views of the path that a star of the mass at the turn-off point evolves along. By the standards of the main sequence time scales, evolution to a red giant is therefore rapid. This is a fate which has yet to befall our Sun! According to these ideas the h and χ Persei system is a very young one, with the brightest stars already evolved into red supergiants. The Pleiades is the next youngest system of our examples, while the M3 and M67 clusters are of particular interest being both very old and highly evolved. The M67 stars are richer in metals than those of M3 and apparently belong to a later generation of stars. It is this fact that accounts for the difference between their giant branches. The colour-magnitude diagram of M3 is typical of many globular clusters and reveals a characteristic feature of the systems not found in open clusters, namely a horizontal branch of stars joining up at the red end with the red giant branch. Variable stars with periods of about half a day are often found in great numbers in globular clusters with average magnitudes and colours which place them in the horizontal branch gap at $B-V \sim 0.3$. We shall return to these so-called RR Lyrae Variables in a later section.

Clusters which have been observed carefully never seem to have a turn-off point redder than $B - V \sim 0.4$ which, if the structure and evolution of a star are correctly assessed, can be used to put a figure to the age of the stellar system which turns out to be not so very different from that of the Sun itself—that is, the Sun is comparatively old as stars go.

All these observations tend to confirm the theory remarkably well, but it does seem rather fortunate that the Sun lies so conveniently near the middle of the main sequence. This in fact raises further questions about stellar evolution. If stars of each mass stand equal chances of being formed, but in some way the process is a continuing one, then at any one time one would expect to find many more intrinsically faint main sequence stars than luminous ones. But even granting that the more luminous stars evolve more rapidly, this does not seem necessarily to provide a reason for seeing less of them unless there were hindrances to their formation which do not exist for stars more like the Sun in mass. In fact, such a hindrance may well exist. The equilibrium of the main sequence star has been calculated with the assumption that gravitational attraction is balanced by gas pressure. For stars with really 'hot' interiors, however, it could be that radiation pressure contributes as well. In fact, radiation pressure is proportional to T^4, while, according to equations (3), (4) and (9), gas pressure is proportional to M^2/R^4. Manipulating these relations using equations (8) and (10) it is found that the ratio of these pressures—radiation pressure to gas pressure—advances with M^2 and radiation pressure becomes dominant at masses of about 50 M. There is thus good reason to suppose that radiation pressure acts as a disruptive influence above this mass and that the kind of equilibrium envisaged breaks down for very bright blue stars. Such stars are therefore more difficult to form, and an explanation can at least be seen for their being comparatively rare.

One further question before leaving this subject—why do main sequence stars evolve into red giants? At first sight this is a rather surprising observation since the theory that has been discussed might lead one to think that the natural course of events would be for a star to maintain the main sequence equilibrium until its fuel were exhausted and then, as at first, seek to generate further energy by gravitational contraction. This, one might imagine, would proceed until the internal temperature is high enough for some heavy-element nuclear reactions to come into play and stabilize the star again. Such a course of events, however, would imply a cycling of all the star's mass through the core where the nuclear reactions occur. This 'convective' picture is somewhat at variance with the 'onion skin' model, and so the fact that stars do not apparently contract off the main sequence may be regarded as indirect evidence in favour of the hypothesis of radiative transfer. It is therefore thought that while a star is on the main sequence an asymmetry in its structure develops due to depletion of the nuclear fuel and consequent change in composition of the material at the star's centre. As this fuel is exhausted the star cannot, without replenishment, supply sufficient L to maintain its equilibrium and so at first it contracts, thereby raising T and accelerating nuclear reactions in a shell of material round the core, whose composition is more like that of the original star than that of the converted core. This inevitably results in an over-compensation of L and a large increase in R. The evolving star is thus confronted with a dilemma—it cannot expand and contract simultaneously, and yet it must do something! What appears to happen is that the stellar core contracts causing the surrounding shell to heat up and produce an increase in the stellar luminosity, which by reason of the very moderate rise in central temperature can only be compensated by a drastic expansion of the stellar envelope. The visible evidence of this is the existence of the red giant phase. Subsequent stages in stellar evolution will be examined in the final section.

The model of stellar interiors produces observable features which are broadly confirmed by photometry of stellar clusters. Moreover, only very simple and natural extensions of this model seem to be needed to account for features not covered by the model. In the next sections, therefore, we shall rely on this model as a first approximation to real stars and only return to examine it in more detail at a later stage.

The nearest stars

There are some 5000 stars brighter than the sixth magnitude and the number brighter than any particular limiting magnitude nearly doubles for each half magnitude fainter. Presented with such numbers it is a formidable task to select the nearest stars from amongst them. In practice there is no certain way of doing this and we have to depend to some extent on luck. At one time it was thought that the brightest stars in the sky were the nearest, but as we have already seen, stars can have one of a wide range of luminosities. In fact the known range of main sequence stars is over 20 magnitudes, or expressed in luminosities, over 10^8. This means that it is possible for a star of any particular apparent magnitude to be within a distance range of 1 to 10,000 units! Apparent magnitude is by itself, then, a very unreliable distance indicator. Nevertheless, astronomers did once seek to determine star distances of most

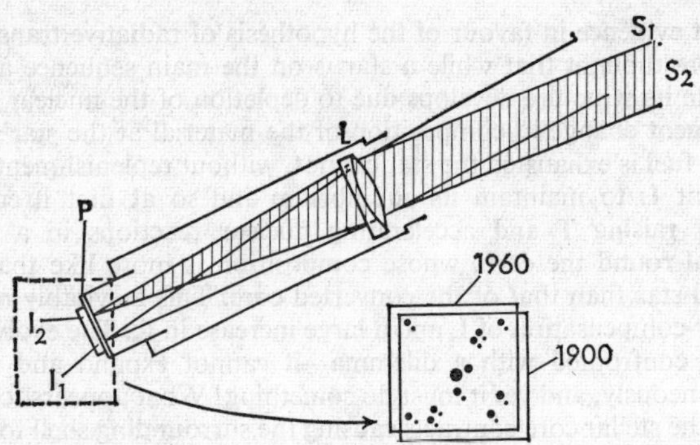

Figure 8.4 The observation of relative proper motions by means of a refracting telescope

of the apparently bright stars, oblivious of the above reasoning, and were, surprisingly enough, more successful than one might have guessed! The reason for this is that the solar neighbourhood is comparatively free of intrinsically luminous stars, most of the nearest of these being sufficiently far away to have apparent magnitudes fainter than six. A more effective way of sorting out the nearer stars is to look for those having large proper motions.

Proper motions It has long been known that the relative positions of stars as seen against the 'celestial sphere' change with the passage of time. This motion is very small and can be confidently measured only after quite long intervals of time. A common method of making such measurements by comparing photographs of the same area of the sky taken with the same telescope at an interval of about 50 years is illustrated in Figure 8.4. This shows how photographic plates are taken with a refractor telescope whose lens L converges the parallel beams of light from different stars S_1, S_2 . . . to a focus on the plate P forming images I_1, I_2. . . . The figure also illustrates the appearance of two plates taken, say, in 1900 and 1960, the former being viewed through the latter and with a slight displacement between them. For illustrative purposes it is supposed that the 1960 plate received a slightly longer exposure so that all the 1960 images are slightly larger than the 1900 ones. The displacement between the pairs of images is very nearly the same for most of the stars but for one star it is markedly different due to the star's big proper motion relative to the others. A more careful inspection of the plates would probably reveal, however, that many of the stars are slightly displaced from their original positions. The displacements may be in any direction and of any size, but typically for a telescope having a focal length of about five metres they are about 0.05 mm for $\sim$ 10th magnitude stars. Brighter stars tend to have displacements larger than this on the average, while fainter ones tend to show smaller movements. The angular motions which give rise to these photographed displacements are called *proper motions* and in this case correspond to 0.03 arc seconds per year. The largest known proper motion is about 10 arc seconds per year, but stars with motions larger than 0.1 arc seconds per year are relatively rare. The movements mean that such photographs at different epochs are not really identical, and it is a matter of some difficulty to match the photographs exactly. What is done is to fit the stars which apparently move least of all with respect to one another, and regard the movement of the other stars as *relative proper motions.* In spite of their minute size, such relative proper motions are comparatively simple to measure under high magnification. So extensive now are astronomers' records of these proper motions that there is no doubt that stars are moving about at random with respect to each other. The movements are too small for us to tell whether they are moving in curved orbits or in straight lines, except in a few cases of well observed binary systems. Since stars are a long way apart in relation to the range of their gravitational fields, however, it is reasonable to regard the proper motions as essentially straight across the line of sight. In general, there is no reason to believe the stars in any one part of the sky are really very different from any others and, therefore, as a working hypothesis, it is reasonable to suppose that all stars have the same typical speed. As we shall see soon, this is not in fact the case, but as an initial assumption it certainly serves. Straight away this means that small proper motions correspond to great distance and larger proper motions to relatively close proximity to the Sun. These motions are therefore a very useful tool in selecting nearby stars, even though there are limitations. Thus, stars moving with the typical speed *along* any line of sight would show no proper motion, and likewise, since the speeds are in fact distributed randomly about a mean value, it is quite possible for a star to have zero transverse velocity with respect to the Sun and again show zero proper motion.

Photographic surveys of the sky have been made looking for high proper motion stars down to about 20th magnitude, and many candidates for the immediate solar neighbourhood are known. However, the list might be only 60 per cent complete for the reason given. Of course, proper motion does not of itself tell us how far away a star is—it simply gives an indication of relative distance. Rough distances can only be calculated from the average proper motion if the random speed is known, and this technique is often used. We shall return to the question of distance determination shortly.

Star positions Turning aside for a while, we should note that the assumption by which two photographs are fitted together in determining proper motions does beg a question. It is not necessarily known whether the stars of *zero relative proper motion* have really got *zero proper motion*. It is of course possible to argue that they might be so far away that, whatever reasonable velocity they have with respect to the Sun, their apparent systematic motion would be negligible. This is in fact the case usually and is the reason why relative proper motions are as useful as they are. However, astronomers cannot rely on this, and have to devise ways of measuring proper motions *absolutely*. An important technique which will be used increasingly in the future, but which has not yet been successfully established, is to compare photographs taken with 'fast' telescopes capable of detecting the so-called extragalactic nebulae (Chapter 10). Many of these have star-like images on photographic plates and can therefore be measured in the same way as the star images themselves. These objects are believed to be so remote that even with huge unrealistic velocities their absolute proper motions would be too small for measurement ($\sim$ 0.00001 arc second per year). In any particular area of the sky these objects therefore serve as an excellent reference frame of effectively zero motion to which stellar proper motions can be referred absolutely. Even when perfected, this method will not be of universal application because extragalactic nebulae cannot be seen through obscuring dust in the Milky Way, and here it will be necessary to fall back to some extent on the technique still used at the present time.

The problem is to establish a reference framework over the whole sky which is invariant with the passage of time and to which the motion of any star can be referred. Astronomers choose to do this by observing positions of stars visible to the naked eye, as well as some others, largely because these stars have a longer history of observation than others, and to define the system with respect to them. The instrument commonly used for this purpose is the transit circle, the principle of which is shown in Figure 8.5. A telescope, T, is set up to rotate about a horizontal axis so as to sweep out the plane NZT containing the Earth's axis of rotation and the zenith point, Z, vertically above T. As the Earth rotates this 'meridian plane' sweeps through the line of sight to every star. At the

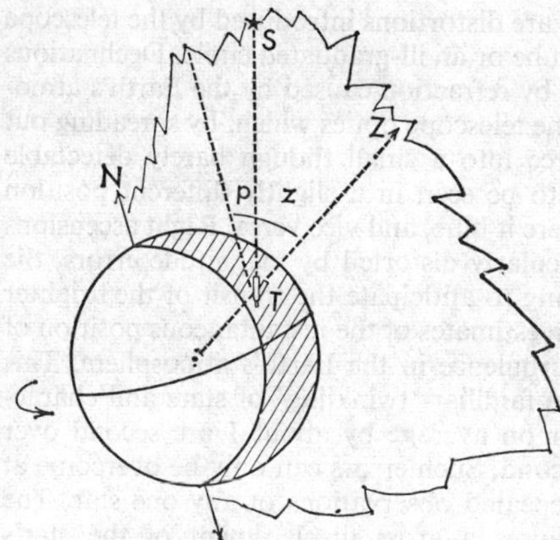

Figure 8.5 The principle of the transit circle for the observation of star positions

instant to which the figure refers a star, S, is in this meridian plane at a 'zenith distance', z, and a 'north polar distance', p. Star positions are observed directly as times of transit across the meridian and zenith distances from the vertical defined with respect to a mercury bath underneath the instrument. The times are converted to a scale such that successive crossings of the meridian by the same star are separated by 24 hours—that is, independently of variations in the Earth's rotation—and referred to an arbitrary zero-point (for example a selected star). The zenith distances are measured on a graduated circle and converted to polar distances, the position of the pole being determined for the transit circle from the mean zenith distance at upper and lower culminations of stars around the pole. Polar distances are then subtracted from 90° to give declinations. The instantaneous position of any bright star can thus be specified by its right ascension, α, the time of transit referred to the arbitrary zero-point and its declination, δ, each of which is in principle independent of the apparatus used to record it. The right ascension depends on the accuracy of the clock used and the declination on that of the circle graduations. In practice both of these are now much better than the setting errors associated with α and δ. These are of the order of 0.3 arc seconds in each coordinate or somewhat less, but before this century, errors could be much larger. It might be thought that (α, δ) for every star could now be determined by extending observations indefinitely and allowing statistics to do the rest, but unfortunately the apparent (α, δ)s are subject to various kinds of secular changes which are quite unavoidable.

The most obvious of these are distortions introduced by the telescope itself, such as flexure of the tube or an ill-graduated circle. Declinations in particular can be affected by refraction caused by the Earth's atmosphere and inadequacies in the telescope optics which, by spreading out the light from a point source into a small though barely detectable spectrum, make a red star to be seen in a slightly different position from that it would occupy were it blue, and vice versa. Right ascensions on the other hand are particularly distorted by magnitude errors, the tendency of the observer being to anticipate the transit of the brighter stars. Large random errors in estimates of the instantaneous position of a star are also caused by turbulence in the Earth's atmosphere. This phenomenon is related to the familiar 'twinkling' of stars and characteristically displaces the star on average by about 1 arc second over times of the order of one second. Such errors can only be overcome at sea level observatories by repeated observations of any one star. The Earth's atmosphere also causes a gross displacement of the star's apparent direction in the sky by refraction. The correction needed may be evaluated empirically by comparing transit circle observations of the same star at different latitudes. Indeed, it is vitally necessary in obtaining a set of (α, δ)s to observe stars with different telescopes at different locations and epochs with different observers, in order to reduce the effect of most of these hazards. In any case, it is necessary to use at least two telescopes to observe positions in both the northern and the southern hemispheres! Even supposing all these troubles can be overcome, unpredictable movements of the Earth's crust also have to be disentangled from the observations—such as latitude variation due to polar wandering.

If these were the only problems astronomers had to contend with, star positions would now be measured on a 'celestial sphere' whose axis coincides with the Earth's rotational axis but whose origin of right ascensions could move. However, star positions also reflect the large-scale motions of the Earth within the Solar System. The orientation of the polar axis in space moves among the stars steadily due to the gravitational action of the Sun and Moon on the Earth's equatorial bulge (luni-solar precession) and, more slightly, the other planets. The axis also 'nutates' due to resonances set up between the Earth's rotation and the Moon's orbital period. In addition, the star positions suffer 'aberration' due to the 'velocity triangle' between the telescope velocity vector and the incoming light vector, the 'telescope velocity' relative to the centre of mass of the Solar System being caused mostly by the Earth's rotation about its own axis and around the Sun. Since our device for measuring star positions is thus recognized to be a shifting base, we

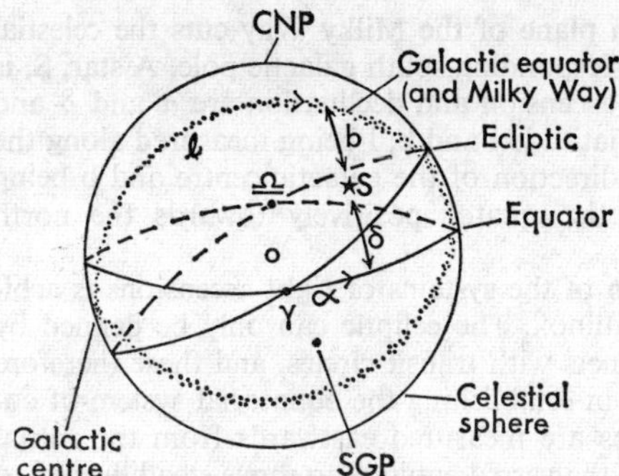

Figure 8.6 Coordinate systems for defining positions on the celestial sphere

refer them, admittedly with some difficulty, to a framework which we believe to be more likely to be invariant. This framework is a celestial sphere centred on the 'centre of mass' of the Solar System.

Basically what we now do is to express these phenomena by a physical model in which the observables at the transit circle (a time and a zenith distance for each star) are related to (α, δ) through a very complicated equation involving unknown parameters describing each of these phenomena. Our knowledge of the size of these effects only comes through a solution of such equations for many star observations. In practice, such solutions are made only occasionally and with some of the unknowns arbitrarily fixed, like the obliquity between the Earth and Solar System axes of rotation. These solutions give the positions of the bright stars at the mean epoch of the observations, as equatorial co-ordinates (α, δ) observed from a rigid Earth rotating at constant speed about an axis fixed in space, with respect to the centre of mass of the Solar System.

Figure 8.6 illustrates the various coordinate systems for defining positions on the celestial sphere. CNP denotes the celestial north pole which is the direction of the north end of the Earth's axis of rotation and the pole of the 'celestial equator' which is the great circle in which the plane of the Earth's equator cuts the celestial sphere. Similarly the 'ecliptic' is the great circle in which the mean plane of the Earth's rotation about the Sun cuts the celestial sphere. The ecliptic is inclined at approximately $22\frac{1}{2}°$ to the equator and crosses it at the equinoctial points, that at the ascending node being the 'First Point of Aries', ♈, or the 'vernal equinox' for the northern hemisphere, while that at the descending node, twelve hours of right ascension later, is the 'autumnal equinox', ♎. Also illustrated is the 'galactic equator' which is the great circle in which the median plane of the Milky Way cuts the celestial sphere. SGP marks the corresponding south galactic pole. A star, S, is shown, of which the right ascension and declination are α and δ and the galactic longitude and latitude l and b, l being measured along the galactic equator from the direction of the galactic centre and b being measured from this galactic equator positively towards the north galactic pole.

The instantaneous origin of the systems of right ascensions is arbitrarily set at the vernal equinox. The ecliptic can only be defined by observing the Sun and planets with transit circles, and these therefore become vital observations in establishing the equatorial system of coordinates. Right ascensions are measured eastwards from the vernal equinox. Precession causes the vernal equinox to move steadily, and so for convenience star positions are generally reduced to a standard equinox close to the epoch of observation.

However, the situation is complicated further by the fact that the stars themselves move. Any set of star positions refers to a particular epoch of observation. Since an astronomer's main interest is in securing positions at different epochs in order to measure their proper motions he immediately comes up against a conceptual difficulty which now reflects itself in determining some features of the above physical model. Suppose the average behaviour of the stars reveals a rotational motion about the axis of the Solar System—does he regard this as due to precession or as a real motion of the stars? Since he does not know *a priori* how stars move, he cannot fully determine the constants of precession and so cannot—even in principle—specify coordinates exactly with respect to the centre of mass of the solar system. Consequently the absolute motion of individual stars is unknown. There are, however, two ways out of this dilemma; one line is to attempt to determine the internal structure of the Earth so exactly that its precessional motion can be calculated, and the other is to make some assumption about the mean motion of the stars. Insufficient information is available about the Earth's moment of inertia to permit the former method at present. Using the latter method the common assumption now made is that the stars as a whole rotate only in the plane of the Milky Way, and by good fortune the plane of the Milky Way is nearly perpendicular to that of the ecliptic. This means that any rotation in the plane of the ecliptic is attributed mostly to precession, but there is still uncertainty about how much to attribute to the stars, and how much to the Earth in the perpendicular planes. The uncertainty may only amount to about 0.003 arc seconds per year, but it is very critical to theories of the Galaxy and of the Earth.

At the end of this long aside we find that it is in practice very difficult to quote proper motions absolutely. This uncertainty does not seriously affect either the identification of *nearby* stars or the determination of their space velocities, but the consequences become more marked for distant stars with smaller proper motions—say less than 0.02 arc seconds per year. In extending our knowledge of these more remote stars it is necessary to solve this problem, and this is why astronomers are now interested in using extragalactic nebulae as a more suitable reference frame.

The fundamental catalogue of star positions contains about 1500 bright stars more or less uniformly distributed over the sky. They are separated from their nearest neighbours on average by about 5°. Few telescopes have a working field as large as this, which means that positions of other stars cannot necessarily be linked to the system of bright stars directly by photography. Many stars ($\sim$ 300,000) fainter than 6th magnitude have their positions observed with transit circles on the same system as the bright stars, and these are then used as secondary standards for interpolating the system at each epoch over every part of the sky, but usually to a somewhat lower accuracy than for the 'fundamental' stars themselves. In principle, then, the motion of any star can be expressed relative to that of a star (or stars) on the fundamental system, and hence absolutely—nevertheless, with an error due ultimately to ignorance of the overall motions of the Earth on the one hand and all the stars on the other. This subject has been discussed somewhat at length, not so much because it is more important than others covered more briefly, but to illustrate the kind of analysis which is often involved even in securing observations of stars let alone using them.

Parallaxes We now return to consider how distances of the nearby stars are determined. Essentially this is done by observing the apparent motion of such stars against the background of more remote stars. This motion is made up of a constant component, the proper motion resulting from the relative motion of the star and the centre of mass of the solar system, and an annual parallactic component arising from motion of the Earth around the centre of mass. Figure 8.7 illustrates this annual parallactic motion. Just as the Earth moves round the Sun, so a nearby star appears to move relative to the stellar background and annually describes a parallactic ellipse. Simple geometry shows that the angular size of the semi-major axis of this ellipse is equal to the radius of the Earth's orbit divided by the distance of the star.

In general, the projected motion on the sky is an ellipse going from a circle for stars near the poles of the ecliptic, to a straight line for stars

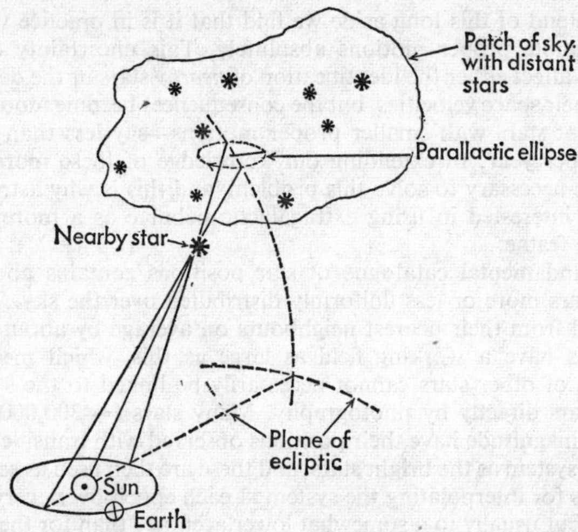

Figure 8.7 The trigonometric method of determining stellar distances

near the ecliptic. The ellipse is always very small owing to the comparatively small scale of the Earth's orbit against the distance of the nearest stars, and has to be measured for greatest accuracy on a series of photographic plates taken with long focal length telescopes over a period of at least one year. Generally speaking, the very nearest stars have a parallactic ellipse whose semi-major axis is about 0.1 arc second, equivalent to only a few microns on the photographic plate. The parallactic ellipse of a nearby star is not measured absolutely, but with reference to more distant stars on the same photographic plate—strictly speaking, therefore, parallaxes are relative but corrections are usually fairly negligible. Measurements have to be conducted with the utmost care, and the limiting accuracy does not permit parallaxes smaller than about 0.04 arc seconds to be determined successfully. The parallactic semi-major axis p is the angle subtended by the radius of the Earth's orbit round the Sun at the star, and since the scale of this orbit is known accurately, the distance D of this star can be found from

$$p = (\text{Earth–Sun distance})/D$$

or

$$D = 1/p \text{ parsecs} \qquad (17)$$

where p is measured in seconds of arc and the unit of 1 parsec is conventionally used for stellar distances. Trigonometric parallaxes of this kind can be measured successfully to distances of 25 parsecs at the most, and the method has been applied to some 7000 stars in all—notal ways with significant results. The effort involved in such work is quite considerable, however, and astronomers do not appreciate wasting it on unlikely stars—this is the reason for using a proper moiton sieve to select probable candidates.

The Sun's nearest stellar neighbours as far as is known are the α Centauri System with a parallax of 0.75 arc seconds, corresponding to a distance of 1.3 parsecs. The brightest visible star is Sirius and this is at a distance of 2.7 parsecs. The nearest star clusters are the Pleiades and Hyades which are at distances of 130 and 40 parsecs respectively and therefore beyond the reach of trigonometric parallax determinations. Their distances have to be found in other ways, and we shall consider these later.

Magnitudes The importance of determining the distances of nearby stars lies in the subsequent calibration of their individual absolute magnitudes—that is, the apparent magnitudes they would have if placed at the same arbitrary distance of 10 parsecs—and of their transverse velocities. The absolute magnitudes are calculated as before from

$$\mathrm{m - M = 5 \log D - 5}$$

assuming there is no absorption between the Sun and the nearest stars. Thus

$$\mathrm{M = m + 5 + 5 \log p} \tag{18}$$

In order that such absolute magnitudes should be on the same scale, it is necessary to ensure that apparent magnitudes are referred to the same zero-point and are on the same scale over the whole sky. This causes greater difficulty than in the case of clusters where all the stars are close together in the sky and the transfer of errors is likely to be small. The main source of trouble is the Earth's atmosphere, which transmits only part of the incoming starlight, and by different fractions in different parts of the spectrum according to the thickness traversed. Allowances are made in practice for this either by making all photometric observations at the same altitude above the horizon, thereby ensuring the same thickness of atmosphere applies all the time, or by reducing observations at any altitude to the zenith by applying empirical corrections derived from observations of the same star at different altitudes. Early this century such work was carried out photographically by directing a telescope first to the field of interest when it was at the same altitude as

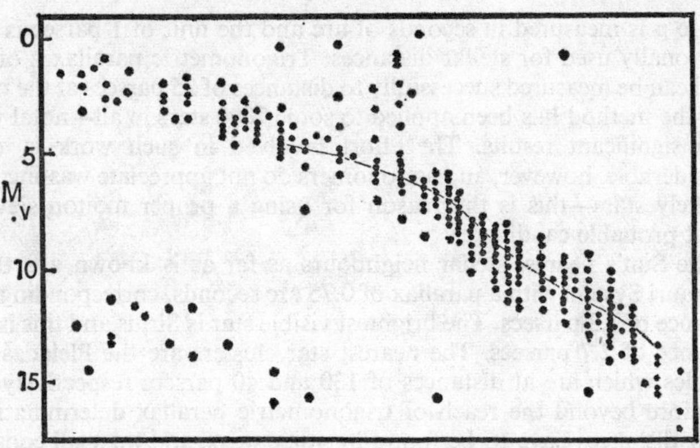

Figure 8.8 Absolute magnitude-intrinsic colour diagram for stars within 10 parsecs of the Sun. After W. Gliese

the north celestial pole and then superimposing on the same exposure a picture of the polar region. This enabled stars in the test field to be standardized against a sequence of 'standard stars' in the polar region. A framework of standards could thus be established over the sky. The work has since become obsolete following the introduction of photo-electric photometry, to which the same principles of observation are, however, applied. Increasingly now, photometry is being carried out from high altitude observatories, balloons, and earth satellites, thereby obviating many of the difficulties experienced at sea-level observatories. Not only are zero-point problems reduced in this way but, more important, other parts of the spectrum become accessible to observation.

Most of the bright stars and many other stars of astrophysical interest have now been observed on the standard U, B, V, photometric system, giving magnitudes in three specified wavelength bands of the spectrum, ultraviolet, blue and visual (or yellow).

Colour-magnitude diagram of the nearest stars Figure 8.8 shows a plot of the absolute visual magnitude M_V against the intrinsic colour B-V for stars which are believed to be within 10 parsecs of the Sun. It resembles the colour-magnitude diagrams found for some of the clusters, particularly as regards the appearance of a main sequence. This is extremely narrow but there are one or two stars which stand above it and which may be evolving away from it. It is important to realize, however, that even if the nearby stars were identical to those in clusters a difference in these diagrams could still be caused by some unsuspected discrepancy between the system of trigonometric parallaxes and the distance determination of the Hyades. There is, in fact, still some uncertainty about the conformity of these distance scales. To all intents and purposes, however, the main sequences are identical, suggesting that the stars of the solar neighbourhood are largely of the same type as seen in open clusters. True, there are many more at the fainter end of the sequence, near the Sun, but this is only to be expected since we are much nearer to them and such stars will therefore be more conspicuous. However, there are certainly fewer of the luminous stars, suggesting that our neighbours are quite evolved and possibly older than the typical open cluster.

In addition, there is a sequence of stars with faint absolute magnitudes ($M_V \sim 14$) running from the blue and possibly joining up with the faint end of the main sequence. Since these stars have more or less the same luminosity, the blue ones with high surface temperatures are much smaller than the red ones. In fact, at the colour of the Sun, stars on this sequence are 10 magnitudes fainter than those on the main sequence—corresponding to a relative luminosity of 10^{-4} and hence a relative radius of 10^{-2}. Since these stars are 100 times smaller than the Sun or less, they have come to be known as *white dwarfs*, and are regarded as an important phase in the evolution of the stars. They are obviously a fairly common type of star even though, for example, they are not conspicuous in stellar clusters—but this is only because of their low intrinsic luminosity which makes them about 20th apparent magnitude even for the nearest clusters. Since they are so common and the immediate solar neighbourhood does not contain excessive quantities of interstellar gas or dust out of which new stars may at present be born, astronomers are inclined to regard white dwarfs as a late stage in the evolution of stars, and it is a matter of some interest to determine their masses so as to identify the part of the main sequence from which they have evolved, and also to enquire how they reached this state from the red giant phase some 10^6 times brighter.

Spectra of stars An important means of examining stars in greater detail than we have presented so far, is provided by spectroscopy. Spectra are normally obtained by attaching an objective prism to a telescope, thereby enabling many stars to be recorded photographically in the focal plane at the same time; or by sending the light from the star image through a slit at the focal plane of the telescope into a dispersing system, prism or diffraction grating, to form a spectrum in a secondary

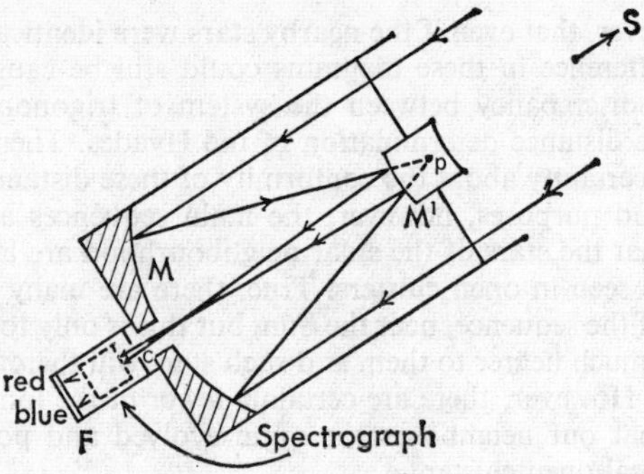

Figure 8.9 The observation of a stellar spectrum with a large reflector

focal plane. This too may be recorded photographically, but an important development in this field is the image-tube, in which the spectrum is formed on a semi-transparent cathode of high quantum efficiency, thereby releasing electrons which are accelerated and brought to yet another focus in an evacuated chamber. As yet, this arrangement works successfully only over a very limited angular field, but exposure times are reduced by factors of the order of 100. Conversely the working limit of a telescope may be improved by 5 magnitudes.

Basically, objective prism spectra are 'seeing' images at each wavelength and details in the spectra are smeared out over about 1 arc second–2 arc seconds. If the dispersion of the spectrum is such that absorption lines are much narrower than 1 arc second, these lines are smeared out and cannot be detected. Objective prism spectra are often secured with a telescope giving a scale of about 100 arc seconds per mm at the focal plane, and with a prism giving a dispersion not better than about 100 Å per mm. Since only the broadest stellar absorption lines are $\sim$ 1 Å in width, only these lines tend to be visible in such spectra. With slit spectra, however, the slit may be narrower than the seeing disk and details comparable with the slit width can be seen. In both cases, however, exposure times are much longer than with direct photographs of the sky because the total star light has to be used to activate a much larger area of emulsion. In order to collect as much light as possible for stellar spectroscopy, one has to use large reflecting telescopes, such as that shown diagrammatically in Figure 8.9. The telescope consists essentially of an aluminized mirror M which reflects light from a star S towards the prime focus P. It would be possible to examine the star image here but, except when very faint objects are being observed, it is usually more convenient to use a Cassegrain mirror M′. This reflects the star light back through a hole in the main mirror to form an image of the star on the slit of the spectrograph. The spectrograph has three essential elements: a collimator, for rendering the light from the star S that gets through the slit into a parallel beam, a dispersing device placed in this parallel beam and an optical system for focusing the dispersed light on to a photographic emulsion, F, or possibly, an array of photocells for monitoring particular regions of the spectrum. The dispersing device may be a prism or, what is now more usual, a blazed diffraction grating.

Spectrophotometry is the measurement of the light intensity at each wavelength of a stellar spectrum. Generally speaking, such measurements show that the *continuous spectra* of main sequence stars are 'black body'-like, consistent with the assumption of Stefan's radiation law earlier on. This means that the peak intensity and colour advance from the red to blue with increasing temperature. It is also found that most stars have absorption lines in their spectra, as does the Sun, and that the character of these lines also changes with colour. Conspicuous in the spectra of many of the main sequence stars are the Balmer lines of hydrogen. When absorption spectra were first discovered, stars were classified according to the strength of their Balmer lines into a sequence A, B, C . . . and so on, but it was subsequently found that this order did not correlate too well with colour. It is now realized that the strength of these lines is primarily dependent on the number of hydrogen atoms in the first excited state in the stellar atmosphere, and this in turn depends on its temperature θ. At $\theta \lesssim 5000°K$, there are very few such atoms; at $\theta \sim 10{,}000°K$, the number has risen to a maximum, but as θ rises to 20,000°K and beyond, the number diminishes again because of increasing ionization of hydrogen atoms. Paucity of hydrogen lines can therefore correspond to either very high or very low temperatures, and is not an unambiguous indicator of temperature. In the Sun's spectrum, for example, the hydrogen Balmer lines are fairly weak, whereas those due to ionized calcium are strong. Helium lines are comparatively rare in stellar spectra while the appearance of ionized helium lines corresponds to surface temperatures higher than 25,000°K. On the other hand, at very low surface temperatures, it is possible for molecular lines to be formed—for example, the appearance of titanium oxide bands indicates a temperature below 3600°K. Table 8.1 gives the principle absorption features which help to classify spectra into a temperature sequence. The main sequence spectral types are

O, B, A, F, G, K, M

TABLE 8.1 PRINCIPAL ABSORPTION FEATURES THAT CLASSIFY SPECTRA INTO A TEMPERATURE SEQUENCE

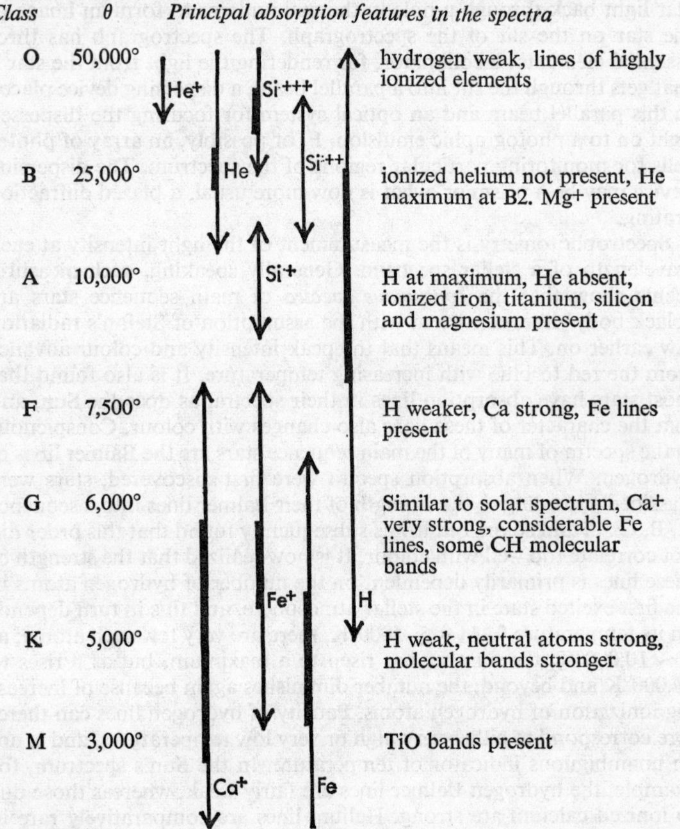

Class	θ	*Principal absorption features in the spectra*
O	50,000°	hydrogen weak, lines of highly ionized elements
B	25,000°	ionized helium not present, He maximum at B2. Mg^+ present
A	10,000°	H at maximum, He absent, ionized iron, titanium, silicon and magnesium present
F	7,500°	H weaker, Ca strong, Fe lines present
G	6,000°	Similar to solar spectrum, Ca^+ very strong, considerable Fe lines, some CH molecular bands
K	5,000°	H weak, neutral atoms strong, molecular bands stronger
M	3,000°	TiO bands present

each interval being divided into tenths. It must be emphasized that the relative strengths of absorption lines are mostly due to temperature, and not to the abundance of chemical elements. The principle absorption features by which stellar spectra are classified are shown in Table 8.1.

H-R diagram of nearby stars The main features of the M_V/Spectral Type diagram for the nearby stars are identical to the colour-magnitude plot, which is not surprising in view of the known colour-temperature correlation. Such a plot is called an H-R diagram after its originators Hertzsprung and Russell, and has proved an invaluable tool in unravelling the stellar universe, primarily because it exposes a relationship between spectrum and absolute magnitude. With its aid the distances of faint stars can be estimated by classifying their spectra and reading off their 'spectroscopic absolute magnitudes'. Such estimates however would clearly be incorrect for stars not on the main sequence and this means it is necessary to identify luminosity criteria in the spectra. The search for such indicators has been an important part of stellar spectroscopy and we shall return to it later. For the moment, we simply note that the spectra of white dwarfs differ from those of main sequence stars in that the former have lines which are extremely broad. Although there are many physical processes capable of broadening spectral lines, it is suspected in this case that the energy levels of atoms in the atmospheres of white dwarfs are heavily perturbed and broadened by proximity to neighbouring atoms. The implication is that the surface density is extremely high, which is in keeping with the very small radius already attributed to these stars. The converse is that very sharp lines are to be expected from atmospheres of very low density as in the case of the giant stars. Line width is therefore also an important parameter.

The formation of spectrum lines in the solar atmosphere has been considered in Chapter 7, and since the same principles apply in the case of stellar atmospheres there is no need to repeat them in detail here. To summarize, however, the observed black body spectrum emerges from a level in the stellar atmosphere roughly where the final absorption and emission occurs for a typical photon anywhere in the spectrum. The effective temperature θ of the stellar atmosphere is that which corresponds to this level rather than the outermost boundary. However, besides continuous absorption, which is largely responsible for the black body spectrum, the state of the stellar atmosphere and the atoms therein is such that at certain frequencies characteristic of these atoms absorption and emission of photons continue out to the very edge of the star. Photons emitted right at the outermost edge of the atmosphere correspond to the lowest possible temperatures, and so the brightness at frequencies where the preferential absorption and emission occur is less than that of the continuous spectrum. In other words, an absorption line is seen. The strength of these lines thus depends on the physical state—temperature and pressure—and composition of the atmosphere, and given a theory of the formation of the lines, it is possible to calculate the numbers of atoms along the line of sight responsible for each line. This in turn enables one to determine the relative abundances of the elements involved in their formation. Such studies are now another important aspect of stellar spectroscopy, since it is believed that chemical abundances provide a clue to the history of the stellar system as a whole. Amongst the nearby stars, however, it is found that most stars have much the same chemical composition. The mixture is dominated by hydrogen (74 per cent by weight) and helium (24 per cent) with a slight peppering of heavier elements.

Radial velocities Besides giving information about the state of stellar atmospheres spectral lines are also displaced in wavelength by small amounts from their laboratory values. These displacements are attributed to relative motion between the star and the telescope along the line of sight. The most direct way of checking this Doppler shift hypothesis is by measuring line displacements throughout the year for selected stars near the plane of the ecliptic. The relative motions of such stars are found to reflect the orbital motion of the Earth round the Sun of about 27 km s^{-1}, and it is therefore usual to make a correction for this motion to all observed displacements dependent on the time of observation. The corrected velocity is called the star's *radial velocity*. Unlike proper motion, this measure of a star's motion is independent of distance. For spectra with a dispersion of 100 Å per mm for example, a radial velocity of 30 km s^{-1} corresponds to 5 microns on the photographic plate. With powerful telescopes and slit spectrographs it is possible to improve on this dispersion, but given a measuring accuracy little better than 1 micron there are very few stars for which an accuracy of 1 km s^{-1} can be bettered. This accuracy is in fact not so very different from that which can be achieved from proper motions and parallaxes of nearby stars, and so total space velocities for stars within, say, 20 parsecs of the Sun are usually determined to about 1 km s^{-1} in any direction.

On the whole, the nearby stars have radial velocities which range over something like 100 km s^{-1}, with a representative value of 30 km s^{-1} in any direction. There are two exceptions, however; the two extreme velocities are those of Barnard's star ($-$ 108 km s^{-1}) which is an M5 dwarf with apparent magnitude $m_V \sim 9.5$, and Kapteyn's star (+ 242 km s^{-1}) which is an M0 dwarf with $m_V \sim 8.8$, the sign in front of the radial velocity indicating whether the star is approaching ($-$) or receding (+). The representative value of 30 km s^{-1}, is in close accord with that derived from transverse velocities of the same stars, and this is taken as strong indirect evidence that no error is made in regarding the displacements of spectral lines as mainly due to radial velocity.

Space velocities From the earliest times when stellar proper motions were first discovered, it has been known that their *directions* of motion tended to be towards the same point in the sky. Although subsequent more refined observations have never dispelled this as a general picture, it is far from true for many individual stars. The rough and ready explanation of this effect is that the Sun's neighbours are moving about in all directions with respect to each other, but nevertheless, on the average, define a standard of rest with respect to which the Sun is found to move. The solar motion results in the observed trend of proper motions and is towards a specific *area* of the sky. By common practice, this area is often specified by the coordinates of a point and called the solar apex, and it is thereby inclined to be given a somewhat greater significance than it really has.

Radial velocity observations show the same tendency as proper motions, with maximum velocities of approach seen amongst stars in the general direction of the solar apex. The solar motion is about 20 km s^{-1} towards R.A. 18h, Dec. + 30° which is in the constellation of Hercules. The custom nowadays is to illustrate the motion of the nearby stars by resolving their total space velocity with respect to the Sun into three components which are considered to be significant in the Galaxy. These components are perpendicular and in the directions of the galactic centre (u), galactic rotation (v) and galactic north pole (w). The first two components are in the plane of the Milky Way and, very roughly, this plane also includes the direction of the solar apex. To a large extent, then, the position of the solar apex may be adequately illustrated in a plot of space motion components u against v, If such a plot for the nearby stars is examined it is seen that the bulk of the stars do indeed stand off by about 20 km s^{-1} from the Sun at the origin. There are, however, many stragglers, who are by no means so exceptional that they can be disregarded. For example, going to stars outside the immediate solar neighbourhood, velocities up to about 500 km s^{-1} relative to the Sun may be encountered.

Stars nearer than five parsecs Table 8.2, which is based on data recently collated by Professor Peter van de Kamp of the Sproul Observatory, lists all stars having measured parallaxes of 0.192 arc seconds or greater, that is all stars whose measured distance from the Sun does not exceed 5.2 parsecs or 17 light years. The uncertainties in the distance measures are such that a limit of 5.2 parsecs should ensure that all stars whose true distance is less than 5.0 parsecs will be included in Table 8.2, which will also contain some whose true distance exceeds this limit.

[*continued on page 320*

TABLE 8.2 SOME OF THE NEAREST STARS

No.	Name	RA 1950	Dec 1950	m_v	SpT	PM (arc sec)	Distance ly	Distance pc	M_v	L
1	*2*	*3*	*4*	*5*	*6*	*7*	*8*	*9*	*10*	*11*
1	Sun			−26.8	G2				4.8	1.00
2A	Alpha Centauri	14h36m	−60°38′	0.1	G2	3″.68	4.3	1.3	4.5	1.30
B				1.5	K5				5.9	0.36
C	Proxima Centauri	14 26	−62 28	11	M5e				15.4	0.00006
3	Barnard's Star	17 55	+ 4 33	9.5	M5	10.30	5.9	1.8	13.2	0.00044
4	750	10 54	+ 7 19	13.5	M6e	4.84	7.6	2.3	16.7	0.00002
5	756	11 01	+36 18	7.5	M2	4.78	8.1	2.5	10.5	0.0052
6A	Sirius	6 43	−16 39	− 1.5	A1	1.32	8.6	2.6	1.4	23
B				7.2	wd				10.1	0.008
7A	144	1 36	−18 13	12.5	M6e	3.35	8.9	2.7	15.3	0.00006
B	145			13.0	M6e				15.8	0.00004
8	1437	18 47	−23 53	10.6	M5e	0.74	9.4	2.9	13.3	0.0004
9	1816	23 39	+43 55	12.2	M6e	1.82	10.3	3.2	14.7	0.00011
10	Epsilon Eridani	3 31	− 9 38	3.7	K2	0.97	10.7	3.3	6.1	0.30
11	1729	22 36	−15 36	12.2	M6	3.27	10.8	3.3	14.6	0.00012
12	852	11 45	+ 1 06	11.1	M5	1.40	10.8	3.3	13.5	0.00033
13A	61 Cygni	21 05	+38 30	5.2	K5	5.22	11.2	3.4	7.5	0.083
B				6.0	K7				8.3	0.040
14	Epsilon Indi	22 00	−57 00	4.7	K5	4.67	11.2	3.4	7.0	0.13
15A	Procyon	7 37	+ 5 21	0.3	F5	1.25	11.4	3.5	2.6	7.6
B				10.8	wd				13.1	0.0005
16A	1431	18 42	+59 33	8.9	M3.5	2.29	11.5	3.5	11.2	0.0028
B	1432			9.7	M4				12.0	0.0013
17A	31	0 16	+43 44	8.1	M1	2.91	11.6	3.5	10.4	0.0058
B	32			11.0	M6				13.3	0.0004
18	1758	23 03	−36 09	7.4	M2	6.87	11.7	3.6	9.6	0.012
19	Tau Ceti	1 42	−16 12	3.5	G8	1.92	11.9	3.7	5.7	0.44
20	527	7 25	+ 5 23	9.8	M4	3.73	12.2	3.8	11.9	0.0014

21	1617	21 14	−39 04	6.7	M1	3.46	12.5	3.8	8.8	0.025
22	Kapteyn's Star	5 10	−45 00	8.8	M0	8.79	12.7	3.9	10.8	0.0040
23A	Kruger 60	22 26	+57 27	9.7	M4	0.87	12.8	3.9	11.7	0.0017
B	1720			11.2	M6				13.2	0.00044
24A	473	6 27	− 2 46	11.3	M5e	0.97	13.1	4.0	13.3	0.0004
B				14.8					16.8	0.00002
25	1283	16 28	−12 32	10.0	M5	1.18	13.1	4.0	12.0	0.0013
26	van Maanen's Star	0 46	+ 5 09	12.4	wdF	2.98	13.9	4.3	14.2	0.00017
27A	923	12 31	+ 9 18	12.6	M6e	1.87	14.2	4.4	14.4	0.00014
B				12.6	M6e				14.4	0.00014
28	5	0 02	−37 36	8.6	M3	6.09	14.5	4.4	10.4	0.0058
29	696	10 08	+49 42	6.6	M0	1.45	15.0	4.6	8.3	0.040
30	1351	17 25	−46 51	9.4	M4	1.15	15.1	4.6	11.1	0.0030
31	1640	21 30	−49 13	8.7	M3	0.78	15.2	4.7	10.4	0.0058
32	1358	17 34	−44 17	11.2	M5	1.14	15.3	4.7	12.8	0.00063
33	171	1 57	+12 51	12.3		2.08	15.4	4.7	13.9	0.00023
34	1034	13 43	+15 10	8.5	M2	2.30	15.7	4.8	10.1	0.0076
35	1364	17 37	+68 23	9.1	M3.5	1.31	15.7	4.8	10.7	0.0044
36	844	11 43	−64 33	11	wd	2.69	15.8	4.9	12.6	0.0008
37	1745	22 51	−14 31	10.2	M5	1.17	15.8	4.9	11.8	0.0016
38A	Omicron^2 Eridani	4 13	− 7 44	4.4	K0	4.08	15.9	4.9	6.0	0.33
B				9.9	wdA				11.2	0.0027
C				11.2	M4e				12.8	0.00063
39	BD+20° 2465	10 17	+20 07	9.4	M4.5	0.49	16.1	5.0	10.9	0.0036
40	Altair	19 48	+ 8 44	0.8	A7	0.66	16.6	5.1	2.3	10.0
41A	70 Ophiuchi	18 03	+ 2 31	4.2	K1	1.13	16.7	5.1	5.7	0.44
B				6.0	K6				7.5	0.083
42	849	11 45	+78 58	11.0	M4	0.87	16.8	5.2	12.4	0.0009
43	1737	22 45	+44 05	10.1	M5e	0.84	16.9	5.2	11.5	0.0021
44A	Stein 2051	4 27	+58 53	11.1		2.37	17.0	5.2	12.5	0.0008
B				12.4	wd				13.8	0.0003

In Table 8.2 each star is identified by its name or by its LFT number, which is its number in a catalogue prepared a few years ago by Professor Luyten of about 1850 stars whose annual proper motion is believed to exceed five-tenths of an arc second per year. The stars are also identified by their positions for 1950 given in columns three and four and by their apparent visual magnitudes given in column five. The spectral types and the total annual proper motions expressed in arc seconds are given in columns six and seven, and the measured distances expressed in light years and in parsecs in columns eight and nine. Column ten gives the absolute visual magnitudes and column eleven the corresponding visual luminosities on the assumption that the visual absolute magnitude of the Sun is 4.8. The table contains 59 stars of which 31 are single, 22 components of double stars and 6 components of triple systems. In addition, six of the single stars and one of the components of the double stars are believed from their observed orbital motions to have unseen companions whose masses range from about 0.0016 to 0.026 that of the Sun, that is, masses intermediate between those of Jupiter and the least massive stars known. The stars in question are Barnard's Star, LFT 756, LFT 527, LFT 1364, BD + 20° 2465, LFT 1737 and 61 Cygni A.

We do not know how complete Table 8.2 is for we cannot tell how faint to go before no further stars appear. Proper motion surveys, for example, are not complete at the faintest apparent magnitudes and may still yield some new faint nearby stars. We can get some idea of the completeness of Table 8.2 by dividing the volume it covers into two equal parts, that contained within a sphere radius 4.2 parsecs, and that contained between this sphere and an outer one radius 5.2 parsecs, and comparing the number of stars found in each. These numbers should be approximately equal if all the stars in the two volumes have been found, for there is no reason to believe that the region of space five parsecs from the Sun is markedly different from that closer to it. Ignoring the unseen companions, the numbers of stars actually found are 35 arranged in 22 systems in the inner volume and 24 arranged in 19 systems in the outer. Including the unseen companions the numbers of 'bodies' are 39 and 27 respectively. This strongly suggests that Table 8.2 is not complete, especially for the fainter stars, since it seems less likely that any of the brighter stars can have been overlooked.

There are no giants or supergiants in the sample of stars contained in Table 8.2 but there are 6 white dwarfs distinguishable by the spectral type 'wd'. All the other stars belong to the main sequence and are distributed amongst the different spectral divisions as follows: 2 in A, 1 in F, 3 in G, 8 in K, and 39 in M, if we can assume that the two stars without observed types are really Ms. The faint M stars are much the most numerous but it is worth noticing that they are far outshone by the less numerous bright stars. Sirius, for example, with a luminosity 23 times that of the Sun, actually outshines all the rest of the stars in the list put together, which have a total luminosity of 21.8. The numerical distribution of the stars in Table 8.2 with absolute visual magnitude is shown in Table 8.3.

TABLE 8.3 THE OBSERVED LUMINOSITY FUNCTION

Range of M_V		*Number of Stars*	*Percentage of Total*
+ 1.3 to	+ 2.4	2	3
2.5	4.9	3	5
5.0	7.4	6	10
7.5	9.9	6	10
10.0	12.4	19	33
12.5	14.9	18	31
15.0	16.7	5	8
All		59	100

The distribution shown in Table 8.3 is known as the *luminosity function* and it can be regarded as fairly typical, at least as far as field stars are concerned. The number density of intrinsically faint stars appears to reach about seven or eight times that of those with the Sun's luminosity at $M_V \sim 15$ and then falls off again at fainter levels, though the fainter end of the luminosity function is not well known.

If we can estimate the masses of the fainter stars from the mass-luminosity relationship, we can estimate the average density of matter condensed into stars in the solar vicinity; their relative velocities and likely ages mean of course that they have not all necessarily condensed out of the same 'piece' of gas, but we shall consider this point in a later section. For the moment, we can calculate an average density of about 50×0.1 solar masses in 500 cubic parsecs or 0.01 M. pc^{-3}. This is equivalent to 10^{-24} g cm^{-3}, which is not so very different from a mass of one hydrogen atom per cubic centimetre. This, in turn, is quite close to the density of hydrogen gas near the Sun derived from 21 cm radio emission (Chapter 9). Matter in the solar neighbourhood is thus fairly evenly divided between stars and hydrogen gas.

Nearly half of the stars in Table 8.2 are members of a multiple system. It is therefore reasonable to conclude that stars with companions are as much the rule as not, and any theory of stellar evolution must explain why such systems are so common. It is fairly easy to see that they are not formed by chance capture by considering this particular sample. The stars have proper motions of the order of 1–2 arc seconds per year. With an average distance of four parsecs this corresponds to velocities relative to the Sun of about 30 km s^{-1} or about 4×10^{-5} parsecs per year. Thus in the lifetime of the Sun the average star will move about 4×10^{5} parsecs relative to the neighbouring stars. Since the Earth's velocity round the Sun is about 30 km s^{-1}, the gravitational interaction between two stars with relative velocities of this order may be expected to be significant only within about the radius of the Earth's orbit round the Sun, that is, within about 10^{-5} pc. In its own lifetime, therefore, a star traverses a volume through which its gravitational influence extends equal to about $(4 \times 10^{5}).(\pi \times 10^{-10}) \approx 10^{-4}$ cubic parsecs. This is so very much smaller than the typical volume associated with each star in the solar neighbourhood, which approximates to 10 cubic parsecs, that the chance of one star meeting another and providing the opportunity for a multiple system to be created, however this could happen, is remote. It is thought, therefore, that the number of multiple systems in the solar neighbourhood is evidence that stars are formed in groups, and it seems very likely that they are formed in clusters. Such an idea is in fact quite plausible because the large number of 'free' stars, or field stars as astronomers call them, can be attributed to the instability of the average cluster against the tidal action of the Milky Way.

Distant stars

An obvious way of exploiting the information that has been gathered about nearby stars is to obtain spectra of more distant stars hoping thereby to classify them and so determine their absolute magnitudes and distances with the H-R diagram. A comparison of the colour magnitude diagrams for the solar neighbourhood and stellar clusters shows, however, that there are many parts of the H-R diagram which can be occupied by stars, but for which there are no 'local' examples. It is therefore necessary to find out whether there are any clues or indications in the observed spectra which tell one whether distant stars are on the main sequence or not. Such clues do in fact exist and are called luminosity criteria. But having found these, it is not possible to place the exceptional stars exactly on the H-R diagram without further information. There is a need to develop methods of calibrating absolute magnitudes for some stars which are beyond the range of trigonometrical parallaxes.

A guide to these is provided by fitting the main sequences of clusters to the main sequence of nearby stars, though unfortunately this cannot be done very accurately because most of the observed stars are at opposite ends of the main sequence in the two cases. It is obviously useful, however, to obtain spectra of the brightest cluster members to compare with those of field stars.

Luminosity criteria The first steps that were taken in this problem were to compare the spectra of pairs of stars of similar magnitude and spectral type, one of which had a much larger proper motion than the other. This was done on the grounds that the low proper motion star was likely to be further off and therefore intrinsically brighter. It turned out that some metal lines are stronger in stars of high luminosity, while others are weaker. The intense ones are lines of ionized atoms such as strontium, titanium and iron. The existence of ionized lines points to an atmosphere which is relatively collision free, that is, one of very low density, and since giant stars have highly tenuous atmospheres as well as being highly luminous, the correlation of ionized line strength with luminosity is entirely plausible. A corresponding reduction in the strength of lines of some neutral atoms, as observed, is also to be expected. This phenomenon can be expressed quantitatively by calculating the intensity ratio of a luminosity sensitive line to an insensitive one for each star. It is sometimes found that there is a smooth relationship between intensity ratio and absolute magnitude, and so this measure can be used for determining 'spectroscopic magnitudes'. Such luminosity criteria, though in this case not necessarily calibrated exactly, are also used in establishing the M-K system. This system is so named because it was originated by Drs Morgan and Keenan of the Yerkes Observatory. In this system, stellar spectra are classified into a two-dimensional array of spectral type against luminosity class, where spectral type no longer bears an unambiguous relation to surface temperatures. There are five main luminosity classes and these tend to run together at spectral type O, but are well spaced out at types K and M. The classes and their appropriate absolute magnitudes at K0 are:

I	Supergiants	$M_V < -5$
II	Bright Giants	$M_V \sim -2$
III	Normal Giants	$M_V \sim 0$
IV	Subgiants	$M_V \sim +3$
V	Main Sequence	$M_V \sim +7$

Two further classes are recognized: the so-called *subdwarfs* which run below the main sequence in absolute magnitude but more or less parallel, and the *white dwarfs*. Stars which can be placed without doubt in this array are regarded as normal, but there are many kinds of *peculiar* stars which are not so easy to place. For example, A stars show a variety of peculiarities, such as extremely shallow lines in some, which are attributed to stellar rotation broadening the lines by 'Doppler' recession at one limb and approach at the other, and abnormal intensities in others caused by the action of powerful magnetic fields. Late-type stars, on the other hand, occasionally show distinctly unusual strengths of lines involving the element carbon—CN and CH bands for example—which are difficult to account for save through varying abundances of carbon.

Statistical parallaxes The best way of finding the absolute magnitude of the intermediate species of luminous stars in the two dimensional array is by determining their statistical parallaxes. Supposing that sufficient stars of one kind can be found more or less uniformly distributed around the sky, the essential data required are their apparent magnitudes, radial velocities and proper motions. Although it is realized that these stars will be moving at random with respect to each other, the assumption is made that they belong to one population which is moving as a whole with respect to the Sun, and that each star is equally likely to be moving with the mean motion of the group. Each proper motion is scaled up or down to a standard apparent magnitude so that all the stars can be regarded as being at the same distance. This distance is then adjusted until the radial velocities and the transverse motions separately imply the same mean motion with respect to the Sun and the same dispersion of velocities about the mean. This adjusted distance is the inverse of the statistical parallax and when applied to the chosen apparent magnitude gives the absolute magnitude of the group. For distant stars, using this method, it is necessary to make corrections for absorption as judged by reddening of main sequence stars along each line of sight. Although sound enough in principle, the technique suffers from two disadvantages. First, the stars are usually so remote that there is some uncertainty in their proper motions, and secondly, it is often very doubtful whether the selected stars can safely be regarded as members of one kinematic group. Whilst it is not really possible to test this for distant stars, there is sufficient evidence amongst stars out to say 100 pc from the Sun to throw considerable doubt on the hypothesis as far as young stars are concerned. Nevertheless, the technique has been used for finding the absolute magnitudes of A-stars and subgiants and confirming those of intermediate spectral type on the main sequence.

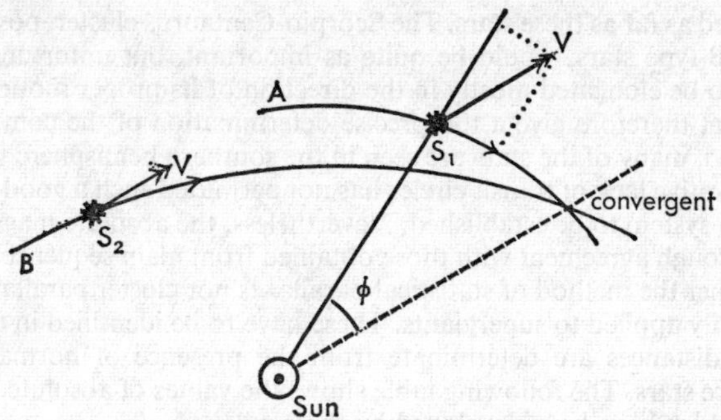

Figure 8.10 The assumed motion of cluster members whose proper motions are directed towards a common convergent point

Cluster parallaxes A very powerful though rather special method using the same kind of observational data finds application in determining the distance of the Hyades and Scorpio-Centaurus clusters. The latter is a prominent part of Gould's Belt at fairly southerly declinations. Both of these clusters are sufficiently close to the Sun for each to cover a substantial portion of the sky, and to have significant proper motions. Considering the Hyades cluster in particular, the proper motion vectors point to a common convergent wherever the members are in the sky, thereby suggesting a community motion in parallel. In much the same way as parallel railway lines converge to a point at infinity, so we can now suppose that each member of the cluster is travelling more or less parallel to the line of sight of the convergent with respect to the Sun, at the same speed V, say. In Figure 8.10, S_1, S_2 represent typical cluster stars and A, B, arcs of the great circles joining them to the convergent point and along which their proper motions lie. If the angle between S_1 and the convergent point is ϕ, the observed radial velocity of S_1 will be $V \cos \phi$ and the transverse velocity $V \sin \phi$. Plotting the observed radial velocities of Hyades members against $\cos \phi$ confirms the model and gives a precise value for V ($\approx$ 40 km s^{-1}) which in turn gives a precise value for the transverse velocity in each case. Dividing this by the observed proper motion enables the distance of each star to be found, thereby permitting the derivation of absolute magnitudes of good accuracy. The importance of the Hyades lies in the presence of late A-type stars, thus allowing the calibration of the main sequence to be extended as far as these stars. The Scorpio-Centaurus cluster, possessing many B-type stars, would be quite as important, but unfortunately it tends to be elongated mostly in the direction of its proper motions and does not therefore give a too precise determination of the convergent, and also, many of the stars are seen in the southern hemisphere where a comparative lack of transit circles has not permitted such a good proper motion system to be established. Nevertheless, the absolute magnitudes are in rough agreement with those obtained from main sequence fitting.

Neither the method of statistical parallaxes nor cluster parallaxes can be readily applied to supergiants. These have to be identified in clusters whose distances are determinate from the presence of normal main sequence stars. The following table shows the values of absolute magnitudes which have been developed by these means:

TABLE 8.4 TEMPERATURES AND ABSOLUTE MAGNITUDES OF STARS

Class / *Type*	V	IV	III	II	Ib	Ia	*Surface temperatures*
B0	−3.9	−4.2	−4.5	−5.2	−6.0	−6.7	
							20,000°
B5	−1.3	−2.2	−3.2	−4.5	−5.7	−7.0	
							12,500
A0	0.3	−0.4	−1.1	−3.0	−4.8	−7.0	
							10,000
A5	2.2	1.4	0.0	−2.0	−4.5	−7.0	
							8,000
F0	3.0	2.0	0.6	−2.0	−4.5	−7.0	
F5	3.5	2.7	1.0	−2.0	−4.5	−7.0	
							6,000
G0	4.4	3.2	0.7	−2.0	−4.5	−7.0	
							5,000
G5	5.1	3.4	0.2	−2.0	−4.5	−7.0	
							4,000
K0	6.0	3.4	0.2	−2.1	−4.5	−7.0	
K5	7.8		−0.3	−2.4	−4.5	−7.0	
M0	9.2		−0.4	−2.4	−4.5	−7.0	
							3,000
M5	12.3						

Stellar kinematics The general study of stellar kinematics remains extremely confused and is largely hindered from progressing by the

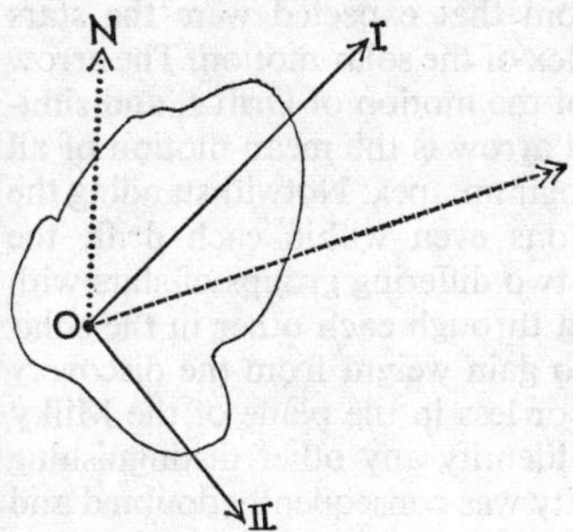

Figure 8.11 The distribution of the proper motions of the brighter stars in a typical area of the sky

limited accuracy with which proper motions and absolute magnitudes can at present be determined. We have already seen that the space motions of stars out to 20 pc can be measured to about 1 km s^{-1}. At 100 pc the corresponding accuracy is nearer 3 km s^{-1}. and at 300 pc, getting on for 10 km s^{-1}. Although there are particular studies where an improvement on these accuracies may be claimed, some doubt usually lingers. Since 10 km s^{-1} is beginning to approach the kind of velocities which systems of stars apparently have with respect to one another, it is not surprising to find some confusion coming in at the distance of 300 pc. At the same time, however, there are some stars at even greater distances which have such high velocities that this confusion does not necessarily arise. To a large extent, in understanding stellar kinematics, observational accuracy obliges one to confine investigations to within 300 pc of the Sun. In practice there is the further limitation of apparent magnitude, for which suitable proper motions and radial velocities are available. This meant that early investigators had material pertaining only to the brightest stars in the sky, mostly those visible to the naked eye. However, the broad features of the results of their investigations have generally been confirmed by going fainter, possibly only because fainter stars in the same volume of space have the same kinematic properties as the intrinsically brighter stars.

Figure 8.11 illustrates the distribution of the proper motions of the stars in a typical area of the sky. The diagram is formed by plotting the number of stars with proper motions in each small interval of position angle in a polar diagram relative to the standard of rest O. The distribution has two fairly substantial 'lobes' which were originally interpreted as two 'drifts' to which the bulk of the stars in each area belonged. This distribution is distinctly different from that expected were the stars simply moving as a whole with the reflex of the solar motion. The arrow I indicates the direction of the apex of the motion of Drift I, and similarly for arrow II; the double-headed arrow is the mean motion of all the stars and is directed towards the solar antapex. Notwithstanding the considerable scatter of proper motions even within each drift, the explanation of this seemed to be that two differing groups of stars with different space velocities were moving through each other in the solar neighbourhood. The idea appeared to gain weight from the discovery that their relative velocity was more or less in the plane of the Milky Way, but it proved very difficult to identify any other distinguishing features between the drifts. Their reality was consequently doubted and it was thought best just to regard the axis of relative velocity between the drifts as a significant direction of maximum 'mobility' amongst the stars. This notion was established further by the later discovery that the axis pointed more or less in the direction of the galactic centre, and the idea arose that the local velocity dispersion of stars was largely controlled by the Galaxy's gravitational field—in such a way that the greatest dispersion was to be seen in the radial direction. It became customary to represent the stellar motions in the solar neighbourhood by a 'velocity ellipsoid' of dispersion with the major axis orientated towards the galactic centre and the other principal axes towards the galactic rotation and galactic pole directions. According to this concept, the solar motion is just the motion of the Sun with respect to the centre of the velocity ellipsoid. As a means of representing the local stellar velocities, the velocity ellipsoid has great simplicity and convenience, but whether it has any physical significance in all cases is rather questionable. However, on the assumption that it is significant for most stars, a considerable amount has been deduced about the gravitational field of the Galaxy from the properties of the velocity ellipsoid.

At the same time, it is recognized that the separation into proper motion drifts in any one part of the sky is rather more marked than an accidental clumping of stars in a velocity ellipsoid would produce. Unfortunately, without any distinguishing characteristics other than their motion, the identification of a drift in one part of the sky as part of the same group of stars represented by a drift in another part of the sky is attended by some uncertainty. Indeed, if the drifts are wrongly matched, an incorrect apex is deduced. Most early work on drifts was governed by the idea that there were two drifts and that one of them had more stars in than the other, and it was this factor that was allowed to dominate the matching. However, there is good reason to believe that there are more than two drifts—a third prominent one, not recognized at first, is mostly evident in the southern sky. This has a velocity more or less at right angles to the axis between the other drifts, and its constituent members, mostly early type stars, are distributed along the feature already mentioned known as Gould's Belt. The fact that this third drift contains a large fraction of the early type stars in the solar neighbourhood means in fact that they are among the most distant stars within 300 pc, while the two other drifts made up mostly of later type stars are much nearer at hand. It seems that, in examining stellar kinematics, some distinction in spectral type must be made to avoid confusion. Such subdivisions are now normally made.

The B-stars in the solar neighbourhood are mostly concentrated in Gould's Belt. Their space motions are such that those in Gould's Belt, which are largely in the third and fourth quadrants of galactic longitude, are moving roughly towards the solar antapex with a velocity of 30 km s^{-1}. The others, mostly in the first two quadrants, have a smaller velocity nearly in the same direction of about 15 km s^{-1}, but with much more scatter about the mean. Gould's Belt appears to be an elongated system about 150 pc wide and 400 pc long in which the Sun is immersed though very much to one side. The space motions of its members suggest that it is expanding along its main axis at about 3 km s^{-1} per 100 pc roughly towards the galactic centre. It is probably not a coincidence that the characteristic time scale of a few 10^7 years related to this kinematic expansion is very close to the evolutionary age of the B-stars concerned.

The A-stars in the immediate solar neighbourhood less than 100 pc from the Sun have space velocities which show a most remarkable clumping into four substantial groups. One of these has the velocity of the Hyades cluster, another that of the Pleiades, yet another has that of the Ursa Major cluster to which the star Sirius apparently belongs, while the remainder are somewhat less exactly grouped but have a velocity like that of the Coma cluster. All the groups are moving roughly within the plane of the Galaxy with the velocities indicated in Figure 8.12 in which the u-axis is directed towards the galactic centre and the v-axis in the direction of galactic rotation. The scale of the diagram is indicated by the marks on the axes which correspond to velocities of 30 km s^{-1}. The velocities plotted are those relative to the Sun, and the well defined blocks into which the velocity points tend to congregate are the Hyades group denoted by H, the Pleiades group by P, the Coma group by C and the Ursa Major or Sirius group by U.M. It would appear that each of the nearest clusters has attendant members in larger surrounding haloes and that each of these haloes is passing through the others in the solar neighbourhood to produce the

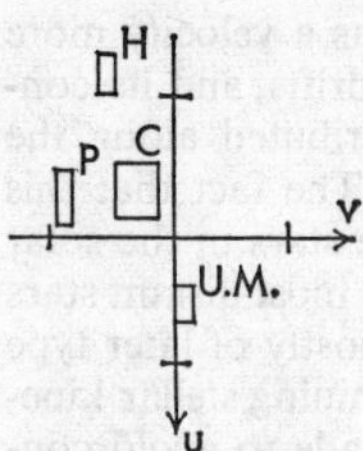

Figure 8.12 The relative motions in the plane of the Galaxy of A stars within 100 parsecs of the Sun

observed groups. There can be little doubt that it is this phenomenon, confused undoubtedly with stars which do not reveal it so readily, that is responsible for the proper motion drifts. The Hyades and Coma groups, moving more or less in the same direction—towards the galactic anticentre—with respect to the Sun, make up one of the drifts, while the Sirius group in the opposite direction towards the galactic centre is another. These together define an axis approximately along a galactic radius. The Pleiades group is the third drift and has a motion identical to that of Gould's Belt as a whole—in fact the Pleiades cluster appears at one end of Gould's Belt and is part of it.

The young stars near the Sun thus separate into distinct groups and, amongst these, it looks as if the luminosity function varies. Thus the Gould's Belt system possesses more intrinsically luminous stars than the Sirius group and is therefore less evolved. It follows that we do not necessarily expect these groups to be represented by late type stars in the same proportion. Indeed, the situation amongst late type stars is much more difficult to unravel because, as pointed out earlier, the main sequence stars could be young or old, and if the latter, then not with the same space velocities as the young clusters. Nevertheless, amongst the spectral types G, K and M within about 50 pc of the Sun, there are still signs of the four groups, but superposed on a 'substratum' of field stars with a much larger velocity dispersion. This substratum does in fact have the characteristics of a velocity ellipsoid, and can be used more appropriately in deriving properties of the Galaxy's gravitational field, since the individual stars are presumably moving in orbits under the controlling influence of this field and do not have a common origin like stars in a cluster or group. Of particular interest are dwarf M-stars, some of which have strong emission lines, notably in ionized calcium: these latter Me stars tend to concentrate at the familiar group velocities, and such emission is now regarded as a sign of youth and a very active chromosphere in these stars. The search for similar indicators of age amongst nearby late stars is obviously of great importance.

Stellar population In the search for indicators of age, accurate photoelectric photometry has played a significant role. For many open star clusters which have been observed photometrically in U, B and V, it is possible to make a meaningful plot of U − B against B − V. Such a two-colour diagram shows a characteristic and common pattern for all main sequence stars. The pattern—a curved line—simply describes the detailed way in which the observed continuous spectrum varies with surface temperature. The relative positions of cluster members in such diagrams is altered, however, by interstellar absorption, but once again it is possible to evaluate an empirical relationship between the effects on U−B and B−V and so apply a correction in reducing these diagrams to absolute. Many of the nearby stars lie on the same curve in the two-colour diagram but there are exceptional stars which show an ultraviolet excess in that their observed U − B is brighter than what would be deduced from the normal curve as corresponding to their observed B − V. It is possible that the Sun itself is amongst such stars. This ultraviolet excess is believed to originate in a redistribution of the spectrum's energy resulting from the relative abundance of metals in the stellar atmosphere. The examination of individual spectrum lines shows that the high ultraviolet excess stars are the ones less abundant in metals. Indeed, the strength of certain metal lines is an even better parameter for isolating metal weak and metal rich stars, but is not necessarily so readily measured as ultraviolet excess is for fainter stars. It turns out that the stars with large velocity dispersion are those with significant ultraviolet excesses or weak metal lines. About half the late-type stars fall into this category. Since the more 'normal' colours are associated with the younger groups of stars, the incidence of ultraviolet excess and high velocity dispersion is now associated with great age. This idea does however create problems, for since all the stars concerned are main sequence stars, they are unevolved in the sense that their fuel at the core has not yet been used up. Since an essential feature of our explanation of the existence of red giants is substantially one of no mixing, the observed stellar atmosphere must have the qualities of the mixture out of which each star formed. The conclusion is that older stars appear not to have been created out of such a metal rich mixture as those which are currently being formed. The general explanation of this is that nuclear reactions inside stars transform hydrogen into elements of higher atomic number during their evolution, and somehow the products of this evolution are distributed amongst the material out of which subsequent generations of stars are formed. It seems that the only reasonable way to cause this to happen is for the highly evolved stars to explode and scatter their contents through the interstellar medium. Such an idea undoubtedly conditions present-day attitudes to the various kinds of explosive stars which have been observed in the sky.

The great age of stars with high ultraviolet excess is confirmed by photometry of globular clusters. These objects have colour-magnitude arrays displaying the reddest of turn-off points, pointing to long periods of time in which evolution could occur, and at the same time, the constituent stars have very large ultraviolet excesses compared to stars of similar B−V in other clusters. Globular clusters are known to reach very great heights above and below the galactic plane, suggestive of extremely high space velocities—as indeed are confirmed by their radial velocities. These old objects with high velocity dispersion are entirely in keeping with the above picture. Globular clusters usually contain two types of star of such a recognizable type that special efforts have been made to search them out in the solar neighbourhood and study their properties. These are the so-called *RR Lyrae variables* and the *subdwarfs*, and we shall return to examine their kinematics shortly.

For the moment, we summarize the picture of stellar kinematics so far uncovered in the solar neighbourhood. There are apparently a few recently formed groups of stars around the Sun which are presumably fairly close to their points of origin. With ages of about 10^8 years and relative velocities of the order of 10 km s^{-1} or so, it seems that the events responsible for the creation of these groups may be located in space at a distance of the order of 1000 pc from the Sun—sufficiently near for our telescopes to examine in some detail if they can be identified. It seems quite likely that the nearby Orion and Sagittarius spiral arms are possible places for such events to occur. Mixed in with the young population—named Population I—there is an older *intermediate* population whose velocity dispersion is typically of the order of 25 km s^{-1} and to which the Sun probably belongs. As we shall see, there is an even older population, less well represented, which has a very large characteristic velocity dispersion—the so-called Population II.

Globular clusters have, as we have already remarked, colour magnitude diagrams with some distinct differences from those of the less evolved open clusters. Notable among these is the appearance of the *horizontal branch* stars (Figure 8.2): a sequence at constant luminosity joining up at the red end with the giant branch which itself extends downwards to the main sequence, and tailing off at the blue end near $B - V \approx 0$. The horizontal branch runs through a zone of the H-R diagram in which variable stars occur. The variables which are present in the horizontal branches of globular clusters are known as RR Lyrae variables after the brightest star of this type in the general field. They

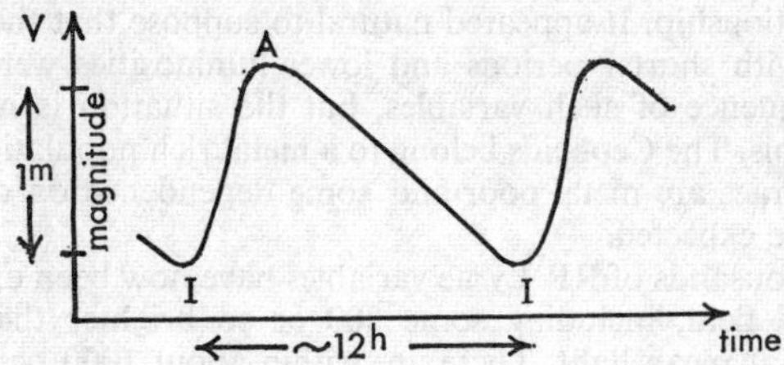

Figure 8.13 Light curve of a typical a-type RR Lyrae variable

have periods of the order of $\frac{1}{2}$ day and vary through a magnitude or so: they are as a result very conspicuous members of globular clusters, being readily identified on a series of photographs by their considerable luminosity and rapid variation. A typical light curve for an a-type RR Lyrae variable is shown in Figure 8.13 in which magnitude is plotted against time. The points A and I indicate maximum and minimum light, which recur regularly with periods that remain sensibly constant to one part in 10^6 over intervals as long as 50 years. The part IA is known as the rising branch and usually takes about ten per cent of the cycle time. These stars which are intrinsically fairly luminous and which can be easily recognized by their characteristic light variation can be used as distance indicators if it can be established that stars having similar periods also have similar absolute magnitudes. For this reason, considerable interest has been shown in the properties of the nearby RR Lyrae type variables. The structure of these stars is also a subject of some interest, since they represent a phase in the evolution of stars of about solar mass—judging by the position of the turn-off point. It is not known for certain whether red giant stars evolve further by passing from right to left along the horizontal branch through the 'variable gap', or whether some more complicated path is likely to be true. RR Lyrae type variables are not found in the younger clusters, suggesting that this phase does not occur in the evolution of the more massive stars. However, there are a few open clusters containing single variables of the so-called *Cepheid* type. These have periods of the order of 20 days or so and are distinctly more luminous than RR Lyrae variables. In fact, it is known from the identification of such stars in extragalactic star systems that there is a period-luminosity relationship amongst stars of this type, in the sense that both increase together. The distances of the clusters in which these stars are seen in our Galaxy confirm such a relationship. It appeared natural to suppose that the RR Lyrae variables with shorter periods and lower luminosities were part of a natural sequence of such variables, but the situation is not quite so simple as this. The Cepheids belong to a metal rich population, whereas the RR Lyraes are metal poor and some dependence on composition may well be expected.

Many thousands of RR Lyrae variables have now been discovered in the general field, including some 300 or so brighter than the 12th magnitude at mean light. These are within about 1000 pc of the Sun, and have periods in the range 0.2 to 1 day. They often have relatively large proper motions and very high radial velocities (averaged over the whole cycle of variation) which can be considered as before to determine their statistical parallax. This gives them an absolute magnitude of about $M_V \sim 0.5$, from which the distances of the individual globular clusters can be found. These turn out to be considerable, going up to many thousands of parsecs, and were in fact the first indication that the Galaxy is very large indeed compared to the small volume of space we have been looking at so far. However, some care has to be taken in selecting the stars, because spectroscopic evidence based mostly on the strength of an ionized calcium line suggests different metal strengths for different RR Lyrae variables. It appears that the metal poor ones have especially large amplitudes and move as a whole with respect to the Sun at about 200 km s^{-1}, more or less dragging behind the Sun as it circles round the Galaxy. Individual RR Lyrae stars are moving about at speeds of this order of magnitude relative to their mean. The other less metal weak stars, on the other hand, have kinematic properties more akin to those of the intermediate population, and are possibly intrinsically fainter. The metal poor RR Lyraes are regarded as members of a widely dispersed Population II, and it is reasonable to expect other members of the same population—for example red giants and main sequence stars—to be found in the solar neighbourhood, even though they are more difficult to identify. There are indeed some high-velocity metal deficient red giants known, and high ultraviolet excess main sequence stars have also been found with large proper motions and radial velocities. These latter seem to have absolute magnitudes lower than the standard main sequence, and are therefore called subdwarfs. Likewise, metal deficient blue stars belonging to the horizontal branch at great distances from the galactic plane are the subject of considerable interest.

In this section we have seen how much of the observational data on nearby stars synthesizes into a fairly consistent general picture with the more distant stars. In Chapter 9 we see how this local picture fits into the wider pattern of the Galaxy as a whole. There are still many other features of stars which demand explanation, however, some of which may be treated as exceptional quirks and others of which represent an important phase in the overall picture which has now been drawn.

Stars with a difference

Binary stars The existence of physically connected binary systems of stars is evident in two ways. The first is from astrometric measurements of close doubles which are orbiting round each other. These measurements are made photographically for widely separated pairs, but are made visually when they are so close that photography causes the two star images to merge: the human eye can catch instants of good seeing which are lost in the longer exposures associated with photography. The second is from spectroscopic binaries, which are close doubles too remote to be separated by eye, but whose spectra vary in a way that can only be explained by two stars orbiting around each other in a plane not at right angles to the line of sight. Special cases of spectroscopic binaries arise when the line of sight lies in the orbital plane and regular partial or total eclipses of each component occur. The discovery of spectroscopic binaries is largely accidental, though it does seem that there is a greater frequency amongst early-type stars, while that of visual binaries depends on the relative orbital velocity of the pair and the care with which positional observations are made. In this latter case, the range of choice is so extensive—owing to accidental alignments—and the difficulty of observation so great that, as before, some care in selecting likely candidates has to be taken. Some 300 systems have in fact moved sufficiently to enable an orbit to be determined. The observation of binary systems is important since they provide the only direct means of determining stellar masses.

The interpretation of binary systems is based entirely on gravitational theory. According to this, the semi-major axis a and period T are related to the total mass M of the system by

$$GM = \frac{4\pi^2 a^3}{T^2}$$

Expressing a in astronomical units, T in years, and M in units of solar mass, this relation becomes:

$$M T^2 = a^3 \qquad (19)$$

In special cases where the relative orbits of each member of the system can be measured with respect to their centre of mass, it is relevant to note the following extra relationships:

$$m_1 a_1 = m_2 a_2$$
$$M = m_1 + m_2$$
$$a = a_1 + a_2$$

which enable the individual masses of the components to be found. In Table 8.2 we see that the nearest star, for example, is a binary system and that it has a semi-major axis of about 18 arc seconds, which at its known parallax corresponds to some 23 astronomical units. The period of revolution is 80 years, and so the mass of the system is about 1.9 solar masses. Most observed systems have masses of this order running as low as one-tenth to about ten times the solar mass—establishing without much doubt that the Sun is a very average kind of star. In many cases the observed orbit is not perpendicular to the line of sight and a geometrical transformation has to be applied to place the centre of attraction at the focus of each orbit. An important nearby star to which these methods have been applied is Sirius, which has a faint companion. The existence of this faint companion was in fact surmised from the roughly sinusoidal deviation of Sirius from a straight line proper motion long before it was actually seen in a telescope. The companion is a typical white dwarf—the first to be discovered—and the system provides sufficient data for its mass to be determined as well as that of Sirius itself. The white dwarf has a mass roughly equal to that of the Sun, which, in view of the earlier discussion, suggests that these stars represent a highly evolved state following the red giant phase.

Spectroscopic binaries are recognized by periodic variations in the positions of the spectral lines resulting from successive approach and recession of the star in its orbit. If the components of the system are comparable in magnitude, the absorption lines are double and the velocities of each component can be measured; however, it is usually only the brighter component whose motion can be detected. There is, nevertheless, an essential uncertainty about the orbit, since its inclination to the line of sight is not known. As the mass of the system is proportional to the cube of the observed orbital scale, the cube of the inclination factor is involved, and only a statistical estimate of the masses of such systems is possible unless the system is an eclipsing one, in which case the orbital plane could include the line of sight. In fact, such systems are more readily discovered than others, because the periodic eclipse results in a light variation which can be detected. The

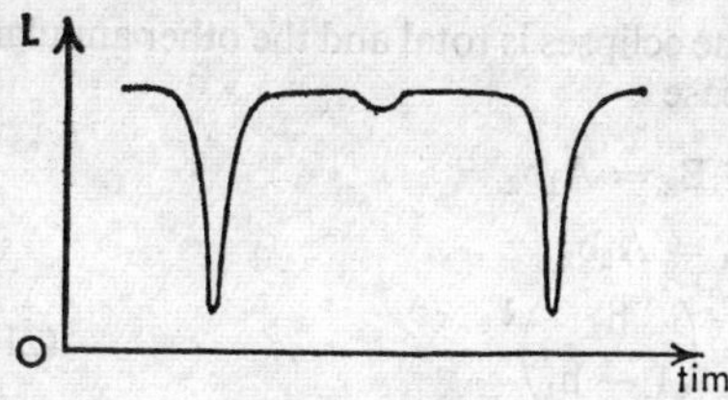

Figure 8.14 Light curve of a typical Algol-type variable

best known star of this type is Algol (Beta Persei) whose light curve is shown schematically in Figure 8.14. The alternating deep and shallow dips in the curve correspond to the alternating eclipses of the bright and faint components.

The light curves of eclipsing binaries have two minima, separated by about $\frac{1}{2}$T, arising from the eclipse of part or all of the light from one component by the other. Suppose each star presents a surface area A of radius R and brightness b to the observer and that an area A_0 is eclipsed when the stars are aligned. Denoting the stars by subscripts 1 and 2, we can write down expressions for the total light out of eclipse B_0 and at each eclipse B_1 and B_2.

$$B_0 = b_1A_2 + B_2A_2$$
$$B_1 = b_1(A_1 - A_0) + b_2A_2$$
$$B_2 = b_1A_1 + b_2(A_2 - A_0)$$

Therefore

$$B_0 - B_1 = A_0b_1$$
$$B_0 - B_2 = A_0b_2$$

If the depth of each minimum below the maximum level of light normalized to unity is given by h, then

$$h = 1 - \frac{B}{B_0}$$

and

$$\frac{h_1}{h_2} = \frac{b_1}{b_2} \qquad (20)$$

In other words, the ratio of the surface brightness of each star is equal to the ratio of the loss of light at each minimum. It follows that the ratio of the surface temperatures of each star is given by:

$$\frac{\theta_1}{\theta_2} = \left(\frac{h_1}{h_2}\right)^{\frac{1}{4}}$$

In the simple case where one of the eclipses is total and the other annular we can put $A_0 = A_1$, in which case

$$B_0 - B_2 = A_1 b_2$$

and

$$B_1 = A_2 b_2$$

and therefore,

$$\frac{R_1}{R_2} = \left(\frac{h_2}{1 - h_1}\right)^{\frac{1}{2}} \tag{21}$$

If the period and velocity curves of each component are known, the length of the orbit, C, can obviously be calculated. At the instants when the minima begin and end, the stars would be seen tangential to each other. Supposing the time interval between these instants is t, then for an orbit whose plane includes the line of sight

$$2\,R_1 + 2\,R_2 = \frac{t}{T}\,C$$

The radii of the stars are thus determined as well as their masses, and if the distance of the star can also be found, as it can be for members of open clusters for example, then so can the surface temperatures and luminosities. Although such systems therefore appear to be extremely useful for checking the theory of stellar structure, it usually turns out that the known eclipsing binaries are the ones whose orbits are fairly small in relation to the size of the components, thereby producing partial eclipses in a large number of possible inclinations to the line of sight. Because the stars are near together in this way, there is considerable interaction between them, thereby upsetting the normal equilibrium conditions. This interaction may take the form of tides, even resulting in the streaming of gas from one to the other, or it may lead to a significant reflection of light from one star by the other.

Eclipsing binary systems also provided the first definite information about stellar rotation. For periods of time immediately preceding and following total eclipse, it is observed in quite a number of cases that there is a sharp change in the observed velocity of the system by opposite and equal amounts. This effect is, very reasonably, attributed to the preponderating velocity at each side of the partially exposed star, and suggests that this star is rotating. It is always found that the star is rotating in the same sense as the binary system itself, and in close systems, with the same period as the orbital revolution.

Stellar rotation When a rotating star which passes behind the other during orbit is not eclipsed, the integrated light from this star produces a spectrum with broad shallow lines. This broadening is caused by Doppler effect and arises from the compounding of profiles due to one limb receding from the observer and the other approaching. Such shallow lines can be observed in other stars which are not members of binary systems, and in general the line widths can be measured to give a value for the rotational velocity. Unfortunately, it is only in the case of eclipsing systems that one can determine the true equatorial rotation velocity; otherwise, one does not know the inclination of the polar axis of the star to the line of sight. Indeed it is quite possible to observe stars pole-on, and in these the lines would be sharp and there would be no evidence of rotation in the spectrum even though the star is in fact rotating. Some of the 'peculiarities' in A-stars may arise from this phenomenon. Thus, weak metal lines may be clearly visible in an A-star seen pole-on, but in other orientations are broadened by rotation to such an extent that they are indistinguishable from the continuum. It is possible to make statistical allowances for the random orientation of polar axes among the classes of rotating stars, and it is found, in general, that the equatorial velocities of early type stars on the main sequence are large, whereas those later than F5 have very little rotation. The reason for this is not known, but it is often speculated that it has something to do with the formation of planetary systems. Thus the Solar System as a whole has a considerable quantity of angular momentum of which only a small fraction is in the Sun itself. It is possible that the contraction of stars on to the lower main sequence gives rise to an instability of a kind that does not arise on the upper main sequence, and which causes the conserved angular momentum to be redistributed. B-stars have equatorial velocities typically of about 100 km s^{-1}, and there are some which are as large as 500 km s^{-1}. The Sun, for example, would suffer rotational instability if the equatorial velocity V were such that

$$V^2 > \frac{G.M}{R} \tag{22}$$

or if V were greater than about 450 km s^{-1}. Since, as we have seen already, M/R increases only slightly for more massive stars, the comparatively rare equatorial velocity of 500 km s^{-1} probably represents an upper limit governed by stability considerations. It also follows that stars with the more typical value of 100 km s^{-1} are quite stable against rotation, and, to a first approximation, the neglect of this issue as in our preliminary treatment of stellar equilibrium is generally permissible. So far as late main sequence stars like the Sun are concerned, rotation is of no importance at all in considering their equilibrium. The Sun's actual equatorial velocity is only about 1 km s^{-1}. It may be shown that the observed equatorial velocities of B-stars are not at variance with the idea that they have condensed as separate units from the interstellar medium conserving angular momentum. For main sequence stars, M/R is roughly constant, which means in turn that the quantity ρR^2 is roughly constant, where ρ is the mean density of the star. A star 15 times more massive than the Sun, for example, has a radius of about 10^{12} cm and a mean density some 200 times smaller and of the order of 10^{-2} g cm^{-3}. Since the density of the interstellar medium is, as we have seen, in the region of 10^{-24} g cm^{-3}, the approximate scale of the element of interstellar medium out of which such a star condenses is

$$\left(\frac{10^{-2}}{10^{-24}}\right)^{\frac{1}{3}} \times 10^{12} \approx 2 \times 10^{19} \text{ cm}$$

The rotational velocity at the edge of such an element, assuming conservation of angular momentum, would thus be about

$$\left(\frac{10^{12}}{10^{19}}\right) \times 100 \approx 10^{-5} \text{ km s}^{-1}$$

This corresponds to a rotational shear across the element of something like 10^{-5} / 2.10^{19} km s^{-1} cm^{-1} or 10^{-3} km s^{-1} per 1000 pc. Such a shear is three or four orders of magnitude less than that which apparently exists in the gravity field of the Galaxy, and so the possession of such angular momentum by stars is in no way implausible. Indeed it might be argued that these stellar angular momenta 'err' on the side of being too small, and that this is the reason why contracting gas clouds must be so frequently 'forced' to form multiple systems—or planetary systems—as they evolve. The Alpha Centauri system has an orbital velocity of about 10 km s^{-1} around a radius of about 3×10^{14} cm, and thus carries about 300 times more angular momentum per unit mass than the isolated massive main sequence star.

Among the rapidly rotating B-stars with equatorial velocities in excess of 200 km s^{-1}, there are some with emission lines rather like the chromospheric lines in the solar spectrum. These are rotationally broadened like the absorption lines but not to the same extent. The Be stars so-called are thus believed to have extensive envelopes rotating with comparable angular momentum to that of the star itself and out to two or three stellar radii. It is reasonable to suppose that such envelopes have been expelled from the star by rotational instability and that their presence is most likely amongst those with large equatorial velocities. Stars with surrounding shells of gas will be examined further in a subsequent section.

Mass-luminosity relationship There is one spectroscopic binary (HD 47129) made up of two similar O-stars orbiting round each other in 14 days. The spectrum also has very broad emission lines, indicating the presence of a large shell of ejected gas. The velocity of each component is some 200 km s^{-1} around the centre of mass. The scale of the orbit is thus such that a $\sim \frac{1}{2}$ while T $\sim$ 1/25 years. The mass of the system is therefore at least 160 times the mass of the Sun (since no eclipses are seen, the line of sight is not in the plane of the orbit, and this figure is a lower limit). These stars are amongst the most massive known, but, by reason of the extensive envelope, are clearly not very stable.

Stable binary systems have provided data on stellar masses from one-tenth to about fifty solar masses ranging over about 20 magnitudes of luminosity. The relationship is, broadly speaking, a straight line one for log L against log M, and the slope corresponds quite closely to the predicted L $\propto$ M^3. There is nevertheless a fairly considerable scatter about the best line, much of which may well be due to observational errors, but some of which is probably real and caused by differing stellar abundances of chemical elements. There are two notable kinds of star which deviate a great deal from the general relationship. The first of these is the white dwarfs, which are underluminous by some seven or eight magnitudes, thereby indicating a major structural difference in these stars from ordinary main sequence stars. In fact the luminosity difference is such that stars of solar mass are about fifty times smaller than main sequence stars, and therefore have mean densities of the order of 10^5 g cm^{-3}. Such densities are approaching the limit to which hot ionized matter can be compressed, and these stars appear to be in a state of cooling down after using up their nuclear fuel. Their low luminosity is such, however, that they can remain in this state for extremely long periods. It still remains to inquire how stars reach the white dwarf phase from the red giant phase. The second kind of star deviating from the mass-luminosity relationship is believed to occur only in binary systems, whence our only information about stellar masses inevitably comes. Many close binaries turn out to have one component which is overluminous for its mass—this component may have a mass of a few tenths of a solar mass and yet be brighter than its heavier companion. The explanation of this curious phenomenon is that both components start off as main sequence stars, but the more luminous and massive star evolves more rapidly, and at some stage begins to expand into a red giant star. Normally this process would continue unhindered, but in a binary system the expanding envelope comes under the gravitational influence of the companion star. Beyond a certain radius, in fact, mass is rapidly transferred from the heavier to the lighter star. The result is that the first star to evolve is seen eventually as the less massive yet more luminous component.

Explosive stars There are stars which can be seen as greenish *extended* objects under high magnification, and it was this that led to their being incorrectly identified and subsequently acquiring a quite misleading name. These stars possess vast gaseous envelopes, emitting discrete line spectra, round a central and sometimes invisible star. Many *planetary nebulae*, as they were first called by Sir John Herschel, have a somewhat incoherent structure, but others appear in the form of a fairly symmetrical ring. A good example of the latter in NGC 7293 in Aquarius. The envelope is in fact presumed to surround the central star completely, but being very thin is seen most conspicuously only in the tangential lines of sight round the rim. Planetary nebulae can be seen to great distances in the Galaxy, the most remote only being known as such from their quite distinctive spectra. The bulk of their radiation is concentrated in a few lines: some of these, in fact, proved very difficult to identify at first and were attributed to an unknown element 'nebulium'. It is now known that they originate from doubly ionized oxygen in a highly tenuous envelope, excited by ultraviolet radiation from the central star. The central star can often not be seen because most of its radiation is in the ultraviolet. This radiation is absorbed into high excitation levels of atoms in the surrounding nebula and re-emitted by these 'cascading' down to the ground level, giving light at lower frequencies than that at which it was absorbed. By measuring the intensities in sets of visible lines like the Balmer series, it is possible to calculate the total amount of ultraviolet energy absorbed and cascading down—and hence the temperature of the central star. This is often in the region of 50,000°K.

Planetary nebulae are not common objects and only one is known to exist in a globular cluster: M 15. However, they are not to be found in young systems either, and seem to be most generally associated with the Intermediate Population. They clearly represent a phase in the evolution of stars, but it is not clear whether their relative infrequency is due to the short time-scale of the phase or to the phase being peculiar to a particular kind of star. The surrounding shell is usually expanding with velocities up to about 50 km s^{-1}, judging by displacements of spectrum lines, and is visible evidence of material ejected from the central star. Approximate distances of planetary nebulae are known from four sources: NGC 7293 has a measurable parallax of about 0.04 arc second; nearby ones with significant proper motions have permitted the determination of a crude statistical parallax; NGC 246 has a common proper motion with a nearby main sequence star to which a rough distance can be put; the proper motion expansion of the shell round NGC 6720 has been measured and compared with its radial velocity. All of these give only a very approximate guide to their distances and hence their size, which is of the order of a few tenths of a parsec. The observed expansion velocity thus points to a time scale for planetary nebulae in the region of 10^{18} cm/50 km s^{-1} $\approx 10^4$ years, which is indeed a very short time on an astronomical scale.

Suppose that planetary nebulae do in fact represent a phase in the evolution of all stars towards the white dwarf phase. The question arises whether the total number of planetary nebulae seen in the Galaxy is consistent with the total number of white dwarfs. From a count of the known planetaries, and their approximate luminosity function, it looks as if the total number of planetaries in the Galaxy at the present time is about 10^4. If 10^4 planetaries exist and each lasts 10^4 years, and if the rate of their formation has remained much the same through the lifetime of the Galaxy, 10^{10} years or so, then some 10^{10} stars will have passed through the planetary phase and become white dwarfs. The volume of the Galaxy within which planetaries are seen is approximately $\pi \times 12000^2 \times 1000 \approx 5 \times 10^{11}$ cubic parsecs. Each white dwarf seen now would thus have a volume of 50 cubic parsecs associated with it. In the vicinity of the Sun there are three white dwarfs within 5 pc. The least that can be said following these very rough calculations is that the relatively small number of observed planetaries is not inconsistent with their being a rapid phase in the evolution of a large proportion of all stars.

Planetary nebulae clearly represent an explosive phase in the evolution of stars, but they are really quite sedate in comparison with some others. Amongst these is the class of stars known as *novae*. Novae are stars that explode suddenly accompanied by an enormous increase in brightness over a period of some hours. Spectroscopic studies reveal that the explosion causes a shell to be ejected from the star at speeds as large as 1000 km s^{-1}—possibly two or three in rapid succession with the later ones overtaking the first outburst. After the maximum brightness has been reached, there is a slow decline in luminosity over a number of years, returning the star to its original state perhaps some 10 magnitudes or more fainter. Some novae are recurrent in that they have been observed to explode again after an interval of a century or so, and it is even suspected that all novae possess this characteristic, but with differing periods. It is possible that the novae with the brightest explosions are the ones that recur least frequently and vice versa. There are, for example, nova-like stars with outbursts every few years which increase in brightness by only a magnitude or so.

The distance and absolute magnitude of any nova are rather difficult to estimate. Most of them in the pre-nova stage are not well observed because they are very faint objects and difficult to distinguish from other faint stars until the explosion has occurred. Nevertheless, in their 'normal' state, they appear to be bluish stars ($B - V \sim 0$) with absolute magnitude between the horizontal branch and white dwarf regions of the H-R diagram. Perhaps the best estimates of absolute magnitude come from the visibly expanding shell round nearby novae in the years after the explosion. Nova Aquilae, for example, expands in radius by 1 arc second per year, while spectroscopically the outgoing gas is moving at 1700 km s^{-1}, thus placing it at some 300 pc from the Sun. When this star exploded it brightened by about 13 magnitudes from about + 5 to − 8 absolute magnitude. Most other novae are at very great distances, however, and are distributed in the Galaxy as if members of the Intermediate Population. Novae are thus comparatively old stars, and their position in the H-R diagram encourages the idea that they are a phase passed through by some stars on their way to the 'stellar graveyard' of white dwarfs.

The explanation of novae phenomena is far from clear, but it is generally believed to be related to some kind of cataclysmic readjustment between the core and the surface layers of an old star. In much the same way as the red giant phase of a star can be regarded as a gentle readjustment or explosion from the main sequence following the depletion of the hydrogen fuel in its core, so it is believed much more violent explosions are generated from other nuclear reactions involving helium when the core contracts to even higher temperatures. In these cases, the increase in core luminosity is so rapid that the outer layers have to expand at enormous speeds in order for the star to restore some kind of equilibrium.

The outburst of energy in a typical nova is about 10^{45} ergs, but there are a few cases of stellar explosions which are even more violent, involving the expenditure of about 10^{49} ergs, a big fraction of the total energy supply of a star. The spectra of these objects seen in the extragalactic nebulae suggest velocities of ejection in the region of 10^4 km s^{-1}. Three possible *supernovae* in our own Galaxy are identified with events that occurred in 1054, 1572 and 1604. The first of these, the Crab Nebula (Plate 32*b*) reached an apparent magnitude several times brighter than Venus and could be seen in broad daylight. Its absolute magnitude must have been −16 at maximum. This and Kepler's Nova of 1604 both leave visible evidence of the explosion now: the Crab

Nebula in particular has been extensively examined. This object is a vast region of expanding nebulosity with filamentary structure possessing radial motions of about 0.2 arc second per year. Since the nebula has a diameter of something like 6 minutes of arc, it has been expanding like this unhindered for about 900 years. This certainly confirms the epoch of the explosion chronicled by the Chinese observers in 1054. At the same time, the radial velocity of these filaments is in the region of 1000 km s^{-1}, from which the distance of the Crab Nebula is put at about 1000 pc. The nebulosity has a continuous spectrum with emission lines in many ways similar to those of planetary nebulae, and early calculations using the same kind of model for the continuum suggested the existence of a small central star with a surface temperature of 5×10^5 °K, and a mass for the nebulosity of some 20 solar masses. Subsequent observations have shown that the nebulosity is highly polarized in such a way that it probably has strong magnetic field lines which lie along the visible filaments. The observed continuum emission is thus attributed to synchrotron radiation from fast electrons spiralling round the magnetic field lines. Such a mechanism involving less energetic electrons undoubtedly accounts for the strong radio emission from the object. If each high energy electron has an associated positively charged nucleon, such particles would have the energies of cosmic rays, and it has been suggested that galactic supernovae are responsible for the high energy cosmic rays striking the Earth, and which may pervade the whole Galaxy. The explanation by synchrotron emission gives only a small mass to the nebulosity but does not of itself provide any source for the electrons. Presumably, however, these originate in some way in the central star. A likely candidate for the central star at 18th magnitude has long been suspected, but only recently this object has been shown to be a pulsar—a small dense object with very high frequency brightness changes in both visible and radio wavelengths. The physical processes occurring in these objects, of which quite a number are now known, are the subject of much speculation at present.

Shell stars Most of the explosive stars so far discussed appear to be old, if only because they occur in regions of the Galaxy which are comparatively empty of interstellar material. The only strong concentration of gas is that which has come from the exploding star itself. There are, however, other kinds of stars possessing luminous shells, but these are mostly embedded to a greater or lesser extent in absorbing material, and the presumption is that the associated stars are young objects either newly arrived on the main sequence or even still in the process of condensing on to it.

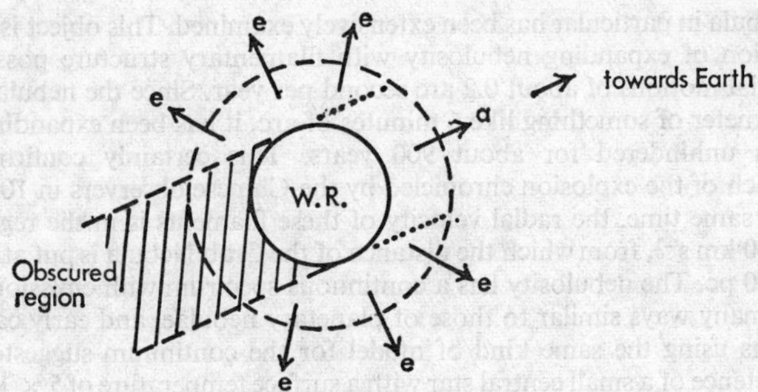

Figure 8.15 Model of a Wolf-Rayet star. The portion of the extended atmosphere marked 'a' is where the absorption lines observed in the spectrum are formed, whereas the observed broad emission lines are formed in those portions marked 'e'

One such star is Pleione, a member of the Pleiades cluster. This is a typical rapidly rotating early-type main sequence star showing the familiar absorption lines of hydrogen and helium. But twice this century the spectrum of this star has developed emission lines in pairs on either side of the absorption lines. These are believed to be due to an expanding shell blown off from the unstable equatorial regions of the star. The shell emission lines are displaced by about 100 km s^{-1} from the absorption line centre, which itself has a broadening of about 200 km s^{-1}. This suggests that the shell is in the form of a ring situated, when observed, at about twice the star's radius. Other shell stars of early type are not necessarily associated with rapid rotation: these are the so-called *Wolf-Rayet* stars which are intrinsically very bright ($M_V \sim -6$), and even in spite of their being usually immersed in strong concentrations of obscuring dust and gas are visible to very great distances. Their absolute magnitudes are best known from their identification in the Magellanic Clouds. Wolf-Rayet stars have surface temperatures of up to 100,000°K and characteristic spectra which include broad emission lines of highly ionized atoms with weak absorption lines on the shorter wavelength side. Figure 8.15 indicates how this spectrum may be formed by a hot central star surrounded by a tenuous expanding shell of gas. The emission lines come from the rim of the shell where it is seen in greatest depth and are broad owing to the rapid velocity of expansion of the shell in all directions, while the absorption line towards shorter wavelengths is attributed to absorption by that part of the expanding shell which is in front of the star and coming towards the observer.

Embedded in large gas-dust complexes where many young main-sequence stars are also present are later-type stars with emission spectra suggestive of a surrounding shell. Particularly strong is the Ca II emission which we have already associated with relative youth amongst dwarf M-stars. These stars are the so-called T Tauri stars after a 'prototype' which is observed with others in the nearby Taurus cloud, some 100 pc away. T Tauri stars show irregular light variations, have broad absorption lines in their spectra possibly caused by rotation, and are several magnitudes brighter than main sequence stars. Apparently similar stars are found in the young cluster NGC 2264 in the Orion Nebula. It is suspected that these objects are stars contracting on to the late main sequence, whose angular momentum has yet to be redistributed. Also embedded in the brighter nebulosity which may be found in the vicinity of such stars are small dark 'globules' whose dimensions correspond to about a parsec diameter, and whose total absorbing power corresponds to roughly a solar mass. It seems very likely that both these phenomena are the visible signs of stars in the early stages of creation. It perhaps seems a little unsatisfactory that, with so much now known or guessed about stellar evolution, astronomers cannot point to more precise evidence of stars in creation. However, this state of affairs is probably in the very nature of things because stars are likely to be formed where matter is already very concentrated. The concentration is bound to obscure the early stages of star formation, and it is believed that we only see what we do see because, when a contracting star eventually becomes sufficiently luminous, its radiation blows away the surrounding dust, possibly in the same way as the solar wind does the tail of a comet, and clears the way for us to see the star. In cases of a very bright and massive O star, it is even thought that the enormous radiation pressure expels the surrounding gas with such force that it impinges on more distant gas, thereby increasing its density and accelerating star formation therein. This could well be the reason for the existence of 'star rings' which can be observed clearly in the Magellanic Clouds, for example, and which have now recently been detected in our own Galaxy. There are also the so-called 'runaway stars', which are very high velocity young stars in the solar vicinity and which, it is suspected, have condensed out of gas accelerated and compressed by the action of this kind of radiation pressure. It may even be this process that causes most stars ultimately to move away from the concentration of gas out of which they originally condense. On the other hand, this is not certain because gas moves under the combined constraints of the

Galaxy's magnetic and gravitational fields, whereas stars are only affected by the latter, and this difference could be the reason for the rapid segregation that is observed.

Pulsating stars Some of the stars which have now been discussed are in the general category of variable stars. Variable stars have always attracted attention, simply because it is their variation which distinguishes them from the great number of stable stars. Astronomers have therefore collected a vast amount of data about these stars, though it must be admitted that they are as often as not much more difficult to explain than non-variable stars. The number of known variables runs to well over ten thousand, and many more are discovered year by year. No two variables are exactly alike, but nevertheless a fair number of characteristic types of variation are now recognized. Among these are eclipsing binaries, which have already been described. Most variables are, however, intrinsic variables caused by some kind of pulsation in the stars themselves. Extreme examples of these are the exploding variables where the velocity of expansion is sufficient to carry the 'atmosphere' away from the gravitational influence of the star. Such stars are novae, supernovae, and shell stars, which have also been described already. Other more regular pulsating variables are classified, broadly speaking, according to the length of their period and amplitude of their light variation. The stars of very small amplitude are the ones about which least is known, generally, because their variation is such that attention has not readily been drawn to them. Some of these have been discovered, for example, from conspicuous variations in their spectra, and this has been followed by detailed photometry revealing luminosity changes which amount to a very small fraction of a magnitude—variations which in the ordinary course of events would not be discovered. These 'spectrum variables' show changes in intensity of absorption lines and are often magnetic variables as well. Other more obvious variables are also thought to be magnetic variables (e.g. RR Lyrae) and small amplitude variables are therefore taken to be a profitable line of investigation for understanding these other more complicated stars. The categories of well-known pulsating variables are summarized in Table 8.5, but the particulars are only representative and cannot be taken too literally. We shall discuss the properties of these groups in greater detail after considering why the pulsations occur.

Let us first consider the behaviour of regular variables like 'normal Cepheids' and 'RR Lyraes'. Although belonging to quite different kinematic populations, members of each of these groups have some distinct similarities in their variations. There are in fact two

TABLE 8.5 PULSATING STARS

Name of variable	*Amplitude (in magnitudes)*	*Approx. period (in days)*	*Average spectral type*
Beta Canis Majoris . .	0.1	0.17	B
Dwarf Cepheids . .	1	0.17	A
RR Lyrae . . .	1	0.5	A
Cepheids . . .	1	20	F
Semi-regular . . .	1	75	M
Long period . . .	5	300	M

characteristic types of RR Lyrae variable which occur together in globular clusters. They are called a-type and c-type, the former having asymmetric light curves with a rapid rise to a maximum which is typically about a magnitude brighter than its minimum, while the latter have a fairly symmetrical sinusoidal light variation of amplitude about $0^{m}.5$. The a-type variables are very similar to the normal Cepheids both in the shape of their light curves and in the periodic variations of their spectra. Thus, at maximum, the star's atmosphere is brighter, of earlier spectral type, and advancing towards the observer, whereas at minimum the atmosphere is cooler and receding. Other stars, however, do not necessarily have this phase relationship between their light and velocity variations,

Integrating over a number of identical cycles, it is still possible to specify the equilibria of these stars by formulae of the kind which were given for a stable star. At some stage, however, in the evolution of a star it is supposed that its outer layers reach a state which renders them more opaque to the passage of radiation. The inner parts of the star thus begin to heat up and the pressure rises. This pressure eventually has the effect of blowing the upper layers outwards, reducing the opacity and permitting the passage of 'bottled up' radiation. This relieves the pressure, permits the expanded atmosphere to fall back, and so the cycle is started again. The cycle is in fact very similar to that of a loose lid on a kettle of boiling water: the lid acts as a valve which periodically releases the pressure built up inside by newly generated steam. The characteristic cycle time in the case of a star is taken to be roughly the time for a pressure wave to be transmitted through the pulsating layers. Appealing once again to the kinetic theory of gases as for equations (3) and (4), we know that for stars of much the same composition the velocity of pressure waves V is such that

$$\frac{1}{2}(xH)\,V^2 = \frac{3}{2}\,k\,T \tag{23}$$

while the period P of a cycle is given by

$$P \sim R\,/\,V \tag{24}$$

However, the situation is not quite so simple as this because the most significant contribution to the period comes from the slowest velocity near the surface. This can only be allowed for by an exact stellar model, but we shall assume for the sake of example that the surface temperature is three orders of magnitude lower than the mean interior temperature, and that the appropriate range of radius over which this temperature is relevant is one order of magnitude down on R. The above equations then become

$$\frac{1}{2}(xH)\,V^2 = \frac{3}{2}\,k\,(T/1000)$$

and $$P \sim \frac{1}{10}R\,/\,V$$

Whence we deduce $$P^2 \sim R^2 \,.\, \frac{10 \times H}{3\,k\,T}$$

and substituting from equation (6) we find

$$P \sim (G\rho)^{-\frac{1}{2}} \tag{25}$$

where ρ is the mean density of the star. This important result is usually expressed in the form

$$P\sqrt{\rho} = \text{a constant.}$$

An implication of this result is that, were the Sun to have the special atmospheric properties we have been considering it would oscillate with a period of about one hour.

Let us now extend our preliminary analysis of stellar structure by writing down a relation between the star's luminosity L and the mass of the core in which nuclear reactions are contributing to the generation of L. For stars of similar structure, that is with cores a certain fraction by mass of the whole and having the same temperature-dependent energy generating processes,

$$L \propto M\,.\,T^y \tag{26}$$

where y is an index appropriate to the particular kind of nuclear reactions involved. Combining equation (26) with equations (8), (9), and (10), we can with a little algebra find $M \propto L^{\frac{1}{4}}$ and $R^3 \propto L^{1-2/y}$. Thus it follows that the square root of the mean density, $\rho^{\frac{1}{2}} \propto L^{1/y-\frac{1}{8}}$. Substituting this result in equation (25) we obtain

$$P \propto L^{\frac{1}{8}-1/y}$$

Now nuclear reactions are extremely sensitive to temperature, and the index y is certainly of the order of 18 for the carbon cycle. Presumably we can, without making any great error, simplify this result further and write

$$P \propto L^{\frac{1}{3}} \qquad (27)$$

This result indicates that a set of variables of similar structure are expected to pulsate with periods which are strictly related to their luminosities. Cepheids and RR Lyraes, however, lie in a region of the H-R diagram well away from the main sequence, and cannot be assumed to have the same internal structure as the Sun. Their periods cannot therefore be calculated simply by relating their luminosities to that of the Sun through equation (27). Beta Canis Majoris stars, on the other hand, lie quite close to the main sequence and have luminosities some 1000 times that of the Sun. This would suggest natural periods some 10 times that of the Sun. These stars do in fact range over something like 3- to 6-hour periods with luminosities in accord with equation (27). Indeed, the behaviour of Beta Canis Majoris stars may be taken as confirmation of the assumed process of energy generation. It has been known for a considerable time, nevertheless, that Cepheid variables in the Magellanic Clouds show a dependence of absolute magnitude on periods, but the relationship is not that given by equation (27). Regardless of its explanation, the chief value of this period-luminosity relationship lies in its empirical use as a means of determining the absolute magnitudes and hence distances of luminous Cepheids in extragalactic systems. However, it is found that very approximately

$$P \propto L \qquad (28)$$

which is difficult to account for in terms of equation (26). This suggests that the adopted energy generating process is not appropriate, and that the onset of the variable phase occurs when the star is producing energy primarily by other means. A suggested explanation for this is that when a star has evolved to the 'top' of the giant branch enhanced convection in the stellar interior sets in and causes its contents to be thoroughly mixed. As a result the well-mixed star contracts under its own gravity to take up a new 'stable' position near the main sequence, but at a considerably higher luminosity than previously because its mean particle weight is now larger than before. The horizontal branch thus represents a contraction phase, and the instabilities responsible for us seeing Cepheid variables and RR Lyrae variables occur during this phase. The instability can only arise when sufficient of the material in the outer layers is in a physical state which behaves in the way already described. Assuming that the stars in question have similar structure and composition, the appropriate condition is that the thermal content of the outer layers had reached a particular value. Expressing this in symbols, the approximate condition for the onset of variation is

$$M . T = \text{some constant} \qquad (29)$$

Combining equation (29) with equations (8), (9) and (10) as before, we find that

$$M \propto L^{\frac{1}{3}} \text{ and } R \propto L^{\frac{2}{3}}.$$

Whence it follows from equation (25) that

$$P \propto L^{5/6} \qquad (30)$$

much more in keeping with the observed period-luminosity relationship. The cause of the opacity is at present believed to be substantially the zone through which helium changes from the non-ionized to the ionized state.

Now, a-type RR Lyrae variables have an absolute magnitude about 4 magnitudes brighter than the Sun, although they are not quite the same colour. If we assume that their outer layers have much the same composition as the Sun, as could be the case in view of the fact that they belong to an older generation of stars, then equation (30) would give them periods some 20 times longer. This result is in very good accord with their observed periods of up to about 20 hours. It does seem then that plausible models of pulsating stars can be constructed without any very radical alteration in the general ideas of stellar structure.

It is now known that stars belonging to different populations and presumably with different compositions can display quite similar kinds of variation. Cepheid variables, for example, are so classified, by the general similarity of their light curves and periods to that of the star Delta Cephei—which has a period of 5.4 days. Stars with such light curves occur up to periods of about 50 days, but within this range there are some stars which have markedly different spectroscopic features. These are the W Virginis stars, named after one particular star of their kind. These stars reveal 'double' absorption lines in their spectra during the rising branch of the light curve, which may be attributed to different parts of the stellar atmosphere, one rising and the other falling. By their radial velocities these stars seem to belong to a different age group—the Intermediate Population—from other Cepheids which are among the youngest stars in the sky. Cepheids generally are of spectral type F, somewhat earlier in type than the Sun, and merge at the longer period end into a population of semi-regular variables of later spectral type. The amplitudes and periods of these semi-regulars vary in an unpredictable fashion, though remaining more or less in the same range, with characteristic periods of about 50 to 100 days and amplitudes of about a magnitude. These variables probably occur amongst stars of all ages, but there does seem to be at least one well-defined group with periods intermediate between those of Cepheids and most semi-regulars, which are known as RV Tauri stars. These are found in globular clusters with rare examples in the general field and have spectral types of G and K. Their absolute visual magnitudes are about − 3, comparable with those of the brightest metal-poor giants.

Stars with periods longer than 100 days come in the general category of long period variables. They are red giant stars of spectral type M. Broadly speaking, they can be classified into the so-called long period variables with amplitudes less than 2.5 magnitudes and the so-called Mira variables which have much larger amplitudes. The former group may be identified by their very bright emission lines in hydrogen at maximum and are probably very much older than the Miras. The star Mira Ceti after which this latter group is named has a period which varies from about 320 to 370 days and its apparent brightness rises from about ninth to first magnitude at maximum. This star, like others of its kind, has very strong titanium oxide bands in its spectrum, indicative of surface temperatures as low as 2000°K. Stars of this type are found with periods up to nearly 1000 days, but it is exceedingly difficult to determine their absolute magnitudes. Few have had any accurate photometry throughout their cycles, and the magnitude of most of them is known best only at maximum. Since this magnitude often varies from cycle to cycle, statistical parallaxes of these stars are very uncertain. Measurements of the bolometric intensity of Mira Ceti indicate that the total radiation at maximum is only three to four times stronger than at minimum, whereas the amplitude in visual light indicates a very much larger ratio. The reason for this is that the bulk of the radiation is infrared with a peak intensity at about 1.5μ. In addition, the star is heavily veiled at minimum light by strong atmospheric condensations into liquid and solid particles. Although the enormous size of Mira variables is consistent with extremely low densities and therefore long period pulsations, the variability is very irregular and suggests that atmospheric phenomena in these stars are only very loosely coupled to the underlying oscillations.

Stellar evolution

In this chapter we have now taken a look at many of the observed properties of stars. The features which have been emphasized are necessarily those which seem to fit into some kind of general pattern—else, otherwise, the story would be a long list of loose ends. An underlying theme of the pattern is the idea that stars evolve, and a wide variety of observations are now interpreted with this in mind, hoping thereby to trace the life history of stars from birth to death.

The main difference between Population I and Intermediate Population stars on the one hand, and Population II stars on the other, is the abundance of metals—that is elements of high atomic number generally—in their atmospheres. Population II stars have a large velocity dispersion typified by most RR Lyrae variables, but are weak in metals. These stars are thought to be among the earliest created in the Galaxy, and the high velocity dispersion is believed to reflect the fact that they were formed while the mass of gas of perhaps about 10^{11} solar masses was still collapsing more or less radially under its own gravity to form the Galaxy as we now see it. Later generations of stars have been formed out of the gas which, by reason of the angular momentum it possessed before contraction started, is now found in a rapidly rotating disk. These later generations of stars are formed with greater concentrations of metals, due, it is supposed, to the enrichment of the gas by the products of evolution in the interiors of massive first generation stars.

Stars like the Sun have a composition by mass of hydrogen 74 per cent, helium 24 per cent, and other elements 2 per cent, in which carbon, nitrogen, oxygen and iron predominate. Although the abundance of heavier elements is some hundred times less in Population II stars, it is not known how much helium they contain. Was the material out of which the Galaxy formed pure hydrogen, or did it possess a significant fraction of helium as well? Perhaps we shall have to learn more about galactic evolution as a whole before we can answer this question. The formation of heavier elements in stellar interiors is believed to occur in the following way. Main sequence stars produce their luminous energy by hydrogen core burning. At temperatures of 10×10^6 °K or so, such as are found in later-type main sequence stars, hydrogen is converted to helium by the proton-proton reaction. This reaction is very much less sensitive to temperature ($\propto T^4$) than the carbon cycle which predominates at higher temperatures of say 25×10^6 °K or more ($\propto T^{18}$). In this reaction hydrogen is also converted to helium with the release of rest mass energy, but through a process involving carbon as a catalyst. The sequence of reactions in the two cases is:

(1) Proton-proton reaction. Two hydrogen nuclei combine to form a deuteron with the simultaneous emission of a positron and a neutrino. The neutrino is unhindered by passage through the star and carries away a small fraction of the nuclear energy. Attempts are now being made to measure this outflow from the Sun, though as yet with no great precision. In fact, this reaction does not occur very readily for any one hydrogen nucleus (once in about 10^{10} years!) but there are so many such nuclei that it proceeds rapidly enough to account for the luminosity of dwarf main sequence stars. The reason why it is so slow is that the reaction really only occurs when one of the protons (H^1) is temporarily turned into a neutron, thereby eliminating the electrostatic potential barrier which normally keeps them apart. In symbols, the reaction is

$$_1H^1 + {_1H^1} \rightarrow {_1H^2} + e^+ + \gamma$$

The deuteron is very short lived (some five seconds) in the stellar interior, but lasts sufficiently long for some to undergo further interaction with protons, releasing electromagnetic radiation as gamma rays and forming helium:

$$_1H^2 + {_1H^1} \rightarrow {_2He^3} + \gamma$$

The next step in the chain is for two He^3 nuclei to collide to form a stable helium isotope He^4 with the further release of radiation

$$_2He^3 + {_2He^3} \rightarrow {_2He^4} + 2{_1H^1} + \gamma$$

In this reaction it is seen that four hydrogen atoms are transformed to one helium atom. Since each of the former has an atomic mass of 1.008 units and the latter has a mass of 4.004 units, the conversion has resulted in a mass loss of 0.028 units. Each gram of converted hydrogen thus results in a mass loss of about 0.7 per cent, or an equivalent energy output of $\Delta\, m.c^2 = 0.007 \times (3 \times 10^{10})^2 \approx 6.10^{18}$ ergs/gm, more than enough to account for a star's luminosity as we have already noted.

(2) Carbon cycle reaction. At the temperature of stellar interiors, all light nuclei from lithium onwards are rapidly burnt up in reactions with protons. Carbon^{12}, however, is stable and lasts sufficiently long to be

involved in reactions with protons in which it behaves like a catalyst. C^{12} first reacts with a proton to produce nitrogen N^{13}, which is unstable and decays by neutrino and positron emission in seven minutes to C^{13}. This product in turn also reacts with protons to form oxygen O^{15} in two stages, which then decays in just over a minute to N^{15}. The final stage involves a reaction between N^{15} and a proton to form C^{12} again, and He^4. In symbols these steps are:

$$_6C^{12} + {_1H^1} \rightarrow {_7N^{13}} + \gamma$$
$$_7N^{13} \rightarrow {_6C^{13}} + e^+ + \nu$$
$$_6C^{13} + {_1H^1} \rightarrow {_7N^{14}} + \gamma$$
$$_7N^{14} + {_1H^1} \rightarrow {_8O^{15}} + \gamma$$
$$_8O^{15} \rightarrow {_7N^{15}} + e^+ + \nu$$
$$_7N^{15} + {_1H^1} \rightarrow {_6C^{12}} + {_2He^4} + \gamma$$

The release of energy in this sequence of reactions is slightly less than in the proton-proton reaction, due to a more energetic emission of neutrinos.

Knowledge of possible nuclear reactions can in fact throw important light on stellar structure. Lithium, for example, is found to be much less abundant on the surface of the Sun than in meteorites, whereas the abundance of beryllium is about the same. Presuming that the abundances of these elements would otherwise be the same, the lack of lithium may be attributed to the existence of deep convection currents which carry the lithium to low levels, where the temperature is so high that the element is virtually destroyed in the reactions

$$_3Li^7 + {_1H^1} \rightarrow 2\,{_2He^4}$$

or

$$_3Li^6 + {_1H^1} \rightarrow {_2He^3} + {_2He^4}$$

At the same time, however, the currents do not go low enough for beryllium to suffer the same kind of fate in the reactions

$$_4Be^9 + {_1H^1} \rightarrow {_1H^2} + 2\,{_2He^4}$$

or

$$_4Be^9 + {_1H^1} \rightarrow {_2He^4} + {_3Li^6}$$

The relative proportions of these elements therefore give some indication of the depth to which the convection reaches. The critical temperature seems to be about 3×10^6 °K and in the Sun, for example, the convection zone thus reaches down to about half the radius. Above this level, mixing is expected to be fairly complete. The search for lithium lines in stellar atmospheres thus becomes extremely important and can give a strong indication of the structure of some stars.

Main sequence stars continue to burn hydrogen for as many as 10^{12} years in the case of stars one-tenth the mass of the Sun and for as few as 10^6 years for those one hundred times more massive, until the core is exhausted. At this stage, the core contracts and a hydrogen burning shell develops which causes the outer layers to expand into a 'red giant'. The core continues to contract until it reaches a temperature of about 100×10^6 °K when helium burns, forming carbon and oxygen:

$$3\ {}_2\mathrm{He}^4 \rightarrow {}_6\mathrm{C}^{12}$$
$${}_6\mathrm{C}^{12} + {}_2\mathrm{He}^4 \rightarrow {}_8\mathrm{O}^{16}$$

The energy per gram of material is not so great for these reactions as it is for hydrogen burning, and since the luminosity of the star at this stage is very high, the energy is rapidly radiated off and the phase passes relatively quickly. Continued contraction of the core then leads to further rises in temperature and the build up of even higher elements. Thus, by 600×10^6 °K, carbon has by various reactions with alpha particles (${}_2\mathrm{He}^4$) produced elements up to Si^{28} with Mg^{24}, in particular, predominating. Surrounding the core are shells of lower temperature in which light nuclei reactions are occurring, the 'hydrogen shell' being outermost. Beyond this stage further contraction then ensues, until at 2000×10^6 °K oxygen converts to sulphur, which then reacts with helium to form iron Fe^{56}. In these reactions, neutrinos carry away most of the energy and the radiated energy per gram is so small that the phase can last only about 24 hours. By the time iron has been created in the stellar core another fundamental turning point has been reached in the life history of the star. Iron nuclei are the most stable, and higher elements can only be formed by the addition of energy rather than its release as in the case of light nuclei. For a while the star's luminosity continues to be supplied by outer shells as the core contracts—until a temperature of about 6000×10^6 °K is reached and Fe^{56} atoms begin to break up under thermal bombardment. The core of the star then collapses catastrophically, as thermal energy, generated by gravitational contraction and the break-up of some Fe^{56} nuclei, is 'sucked up' in the formation of nuclei of even higher atomic number. This catastrophic phase probably corresponds to nova-like events in a star and leads to the violent ejection of the massive nuclei which exist in various layers around the core of the star.

This sequence of events is believed to occur in the less dense and more massive stars. In smaller stars the central density is so high that the core eventually becomes degenerate as it collapses. In this state the pressure of a gas is virtually independent of temperature. A rise in temperature caused by gravitational contraction of a degenerate core does not therefore produce a rise in pressure to balance further contraction, and the collapse continues unchecked. The core overheats and nuclear reactions proceed explosively. The same kind of fate thus seems to befall both high and low mass stars.

The understanding of stellar evolution is not complete until the processes leading up to the main sequence stage have been discovered. Our knowledge in this respect is still quite fragmentary, however, and it is perhaps appropriate to end this chapter by emphasizing a weakness in the story. Our Galaxy evidently contains many clouds of interstellar gas whose sizes seem to range from about 10 to 100 solar masses, with densities of the order of 10^{-23} g cm^{-3}. In between these clouds the density is lower, being nearer to 10^{-25} g cm^{-3}. There is considerable evidence that stars are formed in groups or clusters, and what is believed to be the visible sign of the initial stages of this process is seen in dark globules with individual densities of some 10^{-20} g cm^{-3}. Simple reasoning from equation (15) shows that any concentration of density in the interstellar gas could gravitate over a shorter time interval than the remainder—that is, once fragmentation has started, it will continue—but how do masses of the appropriate stellar size and distribution condense out of the initial cloud? And even granting that they can, how do these objects shed their excess angular momentum? These questions have no clear answers at present, possibly because of the not insignificant part played by magnetic fields and turbulence in the process.

However, the observed density of many interstellar clouds is rather close to a value which is stable against the tidal action of the Galaxy as a whole. The critical density is in the region of M/R^3, where M is the mass of the Galaxy and R is the Sun's distance from the galactic centre. Putting $M = 2.10^{11}$ solar masses and $R = 10$ kpc, the critical density becomes $\sim 10^{-23}$ g cm^{-3}, strongly suggesting that these clouds are close to contracting under their own gravity. But why haven't they? Presumably because they have only recently been created. How then are they created?

The observation of galactic radio emission from neutral hydrogen indicates a temperature of about 100°K for interstellar hydrogen, equivalent to a particle velocity dispersion of about $V = 1$ km s^{-1}. What size must a lump of gas be in order that its self gravity overcomes this dispersion? Roughly speaking, if m is its mass and r its scale, then:

$$\frac{G.m}{r} \sim V^2$$

If the density of the interstellar gas is ρ, it follows that

$$m = \frac{4}{3}\pi r^3 \rho$$

and

$$V^2 \sim G m^{\frac{2}{3}} \rho^{\frac{1}{3}}$$

We thus see that for densities of around 10^{-23} g cm^{-3} the appropriate m is in the region of 10^3 solar masses or more. Thus, unless some additional forces compress the interstellar medium to higher densities, only very large masses, bigger than any typical star, can condense out of it. Such masses would be initially some 10 to 100 parsecs across. If such masses do indeed form and collapse under their own gravity, there will eventually come a stage with conservation of angular momentum when rotational instability sets in. Possibly this results in the formation of an extensive disk around a massive central 'star'. Such a massive object may be expected to be extremely short lived and highly luminous. The radiation pressure resulting from the 'star' in turn forces the disk of gas outwards and compresses it to higher densities, thereby accelerating the formation of stars of smaller size. In this way one might expect to find new stars of normal masses being formed in chains or rings or, quite generally, in expanding associations. Such objects can, it is believed, be identified in the sky and are naturally the subject of considerable investigation. Perhaps the small interstellar clouds are sections of such expelled gas which have not been sufficiently compressed to withstand the galactic tide and so contract.

Chapter Nine

The Milky Way

V. C. Reddish

The stars are not distributed uniformly throughout space but are gathered together in galaxies, each containing many thousands of millions. Our Galaxy is typical of many. It contains about a million million stars, most of which are concentrated into a disk-shaped volume some 100,000 light years in diameter and 2,000 light years thick. This disk is embedded in a spheroidal distribution of the remainder of the stars—the galactic halo. The diameter of the halo is uncertain but it is certainly larger than that of the disk. Figures 9.1 and 9.2 illustrate schematically the structure and size of the Galaxy.

Ten thousand million years ago the Galaxy was no more than a vast spherical cloud of hydrogen gas, filling a volume a million light years in diameter. Despite the low density of the gas—only 10^{-27} g cm^{-3}—the large volume contained enough mass to make two hundred thousand million suns. The gas cloud was rotating slowly, so we may picture it having a pole and an equator. As it contracted under the pull of its own gravitation it rotated faster, and centrifugal force prevented the equator from contracting as much as the poles: thus the sphere began to flatten. Density fluctuations occurred in the gas and denser fragments contracted to form stars, most of them only a tenth as massive as the Sun. Star formation quickly reached a high rate, and then declined slowly as less and less of the gas remained uncondensed into stars.

During the course of their evolution some stars explode. These are the supernovae, and they eject back into the gas atoms of elements heavier than hydrogen, produced in nuclear reactions in their deep interiors, thus gradually enriching the remaining interstellar gas with these elements.

The first stars were formed when the gas cloud was still nearly spherical, and now form the galactic halo. By the time the latter half of the stars were formed out of the gas, it had already contracted to an equatorial disk spinning at a rate of one complete rotation every three hundred million years. Only a few per cent of the mass of the Galaxy now remains in the interstellar gas clouds uncondensed into stars. The clouds are still predominantly hydrogen, but some 30 per cent of the mass is helium, and the heavier elements such as carbon, oxygen, and iron contribute no more than 2 per cent altogether. One effect of the rotation of the Galaxy is to cause these gas clouds to be strung into arms spiralling outwards from the galactic centre.

Stars form in clusters, the smallest containing a few stars, the largest several millions. Most of the clusters have dispersed and contributed to the general distribution of field stars, but some of the more massive ones, tightly held together by their own gravitational attraction, have survived disrupting forces: such are the globular clusters observed predominantly in the halo. Clusters of all sizes, bound and dispersing, are still forming out of the clouds of interstellar gas in the disk: the youngest, especially those known to be dispersing, are given the name 'associations'.

The Sun is one of the stars in the disk, situated about 30,000 light years from the centre; thus we view the disk edgewise, and see the vast numbers of stars of which it is composed as a faintly luminous band of light—the Milky Way.

Photographs of the Milky Way show more detail than is visible to the eye. Plate 36–7 is a composite picture, based on photographs, showing the whole extent of the Milky Way from both northern and southern hemispheres. It was produced by astronomers at the Lund Observatory in Sweden.

The dark patches on the picture are caused by interstellar dust obscuring the light of the distant stars. This dust appears in the clouds of interstellar gas in the disk of the Galaxy and accounts for about 1 per cent of the mass of the clouds. It is out of these gas clouds that new stars are still being formed in the spiral arms. Some of these are very bright, short-lived stars and, irradiating the gas around them, cause the spiral arms to stand out prominently on photographs of spiral galaxies.

The spiral arms are threaded by a magnetic field, which probably helps to maintain their stability and, by interacting with the interstellar dust particles which dim the light of distant stars, causes the starlight to be polarized. Weaker magnetic fields are also believed to exist in the halo.

Diffusing throughout the Galaxy are the cosmic rays—atomic nuclei and electrons moving with speeds close to that of light. They interact with the magnetic fields to produce radio waves detected by radio telescopes. The remnants of supernovae explosions, and gas clouds ionized by hot young stars, are also strong sources of radio wave emission.

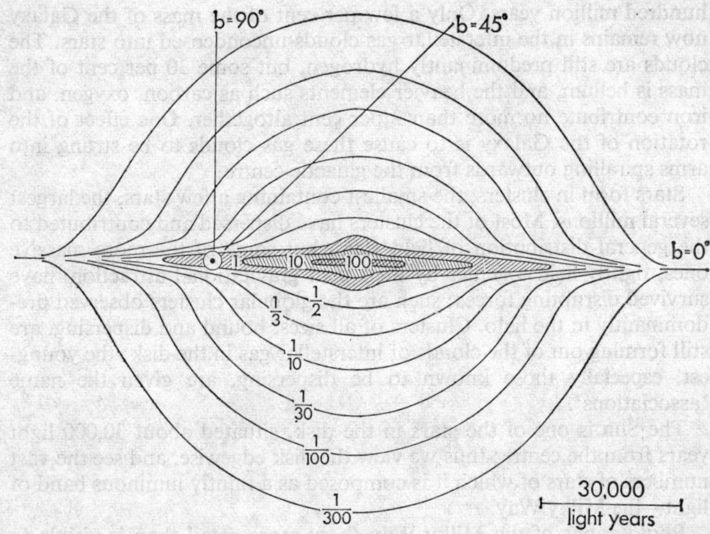

Figure 9.1 Cross-section of the Galaxy showing lines of constant mass density relative to that near the Sun, and angles of galactic latitude

In considering these various features of the Galaxy in more detail it will be convenient to deal separately with the stars and the gas in the disk and halo, but to treat them together in the spiral arms where new stars form from the gas. But before doing so it is useful to recall briefly the kinds of measurements an astronomer may make in his explorations of the Galaxy.

Exploring the Milky Way All the information which an astronomer obtains about the Milky Way is gained by measuring the radiations received from it. The stars and gas clouds in it are at such great distances that this is the only method open to him. He can measure the direction from which radiation comes, its quantity and its quality. For any particular object such as a star this means that he measures its position in the sky, its brightness and its spectrum. These are the sciences of astrometry, photometry and spectrophotometry.

Starlight is weak and large telescopes are required to collect enough

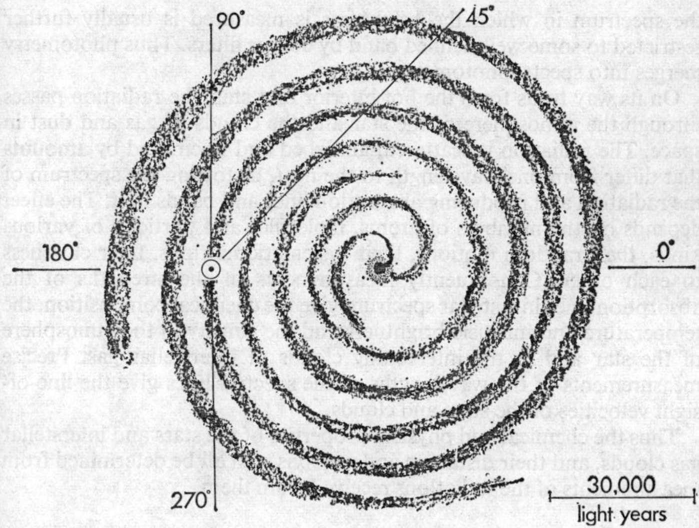

Figure 9.2 Plan of the Galaxy showing spiral arms and angles of galactic longitude

of it to disperse into spectra. Measurements of the directions of stars and of their brightnesses, of the strengths and wavelengths of features in their spectra, have to be made with high precision and require telescopes, spectrographs and measuring instruments equally precise.

By measuring the position of a star at different times any angular motion in the interval can be determined. If the distance of the star is known the velocity transverse to the line of sight can then be obtained. Thus astrometry gives the apparent distribution and angular motions of the stars, and the true space distribution and transverse velocities of some of them.

If the intrinsic brightness of a star is known, comparison with the apparent brightness allows the distance to be estimated. Measurements of the brightness at different times enable variable stars to be found and their periods of variability determined. In practice the total amount of radiation emitted by a star cannot be measured from the ground because only part of it passes through the Earth's atmosphere, and the region of the spectrum in which the brightness is measured is usually further restricted to some well-defined band by colour filters. Thus photometry merges into spectrophotometry.

On its way to us from the hot interior of a star, the radiation passes through the atmosphere of the star and the clouds of gas and dust in space. The radiation is scattered, absorbed and re-emitted by amounts that differ from one wavelength to the next, distorting the spectrum of the radiation and producing absorption lines and bands in it. The effect depends on the numbers of atoms, molecules and particles of various kinds, their random motions, their systematic motions, their closeness to each other. Consequently measurements of the strengths of the absorption lines in a stellar spectrum give the chemical composition, the temperature and intrinsic brightness and the density in the atmosphere of the star and in the intervening clouds of interstellar gas. Precise measurements of the wavelengths of the spectral lines give the line-of-sight velocities of the stars and clouds.

Thus the chemical and physical properties of the stars and interstellar gas clouds, and their distances and motions, can all be determined from measurements of the radiations received from them.

The halo

The globular clusters, first resolved into stars by Sir William Herschel, are the most striking objects in the galactic halo. The most massive clusters in the Galaxy, containing millions of stars, they range in size from twenty to a hundred light years, in distance from ten thousand to two hundred thousand. 'Beacons lighting the way to the edges of the Galaxy', they were described and used as such by H. Shapley, who pioneered and developed the most extensive observations of them at Harvard. One of the nearest globular clusters is shown in Plate 31*a*.

Many of the globular clusters contain RR Lyrae variable stars easily recognized on account of their short periods of regular variability—less than a day. These variables all have about the same intrinsic brightness, their absolute magnitudes being close to $M_V = +0.5$. Shapley used measures of their apparent magnitudes to estimate the distances to many of the globular clusters. He also noted that most of the brightest stars in the clusters are red giants always some three magnitudes brighter than the RR Lyrae variables, and used these to estimate distances to those clusters too far away for the variables to be observed.

The properties of the globular clusters are indeed so uniform that he was able to use the apparent diameters of many of them for distance estimates. Thus the distribution of the globular clusters was determined, and has been progressively improved by more and better data; they are found to form a spheroidal system over a hundred thousand light years in diameter with the centre some thirty thousand light years away in the direction of Sagittarius. Shapley concluded, and many other investigations have since confirmed, that this is the centre of the Galaxy.

More than a hundred globular clusters are known, and many others must be hidden by the interstellar dust clouds which obscure much of the view of the Galaxy. There may be as many as five hundred of them. Some globular clusters, such as Omega Centauri, are relatively near to us at ten thousand light years. Others such as NGC 2419 are so distant, possibly 175,000 light years, that they may not really be part of our Galaxy at all, and have been referred to as 'intergalactic tramps'.

Although globular clusters are closely similar to each other in many of their features, there are some differences. The most significant of these is probably in the relative abundances in the cluster stars of the heavier atomic elements, that is elements heavier than hydrogen and helium. The abundance of metallic elements in the globular cluster 47 Tucanae is about one-quarter that in the Sun, in M5 about a twentieth, in M15 and M92 only two-thousandths. The differences are believed to be connected with the times and places at which globular clusters formed; galactic fossils, telling us of conditions in distant parts and past times when the Galaxy was just beginning. Measurements of the colours and brightnesses of their stars, displayed on colour-magnitude arrays and interpreted by theories of stellar evolution (Chapter 8) show that all the halo globular clusters are old—several thousand million years. Some of them may be the oldest objects in the Galaxy. This aspect is considered further in the later section on the evolution of the Galaxy.

Globular clusters concentrated towards the centre of ths Galaxy, and those near the disk or 'plane', have the highest metal abundances; those farthest from the plane and the centre have the lowest. Clusters more than 60,000 light years from the centre, whatever their metal abundances, are also larger and less dense, indicating that the stars are following more eccentric orbits in their motions within them.

Although massive and dense enough to have held together against disrupting forces for several thousand million years, the globular clusters are nevertheless losing stars into the surrounding space—slowly evaporating. Calculations indicate that, independent of the mass or age of the cluster, each globular cluster loses some twenty thousand stars every thousand million years. It has been estimated that 20 per cent of all the RR Lyrae variable stars in the halo may have been lost from globular clusters; indeed their numbers show a concentration towards some at least of the clusters.

The *field stars* compose the greater number and the greater part of the mass in the halo. Their distribution is difficult to determine because they are mostly faint, and thinly spread over great distances; once again the RR Lyrae variables have played an important role in the investigations, because they are plentiful in the halo, bright enough to be observed to distances of tens of thousands of light years, and relatively easy to pick out from among the other stars. They are found to extend to distances more than 50,000 light years above and below the galactic plane, spread through a spherical volume similar in shape and extent to that occupied by the globular clusters.

Equidensity surfaces of the RR Lyrae variables are flattened spheroids out to distances of some 20,000 light years from the galactic centre, thereafter becoming less and less flattened and finally almost spherical.

The kinds of field stars which occur in the halo are very similar to those in globular clusters, although there are differences. One of them, rather odd and not yet explained, concerns the RR Lyrae stars. The period of variability of these stars bears some relation to their metal abundance; those with periods greater than 0.54 days have very low abundances; they are found to great heights above the galactic plane, that is far out in the halo, and also in those globular clusters whose stars in general are deficient in metals. On the other hand RR Lyrae variables with periods less than 0.44 days are metal rich—their metal abundances are similar to those in the Sun. They are found in large numbers among the field stars in the Galaxy, concentrated towards the disk, but are absent from metal-rich globular clusters. It is possible that the metal-deficient RR Lyrae variables and globular clusters, the metal-rich globular clusters, and the metal-rich RR Lyrae stars, represent three separate phases of star formation. This intriguing problem will be considered again later.

How many of the stars and how much of the mass of the Galaxy as a whole are to be found in the halo is still very uncertain. About 5 per cent of the mass of the Galaxy is accounted for by K and M dwarf halo stars; fainter stars are difficult to find directly, but estimates of the total amount of mass that may be contained in very faint stars can be made indirectly. This is done by determining the average mass per unit volume in the solar region of the Galaxy from dynamical arguments, subtracting all known contributions to this mass in terms of observed stars and interstellar matter, and supposing that the remainder may consist of very faint unobserved dwarf stars. This 'remainder' accounts for 40 per cent of the mass of matter in the local region. It may be due to very faint halo stars; but on the other hand it may be due to stars confined to the disk, or due to large unobserved quantities of gas. We still do not know, therefore, whether the halo forms a major or a minor part of the total mass of the Galactic system.

This uncertainty in the mass of the halo causes corresponding uncertainties in deductions made from the motions of stars in it. For instance, it has been estimated that a fifth of all RR Lyrae stars in the halo are moving with speeds high enough to escape from the gravitational pull of the Galaxy, implying that the halo is evaporating into intergalactic space. Although this is bound to happen to some extent, the rapidity of the loss cannot be determined with any certainty at present.

There is no distinct boundary between the halo and the disk; the disk is, in effect, embedded in the halo. How large a change in density occurs going from disk to halo will, however, remain unknown until the question of the mass density in the halo is answered.

The disk

Field stars The increasing density of stars towards the galactic plane is a prominent feature of the distribution of stars in the Galaxy as a whole; indeed it is this concentration which gives rise to the visible Milky Way and the concept of the galactic plane itself. However, the concentration is more pronounced with some kinds of stars than with others. This has already been noted in the case of the RR Lyrae stars. The hot young O and B stars are highly concentrated in the plane of the Milky Way and account for much of its brightness.

The differences in the distributions of various kinds of stars and other components of the Galaxy, and the smooth transitions from those forming a thin disk to those spread throughout a sphere, are shown in Table 9.1. This gives the average thicknesses of the flattened spheroidal volumes occupied by various objects, and the average speeds of motion of the objects in directions perpendicular to the galactic plane.

The last part of the table gives objects found out to great distances from the plane—the halo objects considered in the previous section.

The first part of the table contains those objects concentrated into a thin layer; they are in fact largely confined to the spiral arms which are considered in a following section. Here we are concerned with those objects listed in the central part of the table, forming the thick disk of the Galaxy and its central bulge.

TABLE 9.1 THE GALACTIC DISTRIBUTION OF VARIOUS OBJECTS

Object	*Average thickness in light years*	*Average perpendicular speed in km s⁻¹*
O-associations	260	
O and B stars	360	5
Cepheid variables	460	5
Galactic clusters	520	6
Interstellar gas	800	6.5
A-stars	740	9
F-giants	1,200	11
White dwarfs	1,800	18
G and M giants	2,200	15
Planetary nebulae	2,200	20
RR Lyrae variables ($P < 0\overset{d}{.}5$)	6,000	35
Subdwarfs	20,000	55
RR Lyrae variables ($P > 0\overset{d}{.}5$)	20,000	70
Globular clusters	26,000	70

A-stars have lifetimes of a few hundred million years, whereas the planetary nebulae are most probably produced by stars some ten times older. Thus the thickness of the layer in the disk occupied by various kinds of stars is related to their age. There are two effects operating to cause this. Old stars were formed from the gas clouds when they were not so highly concentrated to the galactic plane as they are now; and stars formed from the gas close to the plane not so long ago have their speeds of motion perpendicular to the plane increased through interacting dynamically with the remaining gas clouds, so that they move to greater distances from the plane than the gas out of which they formed.

The majority of stars have masses only about a tenth that of the Sun, but although there are so many of them—possibly 100 within 10 light years of the Sun—they are so faint that few of them are seen; conversely, massive stars are comparative rarities, but many of them are observed because their great intrinsic brightness enables them to be seen to great distances. Table 9.2 shows the relative numbers of stars of different types and masses in a given volume of space, in the region of the disk near the Sun.

TABLE 9.2 RELATIVE MASSES AND SPACE DENSITY IN THE SOLAR NEIGHBOURHOOD

Object	*Mass* (*Sun's mass = 1*)	*Relative number per unit volume*
O stars	40	0.05
B stars	8	0.15
Solar type stars	1	1
Dwarf M stars	0.2	7
RR Lyrae variables	1	2×10^{-6}
Planetary nebulae	1	1×10^{-6}

Measurements of the space density of planetary nebulae show that their number per unit volume does not appear to change substantially along the disk, from the solar region to the edge of the central bulge.

The stars are not, however, spread uniformly throughout the disk; as in the halo, some of them occur in clusters, but almost all of these contain many fewer stars and are much less dense than the globular clusters. On account of their appearance they are called open clusters.

Open clusters typically contain a few hundred stars in a volume several light years across. The Pleiades cluster (Plate 40*b*) is a well-known example visible to the naked eye. The youngest open clusters are to be found in the spiral arms, but the older ones are more widely distributed in the disk. During the last two decades observations of them have provided much of the information on which theories of the evolution of stars have been based and developed (Chapter 8), and these theories have enabled the ages of the clusters to be determined. They range from a few million to a few thousand million years. The Pleiades is about 60 million years old.

The clusters do not have indefinite lifetimes. The stars are moving about inside the clusters, each being alternately speeded up and slowed down by the changing gravitational pull of the other stars moving in its neighbourhood. Occasionally a star thus gains sufficient speed to escape from the gravitational pull of the cluster as a whole. This process is speeded up whenever a cluster passes near to one of the massive clouds of interstellar gas, the gravitational interaction causing an increase in the energy of motion of all the stars in the cluster, and as a result more of them are able to escape. Stars which escape from the clusters become field stars in the disk. The majority of open clusters probably lose al their stars in this way in a period of about a thousand million years: we see few of them older than this.

It is possible that many, or all, of the field stars in the disk were formed in clusters, because in addition to this slow evaporation of stars from them there may be a very substantial rate of loss at the time the clusters are formed. Thus many of the small older clusters we observe may be the remnants of much richer gatherings in the past, and many more may have dispersed and left no trace at all. There is indeed evidence that many of the field stars in large volumes of space around the clusters are moving through the Galaxy at about the same speed and in the same direction as the clusters, indicating a common origin. A substantial proportion of the brighter stars in the solar neighbourhood may be associated in this way with the Pleiades cluster.

The central bulge cannot be observed directly; it is heavily obscured by dust clouds; but attempts to observe the fringes of it have met with some success, and measurements of the motions of gas in it from radiations at radio wavelengths—which penetrate the dust clouds—have given important information about the dynamics, and hence indirectly about the total mass density.

When the various pieces of information are put together, a picture of the bulge begins to emerge. It is a flattened spheroid about 6,000 light years in diameter and 3,000 light years thick, composed predominantly of old stars. The great majority of the stars are metal rich and are probably younger than those in the globular cluster 47 Tucanae, but older than most of the stars in the galactic disk. They include an unusually high proportion of RR Lyrae variables. The number of stars per unit volume increases rapidly towards the centre: at 1500 light years it is fifty times the number near the Sun, at 300 light years a thousand times, at 30 light years more than twenty thousand times. At the centre the stars are separated from each other by distances of a few light months. An observer at the centre would see a brilliantly starry sky.

The spiral arms

The spiral arms are embedded in the disk in much the same way that the disk is embedded in the halo. They are composed predominantly of clouds of interstellar gas and groups of young stars, and because the techniques used for investigating these two components have been largely very different from each other, it is convenient to deal with them separately before considering how they are related to each other.

Spiral arms of gas Atomic hydrogen is the most abundant element in the Universe. It comprises about 70 per cent of the mass of matter in the stars, where it produces strong absorption lines in the spectra of the light coming from their interiors. It produces strong emission lines in the spectra of interstellar gas clouds heated to 10,000°K by bright hot stars near to them, indicating a similar abundance. But most of the interstellar gas clouds are cool, with temperatures of about 120°K (– 150°C). At this temperature hydrogen does not emit radiation in the visible region of the spectrum. The theoretical prediction by H. C. van de Hulst at Leiden in 1944, that it emits radio waves with a wavelength of 21 cm, opened up a whole new field of observational astronomy, one that has been vigorously pursued by J. H. Oort and his colleagues at the Leiden Observatory. Its pursuit has provided some of the most outstanding contributions made by radio astronomy to our astronomical knowledge.

The 21 cm hydrogen line radiation possesses three important advantages as compared with radiation in the optical region of the spectrum. First, it enables us to observe the major constituent of the interstellar gas: at the temperatures concerned, the strength of the radiation received measures directly the amount of atomic hydrogen emitting it. Secondly, it passes unaffected through clouds of interstellar dust, and we can thus measure the amounts of hydrogen in all regions of the Galaxy, including the central regions which are completely obscured at visible wavelengths. Thirdly, the motions of clouds of interstellar atomic hydrogen, towards or away from us, respectively compress or stretch the waves—the Doppler effect—and these changes in wavelength can be measured precisely by the radio receivers employed, giving correspondingly precise measures of the radial velocities of the clouds.

The work of the Netherlands astronomers has been supplemented by similar work in Australia, covering that part of the Galaxy only visible from the southern hemisphere. Between them they have succeeded in producing a map, shown in Plate 34, showing the distribution of hydrogen throughout the disk of the Galaxy.

At the centre of the Galaxy is a rotating disk of hydrogen 5000 light years in diameter. It is very thin and the angular velocity increases steeply towards the centre. It contains 5 million solar masses of interstellar atomic hydrogen, and probably many times this mass in stars. Two spiral arms wind out from the edges of this disk. They are rotating with a speed of about 50 km s^{-1}, and expanding outwards, the one on the near side with a speed of 53 km s^{-1}, the one on the far side at 135 km s^{-1}; at about 10,000 light years from the centre they merge into the more tightly wound pattern of arms.

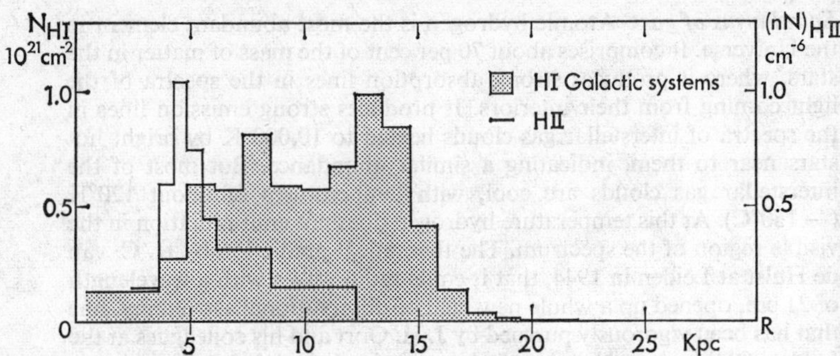

Figure 9.3 The amount of interstellar hydrogen in the disk, against distance from the galactic centre

The grey parts show the numbers of hydrogen atoms in columns of 1 cm² cross-section perpendicular to the equatorial planes of the system. Abscissae are distances from the centre in kpc. The curve with the sharp maximum at R = 5 gives the distribution of ionized hydrogen (after G. Westerhout and an unpublished investigation by H. van Woerden)

The amount of gas in these arms increases outwards, reaching the beginning of a flat maximum about 15,000 light years from the centre, as shown in Figure 9.3. The Perseus spiral arm, 40,000 light years from the centre, appears to have the most hydrogen in it.

Moving outwards from the centre the arms appear at intervals of about 6,000 light years; they are not smooth, but are broken up into clouds about 2,000 light years in diameter and a few hundred light years thick, each containing enough hydrogen to make a million stars. These clouds are in turn broken up into subclouds 50 to 100 light years across, filling altogether only 1 per cent of the volume of the parent cloud and each containing some hundreds or thousands of solar masses of hydrogen. Some of the denser clouds are cooler than average—only 50°K. These vast quantities of gas are the result of the large volumes; the densities are low—only a few atoms per cubic centimetre, a few 10^{-24} g cm^{-3}—a thousand million million millionth of the density of the Earth's atmosphere.

The distribution of clouds forms a layer of remarkably uniform thickness about the plane of the Galaxy. At a distance of 1500 light years from the centre the thickness is 250 light years; by 10,000 light years i has risen to 350 light years, and at the distance of the Sun to 500 light years. Thereafter it increases more rapidly, to perhaps as much as 3,000 light years at 50,000 light years from the centre. In the inner regions it stays close to the galactic plane—within 100 light years of it everywhere, but the outer edges deviate markedly from the plane, curving upwards at one side and downwards at the other; rather like the brim of a hat curled up at the back, pulled down over the eyes, with the Sun sitting on the brim over the right ear.

The whole system of spiral arms is rotating, with the arms trailing. The rotation of the Galaxy is considered in a later section, but one aspect of it is of particular interest here. The period of rotation of the spiral arms in the solar neighbourhood is about two hundred million years; the inner parts rotate faster than this—the outer parts more slowly. The Galaxy is at least ten thousand million years old—enough time for fifty rotations: yet there are only half a dozen turns on the spiral. The solution to this puzzle has still not been found with certainty, but a clue may be found in the motions of the spiral arm winding out from the central disk—its speed of rotation, 50 km s^{-1}, is only a fifth of the orbital speed at that point, yet the arms are moving outwards as if they had too much orbital energy.

Spiral arms of stars Photographs of other galaxies show their spiral arms to be traced out by bright, hot O-stars—young stars—associated with the clouds of gas. It was therefore natural to look for a similar situation in our Galaxy. This is much more easily said than done; great difficulty lies in determining the distances to these stars with sufficient accuracy to be able to see if they form arms. The first successful attempt was made by W. W. Morgan, S. Sharpless and D. Osterbrock in 1952; they found the distances to O and B stars by comparing spectrophotometric estimates of intrinsic brightnesses with apparent brightnesses, having estimated the dimming by interstellar dust from the reddening it produces. These early results have been added to and improved; Figure 9.4 shows how they delineate spiral arms largely coinciding with the arms of gas clouds found from 21 cm hydrogen line measures.

This coincidence between the star and gas arms is not found, however, in the case of older stars of type B8 and later; these appear to be nearer to the centre of the Galaxy than the gas arms. A similar feature is found in the case of the Cepheid variables: the very bright young ones are located in the arms, whereas the older ones occur along the inner edge of the arms, nearer the galactic centre. This suggests an interesting possibility. It was noted earlier that the gas arms within 10,000 light years of the centre are expanding outwards although they have much less than orbital circular velocity; thus there may be some force acting on the gas, pushing it out from the centre, which more than compensates for the lack of centrifugal force. If this outward force acts only on the gas and not on the stars, when stars form out of it they will fall towards the centre, following an elliptical orbit lying inside the gas arm. The existence of such an outward force, resulting in much smaller circular velocities of the gas nearer the galactic centre, may account for there being so few turns of the spiral arms.

Another method of tracing spiral arms has been developed by W. Becker. He has used observations of a large number of open clusters for this purpose; the distances to these can generally be determined more precisely than for single stars. The young clusters, those with ages less than about twenty million years, clearly show three spiral arms and possibly a fourth, as may be seen in Figure 9.5; clusters older than two hundred million years show little trace of grouping in the spiral arms. This is to be expected: the random velocities of the clusters are about 10 km s^{-1}; the older ones have had enough time to move out of the spiral arms where they were formed. Sometimes this kind of investiga-

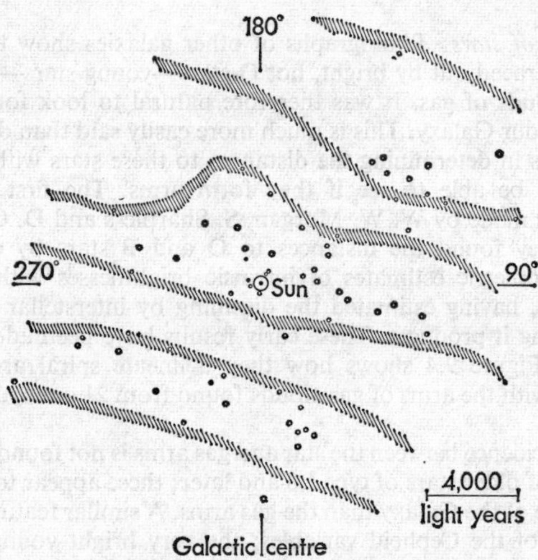

Figure 9.4 Parts of spiral arms delineated by O-stars visible from Earth, and corresponding parts of the hydrogen gas distribution

tion can be worked in reverse. For instance, giant stars of types M2 to M4 are concentrated to the spiral arms, whereas those of spectral types later than M4 are more uniformly distributed; from this it may be concluded that the former evolve rapidly from young stars—most probably O-stars—and the latter are related to older types of stars. A similar argument applies to the carbon stars and S stars, which are also concentrated to the arms.

The thickness of the arms in a direction perpendicular to their plane can be judged from the data given in Table 9.1 for O-stars, Cepheids and open clusters. The width of the arms, normal to their length, in the plane, is more difficult to determine. Becker's distribution of young open clusters indicates that they are about 1800 light years across, a value in agreement with that for the width of the Orion arm determined from measurements of 1000 stars in it.

O-associations In 1949 the Soviet astronomer V. A. Ambartsumyan noted that many of the O and B stars are gathered together in groups, and called them O-associations. He pointed out that, although these associations represent dense concentrations in the distribution of O and B stars alone, they appear to add little to the density of stars of all kinds in their neighbourhood; if the distribution of O-stars alone is plotted out the groupings stand out clearly; if all kinds of stars are plotted, the O-

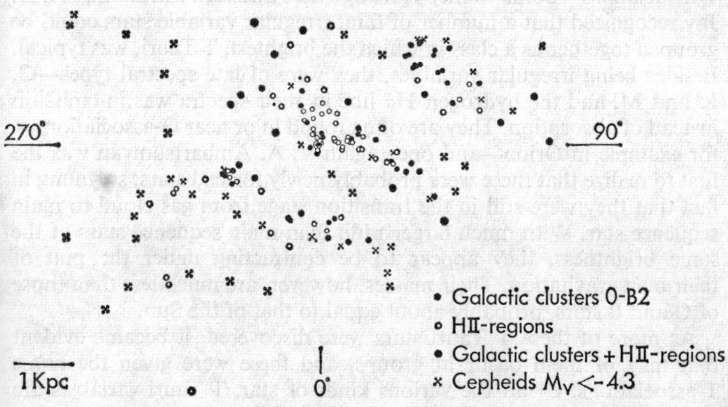

Figure 9.5 The spiral arms formed by young open clusters, from the work of W. Becker

stars are lost in the general background. Ambartsumyan argued that the gravitational attraction of the O-associations would not therefore be large enough to hold them together against the disruptive forces caused by the varying pull of other stars and gas clouds, and that they must therefore be dispersing. As this dispersion would occur relatively quickly he argued that they must have formed comparatively recently—not more than a few million years ago.

Measurements of the motions of stars in O-associations show that they are indeed moving predominantly outwards. A leading investigator of these expanding associations has been the Netherlands astronomer A. Blaauw. He has found, for instance, that the stars in the association Perseus II are moving outwards with an average speed of 12 km s^{-1}. If they were all found close together in space at the centre of the association it will have taken them a little over a million years to reach their present positions: similarly young ages have been found for other associations. The central part of the Orion association appears to be no more than 300,000 years old.

So Ambartsumyan's argument that the O-associations are dispersing systems of recently formed stars has been confirmed, and his belief that they are of great importance to theories of star formation has been amply justified. They are, indeed, amongst the youngest known systems of stars, matched only by the T-associations.

T-associations Some twenty years ago the American astronomer A. H. Joy recognized that a number of faint irregular variable stars could be grouped together as a class in which the brightest, T Tauri, was typical. Besides being irregular variables, they were of late spectral types—G, K and M, and the hydrogen Hα line in their spectra was in emission instead of absorption. They are often found in or near O-associations—for example in Orion—and once again V. A. Ambartsumyan was the first to realize that these were probably newly formed stars, so young in fact that they were still in the transition stage from gas cloud to main sequence star. With much larger radii than main sequence stars of the same brightness, they appear to be contracting under the pull of their own gravitation. Their masses, however, are much less than those of O and B stars, probably about equal to that of the Sun.

As more of these T Tauri stars were discovered, it became evident that may of them occur in groups, and these were given the name T-associations. Of all the various kinds of star, T Tauri variables are the most highly concentrated to the interstellar clouds and their further study can be expected to play a major part in answering the question 'How do stars form out of the interstellar gas?'

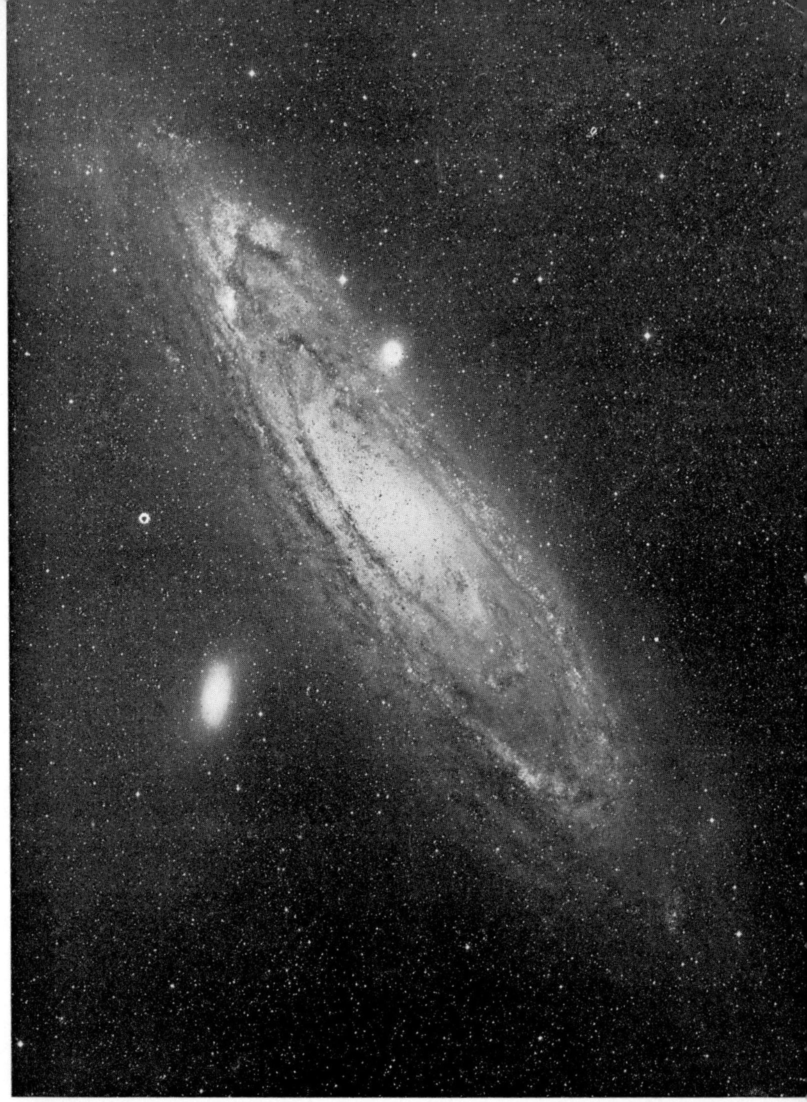

Plate 33 M 31, the Great Spiral Nebula in Andromeda and two companion ellipsoidal nebulae. This system probably bears a considerable resemblance to our Milky Way and indicates how it might look when viewed nearly side-ways on. Hale Observatories photograph (1cm = 10′ of arc)

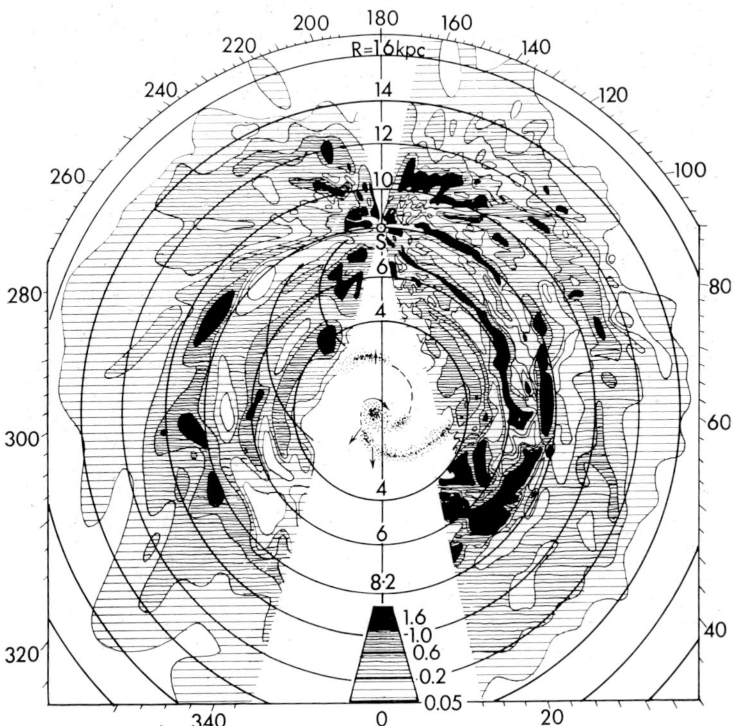

Plate 34 The structure of our Galaxy as indicated by the distribution of hydrogen in its central plane deduced from observations of the 21 cm line of hydrogen made in the Netherlands (Northern Milky Way) and at the Radio Physics Laboratory, CSIRO, Australia (Southern part). (Plate 47)

The different shadings show the density of hydrogen atoms per cm^3. Distances are indicated in kiloparsecs (1 kiloparsec = 3262 light years). The Sun is at S, there are two empty sectors in the direction towards and away from the centre where the hydrogen distribution cannot be unravelled from radio data. The distribution drawn for the central part is highly schematical. It shows arms expanding away from the centre

Plate 35 M 83 or NGC 5236, a spiral nebula in Hydra which might indicate how our Milky Way looks when viewed square-on. The Sun would be located near the outer edge. Hale Observatories photograph (1 cm = 1′.5 of arc)

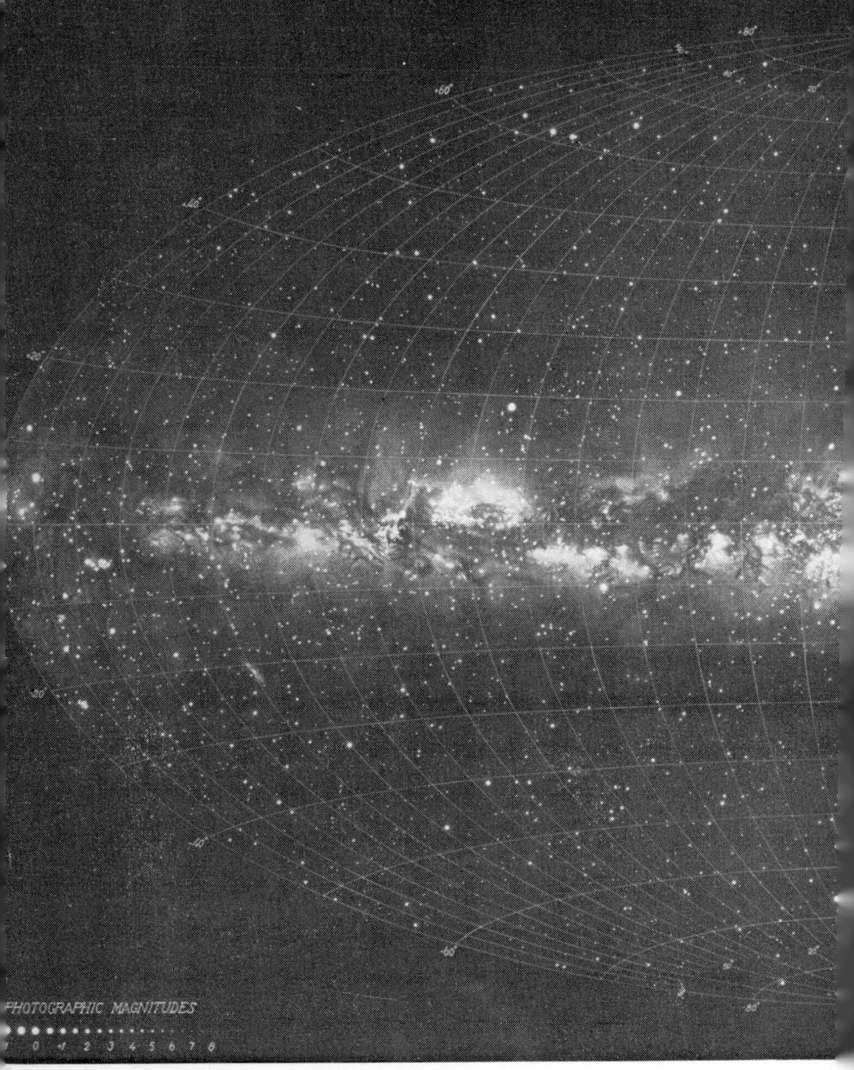

Plate 36–7 The Milky Way

This chart was prepared at the Lund Observatory by plotting 7,000 of the brightest stars in the sky according to their photographic magnitude and then drawing in the general structure of the Milky Way from photographs. It is on an equal area Aitoff projection of galactic co-ordinates; distances are scarcely distorted along the equator but are markedly so towards the poles as may be seen from the 10° × 10° grid

The Cygnus-Aquila dark rift is conspicuous to the left of centre. Auriga and Perseus are on the far left, Sagittarius in the centre and to the right of it Centaurus, Crux, Puppis and Canis Major. Sirius, with the Orion area below and to the right of it, is conspicuous about 50° from the right of the chart while the Large and Small Magellanic Clouds are the two bright patches in the lower right that look like detached fragments of the Milky Way. The Great Nebula in Andromeda is also shown in south galactic latitude 20° and 50° from the left of the chart.

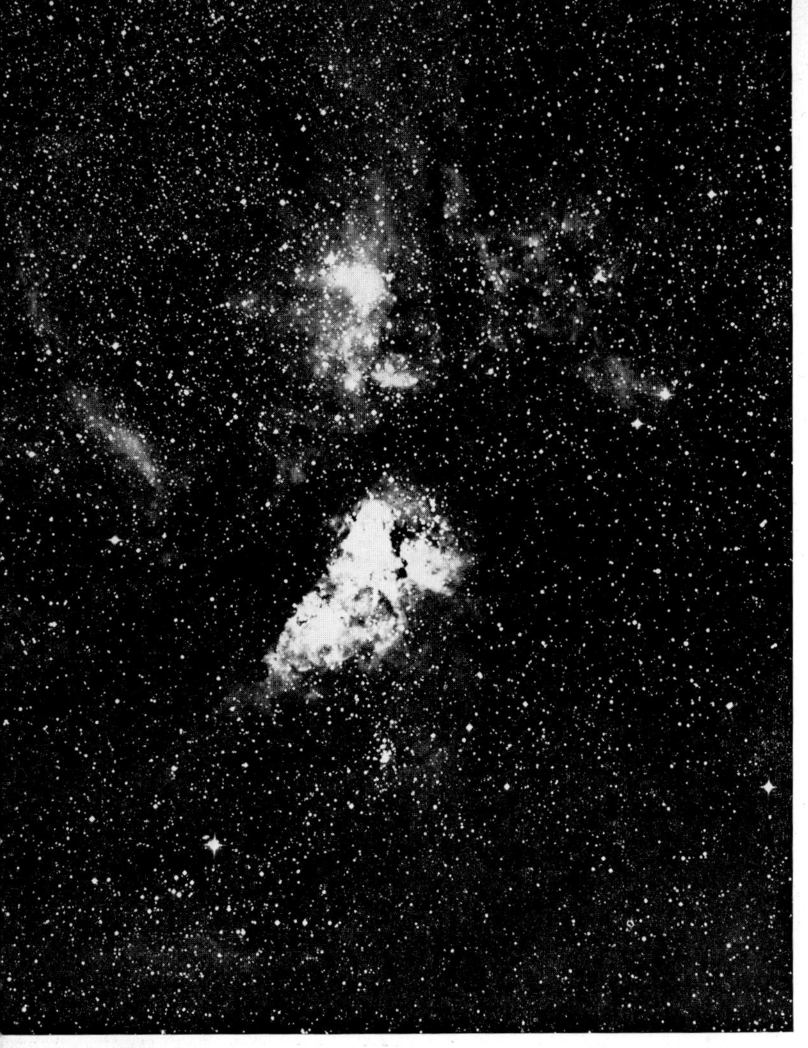

Plate 38 The region surrounding Eta Carinae is one of the most interesting portions of the southern Milky Way and contains many bright diffuse and dark nebulae in addition to numerous star clusters. The dark marking superimposed on the lower bright mass is sometimes called the 'Keyhole Nebula'. This was one of the first photographs taken with the Elizabeth Telescope (Plate 46)

Plate 39*a* Eta Carinae and the densest part of the surrounding nebulosity as seen in the light of Hα. Radcliffe Observatory photograph (1 cm = 1′.4 of arc)

Plate 39*b* NGC 6193, an example of a bright rim to a dense interstellar cloud caused by the radiation from an O-type star. The exciting star in this case is the very bright one at the top of the plate. Radcliffe Observatory photograph (1 cm = 1′.9 of arc)

Plate 40*a* M 42, the Great Nebula in Orion. This is a region where stars still seem to be forming out of clouds of nebulous matter. Lick Observatory photograph (1 cm = 10′.7 of arc)

Plate 40*b* M 45, the Pleiades showing how clouds of dusty gas round the brighter stars form a reflection nebula. Lick Observatory photograph (1 cm = 10′ of arc)

HII regions and emission nebulae The temperatures of the surface layers of O-stars exceed 20,000°K. Radiation from them heats the surrounding gas cloud; when the temperature reaches 10,000°K collisions between the atoms are sufficiently energetic to knock the electrons out of many of them. These ionized atoms recapture the free electrons moving through the gas and in doing so emit radiation particularly strongly at wavelengths corresponding to differences between the electron energy levels in the atom. Photographs taken through filters isolating the Hα radiation of hydrogen show O stars to be surrounded by glowing clouds of hydrogen; these are the HII regions, sometimes a hundred light years across. Plate 39*a* shows the HII region surrounding Eta Carinae. The hotter the star, the larger the HII region. In the space occupied by O-associations, the individual HII regions merge into a vast glowing cloud, thus forming an emission nebula which may contain more than 10^4 solar masses of gas.

The HII regions are not static: the energy pouring into them from the exciting stars causes them to expand. Sometimes the rate of expansion is faster than the speed of sound in the surrounding gas—about a kilometre per second—and the moving edge of the HII region becomes a shock wave. These edges, the transition from the ionized to the neutral hydrogen, are in any case sharp, only a few hundredths of a light year thick.

Where the radiation from an O-star falls on a particularly dense interstellar cloud containing perhaps 10^6 atoms cm^{-3}, it causes the cloud to develop a bright rim, such as those shown in Plate 39*b*, and heated gas streams off the cloud towards the star at the speed of sound —about 13 km s^{-1} at the temperature of 10,000°K. The effect may be compared to that of a rocket exhaust, and accelerates the cloud in the opposite direction.

In addition to the radiation from hot hydrogen, the oxygen and nitrogen atoms also radiate strongly: the radiations by oxygen in the violet and green regions of the spectrum are responsible for a large part of the energy radiated by the HII regions, the oxygen thus acting as a coolant among the hot hydrogen.

Since the interstellar gas clouds and the O-stars are concentrated to the spiral arms, HII regions, being the result of a combination of the two, provide excellent 'tracers' of spiral arms, and have been used with success for this purpose both in our own and other galaxies. Photographs taken through filters isolating the light of Hα, for instance, show HII regions strung like beads along the spiral arms.

In addition to the visible radiation emitted by the atoms, the electrons in HII regions emit radio waves as their motions are changed by the attractions of the ionized atoms. This radiation has the same intensity at all radio frequencies; unlike the 21 cm wavelength radiation by neutral hydrogen it is not restricted to a narrow range of frequency. Since it results from the gas being hot it is called thermal radio emission. The larger the number of electrons and ions the stronger the radiation. Since these radiations are able to pass through interstellar dust clouds unhindered, receivers attached to radio telescopes are able to measure their strength, and enable the density of ionized hydrogen to be estimated in distant parts of the Galaxy. The measurements have shown that the density reaches a maximum about 15,000 light years from the centre just where the density of neutral hydrogen is rising rapidly towards its maximum. Further out from the centre the density of ionized hydrogen falls substantially whereas that of neutral hydrogen continues to rise slowly. Over the Galaxy as a whole, a few per cent of all the hydrogen is ionized.

Measurements of Doppler shifts of lines in the spectra of emission nebulae give the motions of the emitting atoms. Within any one cloud these motions are due to the thermal kinetic energy of the atoms, and, being random, broaden the spectrum line without changing its average wavelength. The breadth of the line then provides a measure of the temperature of the cloud. The bodily motions of the clouds as a whole, however, change the average wavelength of their emission lines. Thus it is found that the average temperature of the gas in the emission nebulae in Orion is 9,600°K, and the temperature everywhere in the nebula is within 300°K of this average; that the gas is turbulent, elements not more than 1/30 light year across moving relative to each other at speeds of 25 km s^{-1}.

Interstellar dust grains

Although composed primarily of hydrogen, and to a lesser extent of helium, the interstellar clouds contain small solid particles, a few millionths of a centimetre across, which have come to be called interstellar dust grains. If the clouds were composed purely of gas they would be very transparent; the dust causes them to be foggy, dimming the light of stars observed through them. About 1 per cent of the mass of a cloud is dust. Some of the clouds are dense enough to be nearly opaque, hiding the stars behind and looking like holes in the distribution of stars; this is what Sir William Herschel (1784) thought them to be. Barnard's *Atlas of Selected Regions of the Milky Way*, 1927, showed many of them, and detailed examination of their shapes and distribution provides convincing evidence that they are obscuring clouds and not holes.

Many of the clouds are illuminated by bright stars near to them. If the illuminating star is very bright and hot, the gas is heated to luminescence, and the cloud becomes an *emission nebula* radiating light in wavelengths typical of the atoms it contains. If the star is not so bright and hot the cloud merely reflects the starlight, and is termed a *reflection nebula*. Sir William Huggins, in 1867, noted the differences between the spectra of emission and reflection nebulae, but it was not until 1912 when V. M. Slipher photographed the spectrum of the brighter regions of the Pleiades nebulosity that the spectrum was shown to have the same absorption line pattern as that of the illuminating star.

The presence of a distribution of dust more widespread than that in the distant clouds was suspected for some years before 1930. For instance, distant stars were redder than nearby ones with similar line spectra, an effect which could be explained if the light was dimmed by interstellar dust more strongly in the blue than in the red. In that year its existence was established by R. J. Trumpler in the following way. He estimated the relative distances to various open clusters of stars by the apparent brightnesses of the stars in them, and then calculated the linear sizes of the clusters from their distances and angular diameters. The sizes appeared to increase with distance; the most probable explanation of the effect was that the distances had been wrongly estimated, part of the decrease in the apparent brightnesses of the stars with increasing distance being due to dimming by interstellar dust. This conclusion has been fully confirmed in succeeding years.

Measurements of the relative brightnesses of dimmed and undimmed stars showed that the dimming was stronger for blue light than for red. Measurements at several wavelengths from about 0.1 microns in the ultraviolet to about 22 microns in the infrared have shown that the amount of dimming is closely proportional to the frequency of the light waves, with a hump at a wavelength of 0.2 microns.

Few chemical elements are abundant enough to provide the major constituent of the dust; hydrogen, helium, oxygen, neon, carbon, nitrogen, silicon, magnesium, sulphur, iron, are the more abundant; iron, ice (hydrogen and oxygen), graphite (carbon) and silicates have been proposed as possible dust grains. The dimming (or so-called obscuration) results from starlight being scattered out of the line of sight by the grains; the particular chemical composition of the grains affects the way in which the obscuration depends on the wavelength of the light, and measurements of this dependence provide a means of investigating the chemical composition of the dust.

Recently, very precise measurements of the way in which interstellar obscuration depends on wave number have been made by J. W. Harris at the Royal Observatory, Edinburgh. They show that there is a sharp change at wave number $2.30\mu^{-1}$; this indicates that much of the obscuration is due to absorption of light rather than to scattering, but the kind of grain which can produce just such an effect has still not been determined. It may be the result of complex molecular structures formed on the surfaces of the dust grains.

Measurements by K. Nandy show distinct differences in the optical properties of the dust grains in different directions in the Galaxy, implying differences in the chemical composition or structure of the grains.

A remarkable feature of the grains is their ability to survive in some of the more dense HII regions in which the temperature of the gas approaches 10,000°K. It had been expected that the grains would be evaporated in such hot clouds, but not only do they survive, they are so abundant in some of the more compact HII regions that they completely obscure the light of the stars embedded in the clouds. On the other hand, light of wavelengths shorter than 0.1 micron is able to penetrate the dusty regions and ionize the surrounding gas, indicating that the grains must absorb little light of such wavelengths. And yet at twice that wavelength, the failure to detect light scattered by the grains shows that they must absorb most of it.

None of the 'models' of interstellar dust grains which have so far been proposed accounts for even most of the various features observed at different wavelengths. The detailed composition and structure of the grains remain a mystery.

There are two other effects on the light from stars which are believed to be due to the dust—polarization, and the interstellar bands.

Polarization In 1949 the American astronomers W. A. Hiltner and J. S. Hall discovered that starlight is polarized; light waves vibrating perpendicular to the Galactic plane are dimmed rather more than those vibrating parallel to it.

Explanations of the interstellar polarization have been sought in the idea that the dust particles are elongated and aligned by a magnetic field along the spiral arms. Looking along the magnetic field—along the spiral arm towards Cygnus—polarization is weak; looking perpendicular to the magnetic field and the arm, towards Perseus, polarization is a maximum. Theory and observation agree so far as this feature is concerned. The strength of the magnetic field required is similar to that invoked to explain other phenomena, such as the stability of the spiral arms and the non-thermal radio emission by the Galaxy.

Interstellar bands In 1936, P. W. Merrill discovered a shallow dip in the spectrum of a reddened star, some twenty angstroms wide at a wavelength of 4430Å. This has been observed in a considerable number of stars since then and has become known as the 4430Å band. It is stronger in stars more heavily reddened by interstellar dust and is therefore believed to be caused by that dust, or by something distributed in space with the dust. Merrill also discovered six narrow bands, diffuse lines, in the yellow-red region of the spectrum. Three more interstellar bands were discovered by R. Wilson in 1958. The strengths of all these lines and bands appear to be roughly related to each other and to the interstellar obscuration.

So far no generally accepted theory of the cause of them has been put forward. It would not be surprising if the dust particles in interstellar space, at low temperatures and low densities, irradiated by ultraviolet and X-radiation and bombarded by cosmic rays, behave in unexpected ways. The interstellar bands may contain important information for us if only we can understand it.

Interstellar absorption lines

The spectra of distant stars often show very narrow absorption lines, much narrower than those due to absorption of light in the atmosphere of the star itself. They are caused by atoms in the interstellar gas. Their narrowness results from two causes. Firstly, the gas is at a low temperature, which means that the speeds of the atoms within any one cloud of gas are relatively slow. Their speeds in the line of sight are spread over a very narrow range, and consequently the changes in frequency of the radiation they absorb or emit, due to these motions, are restricted to a correspondingly narrow range. That is to say, the Doppler broadening of the absorption lines is small. Secondly, the density is low, so the atoms are far apart and their energy levels are not disturbed by interactions with their neighbours.

Absorption lines due to atoms of sodium, potassium, calcium, titanium and iron, and molecules of CH and CN have been observed.

It is probable that there are large quantities of molecular hydrogen, H_2, in the cooler clouds, but it does not produce absorptions of measurable strength in the visible region of the spectrum. Measurements in the ultraviolet part of the spectrum made by orbiting astronomical observatories above the Earth's atmosphere will some day tell us how much H_2 there is.

The most efficient way of producing molecular from atomic hydrogen in the interstellar clouds is by the capture of hydrogen atoms on the surfaces of dust grains, and it is likely that virtually all the H_2 is produced in this way. The larger the grains the more H_2 will be produced; thus measurements of its abundance will indirectly give useful information about the dust which may be compared to that obtained by measuring the wavelength dependence of the obscuration.

Although the atoms have small speeds relative to each other within a cloud, the clouds themselves sometimes have considerably larger speeds, and the Doppler shifts of the interstellar absorption lines are used to determine their motions in the line of sight. Unfortunately, because of their narrowness and because very little of the starlight is included within them, they can only be measured with sufficient precision on highly dispersed spectra, and this restricts the measurements to the brighter stars. Nevertheless such measurements have given a good deal of information about the motions of gas in cool interstellar clouds. They have shown that the gas surrounding the brighter stars in the Pleiades is falling in towards them, perhaps indicating that those stars have not yet completed their process of formation; in the spectrum of the star α Cygni they are so narrow that the intrinsic hyperfine structure of the sodium D_2 line can be seen, showing that turbulent velocities in the gas between us and the star are less than 0.64 km s^{-1}; this may be compared with the 25 km s^{-1} turbulent velocities in the hot nebula in Orion (see the section on HII regions and emission nebulae), which therefore has more than a thousand times as much turbulent kinetic energy per unit mass.

Observations of interstellar absorption lines have also provided a means of searching for gas clouds in the halo.

Interstellar gas in the halo Measurements of interstellar absorption lines in the spectra of stars in the halo, by G. Munch and H. Zirin, have revealed the existence of interstellar gas clouds up to distances of at least 1 kpc from the galactic plane, moving with speeds of up to 50 km s^{-1}. Once again, however, most information about gas in the halo has come from the 21 cm wavelength radio emission by neutral hydrogen, and once again astronomers at the Leiden Observatory have played a leading part. They found streams of gas moving inwards from the halo towards the galactic plane, at speeds up to 175 km s^{-1}, a large amount in galactic longitude 120°. The average speed of flow is much lower than this, about 6 km s^{-1}. Observations made using the big 210 ft radio telescope in Australia indicate that gas is flowing away from the polar region in the galactic plane, towards the centre and anticentre, at a similar speed.

Blaauw has constructed a model of the halo gas clouds to fit the radio measurements. These are given in Table 9.3, where they are compared to an interpretation of the measurements of absorption lines in the optical spectra.

TABLE 9.3 HALO GAS CLOUDS

	Radio	*Optical*	
Average diameter	8	80	light years
separation	30	100	light years
density	47	10	atoms cm^{-3}

It is of interest that recent measurements by B. Strömgren of the sizes of interstellar clouds within 500 light years of the Sun, made by examining the distribution of the interstellar obscuration caused by their dust content, show them to have diameters of about 130 light years. The difference in the results produced by the various methods may not be real; they may be due to the difficulty of interpreting the data.

Magnetic fields in the Galaxy

There are a number of indications of the existence of a large-scale magnetic field in the Galaxy: the polarization of starlight and radio waves, the origin of the non-thermal radio waves, the possibility of non-gravitational forces acting on the gas clouds.

It was mentioned on page 380 that theories attempting to account for the polarization of starlight have been largely based on the idea that the interstellar dust particles are elongated, and aligned by a magnetic field along the spiral arms. Because of collisions between the dust particles and atoms in the interstellar gas moving with thermal velocities, the grains would continually be getting knocked out of alignment; only a proportion of them would be aligned at any time. How large this proportion would be depends on how strongly the particles are affected by magnetic fields—iron would be affected more than ice, for instance—and on how frequent and violent the collisions with other atoms are, factors which depend on the density and temperature of the interstellar gas. The greater the degree of alignment, the more the starlight will be polarized. The efficiency of polarization by the particles depends also on their optical properties and hence on their chemical composition. Thus if we know the chemical and physical properties of the dust grains, and the temperature and density of the interstellar gas, we can estimate the strength of the magnetic field required to give the degree of alignment necessary to account for the observed polarization. Such calculations lead to a value of about 10^{-6} gauss. Having regard to the uncertainty in the chemical and physical properties of the grains, however, this result has to be viewed with caution.

The polarization shows extremely high uniformity along the Milky Way. In Perseus especially the planes of vibration of light coming from different stars are aligned to within a few degrees of each other, and the strength of the polarization is correlated with the amount of interstellar dimming. This is evidence of considerable uniformity in the direction and strength of the magnetic field over great lengths of the spiral arms.

The origin of those radio waves not emanating from HII regions is believed to be due to interaction between cosmic ray electrons and magnetic fields. This radio emission comes from the halo as well as from the disk. It is considered in more detail in the section dealing with radio emission; here it is just sufficient to point out that the strength of the magnetic field required is again about 10^{-6} gauss—rather more for radio waves produced in the disk, rather less for those in the halo. It is the strongest evidence of the existence of magnetic fields in the halo.

The radio waves are polarized, but not so much as they would be if they came to us through empty space. Their planes of polarization are rotated as they pass through regions in which there are free electrons in magnetic fields, the amount of rotation, Faraday rotation as it is called, depending on the density of the electrons and the strengths of the magnetic fields. Different sets of waves reaching us from different distances in a given direction suffer different amounts of rotation, and arrive with their planes of vibration in disarray; their polarizations mutually cancel to some extent, this depolarization leaving a smaller net polarization. Thus the higher the density of interstellar electrons the more the rotations differ with distance and the smaller the net polarization. If there were no differential Faraday rotation, the polarization would be 50 per cent; it is at most a few per cent. This exceptionally low value cannot be explained by the different distances which the waves have traversed; the electron density has been determined from the strength of the *thermal* radio emission, page 388, and it is not high enough. The depolarization can only be explained by supposing that the magnetic fields are very tangled. This would seem to contradict the earlier conclusion from the uniformity of the polarization of starlight that the magnetic fields are very uniform. It does not. The starlight is polarized by dust grains and these are in the cool interstellar clouds; the radio waves are polarized by electrons and these are in hot ionized clouds. Thus the observations tell us that in the cool clouds the magnetic field is neatly aligned along the spiral arms, in hot regions it is chaotically entangled. This is in accord with our knowledge of the state of motion in the gas clouds referred to on pages 372 and 378; the turbulent velocities in the hot clouds are some forty times larger than in the cool ones; that is to say, the turbulent energy per unit mass is more than a thousand times larger.

A more direct measure of the strength of the magnetic field has been made by R. D. Davies and his colleagues using the 250-ft radio telescope at Jodrell Bank. They received radiation, from a distant non-thermal source, which had passed through cool clouds of hydrogen gas, and observed the 21-cm hydrogen line in *absorption*. Because the radiation is received in a narrow cone from the distant source, it passes through only a few cool and dense clouds, and these produce deep and narrow absorption lines. The lines are split by the action of the magnetic field on the hydrogen atoms in the cloud, into two overlapping lines whose planes of polarization are rotating in opposite senses. The amount of separation of the two component lines is proportional to the strength of the magnetic field, but it is very small and the measurement presented exceedingly difficult problems. They finally succeeded, however, in measuring a magnetic field in one cloud which has a strength of 5×10^{-5} gauss. Measurements in other clouds failed to detect magnetic fields, setting an upper limit of about 5×10^{-6} gauss on their strengths. Later measurements, however, have detected magnetic fields in several clouds with strengths of about 10^{-5} gauss.

If they are sufficiently strong, magnetic fields have an important effect in clouds containing free electrons. The electrons can move freely along the magnetic lines of force, but not across them. Wherever the lines of force go the electrons go, and vice versa. If the gas cloud contracts it compresses its magnetic field; if the field is the stronger and expands, taking the electrons with it, they sweep the atoms outwards with them. There is some slippage if the atoms far outnumber the electrons, but if the ionization is at all substantial, the magnetic field is inextricably embedded in the cloud. Thus magnetic fields can exert a force on the gas. They resist compression and hence may prevent a cloud contracting to become a star. They may link a cloud to surrounding clouds and prevent it rotating, holding it like a fly in a spider's web. Threading the spiral arms of the Galaxy they may help to hold them together. They may be the force acting on the gas in the spiral arms which prevents them from falling towards the centre of the Galaxy despite their lack of orbital velocity. All these are possibilities but none of them are certainties; the methods used to investigate the interstellar magnetic fields have perforce been so indirect as to make it almost impossible to reach absolutely firm conclusions about them.

Cosmic rays

The cosmic rays are nuclei of atoms hurtling through space at speeds close to that of light. At these speeds their energy is enormous. Any that enter the Earth's atmosphere smash the atoms in their path, creating a shower of fundamental particles, some of which can be detected at ground level. The study of these cosmic ray showers has been a valuable aid to the nuclear physicists investigating the structure of the atom.

Those cosmic ray particles which are electrically charged, such as electrons and protons, have their directions of motion changed by the Earth's magnetic field as they approach. When allowance has been made for this it is found that with one exception the particles come equally from all directions. The exception is those particles coming from the Sun (Chapter 7). This isotropy in their distribution indicates either that the cosmic rays come from many sources distributed isotropically about us, or that their directions of motion are quickly randomized, such as may happen through the existence of strong interstellar magnetic fields.

The energy gained by an electron falling through a potential of 1 volt is termed an electron volt. In the atmospheres of most stars with temperatures of several thousand degrees, the hydrogen atoms are moving with speeds of about half a kilometre per second, their kinetic energies being about an electron volt. Cosmic ray particles have energies as high as 10^{19} electron volts. These are a minority, however The number of cosmic ray particles with energy greater than E is given by the formula

$$N(>E) \propto E^{-\gamma}$$

where γ is about 1.7.

The higher the energy of a cosmic ray particle, the stronger the magnetic field required to curve its path sufficiently to retain it within a given volume of space. 10^{17} electron volts particles can only be confined to the disk of the Galaxy if the magnetic fields are greater than 10^{-} gauss. It would take less than 2×10^{6} years for such particles to escape from the disk, while a photon, which travels in a straight line, would take 10^{3} years to traverse half the thickness of the disk. The energ density of the cosmic rays in space is similar to that of the light from the stars. Since a cosmic ray particle of 10^{17} electron volts is confined to the disk for 2,000 times as long as a photon, the efficiency with which energy is put into cosmic rays need only be 1/2000 as high as for light.

Similar results come in considering cosmic ray particles confined to the galactic halo, except that because of the larger volume particles with energies not greater than 10^{19} electron volts can be confined provided the magnetic field is greater than 5×10^{-6} gauss.

Magnetic fields of 10^{-5} gauss in the disk and 5.10^{-6} in the halo are larger than those indicated by some of the investigations reported in an earlier section. If the fields are indeed much less than this, the cosmic rays must be truly cosmic, in the sense that they are free to travel through space in the Universe at large.

It has been mentioned that the energy density of the cosmic rays in space is about equal to that of starlight. The kinetic energy per unit volume of the interstellar gas also has about the same value. If it is linked to the magnetic field as described previously then, since the cosmic rays are also linked to the fields, they will exert a pressure on the gas, influencing its distribution and motions.

The abundances of the various chemical elements among the atoms of the cosmic rays are similar to those in the stars, but there are important differences; for a given amount of hydrogen the abundances of the medium and heavy elements, carbon, oxygen, iron and so on, decrease with increasing atomic weight in both cases, but are 10 to 100 times greater throughout in the cosmic rays, and the abundances of the light elements such as lithium are nearly a million times greater. The abundance of lithium in the interstellar gas and in T Tauri stars—new stars—is midway between these extremes.

The origin of cosmic rays is still not known with certainty. There are various possibilities and they may all play a part; the acceleration of interstellar particles by shockwaves in the interstellar gas or by the motion of interstellar gas clouds causing waves in the magnetic fields; ejection of high speed particles by supernovae; emission by quasars (page 423).

The cosmic rays are responsible, indirectly, for much of the radio wave emission of the Galaxy. These waves are produced by the motion of high speed electrons through the interstellar magnetic fields, and the high speed electrons in their turn are produced through the break-up of interstellar hydrogen atoms hit by cosmic rays. The high energy electrons ($E > 10^9$ electron volts) do not penetrate the Earth's atmosphere; their flux has been measured by geiger and scintillation counters flown in balloons; it is about 8×10^{-3} electrons per square centimetre per second per unit solid angle, and, if the interstellar magnetic fields are about 5×10^{-6} gauss, is just sufficient to account for the strength of the non-thermal radio emission.

Galactic radio emission

Thermal radio emission, that is the radio waves emitted by electrons moving with thermal energies in clouds of ionized gas, has been discussed in the section on HII regions.

Non-thermal radio emission is produced by cosmic ray electrons moving with speeds close to that of light through interstellar magnetic fields. In these conditions the electrons travel a spiral path and behave as they do in a laboratory synchrotron, spraying out radiation. The energies of the cosmic ray electrons and the strength of the interstellar magnetic fields result in much of this radiation occurring as radio waves. The higher energy electrons produce the higher frequency, shorter wavelength, radiation. Since there are fewer of them, the intensity of the radio emission is less at the shorter wavelengths, in contrast to the thermal radio emission which has the same intensity at all wavelengths. This difference in spectrum provides the means by which the thermal and non-thermal components of the radio emission may be separated; at short wavelengths it is predominantly thermal, at long wavelengths predominantly non-thermal.

The thermal radio emission comes predominantly from HII regions, and their distributions are therefore similar, both being concentrated towards the Milky Way and both being patchy. The non-thermal emission, on the other hand, picks out the distribution of high energy electrons and magnetic fields. There is a broad background component coming from the galactic halo, a narrower one from the disk. In addition there are a large number of discrete sources of radio emission. Many of them are extragalactic, but a proportion are in our Galaxy and are strongly concentrated towards the central plane. Some are remnants of supernovae explosions such as the Crab Nebulae shown in Plate 32*b*. Many are hidden from view by the dust clouds. There is a group of strong discrete radio sources at the centre of the Galaxy whose origin is unknown.

The synchrotron process produces radiation over a wide range of frequencies. Some of the light coming from the Crab Nebula is produced in this way, and recently X-rays have been detected by instruments mounted in space rockets, from an area about a minute of arc across near its centre. X-rays have been detected from several other regions, some of which have also been identified with supernova remains.

The rotation of the Galaxy

The Galaxy rotates about an axis perpendicular to the centre of its disk. The effect of this rotation can be seen in the motions of the stars within a few thousand light years of the Sun. Most of them are following fairly circular orbits; those nearer to the centre are moving faster and overtaking the stars in our immediate vicinity; those further out are moving more slowly and falling behind. This differential rotation indicates that the mass of the Galaxy is concentrated towards its centre. Observations of the angular and radial motions of stars, by astrometry and spectrometry, are limited by the obscuring clouds of interstellar dust to a region around the Sun representing only a few per cent of the galactic disk. The most extensive information about the rotation of the disk of the Galaxy has come from measurements of the radial velocity of neutral hydrogen, by the Doppler shifts in the wavelengths of the 21-cm wavelength radio emission. From these a picture has been built up of the differential rotational velocity of the disk from the centre out to the distance of the Sun. Spiral arms further out from the Sun cannot be viewed tangentially and the interpretation of the observations becomes difficult.

Some of the results for the central regions have been referred to earlier. A central region 1300 light years in radius, rotating very quickly, is surrounded by a system of expanding spiral arms of gas, the velocity of rotation of which falls far short of orbital circular velocity. We know nothing of the speeds of the stars in this region. The speed of rotation increases steeply as we move outwards, reaching 210 km s^{-1} at 13,000 light years from the centre, and then increasing more slowly and reaching a broad flat maximum of about 240 km s^{-1}. This includes the solar region 30,000 light years from the centre. Calculations of the speed of rotation at the distance of the Sun based on measurements of stellar radial velocities give 250 km s^{-1}.

When the 21-cm hydrogen line velocities are plotted against distance from the centre, they show two humps, 10–15 km s^{-1} high, at 18,000 light years and 26,000 light years from the centre; these may be due to mass concentrations at these distances causing variations in the radial gravitational field.

Not all the stars are travelling in circular orbits; some move in elliptical orbits and, passing through the solar region, are travelling faster or slower than the Sun according to whether their orbits lie largely outside or inside our distance from the galactic centre. None, however, are observed to have speeds greater than 313 km s^{-1} and it is believed that this may represent the velocity of escape from the Galaxy in this region. Calculations of the velocity of escape based on the gravitational attraction of the mass distribution lead, however, to values ranging from 336 to 380 km s^{-1}, a puzzling discrepancy between theory and observation.

The halo is rotating more slowly than the disk. It follows that the objects in it do not have circular velocity and are in general following highly elliptical orbits which carry many of them quite close to the centre of the Galaxy. At the solar distance from the centre, the system of globular clusters, halo RR Lyrae variables and metal deficient subdwarf field stars, is rotating about the centre with a speed of 50 to 60 km s^{-1}; this speed increases by about 10 km s^{-1} per 3,000 light years towards the centre.

An important deduction may be drawn from this. If angular momentum had been conserved as the various star systems that make up the Galaxy formed out of the gas, then the fact that the velocity of rotation of the halo is only a fifth that of the disk implies that the halo has about five times the extent of the disk: that is to say, its diameter is half a million light years or more.

Star formation

There is a close relationship between new stars and interstellar gas. This is evident in a general way from the concentration of bright stars and gas clouds to the spiral arms, more particularly in the bright nebulae, and from the existence of O- and T-associations in large dense cloud complexes such as Cygnus, Taurus and Orion. This relationship, together with the similarity in chemical composition of new stars and interstellar gas, leads to the view that stars form out of the interstellar gas. The wide range in the ages of stars, deduced especially from observations of star clusters and associations, shows that star formation is a continuous process, still going on. The region of Orion, which is illustrated in Plate 40*a*, is rich in O and T Tauri stars and contains several groups of stars with ages ranging from twenty million to three hundred thousand years or less; it is almost certain that stars are currently being formed from the gas clouds there.

Most stars probably form in clusters or associations, containing anything from several hundred to a million stars. In the majority of cases, however, the gravitational self-attraction is not sufficient for the group of stars to hold itself together, and the stars disperse into the general field in a relatively short time, measured in tens of millions of years. This appears to be the case for many of the O-associations. In some cases, however, where the stars are formed with unusually low relative velocities and cannot overcome their combined gravitational attraction, a bound cluster is formed. Such are the globular clusters. Sometimes both cases occur together; some dispersing O-associations contain within them small, apparently stable clusters. The Cas OB5 association contains a string of several of these.

The details of the processes by which stars form are not known. It is evident that a massive cluster must form out of a massive cloud, and that the cloud must have broken into fragments to form the stars. The average 'smoothed out' density of interstellar gas in our region of the Galaxy is about 10^{-24} g cm^{-3}. Most theories predict that a cloud must have contracted until its density has increased to 10^{-16} g cm^{-3} or even to 10^{-12} g cm^{-3} before fragments of a size corresponding to the mass of a star can hold themselves together against disrupting forces—collisions, magnetic fields, heating by stars and cosmic rays. Nature does not, however, appear to agree; the average density of matter in most new star groupings is only about 10^{-22} g cm^{-3}; even the most dense of them do not exceed 10^{-18} g cm^{-3}. One possibility is that in some clouds the dust grains become so cold, close to the 3°K background temperature of the Universe, that the interstellar hydrogen freezes on to them. The rate at which hydrogen freezes depends very, very sensitively on temperature, and would vary from one part of a cloud to another. It has been shown that this could cause the clouds to break up into fragments of stellar mass, which would contract to form stars. Some of the matters discussed below, such as the rate of star formation and the numbers of stars formed with various masses, would be satisfactorily explained. Doubts chiefly centre upon the temperature of the grains—can they become cold enough? The abundances of various species of interstellar molecules such as water vapour, ammonia and formaldehyde which must be formed on the grain surfaces, have been found from their radio emissions to be unexpectedly large, and it is possible that hydrogen freezes on to grains more easily than has been believed.

Another unsolved problem concerns the way in which a pre-star cloud fragment loses its angular momentum. As the fragments collide with each other, with speeds about equal to the turbulent velocities in the cloud, they will be set tumbling with similar speeds, several tenths of a kilometre per second. If centrifugal force is not to prevent their contracting to become stars they must lose all but one part in a million of this angular momentum. Several ways in which this might happen have been suggested. Perhaps most of the angular momentum of a fragment goes into a planetary system formed with the star; our own planetary system contains 200 times as much angular momentum as the Sun, and a great deal more may have been lost in matter not retained. Another possibility is that the fragments are linked by magnetic fields to the gas surrounding them, and these effectively brake the rotation of the fragment, transferring the angular momentum to the greater surrounding mass.

Small faint stars are formed in much greater numbers than bright massive ones. Indeed the relative numbers of stars formed decrease steadily with increasing stellar mass. This so-called mass function shows such surprising uniformity from one group of stars to another that it has every appearance of being the result of something quite fundamental in the processes of star formation. There is no generally accepted explanation of this phenomenon.

Counts of the numbers of young stars and measurements of the strength of the 21-cm hydrogen line emission have been made for several parts of the Galaxy and for a number of other galaxies. They indicate that the rate of star formation is roughly proportional to the amount of interstellar gas available. Thus the rate of star formation in the Galaxy must have decreased exponentially after rising to a maximum early in its life. At present, stars are being formed at the rate of ten a year; their average mass is a tenth that of the Sun. O and B stars are formed at the rate of one a century. Since interstellar dust limits our view to a few per cent of the total extent of the spiral arms, we will be lucky to observe a really new bright star.

Abundances of the chemical elements

The abundance of metallic elements varies widely among the various sub-systems of stars which make up our Galaxy. Stars in globular clusters far out in the halo have as little as a thousandth of the abundance of metals in the Sun (Chapter 7). Those in globular clusters nearer the Milky Way are deficient only by factors of ten. On the other hand stars in open clusters, most of which are very much younger than globular clusters, do not show substantial deficiencies and some have up to one and a half times the solar abundance. In so far as some of the oldest stars are very metal deficient, but none of the young ones are, there appears to be a general increase of metal abundance as one goes from the earliest stars formed to the most recent ones: that is to say, the abundance of metals in stars (this applies also to other heavy elements) has increased with time. This is to be expected as a result of element synthesis in nuclear reactions in stars and the ejection of the metal-enriched gases so produced back into the interstellar gas out of which stars form—ejections which occur violently in supernovae explosions.

The increase does not appear to have occurred smoothly and uniformly with time. A picture of what may have happened has been built up by M. E. Dixon from measurements of the abundances of metals in stars with various ages and galactic orbits; it is as follows. When the first stars formed they did so out of gas consisting of hydrogen and possibly some helium, but almost, or completely, devoid of heavy elements. The heavy elements produced by nuclear synthesis in the hot interiors of some of them were returned to the interstellar gas in explosions; this interstellar gas was very turbulent and hence the heavy elements were well mixed in it so that its composition was kept fairly uniform. About the time when the abundance of heavy elements had reached about two-thirds of the solar value the mixing became inefficient; at this time the abundances in the gas clouds throughout the Galaxy lay within the narrow range from a half to three-quarters those in the Sun. Thereafter, in the absence of efficient mixing, the composition of the interstellar gas became more patchy, more dependent on the amounts of heavy elements ejected by local supernovae, so that now the abundance of heavy elements in interstellar clouds lies in the wider range from a half to one and a half times the Sun's value.

The absence of heavy elements at the time the first stars in the Galaxy formed implies the absence of interstellar dust. Thus those theories of star formation which require the presence of dust to radiate heat and cool the clouds sufficiently for them to contract and become stars find themselves in difficulty when trying to account for the formation of first generation stars. If dust were required to produce stars, and stars are required to produce dust, our Galaxy would never have got started! But observations show that the youngest stars in the Milky Way are embedded in dense dust clouds, while it is known that the formation of molecules, and possibly of solid layers of hydrogen on grains, affects the physical conditions in the clouds in such a way as to make star formation in them much easier. Indeed there is growing evidence that in this way dust grains exert a profound control over the processes of star formation and hence over the evolution of galaxies.

It is not known if the abundance of helium has changed with time. Most of the energy radiated by stars comes from nuclear reactions in which hydrogen is converted into helium. Ten per cent or more of the mass of a star becomes helium in this way. Its production in the interior of a star precedes that of heavier elements. It is therefore to be expected that if material ejected by a star is enriched in heavy elements it will be enriched in helium also. Measurements of the abundance of helium in clouds of interstellar gas in our Galaxy show that 30 per cent of their mass is helium; the same value, within a few per cent, is obtained for several different clouds. To find out if the helium abundance is increasing with time, it is necessary to determine it in old stars formed out of the gas long ago. However, the stars chosen must not have evolved so much that their atmospheres have become enriched by helium synthesized in their interiors. Unfortunately, this restricts the observations to faint cool stars and it has not so far proved to be possible to determine their helium abundance. Their spectra are too cool to show lines due to helium. It may be possible to estimate the helium abundance in a few old dwarf stars from the effect it is calculated to have on their luminosities, but the method is full of uncertainties and the data are as yet inadequate.

Determinations of the helium abundances in planetary nebulae show that they range from 30 per cent to 45 per cent, averaging 38 per cent. Planetary nebulae are formed of gas ejected by fairly old stars in the disk of the Galaxy. It may be that they are enriched by helium produced in their parent stars.

A knowledge of the abundance of helium at various times is vital to our understanding of how the Galaxy has evolved; it has so far largely eluded us.

The evolution of the Galaxy

In the present state of our knowledge of the Galaxy, it is not possible for us to say with certainty how it has evolved. Nevertheless it is of interest to attempt to piece together the information in the preceding pages to construct an overall picture which, despite all its doubts and uncertainties, will still give us a view of the Galaxy as a whole.

About ten thousand million years ago, stars had not yet begun to form in the slowly contracting cloud of gas which was ultimately to form the Galaxy. The cloud, some million light years in diameter and with a density of only 10^{-27} g cm^{-3} (one atom per 10 cm cube), was rotating slowly, its outer edge moving with a speed of about 15 km s^{-1}. The gas was composed mainly, or entirely, of hydrogen. There may have been a few per cent of helium; there were no heavier elements.

Similar clouds of gas, later to form other galaxies such as the Magellanic Clouds and M 31, were close by in the surrounding space. Their gravitational attraction raised tides in the pre-Galaxy cloud, tides which caused the rotating cloud to develop currents of flowing gas. These would flow with supersonic speed, creating shock waves, turbulence and consequent density fluctuations.

As the contraction proceeded, some of the denser portions reached 10^{-22} g cm^{-3} and broke into clusters of pre-star fragments. Most of the clusters so formed were not stable and the stars dispersed into the surrounding gas; a minority held together and became the first globular clusters.

These early stars contained no heavy elements. The brightest of them evolved rapidly, synthesizing elements in their hot interiors, and within a million years had exploded and ejected enriched material back into the gas. Elements heavier than helium constituted about 3 per cent of the mass of this ejected material. The explosions caused violent turbulence, stirring up the gas and causing large density variations. Star formation reached a high rate. A hundred million years after stars had started to form (1 per cent of the present age of the Galaxy), 4 per cent of all the stars had formed, and the abundance of heavy elements in the interstellar gas had risen from zero to a hundredth of 1 per cent. Supernovae flared at the rate of one a year. When five hundred million years had passed, still only a twentieth of the present age of the Galaxy, a fifth of all the stars had formed, and the abundance of heavy elements exceeded a tenth of 1 per cent. By this time most of the halo stars and globular clusters were in existence. Interstellar dust had formed. It was beginning to look like a galaxy.

As stars shrank from the gas they were no longer supported by the pressures—thermal, magnetic, turbulent—which held it up against the gravitational pull of the Galaxy as a whole, and they fell inwards on long elliptical orbits passing close to the galactic centre. As the remaining gas slowly continued to contract, angular momentum prevented it from contracting as quickly in the plane of its equator as in the direction of its axis of rotation. Now it had become a flattened spheroid twenty thousand light years thick and a hundred thousand in diameter. It was rotating faster as angular momentum had been conserved during contraction, and stars forming out of it were following more circular orbits.

When the Galaxy had reached a quarter of its present age, two-thirds of the stars had been formed: all the stars in the halo and more than half of those in the disk; the abundance of heavy elements had reached nearly 1 per cent, that of helium 12 per cent. The stars which had formed first from hydrogen gas only had swept up enough of the enriched gas to give their atmospheres a small abundance of heavy elements. The metal rich clusters, the stars in the central 'bulge', those which today have evolved to become the shorter period 'metal rich' RR Lyrae variables and the planetary nebulae—all were there. So were the spiral arms, ten times as rich in O stars as they are today, abounding in emission nebulae, glowing red with hydrogen and green and violet with oxygen. Supernovae burst and blazed through the dust clouds. The Milky Way gleamed brightly in the heavens. The gases swirled and stars and planets formed. But already the long decline had begun.

Five thousand million years had elapsed and only a tenth of the original pre-Galaxy gas cloud remained uncondensed into stars, when a loose cluster of stars containing the Sun and its planets formed in a dusty cloud of gas near to the equatorial plane of the Galaxy, 33,000 light years from the centre. Heavy elements now constituted 1.3 per cent of the mass of the interstellar gas, helium 20 per cent. The Sun's cluster was not rich enough in stars to hold together against the disrupting gravitational pulls of other clusters and clouds of gas. It gradually dispersed among the surrounding stars.

The Galaxy had reached middle age; the speed of rotation of the spiral arms and disk of gas had increased to about its present value, but everything else happened more slowly; time is now more conveniently measured in units of a thousand million years.

Today the Galaxy is a little less bright; stars form, but much less often; supernovae shine once a century, but most cannot be seen through the dust clouds; bright stars are rarer, faint ones abound, the abundance of heavy elements has climbed to 2 per cent of the mass of the interstellar gas, helium to 30 per cent; and on the planet Earth formed with the star Sun five thousand million years ago, creatures of curiosity collect the photons of light from the stars, read the messages they carry, and seek to construct from them a story of the Milky Way.

In a sense it is easier to predict the future than it is to reconstruct the past. As the gas is consumed, stars will form less and less often and ultimately not at all. The brighter stars will run through their energy supplies and fade; only faint dwarfs will be left. The spiral arms will have gone. As the hundreds of thousands of millions of years roll by, the Galaxy will become dimmer and dimmer. Nothing will be visible to the eye; the most sensitive instruments would be required to detect that it was still there at all. Only its gravitational field will remain largely unchanged. The possibility of a cataclysmic end to some final shrunken state cannot be ruled out, but all that the future appears to hold for us is an endless decline to obscurity.

Chapter Ten

The extragalactic nebulae

David S. Evans

Nomenclature With the development of systematic telescopic observation came the realization in the late 18th and early 19th centuries that the sky contained a number of diffusely luminous objects, which could be differentiated from the planets, since they showed no motion, and from the stars, since they were of perceptible extent. All were, at first, lumped together under the name 'nebula' (Latin = cloud), and this word is often used without qualification when it is thought that the kind of nebula meant is clear from the context. It is now known that the objects originally classified as nebulae included several different types, of utterly different natures and dimensions. They included the planetary nebulae (a more misleading choice of name could hardly be imagined), which are luminous clouds of gas surrounding a single hot star; diffuse nebulae, which are gas clouds illuminated by light from a number of stars; and the extragalactic nebulae, with which we are now concerned. The members of the two first-named classes are relatively small objects which are details in our own Milky Way system: those in the last-named are entirely independent and separate systems containing stars and gas and, incidentally, planetary and diffuse nebulae of their own. They are of dimensions similar to our own Milky Way and entirely separate from it. Our own Milky Way is, in fact, just one among a myriad of extragalactic nebulae.

We use the term 'Milky Way' to describe either the appearance as seen from the Earth of the innumerable stars in our own stellar system, or its structure as we should see it were we able to view it from some point in space. The term 'Galaxy', or 'our own Galaxy', is used in the same sense. The term 'extragalactic nebula' means a system of a similar kind and size, such as we find scattered throughout space. We use the adjective 'extragalactic' to emphasize the fact that it is entirely divorced from our own system. We shall also find in the literature the terms 'galaxy' and 'nebula' used to mean the same thing as 'extragalactic nebula'. Many extragalactic nebulae show a spiral structure, and we sometimes find the term 'spiral nebula' used, though by no means all extragalactic nebulae are spirals. The most expressive term of all, 'island universe', which perhaps conveys most exactly the concept of a vast archipelago of discrete entities, has unfortunately fallen into disuse.

This confusion of nomenclature arose almost inevitably. Extragalactic astronomy only became possible with the introduction of the telescope, since only three extragalactic nebulae, the Great Nebula in Andromeda, and the Large and Small Magellanic Clouds, are visible to the naked eye. When telescopes adequate for the visual observation of the brightest extragalactic systems were first introduced nothing whatever was known of the nature of these systems. Indeed there was no realization of the essential structure of our own Galaxy, and all diffuse extended objects were listed together in early catalogues, including not only various nebulae, but also galactic and globular star clusters.

The first observations of these objects consisted merely in the record of their positions in the sky with brief descriptions. Charles Messier, a French observer of comets, published, in the *Connaissance des Temps, Ephémérides astronomique pour l'An*, 1784, a catalogue of 103 nebulous objects and clusters. Some of the entries were erroneous: many refer to globular clusters or clusters of other kinds: some are gaseous or planetary nebulae. About 30 per cent are true extragalactic objects. Messier's designations are still in fairly common use, and, for example, the Andromeda Nebula, which was No. 31 in his catalogue, is frequently referred to as Messier 31 or, more simply, M 31. Sir William Herschel systematically surveyed the northern sky, and his son, Sir John, both the northern and the southern skies. A catalogue of nebulae and clusters resulted from this and formed the main basis of the compilation by Dreyer of *A New General Catalogue of Nebulae and Clusters of Stars* comprising 7840 objects, including many clusters and gaseous nebulae, and a fair proportion of extragalactic nebulae. This was published in 1888, and was supplemented, in 1895 and 1908, by Dreyer's rather oddly named First and Second Index Catalogues of nebulae and clusters. Designations from these catalogues are in frequent use, and, in this terminology, the Andromeda Nebula is referred to as NGC 224, while nebulae in the Index Catalogues are denoted by the prefix IC with a number. The first catalogue covering the whole sky, devoted to extragalactic nebulae only, was that by Harlow Shapley and Adelaide Ames, published in 1932. This was intended to be complete down to the 13th magnitude, and listed 1249 objects. In 1964, G. and A. de Vaucouleurs produced their *Reference Catalogue of Bright Galaxies* intended as a revision of the Shapley-Ames catalogue. This contains data for 2599 galaxies. Subsidiary investigations have shown that the Shapley-Ames catalogue was 50 per cent complete near magnitude 12.5. In the revision, the 50 per cent completeness level is thought to lie near blue magnitude 13. Fainter and more distant nebulae have been counted in vast numbers: in early days special area surveys were made. At the present time the principal source of information about numbers and distribution of galaxies is the National Geographic Sky Survey made with the Palomar Schmidt telescope which covers the northern two-thirds of the sky and goes to well past the 20th magnitude. As fainter magnitudes are reached more and more galaxies are discovered, and in the purely optical field there are no firm indications that a limit is being reached.

As a supplement to all-sky catalogues, which are useful only for brighter objects, special catalogues devoted to particular areas (e.g. Zwicky), to unusual forms (Vorontsov-Velyaminov), and correlation with radio sources (Arp), have been produced.

Photography The problem of photographing faint extended objects like extragalactic nebulae is different from that of photographing faint stars. For nebulae it is the focal ratio of the instrument that is important while for stars it is the aperture of the objective. It is not difficult to see why this is so. Consider first the case of the stars. If the diameter of the objective is, say, doubled, four times as much light will be caught from a given star, and, assuming a perfect instrument, packed into the image being built up on the photographic plate. Thus, the larger the telescope, the fainter will be the faintest star which can be recorded, or the quicker any given star can be recorded. The scale of the plate depends on the focal length of the telescope. Clearly if we double all the dimensions of a telescope we shall double the scale of the picture, i.e. the distance between any two star images will be doubled and, since we have quadrupled the area of the objective, four times as much light as before will go into every point image. Now consider photography of an extended object, such as a nebula, by means of two telescopes, similar in every way, except that one has twice the dimensions of the other. The larger instrument will collect four times as much light from the nebula as the smaller: it will put this into an image which is twice as long and twice as broad in the larger telescope as in the smaller. That is, four times as much light will have gone into an image having four times the area. In other words the brightness of the image in the larger telescope will be no greater than in the smaller, so that, so far as registering faint extended objects is concerned, we shall have gained nothing. This is a rule perfectly familiar to amateur photographers who judge exposures simply in terms of the light intensity and the focal ratio: the lens aperture itself does not enter, except that, as every amateur photographer knows, a larger lens of the same quality will give better resolution. How then are we to photograph faint extended objects? The amateur photographer will rightly tell us to increase the exposure, and we can do this, and employ exposures of several hours; but practical considerations, and the fact that even the darkest night sky is not perfectly black, set limits to the useful exposure time. The next alternative is to use a larger stop, that is, to make the aperture larger while keeping the same focal length. Astronomical telescopes are, in most cases, built with a certain fixed aperture-ratio, and for very large instruments there are limits to what can be achieved. Let us now build a telescope with an aperture as large as possible, to put up the total light-gathering power, and a focal length as short as possible, to pack the light we have collected into an image as small and bright as possible. Since we also want as much detail as possible, we can use high resolution photographic plates and enlarge the negative once we have obtained it. The limit for 'normal' telescopes so far attained is the 200-inch telescope (Plate 45*b*) which has a focal ratio of f/3.3.* We thus have the surprising conclusion that an ordinary good-class camera of focal ratio f/2.8 will photograph a faint object faster than the 200-inch telescope, provided it is big enough to register on both as an extended object. Since there is such a vast disparity of scale this would only be the case for enormous objects, and the 200-inch will, of course, score hands down in revealing detail.

Thus we can see why it was that practically no detailed studies of nebulae were made at all until the advent of large reflecting telescopes working at f/5 or better, since the refractors usually had ratios of f/10 or worse. The era of extragalactic research is less than a century old; particularly useful have been such instruments as the Hale Observatories' 60-inch, 100-inch and later the 200-inch telescopes, which between them have probably done more for extragalactic research than almost all other telescopes put together. Later contributors in the north have been the Lick 120-inch and the Kitt Peak 84-inch, and, in the south, the 74-inch telescopes at Canberra and Pretoria, the latter outstanding for work on the Magellanic Clouds. Success has, however, not always been on the side of size, and, in the hands of Keeler, Curtis and Mayall, the 36-inch Crossley reflector at

* At the time of writing the new Russian 6-metre telescope had not come into operation.

Lick produced results which would do credit to much larger instruments.

The search for higher light intensities at the focal surfaces of telescopes led to the development of the Schmidt camera, where focal ratios as small as f/1, exceptionally still smaller, are attainable. Outstanding has been the Palomar Schmidt, already mentioned, which has an aperture of 48 inches, a main mirror of 72 inches, and an effective focal ratio of f/2.44. In the design of these instruments which usually record a large area of sky on a small scale, every effort has to be made to preserve the resolution of the photographs, that is, the finest detail must be faithfully represented, so that, by photographic enlargement or microscopic examination, this detail may be brought up to a convenient size when it is later examined.

The enhancement of light intensity by purely optical means has probably been brought almost to the practical limit, and, in recent years, several techniques of electronic enhancement have been introduced. The first of these was the electronic telescope of Lallemand and his collaborators. Here the initial image was formed on the end of a tube coated internally with a photo-sensitive surface emitting electrons. The tube was highly evacuated and the emitted electrons accelerated and focused by electromagnetic and electrostatic devices, until they impinged on a photographic surface within the vacuum, which then recorded a reproduction of the original image at enhanced intensity. This device is still in use, but the technique requires the utmost experimental virtuosity, and is extremely demanding under conditions of astronomical observing. It has tended to be replaced by the image tube, a device which owes its origin to the development of the television industry. Here, the enhanced image is reproduced on a phosphor-coated screen, which is imaged by a transfer lens on to a photographic plate. Although this too is a piece of equipment requiring high skill, the fact that the interior of the vacuum does not have to be accessible is a simplifying factor. The enhanced image is in monochrome corresponding to the emissivity of the second phosphor, so that one has the curious result that, for example, red light can be photographed on a blue-sensitive plate. It is usually difficult to combine the highest conventional optical speed with these enhancement devices, since there is no room to get the image tube into the fastest kind of purely optical camera. However, an overall gain approaching one hundred times seems to be perfectly practical and wide use is being made of equipment of this kind, both for direct photography and spectroscopy.

With any purely optical instrument the following general rules will apply: a certain minimum focal ratio, probably about f/5, is necessary before any effective extragalactic photography can be carried out; once a few systems are accessible, large numbers will be accessible, for the surface brightness of a nebula is independent of its distance from us. We can prove this by an argument similar to that used above: consider a nebula of a given linear size emitting a certain total light. If we could double its distance we should reduce the light received to one quarter, but since the angular or apparent size of the nebula would be halved in length and halved in width, i.e. the angular area from which the light came would be reduced also to one quarter of the original value, the surface brightness would remain unchanged. We thus obtain photographs showing nebulae of all apparent sizes, the larger ones being usually those nearest to us, the smaller the more remote. Very distant nebulae will look very small, and, depending on the resolution of the telescope (i.e. on its aperture), at a certain size they will become rather fuzzy points, hardly distinguishable from stars. At this point the foregoing arguments break down and the limiting faintness attainable will depend on the aperture of the telescope, just as in the case of stars.

The distribution of nebulae in the sky If, with a given telescope and photographic emulsion, we make an exposure on two areas of sky selected at random, we shall find that the resulting photographs do not show the same number of external galaxies. There is a two-fold reason for this. In the first place, we ourselves live on a planet attached to a star which is itself a member of a galaxy, and this alone would produce a non-uniform apparent distribution, even if the real distribution were uniform; secondly, the spatial distribution of galaxies is not itself uniform.

Our Milky Way, the galaxy in which we live, has a structure which is typical of that shown by many other galaxies. Seen in plan, the system is of a roughly circular outline, with a diameter of the order of 30 thousand parsecs. This figure, like most others connected with the sizes of galaxies, is indefinite, since galaxies are assemblages of stars which have no definite boundaries. All we mean by the given figure is that, at a distance of about 15 thousand parsecs from the centre, the star density is only a very small fraction of that at the centre of the system. Seen in side elevation the system is a very elongated oval, and along the major axis there runs a band of absorbing material and gas, relatively very thin and very nearly plane. The Sun lies near this plane (a matter of sheer chance) and at a distance from the centre of about ten thousand parsecs. Seen in plan our galaxy probably shows a spiral structure, but evidences of this are hard to gather by the methods of optical astronomy. The whole system is rotating, not as a solid body, but much faster at the centre than at the outer parts, and the period of rotation

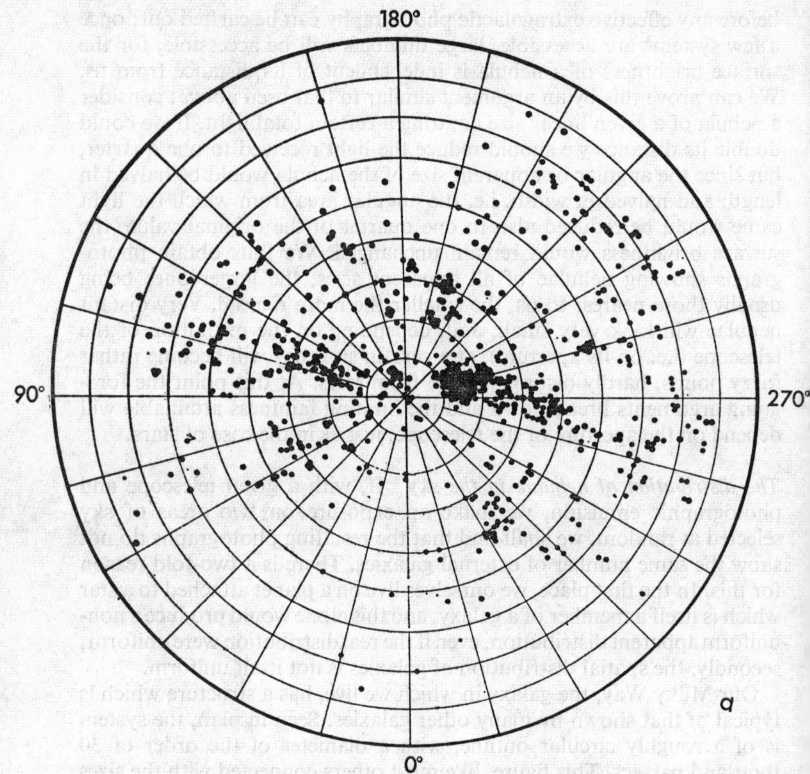

Figure 10.1 The observed distribution of the brighter galaxies *a* in the northern galactic hemisphere and *b*, opposite, in the southern galactic hemisphere. After Shapley and Ames, Harvard College Observatory.

at the Sun's distance is about 250 million years, corresponding to a linear velocity for the stars in the solar neighbourhood of about 250 kilometres per second. We must always remember that the structure of any galaxy is determined by dynamical considerations. The stars are not fixed in space: all of them are in motion, some at very high speeds, and the overall structure of any extragalactic nebula is the outcome of these motions.

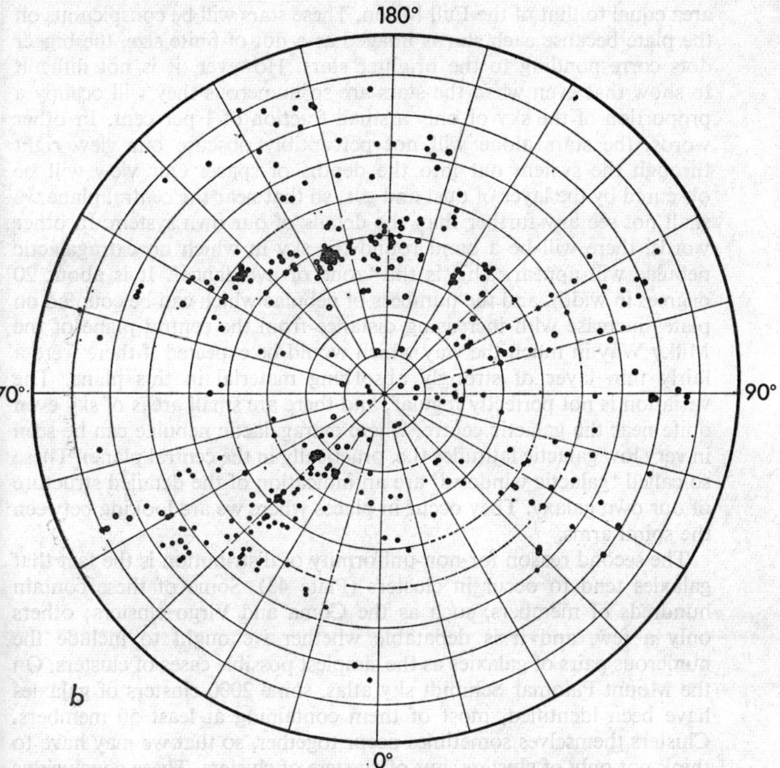

The clustering of the nebulae and the effect of the 'Zone of Avoidance', which occupies the outer ten degrees of the two hemispheres, can be clearly seen.

We may, for the moment, ignore the dynamical aspects of our own galaxy, and consider how the external Universe will appear to us from our present position in the median plane of a fairly typical galaxy somewhere near its outer borders. We shall see the vast assemblage of stars which it contains as a band of faint light encircling the sky. This is the Milky Way. A photograph of part of the Milky Way taken with a powerful telescope may show hundreds of thousands of stars in an area equal to that of the Full Moon. These stars will be conspicuous on the plate because each star is imaged as a dot of finite size, the bigger dots corresponding to the brighter stars. However, it is not difficult to show that even when the stars are so numerous they will occupy a proportion of the sky of only a small fraction of 1 per cent. In other words, the stars alone will not perceptibly obscure our view right through the system out into the depths of space. Our view will be obscured by the layer of dust and gas, so that near the central plane we shall not see any further than the details of our own system. In other words, there will be a band round the sky in which no extragalactic nebulae will appear. This is the 'zone of avoidance'. It is about 20 degrees in width, and the numbers of nebulae which can be counted on plates increase with increasing distance from the central plane of the Milky Way in much the way which would be expected if there were a fairly thin layer of strongly absorbing material in this plane. The variation is not perfectly regular, and there are small areas of sky even quite near the galactic centre, where extragalactic nebulae can be seen in very low galactic latitudes (i.e. practically in the central plane). These so-called 'galactic windows' are an indication of the detailed structure of our own galaxy. They occur in places where we are looking between the spiral arms.

The second reason for non-uniformity of distribution is the fact that galaxies tend to occur in clusters (Plate 43). Some of these contain hundreds of members, such as the Coma and Virgo clusters; others only a few, and it is debatable whether we ought to include the numerous pairs of galaxies as the simplest possible cases of clusters. On the Mount Palomar Schmidt sky atlas, some 2000 clusters of galaxies have been identified, most of them containing at least 50 members. Clusters themselves sometimes occur together, so that we may have to think not only of clusters, but of clusters of clusters. These conclusions have been reached by counting galaxies on photographic plates and making statistical studies of the results. A fairly sophisticated approach is necessary, for it is clear that random placing of galaxies on the sky would lead to the occasional occurrence of many galaxies close together, but it is now certain that clusters whose members are near to each other in space do occur with greater frequency than can be accounted for by mere chance. So far, little has come of this discovery, but an explanation of why galaxies exhibit this clustering tendency may be of the greatest cosmological significance.

Types of extragalactic nebulae Galaxies were classified according to their forms and structure by Hubble during the 'thirties. In recent years

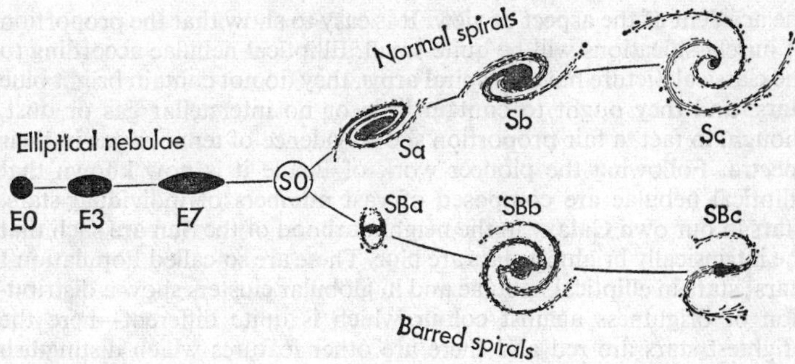

Figure 10.2 The sequence of nebular types used by Hubble in his earlier work

efforts have been made to improve on Hubble's system, possibly not entirely successfully, firstly because, even now, we are not sure which are the most significant features of a galaxy from the evolutionary point of view, and secondly because, if a classification is to be successful, different astronomers must find no ambiguity in assigning objects to the various classes.

Towards the end of his life, Hubble himself was in process of modifying his classification system. Using these notes and adopting extensive modifications of his own, Sandage has produced the lavishly illustrated *Hubble Atlas of Galaxies*. A more elaborate classification system has been produced by de Vaucouleurs, while W. W. Morgan and Sidney van den Bergh have both worked extensively on galaxy classification, in the latter cases with attention to idiosyncrasies of intrinsic luminosity.

Hubble's system distinguished elliptical nebulae, ordinary spirals, barred spirals, and irregular galaxies. Within each category there were subdivisions. Thus, elliptical nebulae are objects, round or elliptical in outline, showing a smooth diminution of brightness from the centre outwards, with little or no surface detail. The circular ones were designated E0, while those of greater elongation ran from E1 up to E7, in order of increasing elongation. If the largest and smallest diameters were a and b, the designation was E n, where $n/10 = (a - b)/a$. Round about E7 the elliptical outline was replaced by a lens or spindle shape. Since most isolated galaxies are presumed to have a nearly circular outline when seen in plan view, it is clear that some systems, though in truth very flattened, might be erroneously called E0, through the accident of the aspect of view. It is easy to show that the proportion of misclassifications will be quite small. Elliptical nebulae according to the classical picture have no spiral arms, they do not contain bright blue stars, and they ought to contain little or no interstellar gas or dust, though, in fact, a fair proportion show evidence of tenuous gas in their spectra. Following the pioneer work of Baade it is now known that elliptical nebulae are composed of vast numbers of individual stars. Stars in our own Galaxy in the neighbourhood of the Sun are such that the intrinsically brightest stars are blue. These are so-called Population I stars; stars in elliptical nebulae and in globular clusters show a distribution of brightness against colour which is quite different—here the brightest stars are red and there are other features which distinguish what is called Population II. In general, Population II stars are very much older than Population I. Many nebulae of other types have central regions (nuclei) which strongly resemble elliptical nebulae, and, indeed, in cases where the outer parts are very faint, such a nebula might easily be wrongly classified as elliptical. Careful photography of many so-called elliptical nebulae demonstrates the existence of exceedingly faint outer structure, and it is debatable what proportion of 'elliptical' nebulae really deserve that appellation. Sometimes classified as 'dwarf ellipticals' are the two systems in the constellations of Sculptor and Fornax which belong to the Local Group of Galaxies (see below) and are relatively very near to us. They are close enough to be readily resolved into stars, and have an extremely low surface brightness. There may well be a high proportion of systems like this in space which are as yet unknown, since they are exceedingly hard to detect.

Between the ellipticals and the spiral nebulae lies an intermediate form, the S0 nebulae, which look like ellipticals but have a bright nucleus, surrounded by a featureless outer zone of lower luminosity. The remaining types of nebulae are classified from the appearance of their spiral structure. Barred spirals are those which possess a line or bar of luminous material passing through the nucleus. From the ends of this bar spring a pair of spiral arms which extend outwards. Normal spirals are those in which there is no bar, and the arms spring directly from the nucleus. In the Hubble system these two main types are denoted as SB nebulae and S nebulae, and each is subdivided into a, b and c. Assignment to these subdivisions depends on the degree of openness of the arms and the extent to which star clusters, as against clouds of dust and gas, can be seen. Irregular nebulae are ones not falling into the preceding categories. Spiral nebulae are classified on the basis of the appearance we think they would have if we could view them in plan, and there are inevitably some difficulties in inferring this from the actual aspect of view. A rough guide to proportions is that some 3 per cent to 5 per cent are irregular or peculiar, one-fifth to one-quarter (possibly more in some clusters) are elliptical, and the remainder about equally divided between normal and barred spirals.

The structure of spiral nebulae Although used as the basis of classification, the physical origin of spiral structure still lacks adequate explanation. The typical spiral nebula may be described in terms closely similar to those used in describing our own Galaxy, and this is no surprise, for we believe that the latter is a typical normal spiral nebula. All possess a central nucleus where the star density is high, traversed by a bar structure in the case of barred spirals. In some cases closed rings may be detectable either close to the nucleus or at some diameters away. The spiral arms are usually in almost symmetrical pairs, springing from opposite ends of the bar, or from opposite points of the nucleus. They can vary greatly in appearance and structure. In some nebulae the arms are not continuous but are composed of a series of more or less aligned blobs of luminous gas (probably mainly hydrogen) which owe their light to very bright blue stars enveloped in them. There may be lanes of dark absorbing material between the lines of luminous blobs and the details of the structure may be very complex indeed. The arms may be superposed on a bright background of a generally circular outline, or they may have the appearance of extending out into empty space. Whatever the mechanism which produces spiral arms it is one which can operate in almost all circumstances, for nebulae of all degrees of surface brightness and all varieties of structural content can show spiral arms.

The stars which make the spiral arms so prominent a feature are bright blue giant stars, which, so modern theory tells us, can only have an age of a few million years. The mechanism of the formation of these young stars (Population I) from the dust and gas in the nebulae is not fully understood, but that this is their origin there is no doubt. We generally use the word 'early' to describe an Sa or SBa nebula, and the word 'late' to describe the c-subdivision. These adjectives are probably legitimate in the temporal sense, for the early-type spirals are the ones where the blue giants have been relatively recently formed and there is still plenty of raw material left in the form of interstellar dust and gas. In the late-type spirals the arms are now marked not by clouds of gas but by clusters of stars, and the impression is given that there has been some dispersion of the structure due to interaction between stars in the clusters and other passing stars in the galaxy. It is tempting to think of the elliptical nebulae as an early stage in the formation of a spiral galaxy; that the arms are somehow ejected from the nucleus; that the gas and dust in them condense into clusters of stars and that the clusters disperse. This would make the sequence of types a sequence of ages throughout, but this is unlikely to be true since the Population II stars of the elliptical nebulae are not the youngest but the oldest of stars. Seen in profile, an extragalactic nebula looks extremely elongated, rather like a narrow luminous band, with, at the centre, a bulbous, more or less spherical, nuclear region. The band may sometimes be seen to have a dark line running down it, dividing it into two: this is the absorbing material of the nebula consisting of solid particles of some kind, sometimes, possibly in a rather misleading way, called 'dust', which is concentrated into an extremely thin plane layer dividing the nebula into two. We can thus enumerate the parts of a nebula as follows.

The nucleus: a generally spherical cloud of stars with some gas and dust, which in some cases looks like a small elliptical nebula.

The absorbing layer: the 'paper-thin' 'paper-flat' layer of dust and gas.

The disk: the distribution of stars and gas clouds, which are the most striking feature of a nebula on a photograph. The spiral arms occur in this very flattened circular system. The more dust and gas the nebula contains, the more numerous the bright blue stars it contains, and the more striking is its arm structure. In nebulae very close to us, in which we can make out detail, we find volumes of luminous gas stimulated by the ultraviolet and blue light from very hot stars, which are of the same kind as similar structures (gaseous nebulae, planetary nebulae and Strömgren spheres) in our own Galaxy.

The halo: the absorbing layers and disk are both very flattened structures. Studies of the faintest outer parts of nebulae show in many cases what are presumed to be large numbers of exceedingly faint stars forming a more or less spherical system extending out to very large distances, often several times as far as the visual appearance which can be captured on a photographic print. Within the disk-structure stars often occur in groups or clusters, containing perhaps several hundred members, which are presumed to have been formed relatively recently and contemporaneously. Associated with the halo is a distribution of a different kind of star cluster (the globular clusters), each of a nearly spherical shape, having the same kind of star population (Population II) as the elliptical nebulae. It is presumed that these clusters are very old and were formed very early in the history of the system when it may have had a far less flattened shape than it now has, and at a time before the formation, presumably through nuclear processes in stars, of the metallic elements out of primordial hydrogen. It is certainly a characteristic of some globular cluster stars, and of other very old stars in our Galaxy, that they contain a far smaller proportion of metallic elements than do more recently formed stars.

The local group and some individual galaxies Our own Galaxy is a member of a group of about twenty galaxies usually referred to as the local group. All these nearby galaxies show a good deal of detail, and form a sample of objects which are available for close study, and influence our ideas of the nature of more distant objects.

The nearest are the Magellanic Clouds at a distance of about 70,000 parsecs. The Large Cloud (Plate 42*a*) has a visual magnitude of about 0.3 (about the same as a bright star), and dimensions out to extreme limits of about 17° × 15°. The extent as seen with the unaided eye is far smaller than this and about half the light comes from an area about 5° across. The brightest area is in the form of a bar with a protuberance at one end. The Small Cloud (Plate 42*b*) has an integrated magnitude of about 2.4 from a total area of about 8° × 4° and half the light comes from an area about 2° across. The Small Cloud is of a roughly circular form. Claims have been made that the two clouds differ one from another in the composition of the star material, and that the Cepheids in them are systematically of a different colour from those in our own Galaxy. Neither of these claims seems to be well founded. Radio studies put the mass of hydrogen in the Large Cloud at about 6×10^8 solar masses, and in the Small Cloud at about 4×10^8 solar masses. Radio and optical studies have suggested that the Clouds are rotating, and it has been claimed that their appearance can be interpreted in terms of a spiral structure which trails on the rotation. On this hypothesis the radio and visual observations lead to estimates of about 3×10^9 solar masses for the Large Cloud and about one-third of this for the Small Cloud.

The Andromeda Nebula (Plate 33) is the most famous of all extra-galactic systems. It is a normal spiral which, on photographs, shows a length of about $2\frac{1}{2}°$ and a width of about $\frac{2}{3}°$. By photographic or photoelectric surface photometry the system can be traced out to a length of over 4°. It has two elliptical systems near it, one of which, NGC 205, was the first to be resolved into stars by Baade. The total apparent visual magnitude is about 3.4, including the companions. The preceding (western) side of the nebula is both reddened and obscured and has been identified by de Vaucouleurs as the nearer one. The system is rotating with the arms trailing. The distance is about 700,000 parsecs or about ten times that of the Magellanic Clouds. Its total mass and luminosity are about 34×10^{10} and 1.4×10^{10} those of the Sun.

There is a central region about 15 parsecs in diameter and with a mass 13×10^6 that of the Sun which rotates in a period of 0.5×10^6 years, in striking contrast with the outer regions where the period of rotation varies from 20×10^6 to 200×10^6 years.

Of the remaining certainly identified members of the Local Group, only M 33 in Triangulum is not elliptical or irregular. M 33 is a rather later and more open system than the Andromeda Nebula and about one-third of its angular size. Its velocity has been very well determined and its mass distribution inferred. Two of the members of the Local Group are the Fornax and Sculptor systems, so-called 'dwarf ellipticals', each completely resolved into a vast number of faint stars, giving a faint patch of light about 1° across. The Sculptor system shows some 10,000 stars brighter than magnitude 19.5. NGC 300 is a possible member of the Local Group. It is a very extended, late-type spiral, with arms resolved into stars, which is seen almost face on.

There are only about half a dozen galaxies outside the Local Group which have an apparent diameter more than one-third of a degree across. Studies of these and of other relatively bright galaxies suggest that the Local Group forms part of a super-cluster of galaxies whose centre lies in the Virgo cluster. This super-cluster appears to be flattened and this may be a sign that it is rotating. The observational data are still uncertain but it does seem possible that the Local Group has a rotational velocity of about 300 km s^{-1} about the Virgo cluster. The individual nebulae do, of course, have considerable random motions relative to that of the cluster as a whole; thus relative to the Local Group our Galaxy has a velocity of about 100 km s^{-1}.

The motions of the nebulae In an earlier section we spoke of nebular evolution. Since this will be on a time scale of hundreds or thousands of millions of years, we cannot observe its progress in one nebula, but must infer it from examples in which the processes have attained different stages. A similar obstacle prevents us from studying the rotation or linear motion of nebulae from observations of changes of position in the sky. We can, however, observe and measure velocities of stars and nebulae in the line of sight, i.e. towards or away from us, or, in technical parlance, radial velocities. Such velocities are measured by means of the spectrograph: if the source of light is receding, then any wavelength, or any spectrum line marking a definite wavelength, which is received from the source, will occur not in its normal position but displaced to longer wavelengths (to the red) by an amount proportional to the velocity of recession. The amount of the displacement is determined by comparison with a spectrum produced by a terrestrial source and fed into the spectrograph, such as that of the iron arc, or a gas discharge tube containing hydrogen, helium or argon, etc. For velocities small compared with the velocity of light, there is a proportionality between the wavelength displacement and the velocity: thus if the source has a velocity of recession of 1 per cent of 1 per cent of the velocity of light (i.e. 30 kilometres per second) there will be a change in wavelength or frequency of any spectrum line of 1 per cent of 1 per cent to the red. For a typical wavelength of 4000 angstroms the change will be 0.4 angstroms, to the red (greater wavelength) for a velocity of recession, and to the blue (shorter wavelength) for a velocity of approach.

The accuracy of measurement of a radial velocity is mainly determined by the scale, or dispersion, of the spectrum. In stellar work, dispersions of 30 to 100 angstroms per millimetre are fairly common, and velocities, which rarely exceed one or two hundred kilometres per second, can be determined from a batch of three or four plates with an accuracy of one kilometre per second or better. The problem of determining the radial velocity of an extragalactic nebula, or of some feature in it, is that of lack of light. The observer with purely optical equipment could not afford to spread out the light to make a high dispersion spectrum if he were to obtain any photograph at all. Thus, when nebular work was first undertaken, dispersions of 300 angstroms per millimetre were commonly used, and the observer often had to be content with one spectrum, which might have occupied a whole night's exposure. From a single low-dispersion spectrum obtained on a minute scrap of film or plate, an accuracy of velocity measurement of only 50 to 100 km s^{-1} might be obtainable, but this would be quite good enough for many applications.

The application of image-tube techniques is changing things rapidly. Development has mainly been towards observation of fainter and fainter galaxies, without very much change of dispersion. Exposures are very much shortened, and, although it is difficult to generalize, they would now be mostly of the order of an hour. The limiting exposure is determined by the sky brightness rather than the contribution of the nebula itself.

Some galaxies are near enough to permit us to distinguish the details of their structure. In such a case, the velocity of the nucleus gives the general transport velocity for the whole system. However, galaxies are not rigid structures. Every star, gas molecule and dust particle in a galaxy is in motion under the gravitational attraction of everything else in the galaxy, combined sometimes with magnetic forces and the effects of gas and radiation pressures. The forms assumed by galaxies are the result of all these forces acting on its component parts. All galaxies seem to be in rotation round an axis through the nucleus and perpendicular to the median plane, i.e. perpendicular to the thin gas and dust layer. If we pick a galaxy which is seen exactly edge-on, the velocity of the nucleus will as usual give us the rate at which the galaxy as a whole is receding from us or approaching us. Velocities measured at regions removed from the nucleus will enable us to deduce the speed of rotation of the region observed, because the rotational component will be given by the difference between this velocity and that found for the nucleus. Of course, there are complications of interpretation, for only the line-of-sight velocity is measurable, and in any given galaxy which is not seen precisely edge-on it is difficult to make the necessary allowances for foreshortening. In general the results found have confirmed the early work carried out in the late thirties and early forties for M 31 by Babcock, and for M 33 by Aller and Mayall. Galaxies do not rotate as solid bodies but more in the manner of the planets moving round the Sun, that is, the outer parts move much more slowly than the central parts. For matter moving in a circle round the nucleus the centrifugal force due to rotation must balance the gravitational attraction of the whole galaxy at that distance. In other words observed curves of velocity against distance from the nucleus can be used to determine the distribution of mass within the system. To obtain the results in terms of the usual unit, the mass of the Sun, we need to know the distance of the system, so that measures of angular distances on the sky can be converted into linear distances, and corrections for foreshortening depending on the inclination of the plane of the galaxy must be applied. In recent years significant contributions to our knowledge of the rotational properties and mass distribution of nebulae have been made by the Burbidges and others. New methods, such as the observation specifically of clouds of gas emitting line spectra, have been introduced by Courtès. And, in addition, considerable attention has been paid to the extent to which features in galaxies are moving in paths which are non-circular. One important discovery is that the central region of M 31, only about 8 parsecs in diameter, that is, the very innermost part of the nucleus, is spinning extremely rapidly.

A controversial question in extragalactic astronomy has been the origin of the spiral arms and their relation to the direction of rotation. Do the spiral galaxies rotate so that the arms lead or trail in the rotation? To decide this observationally we need to observe galaxies seen nearly edge-on, so that the effects of the rotation, expected to be of the order of 300 km s^{-1}, will be appreciable. On the other hand, the cases selected for observation must not be exactly edge-on, since otherwise the arms would not be seen, and there must be well-defined arms. Finally, we need to be able to decide which edge of the galaxy is nearer to us in space. There are not many large galaxies which satisfy all these conditions. Identification of the nearer edge is a contentious matter. Some say that the nearer edge of a galaxy is the one showing more absorption, on the ground that the absorbing matter is there projected against the rest of the galaxy, while at the other edge it is invisible, because it is not then distinguishable from the blackness of space. Others prefer a diametrically opposite view. Modern opinion seems to favour the view that the arms must be trailing. This, however, does not solve the problem of their origin, for the fact that material at different distances from the centre is going at different speeds would mean that a straight line arm would be wound up into a great many turns round the centre in a few hundred million years, and would not persist in a recognizable form. This follows from the fact that a typical rotation period, for example for the Sun round the centre of our own Galaxy, is about 250 million years. A complication is that it is the young blue stars, which have ages less than, say, 10 million years, which mark the arm structure, so we may have to deal with a pattern which is continually being regenerated rather than a form which is being carried round by the gross rotation of the galaxy. At one time it was thought that no amount of manipulation of a purely gravitational model could produce the observed effects, and all kinds of non-gravitational forces such as magnetic effects and radiation pressure were considered. Now opinion seems to be swinging the other way, and the possibility of density waves produced almost entirely by gravitational effects and moving more slowly than the rotation is under consideration. Extensive work on computer simulation of galaxies by the investigation of models, involving up to several thousand mutually gravitating masses under various initial conditions, has recently been undertaken, and configurations strikingly similar to many observed galaxies have been produced.

So far we have been concerned only with nearby nebulae of large angular size, in which specific features such as bright knots, star clusters and gas clouds can be observed separately. In smaller galaxies with the spectrograph slit along the longer diameter, a tilt of the spectrum lines can sometimes be observed, due to the fact that rotation makes one end of the galaxy image recede faster than the other.

Finally we come to more distant galaxies which may appear as no more than a fuzzy patch or even have a nearly stellar appearance. These, no doubt, possess all the features of nearer galaxies, but are too far away for us to distinguish them. Now we have a spectrum from all parts of the galaxy mixed together, with the nucleus predominating, but, because of rotation, some parts may have line-of-sight velocities differing by nearly 1000 km s^{-1} from others. There will be a tendency to blurring of the lines, which reduces the number which are measurable, but the figure obtained will be a fair approximation to the total translational velocity of the system observed.

The red shifts of distant nebulae The velocities of large numbers of extragalactic nebulae have been measured, almost all in the part of the sky accessible from the north. Following the pioneer work of V. M. Slipher, the bulk of the early measures were made by Hubble and Humason at Mount Wilson, and by Mayall at Lick. The more recent work of the Burbidges, the de Vaucouleurs and Sandage has added to this total. Only a few have been measured in the south, mainly by Evans and his collaborators in South Africa, by Shobbrook in Australia and more recently by American astronomers in Chile. Special studies of the Magellanic Clouds have been made by Thackeray, de Vaucouleurs, Feast and others.

It is far from being strictly true that all galaxies have the same linear dimensions, but the range is not inordinately great, so that apparent size does give some indication of distance. It became clear very early on that there was a relation between the measured radial velocity and the apparent size, or by inference, the distance, of the galaxy to which it referred (Plate 44). Out to vast distances the relation is a linear one, and may be expressed in the form that distant nebulae show velocities of recession, the velocity being proportional to distance, at about 55 km s^{-1} for every million parsecs of distance from us. This is a statistical relation: any individual galaxy can show a value which differs from the figure predicted from this relation by some hundreds of kilometres per second. Many galaxies occur in clusters which, as a whole, may obey this relation, but, within the cluster, deviations of the order of 500 km s^{-1} can occur. The measured velocities are affected by the motion of the Sun in our own Galaxy. For certain nearby galaxies this is enough to convert a motion of recession from the centre of the Galaxy into a motion of approach relative to the Sun. By and large, however, the motion is one of recession, and all the galaxies at distances greater than 10 million parsecs, which in the present context is small, have motions of recession, and the deviations from linearity become progressively less significant at greater and greater distances. At large distances enormous velocities are observed, and some theoreticians have been reluctant to interpret them as true velocities of recession, and speak of the values derived as 'symbolic velocities', but this does not seem to be a general view.

Plate 41 NGC 5128 as photographed in blue light at the Hale Observatories. This peculiar galaxy marks the centre of the strong Centaurus A radio source. Scale 1 cm = 1′

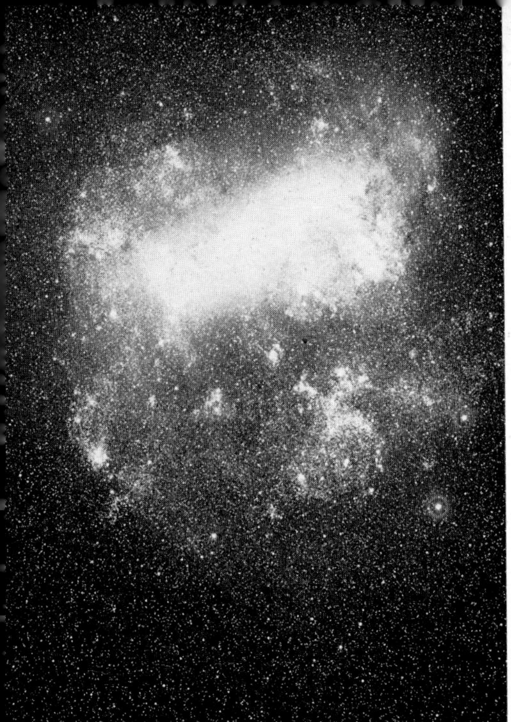

Plate 42

a The Large Magellanic Cloud as photographed with the 10-inch Metcalf Telescope of the Boyden Observatory. Most of the light visible to the naked eye comes from the bright 'bar' whose bent ends may be indications of spiral arms. Scale 1 cm = 59′

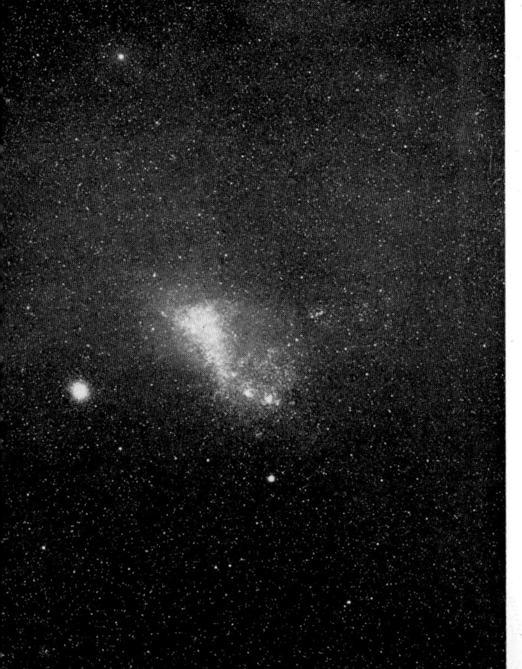

b The Small Magellanic Cloud as photographed with the 10-inch Metcalf Telescope. The bright object close to it is the galactic globular cluster 47 Tucanae. Scale 1 cm = 65′

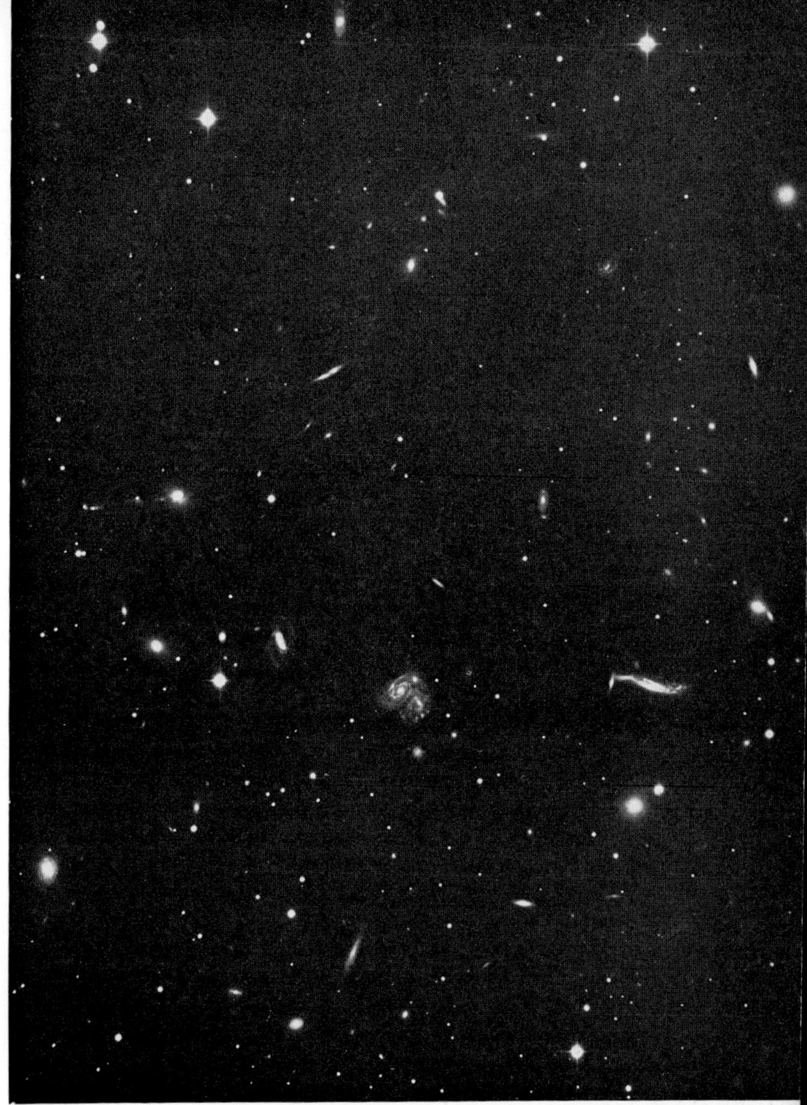

Plate 43 A cluster of galaxies in Hercules as photographed with the 200-inch telescope of the Hale Observatories. Scale 1 cm = 1′.5

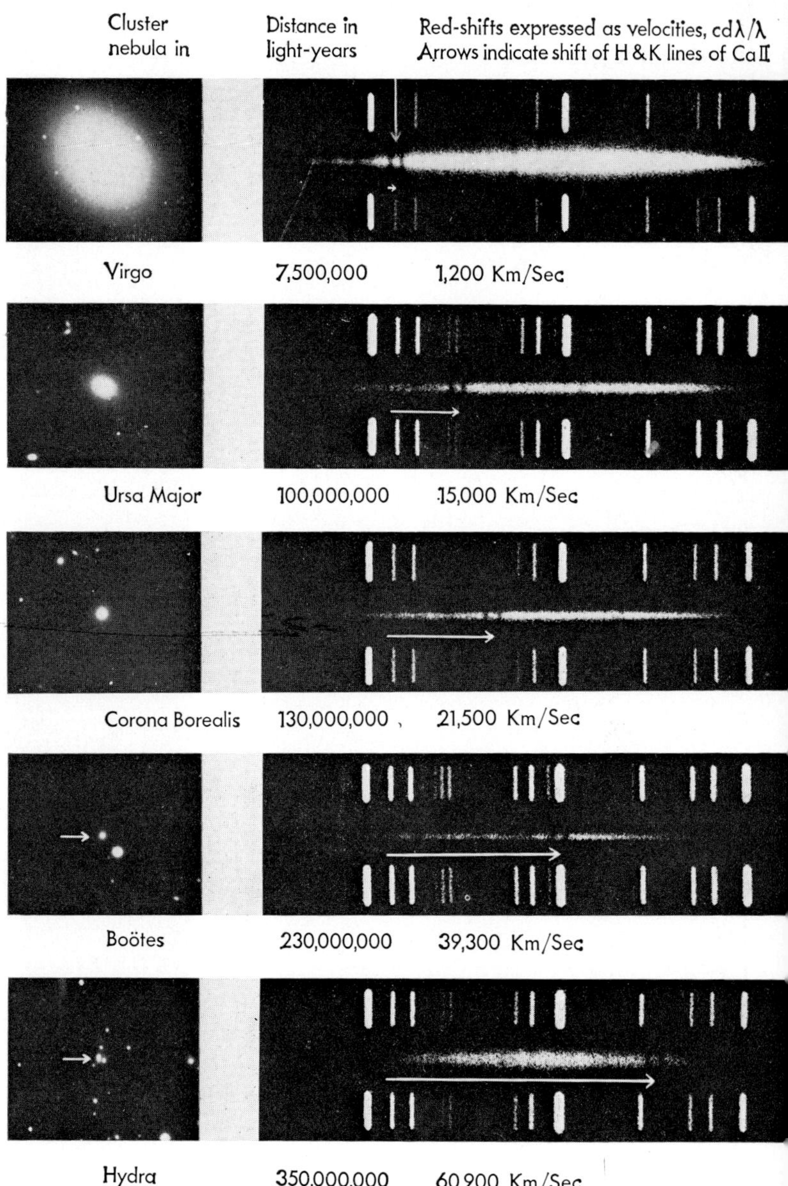

Plate 44 The red-shift distance relationship for galaxies. This composite diagram was prepared at the Hale Observatories

It is a fundamental tenet of the theory of relativity that the relative velocity of two material bodies cannot ever attain the velocity of light, so that there is tremendous pressure to observe galaxies at greater and greater distances, for which relative velocities approaching that of light can be measured. To describe high velocities of recession it has become customary to use a parameter z which is the ratio of the observed wavelength to its undisplaced value. For velocities of pure recession, v, approaching that of light, c, the relation $1 + z = (1 + v/c) / (1 - v^2/c^2)^{\frac{1}{2}}$ holds, based on the restricted theory of relativity. The advantage is that z has an open scale and can, in principle, be as large as one pleases. The largest observed value of z at the time of writing is just below 3, interpretable as a recession velocity of almost 90 per cent that of light. The effect of thc enormous red shifts on the spectra is dramatic. Wavelengths normally in the far ultraviolet are transported into the red region of the spectrum, so that the spectra of distant objects are completely different from those of nearby ones. The colour of the remote galaxies is heavily reddened by this effect, and measures of reddening of faint galaxies have been used to determine recession velocities. In addition, because of the immense distances of these remote objects, the light time required for the radiation to arrive at the Earth is very great, the largest values being comparable with the age of the solar system. Thus, as astronomers reach out into space, they also reach back in time, and should be able to make deductions about the appearance of the universe in the remote past.

We shall consider some further implications of this situation later. For the moment it need only be remarked that it is incorrect to deduce, from the fact that all galaxies seem to be running away from us, the conclusion that we are in a unique situation in the Universe. There is a general expansion, rather like the steady stretching of a picture drawn on an indiarubber sheet, in which all points recede from each other at a rate proportional to the distance between them. Any other observer in the Universe would find all the galaxies receding from himself, and no single observer is in a privileged position.

Nebular distances We have already quoted a figure involving distances of galaxies, namely the red shift, or Hubble constant, now taken as 55 km s^{-1} per million parsecs, with a considerable uncertainty. It is an indication of the extraordinary difficulties encountered in estimating very large distances that, two or three decades ago, the value given for this constant was several times larger. All estimates of nebular distances are very indirect and uncertain and involve complex chains of deduction which can only be sketched here.

Very small distances can be determined by trigonometrical methods. These are reliable up to twenty parsecs, and of some value for statistical purposes up to one hundred parsecs. Within this range stars occur in sufficient numbers to enable us to recognize those with particular physical characteristics from their spectra or from photometric measures of magnitudes and colours. Photoelectric photometry is now sufficiently advanced to permit corrections for absorption and reddening of starlight by interstellar matter to be reliably made. We are thus able to apply a method of very general validity, that is, to find some object whose intrinsic brightness in terms of the Sun we know, and to find out how far off that object must be, taking absorption and reddening into account, to make it appear as faint as it does. The sample of stars near to the Sun contains few stars of great intrinsic brightness; however, fairly remote clusters (still in our own Galaxy) are known which contain both stars similar to ones in our local sample and very bright giant stars. Since all the stars in a cluster are at effectively the same distance, we can thus infer the intrinsic brightness of some very luminous stars. The brightest accessible are about 10,000 times as bright as the Sun, or in correct professional terms, 10 magnitudes brighter than the Sun. We can specify the distance of an object either by means of a number of parsecs or in terms of the distance modulus. This is the difference between the magnitude the object would have at the standard distance of 10 parsecs and the magnitude it has as seen from its actual distance. For a telescope of moderate size, say 74 inches in diameter, the limit for spectroscopic work is an apparent magnitude of 12 and for precise photographic photometry about 19. Thus a star of absolute magnitude − 5 is observable spectroscopically up to a distance modulus of 17 (or 25,000 parsecs) and photometrically up to a distance modulus of 24 (630,000 parsecs). In other words we can attain far greater distances if we can find a type of bright star recognizable photometrically than if we had to rely on spectroscopic criteria. Nature has provided bright stars satisfying our requirements in the shape of the Cepheid variables. These, so-called from the prototype of the class, Delta Cephei, are variable stars which owe their variability to a pulsation accompanied by a variation in light output, and are recognizable from the characteristic way in which the light varies in each cycle. Many years ago Miss Leavitt of Harvard recognized them in the Small Magellanic Cloud (Plate 42*b*) and found that the period of pulsation was longer the brighter the Cepheid. Since all the Cepheids in the Small Cloud could be considered to be at the same distance, this could be recognized as an intrinsic property of the Cepheids. At this time the distance of no Cepheid was known, and none occur near the Sun. Now a variety of lines of attack, including the discovery of Cepheids in galactic star clusters (a rare phenomenon), and a discussion of the motions of Cepheids in the galaxy, have suggested that the visual absolute magnitude of a Cepheid with a period of 100 days is about − 7.5 and of a 10-day Cepheid is about − 4.2. Although there is still some uncertainty concerning the zero point of the calibration, this result enables us to infer our first extragalactic distance, namely that the distance modulus of the Magellanic Clouds lies between 18.7 and 19.2 magnitudes, i.e. they lie at between 55,000 and 69,000 parsecs. The history of this topic is complex, and much lower values were quoted until recently. These rested on the assumption that certain short-period variable stars, known as the RR Lyrae or cluster-type variables, formed a series continuous with the classical Cepheids. This has been shown to be incorrect: RR Lyrae stars found in globular clusters in the Large Cloud by Thackeray and his associates turned out to be fainter than Cepheids of the same period would have been, by an amount which just about doubled the previous estimates of distance.

Cepheids have been identified in a number of other galaxies and used along with other methods to estimate distances, including that of the Andromeda Nebula with a distance modulus of 24.2 magnitudes. However, beyond the nearest galaxies, even the brightest Cepheids fail as distance indicators. It is true that individual bright stars with absolute magnitudes of about − 9 have been recognized in the Magellanic Clouds (Plate 42) but the difficulty is to identify a particular bright object as a star of a given type. The gap can be partially filled by observations of novae and supernovae. Novae occur rather frequently in galaxies and may reach an absolute magnitude at maximum of − 8 or − 9 which makes them somewhat brighter than the brightest Cepheids. They are recognizable purely photometrically by the fact that their light increases catastrophically in a matter of days or hours and fades away, after the maximum, in a matter of weeks or even months. The supernova phenomenon is superficially similar to that of the ordinary nova, on a larger scale, in that a star suddenly increases in brightness to a maximum, emitting a characteristic spectrum, and fades away slowly. Supernovae are now generally divided into two types. In a Type I supernova the absolute magnitude at maximum may reach something of the order of − 18, and at such a time the emission from the supernova is comparable with the total emission from the galaxy in which it occurs. Type II supernovae resemble ordinary novae more closely and may reach an absolute magnitude of about − 16 at maximum light. The origin of the phenomenon, and the type of star likely to undergo a supernova outburst, are both obscure and the rate of occurrence is very small, possibly of the order of one supernova of Type I per galaxy every 500 years. Even so, the number of available galaxies is so large that several supernovae per annum are now being detected, and they are of some value for the estimation of the distances of the systems in which they occur.

Perhaps the best distance criterion for any given galaxy is its integrated magnitude, for from studies of nearby galaxies it is now thought that the integrated absolute magnitude of the average galaxy is of the order of -20, corresponding to a luminosity of about 10^{10} stars equal to the Sun. The measured magnitude of any galaxy then depends on its distance and the amount of reddening due to its red shift. The complicated effects involved can be disentangled and the value of the Hubble constant can be established at the figure of 55 kilometres per second per megaparsec, quoted above. Assuming this figure, the measured velocity of a nebula is often itself used as a means of estimating its distance. At the same time the establishment of a distance scale gives linear diameters, which come out at values of the order of 20 thousand parsecs, and permit determinations of mass, yielding total masses for normal galaxies of the order of some 10^{11} times the solar mass.

Cosmological implications of the red shifts Cosmology is the attempt to give an account of the Universe on the grand scale. The discovery of the red-shift law has been one of the most important observational facts of cosmology and has precipitated more, and more acrimonious, discussion than any other. It is impossible to do more than summarize the present theoretical situation very briefly. The General Theory of Relativity can account for a general dispersion of nebulae with three possible cases: expansion at a constant rate, at an increasing rate, or at a rate which is slowing down. If this theory is the correct one, then according to one discussion of the observations, the last possibility is the correct one, but to arrive at this conclusion the observational results must be pushed to the limit. There are other alternative theories: some, like that of the Belgian cosmologist, Lemaître, imagine that there was a catastrophic beginning to the Universe which exploded from a single exceedingly massive particle: others, like that of Milne, elaborated the idea that the velocity/distance relation arose as the result of the dispersion of a large number of nebulae moving with velocities directed at random and having all kinds of numerical values. Thus after a lapse of time the fast-moving objects would be on the outside of the assemblage and a nearly linear relation between velocity and distance would arise. In opposition to all these theories is the steady state theory. As we have seen, the expansion of the Universe gives no special privilege to an observer at any particular place: the proponents of the steady state theory wish to extend this to the denial of any special significance to any moment of time: the Universe on the grand scale looks the same as it always has, and there is no beginning or end. This is found to imply the creation of matter out of nothing in empty space, but at a rate likely to be forever undetectable. The steady state theory does not now seem to be maintained with the same fervour as at one time, but it is not clear whether it has been entirely abandoned or only considerably modified in the face of observational evidence which appears to be in conflict with it.

Extragalactic radio sources In the 'thirties, Reber and Jansky made the discovery that radio waves were being emitted from sources external to the Earth in the form of noise or static. Since World War II radio astronomy has grown enormously in stature, and now rivals optical astronomy as a branch of the science, each forming an essential complement to the other. It is now known that some of the planets, the Sun, some stars, some gaseous objects in the Galaxy, especially hydrogen clouds and supernova remnants, most late-type galaxies and, most important of all, the objects known as quasars, are emitters of radio waves. These can be classified into three groups. First is line emission, produced at a particular intrinsic wavelength by certain specific atoms and molecules, of which the best known is the 21-centimetre wavelength produced by a configuration change in the neutral hydrogen atom. Thermal radiation comes from the motion of electrons due to the temperature of the environment in which they find themselves. Synchrotron radiation is due to very high-speed motion of electrons, at speeds at which relativity effects are important, in a magnetic field.

Because the hydrogen emission is in a line frequency, measures of the actual received frequency give an indication of the line of sight velocity of the source, as well as of the space density of the atoms producing the observed intensity. Adopting a particular model for the speed of circular motion about the centre of our own Galaxy at various distances from the centre, the radio astronomers have been able to plot out maps showing the distribution of hydrogen clouds in our own Galaxy. These have revealed a general spiral structure, almost impossible to delineate by any other method, and have demonstrated that, in general, the gaseous layer is very thin and flat. The conclusions have not gone entirely uncontested, but have shown the close similarity between our own Galaxy and others in the heavens. Studies of the polarization of radio waves have given information about magnetic fields in the Galaxy, again, not without controversy about the results.

Observations of highly localized sources such as the Crab Nebula

(Plate 32*b*), a known supernova remnant within our Galaxy, show evidence of strong magnetic effects in this class of object. Observations of other galaxies show that at certain frequencies the source for radio waves is much larger than the visual extent of the object, and forms a kind of halo of roughly spherical shape. For normal galaxies of later type, that is, the spirals, there is a fairly close correlation between radio emission and optical brightness. Normal ellipticals radiate very weakly, if at all.

In recent years interest has tended to concentrate on galaxies which show radio emission of an intensity far greater than might be expected from the observed visual brightness. Some of these objects, which are near enough for details to be visible, are of unusual form. The intense radio sources in Fornax and in Centaurus have been identified with the peculiar galaxies NGC 1316 and NGC 5128 (Plate 41). Both of these have the general appearance of elliptical galaxies with the abnormality that they include pronounced clouds of absorbing material. There seems a general tendency for giant elliptical galaxies to be associated with radio sources, though in many cases the distance is too large for possible abnormalities of structure, such as are found in these cases, to be detected. An enormous amount of thought has been expended on attempts to explain the strong radio emission of cases such as this. The strong radio source, Cygnus A, has been accounted for by the hypothesis of a collision between two galaxies, but observations of the relative motions with NGC 5128 suggest that this is not a tenable hypothesis in this case. The strikingly irregular galaxy NGC 3034 (M 82) has been examined in detail, and its strange form attributed to some kind of enormous explosion. So far, no one has produced a satisfactory explanation, although many hypotheses have been considered. All face the problem of producing a vast quantity of energy in a short time in a small space, and this explains the attractions of such ideas as the almost simultaneous explosion of a series of supernovae.

When intense radio sources were first discovered, the resolving power of available radio antennae was so small that only very rough positions could be given. Now, with increasing size of steerable dishes and fixed transit instruments, and the development of aperture synthesis and interference instruments, it is possible not only to determine positions with great accuracy but also to analyse with great precision the fine structure of extragalactic sources. In the case of the peculiar galaxies already known it has been established that, in addition to relatively extended sources, there are also point sources, usually in pairs, very often located at positions such that no visible feature coincides with the source. In the early days identification with an optical feature usually proceeded by the method, very crudely expressed, of searching in the area identified by the radio position for the oddest looking optical object. As we have indicated, this method sometimes works: peculiar galaxies are often radio sources, or are associated with pairs of point sources. The study of the relation between peculiar galaxies and radio sources has been pushed further by Arp, who has compiled a catalogue from the galaxies shown in the Palomar sky atlas. Optical identification of radio sources in general has now become a precise science, and, in the north, with big optical instruments available, many identifications have been made, mostly with objects which are optically faint. Some of these are presumably peculiar galaxies. The most interesting of the sources have, however, been found to be stellar in appearance and there is some risk of confusing them with faint stars in our own Galaxy. The name 'quasar' has been adopted for these quasi-stellar sources, and study of them is in the forefront at the time of writing. Photometrically they are characterized by a strong emission in the ultraviolet part of the spectrum which distinguishes them from the general run of stars. A few of them, such as the brightest, known as 3C273, show structure in the form of a kind of jet, rather like a famous radio-emitting giant elliptical galaxy NGC 4486 which has a jet protruding from it. The actual emitting regions are of extremely small angular size, often in the range of a few thousandths of a second of arc. These angular measures have been made with radio interferometers with extremely long, sometimes intercontinental, base lines.

Optical spectra of a number of quasars have been obtained, with emission lines, showing, until recently, an apparent limit of recession with values of z just over 2. An extraordinary feature has been the discovery in many spectra of absorption lines showing high values of z, but less than for the emission lines.

If these red shifts are cosmological in origin, i.e. if they are due to the general expansion of the Universe and not to some extraordinary locally produced effect, the quasars must be among the oldest and most remote objects in the Universe. Their luminosities in the optical range computed from distances based on the measured red shifts come out for the brightest ones at several magnitudes brighter than ordinary galaxies.

A remarkable discovery, first noted for 3C273, but now confirmed for many others, is that quasars are optically variable. The quasar 3C273 is one of the few bright enough to show up on patrol plates taken decades ago, and it was from the study of such historic material that quasar variability was first discovered. The variations give a certain impression of periodicity, and it has been argued that, if a quasar shows a variation in a time of a few hours, then its dimensions must be comparable with the distance travelled by light in such a time. This raised the crucial question not only of the immense output of energy by quasars but also of its production within an astronomically minute volume and the possibility of significant variation within a very short time. Even if the periodic time were as long as the 12 or 13 years suggested for 3C273 the difficulties would be immense, though not as extreme as for the shorter time variations. It now seems clear that the variations are not periodic but are the sum of random events, which perhaps widens the field of speculation concerning physical mechanisms rather than leading more readily to a conclusion.

To illustrate the diversity of speculation one may mention a few of the ideas which have been entertained. These include the explosion at random times of a whole series of supernovae, the random mutual annihilation of matter and anti-matter, complex interaction of massive rapidly rotating material bodies and magnetic fields, and the focusing of light of a more distant galaxy by the Einstein gravitational effects of a nearer one. This by no means exhausts the range of speculation, but the list does serve to illustrate the theoretical difficulties of explaining enormous and variable energy outputs within minute volumes of space.

By way of obviating a possible source of confusion, reference may be made here to another class of radio object, the pulsars, which came into astronomy only a few years ago and have attracted enormous attention. These are presumed to be quite different from the quasars, and so far detectable only within our own Galaxy, They pulsate in very short periods of the order of one second, and are tentatively identified with rapidly rotating superdense neutron stars only a few kilometres in diameter, such as might be left as the remnant of a supernova. Only one, the Crab Nebula pulsar, has at the time of writing been found to vary optically, and it does so in a period of the order of one-thirtieth of a second.

D. S. E.

Postscript In the interval that has elapsed since Professor Evans wrote the preceding paragraphs, work on quasars, or QSOs (quasi-stellar objects) as they are now more usually called, has been intensively pursued; many new observational data have been accumulated and various theoretical ideas have been explored. A concise but delightfully lucid and authoritative account of some of this work is given in *Modern Cosmology* by D. W. Sciama, published in 1971 by the Cambridge University Press. So far, however, the net result of this very considerable activity has been rather to increase the number of unsolved problems and to throw doubt on some ideas which were considered to be well established than to clarify our understanding of these mysterious objects. When finally these particular problems are solved, others will undoubtedly arise, but in the process the bounds of space of which we have some knowledge will probably have been pushed further back. Modern techniques, and particularly those of radio astronomy, have greatly enlarged the volume of the observable universe since Hubble wrote *The Realm of the Nebulae*, but his closing remarks still remain true:

> Thus the explorations of space end on a note of uncertainty. And necessarily so. We are, by definition, in the very centre of the observable region. We know our immediate neighbourhood rather intimately. With increasing distance, our knowledge fades, and fades rapidly. Eventually, we reach the dim boundary—the utmost limits of our telescopes. There, we measure shadows, and we search among ghostly errors of measurement for landmarks that are scarcely more substantial.
>
> The search will continue. Not until the empirical resources are exhausted, need we pass on to the dreamy realms of speculation.

R. H. S.

Chapter Eleven

The tools of an astronomer

H. Seddon

The search for information The essential job of an astronomer, like that of other practising scientists, is to solve riddles, gathering and using any clues available however slender they may appear to be. The commonly held view of an astronomer as sitting night after night looking through long and improbable telescopes at Saturn is far from the truth. Observation is only one of the many links in the chain of reasoning that leads to the solution of a problem; imagination, deduction and rationalization also play their part. Ideally, observation leads to new theories which, in their turn, predict new features which can be checked by observation. Sometimes the observations so indicated require years of hard work to develop the appropriate instruments before any sort of confirmation can be attempted. Observations on the frontiers of the possible are only achieved by the exercise of great ingenuity, extreme meticulousness, and an infinite amount of patience. The observational astronomer is well aware that his efforts are never ending for he knows that every problem successfully solved leads on to two or three more not so susceptible to solution. At the back of his mind, however, is always the hope that in the course of his observations he will discover something that will confound the theoreticians, something which they have not yet even considered and which will lead to the opening up of entirely new lines of work.

As it is quite impossible in the limited space available even to begin to describe all the many and varied instruments that have been and are being developed to solve particular problems, this chapter is devoted to a short account of some of the factors underlying the design of the basic astronomical instruments and of the limitation on observation that these impose.

Electromagnetic radiation Most of the data with which a practical astronomer has to deal come originally in the form of electromagnetic

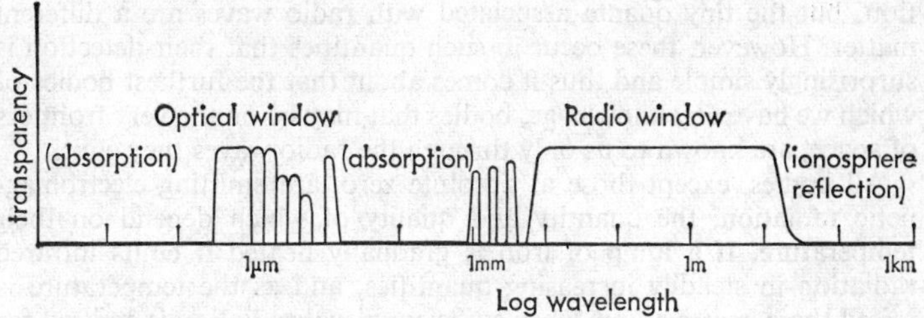

Figure 11.1 The electromagnetic radiations that reach the Earth's surface

radiation, though some are in the form of cosmic rays and other streams of particles such as electrons and neutrinos. Figure 11.1 illustrates the electromagnetic spectrum and indicates those parts of it that are accessible to ground-based observations. These latter, which are sometimes referred to as the optical, infrared and radio windows, account for only a small part of the whole spectrum but contain all the radiations on which our astronomical knowledge had to be based until the coming of rocket and satellite borne instruments.

Electromagnetic radiation travels through empty space with the velocity of light, c, which is independent of the wavelength and approximately equal to 3×10^5 km s^{-1}. The wavelength of the radiation, λ, and its frequency, ν, are connected by the relation

$$\lambda.\nu = c \,,$$

c and λ being in the same units of length and ν in hertz or cycles per second. Thus a radio wavelength of one metre corresponds to a frequency of 3×10^8 Hz, or, as it is more usually written, 300 MHz. Similarly orange-yellow light with a wavelength of 6000 angstroms or 600 nanometres or 0.6 microns corresponds to a frequency of 5×10^{14} Hz.

The energy carried by the radiation can only be interchanged in multiples of small elementary packets or quanta, the energy associated with each individual quantum being $h\nu$, where ν is the frequency expressed in hertz and h is Planck's constant and equal to 6.625×10^{-27} ergs. It follows that quanta of high frequency radiation are very much more energetic than those of low frequency and therefore much easier to detect individually. It is possible to detect a single quantum, or photon as it sometimes called, of visual and higher frequency radiation, but the tiny quanta associated with radio waves are a different matter. However, these occur in such quantities that their detection is surprisingly simple and thus it comes about that the furthest bodies of which we have any knowledge, bodies that may be on the very frontiers of space, are known to us only through the radio waves they emit.

All bodies, except those at absolute zero, are emitting electromagnetic radiation, the quantity and quality of which depend on their temperature. If a lump of iron is gradually heated it emits infrared radiation in steadily increasing quantities, and as the temperature is raised there comes a time when sufficient visual radiation is emitted for the iron to be seen to have a deep red glow. As the temperature is raised still further, the glow gets brighter and brighter and changes its colour from red to yellow, from yellow to white, from white to bluish white, and so on. In the case of a 'black' body or 'perfect radiator', to whose behaviour that of most bodies, liquids, and dense gases tend, it is possible through Planck's law to specify exactly how the emitted radiation depends on the temperature. In terms of wavelength the radiation emitted per unit area per unit interval of wavelength is

$$C_1 / \lambda^5 . (\exp(C_2/\lambda T) - 1)$$

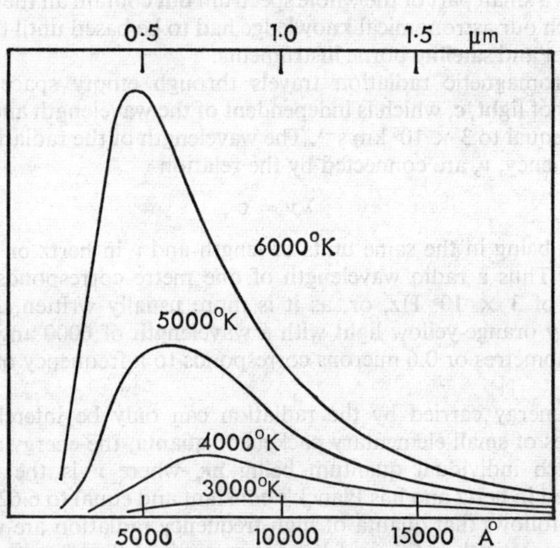

Figure 11.2 Black body radiation: variation of relative intensity with wavelength at various temperatures

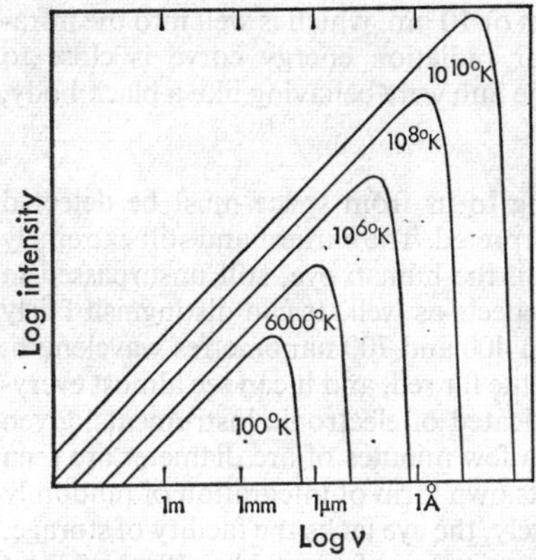

Figure 11.3 Black body radiation: variation of intensity with frequency for a wide range of temperatures

where C_1 and C_2 are constants and T is the absolute temperature. Expressed in frequency and for unit intervals of frequency, this function takes the form

$$C_3 \,.\, \nu^3 / (\exp(C_4\nu/T) - 1) \quad ,$$

C_3 and C_4 being constants. These functions are plotted for various temperatures in Figures 11.2 and 11.3.

The total radiation emitted at any temperature will be proportional to the area under the appropriate curve for that temperature and can be shown to be directly proportional to T^4. This is called the Stefan-Boltzman law and was discovered before that of Planck from which it can be deduced. Expressed in words, it states that the power radiated per unit area by a black body is proportional to the fourth power of the absolute temperature of that body.

It will be noticed from Figure 11.3 that the frequency at which the maximum of the energy curve occurs increases with increasing temperature. The actual relationship is

$$\nu_{\max} = K \,.\, T$$

where K is a constant. This relationship, which is known as Wien's displacement law, can also be written

$$\lambda_{\max} \,.\, T = K'$$

where K′ is a constant and approximately equal to 0.0029 when λ is measured in metres and T in degrees Kelvin. Thus a body at a temperature of 300°K, which is very approximately normal room temperature, radiates most strongly at 0.01 mm or 10 μm, which is well into the infra-red. The maximum of the solar radiation energy curve is close to 5000 Å, which indicates that if the Sun were behaving like a black body, its temperature would be 5800°K.

Detectors The radiation coming to us from space must be detected and assessed before it can be interpreted. The earliest and still extremely valuable receiver and instrument is the human eye, still unsurpassed in versatility and in many other respects as well. It can distinguish fairly fine gradations in colour between 400 and 700 nanometres wavelength, that is between the far violet and the far red, and it can see almost everything visible to the most sophisticated of electronic instruments, given the same conditions. Objects of a few minutes of arc diameter are seen as extended, and the brain does its own form of integration of randomly disappearing images. Unfortunately, the eye lacks the facility of storage, but apart from this the retina compares very favourably with the fastest of photographic emulsions. While storage in the eye is only for the order of a twentieth of a second, a photograph can go on storing and integrating radiation for many hours thus enabling fainter and fainter objects to be observed. In addition, the received information can be treated at leisure by refined measuring machines to yield results that are usually more reliable and of greater refinement than those obtained by the use of the eye alone.

The photographic emulsions used in astronomy differ from those used for more normal photography in a number of ways, particularly as regards sensitivity to faint light and in being available to cover any part of the spectrum between gamma rays and the infrared. Nearly all photographic emulsions are subject to what is called reciprocity failure and are relatively more efficient for high light intensities and short exposures than for low light intensities and correspondingly long exposure times. This drop in efficiency is of little consequence in normal photography, for which the exposures are usually only a fraction of a second, but becomes important when what is being photographed is so faint that exposures of several minutes, or maybe hours, are required. Consequently special steps are taken in the manufacture of photographic emulsions intended for astronomical use to reduce this reciprocity failure to a minimum. Another drawback of the photographic process when applied to photometry, which forms an important branch of astronomical observation, is that the densities of the resulting images on the plate are not linearly related to the quantities of light producing them; moreover, the degree of this non-linearity varies with the wavelength of the incident light. Each plate has therefore to be specially calibrated, the particular method employed depending on the use for which the plate is intended.

In spite of such complications, the photographic plate is so efficient for so many applications that it is unlikely to be completely superseded by any of the current photoelectric devices, convenient and efficient as some of these are for special purposes. These depend on the photoelectric effect, viz. when a sufficiently energetic photon falls on a conducting surface it will cause a photoelectron to be ejected. If this occurs in a vacuum, the photoelectrons can be collected and measured as an electric current, with the very useful property that the effect is linear over very large ranges. Thus if ten photons are needed to eject one electron, then ten million photons will eject a million photoelectrons, the linearity being affected only by randomness in the emission and conduction processes. The resulting current is, of course, small and must be amplified in some way before measurement. One of the most common ways of achieving this amplification with low penalties in the way of added noise is the photomultiplier cell. These are available in many forms, each with its own special features, but having in common a photocathode that emits photoelectrons when light of suitable wavelength falls on it and a dynode structure following, each surface of which emits more than one electron when an electron from the immediately preceding stage falls on it. The first dynode is held at a higher potential than the photocathode and each subsequent dynode at a still higher potential than the one immediately preceding it. The electrons released from the photocathode by the incident light are therefore accelerated towards the first dynode and when they impinge on it release more electrons which, in their turn, are accelerated towards the second dynode, and so on. The end result is a greatly amplified pulse of electrons at the collector for every incident photon, plus a certain amount of unwanted output, called dark current from the fact that this flows even when there is no light falling on the cathode. Figure 11.4 shows four common ways of arranging the dynodes within the photomultiplier to ensure the most efficient degree of amplification.

Photomultiplier cells have been developed to such a stage that they are now more sensitive and efficient detectors than the best available photographic emulsions, and they are available to cover much the same spectral ranges. Various devices are being developed to combine the advantages of photography, of two dimensional storage and fine grain, with the linearity and sensitivity of the photoelectric effect. In some of these devices the photographic emulsion is actually introduced into the evacuated space of the photoelectric tube, while in others it is separated from this evacuated space by a thin electron-transparent membrane.

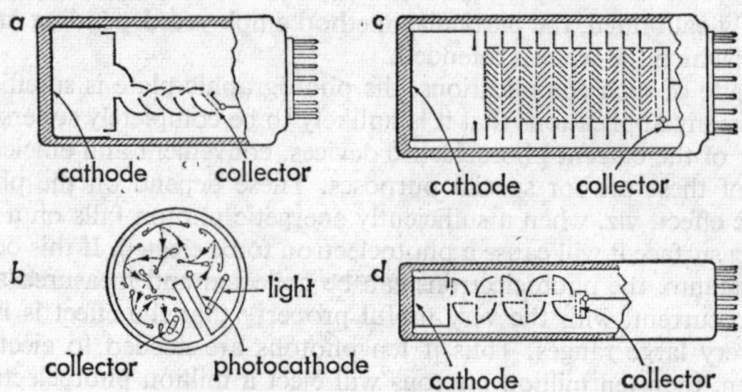

Figure 11.4 Internal geometries of four common types of photomultiplier cells with electrostatic dynode systems: *a*, focused structure; *b*, compact focused structure; *c*, venetian-blind structure; *d*, box and grid structure

The electrons released from the photocathode are accelerated and focused by electric and magnetic fields onto the photographic emulsion and there blacken the sensitive silver grains. This method is highly sensitive and its linearity approaches that of the photoelectric method itself, but the devices so far produced are difficult to handle and are short lived. They will, no doubt, be improved to the point of easy use and availability. In another device the photoelectrons are accelerated as in a TV tube on to a phosphor screen and the image that appears there is focused on to a photographic emulsion by an external camera. Such devices are reliable and fairly sensitive but their response is not linear, a relatively small consideration if it makes the difference between being able, or not being able, to record the spectrum of a faint distant nebula.

Photographic emulsions and photoelectric cells tail off in usefulness as we go further into the infrared than one micron wavelength, becoming insensitive and noisy before their sensitivity disappears altogether at about one and a half microns. Other methods of detection have to be used. One of the earlier devices used for detecting and measuring infrared radiation was the thermocouple in which two fine wires of dissimilar metals are joined and exposed to the radiation. To increase sensitivity many such couples were combined together to form a thermopile. More sensitive, however, is the thermistor bolometer, the thermistor being a small flake of semiconductor with a large negative temperature coefficient of resistivity, that is, its resistance drops as heat

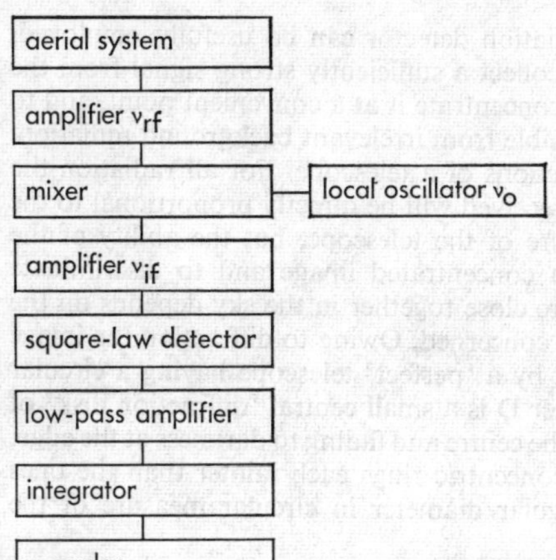

Figure 11.5 Block diagram of a superheterodyne radio-telescope receiver

is absorbed. These bolometers are useful in that they are not particularly colour sensitive. The materials most commonly used are the photo-sensitive semiconductors, in which the absorption of infrared radiation causes electrons in the material to become available for conduction. Peak sensitivity varies from 4 μm for lead sulphide at room temperature to 30 μm for zinc-doped germanium at the temperature of liquid helium, about 4°K. Between 30 μm and the radio region which begins at about 1 mm, we revert to thermopiles and such devices as the Golay cell, in which the infrared radiation is used to heat and expand air in a small cavity and thus cause a silvered diaphragm to bulge. Visible light is focused on to this diaphragm through a grid system in such a way that, when cold, the grid obstructs its own image, and as the diaphragm distorts, more and more light is allowed through.

The commonest form of radio radiation detector is the superheterodyne receiver, typified by the common domestic radio receiver. A block diagram of a superheterodyne radio-telescope receiver is shown in Figure 11.5. Radiation from the aerial is picked up on a simple dipole and fed to an amplifier which increases the power level of the signal at the incoming frequency with a minimum addition of extra noise. The signal is then mixed with a locally generated signal whose frequency is made to differ from that of the incoming signal by a pre-chosen amount. The output from this mixing contains, amongst others, a signal at the chosen frequency difference, which is usually called the intermediate frequency or I.F. This I.F. signal is then amplified and recorded.

Telescopes Before any radiation detector can be usefully employed, however, it is necessary to collect a sufficiently strong signal from the selected celestial source, to concentrate it at a convenient point, and to separate it out as far as possible from irrelevant background radiation. These are the principal functions of a telescope. For all radiation the total strength of the signal received will be directly proportional to the area of the entrance aperture of the telescope, but the ability of the telescope system to form a concentrated image and to discriminate between two sources that are close together in the sky depends on the wavelength of the radiation concerned. Owing to diffraction the image of a point source produced by a 'perfect' telescope having a circular entrance aperture of diameter D is a small central 'diffraction disk' of finite diameter, brightest at the centre and fading to darkness at the edge, surrounded by a series of concentric rings each fainter than the ones within it. The effective angular diameter in circular measure of the central diffraction disk is

$$k . \lambda / D$$

where k is a constant approximately equal to 1.1 and λ and D are expressed in the same units of length.

Consider first the case of an optical telescope for which we can assume an effective wavelength of 5000 Å or 5×10^{-5} cm. The angular diameter of the central diffraction disk is $5.5 / 10^5$ D, or, converting to arc seconds by multiplying by 206265, $11''.3$ / D, where D is the aperture of the telescope in centimetres. This can also be taken as the effective resolving power of the telescope since the images of points closer together than this will not be separated but will appear as a single blur. In the case of the largest optical telescope in operation, the 200-inch (508-cm) reflector, the minimum diameter of the stellar image it can in theory form is only 0.02 arc seconds, but this limit is unlikely to be obtained in practice, since, apart from any optical defects in the telescope itself, the light entering the telescope has to pass through the atmosphere where it suffers various distortions. The effect of these distortions, which are usually referred to as 'seeing', is to cause the image to be partially blurred and to move about rapidly. Seeing varies from place to place and from time to time. Before establishing a new observatory astronomers spend a great deal of time and effort in trying to locate a place where the seeing is very good some of the time and good most of the time. Even at the very best ground-based sites, the seeing disk is rarely as small as a quarter of a second of arc, and more usually it is of the order of one or two seconds. It follows, then, that as regards resolving power little is gained by increasing the aperture of an optical telescope much beyond 40 cm; in fact, as the effect of bad seeing on image size (but not motion) is apt to be larger for the bigger apertures, cutting down the aperture may, in some cases, actually improve the resolving power.

The situation is very different for radio telescopes. For wavelengths of one metre the resolution of a radio dish having an aperture of D metres is 1.1/D radians or 63/D degrees. Thus the largest radio telescope in use, the 1000-foot fixed dish at Arecibo, will have a resolving power at one metre wavelength of about 0°.2 or 720″ arc seconds. To achieve the same sort of resolution as an optical telescope of only 11 cm aperture, viz. one arc second, a radio dish would have to have an aperture of 720,000 feet, that is about 136 miles or 220 kilometres. It is not surprising then that, in radio astronomy, dishes are used for collecting the radiation while resolution is obtained by the application of various ingenious interference techniques.

Telescopes in general can be divided into three main types according to the purposes for which they are principally intended. The first type includes those used simply as flux collectors, i.e. to collect as much radiation as possible from one chosen object and to concentrate it at some convenient point for analysis. The second type includes those instruments in which the main emphasis is on the formation of a high-quality image of the single object under examination, while the third type includes those instruments which may be thought of as celestial cameras and whose function is to photograph as large a field of the sky as possible in good definition. By construction, telescopes can be divided into refractors and reflectors.

Refractors The earliest telescopes were all refractors and this form still has many advantages for small and medium sized instruments. The essential component is the objective, a convex lens that forms an image of a portion of the sky in its focal plane, where, if desired, it can be recorded on a photographic plate. Alternatively, the image of one object can be selected for special examination by a spectrograph, photoelectric photometer, etc., or, in the case of a visual telescope, by an eyepiece. This latter case is illustrated diagrammatically in Figure 11.6. The very earliest telescopes used simple convex lenses for both objective and eyepiece, but the deficiencies in this arrangement soon became apparent, in particular the fact that the images were fringed with colour. This was due to the fact that the amount by which light is refracted is colour dependent, so that the surface over which the red light was in focus was further away from the objective than that at which the blue was in focus. Consequently, if the eyepiece was moved out to focus the

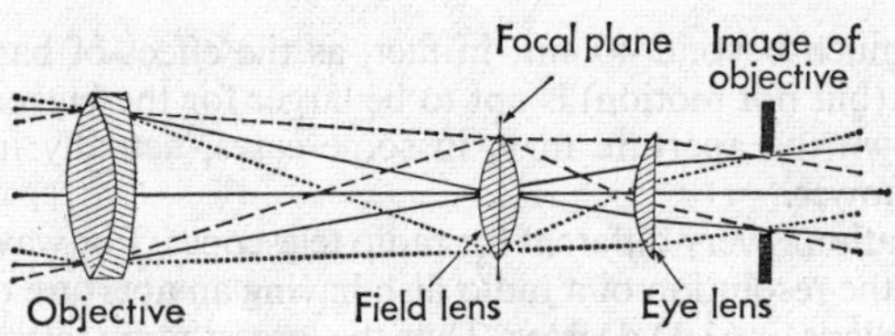

Figure 11.6 Diagram of a simple refracting telescope showing how the angular size of the observed field is determined by the diameter of the field lens of the eyepiece. The parallel light rays that form the beam in the direction of the axis of the telescope are indicated by ———, while those forming the beams that define the edges of the telescope field are denoted by - - - - - - and ...., When the telescope is properly focused the emerging beams are parallel and the eye should be placed at the 'exit aperture', i.e. where the image of the objective is formed by the eyepiece.

red, the image was seen with a blue halo, and vice versa. For a long time this seemed to be a fundamental limitation, so much so that Newton looked for another, colour-free system, and found it in the reflector, which we will be considering later. The subsequent development of glasses with different refractive properties made it possible to construct compound objectives that were effectively achromatic for a limited range of colour. The most usual form for a compound objective is a convex component of crown glass matched with a concave component of flint glass. Before the introduction of the achromatic objective, some observers used small lenses of great focal length to reduce the effects of chromatic aberration. Thus a telescope belonging to Hevelius had a focal length of 150 feet which must have been extraordinarily inconvenient to use, especially as it was very crudely mounted. By contrast, the biggest refractor ever built, and still in use at the Yerkes Observatory, has an objective 40 inches in diameter and a focal length of 60 feet. (Plate 45*a*.)

A typical eyepiece is shown in Figure 11.6 and consists of an eye lens which is responsible for causing the light rays from the focal plane to enter the eye as though from infinity, and a field lens which intercepts rays which would otherwise miss the eye-lens, and so helps to produce a larger field of vision. The field lens is close to the focal plane of the objective and so has little effect on the overall magnification of the telescope which is F/f, where F is the focal length of the objective and f that of the eyepiece. Light that passes through the objective eventually passes through the image of the objective formed by the eyepiece. This is called the exit pupil and it is where the eye should be placed to take full advantage of the light-gathering power of the telescope. The ratio of the size of the objective to that of the exit pupil is also approximately F/f, which is equal to the magnification of the telescope. If no light is to be wasted, the exit pupil must be smaller than the dark-adapted iris of the observer's eye. If this is taken as 8 mm, the minimum power eyepiece that should be used with an objective D cm in diameter is 10 D / 8. In the case of the 200-inch telescope this implies a minimum power of about 630 diameters. The maximum power eyepiece that can be usefully employed in the case of a large telescope depends largely on the state of the seeing; in the case of a small telescope, on its resolving power, i.e. on the diameter of its objective, and may be taken as 20.D, D being in centimetres.

Another important consideration is the brightness of the image formed by the objective. For stellar images the brightness is directly proportional to the aperture, i.e. to D^2, but for an extended surface like a nebula the light collected is spread over an image whose area varies as the square of the focal length, i.e. as F^2. Hence the brightness of the image per unit area will be proportional to D^2/F^2. In the case of a normal camera lens, the f-number is defined as F/D, and if we use the same nomenclature for astronomical objectives, we can say that the brightness of the image of an extended surface formed by an objective is proportional to $1 / f^2$. Most of the early refractors which were built for visual use have an f-number between 15 and 20. These were adapted for photography by the use of colour filters and panchromatic plates and are reasonably efficient for stellar photography but very slow and inefficient for photographing nebulosities. Hence, as photography increased in importance and refractors were built and specially achromatized for the photographic region, the f-number was reduced to about 10, this being the limit if a simple two-component objective is to give a reasonable sized field in good definition. Lenses having several spaced components and smaller f-numbers have been built especially in the smaller sizes where it is hard to discriminate between them and special camera lenses. The fastest camera lenses have f-numbers in the range 1.0 to 1.5, while special lens-mirror systems may have f-numbers down to 0.6.

It is most unlikely that any refractor as big as or bigger than the Yerkes 40-inch telescope will ever be built, partly because of the simplicity, convenience and efficiency of reflectors of equivalent light-gathering power, and partly because of the difficulties of producing large homogeneous disks of optical glass and then of supporting the finished lenses. If the lenses are made thick enough to be sufficiently rigid to be supported at their edges, they will absorb a considerable fraction of the light passing through them, since glass is not perfectly transparent. In addition to the light lost in transmission through the lenses, a certain amount is lost at every surface by reflection. For crown glass this amounts to about 4 per cent per surface, and for flint glass about 5 per cent. Thus for an achromatized two-component objective, 17 per cent of the initial light is lost by reflection alone. Obviously, extra components are to be added only for compelling reasons. For small lenses it is possible to reduce this loss by the process of blooming, in which a coating of a suitable substance is deposited in vacuum on the lens surfaces. The material used should have a refractive index equal to the square root of that of the glass, and be a quarter of a wavelength thick. It is also desirable that it should stand up to the atmosphere and to cleaning. Incidentally, a similar process suitably tailored may be used to increase the reflectivity of mirrors.

Refractors have a number of limitations, the chief of which is that they can only be made to cover a very limited range of wavelength, but they do have a number of advantages which make them particularly useful for visual observations and for making photographs which are intended to be measured accurately. When once set up, refractor systems are very stable and need few subsequent adjustments, nor do they have to be disturbed for anything analogous to the re-aluminizing or re-silvering required by reflector systems. The effect of temperature changes on compound lenses tends to be smaller than on mirrors, as warping on the front surfaces balances out the effect of warping on the back. The use of a closed tube partially eliminates the effects of air currents, while the lack of any obstruction in the beam means that the images have no strong associated diffraction patterns. It is the presence of such obstructions in the reflector systems that leads to star images with spikes, as depicted on Christmas cards!

It is possible to make refracting optics for use in the radio region out of expanded foam and metal inserts, but no practical use seems to have been made of such devices since there are other cheaper ways of performing the same tasks.

Reflectors As was mentioned earlier, Newton concluded (wrongly) that large colour effects were inevitable in the use of refracting optics, and so he designed the first reflecting telescope. From this small instrument has sprung a large family of related reflectors with which the greater part of astronomical observing is now performed. His original choice was based on the fact that reflection is not colour dependent in its geometry, which means that the same basic instrument may be used over the entire spectrum, from the radio region to that of short ultraviolet radiation. There are practical limitations, however, since it is difficult to find suitable reflecting surfaces in and beyond the ultra-violet, while the size of reflectors necessary in the radio region brings us into a new area of major precision engineering.

The paraboloidal surface is ideal for flux collecting since all rays intercepting such a surface from an infinitely distant point source on its axis pass through its focus. The accuracy of the surface of the paraboloid is normally specified as a tenth to a twentieth of a wavelength if the best images are to be achieved. In the case of the 200-inch optical reflector this corresponds to an accuracy of one part in a thousand million. The 100-metre dish of the world's largest steerable radio telescope of the Max Planck Institute for Radio Astronomy in West Germany is figured to an accuracy of 0.3 mm, which is about three parts in a million. The radiation collected by the main or primary paraboloidal mirror may be detected and examined at the prime focus of the mirror, or a secondary mirror may be placed into the beam near the prime focus to bring it to a focus at a more convenient spot. Observing at the prime focus has the merit of simplicity and, as compared with most of the secondary arrangements, the smallest effective f-number. Nearly all large radio paraboloids have the detector at the prime focus, which is quite often within the front aperture of the disk so that the detector is shielded to some extent from the surroundings by the dish itself. In optical telescopes cameras, spectrographs and other detectors are often placed at the prime focus when faint sources are to be observed. Some radiation is blocked on its way to the main mirror, but this loss is inevitable with most reflector systems and is, in any case, relatively small. As can be seen from Plate 45*b*, an observer can actually be housed at the prime focus of the 200-inch Hale Telescope and ride round with it.

Figurc 11.7 shows some of the more usual optical arrangements of a reflecting telescope. In the Newtonian configuration a small diagonal plane mirror slightly inside the prime focus transfers the image plane to the outside of the tube. While this position is very useful for small telescopes, it is inconvenient for large instruments because of the need to support the observer near the upper end of the moving tube. More usual is the Cassegrain arrangement in which a small hyperboloidal mirror intercepts the converging light before the prime focus and returns it through a central hole in the primary mirror to a secondary focus just behind it, where detectors of various sorts can be conveniently attached. The focal length of the combination is several times that of the primary mirror and the f-number is usually between 10 and 20. Some form of coudé arrangement is used when it is desired to feed the light into some heavy or bulky instrument or into an experimental

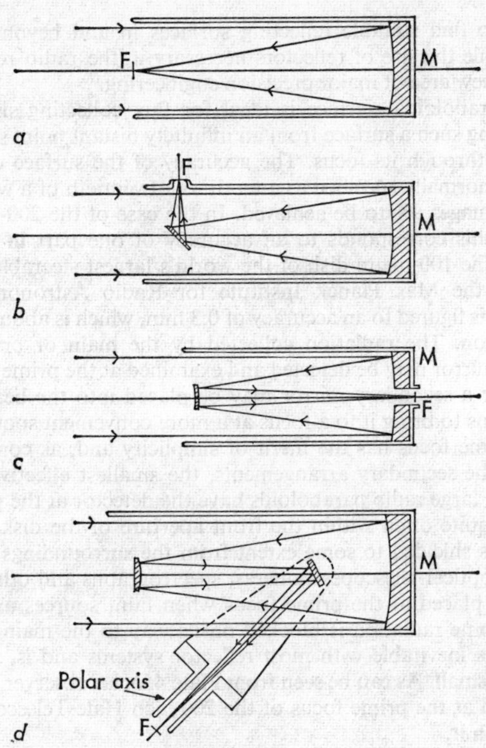

Figure 11.7 Some of the more common arrangements of the parabolic reflector: *a*, prime focus; *b*, Newtonian; *c*, Cassegrain; *d*, coudé. In each case F denotes the position of the effective focus

optical bench set-up. Light returning from the Cassegrain secondary is intercepted by a further mirror placed at the intersection of the axes of the telescope, which deflects the light beam to a fixed focus on the polar axis of the telescope. The image rotates as the telescope follows the diurnal motion of the object, but there are ways of counteracting this rotation if it is undesirable. The focal length of coudé combinations is usually very large, with f-numbers in the range 30 to 50. The light paths for the prime, Cassegrain, and coudé arrangements for the 200-inch Hale Telescope are indicated in Plate 45*b*.

So far we have been considering the relatively simple case in which reflectors are required to observe only one object at a time and can use a single detector at the focus. But there are many investigations in which it is necessary to detect a whole field of objects and which call for an instrument that can give good definition for a fairly wide angle round the principal axis of the telescope. A number of aberrations affect the off-axis images produced by the normal parabolic reflecting systems. Three of these are coma, astigmatism and field curvature. Coma is caused by different annular zones of the mirror (or lens) having different effective magnifications which cause the off-axis star images to have a fan-like shape with a bright pointed end towards or away from the axis. For a given mirror the extent of the coma is proportional to the distance of the image from the plate centre, while from mirror to mirror the coma at the same angle to the axis is proportional to the square of the diameter of the mirror. The effect of astigmatism is to elongate star images radially from the centre of the field outside focus and at right angles to this inside. There is a compromise best surface in between, where the elongated images merge into what is called the 'circle of least confusion'. It is, however, a compromise and the effect of the astigmatism increases with the square of the distance of the star image from the axis. This means that coma is the important aberration near the axis while astigmatism becomes important further off. Field curvature results from the fact that the locus of the best compromise foci of off-axis beams is not a plane through the prime focus but a curved surface approximately spherical in shape. It can sometimes be countered by bending the photographic plate to fit the focal surface or by using subsidiary optics to flatten the field.

The effect of these aberrations on a paraboloidal system is not too serious when the f-number is large. For instance, at f/30 they will not enlarge a star image more than one half a second of arc in a field of diameter 80 minutes of arc. Even at f/10 the images are not enlarged more than this in a field of diameter 9 minutes of arc. But at f/3, the field over which this is true has shrunk to only 48 seconds of arc. Clearly this is unacceptable if we wish to take photographs at the prime focus of a large reflector. Various correcting lenses placed in front of the focus have been designed to improve the field at the prime focus of a reflector but this improvement is obtained at some expense to the on-axis images and the sacrifice of the achromatic properties of an all-reflecting system. When, on account of speed, it is desired to take photographs at a low f-number it is better to use a specially designed instrument.

The Schmidt system Such an instrument became practical with the

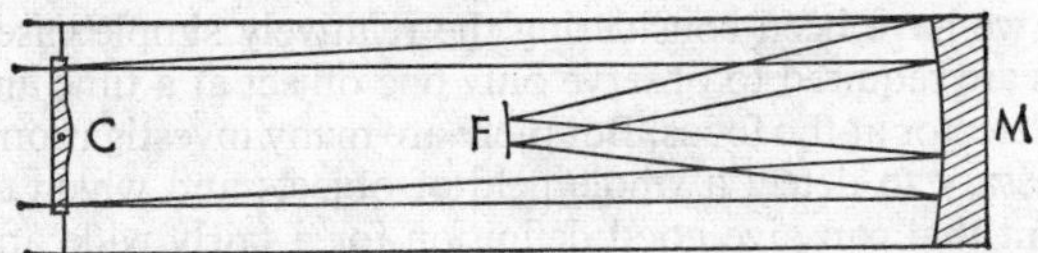

Figure 11.8 Schmidt Camera. M is a spherical concave mirror with its centre of curvature at C, the middle of the aspherical corrector plate. The focal surface F is spherical, concentric with the surface of the mirror and of half its radius

development of the Schmidt camera, the principle of which is shown in Figure 11.8. Basically what Schmidt pointed out was that as a spherical mirror has no particular principal axis, a telescope with a spherical mirror will be free from all aberrations that depend upon the distance from this axis and also, of course, from chromatic aberration. It will, however, suffer from field curvature and from spherical aberration. This latter is illustrated in Figure 11.9 which shows a parallel beam of light falling on to a spherical concave mirror. The central part of the beam that passes through the centre of curvature, C, of the mirror and strikes the mirror at its vertex, V, comes to a focus at F, the point half way between V and C. Similarly the outer parts of the beam that strike the mirror around the circular zones aa′, bb′, etc. come to a focus at F_a, F_b, etc. where F_a, F_b, etc. lie on the mirror side of F. It was to cure this aberration and to make all these focal points coincide that Newton parabolized his mirror. This cure is perfect but works only for beams parallel to the axis of the paraboloid. Newton arrived at his solution from his knowledge of the geometrical properties of parabolas, but the matter can be looked at slightly differently. We could make F and F_a coincide with F_b if we could slow up different parts of the beam by an appropriate amount. This could be done by increasing the path lengths for the rays nearer the axis by making the mirror deeper at the vertex and not quite so deep towards the edges, that is by parabolizing it. Schmidt demonstrated that the path lengths could also be effectively altered by introducing a properly shaped correcting plate before the mirror, and that if this plate were placed at the centre of curvature the correction that it introduced was effective for parallel beams of light approaching the mirror over an angle of several degrees. The resulting focal surface is a sphere concentric with the mirror and half its radius.

In Figure 11.8 the thickness and curvatures of the correcting plate are greatly exaggerated to show its form more clearly. In practice, the

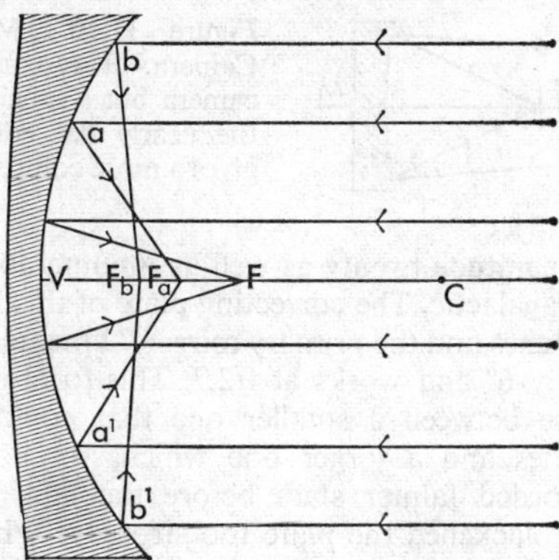

Figure 11.9 Spherical aberration of a concave mirror. Light reflected from the outer zones comes to a focus nearer the mirror than does the light reflected from the inner zones

surface contours of the correcting plate are barely detectable and the manufacture of such aspherical surfaces requires considerable ingenuity. Fortunately, the deviation from a flat surface is usually small so that the plate can be made by working zone by zone. The end result is worth the effort, for a well-adjusted Schmidt camera can give practically perfect images over a field of several degrees.

As the correcting plate acts by refraction it only functions perfectly for one chosen colour. For other colours there is some chromatic aberration and a small degree of spherical aberration that produces some coma well away from the axis, but these are not usually serious. As the focal surface is spherical, the photographic plates must be deformed to fit it, or some special field-flattening optical element must be introduced. The first alternative is usually adopted, although in some special cases, like that of a small Schmidt camera flown in a rocket, the expensive expedient of figuring the surface of the photographic plates to conform with the shape of the focal surface has been employed.

Schmidt and Schmidt-type cameras have been built in many different sizes and forms for many different purposes. One of the largest and most famous is that at the Mount Wilson and Palomar Observatories, with which was made the National Geographic map of three-quarters of the sky. This map, which was made in both red and blue light, shows all

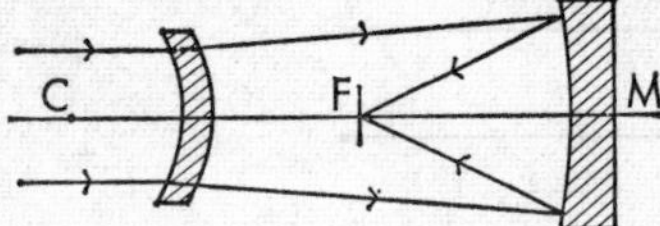

Figure 11.10 Maksutov-Bouwers Camera. It resembles the Schmidt camera but a meniscus lens replaces the nearly flat corrector plate and gives a more compact system

stars down to magnitude twenty as well as innumerable nebulae, both gaseous and extragalactic. The correcting plate of this instrument has a diameter of 48 inches and the primary mirror 72 inches. It covers a field of just over 6° by 6° and works at f/2.7. This focal ratio was chosen as a compromise between a smaller one that could have recorded fainter nebulosities and a larger one which, for a given aperture, would have recorded fainter stars before the light from the night sky background blackened the plate too strongly. What is virtually a duplicate of this fine instrument has been constructed for use in the southern hemisphere by British astronomers working at the Siding Spring Observing Station of the National Australian Observatory.

Where speed of recording faint extended objects or trails becomes paramount, the smallest possible f-numbers must be used. Plate 48*a* shows the Hewitt Camera at the Earlyburn Outstation of the Royal Observatory, Edinburgh, which was specially designed for observing artificial satellites. The camera remains stationary and a precisely timed shutter makes a series of gaps which act as time marks in the recorded trails of the satellites and surrounding stars. The camera has an f/1 Schmidt system with a special field-flattening lens in front of the flat photographic plate; flat because precise measures of position are desired. The correcting plate has an aperture of 63 cm and the spherical mirror one of 80 cm, so that it can reflect a full beam of light from objects lying as far as 10° off the axis. The field-flattening lens consists of three elements cemented together, a flint negative between two components of lanthanum crown.

Several variations of the Schmidt system have been proposed, each with its own special feature. One of the most useful of these for the larger f-numbers is that devised independently by Maksutov and Bouwers which is illustrated in Figure 11.10. It arose from the realization that it was possible to introduce spherical aberration in the opposite sense to that of the main mirror by using a negative meniscus lens instead of the aspherical corrector. By suitably choosing the curvatures of the lens surfaces, the combination could be made free from both spherical and chromatic aberrations. Moreover, the tube length required was shorter than that of the equivalent Schmidt, a considerable advantage when the f-number is large. When the fastest possible cameras are desired, more

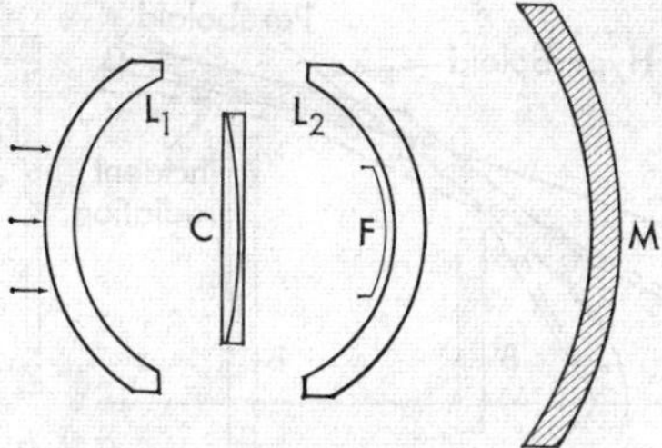

Figure 11.11 A wide field super-Schmidt camera working at f/0.67 which was especially designed for observing meteors. In this instrument the corrector plate, C, is augmented by two lenses, L1, L2, whose spherical surfaces are concentric with that of the mirror M. The inner surface of L2 provides the focal surface against which the plate or film is pressed

transparent components have to be added. Figure 11.11 shows a camera designed for recording meteor trails. It works at f/0.67 and has a large field in sharp focus, though its scale is necessarily small.

Other systems Another optical system which is becoming increasingly popular for general purpose telescopes is the Ritchey-Chrétien, which has a hyperbolic primary mirror and an ellipsoidal secondary used in a Cassegrain configuration. When suitably designed, the combination is relatively free from coma and spherical aberration and, being all-reflecting, from chromatic aberration as well. It has, however, a curved field and some degree of astigmatism, but if the f-number is not smaller than 6, it gives a moderately-sized field in good definition without the use of refracting materials.

The possibility of carrying telescopes out of the Earth's atmosphere has made it necessary to give some thought to X-ray optics. X-rays, except near grazing incidence, penetrate metal reflecting surfaces, making the usual telescope mirror useless. However, near grazing incidence metals reflect fairly well down to the region of soft X-rays, and advantage has been taken of this fact to construct a telescope for observing X-ray sources. Briefly, a section of a paraboloid is used well outside its focus. The rays that are reflected at the almost cylindrical surface intersect at the focal plane and can be detected there by photographic or photoelectric means. An aplanatic image can be obtained with some shortening of the telescope by using a two-curve mirror as shown in

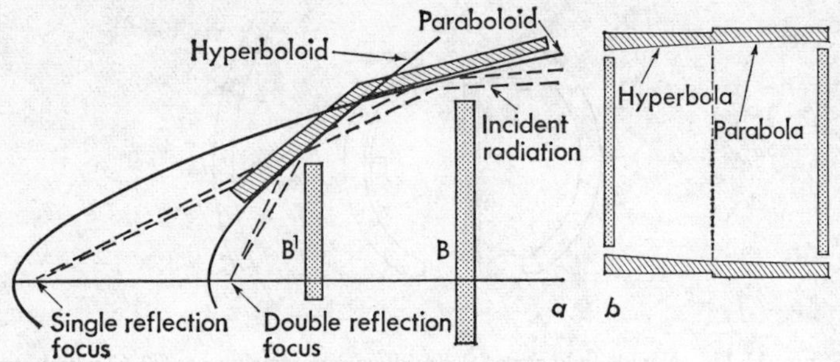

Figure 11.12 A reflecting telescope for observing X-ray sources.

a, how images can be formed using only rays near grazing incidence; *b*, cross-section of an actual telescope made of aluminium. The baffles B and B^1 are used to block out unwanted X-rays and thus increase the contrast of the images formed by the focused light

Figure 11.12. The X-rays are first deflected by the paraboloidal surface and then again by the hyperboloidal surface, the stops shielding the detector from unfocused radiation. Efficiencies of 0.2 per cent at 8–12 Å and 5 per cent at 44 Å are claimed for this system.

Mountings The finest optical components are useless unless they can be properly and conveniently mounted. If they are small there is no great problem involved in doing this, but difficulties quickly escalate as size increases. To mount a large mirror, which can distort appreciably under its own weight, so that it can be turned in all directions without a sensible loss of figure needs a very carefully designed system of support pads and counterpoised levers which taxes to the utmost the skill and ingenuity of the engineer. Nor is it easy to support the secondary optics so that they maintain their precise alignment relative to the primary in all positions of the telescope. Small instruments can be provided with what are virtually rigid tubes, but this is not possible for the larger ones and it becomes necessary to design a tube which is such that as it flexes under gravity, the optics that it supports remain in the same relative positions. The first instrument for which this seems consciously to have been done was the 200-inch Hale Telescope (Plate 45*a*), but it has now become standard practice for all but the smallest optical telescopes. The tube usually consists of a short, fairly rigid central section to which are attached a series of A-frames carrying upper and lower rings. As the tube flexes, these rings, which carry the optical components, remain parallel to one another and the amount of their displacement can be made equal by suitably choosing the sizes of the A-frames in relation to the loads they have to carry.

Most optical telescopes are supported on equatorial mounts in which one of the axes of rotation is parallel to that of the Earth. This gives this form of mount the great advantage of requiring rotation about one axis only to counteract the effects of diurnal motion and to follow the observed object across the sky. Equatorial mounts have been made in many shapes and sizes, the most usual form for refractors and small reflectors being the German mounting illustrated in Plate 45b which shows the Yerkes 40-inch refractor. A more rigid and therefore more satisfactory type of mount which has been used for many medium-sized reflectors is the cross axis or modified English mounting in which the polar axis is supported at both ends. This is illustrated in Plate 46*a* which shows the Elizabeth Telescope of the Cape Observatory. For the biggest telescopes some form of symmetrical mounting is desirable, both for mechanical strength and because for a telescope of given size such a mounting requires the minimum size of dome to cover it—an important consideration, since the cost of a dome increases rapidly with size. One form of symmetrical mounting which is used for instruments of all sizes is the fork mounting, an example of which is illustrated in Plate 46*b*, which shows the Isaac Newton Telescope at the Royal Greenwich Observatory. For larger instruments there is some difficulty in making the tines of the fork sufficiently long and rigid. The type of symmetrical mounting used for the 200-inch Hale Telescope is very much more robust, but also considerably more complicated. As can be seen from Plate 45*b*, the northern end of the polar axis is a large horseshoe, 14 m in diameter, which rests on oil pressure pads, the oil being under sufficient pressure to counterbalance the load. Similar oil pressure pads support the lower end of the axis and are so effective that the whole massive construction of over 500,000 kg is easily rotated by a small 60 W electric motor. The declination axis can be seen midway down the cylinders joining the horseshoe to the south bearing. The reason for the horseshoe is so that the telescope can be pointed directly at the North Pole, a feature which is not shared by some yoke-mounted telescopes such as the 100-inch reflector on Mount Wilson.

The telescope is set on the selected object by means of right ascension and declination scales associated with the two axes of the equatorial mount. On older and on smaller instruments which are set manually, these scales are mounted directly on the axes and read visually. On larger and more modern instruments, particularly those that are set with the help of electric motors, the scales are usually situated on the control panel and are connected with transmitters on the axes by suitable magslip or selsyn systems. Once the object has been located and centred the telescope is made to follow it by a motor whose speed is carefully controlled. However good the mount and the drive may be, it rarely of itself manages to keep the image of the object absolutely steady on the photographic plate, or on the slit of the spectrograph, etc., for more than a very limited period. Apart from inevitable small mechanical defects there are the effects of such things as differential refraction and irregular seeing which cannot be completely predicted. Consequently, for any lengthy exposure means must be provided to monitor the accuracy of the drive and to correct it where and when necessary. Formerly this was done by an observer maintaining a continuous visual watch on a suitable guide star and manipulating the slow motions of the telescope so that the guide star stayed centrally on the cross wires. This tedious manual guiding is now being very largely replaced by automatic devices by which the light of the guide star is monitored by one or more photoelectric cells and any wandering of the star from its mean position quickly corrected by servo mechanisms. One such device developed by Mr Adam of the Royal Observatory, Edinburgh, is illustrated in Figure 11.13.

Although the equatorial mount is undoubtedly the most satisfactory form for most optical and many of the smaller radio telescopes, it is not a practical proposition for radio telescopes of the largest size whose dishes may be more than twenty times the diameter of the 200-inch mirror and which, in addition to their own huge weight, are subject to the stresses imposed by high winds and heavy falls of snow. Only an altazimuth mount, that is one in which the two axes of rotation are horizontal and vertical, can carry such loads, but for it to be able to follow the diurnal motion of an object across the sky it must be driven simultaneously about both axes at ever-varying speeds. In practice this problem has been solved in two ways. In the first, the speeds of the driving motors are computer controlled, a relatively simple matter, but for this method to be effective the axes of rotation must be carefully aligned and completely stable. The second method, which was adopted by the Australian CSIRO for their 210-foot radio telescope (Plate 47*b*) does not require the axes to meet this rather stringent condition. A small optical telescope is mounted equatorially close to the point of intersection of the horizontal and vertical axes. This pilot telescope is accurately adjusted and can be pointed at and follow celestial objects in the normal way. It is linked optically to the huge 210-foot dish, and

Plate 45
a The 200-inch telescope of the Hale Observatories and *b*, below, the 40-inch refractor of the Yerkes Observatory

Plate 46
a The Elizabeth Telescope of the Cape Observatory and *b*, below, the Isaac Newton Telescope at the Royal Greenwich Observatory during construction. Photograph by Grubb-Parsons

Plate 47

a The radio telescope at Dwingeloo, the Netherlands, Leiden Observatory photograph, and *b*, below, the 210-foot radio telescope at Parkes, New South Wales. The smaller telescope in the foreground is used when making interferometric observations. Australian National Radio Astronomy Observatory photograph

Plate 48
a above, the Hewitt Satellite Tracking Camera at the Earlyburn Station of the Royal Observatory, Edinburgh, and *b* the payload of the S 47/2 Skylark rocket

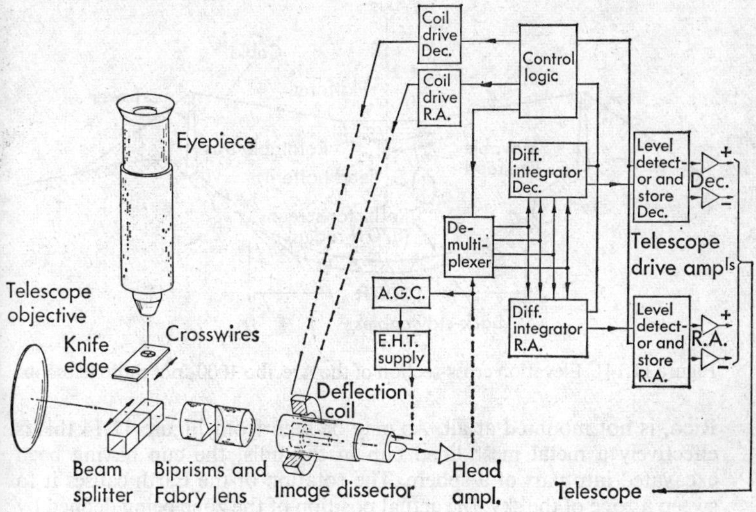

Figure 11.13 General layout of the autoguider devised by G. Adam

servo mechanisms controlled by this link drive the dish so that it points always in the same direction as the small pilot telescope.

An altazimuth mounting has also been adopted for the very large 6-metre optical telescope now being constructed in the U.S.S.R., but here there is a complication not met with in radio telescopes which are used only to observe objects on the principal axis. In optical telescopes the field is also of importance and in an altazimuth mount diurnal motion causes the field defined by the images in the focal plane to rotate relatively to the body of the instrument. As long as this rotation is comparatively slow it can be neutralized by rotating the plate holder by automatic guiding devices. But if the field in question passes near or through the zenith, the speed of rotation becomes very rapid and is, in fact, theoretically infinite at the zenith itself. Consequently no attempt is to be made to use the Soviet telescope closer than 5° to the zenith, which is no great hardship since objects which pass close to the zenith are accessible to observation for some hours before and after their meridian passage. The other limitation on this large telescope is also trivial, namely that it will not be pointed closer to the horizon than 10°.

The largest radio telescope in use, the 1000-foot at Arecibo, Puerto

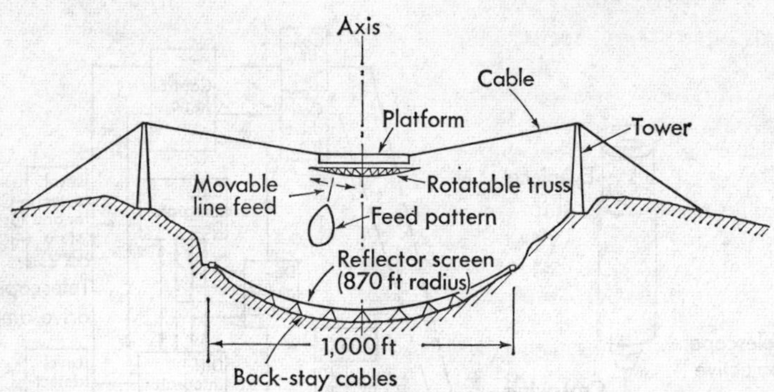

Figure 11.14 Elevation cross-section of the Arecibo 1000-foot radio telescope

Rico, is not mounted at all. As may be seen from Figure 11.14 this is effectively a metal mesh-lined cup in the hills, the cup having been excavated into part of a sphere. The rotation of the Earth causes it to sweep a zone of the sky, the actual position of the zone being defined by the position of the receiver feed point which can be moved from side to side in the focal plane. The off-axis images are degraded, but this is acceptable because of the extra cover it gives in declination, and in any case the aberrations can be counteracted by ensuring that the receiver accepts all the information at the image point in use. By this means this telescope can cover a band 20° on either side of the zenith and, at a wavelength of 0.70 metres, has a beam width of 10 minutes of arc.

Large as this instrument is, it is completely outclassed as regards directional discrimination by the various aerial arrays using interference between two or more individual receiving systems. These usually, but not always, scan in right ascension by the diurnal rotation. Some of them will be described in the next section.

Interference and acuity The earliest deliberate use of the phenomena of interference to increase the resolving power of a telescope seems to have been by Michelson, who based his work on the classical experiments of Young. In 1922, in collaboration with Pease, Michelson added a system of adjustable mirrors to the 100-inch telescope at Mount Wilson. The outer mirrors could be separated by any distance up to 6 metres and the beam on which they were mounted could be rotated about the optical axis of the telescope. This instrument was used for measuring the distances between some close double stars and for obtaining the diameters of seven stars, the largest diameters measured being 0.056 arc seconds for Mira and 0.047 arc seconds for Betelgeuse.

In these experiments the visibility, or otherwise, of the interference fringes was determined by visual inspection: Hanbury Brown and Twiss have now shown that this can be done photoelectrically and Hanbury Brown has developed an apparatus and has used it to measure the diameter of many stars. The instrument, which is situated at Narrabri in New South Wales, Australia, has two optical telescopes mounted on a circular track of 188 metres diameter. Each telescope mirror is 6.5 metres in diameter and is made up of 252 hexagonal spherical mirrors placed side by side. The only specification that the images formed by these compound mirrors have to meet is that all the light from the object observed should pass through a circle 1 cm in diameter at the focus. The images formed by the two mirrors are detected by phototubes, and the outputs from these two tubes, over a bandwidth of 10 to 110 MHz, are multiplied. By suitably varying the positions of the two telescopes on the circular track, the apparent diameters of stars with spectral type earlier than F5 and with blue magnitudes brighter than 2.0 can be measured to better than 0.001 arc seconds. The star's actual linear diameter can then be deduced if its distance is known from trigonometrical parallax observations, and provides an important check on theories of stellar constitution.

Exactly the same interference methods can be used in radio astronomy, except that the telescopes have to be separated by much greater distances, even up to distances comparable with the Earth's diameter. The Mark I 250-foot telescope at Jodrell Bank has been used as early as 1958 for one end of an interferometric method analogous to Michelson's experiment. Other smaller dishes at various distances up to 130 km were used for the other end. The instruments were used in a superheterodyne mode with a common local oscillator producing a beat intermediate frequency signal. There were problems with stability in transmitting these signals over the distances involved but these were eventually overcome and a resolution of 3 arc seconds at 158 MHz was achieved in 1960 and of 0.025 arc seconds at 6 cm wavelength in 1967. This latter is, of course, comparable to what Michelson achieved optically in 1922—a very considerable achievement indeed in so short a time.

The difficulty of communicating stably between the two stations at the end of the base made it impossible to pursue this approach any further, though the need for it was apparent. An alternative method was developed by groups in Canada and the United States who used independent atomic standard oscillators of very high stability to record the intermediate frequencies on tape. The separate records were brought together and the interference pattern produced by a computer. It was possible to use a baseline of 10,600 km between California and Australia with this method, and at a wavelength of 13 cm to achieve a resolution of a little over 0.002 arc seconds. A still higher resolution of just under 0.002 arc seconds was obtained by using a baseline of 6,300 km between West Virginia, U.S.A., and Sweden, and a wavelength of 6 cm. To better these figures significantly the further station will have to be either in orbit or on the Moon.

Another type of aerial system suitable for making surveys of the sky at relatively long wavelengths and at relatively low cost was developed by Mills in Australia. He arranged two lines of aerials at right angles to form a cross, the lines for his first cross being 500 yards long, each containing 500 half-wave dipoles with the received pattern concentrated in front by wire mesh reflectors placed behind them. The pattern of the energy received from a line of simple aerials suitably interconnected is fan shaped, being narrow in the plane containing the line of aerials and wide at right angles to it. Thus if the energy outputs from the two arms of the cross are added the region of the intersection of the two fan-shaped beams will contribute to the output at twice the rate of the remainder of the beams. Conversely, if the outputs from the arms of the cross are subtracted, this region of the intersection will contribute nothing to the total output. Consequently, if the outputs from the arms of the cross are suitably alternated the steady outputs from the outer parts of the beam will cancel out and the only response will be from the narrow intersection of the two beams. Mills's original cross worked at a wavelength of 3.5 m and had a beam width of 48 minutes of arc. The wavelength of operation of such an array cannot be changed significantly since it is mainly defined by the physical length of the individual dipoles. In a second cross, which has arms a mile long, Mills replaced the plane wire mesh reflectors by parabolic cylinders having their focal axes along the lines of the receiving dipoles. The reflectors in the north–south arm are fixed so that the response pattern is confined to the meridian. Those in the east–west arm can be tilted so as to alter the response pattern in altitude, that is in declination. The beam width between half-power points is about 3 arc minutes at 408 MHz.

A relatively cheap method of synthesizing large apertures has been developed by Ryle's group at Cambridge. In this system the east–west arm of the Mills cross is retained, but the north–south arm is replaced by a small aerial array mounted on a north–south railway. Observations are made with this movable array in a number of positions and the resulting records are processed by computer to give a response similar to that obtained with a Mills cross. A further development is to utilize the natural motion of the aerial array produced by the rotation of the Earth to form the aperture that is synthesized, due attention being paid to the varying direction during the observations of the object relative to the aerial array. This array can take many forms, but in all cases the effective collecting area is that of the elements and not that of the synthesized pattern.

Analysis of the radiation The radiation collected by the telescope has to be analysed and the result recorded. The simplest case is, of course, the direct examination of the optical image by the human eye; the next simplest the direct recording on a photographic plate. When suitably measured a direct photograph yields positional, structural and photometric information about the objects observed. The structural and photometric information is often more meaningful if it refers to a definite limited band of radiation defined by some or other colour filter, which may be of glass, perspex, or gelatin suitably dyed and used singly or in combination. Such filters give rather wide, not very sharply defined passbands; narrower, more specific passbands may be obtained by using interference filters which are made by depositing *in vacuo* layers of various dielectric media on a glass base. The thickness and refractive indices of the dielectrics determine the wavelengths of the transmission of the filter; passbands only a few angstroms wide can be produced by depositing many alternating layers. As was mentioned in an earlier chapter in connection with the observation of the solar chromosphere, Lyot developed a filter having a passband less than one angstrom wide. He used alternate layers of quartz and polaroid, each successive layer of quartz being twice as thick as the preceding layer. The temperature of such a filter has to be closely controlled to keep the wavelength of the transmission band constant; alternatively, the filter can be 'tuned' to some extent by altering its temperature.

Originally the only passbands in general use were the very wide and vaguely defined 'visual' and 'photographic'; now the choice of filters is almost unlimited but certain ones have come into fairly general use and are quite often simply denoted by letters. Amongst these are

U for which the effective wavelength of the passband is	3600 Å	(ultraviolet)
B	4400	(blue)
V	5500	(visual)
R	7000	(red)
I	9000	(infrared)
J	12500	
K	22000	
L	34000	

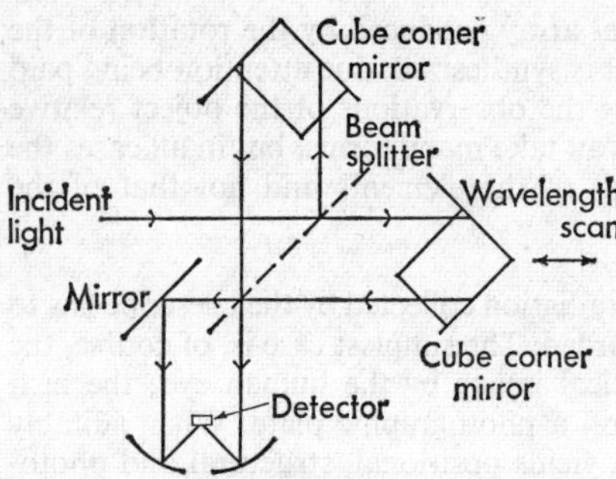

Figure 11.15 Michelson interferometer for infrared spectrophotometry

Where a finer discrimination in colour than that provided by filters is required use can be made of some form of spectrograph. Sometimes, especially for survey purposes, the dispersion produced by a small-angled prism or a coarse grating placed in front of the objective is sufficient, but more frequently greater resolving power than this provides is required. Astronomical spectrographs are, in their essentials, similar to those used in the laboratory, but rather more attention has to be paid to light efficiency since many astronomical sources are very faint, and also to rigidity in the case of those spectrographs that are mounted on and move round with the telescope. Astronomical spectrographs range in size from the very compact low dispersion spectrographs used at the prime focus to observe very faint objects like distant extragalactic nebulae, through medium dispersion instruments mounted at the Cassegrain focus, to the static high dispersion spectrographs used at the coudé focus. Even bigger, specially built spectrographs are used for observing the Sun from which plenty of light is available. Originally in order to conserve light, most astronomical spectrographs used glass or quartz prisms as the dispersing agent, but these have been steadily replaced by diffraction gratings since the development of the technique of 'blazing', by which the profiles of the grooves in the grating are so shaped as to throw most of the light into the spectrum of one order. Grating spectrographs have the advantage that the dispersion they produce is linear with wavelength and, if built with all reflection optics, can be used for a wider range of wavelengths than can a prism instrument.

A form of spectrograph now coming into increasing use, especially for observations in the infrared, is based on interference techniques. Figure 11.15 shows the essential features of the apparatus, which is based on the Michelson interferometer. If, while the instrument is illuminated by constant monochromatic light, one of the cube corner mirrors (which have the property of returning light along the same direction as it arrived) is moved at a steady speed, the intensity of the illumination on the detector will vary because of the varying interference between the split beams as the path length of one of them changes. The precise form of the intensity variation recorded by the detector will depend partly on the speed with which the mirror is moved and partly on the frequency of the incident light. If the apparatus is illuminated simultaneously by light of all colours the intensity variation recorded is the result of the patterns for all the individual colours present compounded according to their relative strengths; moreover different patterns can be produced for the same source by moving the mirror at different speeds. Thus it is possible in principle, and also in practice with some difficulty and using a suitable computer, to analyse out the strength of each component frequency of the incident illumination, i.e. to produce the spectrum of the incident light.

For astronomy this instrument has the great advantage that all the incident light is used; none is wasted on the jaws of a narrow slit. There remains, however, the difficulty that sources are usually faint and subject to scintillation. This difficulty has been overcome by integrating the digitized output for a sufficient number of mirror scans in the computer memory and by moving the mirror by a loudspeaker-type transducer at a higher frequency than that of the scintillation, the motion of the mirror being monitored by a separate interferometer using the monochromatic light from a helium-neon laser. The integration process both strengthens the spectrum and reduces the unwanted noise; it also renders relatively unimportant the accidental loss of light by occasional clouds and faulty guiding. Figure 11.16 shows an interferogram and a spectrum of Antares obtained by M. J. Smyth with the Radcliffe Reflector and a rapid-scanning Fourier spectrometer belonging to Edinburgh University.

Reduction of photographic observations An enormous amount of astronomical data is stored on photographic plates and can be of little use until the photographs have been measured and reduced. A single plate of the denser regions of the Milky Way taken with a large Schmidt camera may well contain over a million star images as well as complicated wisps of bright and dark nebulosity and, if by chance part of the region is fairly transparent, some extragalactic nebulae as well. A single spectrum plate may register the precise positions and intensities of hundreds of lines, some single, some blends of two or more. The exploitation of such material gives rise to two problems: what can be

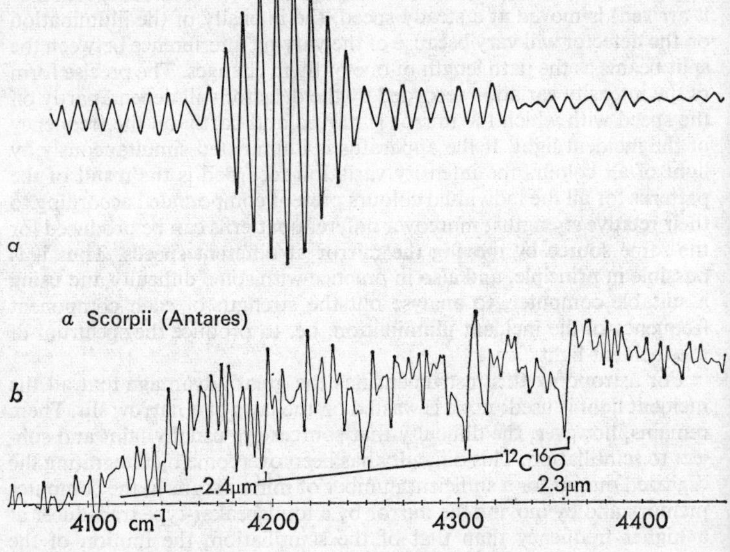

Figure 11.16 Infrared spectrum of Antares (Courtesy of M. J. Smyth, University of Edinburgh)
a, the observed interferogram; *b*, the deduced spectrum

measured and how can the measures be performed on a large number of objects in a reasonable time?

The measurement of the spectral plates is done with exactly the same kind of micrometers and microphotometers as are used for similar work in the laboratory. The processing of the direct photographs calls for machines that are more specifically astronomical. As regards the star images two kinds of measures are immediately possible, positional and photometric: where is the star and how bright is it in the particular coloured light in which the photograph was taken? Measurements of position are made on special machines, either one coordinate at a time or, as is now more usual, both coordinates simultaneously, the measuring scales being either carefully ground and lapped micrometer screws, graduated glass scales, or moiré fringe devices. The accuracy that can be expected from a good machine is rather better than one micron. Several of the larger machines are now semi-automatic in their action and yield their output in a form that is ready for direct computer processing. Accurate measurements of positions on a plate are of little use in themselves. They must in some way be converted into positions in the sky by the aid of stars on the plate whose positions are already known from previous work which, directly or indirectly, depends on observations made with a transit circle.

The brightness of a star is directly related to the size and structure of the photographic image it produces on the plate—the brighter the star, the bigger and blacker its image. Hence we can measure the brightness of the stars by measuring the size of their images, provided we can construct for each plate a calibration curve connecting the size of image with star brightness. This can be done if there is on the plate a selection of stars whose brightness is already known, e.g. from observations made with a photoelectric photometer. Various ways of estimating the image size have been used, such as measuring their diameters with a micrometer, comparing them with a graduated scale of images, and so on. One method that has been widely adopted is to measure the obstructive power of the image when it is placed centrally in a narrow circular beam of light. At first the diameter of the circular beam was kept constant, but it was found that a greater range of image size could be measured if the diameter was varied by means of an iris diaphragm. Figure 11.17 shows the layout of the Becker iris microphotometer. The light beam from the projection lamp is divided into two, the measuring beam and the comparison beam. The latter, on its way to the detecting photomultiplier, passes through a neutral wedge, which is a grey filter of adjustable transmission, and a chopping disk driven by a synchronous motor. The measuring beam illuminates the portion of the plate under examination and projects it in a magnified form onto the ground glass screen where it can be observed by the operator. In the centre of the beam and just in front of the screen is placed the adjustable iris diaphragm. Part of the light passing through this iris is deflected to the chopping disk, which alternately lets through this light and the comparison beam to the photomultiplier detector. When the two beams are equally bright, the photomultiplier will see a steady source; if they are not equally bright, the photomultiplier will give an alternating output at the chopping frequency. The operator centres the image to be measured in the iris diaphragm and then adjusts the iris until the alternating signal, which can be monitored on a cathode ray oscillograph, disappears. The reading corresponding to this opening of the iris is taken as the measure of the obstruction caused by the star image. Such photometers are made

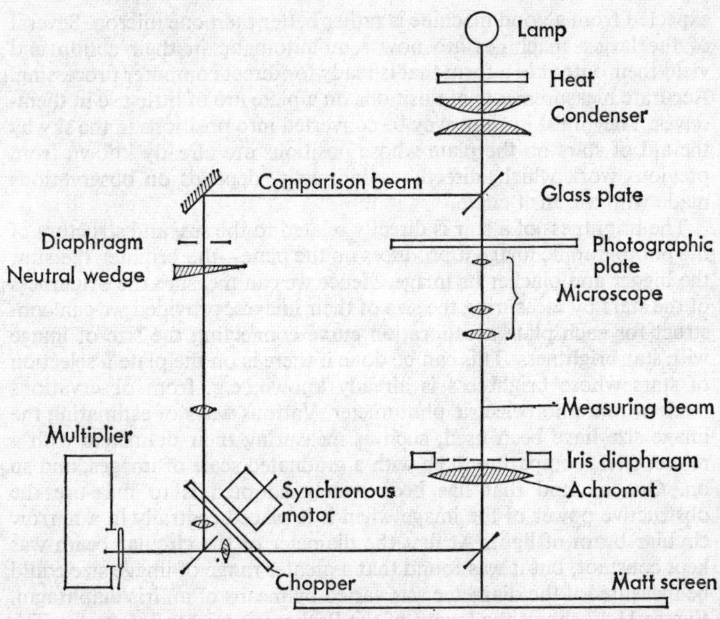

Figure 11.17 The basic design of a Becker iris photometer

in varying degrees of sophistication; the alternating output from the photomultiplier can be used to drive a servo mechanism to make the adjustment of the iris automatic while the readings from the machine, i.e. the iris reading and coordinate readings indicating the position on the plate, can be punched out ready for processing by a computer. One machine at the Royal Observatory, Edinburgh, has been made completely automatic and works on line to the Observatory's main computer.

A machine that has been developed at Edinburgh for high speed scanning and accurate measurement of direct photographs is known as GALAXY, which stands for *G*eneral *A*utomatic *L*uminosity *A*nd *X*, *Y* measuring machine. Its function is to scan an assigned area of a plate, note the position of all images between preassigned limits and then to measure some, or all, of these for magnitude and position. The heart of GALAXY is a highly accurate two-dimensional coordinate table which carries the plate and whose position is read off in units of one micron by two moiré fringe grating systems. Two cathode ray tubes of the micro-spot type with their scanning assemblies and optical systems are rigidly mounted on a heavy casting spanning the carriage. The star images are brought in turn within the optical field of one or other of these systems by the appropriate automatic mechanism. One of the systems is used for the preliminary scanning, the other for precise measurement.

For scanning, the light produced by the first tube is projected down to a small spot (8, 16, 32 and 64 microns in diameter depending on the size of the images under examination), passes through the plate and on to a photoelectric cell. The passage of the spot of light over a star image is detected as a reduction in the brightness of the spot. There is a memory of successive scans over the same image, and when the image has been finally passed its X, Y coordinates are punched out on eight-channel paper tape with a precision about equal to the size of the scanning spot. The plate is scanned in columns 8 millimetres wide by the combination of a line scan on the cathode ray tube and mechanical indexing of the carriage in the orthogonal direction. With a resolution of 16 microns, the Edinburgh Schmidt plates currently being measured are searched at the rate of 30 square millimetres per minute and, on an average, some ten thousand stars found per hour.

The precision measurement of the plate is carried out as a separate operation controlled by a punched tape giving the approximate co-ordinates of the stars to be measured. This tape can be either that produced during the search phase or, if only selected stars are of interest, one prepared quite independently. The projected spot of light produced by the measurement cathode ray tube, only 1 micron across, is scanned in a spiral pattern either 256 or 2048 microns in diameter depending on the range of sizes of the images to be measured. If the approximate setting coordinates do not bring the image precisely to the centre of the spiral pattern, more light passes one side of it than the other. This actuates a servo mechanism which moves the carriage until centring is achieved. At the same time the density-radius profile is compared with 1024 programmed profiles chosen to be appropriate to the particular plate and contained in a core store. The profile matching and the centring are both weighted by a function related to the distribution of information within the image. Finally the coordinates of the image centre and the address of the matching profile, which is a measure of the magnitude, are punched out on eight-channel paper tape ready for subsequent computer analysis.

Observations from above the atmosphere Ground-based observations are subject to severe restrictions imposed by the atmosphere. Celestial radiations of a wide range of frequencies including some of great astrophysical significance are shut out altogether, while those radiations that do penetrate as far as ground level are distorted by selective extinction and by bad seeing. The atmospheric layers that are responsible for much of this bad seeing and for those parts of the extinction that are due to water vapour, suspended dust, etc., are comparatively low, so that their bad effects can, in some cases, be avoided by lifting the receiving apparatus above them in high flying aircraft or in balloons. The layers responsible for shutting out much of the ultraviolet are considerably higher, however, and can only be avoided by observing from sounding rockets or from artificial satellites. Many observations could be better made from these space vehicles than from the ground, but the great expense and complexity of the equipment that would be needed dictate that only observations that can be made in no other way should be made from space. In practice this means observations in the far ultraviolet since those in the infrared can be made from aircraft or from balloons.

The basic principles of astronomical instruments used in unmanned balloons, rockets and satellites are precisely the same as for their ground level equivalents, but their detailed design calls for a much higher degree of imagination, skill and ingenuity to meet the many extra and varied stringent conditions imposed by considerations of size, weight, robustness, reliability, remote control, and the need for the read-out to be in a form that can be telemetered to the ground. Further complications arise in the construction of ultraviolet optical systems because of the scarcity of materials having the right optical properties at the required wavelengths. Moreover, before these optical systems can be used for photometric purposes they have to be calibrated, which brings in further difficulties, partly because suitable standard sources are not easily available and partly because the work has to be done in a vacuum since oxygen becomes opaque below 2000 Å.

Balloons have been used for many years for cosmic ray research, and in particular for carrying up blocks of photographic emulsion to heights where they can register the incoming flux of cosmic ray particles before it has been significantly affected by the atmosphere. During the past twenty years balloons have been used for lifting astronomical apparatus either for making high resolution photographs, e.g. of the granulation of the solar photosphere, or for observing infrared spectra. One of the most ambitious of such projects is the Stratoscope II instrument used by Schwarzschild and his associates in the U.S.A. This consists of a 91-cm aperture telescope which, with its associated spectrograph and control gear, weighs over 2800 kg and which is raised to heights of over 20 km by two unmanned balloons. Balloons have also been used for observations in the near ultraviolet. In a recent experiment to record a high resolution spectrum of the Sun in the region round 2800 Å, a total payload of over 400 kg was lifted to a float altitude of 40 km. This is still a long way short of the top of the ozone layer which is at approximately 50 km; to pass beyond this layer some form of rocket propulsion is essential.

Rockets have been made in all shapes and sizes. The average sounding rocket used for scientific experiments can lift loads of the order of 250 kg to heights of 200 km, the total duration of the useful part of the flight, i.e. the time the rocket is above 100 km, being about five minutes. Many extremely ingenious experiments have been flown in rockets during the past twenty years, but as it is quite impossible to mention them all it is hoped that the following examples will illustrate the possibilities of this method of observation.

Plate 48*b* shows the payload of a Skylark rocket designated S 47/2 in the European Space Research Organization's (ESRO's) sounding rocket programme. This rocket was successfully fired from the Woomera Test Range on 30 September 1971. It will be noticed that the load was made up of a number of standard circular sections each of which carried either a self-contained scientific experiment or an integral part of the equipment needed to enable the rocket to carry out its function. Starting from the stainless steel nose cone, the various sections were:

1. The heat shield
2. The parachute bay
3. The telemetry section
4. Batteries and housekeeping section
5. Magnetometers and Moon sensors
6. Photometer No. 1
7. Photometer No. 2
8. Stellar attitude sensor
9. Photometer No. 3
10. Roll control unit
11. Ring for attaching load to a Raven solid fuel rocket motor

Sections 1–5 were standard rocket equipment, sections 6–10 were provided by the experimenter, in this case J. W. Campbell of the Royal Observatory, Edinburgh. Photometers 1, 2 and 3 were similar except for the band passes which were centred on 1370 Å, 1480 Å and 2150 Å respectively. Each photometer was complete in itself and was fed by a Cassegrain telescope having an aperture of 23 cm, a field of view of one degree and viewing the sky in a direction perpendicular to the long axis of the rocket. The jettisonable covers of the telescope apertures can be seen in Plate 48*b* on the left-hand side of the appropriate sections. The photometers were carefully calibrated both before and after the flight, the main object of the experiment being to measure the absolute flux at the chosen wavelengths of the radiation from the bright early-type stars viewed by the telescopes during the rocket flight. Before any observations were made, the special roll control unit reduced the roll of the rocket from its initial rate of two revolutions per second to a steady rate of 12° per second. The stars observed were identified from the attitude of the rocket at the appropriate moment which was deduced to within about 4° from the readings of the magnetometers and Moon sensors and checked by the stellar attitude sensor.

Because of their great cost there have been relatively few astronomical satellites. Figure 11.18 shows the general layout of Europe's first astronomical satellite, ESRO's TD-1A, which was launched from the Western Test Range in California on 12 March 1972. Its gross weight was 472 kg of which 145 kg was the payload made up of the following seven experiments:

1. S2/68 prepared jointly in Belgium and the United Kingdom to measure for a very large number of stars the absolute flux and spectral distribution of the ultraviolet radiation in the range between 1330 Å and 3000 Å.
2. S59 prepared in the Netherlands to measure the spectra of bright stars with a resolution of about 1Å in three wavelength channels centred round 2100 Å, 2500 Å and 2800 Å.
3. S67 prepared in France to measure the spectrum of charged cosmic ray particles between atomic numbers 2 and 28 in the energy range above 220 MeV/nucleon.

Figure 11.18

1. Hood with apertures for various experiments; 2. compartment housing the experiments; 3, 4, 5, 6. parts of the S133 experiment; 7, 8. S2/68 experiment and aperture; 9, 10. S59 experiment and aperture; 11. aperture for the S77 experiment; 12. aperture for the S67 experiment; 13. S88 experiment; 14. S100 experiment; 15. compartment housing power supplies, control equipment, etc; 16. power supply for attitude control system; 17. gas tank; 18. Y nozzles; 19. X and Z nozzles; 20. reaction wheels; 21. coarse Sun sensor; 22. fine and intermediate Sun sensors; 23, 24. panels carrying arrays of solar cells; 25. battery; 26. inverter supplying regulated AC power to the experiments; 27. pulse width modulated bucking regulator providing stabilized DC voltage to the satellite's own equipment; 28. power control unit containing switching logic, monitoring circuits, etc; 29. selection box controlling action of tape recorders, distributing power to transmitters, receivers, decoders, etc; 30. directional coupler splitting the radio frequency signal into two equal parts but with 90° phase shift; 31. antenna boom; 32. turnstile antenna

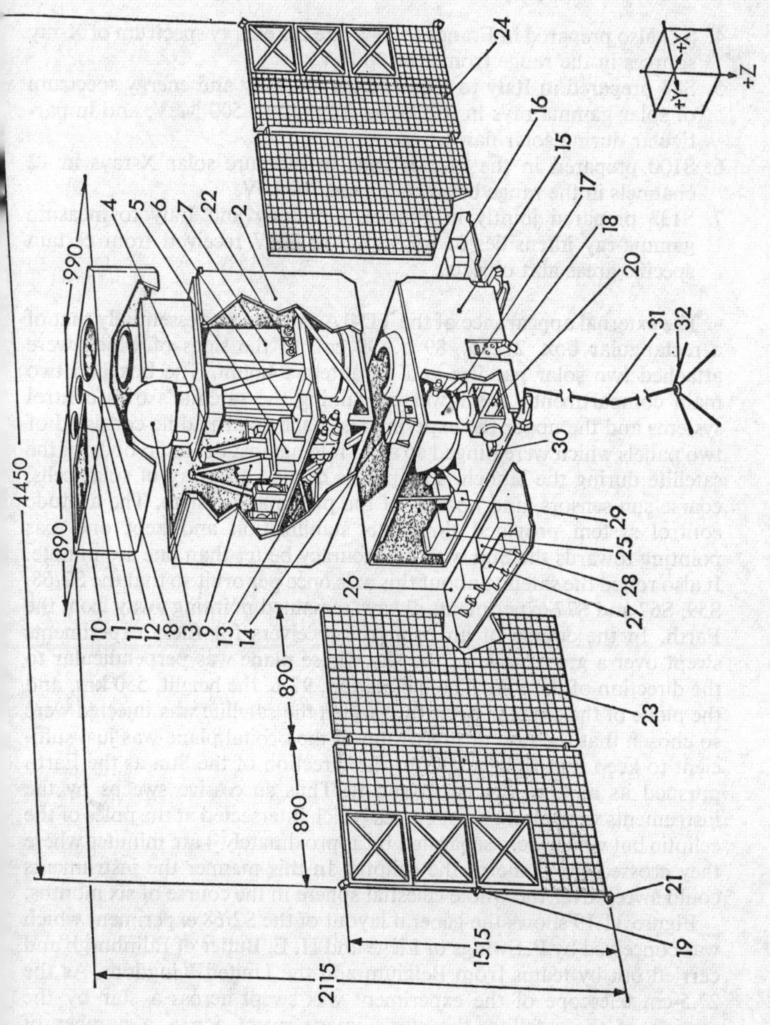

Figure 11.18 Exploded view of the TD-1A satellite of the European Space Research Organization. *Details opposite*

4. S77 also prepared in France to measure the energy spectrum of X-ray sources in the range from 2 to 30 keV.
5. S88 prepared in Italy to measure the intensity and energy spectrum of solar gamma rays in the range from 50 to 500 MeV, and in particular during solar flares.
6. S100 prepared in the Netherlands to measure solar X-rays in 12 channels in the range between 20 and 700 keV.
7. S133 prepared jointly in France, Germany and Italy to measure gamma-ray intensities in excess of 30 MeV received from certain specific areas and objects.

The external appearance of the TD-1A satellite was essentially that of a rectangular box, 212 × 89 × 99 cm, to the sides of which were attached two solar paddles and an antenna boom. The box had two main compartments, the lower containing the satellite's own control systems and the upper the experiments. Each solar paddle consisted of two panels which were hinged so as to fold against the main body of the satellite during the launch. The panels carried an array of solar cells, coarse sun sensors, and nozzles of the pneumatic system. The attitude control system provided three-axis stabilization and kept one axis pointing towards the Sun with an accuracy better than one arc minute. It also rolled the satellite about this axis once per orbit so that the S2/68, S59, S67 and S77 experiments always remained pointing away from the Earth. In the course of an orbit the receivers for these experiments swept over a great circle of the sky whose plane was perpendicular to the direction of the Sun. The inclination, 97°.6, the height, 550 km, and the plane of the circular orbit into which the satellite was injected were so chosen that the rate of precession of the orbital plane was just sufficient to keep it at right angles to the direction of the Sun as the Earth pursued its annual journey round it. Thus successive sweeps by the instruments were along great circles which intersected at the poles of the ecliptic but which were separated by approximately 4 arc minutes where they crossed the plane of the ecliptic. In this manner the instruments could sweep over the whole celestial sphere in the course of six months.

Figure 11.19 shows the general layout of the S2/68 experiment which was conceived by P. Swings of Liège and H. E. Butler of Edinburgh and carried out by teams from Belgium and the United Kingdom. As the 27.5-cm telescope of the experiment was swept across a star by the motion of the satellite, the star's image swept across a number of entrance slots in the off-axis focal plane of the telescope. One narrow slot fed the single-channel photometer, A1, which measured the total flux of the star in the passband 2600 Å–3000 Å. Two adjacent shorter slots which also fed into this photometer were so positioned that they fixed the relative position of the star image as it crossed the slots. A larger slot admitted the star light to a three-channel spectrophotometer, the dispersing element being a plane reflecting grating which sent light of the appropriate frequencies to the entrance slots of three photomultipliers, A2, A3 and A4, which covered the spectral ranges 1330–1790 Å, 1730–2190 Å and 2130–2590 Å respectively. As the star image moved across the entrance slot the dispersed spectrum moved across the exit slot array, thus providing spectrum scanning without the need for any moving parts. Each of the three detector channels yielded approximately 20 data points per scan, the data being in the form of photon counts for integration periods of 0.148 seconds and passbands of approximately 35 Å half width. The field of view of the telescope was 17 arc minutes wide, so that each object was seen at least three times and many more times than this if it happened to be near one of the poles of the ecliptic.

Gravitational waves Finally it may be of interest to mention the current search for gravitational waves. The existence of these was predicted from Einstein's general theory of relativity which indicated that accelerated masses should radiate energy in the form of gravitational fields at the speed of light. Unfortunately, the detection of this energy, which should occur in quanta similarly to electromagnetic radiation, is extraordinarily difficult because of its weakness and its feeble interaction with detecting bodies. As the sensitivity of a detector should be proportional to its mass and size, an obvious first choice for a detector is the Earth itself. Its free modes of oscillation start from a lowest frequency of one cycle in 54 minutes—324 μHz—and range upwards. The Earth's natural seismic noise is too high to make it of real value as a detector, though in conjunction with the much quieter Moon it might be useful. Indeed, a gravimeter was placed on the Moon by the Apollo 17 crew with this application in mind. Laboratory detectors are restricted to masses of the order of tons and have vibration frequencies in the kHz range, which are the sort of frequencies which might be generated by stars in a state of gravitational collapse.

Weber, at the University of Maryland, has been experimenting with detectors consisting of solid cylinders of aluminium, 1.5 m in length and 1 m in diameter and weighing about 3500 kg. These are suspended in complete isolation from all the usual environmental disturbances and their internal vibrations are sensed by piezoelectric crystals fastened round the middle. It is claimed that the sensitivity is such that deformations of the cylinders as great as one part in 10^{16} can be detected, which

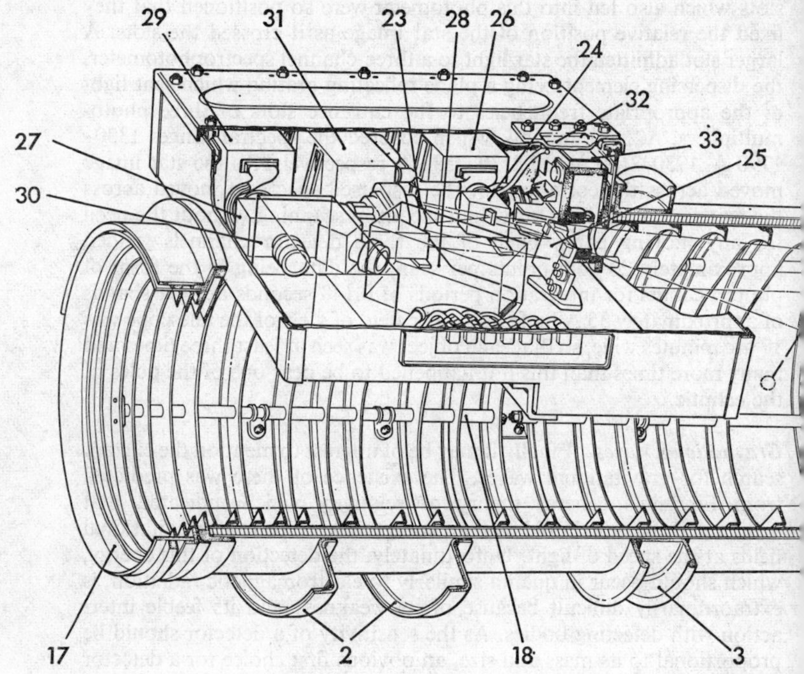

Figure 11.19 Layout of the telescope and photometers for the S2/68 experiment

1. Telescope tube made of reinforced aluminium honeycomb; 2. aluminium stiffening rings; 3. upper antivibration attachment ring; 4. lower antivibration attachment ring; 5. webbed aluminium base machining; 6. aluminium sub-ring; 7. cervit primary mirror; 8. primary mirror stop; 9. primary mirror alignment adjuster; 10. kinematic mount; 11. roller support assembly; 12. epoxy shim; 13. viton pressure pad; 14. monitor mirror access port; 15. aluminium bronze G clamp; 16. purge gas inlet union; 17. Sun baffle assembly;

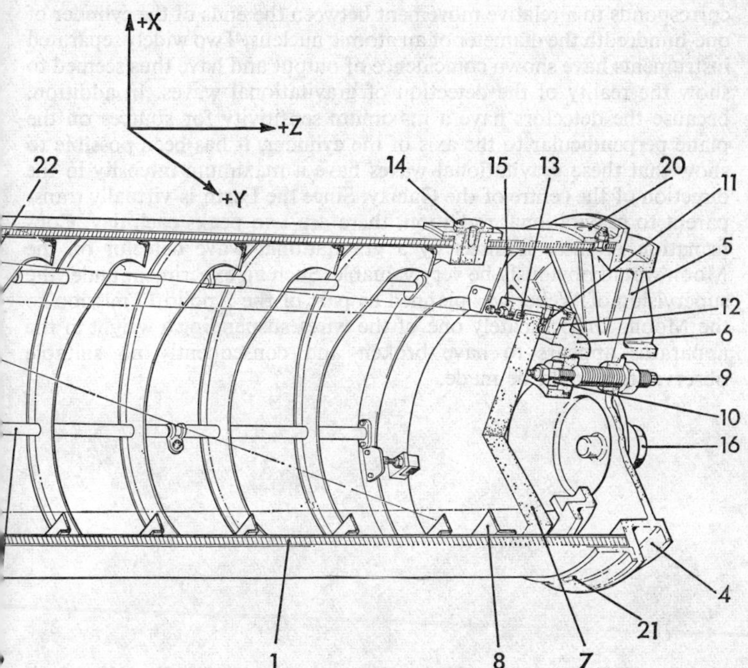

18. upper baffle stack; 19. lower baffle stack; 20. thermistor T1; 21. thermistor T2; 22. thermistor T3; 23. zerodur secondary mirror; 24. prime focus slit unit; 25. plane reflecting diffraction grating; 26. detector for the A1 photometric channel 2600–3000 Å; 27. exit slit and Fabry housing; 28. detector for the A2 spectrophotometric channel 1330–1790 Å; 29. detector for the A3 spectrophotometric channel 1730–2190 Å; 30. detector for the A4 spectrophotometric channel 2130–2590 Å; 31. shutter logic unit; 32. shutter and monitor mirror access panel; 33. shutter arming block

corresponds to a relative movement between the ends of the cylinder of one-hundredth the diameter of an atomic nucleus. Two widely separated instruments have shown coincidence of output and have thus seemed to show the reality of the detection of gravitational waves. In addition, because the detectors have a maximum sensitivity for sources on the plane perpendicular to the axis of the cylinder, it has been possible to show that these gravitational waves have a maximum intensity in the direction of the centre of the Galaxy. Since the Earth is virtually transparent to gravitational radiation, there are two peaks each day. Confirmation of these findings by a gravitational wave detector on the Moon would obviously be very valuable. Such an experiment under the supervision of Weber was planned as part of the Apollo 17 mission to the Moon. Unfortunately one of the wires suspending a weight in the apparatus appears to have broken and consequently no suitable observations could be made.

Glossary of astronomical terms

The meaning of other terms, less frequently used, can be found through the index. Numbers in parentheses indicate pages where fuller explanations are given.

Aberration Displacement of the apparent position of a celestial body caused by the motion of the observer (304); deviation of an optical system from ideal performance. (441)

Absolute Magnitude A measure of the intrinsic brightness of a celestial body; for asteroids and comets (203), for stars and nebulae. (29, 309)

Absolute Temperature This is measured on a thermodynamical scale of which the zero is that temperature at which the constituent molecules of any substance are completely devoid of heat energy. This is approximately -273°C, so that for all practical purposes the absolute temperature corresponding to t°C is (t+273)°K.

Achondrite A stony meteorite with a texture similar to some terrestrial rocks but with a complete absence of the characteristic spherical chondrules present in many meteorities. (228)

Achromatic Used to describe optical systems in which light is not split into its constituent colours. (436)

Adiabatic Used to describe a process in which there is no exchange of heat with the surroundings.

Albedo A measure of the reflecting power of a surface or an object. (145)

Alpha Particle A heavy, positively charged particle emitted during radioactive decay; identified with the nucleus of an ordinary helium atom.

Alpha Rays A stream of fast-moving alpha particles.

Altazimuth An instrument or mounting similar to a theodolite in that it can move in both azimuth and altitude, i.e. about both vertical and horizontal axes.

Altitude The angular height above the horizon.

Angstrom (Å) A unit of length named after a Swedish spectroscopist and chiefly used for measuring the wavelength of light and X-rays. It is equal to 10^{-10}m, or 0.1 nanometres, a unit which is gradually replacing it.

Angular Momentum The product of the angular velocity of a rotating body and its moment of inertia.

Aphelion The point on a circumsolar orbit that is farthest from the Sun.

Apogee The point on a circumterrestrial orbit that is farthest from the Earth.

Apse (pl. apsides) A point on a central orbit at which the tangent is perpendicular to the radius vector.

Asterism A group of stars, not necessarily a complete constellation, that forms an easily recognizable figure in the sky.

Astronomical Unit (A.U.) The mean distance of the Earth from the Sun. It equals 149.6 Gm, i.e. 149.6×10^6 km.

Azimuth The horizontal angle between the direction in question and a chosen initial direction. In astronomy, north is taken as the chosen initial direction and azimuths are measured eastwards from 0° to 360°.

Basalt A dark, fine-grained igneous rock similar to that composing the Giant's Causeway.

Beta Particle A light, negatively charged particle emitted during radioactive decay; identified with the electron.

Beta Rays A stream of fast-moving electrons.

Black Body A theoretical body with radiation properties to which those of actual bodies approximate. It absorbs all the radiation falling upon it, while the quantity and spectral distribution of the radiation that it emits is determined only by its absolute temperature. (428, 429)

Bolometer An instrument for measuring radiation. (423, 433)

Bremsstrahlung Electromagnetic radiation produced when fast-moving charged particles are retarded. (275)

Caldera A crater-like depression within the body of a volcano.

Calorie A unit for measuring the quantity of heat. In astronomy usually taken to be the amount of heat required to raise the temperature of one gram of water through one degree Centigrade.

Celestial Pole Point in the heavens about which the stars appear to circle as the Earth rotates.

Cepheid A type of intrinsically very bright variable star which is useful as a distance indicator. (34, 352, 353)

Chondrites Stony meteorites containing chondrules. (228)

Chondrules Small round globules occurring in many stone meteorites. (228)

Chromosphere A layer of the solar atmosphere immediately above the photosphere. So called because it was first seen during a solar eclipse as a vivid red envelope surrounding the Sun. (247, 248)

Collimation The process of lining up an optical system or of making a beam of light parallel.

Colour Index A convenient way of measuring the colour of a star numerically. (28, 292)

Conjunction The apparent proximity of two heavenly bodies. (136, 137)

Corona The upper tenuous layers of the solar atmosphere, visible to the naked eye at the time of a total solar eclipse as a white, pearly halo surrounding the Sun. (252, 253, 254)

Cosmic Rays Streams of highly penetrating charged particles, atomic nuclei mainly of hydrogen and helium, that appears to permeate all space. (386)

Couple The turning effect produced by the application of two equal and opposite parallel forces. Its torque is measured by the product of the forces and the distance between them.

Culmination The moment when a celestial object is crossing the meridian.

D-Layer The lowest layer of the Earth's Ionosphere. (85, 86)

Declination The celestial equivalent of latitude. (24, 303, 305)

Density The mass per unit volume, but frequently used for 'relative density', i.e. the number of times a volume of a substance is more massive than the same volume of water.

Diffraction An interference phenomenon occurring when a train of waves encounters an obstruction and resulting in non-rectilinear propagation. Thus the shadow cast by monochromatic light passing a straight edge is flanked by a series of light and dark bands. The width of these bands depends on the wavelength of the light so that the phenomenon can be used, as in the diffraction grating, to disperse light into its constituent colours.

Dipole Two opposite magnetic poles or electrical charges separated by a small distance, e.g. a short bar magnet. A form of radio antenna consisting of a straight conductor, one half wavelength long with the lead connected to the centre.

Doppler Effect The apparent change in frequency of wave motion produced by the relative motion of the source and the observer. In sound one of the most familiar examples is the way in which the whish of an approaching fast car turns into a whoosh as the car recedes. In astronomy the important effect is the way in which light from an approaching object is shifted towards the violet, while that from a receding object is shifted towards the red.

Dynode One of the intermediate sensitive surfaces in a photomultiplier cell. (431)

Eccentricity If a and b denote the semi-major and semi-minor axes of an ellipse its eccentricity, e, is given by

$$e^2 = (a^2 - b^2)/a^2.$$

Thus $e = 0$ for a circle and approximates to 1 for a very elongated ellipse.

Ecliptic The circle in which the plane of the Earth's orbit about the Sun cuts the celestial sphere. (24, 305)

Electron-volt A convenient measure of energy when considering atomic transitions. It is the energy acquired by an electron in falling through a potential difference of one volt and is equal to 1.60203×10^{-12} ergs or to the energy of a quantum having a wavelength of 1.2395 microns.

Elongation The apparent angular distance from the Sun. (136)

Equinox The time when day and night are of equal length; sometimes used to denote the points in the heavens where the Sun appears to be on these occasions. (305)

Erg The unit of work in c.g.s. (centimetre, gram, second) units. There are 3.6×10^{13} ergs per kilowatt-hour.

Evershed Effect The radial outflow of material from the lower levels of sunspots. (266)

Fibrilles Fine, complex structures in the chromosphere, especially in the neighbourhood of sunspots.

First Point of Aries The point of zero declination and zero right ascension, defined as the intersection of the ecliptic and the celestial equator corresponding to the position of the Sun at the time of the March equinox.

Flare Sudden, localized burst of intense radiation from the surface of the Sun or other star. (270, 271)

Flare Cycle Periodic fluctuation in the number of solar flares similar to that in the number of sunspots.

Fraunhofer Joseph Fraunhofer (1787–1826) was a German optician and one of the first to observe and to describe carefully the dark absorption lines in the solar spectrum. Such an absorption spectrum is frequently called a Fraunhofer spectrum and the dark lines, particularly the stronger ones, Fraunhofer lines. (244)

Gamma The third letter of the Greek alphabet (γ) used as a symbol for many different things, among others being a measure of the strength of a magnetic field. One gamma $= 10^{-5}$ gauss.

Gamma Rays Very energetic radiation emitted during radioactive decay. It is not corpuscular like the alpha and beta rays but is electromagnetic radiation of extremely short wavelength. (285)

Gauss The c.g.s unit of magnetic flux density named in honour of Carl Friedrich Gauss, 1777–1855. The Earth's normal magnetic field is of the order of one gauss.

Gegenschein A faint glow that can sometimes be seen near the antisolar point on dark, very clear nights. (230)

Half-life A measure of the rate at which spontaneous atomic, nuclear, or other such processes take place. If N is the original number of excited particles and t the corresponding half-life, the number still excited after time t will be $\frac{1}{2}$N; after time 2t the number will have dropped to $\frac{1}{4}$N; after 3t to $\frac{1}{8}$N, and so on.

Hertz A unit of frequency, viz. one cycle per second, named in honour of the German physicist who first demonstrated the physical existence of radio waves.

Hydrogen Alpha (Hα) The red radiation emitted by hydrogen atoms; the first line in the hydrogen Balmer series, wavelength 6563 Å.

Hydrosphere The sphere defined by the water covering the Earth's surface, including not only the oceans but also the seas, lakes, rivers, etc.

Infrared Electromagnetic radiation with wavelengths between about 0.8 μm and 1 mm; sometimes called heat radiation.

Ion An atom or molecule that has gained or lost one or more electrons and thus become negatively or positively charged.

Ionosphere That part of the Earth's upper atmosphere in which a considerable fraction of the constituent atoms and molescules are ionized. (85, 86)

Irradiation The phenomenon of a brightly illuminated object appearing to extend into the dark background; also exposure to radiation, particularly for a given purpose.

Isostasy The theory that the heights of the various portions of the upper crust of the Earth are so adjusted that the mass of a vertical column of given area above a certain layer is approximately constant, i.e. the land masses, ocean floor, etc. behave as though they were floating on a denser layer a few miles beneath the surface.

Kelvin A British physicist, 1824–1907, whose name is used for the unit of thermodynamic temperature. Among the many problems he investigated was that of the source of stellar energy which he attributed to the work done by gravity as the star contracted and became more and more dense. This is now known to be only a phase in the life of a star and is frequently described as the Kelvin contraction phase.

Kerr Cell A device making use of the Kerr electro-optical effect to provide an extremely fast-acting, electrically controlled shutter for light beams.

Kirkwood Gaps Gaps in the asteroid belt named after the American astronomer who first explained them in terms of Jupiter's gravitational influence. (198, 199)

Librations Periodic oscillations, particularly those occurring in the apparent motion of the Moon. (102, 103)

Light Year The distance light travels in a year. 5.88 × 10^{12} km.

Limb The edge of the disk of the Sun, Moon or other celestial object.

Lithosphere The solid, rocky, outer portions of the Earth.

M Standing for Messier, a French astronomer who compiled one of the first lists of nebulae and star clusters, many of which are still known by the number in his list. (399)

Magnetopause The outer boundary of the Earth's magnetosphere. (86)

Magnetosphere Volume surrounding the Earth in which the terrestrial magnetic field is enclosed by the solar wind. It extends to about 10 earth radii in the direction of the Sun and a much greater distance in the opposite direction. (86)

Magnitude A convenient way of expressing the brightness of celestial objects. (27, 28, 292)

Main Sequence The great majority of observable stars whose intrinsic brightness and surface temperature are directly related to their mass; thought to be those stars for which the principal source of energy is the conversion of hydrogen into helium. (29, 293, 296, 357)

Mare (pl. maria) The Latin word for sea and used for describing certain areas of the Moon and Mars once regarded as possible seas.

Meridian The north–south line through the place of observation; the plane defined by the axis of the Earth's rotation and the place of observation; the great circle in which this plane intersects the celestial sphere.

Metamorphic Structural transformation brought about by long exposure to pressure, heat, liquids, etc.

Metastable State In astronomy this term is usually used to refer to atomic states from which radiative transitions to states of lower energy are 'forbidden' by the normal selection rules. These states have half-lives very much longer than the average so that under 'normal' conditions an atom is removed from such a state by particle collision, or by absorbing an appropriate quantum, before it has time to regain a lower state by the emission of radiation.

Microwave Region This spans the gap in the electromagnetic spectrum between the infrared and the normal radio region. The nominal wavelengths and frequencies of the various bands are as follows:

Band	Wavelength (cm)	Frequency (GHz)
L	25	1
S	10	3
C	6	5
J	4.5	6
X	3	10
K	1.2	25
Q	0.8	38

Milky Way The band of faint stars across the sky resulting from our viewing the Galaxy from the inside; sometimes used as an alternative name for the Galaxy. (361)

Millibar The unit used for measuring atmospheric pressure and equivalent to 1000 dynes per square centimetre. Normal sea-level atmospheric pressure is approximately 1000 millibars.

Moment of Inertia The sum of the products of the masses of the constituent particles of a body by the square of their distance from the axis of rotation.

Momentum The product of the mass of a body by its velocity.

Nadir The direction of gravity.

Neutrino A fundamental particle of matter having neither electrical charge nor rest mass. (237, 238)

Nicol Prism A device for producing plane polarized light. It consists of two specially cut pieces of Iceland spar cemented together.

Node The most usual meaning in astronomy is the intersection of an orbit with the ecliptic.
Nova A type of stellar outburst. (343, 344)
Nutation Periodic oscillations of the Earth's axis. (92, 94, 96)

Oblateness Flattening at the poles, or ellipticity, measured numerically in the case of an ellipsoid of revolution by the ratio (a−c) : a, where a and c denote the equatorial and polar semi-diameters.
Obliquity Used in astronomy to denote the angle between the planes of the ecliptic and of the Earth's equator.
Occultation The obscuration of one body by the solid body of another, normally of a star by the Moon.
Opposition A celestial body is said to be in opposition when it crosses the meridian at midnight. (136, 137)

Parallax The apparent displacement in the position of an object when viewed from different points. Used in astronomy to denote the distance of an object, particularly when this is expressed as an angle subtended at the object by the radius of the Earth or of its orbit. (133, 135, 307, 308, 309)
Parsec Unit of distance equal to approximately 3.26 light years or 1.92×10^{13} km.
Penumbra The partly shaded region round the total shadow during an eclipse; the outer part of a sunspot. (266)
Peridotite A coarse-grained igneous rock.
Perigee The point on a circumterrestrial orbit that is closest to the Earth.
Perihelion The point on a circumsolar orbit that is closest to the Sun.
Permafrost A layer beneath the surface which in some parts of the Earth remains frozen indefinitely because the summer heating does not penetrate to it.
Perturbations Small deviations of an actual orbit from one that has been calculated with simplified conditions.
Photon A quantum of light radiation. (427)
Photosphere The visible surface of the Sun or of a star. (241)
Plage A bright area of the solar surface in the neighbourhood of a sunspot. (267, 268)
Planck's Law This gives the quantity and spectral distribution of the radiation emitted by a black body at a specified absolute temperature. (428, 429)
Planetesimals Small hypothetical bodies in space out of which the planets were supposed to have been formed by accretion.
Plasma A state of matter in which many of the constituent particles are electrically charged so that their motions are mainly controlled by electromagnetic interactions. (261)
Plutonic Descriptive of igneous rocks that have been formed deep in the Earth, in contrast to volcanic lavas which have cooled on the surface.
Polarization The process of selecting out that portion of the incident radiation for which the vibrations are in a specified plane. (262)
Polaroid A specially prepared film with the property of polarizing light passing through it.
Position Angle The angle between a given direction and true north, this angle being measured eastwards from 0° to 360°.
Positron A positive electron, one of the fundamental particles of matter having the same mass as an ordinary negative electron but an opposite charge. (237, 238)
Poynting-Robertson Effect This is the way in which finely divided matter orbiting round the Sun gradually spirals inwards under the action of radiation pressure.

Precession A gradual change in the direction of the Earth's axis of rotation caused by the gravitational attraction of the Sun and the Moon on the Earth's equatorial bulge. (90)

Prominences Extended, and sometimes detached, portions of the solar chromosphere seen as huge red flames on the edge of the solar disk at the time of a total eclipse or when the Sun is viewed in the light of Hα. The frequency of their appearance follows a cycle similar to that of sunspots. (268)

Proper Motion The part of the change in the apparent position of a body on the celestial sphere that is due to the actual motion of the body relative to the solar system. (301)

Protonosphere That portion of the Earth's upper atmosphere above about 1000 km in which the dominant particles are protons.

Pulsar A source emitting very short bursts of radiation at regular intervals of the order of a fraction of a second. Pulsars are thought to be rapidly spinning, extremely dense neutron stars. (424)

Quantum (pl. quanta) The unit of energy exchange between radiation and matter. The energy associated with each quantum is hν, where ν is the frequency of the radiation and h is Planck's constant. (427)

Quasar An extremely powerful emitter of radio and optical radiation. The spectra of quasars show large red shifts possibly indicating extreme remoteness but the exact nature of these objects is still unknown. (423, 424)

Radial Velocity The velocity of an object in the line of sight, i.e. either directly towards or away from the observer.

Radiant The point from which the paths of a related group of meteors appear to diverge. (219)

Rayleigh Scattering Scattering of radiation by particles much smaller than its wavelength. The amount of the resulting scattering is proportional to the inverse fourth power of the wavelength.

Redshift The shift to the red of radiation received from distant nebulae, possibly as the result of a Doppler effect due to their recession. (416)

Right Ascension The celestial equivalent of longitude. (24, 303, 305)

Rills Deep, ditchlike depressions in the lunar surface, some of them extending for several tens of km.

Roche's Limit The distance within which a liquid satellite would be pulled apart by the differential gravitational attraction of its primary.

S.I. Units The International System of Units, which has replaced the c.g.s. (centimetre, gram, second) system for general scientific use, takes the metre, kilogram, and second as basic units and tends to use prefixes only in multiples of 1000. Thus:

Multiple	Prefix	Symbol	Multiple	Prefix	Symbol
10^{-3}	milli	m	10^{3}	kilo	k
10^{-6}	micro	μ	10^{6}	mega	M
10^{-9}	nano	n	10^{9}	giga	G
10^{-12}	pico	p	10^{12}	tera	T

Solar Wind Ionized particles streaming outwards from the Sun and having a velocity of about 400 km s^{-1} when they reach the neighbourhood of the Earth. (256, 257)

Space Probes and Artificial Satellites The man-made objects floating round the solar system must now be counted by the thousand, and more are constantly being injected by an increasing number of nations. The principal objects are known by their number in a particular series, each such series having a code name which indicates its main purpose. Amongst those that have included some astronomical observations in their schedule are the Cosmos, Lunik, Zond, Luna, Venus, Vostok, Voskhod, Soyuz series launched by the U.S.S.R. and the Pioneer, Explorer, Ranger, Discoverer, Mariner, Surveyor, Lunar Orbiter, OSO (Orbiting Solar Observatory), OAO (Orbiting Astronomical Observatory), Mercury, Gemini, Apollo series launched by the U.S.A.

Spicules Small rapidly ascending jets rising in large numbers out of the solar chromosphere and persisting for about 30 minutes. (250)

Stefan's Law This states that the rate at which energy is radiated from a black body is proportional to the fourth power of its absolute temperature. (429)

Synchroton Radiation Electromagnetic radiation produced when an electron or other charged particle spirals round under the influence of a magnetic field.

Synodic Period The time required for a body to complete a cycle from a specified position relative to the Sun and the Earth back to the same relative position. (133)

Terminator The dividing line between the illuminated and non-illuminated portions of the Moon or of a planet.

Ultraviolet Electromagnetic radiation with wavelengths between about 4000 Å and 50 Å.

X-Rays Electromagnetic radiation with wavelengths between about 50 Å and 0.01 Å; sometimes referred to as 'soft' or 'hard' according to whether the wavelength is longer or shorter than 1 Å.

Zenith The point immediately overhead as defined by the direction of gravity.

Zodiac The band of the sky in which the Sun, the Moon and the principal planets appear to move. (31, 47)

Index of persons

General index

Objects are given under the general category to which they belong, e.g. cluster, constellation, Sun, Moon, star, etc. Objects of special interest are listed under their most usual name and cross references to them under the appropriate categories are restricted to 'S.E.', indicating a special entry. No references are given either to the Glossary or to the names included in the Index of Persons.